REAL-TIME SYSTEMS

REAL-TIME SYSTEMS

Scheduling, Analysis, and Verification

ALBERT M. K. CHENG
University of Houston

WILEY-INTERSCIENCE

A JOHN WILEY & SONS, INC., PUBLICATION

To My Family and Friends

CONTENTS

PREFACE

This text is based on two rich sources: (1) materials in lecture notes I taught to senior and graduate-level computer science and electrical engineering students at Rice University and at the University of Houston, and (2) my research in the area of timing analysis and verification of real-time systems since the late 1980s, especially in the emerging area of embedded rule-based systems. Condensed forms of key concepts appearing in this text have been presented in my tutorials and seminars at many major international conferences. The focus is on the formal analysis and verification of real-time systems. The text is self-contained in that it includes a presentation of basic real-time scheduling algorithms and schedulability analysis as well as a description of the necessary background in logic and automata theory for understanding the more advanced materials. It provides a clear presentation of the concepts underlying the formal methods for real-time systems design.

Many of the systems and devices used in our modern society must provide a response that is both correct and timely. More and more computer systems are built as integral parts of many of these systems to monitor and control their functions and operations. These embedded systems often operate in environments where safety is a major concern. Examples range from simple systems such as climate-control systems, toasters, and rice cookers to highly complex systems such as airplanes and space shuttles. Other examples include hospital patient-monitoring devices and braking controllers in automobiles. Toward the goal of ensuring that these safety-critical systems operate as specified by the design and safety requirements, we have to develop sound methodologies and apply the corresponding tools to analyze and verify that these systems meet their specifications.

Much has been written in the area of formal analysis and verification of real-time systems in the form of technical papers that assume an advanced mathematical background on the part of the reader. Many of these presentations tend to be narrow in their coverage and many are model, architecture, or implementation dependent. Although they are timely and useful disseminations of state-of-the-art results, often there is little unifying discussion or foundation linking or relating the different results, making it difficult to make use of the results in practice. They are usually written in a formal manner with extensive notation and proofs, and with the assumption that the reader is a knowledgeable researcher in the same field. Since research results must be reported in a timely manner in the scientific field, authors of these papers do not have the time and space to show extensive examples or to provide a more tutorial perspective. Several books are available on the subject of analysis and verification of real-time systems, but they are basically collections of papers in their original form, sometimes with very brief, additional introductions to the papers.

Therefore, the purpose of this text is to make the most significant of these state-of-the-art materials accessible to upper-division undergraduates (juniors and seniors) and first-year graduates while still serving as a resourceful reference for more advanced practitioners and researchers by providing an extensive bibliography and pointers to more detailed papers on selected topics. This text is also a more unified treatment of the different approaches to analysis and verification. It compares these approaches and relates one approach to another so that the reader can decide when to use which approach or combination of approaches. The text does not attempt to be comprehensive but does present the most significant trends in the field. Thus, it also serves as a motivating source to generate interest in the area in order to tackle the many difficult problems awaiting correct or efficient solutions.

EXAMPLES

The text describes the application of the presented techniques and tools to a variety of industrial and toy examples. For easy reference, we list the major examples:

- Automatic air conditioning and heating unit (chapter 2)
- Simplified automobile control (chapters 2, 4, 7)
- Smart traffic light system for a traffic intersection (chapters 2, 8)
- Railroad crossing (chapters 4, 6)
- Mutual exclusion problem for processes (chapter 5)
- NASA X-38 Crew Return Vehicle avionics (chapter 6)
- NASA Mars Odyssey Orbiter (chapter 5)
- Message sending and acknowledgment (chapter 7)
- Airport radar system (chapter 9)
- Object detection (chapter 9)
- Space Shuttle Cryogenic Hydrogen Pressure Malfunction Procedure (chapter 10)
- Fuel cell expert system (FCE) (chapter 10)

- Integrated status assessment expert system (ISA) (chapters 10, 11, 12)
- Seat assignment (chapter 11)
- Analysis of 2D line-drawing representation of 3D objects (chapter 11)
- Space Shuttle Orbital Maneuvering and Reaction Control Systems' Valve and Switch Classification Expert System (OMS) (chapter 11)

TEXT OUTLINE

Common to every chapter is a description of the available design, analysis, and verification tools; a section on historical perspective and related work; a summary; and a set of exercises.

Chapter 1 introduces real-time systems, defines the notion of time and how to measure it, and provides a synopsis of several analysis techniques, including simulation, testing, verification, and run-time monitoring. It also gives pointers to useful resources in the study and design of real-time systems.

Chapter 2 describes the analysis and verification of non-real-time systems using symbolic logic and automata-theoretic approaches. It covers topics in propositional logic, proving satisfiability using the resolution procedure, predicate logic, prenex normal forms, Skolem standard forms, proving unsatisfiability of a clause set with Herbrand's procedure and the resolution procedure, languages and their representations, finite automata, and the specification and verification of untimed systems.

Chapter 3 presents real-time scheduling and schedulability analysis, covering topics in computation time prediction, uniprocessor scheduling, scheduling preemptable and independent tasks, fixed-priority schedulers, rate-monotonic and deadline-monotonic algorithms, dynamic-priority schedulers, earliest-deadline-first (EDF) algorithm, least-laxity-first (LL) algorithm, scheduling nonpreemptable sporadic tasks, nonpreemptable tasks with precedence constraints, periodic tasks with precedence constraints, communicating periodic tasks, deterministic rendezvous model, periodic tasks with critical sections, kernelized monitor model, multiprocessor scheduling, schedule representations, scheduling game board, sufficient conditions for conflict-free task sets, scheduling periodic tasks on a multiprocessor, PERTS, PerfoRMAx, TimeWiz, and real-time operating systems (RTOSs).

Chapter 4 describes model checking of finite-state systems. Topics covered include system specification, Clarke–Emerson–Sistla model checker, CTL, complete CTL model checker in C, symbolic model checking, binary decision diagrams, real-time CTL, minimum and maximum delays, minimum and maximum number of condition occurrences, and state graphs with non-unit transition time.

Chapter 5 presents visual formalism, Statecharts, and Statemate, covering basic Statecharts features, including OR-decomposition, AND-decomposition, delays and timeouts, condition and selection entrances, and unclustering. It also describes activity-charts, module-charts, Statechart semantics, and code executions and analysis.

Chapter 6 describes real-time logic (RTL), graph-theoretic analysis, and Modechart, covering specification and safety assertions, event-action model, restricted

RTL formulas, constraint-graph construction, unsatisfiability check, analysis complexity and optimization, NASA X-38 Crew Return Vehicle X-38 Avionics Architecture, Modechart, verification of timing properties of Modechart specifications, system computations, and computation graphs. It presents techniques for finding the minimum and maximum distance between endpoints, and exclusion and inclusion of endpoint and interval.

Chapter 7 describes verification using timed automata. Topics covered include Lynch–Vaandrager automata-theoretic approach, timed executions, timed traces, composition of timed automata, MMT automata, proving time bounds with simulations, Alur–Dill automata-theoretic approach, untimed traces, timed traces, Alur–Dill timed automata, Alur–Dill region automaton and verification, and clock regions.

Chapter 8 presents untimed Petri nets and time/timed Petri nets. Topics covered include conditions for firing enabled transitions, environment/relationship nets, high-level timed Petri nets (HLTPNs), time ER nets, strong and weak time models, properties of high-level Petri Nets, Berthomieu–Diaz analysis algorithm for TPNs, determining fireability of transitions, deriving reachable classes, Milano Group's approach to HLTPN analysis, and facilitating analysis with TRIO.

Chapter 9 presents process-algebraic approaches to verification, covering untimed process algebra, Milner's Calculus of Communicating Systems (CCS), direct equivalence of behavior programs, congruence of behavior programs, equivalence relations, bisimulation, timed process algebras, Algebra of Communicating Shared Resources (ACSR), syntax of ACSR and semantics of ACSR, operational rules, analysis, and VERSA.

Chapter 10 describes the design and timing analysis of propositional-logic rule-based systems. Topics covered include real-time decision systems, real-time expert systems, EQL language, state space representation, computer-aided design tools, response time analysis problem, finite domains, special form, general analysis strategy, synthesis problem, time complexity of scheduling equational rule-based programs, method of Lagrange multipliers, specifying termination conditions in Estella, behavioral constraint assertions, syntax and semantics of Estella, specifying Special Forms with Estella, context-free grammar for Estella, Estella-General Analysis Tool, selecting independent rule set, constructing and checking the dependency graph, checking compatibility conditions, checking cycle-breaking conditions, quantitative timing analysis algorithms, mutual exclusiveness and compatibility, high-level dependency graph, and rule-dependency graph.

Chapter 11 presents the timing analysis of predicate-logic rule-based systems, covering the OPS5 language, Rete network, Cheng–Tsai timing analysis methodology, static analysis of control paths in OPS5, termination analysis, termination detection, enabling conditions of a cycle, prevention of cycles, program refinement, redundant conditions, redundant extra rules, timing analysis, prediction of the number of rule firings, WM generation, maximizing matching time, maximizing rule firings, complexity and space reduction, ordering of the initial WMEs, Cheng–Chen timing analysis methodology, classification of OPS5 programs, maximal numbers of new matching WMEs number of comparisons, the class of cyclic programs, and removing cycles with programmer's help.

Chapter 12 describes the optimization of rule-based systems. Topics covered include execution model of a real-time decision system based on a state space representation, several optimization algorithms, derivation of an optimized state space graph, synthesis of an optimized EQL(B) program, EQL(B) programs without cycles, EQL(B) programs with cycles, qualitative comparison of optimization methods, constraints over EQL language required by optimization, and optimization of other real-time rule-based systems.

ACKNOWLEDGMENTS

I would like to express my sincere thanks to editor Andrew J. Smith, who first inivited me to embark on this textbook project, to the current senior editor Philip Meyler, who is very supportive and flexible with deadlines, to the anonymous reviewers for providing constructive comments, to my Ph.D. student Mark T.-I. Huang for drawing many of the figures, and to associate managing editor Angioline Loredo, Kirsten Rohsted, and the editorial staff for professional editing. My family and friends have provided continuous encouragement and support for which I am greatly indebted.

ALBERT M. K. CHENG

Houston, TX

LIST OF FIGURES

REAL-TIME SYSTEMS

CHAPTER 1

INTRODUCTION

The correctness of many systems and devices in our modern society depends not only on the effects or results they produce but also on the time at which these results are produced. These real-time systems range from the anti-lock braking controller in automobiles to the vital-sign monitor in hospital intensive-care units. For example, when the driver of a car applies the brake, the anti-lock braking controller analyzes the environment in which the controller is embedded (car speed, road surface, direction of travel) and activates the brake with the appropriate frequency within fractions of a second. Both the result (brake activation) and the time at which the result is produced are important in ensuring the safety of the car, its driver, and passengers.

Recently, computer hardware and software are increasingly embedded in a majority of these real-time systems to monitor and control their operations. These computer systems are called embedded systems, real-time computer systems, or simply real-time systems. Unlike conventional, non-real-time computer systems, real-time computer systems are closely coupled with the environment being monitored and controlled. Examples of real-time systems include computerized versions of the braking controller and the vital-sign monitor, the new generation of airplane and spacecraft avionics, the planned Space Station control software, high-performance network and telephone switching systems, multimedia tools, virtual reality systems, robotic controllers, battery-powered instruments, wireless communication devices (such as cellular phones and PDAs), astronomical telescopes with adaptive-optics systems, and many safety-critical industrial applications. These embedded systems must satisfy stringent timing and reliability constraints in addition to functional correctness requirements.

Figure 1.1 shows a model of a real-time system. A real-time system has a decision component that interacts with the external environment (in which the decision

1

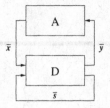

Figure 1.1   A real-time system.

component is embedded) by taking sensor readings and computing control decisions based on sensor readings and stored state information. We can characterize this real-time system model with seven components:

1. A sensor vector $\bar{x} \in X$,
2. A decision vector $\bar{y} \in Y$,
3. A system state vector $\bar{s} \in S$,
4. A set of environmental constraints A,
5. A decision map D, $D : S \times X \to S \times Y$,
6. A set of timing constraints T, and
7. A set of integrity constraints I.

In this model, X is the space of sensor input values, Y is the space of decision values, and S is the space of system state values. Let $\bar{x}(t)$ denote the value of the sensor input $\bar{x}$ at time t, and so on.

The environmental constraints A are relations over X, Y, S and are assertions about the effect of a control decision on the external world which in turn affect future sensor input values. Environmental constraints are usually imposed by the physical environment in which the real-time decision system functions.

The decision map D relates $\bar{y}(t + 1)$, $\bar{s}(t + 1)$ to $\bar{x}(t)$, $\bar{s}(t)$, that is, given the current system state and sensor input, D determines the next decisions and system state values. Decision maps can be implemented by computer hardware and software components. A decision system need not be centralized, and may consist of a network of coordinating, distributed monitoring/decision-making components.

The decisions specified by D must conform to a set of integrity (safety) constraints I. Integrity constraints are relations over X, S, Y and are assertions that the decision map D must satisfy to ensure safe operation of the physical system under control. The implementation of the decision map D is subject to a set of timing constraints T, which are assertions about how fast the map D has to be performed. In addition, timing constraints exist on the environment (external to the decision system) that must be satisfied for the correct functioning of this environment.

There are two ways to ensure system safety and reliability. One way is to employ engineering (both software and hardware) techniques, such as structured programming principles, to minimize implementation errors and then utilize testing techniques to uncover errors in the implementation. The other way is to use formal analysis and verification techniques to ensure that the implemented system satisfy the required safety constraints under all conditions given a set of assumptions. In a real-time system, we need to not only satisfy stringent timing requirements but also guard against an imperfect execution environment, which may violate pre-runtime design assumptions. The first approach can only increase the confidence level we have on the correctness of the system because testing cannot guarantee that the system is error-free [Dahl, Dijkstra, and Hoare, 1972]. The second approach can guarantee that a verified system always satisfies the checked safety properties, and is the focus of this text.

However, state-of-the-art techniques, which have been demonstrated in pedagogic systems, are often difficult to understand and to apply to realistic systems. Furthermore, it is often difficult to determine how practical a proposed technique is from the large number of mathematical notations used. The objective of this book is to provide a more readable introduction to formal techniques that are practical for actual use. These theoretical foundations are followed by practical exercises in employing these advanced techniques to build, analyze, and verify different modules of real-time systems. Available specification analysis and verification tools are also described to help design and analyze real-time systems.

1.1 WHAT IS TIME?

Time is an essential concept in real-time systems, and keeping time using accurate clocks is thus required to ensure the correct operations of these systems. The master source for time is Paris's International Atomic Time (TAI), an average of several laboratory atomic clocks in the world. Since the earth's rotational rate slows by a few milliseconds each day, another master time source called the Universal Coordinated Time (UTC) performs leap corrections to the time provided by TAI while maintaining TAI's accuracy, making the time length of every natural solar day constant [Allan, Ashby, and Hodge, 1998].

UTC is used as the world time, and UTC time signals are sent from the National Institute of Standards and Technology (NIST) radio station, WWVB, in Fort Collins, Colorado, and other UTC radio stations to specialized receivers. Selected radios, receiver-clocks, some phone-answering systems, and even some VCRs have the capability to receive these UTC signals to maintain accurate clocks. Some computers have receivers to receive these UTC signals and thus the time provided by their internal clocks is as accurate as UTC. Note that depending on the location of the receiver-clock, there is a delay in receiving the UTC signal. For instance, it takes around 5 ms for WWVB's UTC signal to get from Fort Collins to a receiver-clock in my Real-Time Systems Laboratory in Houston, Texas.

For computers whose time is kept by quartz-based computer clocks, we must ensure that these clocks are periodically synchronized such that they maintain a bounded drift relative to UTC. Software or logical clocks can be derived from computer clocks [Lamport, 1978]. In this text, when we refer to wall clock or absolute time, we refer to the standard time provided by a bounded-drift computer clock or UTC. Thus there is a mapping *Clock:* real time → standard clock time.

1.2 SIMULATION

Simulation consists of constructing a model of an existing system to be studied or a system to be built and then executing actions allowed in this model. The model can be a physical entity like a scale clay model of an airplane or a computer representation. A computer model is often less costly than a physical model and can represent a non-computer entity such as an airplane or its components as well as a computer entity such as a computer system or a program. A computer model also can represent a system with both computer and non-computer components like an automobile with embedded computer systems to control its transmission and brakes.

This physical or computer model is called the *simulator* of the actual system. A simulator can carry out simulated executions of the simulated system and display the outcomes of these executions. A physical model of an airplane in a wind tunnel shows the aerodynamics of the simulated plane that is close to the actual plane. A software simulator on a single-processor system shows the performance of a network of personal computer workstations under a heavy network traffic condition. A software simulator can also be designed to simulate the behavior of an automobile crashing into a concrete barrier, showing its effects on the automobile's simulated occupants. Sometimes a simulator refers to a tool that can be programmed or directed without programming to mimic the events and actions in different systems. This simulator can be either computer-based (software, hardware, or both) or non-computer-based.

Simulation is an inexpensive way to study the behavior of the simulated system and to study different ways to implement the actual system. If we detect behavior or events that are inconsistent with the specification and safety assertions, we can revise the model and thus the actual system to be built. In the case in which we consider several models as possible ways to implement the actual system, we can select the model that best satisfies the specification and safety assertions through the simulation and then implement it as the actual system.

Different levels of details of the actual system, also called the *target system*, can be modeled and its events simulated by a simulator. This makes it possible to study and observe only the relevant parts of the target system. For example, when designing and simulating the cockpit of an aircraft, we can restrict attention to that particular component by simulating only the cockpit with inputs and outputs to the other aircraft components, without simulating the behavior of the entire aircraft. In the design and simulation of a real-time multimedia communication system, we can simulate the traffic pattern between workstations but need not simulate the low-level signal processing involved in the coding and transmission processes if the performance is not affected by these low-level processes. The ability to simulate a target system at different detail levels or only a subset of its components reduces the resources needed for the simulation and decreases the complexity of the analysis of the simulation.

There are several simulation techniques in use, such as real-time-event simulation and discrete-event simulation. A real-time-event simulator like a physical scale model of an automobile performs its actions in real-time and the observable events are recorded in real-time. An example is the crash testing of the physical model of an automobile. Such a simulator requires recording instruments capable of recording events in real-time. When the physical model is actually an implemented target system, this is no longer a simulation but rather a *testing* of the actual system, as discussed below.

A discrete-event simulator, on the other hand, uses a logical clock(s) and is usually software-based. The variety of systems that can be represented by such a simulator is not limited by the speed at which the hardware executes the simulator since the simulated actions and events do not occur in real-time. Rather, they take place according to the speed of the simulator hardware and the instructions in the simulator program. Examples include the simulation of a network of computers in a single-processor system or the simulation of a faster microprocessor in a slower processor as in the design of popular next-generation personal computer microprocessors. Here, the appropriate actions and events "occur" at a particular logical time (representing real-time in the target system) depending on previous and current simulated actions and events. Entire books have been written that are devoted to discrete-event simulation.

Variations of simulation include the hybrid simulation approach, in which the simulator works with a partial implementation of the target system by acting as the non-implemented part. As in the case of using only a simulator, the simulator here makes it possible to predict the performance and behavior of the target system once it is completely implemented.

One main disadvantage of simulation as a technique to analyze and verify real-time systems and other systems is that it is not able to model all possible event-action sequences in the target system where the domain of possible sequences of observable events is infinite. Even when this domain is finite, the number of possible events is so large that the most powerful computer resources or physical instruments may not be able to trace through all possible sequences of events in the simulated target system.

1.3 TESTING

Testing is perhaps the oldest technique for detecting errors or problems in implemented software, hardware, or non-computer systems. It consists of executing or operating (in the case of a non-computer system) the system to be tested using a finite set of inputs and then checking to see if the corresponding outputs or behavior are correct with respect to the specifications. To test a real-time system, the values as well as the timing of the inputs are important. Similarly, both the output values and the time at which they are produced must be checked for correctness.

Many approaches have been developed for testing software, hardware, and non-computer systems. The simplest technique is of course to perform an exhaustive test run of the system with every possible input and then to check if the corresponding output is correct. This approach is not practical except for small systems with limited input space. For larger systems, the time needed to test is prohibitively long. For systems with an infinite number of possible inputs, this approach is of course not viable. Since relatively little training is required on the part of the testing personnel, testing has been and will continue to be used extensively in industry.

There are three common techniques for software testing in the current state-of-the-practice: functional testing, structural testing, and code reading. *Functional testing* uses a "black box" approach in which the programmer creates test data from the program specification using one or a combination of techniques such as boundary value analysis and equivalence partitioning. Then the program is executed using these test data as input, and the corresponding program behavior and output are compared with those described in the program specification. If the program behavior or output deviates from the specification, the programmer attempts to identify the erroneous part of the program and correct it.

Partition testing is a popular way to select test data, in which the program's input domain is divided into subsets called subdomains, and one or more representatives from each subdomain are chosen as test input. Random testing is a degenerate form of partition testing since it has only one subdomain, the entire program.

Structural testing is a "white box" approach in which the programmer examines the source code of the program and then creates test data for program execution based on the percentage of the program's statements executed.

Code reading by *stepwise abstraction* requires the programmer to identify major modules in the program, determine their functions, and compose these functions to determine a function for the whole program. The programmer then compares this derived function with the intended function as described by the program specification.

1.4 VERIFICATION

The previous two techniques are good for revealing errors in the simulated or actual system but usually cannot guarantee that the system satisfy a set of requirements. To apply formal verification techniques to a real-time system, we must first specify the system requirements and then the system to be implemented using an unambiguous specification language. Since the applications expert (programmer or system designer) is usually not knowledgeable in formal methods, a formal methods expert collaborates with the applications expert to write the requirements and system specification. Both experts work closely to ensure that the specifications reflect the real requirements and system's behavior.

Once these specifications are written, the formal methods expert can verify whether the system specification satisfy the specified requirements using his/her favorite formal verification methods and tools. These formal methods and tools can show the satisfaction of all requirements or the failure to satisfy certain requirements. They may also pinpoint areas for further improvement in terms of efficiency. These results are communicated to the applications expert who can then revise the system specification or even the system requirements. The formal specifications are next revised to reflect these changes and can be analyzed again by the formal methods expert. These steps are repeated until both experts are happy with the fact that the specified system satisfies the specified requirements.

1.5 RUN-TIME MONITORING

Despite the use of the best state-of-the-art techniques for static or pre-run-time analysis and verification of a real-time system, there will often be system behavior that was not anticipated. This unexpected behavior may be caused by events and actions not modeled by the static analysis tools or may be the result of making simplified assumptions about the real-time system. Therefore, it is necessary to monitor the execution of the real-time system at run-time and to make appropriate adjustments in response to a monitored behavior that violates specified safety and progress constraints. Even if the real-time system meets the specified safety and progress constraints at run-time, monitoring may provide information that can improve the performance and reliability of the monitored system.

Here, the monitored real-time system is the target system and its components, such as programs, are called target programs. The monitoring system is the system used to monitor and record the behavior of the target system. It consists of instrumentation programs, instrumentation hardware, and other monitoring modules. Basically, the monitoring system records the behavior of interest of the target system and produces event traces. These event traces may be used on-line as a feedback to the real-time controller or may be analyzed off-line to see if the target system needs to be fine-tuned.

There are two broad types of monitoring techniques: intrusive and nonintrusive. *Intrusive monitoring* uses the resources of the target system to record its behavior and thus may alter the actual behavior of the target system. A simple example is the insertion of print statements in a target program to display the values of the program variables. Another example is the extra statements inserted in the programs of computing nodes to record their states and the exchanges of these state variables in taking a snapshot of a distributed real-time system. A non-computer example is the addition of speed and impact-force sensing instruments in an automobile to record its performance. In all these monitoring cases, the monitoring system's use of the target system's resources (processor, memory, electricity, fuel) may change the target system's behavior. The degree of intrusion varies in different monitoring systems, and different target systems may accept monitoring systems with different degrees of intrusion or interference.

Nonintrusive monitoring, however, does not affect the timing and ordering of events of the monitored target system. This is especially important in the monitoring of real-time systems where both timing and ordering of events are critical to the safety of the real-time systems. An example is the use of additional processor(s) to run monitoring programs used to record the target system's behavior in a real-time environment.

The availability of monitoring systems does not mean that we can relax on the task of stringent pre-run-time analysis and verification of the target system. Rather, monitoring should serve as an additional guarantee on the safety and reliability of the safety-critical target real-time system.

1.6   USEFUL RESOURCES

A comprehensive listing of available formal methods for the specification, analysis, and verification of both untimed and real-time systems can be found in:

`http://www.afm.sbu.ac.uk`

The website of the IEEE Computer Society's Technical Committee on Real-Time Systems (IEEE-CS TC-RTS), which contains useful information on resources, conferences, and publications in all aspects of real-time systems, is:

`http://cs-www.bu.edu:80/pub/ieee-rts/`

Major conference proceedings in the field of real-time systems include:

- Proceedings of the Annual IEEE-CS Real-Time Systems Symposium (RTSS)
- Proceedings of the Annual IEEE-CS Real-Time Technology and Application Symposium (RTAS)
- Proceedings of the Annual Euromicro Conference on Real-Time Systems (ECRTS)
- Proceedings of the ACM SIGPLAN Workshop on Languages, Compilers, and Tools for Embedded Systems
- Proceedings of the International Conference on Real-Time Computing Systems and Applications (RTCSA)

Major conference proceedings in the field of formal verification include:

- Proceedings of the Conference on Computer Aided Verification (CAV)
- Proceedings of the Conference on Automated Deduction (CADE)
- Proceedings of the Formal Methods Europe (FME) Conference
- Proceedings of the IEEE Symposium on Logic in Computer Science (LICS)
- Proceedings of the Conference on Rewriting Techniques and Applications (RTA)
- Proceedings of the Conference on Automated Reasoning with Analytic Tableaux and Related Methods (TABLEAUX)
- Proceedings of the International Conference on Logic Programming (ICLP)
- Proceedings of the Conference on Formal Techniques for Networked and Distributed Systems (FORTE)

Major journals that publish articles on real-time systems include:

- *Journal of Real-Time Systems* (JRTS)
- *IEEE Transactions on Computers* (TC)
- *IEEE Transactions on Software Engineering* (TSE)
- *IEEE Transactions on Parallel and Distributed Systems* (TPDS)

Practice and products-oriented magazines that publish articles on embedded and real-time systems include:

- *Dedicated Systems*
- *Embedded Developers Journal*
- *Embedded Systems Programming*
- *Embedded Linux Journal*
- *Embedded Edge*
- *Microsoft Journal for Developers MSDN*
- *IEEE Software*

CHAPTER 2

ANALYSIS AND VERIFICATION OF NON-REAL-TIME SYSTEMS

A great collection of techniques and tools are available for the reasoning, analysis, and verification of non-real-time systems. This chapter explores the basic foundations of these techniques that include symbolic logic, automata, formal languages, and state transition systems. Many analysis and verification techniques for real-time systems are based on these untimed approaches, as we will see in later chapters. Here, we give a condensed introduction to some of these untimed approaches without providing mathematically involved proofs, and describe their applications to untimed versions of several simple real-time systems.

2.1 SYMBOLIC LOGIC

Symbolic logic is a collection of languages that use symbols to represent facts, events, and actions, and provide rules to symbolize reasoning. Given the specification of a system and a collection of desirable properties, both written in logic formulas, we can attempt to prove that these desirable properties are logical consequences of the specification. In this section, we introduce the *propositional logic* (also called *propositional calculus*, *zero-order logic*, *digital logic*, or *Boolean logic*, the most simple symbolic logic), the *predicate logic* (also called *predicate calculus* or *first-order logic*), and several proof techniques.

2.1.1 Propositional Logic

Using propositional logic, we can write declarative sentences called propositions that can be either *true* (denoted by T) or *false* (denoted by F) but not both. We use an uppercase letter or a string of uppercase letters to denote a proposition.

Example
  P denotes "car brake pedal is pressed"
  Q denotes "car stops within five seconds"
  R denotes "car avoids a collision"

These symbols P, Q, and R, used to represent propositions, are called *atomic formulas*, or simply *atoms*. To express more complex propositions such as the following compound proposition, we use logical connectives such as $\rightarrow$ (*if-then* or *imply*):

"*if* car brake pedal is pressed, *then* car stops within five seconds."

This compound proposition is expressed in propositional logic as:

$$P \rightarrow Q$$

Similarly, the following statement

"*if* car stops within five seconds, *then* car avoids a collision"

is expressed as:

$$Q \rightarrow R$$

Given these two propositions, we can easily show that $P \rightarrow R$, that is,

"*if* car brake pedal is pressed, *then* car avoids a collision."

We can combine propositions and logical connectives to form complicated formulas. A *well-formed formula* is either a proposition or a compound proposition formed accoding to the following rules.

Well-Formed Formulas: Well-formed formulas in propositional logic are defined recursively as follows:

1. An atom is a formula.
2. If F is a formula, then $(\neg F)$ is a formula, where $\neg$ is the *not* operator.
3. If F and G are formulas, then $(F \wedge G)$, $(F \vee G)$, $(F \rightarrow G)$, and $(F \leftrightarrow G)$ are formulas. ($\wedge$ is the *and* operator, $\vee$ is the *or* operator, $\leftrightarrow$ stands for *if and only if* or *iff*.)
4. All formulas are generated using the above rules.

Some parentheses in a formula can be omitted for conciseness if there is no ambiguity.

P	Q	$P \to Q$
F	F	T
F	T	T
T	F	F
T	T	T

Figure 2.1   Truth table of $P \to R$.

P	Q	$\neg P$	$P \vee Q$	$P \wedge Q$	$P \to Q$	$P \leftrightarrow Q$
F	F	T	F	F	T	T
F	T	T	T	F	T	F
T	F	F	T	F	F	F
T	T	F	T	T	T	T

Figure 2.2   Truth table for simple formulas.

Interpretation: An *interpretation* of a propositional formula G is an assignment of truth values to the atoms $A_1, \dots, A_n$ in G in which every A_i is assigned either T or F, but not both.

Then a formula G is said to be true in an interpretation iff G is evaluated to be true in the interpretation; otherwise, G is said to be false in the interpretation. A *truth table* displays the the truth values of a formula G for all possible interpretations of G. For a formula G with n distinct atoms, there will be 2^n distinct interpretations for G. Figure 2.1 shows the truth table for $P \to R$. Figure 2.2 shows the truth table for several simple formulas.

A formula is *valid* iff it is true under all its interpretations. A formula is *invalid* iff it is not valid. A formula is *unsatisfiable* (*inconsistent*) iff it is false under all its interpretations. A formula is *satisfiable* (*consistent*) iff it is not unsatisfiable.

A *literal* is an atomic formula or the negation of an atomic formula. A formula is in *conjunctive normal form* (CNF) if it is a conjunction of disjunction of literals and can be written as

$$(\wedge_{i=1}^{n} (\vee_{j=1}^{m_i} L_{i,j}))$$

where $n \geq 1$; $m_1, \dots, m_n \geq 1$; and each $L_{i,j}$ is a literal.

A formula is in *disjunctive normal form* (DNF) if it is a disjunction of conjunction of literals and can be written as

$$(\vee_{i=1}^{n} (\wedge_{j=1}^{m_i} L_{i,j}))$$

where $n \geq 1$; $m_1, \dots, m_n \geq 1$; and each $L_{i,j}$ is a literal. These two normal forms make it easier for proof procedures to manipulate and analyze logic formulas. Fig-

Idempotency	$(P \lor P) = P$
	$(P \land P) = P$
Implication	$P \to Q = \neg P \lor Q$
Commutativity	$(P \lor Q) = (Q \lor P)$
	$(P \land Q) = (Q \land P)$
	$(P \leftrightarrow Q) = (Q \leftrightarrow P)$
Associativity	$((P \lor Q) \lor R) = (P \lor (Q \lor R))$
	$((P \land Q) \land R) = (P \land (Q \land R))$
Absorption	$(P \lor (P \land Q)) = P$
	$(P \land (P \lor Q)) = P$
Distributivity	$(P \lor (Q \land R)) = ((P \lor Q) \land (P \lor R))$
	$(P \land (Q \lor R)) = ((P \land Q) \lor (P \land R))$
Double Negation	$\neg\neg P = P$
DeMorgan	$\neg(P \lor Q) = (\neg P \land \neg Q)$
	$\neg(P \land Q) = (\neg P \lor \neg Q)$
Tautology	$(P \lor Q) = P$ if P is a tautology (true)
	$(P \land Q) = Q$ if P is a tautology (true)
Unsatisfiability	$(P \lor Q) = Q$ if P is unsatisfiable (false)
	$(P \land Q) = P$ if P is unsatisfiable (false)

Figure 2.3   Equivalent formulas.

ure 2.3 lists the laws stating which formulas are equivalent. These laws are useful for transforming and manipulating formulas.

To show that a statement logically follows from another statement, we first define the meaning of logical consequence. A formula G is a *logical consequence* of formulas $F_1, \ldots, F_n$ (i.e., $(F_1 \land \ldots \land F_n \to G)$) iff for every interpretation in which $F_1 \land \ldots \land F_n$ is true, G is also true. Then $(F_1 \land \ldots \land F_n \to G)$ is a valid formula.

We can use the *resolution principle* to establish logical consequences and this principle can be stated as follows. First, we define a *clause* as a finite set, possibly empty, of literals. A clause can also be defined as a finite disjunction of zero or more literals. The empty clause is indicated by a □. A *clause set* is a set of clauses. A *unit clause* contains one literal.

Resolution Principle: For any two clauses C_1 and C_2, if there is a literal L_1 in C_1 and there is a literal L_2 in C_2 such that $L_1 \land L_2$ is false, then the *resolvent* of C_1 and C_2 is the clause consisting of the disjunction of the remaining clauses in C_1 and C_2 after removing L_1 and L_2 from C_1 and C_2, respectively.

It can be easily proved that a resolvent of two clauses is a logical consequence of these two clauses.

Example. Suppose we have two clauses C_1 and C_2:

$$C_1 : P \vee$$
$$C_2 : \neg Q \vee R \vee \neg S$$

Because literal Q in C_1 and $\neg Q$ in C_2 are complementary (their conjunction is false), we remove these two literals from their respective clauses and construct the resolvent by forming the disjunction of the remaining clauses: $P \vee R \vee \neg S$.

The resolvent, if it exists, of two unit clauses is the empty clause $\square$. If a set S of clauses is unsatisfiable, then we can use the resolution principle to generate $\square$ from S.

Example. Consider the following simplified automatic climate control (air conditioning and heating system. The room temperature can be in one of the following three ranges:

comfortable: thermostat sensor detects the room temperature is within the comfort range, that is, between 68 and 78 degrees F.

hot: thermostat sensor detects the room temperature is above 78 degrees F.

cold: thermostat sensor detects the room temperature is below 68 degrees F.

Let

$$H = \text{the room temperature is hot}$$
$$C = \text{the room temperature is cold}$$
$$M = \text{the room temperature is comfortable}$$
$$A = \text{the air conditioner is on}$$
$$G = \text{the heater is on.}$$

We now specify the climate control system in English. If the room temperature is hot, then the air conditioner is on. If the room temperature is cold, then the heater is on. If the room temperature is neither hot nor cold, then the room temperature is comfortable. Can we prove the following? If neither the air conditioner nor the heater is on, then the room temperature is comfortable.

This English specification of the climate control system and the requirement to be proved can be expressed in propositional logic formulas as follows.

$$F_1 = H \rightarrow A$$
$$F_2 = C \rightarrow G$$
$$F_3 = \neg(H \vee C) \rightarrow M$$

Prove: $F_4 = \neg(A \vee G) \rightarrow M$.

We first prove this proposition with the truth-table technique, shown in Figure 2.4. This technique exhaustively checks every interpretation of the formula F_4 to de-

H	A	C	G	M	F_1	F_2	F_3	F_4	$(F_1 \wedge F_2 \wedge F_3) \to F_4$
F	F	F	F	F	T	T	F	F	T
F	F	F	F	T	T	T	F	F	T
F	F	F	T	F	T	T	F	F	T
F	F	F	T	T	T	T	F	F	T
F	F	F	F	F	T	T	F	F	T
F	F	F	F	F	T	T	F	F	T
F	F	F	T	F	T	T	F	F	T
F	F	F	T	T	T	T	F	F	T
F	T	F	F	F	T	T	F	F	T
F	T	F	F	T	T	T	F	F	T
F	T	F	T	F	T	T	F	F	T
F	T	F	T	T	T	T	F	F	T
F	T	F	F	F	T	T	F	F	T
F	T	F	F	T	T	T	F	F	T
F	T	F	T	F	T	T	F	F	T
F	T	F	T	T	T	T	F	F	T
T	F	F	F	F	T	T	F	F	T
T	F	F	F	T	T	T	F	F	T
T	F	F	T	F	T	T	F	F	T
T	F	F	T	T	T	T	F	F	T
T	F	T	F	F	T	T	F	F	T
T	F	T	F	T	T	T	F	F	T
T	F	T	T	F	T	T	F	F	T
T	F	T	T	T	T	T	F	F	T
T	T	F	F	F	T	T	F	F	T
T	T	F	F	T	T	T	F	F	T
T	T	F	T	F	T	T	F	F	T
T	T	F	T	T	T	T	F	F	T
T	T	T	F	F	T	T	F	F	T
T	T	T	F	T	T	T	F	F	T
T	T	T	T	F	T	T	F	F	T
T	T	T	T	T	T	T	F	F	T

Figure 2.4 Truth table for proving F_4.

termine if it evaluates to T. The truth table shows that every interpretation of F_4 evaluates to T, thus F_4 is valid.

Next we prove this proposition using the equivalency laws.

Prove: $\neg(A \vee G) \rightarrow M$. The premise is $F_1 \wedge F_2 \wedge F_3$, which is

$$(H \rightarrow A) \wedge (C \rightarrow G) \wedge (\neg(H \vee C) \rightarrow M)$$
$$= (\neg H \vee A) \wedge (\neg C \vee G) \wedge (\neg\neg(H \vee C) \vee M) \quad \text{(Implication)}$$
$$= (\neg H \vee A) \wedge (\neg C \vee G) \wedge ((H \vee C) \vee M) \quad \text{(Double negation)}$$
$$= A \vee G \vee M \quad \text{(Resolution twice)}$$
$$= (A \vee G) \vee M \quad \text{(Associativity)}$$
$$= \neg(A \vee G) \rightarrow M \quad \text{(Implication)}$$

Therefore, we have shown that the following is valid: If neither the air conditioner nor the heater is on, then the room temperature is comfortable. However, we cannot conclude the following from the specification: If the room temperature is comfortable, then neither the air conditioner nor the heater is on, that is, $M \rightarrow \neg(A \vee G)$.

Proving Satisfiability Using the Resolution Procedure   Now we describe in detail the approach using the resolution principle to establish validity. Once a propositional formula is transformed into conjunctive normal form, the order of the subformulas joined by $\wedge$ and $\vee$ can be changed without altering the meaning of the formula.

Two clause sets are *equivalent* if any truth-value assignment assigns the same truth value to both. Let S be a clause set. We define

$$R(S) = S \cup \{T : T \text{ is a resolvent of two clauses in } S\}.$$

The procedure using resolution to determine the satisfiability of individual propositional formulas consists of the steps shown in Figure 2.5.

This algorithm is an exhaustive approach to resolution since it forms all possible resolvents even though only a subset of these resolvents is needed to derive the empty

---

Resolution procedure:

(1) Transform the given formula into conjunctive normal form (CNF).
(2) Write this CNF formula in clausal form: a set S of clauses each of which is a disjunction of literals.
(3) Compute $R(S)$, $R^2(S)$, ... until $R^i(S) = R^{i+1}(S)$ for some i.
(4) If $\square \in R^i(S)$, then S is unsatisfiable; else S is satisfiable.

Figure 2.5   Resolution procedure for propositional logic.

clause. Hence, its complexity is exponential in the size of the original size of the clause set S. To attempt to form only the needed resolvents, we define the concept of deduction. Given a clause set S, a *deduction* from S consists of a sequence of clauses $C_1, \ldots, C_n$ where either each $C_i \in S$ or for some $a, b < i$, C_i is a resolvent of C_a and C_b.

Resolution Theorem: A clause set S is unsatisfiable iff there is a deduction of the empty clause $\square$ from S.

Example. Consider again the simplified automatic climate control example. Now we prove $(F_1 \wedge F_2 \wedge F_3) \rightarrow F_4$ using this resolution theorem. We show that the negation of this formula is unsatisfiable. The negated formula is

$$\neg((F_1 \wedge F_2 \wedge F_3) \rightarrow F_4)$$
$$= \neg(\neg(F_1 \wedge F_2 \wedge F_3) \vee F_4)$$
$$= (F_1 \wedge F_2 \wedge F_3) \wedge \neg F_4.$$

Replacing F_1, F_2, F_3, F_4 with the original symbols, we convert this formula into CNF:

$$(\neg H \vee A) \wedge (\neg C \vee G) \wedge (H \vee C \vee M) \wedge \neg A \wedge \neg G \wedge \neg M.$$

Then we convert this CNF formula into clausal form:

$$S = \{\{\neg H, A\}, \{\neg C, G\}, \{H, C, M\}, \{\neg A\}, \{\neg G\}, \{\neg M\}\}.$$

We are ready to derive a deduction of $\square$ from S:

$$C_1 = \{\neg H, A\} \text{ member of } S$$
$$C_2 = \{\neg C, G\} \text{ member of } S$$
$$C_3 = \{H, C, M\} \text{ member of } S$$
$$C_4 = \{\neg A\} \text{ member of } S$$
$$C_5 = \{\neg G\} \text{ member of } S$$
$$C_6 = \{\neg M\} \text{ member of } S$$
$$C_7 = \{\neg H\} \text{ resolvent of } C_1 \text{ and } C_2$$
$$C_8 = \{\neg C\} \text{ resolvent of } C_3 \text{ and } C_4$$
$$C_9 = \{H, C\} \text{ resolvent of } C_5 \text{ and } C_6$$
$$C_{10} = \{H\} \text{ resolvent of } C_8 \text{ and } C_9$$
$$C_{11} = \square \text{ resolvent of } C_7 \text{ and } C_{10}.$$

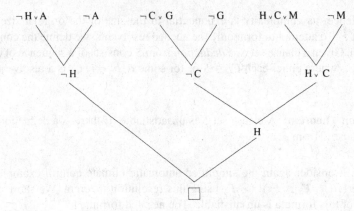

Figure 2.6   Deduction tree 1.

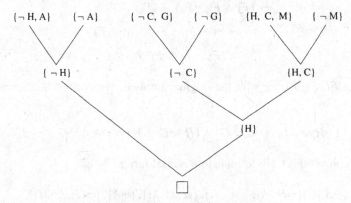

Figure 2.7   Deduction tree 2.

Therefore, the clause set is unsatisfiable. Hence the original (unnegated) formula is valid. Figures 2.6 and 2.7 show two versions of a *deduction tree* corresponding to this deduction.

This resolution theorem forms the basis of most software tools for determining satisfiability of propositional logic formulas. However, the complexity of these tools remains exponential in the original size of the clause set. Chapter 4 presents more efficient representations of boolean formulas using binary decision diagrams (BDDs) that allow faster manipulation of formulas in a number of practical cases. Chapter 6 discusses heuristics for reordering clauses in the decision tree to reduce the search time for determining unsatisfiability.

2.1.2 Predicate Logic

Propositional logic can express simple ideas with no quantitative notions or qualifications, and is also good enough for describing digital logic circuits. For more complex ideas, propositional logic is not sufficient, as shown in the following example.

Example. Consider the following statements:

Every time the car brake pedal is pressed by the driver of the car, the car stops within 8 seconds. Because Mercedes Benz E320 is a car, whenever the driver of the Mercedes Benz E320 presses its brake pedal, the Mercedes Benz E320 stops within 8 seconds.

P denotes "Every time the car brake pedal is pressed by the driver of the car, the car stops within 8 seconds."

Q denotes "Mercedes Benz E320 is a car."

R denotes "Whenever the driver of the Mercedes Benz E320 presses its brake pedal, the Mercedes Benz E320 stops within 8 seconds."

However, R is not a logical consequence of P and Q in the framework of propositional logic.

To handle these statements, we introduce predicate logic, which has the concepts of *terms*, *predicates*, and *quantifiers*. First, we define functions and terms.

Function: A function is a mapping from a list of constants to a constant.

Terms: Terms are defined inductively as follows:

1. Every constant or variable is a term.
2. If f is an n-place function symbol and $x_1, \ldots, x_n$ are terms, then $f(x_1, \ldots, x_n)$ is a term.
3. All terms are generated using the above rules.

Next, we define predicates and atoms.

Predicate: A predicate is a mapping from a list of constants to either T or F.

Atoms or Atomic Formulas: If P is an n-place predicate symbol and $x_1, \ldots, x_n$ are terms, then $P(x_1, \ldots, x_n)$ is an atom or atomic formula.

The special symbol $\forall$ is the *universal quantifier*, and the special symbol $\exists$ is the *existential quantifier*. If x is a variable, then $\forall x$ means "*for all x*," (or "*for every x*") and $\exists x$ means "*there exists an x*." We also need to define the notions of bound and free variables and variable occurrences.

Bound and Free Variable Occurrences: Given a formula, an occurrence of a variable x is a *bound occurrence* iff the occurrence is within the scope of a quantifier over this variable or the occurrence immediately follows this quantifier, that is, x appears in a subformula of the form $(\forall x)F$ or $(\exists x)F$. Given a formula, an occurrence of a variable is a *free occurrence* iff this occurrence is not bound.

Often we omit the parentheses surrounding the quantifier and the quantified variable.

Bound and Free Variables: Given a formula, a variable is *bound* iff at least one occurrence of this variable is bound. Given a formula, a variable is *free* iff at least one occurrence of this variable is free.

Now we are ready to define formulas in predicate logic.

Well-Formed Formulas: Well-formed formulas in predicate logic are defined recursively as follows:

1. An atom is a formula.
2. If F is a formula, then $(\neg F)$ is a formula.
3. If F and G are formulas, then $(F \; op \; G)$ is a formula, where op is $\vee$, $\wedge$, $\rightarrow$, or $\leftrightarrow$.
4. If F is a formula and x is a free variable in F, then $(\forall x)F$ and $(\exists x)F$ are formulas.
5. All formulas are generated using a finite number of the above rules.

Example. Consider the above car example. Let BRAKE_STOP signify "Every time the car brake pedal is pressed by the driver of the car, the car stops within 8 seconds." We have the following predicate logic formulas:

$$(\forall x)CAR(x) \rightarrow BRAKE\_STOP(x))$$

$$CAR(MercedesBenzE320).$$

Since $(\forall x)(CAR(x) \rightarrow BRAKE\_STOP(x))$ is true for all x, replacing x by "MercedesBenzE320," we have

$$(CAR(MercedesBenzE320) \rightarrow BRAKE\_STOP(MercedesBenzE320))$$

is true.

This means that

$\neg(CAR(MercedesBenzE320) \vee BRAKE\_STOP(MercedesBenzE320))$ is true, but

$\neg(CAR(MercedesBenzE320))$ is false since $CAR(MercedesBenzE320)$ is true.

Therefore, $BRAKE\_STOP(MercedesBenzE320)$ must be true.

In propositional logic, an interpretation of a formula is an assignment of truth values to the atoms. Since a predicate-logic formula may contain variables, in order to define an interpretation, we need to specify the domain and an assignment to constants, functions symbols, and predicate symbols in the formula.

Interpretation: An interpretation of a first-order formula F is an assignment of values to each constant, functions symbol, and predicate symbol in F in a nonempty domain D according to the following rules:

1. An element in D is assigned to each constant.
2. A mapping $D^n = \{(x_1, \ldots, x_n) \mid each \ x_i \in D\}$ to D is assigned to each n-place function symbol.
3. A mapping from D^n to $\{T,F\}$ is assigned to each n-place predicate symbol.

A formula can be evaluated to true or false given an interpretation over a domain D as follows:

1. The truth values of formulas involving P and Q with logical connectives are evaluated with the table in the previous section on propositional logic.
2. $(\forall x)P$ is T if the truth value of P is evaluated to T for every element in D; else F.
3. $(\exists x)P$ is T if the truth value of P is evaluated to T for at least one element in D; else F.

Example. Suppose we have the following formulas:

$$(\forall x)IsAutomobile(x)$$

$$(\exists x)\neg IsAutomobile(x).$$

An interpretation is:

   Domain: $D = \{MercedesBenzE320, HondaAccord, FordTaurus, Boeing777\}$.

Assignment:

   $$IsAutomobile(MercedesBenzE320) = T$$

   $$IsAutomobile(HondaAccord) = T$$

   $$IsAutomobile(FordTaurus) = T$$

   $$IsAutomobile(Boeing777) = F$$

   $(\forall x)IsAutomobile(x)$ is F in this interpretation

      since $IsAutomobile(x)$ is not T for $x = Boeing777$.

   $(\exists x)\neg IsAutomobile(x)$ is T in this interpretation

      since $\neg IsAutomobile(Boeing777)$ is T.

Closed Formula: A closed formula has no free occurrences of variables.

The definitions for satisfiable formulas and valid formulas are similar to those for propositional logic.

Satisfiable and Unsatisfiable Formulas: A formula G is *satisfiable* (consistent) iff there is at least one interpretation I in which G is evaluated to T. This interpretation I is said to *satisfy* G and is a *model* of G. A formula G is *unsatisfiable* (inconsistent) iff there is no interpretation I in which G is evaluated to T.

Valid Formula: A formula G is *valid* iff every interpretation of G satisfies G.

To simplify proof procedures for first-order logic formulas, we first convert these formulas to standard forms discussed next.

Prenex Normal Forms and Skolem Standard Forms

We now present a standard form introduced in [Davis and Putnam, 1960] for first-order logic formulas using prenex normal form, conjunctive normal form, and Skolem functions. This form will make it easier to mechanically manipulate and analyze logic formulas. A first-order logic formula can be converted into prenex normal form where all quantifiers are at the left end.

Prenex Normal Form: Formally, a formula F is in prenex normal form iff it is written in the form

$$(Q_1 v_1) \cdots (Q_n v_n)(M)$$

where every $(Q_i v_i)$, $i = 1, \ldots, n$, is either $(\forall v_i)$ or $(\exists v_i)$, and M is a formula with no quantifiers. $(Q_1 v_1) \cdots (Q_n v_n)$ is the *prefix* and M is the *matrix* of F.

The matrix can be converted into a conjunctive normal form (CNF).

The CNF prenex normal form can be converted into a *Skolem standard form* by removing the existential quantifiers using *Skolem functions*. This will simplify the proof procedures since existentially quantified formulas hold only for specific values. The absence of existential quantifiers makes it trivially easy to remove the universal quantifiers as well.

Let Q_i be an existential quantifier in the prefix $(Q_1 v_1) \cdots (Q_n v_n)$, $1 \le i \le n$. If there is no universal quantifier to the left of Q_i, we replace all v_i's in the matrix M by a new constant c distinct from the other constants in M, and remove $(Q_i v_i)$ from the prefix.

If $(Q_{u_1} \cdots Q_{u_m})$, $1 \le u_1 < u_2 \cdots < u_m < i$, are universal quantifiers to the left of Q_i, we replace all v_i in M by a new m-place function $f(v_{u_1}, v_{u_2}, \ldots, v_{u_m})$ distinct from those in M and delete $(Q_i v_i)$ from the prefix. The resulting formula after removing all existential quantifiers is a Skolem standard form. The constants and functions used to replace the existential quantifiers are called *Skolem constants* and *Skolem functions*, respectively.

Example. Transform the following formula into a standard form:

$$(\exists x)(\forall y)(\forall z)(\exists u)(P(x, z, u) \lor (Q(x, y) \land \neg R(x, z))).$$

We first convert the matrix into a CNF:

$$(\exists x)(\forall y)(\forall z)(\exists u)((P(x, z, u) \lor Q(x, y)) \land (P(x, z, u) \lor \neg R(x, z))).$$

Then we replace the the existential quantifiers with Skolem constants and functions. Starting from the leftmost existential quantifier, we replace its variable x by constant a:

$$(\forall y)(\forall z)(\exists u)((P(a, z, u) \lor Q(a, y)) \land (P(a, z, u) \lor \neg R(a, z))).$$

Next we use a 2-place function $f(y, z)$ to replace the existential variable u:

$$(\forall y)(\forall z)((P(a, z, f(y, z)) \lor Q(a, y)) \land (P(a, z, f(y, z)) \lor \neg R(a, z))).$$

Proving Unsatisfiability of a Clause Set with Herbrand's Procedure We can view propositional logic as a special case of predicate logic. By treating 0-place predicate symbols as atomic formulas of the propositional logic, predicate logic formulas become propositional logic formulas with no variables, function symbols, and quantifiers. Thus propositional logic formulas can be easily converted into corresponding predicate logic formulas.

However, we cannot in general reduce predicate logic formulas to single formulas of the propositional logic. However, we can systematically reduce a predicate logic formula F to a countable set of formulas without quantifiers or variables. This collection of formulas is the *Herbrand expansion* of F, denoted by $E(F)$.

A set S of clauses is unsatisfiable iff it is false under all interpretations over all domains. Unfortunately, we cannot explore all interpretations over all domains. However, there is a special domain called the *Herbrand universe* such that S is unsatisfiable iff S is false under all the interpretations over this domain.

Herbrand Universe: The Herbrand universe of formula F is the set of terms built from the constant a and the function name f, that is, $\{a, f(a), f(f(a)), \ldots\}$. More formally, $H_0 = \{a\}$ if there is no constant in the set S of clauses; otherwise, H_0 is the set of constants in S. $H_{i+1}, i \geq 0$, is the union of H_i and the set of all terms of the form $f^n(x_1, \ldots, x_n)$, *each* $x_j \in H_i$, for all n-place functions f^n in S. H_i is the i-level constant set of S, and H_∞ is the Herbrand universe of S.

Example. $S = \{P(x) \lor Q(x), \neg R(y) \lor T(y) \lor \neg T(y)\}$.

Since there is no constant in S, $H_0 = \{a\}$. Since there is no function symbol in S, $H = H_0 = H_1 = \cdots = \{a\}$.

Ground Instance: Given a set S of clauses, a *ground instance* of a clause C is a clause obtained by substituting every variable in C by a member of the Herbrand universe H of S.

Atom Set: Let $h_1, \ldots, h_n$ be elements of H. The *atom set* of S is the set of ground atoms of the form $P^n(h_1, \ldots, h_n)$ for every n-place predicate in S.

H-Interpretation: An H-*interpretation* of a set S of clauses is one that satisfies the following conditions:

1. Every constant in S maps to itself.
2. Each n-place function symbol f is assigned a function mapping an element of H^n to an element in H, that is, a mapping from $(h_1, \ldots, h_n)$ to $f(h_1, \ldots, h_n)$.

Let the atom set A of S be $\{A_1, \ldots, A_n, \ldots\}$. An H-interpretation can be written as a set

$$I = \{e_1, \ldots, e_n, \ldots\}$$

where e_i is either A_i or $\neg A_i$, $i \geq 1$. That e_i is A_i means A_i is assigned true; false otherwise.

A set S of clauses is unsatisfiable iff S is false under all the H-interpretations of S. To systematically list all these interpretations, we use semantic trees [Robinson, 1968; Kowalski and Hayes, 1969]. The construction of a semantic tree for S, whether manually or mechanically, is the basis for proving the satisfiability of S. In fact, constructing a semantic tree for S of clauses is equivalent to finding a proof for S.

Semantic Tree: A semantic tree for a set S of clauses is a tree T in which each edge is attached with a finite set of atoms or negated atoms from S such that:

1. There are only finitely many immediate outgoing edges $e_1, \ldots, e_n$ from each node v. Suppose C_i is the conjunction of all the literals attached to edge e_i. Then the disjunction of these C_is is a valid propositional formula.
2. Suppose $I(v)$ is the union of all the sets attached to the edges of the branch of T and including v. Then $I(v)$ does not contain any complementary pair of literals (one literal is the negation of the other as in the set $\{A, \neg A\}$).

Example. Let the atom set A of S be $\{A_1, \ldots, A_n, \ldots\}$. A complete semantic tree is one in which, for every leaf node L, $I(L)$ contains either A_i or $\neg A_i$, where $i = 1, 2, \ldots$.

A node N in a semantic tree is a *failure node* if $I(N)$ falsifies a ground instance of a clause in S, and for each ancestor node N' of N, $I(N')$ does not falsify any ground instance of a clause in S.

Closed Semantic Tree: A closed semantic tree is one in which every branch ends at a failure node.

Herbrand's Theorem (Using Semantic Trees): A set S of clauses is unsatisfiable iff a corresponding finite closed semantic tree exists for every complete semantic tree of S.

Herbrand's Theorem: A set S of clauses is unsatisfiable iff a finite unsatisfiable set S' of ground instances of clauses of S exists.

Given an unsatisfiable set S, if a mechanical procedure can incrementally generate sets S_1', S_2', ... and check each S_i' for unsatisfiability, then it can find a finite number n such that S_n' is unsatisfiable.

Gilmore's computer program [Gilmore, 1960] followed this strategy of generating the S_is, replacing the variables in S by the constants in the i-level constant set H_i of S. It then used the multiplication method (for deriving the empty clause $\square$) in the propositional logic to test the unsatisfiability of each S_i' since it is a conjunction of ground clauses (with no quantifiers).

Proving Unsatisfiability of a Clause Set Using the Resolution Procedure

The above proof technique based on Herbrand's theorem has a major shortcoming in that it requires the generation of sets of ground instances of clauses, and the number of elements in these sets grows exponentially. We now present the *resolution principle* [Robinson, 1965], which can be applied to any set of clauses (whether ground or not) to test its unsatisfiability. We need several additional definitions.

Substitution: A *substitution* is a finite set of the form $\{t_1/v_1, \ldots, t_n/v_n\}$ where the v_is are distinct variables and the t_is are terms different from the v_is. Here, there are n substitution *components*. Each v_i is to be replaced by the corresponding t_i. The substitution is a ground substitution if the t_is are ground terms. Greek letters are used to denote substitutions.

Example. $\theta_1 = \{a/y\}$ is a substitution with one component. $\theta_2 = \{a/y, f(x)/x, g(f(b))/z\}$ is a substitution with three components.

Variant: A variant (also called a *copy* or *instance*), denoted $C\theta$, of a clause C is any clause obtained from C by a one-to-one replacement of variables specified by the substitution θ. In other words, a variant C can be either C itself or C with its variables renamed.

Example. Continuing the above example, let $C = (\neg(R(x) \wedge O(y)) \vee D(x, y))$. Then $C\theta_1 = \neg(R(x) \wedge O(a)) \vee D(x, a)$.

Unification Algorithm:

(1) $i := 0, \rho_i := \epsilon, C_i := C$.

(2) If $|C_i| = 1$, C is unifiable and return ρ_i as a most general unifier for C. Else, find the disagreement set D_i of C_i.

(3) If there are elements $x_i, y_i \in D_i$ such that x_i does not appear in y_i, go to step (4). Else, return "C is not unifiable."

(4) $\rho_{i+1} := \rho_i\{y_i/x_i\}, C_{i+1} := C_i\{y_i/x_i\}, i := i + 1$, go to step (2). Observe that $C_{i+1} = C\rho_{i+1}$.

Figure 2.8 Unification algorithm.

Separating Substitutions: A pair of substitutions θ_1 and θ_2 for a pair of clauses C_1 and C_2 is called *separating* if $C_1\theta_1$ is a variant of C_1, $C_2\theta_2$ is a variant of C_2, and $C_1\theta_1$ and $C_2\theta_2$ have no common variable.

Unifier: A substitution θ is a *unifier* for a set $C = \{C_1, \ldots, C_n\}$ of expressions iff $C_1\theta = \cdots = C_n\theta$. A set C is *unifiable* if it has a unifier. A unifier for set C is a *most general unifier* (MGU) iff there is a substitution λ such that $\rho = \theta \circ \lambda$ for every unifier ρ for set C.

Example. Let $S = \{P(a, x, z), P(y, f(b), g(c))\}$. Since the substitution $\theta = \{a/y, f(b)/x, g(c)/z\}$ is a unifier for S, S is unifiable.

Unification Theorem: Any clause or set of expressions has a most general unifier.

Now we are ready to describe an algorithm for finding a most general unifier for a finite set C of nonempty expressions (Figure 2.8). The algorithm also determines if the set is not unifiable.

Resolvent: Let C_1 and C_2 be two clauses with no common variable and with separating substitutions θ_1 and θ_2, respectively. Let B_1 and B_2 be two nonempty subsets (literals) $B_1 \subseteq C_1$ and $B_2 \subseteq C_2$ such that $B_1\theta_1$ and $\neg B_2\theta_2$ have a most general unifier ρ. Then the clause $((C_1 - B_1) \cup (C_2 - B_2))\rho$ is the *binary resolvent* of C_1 and C_2, and the clause $((C_1 - B_1)\theta_1 \cup (C_2 - B_2)\theta_2)\rho$ is the *resolvent* of C_1 and C_2.

Given a set S of clauses, $R(S)$ contains S and all resolvents of clauses in S, that is, $R(S) = S \cup \{T : T \text{ is a resolvent of two clauses in } S\}$. For each $i \geq 0$, $R^0(S) = S$, $R^{i+1}(S) = R(R^i(S))$, and $R^*(S) = \cup\{R^i(S)|i \geq 0\}$.

Example

Let $C_1 = \neg A(x) \vee O(x)$ and $C_2 = \neg O(a)$. A resolvent of C_1 and C_2 is $\neg A(a)$. Let $C_3 = \neg R(x) \vee \neg O(a) \vee D(x, a)$ and $C_4 = R(b)$. A resolvent of C_3 and C_4 is $\neg O(a) \vee D(b, a)$.

We are ready to present the resolution theorem for predicate logic.

Resolution Theorem: A clause set S is unsatisfiable iff there is a deduction of the empty clause from S, that is, $\square \in R^*(S)$.

The resolution theorem and the unification algorithm form the basis of most computer implementations for testing the satisfiability of predicate logic formulas. Resolution is *complete*, so it always generates the empty clause $\square$ from an unsatisfiable formula (clause set).

Example. Consider the premise and the conclusion in English. The premise is: Airplanes are objects. Missiles are objects. Radars can detect objects. The conclusion is: Radars can detect airplanes or missiles. We want to prove the premise implies the conclusion.

Let $A(x)$ denote "x is an airplane," $M(x)$ denote "x is a missile," $O(x)$ denote "x is an object," $R(x)$ denote "x is a radar," $D(x, y)$ denote "x can detect y." We are ready to represent the premise and conclusion as predicate logic formulas.

Premise:

$$(\forall x)(A(x) \rightarrow O(x))$$

$$(\forall x)(M(x) \rightarrow O(x))$$

$$(\forall x)(\exists y)(R(x) \wedge O(y) \rightarrow D(x, y)).$$

Conclusion: $(\forall x)(\exists y)(R(x) \wedge (A(y) \vee M(y)) \rightarrow D(x, y))$.

Then we negate the conclusion. Next we convert these formulas into prenex normal form and then CNF.

Premise:

1. $\neg A(x) \vee O(x)$
2. $\neg M(x) \vee O(x)$
3. $\exists y(\neg(R(x) \wedge O(y)) \vee D(x, y))$
    $= \neg(R(x) \wedge O(a)) \vee D(x, a)$
    $= \neg R(x) \vee \neg O(a) \vee D(x, a)$.

Negation of conclusion:

$$\neg(\forall x)(\exists y)(R(x) \wedge (A(y) \vee M(y)) \rightarrow D(x, y))$$

$$= (\exists x)(\forall y)\neg(\neg(R(x) \wedge (A(y) \vee M(y))) \vee D(x, y))$$

$$= (\exists x)(R(x) \wedge (A(y) \vee M(y)) \vee \neg D(x, y))$$

$$= R(b) \wedge (A(y) \vee M(y)) \wedge \neg D(b, y).$$

Therefore, we have three clauses

4. $R(b)$

5. $A(y) \vee M(y)$.

We can easily convert these clauses into clause set form, but here we start the proof by resolution from these clauses.

6. $\neg D(b, y)$

7. $\neg O(a) \vee D(b, a)$ resolvent of (3) and (4)

8. $\neg O(a)$ resolvent of (6) and (7)

9. $\neg A(a)$ resolvent of (1) and (8)

10. $\neg M(a)$ resolvent of (2) and (8)

11. $M(a)$ resolvent of (5) and (9)

12. $\square$ resolvent of (10) and (11)

Thus we have proved the validity of the original conclusion.

Chapter 6 applies some of these concepts to the analysis of safety assertions in relation to specifications expressed in real-time logic (RTL). RTL is a first-order logic that allows formulas to specify absolute occurrence time of events and actions.

2.2   AUTOMATA AND LANGUAGES

An *automaton* is able to determine whether a sequence of words belongs to a specific language. This language consists of a set of words over some finite alphabet. Depending on the type of automaton used, this sequence of words may be finite or infinite. If these sequences of words correspond to sequences of events and actions, we can construct an automaton that accepts correct sequences of events and actions in a system, and thus solve the verification problem as follows.

With the introduction of more concepts, we can use an automaton to represent a process or system. More precisely, a *specification automaton* represents the desired specification of a system, and an *implementation automaton* models an implementation attempting to satisfy the given specification. Our goal is to verify that the implementation satisfies the specification. This problem can now be viewed as the *language inclusion problem* (also known as the *language containment problem*), that is, to determine whether the language accepted by the implementation automaton is a subset of the language accepted by the specification automaton.

This section introduces several classical types of automata and the languages they accept. These automata are deterministic finite automata and nondeterministic finite automata. The languages include regular languages.

2.2.1   Languages and Their Representations

First, we define the terminology for languages. An *alphabet* Σ is a finite set of symbols, which can be Roman letters, numbers, events, actions, or any object. A *string* over an alphabet is a finite sequence of symbols selected from this alphabet. An *empty string* has no symbols and is denoted by e. The set of all strings over an alphabet Σ is written as Σ^*. The *length* of a string is the number of symbols in it. To refer to identical symbols at different positions in a string, we say these are *occurrences* of the symbol, just like saying instances (or iterations) of a process in a computer system.

The *concatenation* of two strings x_1 and x_2, written as x_1x_2, is the string x_1 followed by the string x_2. A *subtstring* of a string x is a subsequence of x. A *language* is any subset of Σ^*. The *complement, union*, and *intersection* operations can be applied to languages since languages are sets. The language operation *Kleene star* (also called *closure*) of a language L, written as L^*, is the set of strings consisting of the concatenation of zero or more strings from L.

Now we describe how to use strings to represent languages. Since the set Σ^* of strings over an alphabet Σ is countably infinite, the number of possible representations of languages is countably infinite. However, the set of all possible languages over a given alphabet Σ is uncountably infinite, and thus finite representations cannot be used to represent all languages. We next focus on languages that can be represented by finite representations. A *regular expression* specifies a language by a finite string consisting of single symbols, $\emptyset$, possibly parentheses, and the symbols $\cup$ and $*$. We now define regular expressions more formally.

Regular Expressions: The regular expressions over an alphabet Σ consist of the strings over the alphabet $\Sigma \cup \{), (, \emptyset, \cup, *\}$ such that:

1. Each member of Σ and $\emptyset$ is a regular expression.
2. If α and β are regular expressions, then $(\alpha \cup \beta)$ is a regular expression.
3. If α and β are regular expressions, then $(\alpha\beta)$ is a regular expression.
4. If α is a regular expression, then α^* is a regular expression.
5. All regular expressions must satisfy the above rules.

Because every regular expression represents a language, we define a function L mapping from strings to languages such that for any regular expression α, $L(\alpha)$ is the language represented by α with the following properties.

1. For each $a \in \Sigma$, $L(a) = \{a\}$, and $L(\emptyset) = \emptyset$.
2. If α and β are regular expressions, then $L((\alpha \cup \beta)) = L(\alpha) \cup L(\beta)$.
3. If α and β are regular expressions, then $L((\alpha\beta)) = L(\alpha)L(\beta)$.
4. If α is a regular expression, then $L(\alpha^*) = L(a)^*$.

2.2.2   Finite Automata

A *deterministic finite automaton* (DFA) belongs to a special class of finite automata in which their operation is completely determined by their input as described below. A DFA can be viewed as a simple language recognition device.

An input tape (divided into squares) contains a string of symbols, with one symbol in each tape square. The finite control is the main part of the machine whose internal status can be specified as one of a finite number of distinct states. Using a movable reading head, the finite control can sense the symbol written at any position on the input tape. This reading head is initially pointing to the leftmost square of the input tape and the finite control is set to the initial state. The automaton reads one symbol from the input tape at regular intervals and the reading head moves right to the next symbol on the input tape. Then the automaton enters a new state depending on the current state and the symbol read. These steps repeat until the reading head reaches the end of the input string. If the state reached after reading the entire string is one of the specified final states, the machine is said to accept the input string. The set of strings accepted by the machine is the language accepted by this machine. We now formally define a DFA.

Deterministic Finite Automaton: A *deterministic finite automaton* A is a 5-tuple $\langle \Sigma, S, S_0, F, \delta \rangle$, in which
   Σ is a finite alphabet,
   S is a finite set of states,
   $S_0 \in S$ is the initial state,
   $F \subseteq S$ is the set of final states, and
   δ is the transition function from $S \times \Sigma$ to S.

We can represent an automaton by a tabular representation called a *transition table*. For example, the transition table shown in Figure 2.9 represents an automaton that accepts strings in $\{a, b\}^*$ with an odd number of bs. ρ is the current input symbol read. s is the current state of the automaton.

A clearer graphical representation of an automata is a *state transition diagram* (or simply *state diagram*), which is a labeled directed graph. In this graph, nodes represent states, and an edge (transition or arrow) is labeled with the symbol ρ from state s to state s' if $\delta(s, \rho) = s'$. The initial state is indicated by a $>$ or $\rightarrow$. Final states, also called fixed points, are represented by double circles. The state transition diagram for the above automaton is shown in Figure 2.10. Figure 2.11 shows the transition table of an automaton that accepts strings in $\{a, b\}^*$ with zero or an odd number of bs followed by zero or an even number of as. Figure 2.12 shows the corresponding automaton.

s	ρ	$\delta(s, \rho)$
s_0	a	s_0
s_0	b	s_1
s_1	a	s_1
s_1	b	s_0

Figure 2.9 Transition table 1.

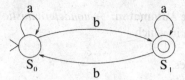

Figure 2.10   Automaton A_1.

s	ρ	$\delta(s, \rho)$
s_0	a	s_1
s_0	b	s_3
s_1	a	s_0
s_1	b	s_2
s_2	a	s_2
s_2	b	s_2
s_3	a	s_1
s_3	b	s_4
s_4	a	s_2
s_4	b	s_3

Figure 2.11   Transition table 2.

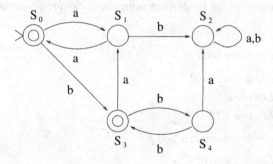

Figure 2.12   Automaton A_2.

To make finite automata more expressive, we introduce the feature of nondeter-minism. A state change in a *nondeterministic finite automaton* (NFA) may be only partially determined by the current state and input symbol, and there may be more than one next state given a current state. Every nondeterministic finite automaton can be shown to be equivalent to a deterministic finite automaton, but this correspond-ing DFA usually contains more states and transitions. Hence, nondeterministic finite automata can often simplify the description of language recognizers.

Nondeterministic Finite Automaton: A *nondeterministic finite automaton* A is a 5-tuple $\langle \Sigma, S, S_0, F, \Delta \rangle$, in which

Σ is a finite alphabet,

S is a finite set of states,

$S_0 \in S$ is the initial state,

$F \subseteq S$ is the set of final states, and

Δ, the transition relation, is a finite subset of $S \times \Sigma^* \rightarrow S$.

The class of languages accepted by finite automata is closed under concatenation, union, complementation, intersection, and Kleene star. We can prove each case by constructing a finite automaton α from one or two given finite automata. A language is *regular* iff it is accepted by a finite automaton. Let $L(\alpha)$, $L(\alpha_1)$, and $L(\alpha_2)$ be the languages accepted by automaton α, α_1, and α_2, respectively.

1. $L(\alpha) = L(\alpha_1) \circ L(\alpha_2)$.
2. $L(\alpha) = L(\alpha_1) \cup L(\alpha_2)$.
3. $\Sigma^* - L(\alpha)$ is the complementary language accepted by deterministic finite automaton α', which is the same as α but with final and nonfinal states interchanged.
4. $L(\alpha_1) \cap L(\alpha_2) = \Sigma^* - ((\Sigma^* - L(\alpha_1)) \cup (\Sigma^* - L(\alpha_2)))$.
5. $L(\alpha) = L(\alpha_1)^*$.

Several important problems can be stated for finite automata, and the solutions to some of these problems can be derived using these closure properties. These problems are:

1. Given a finite automaton α:

    (a) Is string $t \in L(\alpha)$?

    (b) Is $L(\alpha) = \emptyset$?

    (c) Is $L(\alpha) = \Sigma^*$?

2. Given two finite automata α and β:

    (a) Is $L(\alpha) \subseteq L(\beta)$?

    (b) Is $L(\alpha) = L(\beta)$?

The algorithms for solving the above problems are as follows. Suppose automaton α is deterministic. A nondeterministic finite automaton can always be transformed into a deterministic one.

Algorithm 1a executes automaton α on input t for a number of steps equal to the length of t. Because each step of α reads one input symbol, the state at which the automaton ends after length(t) steps determines whether t is accepted.

Algorithm 1b attempts to find, in the (finite) state transition diagram representing the automaton, a sequence of zero or more edges from the initial state to the final state. If there is no such path, then $L(\alpha) = \emptyset$.

Algorithm 1c checks with Algorithm 1b whether the language accepted by the complement of α is the empty set, that is, $L(\alpha') = \emptyset$, where $L(\alpha') = \Sigma^* - L(\alpha)$.

Algorithm 2a determines whether $L(\alpha) \cap (\Sigma^* - L(\beta)) = \emptyset$ using the property of closure under intersection and Algorithm 1b. If it is, then $L(\alpha) \subseteq L(\beta)$.

Algorithm 2b employs Algorithm 2a twice to determine whether $L(\alpha) \subseteq L(\beta)$ and $L(\beta) \subseteq L(\alpha)$.

Simulation is a powerful proof technique to show *preorder*, that an automaton, constructed from one or more automata of the same type, partially imitates the behavior of these other automata. For instance, we can simulate a nondeterministic finite automaton by a deterministic one. *Bisimulation* is another proof technique for checking *equivalence*, that the behaviors of two automata are identical. We describe automata-theoretic approaches for verifying the correctness of real-time systems in chapter 7.

2.2.3 Specification and Verification of Untimed Systems

We now show how an automaton can specify a physical system or a set of processes and how to determine whether a sequence of events or actions is allowed in the specified system. The alphabet of a language can consist of names of events or actions in the system to be specified. We call this alphabet the *event set* of the specified system. Then we can construct an automaton that accepts all allowable sequences (strings) of events in the specified system. This set of allowable sequences of events is the language accepted by this automaton. The following example illustrates these concepts by specifying a simplified automatic air conditioning and heating unit.

Example. The event set (the alphabet Σ) for the automatic climate-control (air conditioning and heating) automaton is {*comfort, hot, cold, turn_on_ac, turn_off_ac, turn_on_heater, turn_off_heater*}. The meanings of these events are as follows:

comfort: thermostat sensor detects the room temperature is within the comfort range, that is, between 68 and 78 degrees F.

hot: thermostat sensor detects the room temperature is above 78 degrees F.

cold: thermostat sensor detects the room temperature is below 68 degrees F.

turn_on_ac: turn on the air conditioner (cooler).

turn_off_ac: turn off the air conditioner (cooler).

turn_on_heater: turn on the heater.

turn_off_heater: turn off the heater.

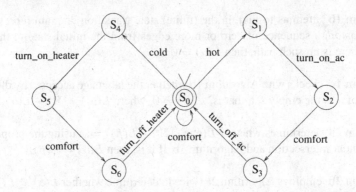

Figure 2.13   Automaton α for automatic air conditioning and heating system.

It is easy to show using Algorithm 1a whether a sequence of events is allowed in the specified system (Figure 2.13). For instance, the sequences

1a. *comfort hot turn_on_ac comfort turn_off_ac* and
1b. *cold turn_on_heater comfort turn_off_heater*

are accepted by the automaton α. Sequence (1a) states that when the sensor detects the temperature is too hot, the system activates the AC until a comfortable temperature is reached and then turns off the AC. Sequence (1b) states that when the sensor detects the temperature is too cold, the system activates the heater until a comfortable temperature is reached and then turns off the heater. However, the sequences

2a. *comfort hot turn_on_heater comfort turn_off_heater* and
2b. *cold turn_on_heater comfort*

are not accepted by the automaton α. Sequence (2a) states that when the sensor detects the temperature is too hot, the system activates the heater until a comfortable temperature is reached and then turns off the heater. Obviously, this should not be allowed since activating the heater makes the temperature even hotter. Sequence (2b) states that when the sensor detects the temperature is too cold, the system activates the heater until a comfortable temperature is reached but does not turn off the heater, which may make the temperature too hot.

Note that automata can only specify acceptable relative ordering of events in a sequence, but cannot specify absolute timing of events. In this example, we cannot specify that the event *turn_on_ac* must occur within, say, 5 seconds of the event *hot*. To handle absolute timing, we need to use *timed automata*, which will be introduced in chapter 7.

We next consider the specification and analysis of a more complex system: a smart traffic light system for a traffic intersection.

Example.   This system has four components, each specified by an automaton: Pedestrian, Sensor_Controller, Car_Traffic_Light, and Pedestrian_Traffic_Light.

When a pedestrian approaches the beginning of the pedestrian crosswalk for the traffic intersection, he/she is detected by a sensor_controller. The sensor_controller then sends a signal to the car traffic light to make it turn to red. This car traffic light turns to yellow and then to red, and in turn sends a signal to the pedestrian traffic light to make it turn on the "walk" sign. This walk sign should turn on before the pedestrian starts crossing the intersection.

Either the time interval for the walk sign to come on (after the pedestrian is detected by the sensor) is less than the time interval it takes to walk from the point the pedestrian is detected by the sensor to the start of the crosswalk, or the pedestrian waits for the walk sign to come on before starting to cross the intersection. Another sensor detects when the pedestrian finishes crossing and the sensor_controller sends a signal to the pedestrian traffic light to make it turn to "don't walk." The pedestrian traffic light then turns to don't walk and sends a signal to the car traffic light to make it turn to green.

The Pedestrian automaton communicates with the Sensor_Controller automaton with the *new_pedestrian* event to indicate a pedestrian approaches the intersec-

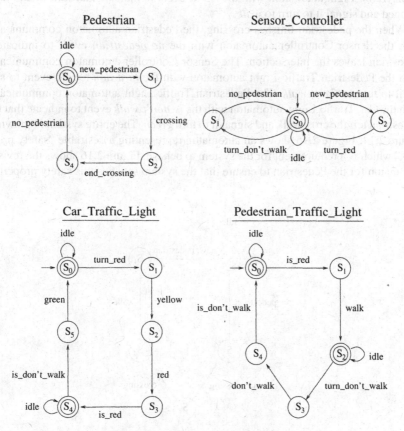

Figure 2.14 Smart traffic light system.

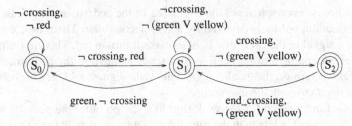

Figure 2.15 Safety property for smart traffic light system.

tion. The events *crossing* and *end_crossing* indicate the beginning and the end of the crossing by the pedestrian. The event of nothing happening is *idle*. The Sensor_Controller automaton communicates with the Car_Traffic_Light automaton with the *turn_red* event to signal it to turn *red*. Note that Car_Traffic_Light turns *yellow* before turning *red*. The Car_Traffic_Light automaton communicates with the Pedestrian_Traffic_Light automaton with the *is_red* event to indicate that cars should have stopped and signal it to turn to *walk*.

When the pedestrian finishes crossing, the Pedestrian automaton communicates with the Sensor_Controller automaton with the *no_pedestrian* event to indicate a pedestrian leaves the intersection. The Sensor_Controller automaton communicates with the Pedestrian_Traffic_Light automaton with the *turn_don't_walk* event to signal it to turn to *don't_walk*. The Pedestrian_Traffic_Light automaton communicates with the Car_Traffic_Light automaton with the *is_don't_walk* event to indicate that the pedestrian left the crosswalk and signal it to turn *green*. The entire system is shown in Figure 2.14. Figure 2.15 shows an automaton representing a desirable "safety property," which is a requirement for the system to behave. Figure 2.16 shows the revised automaton for the Pedestrian to ensure that the system satisfies this safety property.

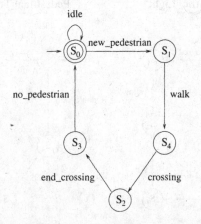

Figure 2.16 Revised pedestrian automaton.

2.3 HISTORICAL PERSPECTIVE AND RELATED WORK

For three centuries, mathematicians and philosophers have attempted to develop a general decision procedure for verifying the validity or inconsistency of a logic formula. Leibniz (1646–1716) [Davis, 1983], the co-inventor of Calculus, first tried to develop such a procedure. Then in the 1900s Peano [Peano, 1889] and in the 1920s Hilbert's group [Hilbert, 1927] again studied the problem and tried unsuccessfully to find a decision procedure. Finally, in 1936 Church [Church, 1936] and Turing [Turing, 1936] independently proved that the problem of determining the validity of first-order logic formulas is undecidable; that is, no general decision procedure for this problem exists.

Turing invented the Turing machine [Turing, 1936] in 1936 to formalize the notion of an algorithm to investigate whether the above satisfiability problem in first-order logic is solvable or not. Turing's machine has one two-way infinite tape and one head. In the same year, Post independently conceived a similar model [Post, 1936]. Mealy in 1955 [Mealy, 1955] and Moore in 1956 [Moore, 1956] were among the first to develop finite automata, also called Mealy and Moore machines, as simplifications of the Turing machine. Also in 1956, Kleene [Kleene, 1956] demonstrated that finite automata accept regular languages. Oettinger [Oettinger, 1961] introduced the pushdown automaton as another simplification of the Turing machine.

In 1930, Herbrand [Herbrand, 1930] proposed an algorithm to find an interpretation that can make a specific first-order logic formula false. A valid formula is by definition true under all interpretations. If the formula to be checked is valid, then Herbrand's algorithm will not find a falsifying interpretation and terminate in a finite number of steps. His algorithm was the first step toward automatic proof procedures or mechanical theorem proving.

In 1960, Gilmore [Gilmore, 1960] implemented Herbrand's algorithm on a computer to determine whether the negation of a formula is unsatisfiable or inconsistent. This was proof by contradiction since a formula is valid iff its negation is inconsistent. His program turned out to be quite inefficient for proving most formulas. Davis and Putnam [Davis and Putnam, 1960] improved Gilmore's computer implementation but their method still was not practical for many formulas. Robinson [Robinson, 1965] made it possible to efficiently perform mechanical theorem proving by introducing the resolution principle.

Several refinements of resolution were introduced in the following years. Slagle [Slagle, 1967] proposed semantic resolution, which unifies hyper-resolution, renamable resolution, and the set-of-support strategy. Boyer [Boyer, 1971] introduced a very efficient lock resolution. Loveland [Loveland, 1970] and Luckham [Luckham, 1970] independently developed linear resolution. Chang [Chang, 1970] showed that a special case of linear resolution called input resolution is equivalent to unit resolution.

Chang and Lee's textbook [Chang and Lee, 1973] is an excellent introduction to symbolic logic (propositional and predicate) and mechanical theorem proving. Hopcroft and Ullman's textbook [Hopcroft and Ullman, 1979] is a classic text introducing automata, languages, and the theory of computation. A simpler introduction to automata, languages, and computation is the text by Lewis and Papadimitriou [Lewis and Papadimitriou, 1981]. Their second edition [Lewis and Papadimitriou, 1998] gives a clearer introduction but omits presentations on symbolic logic.

2.4   SUMMARY

This chapter explores the basic foundations of symbolic logic, automata, formal languages, and state transition systems. These concepts can be used to reason, analyze, and verify the correctness of non-real-time systems. Many analysis and verification techniques for real-time systems are based on these untimed approaches.

Symbolic logic is a collection of languages that use symbols to represent facts, events, and actions, and provide rules to symbolize reasoning. Given the specification of a system and a collection of desirable properties, both written in logic formulas, we can attempt to prove that these desirable properties are logical consequences of the specification. Two popular logics are the propositional logic (also called propositional calculus or zero-order logic, the most simple symbolic logic) and the predicate logic (also called predicate calculus or first-order logic).

Using propositional logic, we can write declarative sentences called propositions that can be either *true* (denoted by T) or *false* (denoted by F) but not both. We use an uppercase letter or a string of uppercase letters to denote a proposition. The basic proof procedure is based on the following principle.

Resolution Principle: For any two clauses C_1 and C_2, if a literal L_1 in C_1 and a literal L_2 in C_2 such that $L_1 \wedge L_2$ is false, then the *resolvent* of C_1 and C_2 is the clause consisting of the disjunction of the remaining clauses in C_1 and C_2 after removing L_1 and L_2 from C_1 and C_2, respectively.

Propositional logic can express simple ideas with no quantitative notions or qualifications and is also good enough for describing digital (Boolean) logic circuits. For more complex ideas, propositional logic is not sufficient, so the predicate logic is needed. Predicate logic allows the use of quantifiers to specify whether a logic formula holds for at least one or for all objects or persons in a universe. The basic proof procedure is also based on the resolution principle.

Resolution Theorem: A clause set S is unsatisfiable iff there is a deduction of the empty clause from S, that is, $\square \in R^*(S)$.

The resolution theorem and the unification algorithm form the basis of most computer implementations for testing the satisfiability of predicate logic formulas. Resolution is *complete*, so it always generates the empty clause $\square$ from an unsatisfiable formula (clause set).

An automaton is able to determine whether a sequence of words belongs to a specific language. This language consists of a set of words over some finite alphabet. Depending on the type of automaton used, this sequence of words may be finite or infinite. If these sequences of words correspond to sequences of events and actions, we can construct an automaton that accepts correct sequences of events and actions in a system, and thus solve the verification problem.

With the introduction of more concepts, we can use an automaton to represent a process or system. More precisely, a *specification automaton* represents the desired specification of a system, and an *implementation automaton* models an implementation attempting to satisfy the given specification. Our goal is to verify that the implementation satisfies the specification. This problem can now be viewed as the *language inclusion problem* (also known as the *language containment problem*), that is, to determine whether the language accepted by the implementation automaton is a subset of the language accepted by the specification automaton.

A DFA belongs to a special class of finite automata in which their operation is completely determined by their input as described below. A DFA can be viewed as a simple language recognition device.

To make finite automata more expressive, we introduce the feature of nondeterminism. A state change in a *nondeterministic finite automaton* (NFA) may be only partially determined by the current state and input symbol, and there may be more than one next state given a current state. Every nondeterministic finite automaton can be shown to be equivalent to a deterministic finite automaton, but this corresponding DFA usually contains more states and transitions. Hence, nondeterministic finite automata can often simplify the description of language recognizers.

An automaton can specify a physical system or a set of processes, and how to determine whether a sequence of events or actions is allowed in the specified system. The alphabet of a language can consist of names of events or actions in the system to be specified. We call this alphabet the *event set* of the specified system. Then we can construct an automaton that accepts all allowable sequences (strings) of events in the specified system. This set of allowable sequences of events is the language accepted by this automaton.

EXERCISES

1. Specify the following English statements in prepositional logic formulas:
    (a) Traffic light system: If the car traffic light turns red, then the pedestrian traffic sign changes from "don't walk" to "walk." If the pedestrian "walk" sign turns on, pedestrians cross the street; otherwise, pedestrians wait at the sidewalk.
    (b) Gate controller: The gate to the building remains closed unless the gate controller receives an "open gate" signal from a wireless transmitter or a wired transmitter.
    (c) Pipeline valve: Valve labeled "A" is closed if and only if the pressure of the pipeline is between 20 and 50 psi (pound per square inch).
2. Consider the specification in exercise 1(a). Prove the following using equivalent formulas and then using a truth table: If the car traffic light turns red, then pedestrians cross the street.
3. Specify the following English description of an automobile automatic cruise control system in prepositional logic formulas. *Automobile automatic cruise sys-*

tem: If the "auto-cruise on" button is lighted, the automatic cruise system is turned on; otherwise, it is turned off. Pressing the "auto-cruise on" button once turns its light on. Pressing the "auto-cruise off" button once turns the "auto-cruise on" button's light off. If the distance between the car and the obstacle in front is less than a safe distance d, the automatic cruise system applies brake slowly to slow the car. If the distance between the car and the obstacle in front is less than a short distance e, the automatic cruise system applies brake quickly to slow the car more quickly and turn on an "unsafe distance" warning light. If the distance between the car and the obstacle in front is d or more, the automatic cruise system does nothing and is in the monitoring mode; otherwise, it is in both monitoring and control modes.

4. Suppose $R(x)$ represents "task x is schedulable by the rate-monotonic scheduler" and $E(x)$ represents "task x is schedulable by the earliest-deadline scheduler." Specify the following English statements in predicate logic formulas:

   (a) Every task schedulable by the rate-monotonic scheduler is schedulable by the earliest-deadline scheduler.

   (b) Not every task is schedulable by the earliest-deadline scheduler.

   (c) Some tasks not schedulable by the rate-monotonic scheduler are schedulable by the earliest-deadline scheduler.

5. Using the specifications in 4(a), (b), and (c), prove the validity of the following statement: If a task is not schedulable by the earliest-deadline scheduler, then this task is not schedulable by the rate-monotonic scheduler.

6. Prove by resolution whether the following clauses are satisfiable:

   $$A, B, C, D, E, F \vee G, \neg F \vee \neg G, \neg B \vee \neg D \vee \neg F, \neg A \vee \neg C \vee \neg G \vee \neg E.$$

7. Show the DFA accepting the language represented by the following regular expression: *(message ack)**.

8. Describe the difference between a deterministic finite automaton and a nondeterministic finite automaton. Are they equivalent in terms of expressive power?

9. Consider the smart traffic light system in Figure 2.14 and the safety property shown in Figure 2.15. Show why this safety property is not satisfied. Describe how the revised Pedestrian automaton in Figure 2.16 corrects the problem.

10. Consider a smart airbag deployment system in an automobile. A sensor that detects the distance between the driver and the steering wheel is attached to the driver's seat. This distance depends on the shape and size of the driver, and the position of the steering wheel. Based on this distance, the airbag computer determines the force of the airbag inflation to minimize harm to the driver. The airbag will deploy when a collision impact with a speed exceeding 30 mph occurs; otherwise, it will not deploy. If the distance is far (> 1.5 ft), the airbag will be inflated with maximum force. If the distance is average (between 1.0 ft and 1.5 ft), the airbag will be inflated with regular force. If the distance is near (< 1.0 ft), the airbag will be inflated with minimum force. Specify this system as a deterministic finite automaton.

CHAPTER 3

REAL-TIME SCHEDULING AND SCHEDULABILITY ANALYSIS

As in preparing a schedule of to-do tasks in everyday life, scheduling a set of computer tasks (also known as processes) is to determine when to execute which task, thus determining the execution order of these tasks; and in the case of a multiprocessor or distributed system, to also determine an assignment of these tasks to specific processors. This task assignment is analogous to assigning tasks to a specific person in a team of people. Scheduling is a central activity of a computer system, usually performed by the operating system. Scheduling is also necessary in many non-computer systems such as assembly lines.

In non-real-time systems, the typical goal of scheduling is to maximize average throughput (number of tasks completed per unit time) and/or to minimize average waiting time of the tasks. In the case of real-time scheduling, the goal is to meet the deadline of every task by ensuring that each task can complete execution by its specified deadline. This deadline is derived from environmental constraints imposed by the application.

Schedulability analysis is to determine whether a specific set of tasks or a set of tasks satisfying certain constraints can be successfully scheduled (completing execution of every task by its specified deadline) using a specific scheduler.

Schedulability Test: A *schedulability test* is used to validate that a given application can satisfy its specified deadlines when scheduled according to a specific scheduling algorithm.

This schedulability test is often done at compile time, before the computer system and its tasks start their execution. If the test can be performed efficiently, then it can be done at run-time as an on-line test.

Schedulable Utilization: A *schedulable utilization* is the maximum utilization allowed for a set of tasks that will guarantee a feasible scheduling of this task set.

A hard real-time system requires that every task or task instance completes its execution by its specified deadline; failure to do so even for a single task or task instance may lead to catastrophic consequences. A soft real-time system allows some tasks or task instances to miss their deadlines, but a task or task instance that misses a deadline may be less useful or valuable to the system.

There are basically two types of schedulers: compile-time (static) and run-time (on-line or dynamic).

Optimal Scheduler: An *optimal scheduler* is one which may fail to meet a deadline of a task only if no other scheduler can.

Note that "optimal" in real-time scheduling does not necessarily mean "fastest average response time" or "shortest average waiting time." A task T_i is characterized by the following parameters:

   S: start, release, ready, or arrival time
   c: (maximum) computation time
   d: relative deadline (deadline relative to the task's start time)
   D: absolute deadline (wall clock time deadline).

There are three main types of tasks. A *single-instance* task executes only once. A *periodic* task has many instances or iterations, and there is a fixed period between two consecutive releases of the same task. For example, a periodic task may perform signal processing of a radar scan once every 2 seconds, so the period of this task is 2 seconds. A *sporadic* task has zero or more instances, and there is a minimum separation between two consecutive releases of the same task. For example, a sporadic task may perform emergency maneuvers of an airplane when the emergency button is pressed, but there is a minimum separation of 20 seconds between two emergency requests. An *aperiodic* task is a sporadic task with either a soft deadline or no deadline. Therefore, if the task has more than one instance (sometimes called a job), we also have the following parameter:

   p: period (for periodic tasks); minimum separation (for sporadic tasks).

The following are additional constraints that may complicate scheduling of tasks with deadlines:

1. frequency of tasks requesting service periodically,
2. precedence relations among tasks and subtasks,
3. resources shared by tasks, and
4. whether task preemption is allowed or not.

If tasks are preemptable, we assume that a task can be interrupted only at discrete (integer) time instants unless we indicate otherwise.

3.1 DETERMINING COMPUTATION TIME

The application and the environment in which the application is embedded are main factors determining the start time, deadline, and period of a task. The computation (or execution) times of a task are dependent on its source code, object code, execution architecture, memory management policies, and actual number of page faults and I/O.

For real-time scheduling purposes, we use the worst-case execution (or computation) time (WCET) as c. This time is not simply an upper bound on the execution of the task code without interruption. This computation time has to include the time the central processing unit (CPU) is executing non-task code such as code for handling page faults caused by this task as well as the time an I/O request spends in the disk queue for bringing in a missing page for this task.

Determining the computation time of a process is crucial to successfully scheduling it in a real-time system. An overly pessimistic estimate of the computation time would result in wasted CPU cycles, whereas an under-approximation would result in missed deadlines.

One way of approximating the WCETs is to perform testing of the system of tasks and use the largest value of computation time seen during these tests. The problem with this is that the largest value seen during testing may not be the largest observed in the working system.

Another typical approach to determining a process's computation time is by analyzing the source code [Harmon, Baker, and Whalley, 1994; Park, 1992; Park, 1993; Park and Shaw, 1990; Shaw, 1989; Puschner and Koza, 1989; Nielsen, 1987; Chapman, Burns, and Wellings, 1996; Lundqvist and Stenstrvm, 1999; Sun and Liu, 1996]. Analysis techniques are safe, but use an overly simplified model of the CPU that result in over-approximating the computation time [Healy and Whalley, 1999b; Healy et al., 1999]. Modern processors are superscalar and pipelined. They can execute instructions out of order and even in parallel. This greatly reduces the computation time of a process. Analysis techniques that do not take this fact into consideration would result in pessimistic predicted WCETs.

Recently, there are attempts to characterize the response time of programs running in systems with several levels of memory components such as cache and main memory [Ferdinand and Wilhelm, 1999; Healy and Whalley, 1999a; White et al., 1999]. Whereas the studies make it possible to analyze the behavior of certain page replacements and write strategies, there are restrictions in their models and thus the proposed analysis techniques cannot be applied in systems not satisfying their constraints. More work needs to be done before we can apply similar analysis strategies to complex computer systems.

An alternative to the above methods is to use a probability model to model the WCET of a process as suggested in [Burns and Edgar, 2000; Edgar and Burns, 2001]. The idea here is to model the distribution of the computation time and use it to compute a confidence level for any given computation time. For instance, in a soft real-time system, if the designer wants a confidence of 99% on the estimate for WCET, he or she can determine which WCET to use from the probability model. If the designer wants a 99.9% probability, he or she can raise the WCET even higher. In chapters 10 and 11, we describe techniques for determining the WCET of rule-based systems.

3.2   UNIPROCESSOR SCHEDULING

This section considers the problem of scheduling tasks on a uniprocessor system. We begin by describing schedulers for preemptable and independent tasks with no precedence or resource-sharing constraints. Following the discussion on these basic schedulers, we will study the scheduling of tasks with constraints and show how these basic schedulers can be extended to handle these tasks.

3.2.1   Scheduling Preemptable and Independent Tasks

To simplify our discussion of the basic schedulers, we assume that the tasks to be scheduled are preemptable and independent. A preemptable task can be interrupted at any time during its execution, and resumed later. We also assume that there is no context-switching time. In practice, we can include an upper bound on the context-switching time in the computation time of the task. An independent task can be scheduled for execution as soon as it becomes ready or released. It does need to wait for other tasks to finish first or to wait for shared resources. We also assume here that the execution of the scheduler does not require the processor, that is, the scheduler runs on another specialized processor. If there is no specialized scheduling processor, then the execution time of the scheduler must also be included in the total execution time of the task set. Later, after understanding the basic scheduling strategies, we will extend these techniques to handle tasks with more realistic constraints.

Fixed-Priority Schedulers: Rate-Monotonic and Deadline-Monotonic Algorithms   A popular real-time scheduling strategy is the *rate-monotonic* (RM) scheduler (RMS), which is a fixed-(static-) priority scheduler using the task's (fixed) period as the task's priority. RMS executes at any time instant the instance of the ready task with the shortest period first. If two or more tasks have the same period, then RMS randomly selects one for execution next.

Example.   Consider three periodic tasks with the following arrival times, computation times, and periods (which are equal to their respective relative deadlines):

$$J_1: S_1 = 0, c_1 = 2, p_1 = d_1 = 5,$$

$$J_2: S_2 = 1, c_2 = 1, p_2 = d_2 = 4, \text{ and}$$

$$J_3: S_3 = 2, c_3 = 2, p_3 = d_3 = 20.$$

The RM scheduler produces a feasible schedule as follows. At time 0, J_1 is the only ready task so it is scheduled to run. At time 1, J_2 arrives. Since $p_2 < p_1$, J_2 has

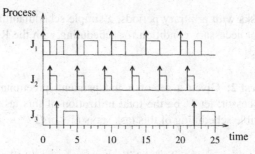

Figure 3.1   RM schedule.

a higher priority, so J_1 is preempted and J_2 starts to execute. At time 2, J_2 finishes execution and J_3 arrives. Since $p_3 > p_1$, J_1 now has a higher priority, so it resumes execution. At time 3, J_1 finishes execution. At this time, J_3 is the only ready task so it starts to run. At time 4, J_3 is still the only task so it continues to run and finishes execution at time 5. At this time, the second instances of J_1 and J_2 are ready. Since $p_2 < p_1$, J_2 has a higher priority, so J_2 starts to execute. At time 6, the second instance of J_2 finishes execution. At this time, the second instance of J_1 is the only ready task so it starts execution, finishing at time 8. The timing diagram of the RM schedule for this task set is shown in Figure 3.1.

The RM scheduling algorithm is not optimal in general since there exist schedulable task sets that are not RM-schedulable. However, there is a special class of periodic task sets for which the RM scheduler is optimal.

Schedulability Test 1: Given a set of n independent, preemptable, and periodic tasks on a uniprocessor such that their relative deadlines are equal to or larger than their respective periods and that their periods are exact (integer) multiples of each other, let U be the total utilization of this task set. A necessary and sufficient condition for feasible scheduling of this task set is

$$U = \sum_{i=1}^{n} \frac{c_i}{p_i} \leq 1.$$

Example. There are three periodic tasks with the following arrival times, computation times, and periods (which are equal to their respective relative deadlines):

$$J_1: S_1 = 0, c_1 = 1, p_1 = 4,$$

$$J_2: S_2 = 0, c_2 = 1, p_2 = 2, \text{ and}$$

$$J_3: S_3 = 0, c_3 = 2, p_3 = 8.$$

Because the task periods are exact multiples of each other ($p_2 < p_1 < p_3$, $p_1 = 2p_2$, $p_3 = 4p_2 = 2p_1$), this task set is in the special class of tasks given in Schedulability Test 1. Since $U = \frac{1}{4} + \frac{1}{2} + \frac{2}{8} = 1 \leq 1$, this task set is RM-schedulable.

For a set of tasks with arbitrary periods, a simple schedulability test exists with a sufficient but not necessary condition for scheduling with the RM scheduler [Liu and Layland, 1973].

Schedulability Test 2: Given a set of n independent, preemptable, and periodic tasks on a uniprocessor, let U be the total utilization of this task set. A sufficient condition for feasible scheduling of this task set is $U \leq n(2^{1/n} - 1)$.

However, using this simple schedulability test may under-utilize a computer system since a task set whose utilization exceeds the above bound may still be RM-schedulable. Therefore, we proceed to derive a sufficient and necessary condition for scheduling using the RM algorithm. Suppose we have three tasks, all with start times 0. Task J_1 has the smallest period, followed by J_2, and then J_3. It is intuitive to see that for J_1 to be feasibly scheduled, its computation time must be less than or equal to its period, so the following necessary and sufficient condition must hold:

$$c_1 \leq p_1.$$

For J_2 to be feasibly scheduled, we need to find enough available time in the interval $[0, p_2]$ that is not used by J_1. Suppose J_2 completes execution at time t. Then the total number of iterations of J_1 in the interval $[0, t]$ is

$$\left\lceil \frac{t}{p_1} \right\rceil.$$

To ensure that J_2 can complete execution at time t, every iteration of J_1 in $[0, t]$ must be completed and there must be enough available time left for J_2. This available time is c_2. Therefore,

$$t = \left\lceil \frac{t}{p_1} \right\rceil c_1 + c_2.$$

Similarly, for J_3 to be feasibly scheduled, there must be enough processor time left for executing J_3 after scheduling J_1 and J_2:

$$t = \left\lceil \frac{t}{p_1} \right\rceil c_1 + \left\lceil \frac{t}{p_2} \right\rceil c_2 + c_3.$$

The next question is how to determine if such a time t exists so that a feasible schedule for a set of tasks can be constructed. Note that there is an infinite number of points in every interval if no discrete time is assumed. However, the value of the ceiling such as

$$\left\lceil \frac{t}{p_1} \right\rceil$$

only changes at multiples of p_1, with an increase at c_1. Thus we need to show only that a k exists such that

$$kp_1 \geq kc_1 + c_2 \quad \text{and} \quad kp_1 \leq p_2.$$

Therefore, we need to check that

$$t \geq \left\lceil \frac{t}{p_1} \right\rceil c_1 + c_2$$

for some t that is a multiple of p_1 such that $t \leq p_2$. If this is found, then we have the necessary and sufficient condition for feasibly scheduling J_2 using the RM algorithm. This check is finite since there is a finite number of multiples of p_1 that are less than or equal to p_2. Similarly for J_3, we check if the following inequality holds:

$$t \geq \left\lceil \frac{t}{p_1} \right\rceil c_1 + \left\lceil \frac{t}{p_2} \right\rceil c_2 + c_3.$$

We are ready to present the necessary and sufficient condition for feasible scheduling of a periodic task.

Schedulability Test 3: Let

$$w_i(t) = \sum_{k=1}^{i} c_k \left\lceil \frac{t}{p_k} \right\rceil, \quad 0 < t \leq p_i.$$

The following inequality

$$w_i(t) \leq t$$

holds for any time instant t chosen as follows:

$$t = kp_j, j = 1, \ldots, i, k = 1, \ldots, \left\lfloor \frac{p_i}{p_j} \right\rfloor$$

iff task J_i is RM-schedulable. If $d_i \neq p_i$, we replace p_i by $\min(d_i, p_i)$ in the above expression.

The following example applies this sufficient and necessary condition to check the schedulability of four tasks using the RM algorithm.

Example. Consider the following periodic tasks all arriving at time 0, and consider every task's period is equal to its relative deadline.

$$J_1: c_1 = 10, p_1 = 50,$$

$$J_2: c_2 = 15, \ p_2 = 80,$$

$$J_3: c_3 = 40, \ p_3 = 110, \text{ and}$$

$$J_4: c_4 = 50, \ p_4 = 190.$$

Using the above schedulability test, we proceed to check whether each task is schedulable using the RM algorithm, beginning with the task having the smallest period.

For $J_1, i = 1, j = 1, \ldots, i = 1$, so

$$k = 1, \ldots, \left\lfloor \frac{p_i}{p_j} \right\rfloor = 1, \ldots, \left\lfloor \frac{50}{50} \right\rfloor = 1.$$

Thus, $t = kp_j = 1(50) = 50$. Task J_1 is RM-schedulable iff

$$c_1 \leq 50.$$

Since $c_1 = 10 \leq 50$, J_1 is RM-schedulable.

For $J_2, i = 2, j = 1, \ldots, i = 1, 2$, so

$$k = 1, \ldots, \left\lfloor \frac{p_i}{p_j} \right\rfloor = 1, \ldots, \left\lfloor \frac{80}{50} \right\rfloor = 1.$$

Thus, $t = 1p_1 = 1(50) = 50$, or $t = 1p_2 = 1(80) = 80$. Task J_2 is RM-schedulable iff

$$c_1 + c_2 \leq 50 \quad \text{or}$$

$$2c_1 + c_2 \leq 80.$$

Since $c_1 = 10$ and $c_2 = 15$, $10 + 15 \leq 50$ (or $2(10) + 15 \leq 80$), thus J_2 is RM-schedulable together with J_1.

For $J_3, i = 3, j = 1, \ldots, i = 1, 2, 3$, so

$$k = 1, \ldots, \left\lfloor \frac{p_i}{p_j} \right\rfloor = 1, \ldots, \left\lfloor \frac{110}{50} \right\rfloor = 1, 2.$$

Thus, $t = 1p_1 = 1(50) = 50$, or $t = 1p_2 = 1(80) = 80$, or $t = 1p_3 = 1(110) = 110$, or $t = 2p_1 = 2(50) = 100$. Task J_3 is RM-schedulable iff

$$c_1 + c_2 + c_3 \leq 50 \quad \text{or}$$

$$2c_1 + c_2 + c_3 \leq 80 \quad \text{or}$$

$$2c_1 + 2c_2 + c_3 \leq 100 \quad \text{or}$$

$$3c_1 + 2c_2 + c_3 \leq 110$$

Since $c_1 = 10$, $c_2 = 15$, and $c_3 = 40$, $2(10) + 15 + 40 \leq 80$ (or $2(10) + 2(15) + 40 \leq 100$, or $3(10) + 2(15) + 40 \leq 110$), thus J_3 is RM-schedulable together with J_1 and J_2.

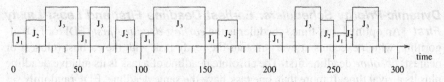

Figure 3.2   RM schedule.

For $J_4, i = 4, j = 1, \ldots, i = 1, 2, 3, 4$, so

$$k = 1, \ldots, \left\lfloor \frac{p_i}{p_j} \right\rfloor = 1, \ldots, \left\lfloor \frac{190}{50} \right\rfloor = 1, 2, 3.$$

Thus, $t = 1p_1 = 1(50) = 50$, or $t = 1p_2 = 1(80) = 80$, or $t = 1p_3 = 1(110) = 110$, or $t = 1p_4 = 1(190) = 190$, or $t = 2p_1 = 2(50) = 100$, or $t = 2p_2 = 2(80) = 160$, or $t = 3p_1 = 3(50) = 150$. Task J_4 is RM-schedulable iff

$$c_1 + c_2 + c_3 + c_4 \leq 50 \qquad \text{or}$$

$$2c_1 + c_2 + c_3 + c_4 \leq 80 \qquad \text{or}$$

$$2c_1 + 2c_2 + c_3 + c_4 \leq 100 \qquad \text{or}$$

$$3c_1 + 2c_2 + c_3 + c_4 \leq 110 \qquad \text{or}$$

$$3c_1 + 2c_2 + 2c_3 + c_4 \leq 150 \qquad \text{or}$$

$$4c_1 + 2c_2 + 2c_3 + c_4 \leq 160 \qquad \text{or}$$

$$4c_1 + 3c_2 + 2c_3 + c_4 \leq 190.$$

Since none of the inequalities can be satisfied, J_4 is not RM-schedulable together with J_1, J_2, and J_3. In fact,

$$U = \frac{10}{50} + \frac{15}{80} + \frac{40}{110} + \frac{50}{190} = 1.014 > 1.$$

Therefore, no scheduler can feasibly schedule these tasks. Ignoring task J_4, the utilization is $U = 0.75$, which also satisfies the simple schedulable utilization of Schedulability Test 2. The RM schedule for the first three tasks is shown in Figure 3.2.

Another fixed-priority scheduler is the *deadline-monotonic* (DM) scheduling algorithm, which assigns higher priorities to tasks with shorter *relative* deadlines. It is intuitive to see that if every task's period is the same as its deadline, then the RM and DM scheduling algorithms are equivalent. In general, these two algorithms are equivalent if every task's deadline is the product of a constant k and this task's period, that is, $d_i = kp_i$.

Note that some authors [Krishna and Shin, 1997] consider deadline monotonic as another name for the earliest-deadline-first scheduler, which is a dynamic-priority scheduler described in the next section.

Dynamic-Priority Schedulers: Earliest Deadline First and Least Laxity First   An optimal, run-time scheduler is the *earliest-deadline-first* (EDF or ED) algorithm, which executes at every instant the ready task with the earliest (closest or nearest) *absolute* deadline first. The absolute deadline of a task is its relative deadline plus its arrival time. If more than one task have the same deadline, EDF randomly selects one for execution next. EDF is a dynamic-priority scheduler since task priorities may change at run-time depending on the nearness of their absolute deadlines. Some authors [Krishna and Shin, 1997] call EDF a deadline-monotonic (DM) scheduling algorithm whereas others [Liu, 2000] define the DM algorithm as a fixed-priority scheduler that assigns higher priorities to tasks with shorter *relative* deadlines. Here, we use the terms EDF or DM to refer to this dynamic-priority scheduling algorithm. We now describe an example.

Example.   There are four single-instance tasks with the following arrival times, computation times, and absolute deadlines:

$$J_1: S_1 = 0, c_1 = 4, D_1 = 15,$$

$$J_2: S_2 = 0, c_2 = 3, D_2 = 12,$$

$$J_3: S_3 = 2, c_3 = 5, D_3 = 9, \text{ and}$$

$$J_4: S_4 = 5, c_4 = 2, D_4 = 8.$$

A first-in-first-out (FIFO or FCFS) scheduler (often used in non-real-time operating systems) gives an infeasible schedule, shown in Figure 3.3. Tasks are executed in the order they arrive and deadlines are not considered. As a result, task J_3 misses its deadline after time 9, and task J_4 misses its deadline after time 8, before it is even scheduled to run.

However, the EDF scheduler produces a feasible schedule, shown in Figure 3.4. At time 0, tasks J_1 and J_2 arrive. Since $D_1 > D_2$ (J_2's absolute deadline is earlier than J_1's absolute deadline), J_2 has higher priority and begins to run. At time 2, task J_3 arrives. Since $D_3 < D_2$, J_2 is preempted and J_3 begins execution. At time 5, task J_4 arrives. Since $D_4 < D_3$, J_3 is preempted and J_4 begins execution.

At time 7, J_4 completes its execution one time unit before its deadline of 8. At this time, $D_3 < D_2 < D_1$ so J_3 has the highest priority and resumes execution. At time 9, J_3 completes its execution, meeting its deadline of 9. At this time, J_2 has the highest priority and resumes execution. At time 10, J_2 completes its execution two

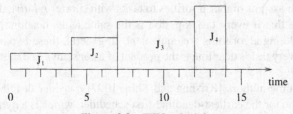

Figure 3.3   FIFO schedule.

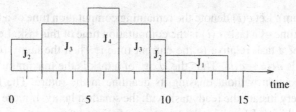

Figure 3.4 EDF schedule.

time units before its deadline of 12. At this time, J_1 is the only remaining task and begins its execution, finishing at time 14, meeting its deadline of 15.

Using the notion of optimality that we have defined in the introduction, the EDF algorithm is optimal for scheduling a set of independent and preemptable tasks on a uniprocessor system.

Theorem. Given a set S of independent (no resource contention or precedence constraints) and preemptable tasks with arbitrary start times and deadlines on a uniprocessor, the EDF algorithm yields a feasible schedule for S iff S has feasible schedules.

Therefore, the EDF algorithm fails to meet a deadline of a task set satisfying the above constraints only if no other scheduler can produce a feasible schedule for this task set. The proof of EDF's optimality is based on the fact that any non-EDF schedule can be transformed into an EDF schedule.

Proof. The basis of the proof is the fact that blocks of different (independent and preemptable) tasks on a uniprocessor can be interchanged. Given a feasible non-EDF schedule for a task set S on a uniprocessor, let J_1 and J_2 be two blocks corresponding to two different tasks (or parts of these tasks) such that J_2's deadline is earlier than J_1's, but J_1 is scheduled earlier in this non-EDF schedule.

If J_2's start time is later than the completion time of J_1, then these two blocks cannot be interchanged. In fact, these two blocks follow the EDF algorithm. Otherwise, we can always interchanged these two blocks without violating their deadline constraints. Now J_2 is scheduled before J_1. Since J_2's deadline is earlier than J_1's, this exchange of blocks certainly allows J_2 to meet its deadline since it is now scheduled earlier than in the case of the non-EDF schedule.

From the original feasible non-EDF schedule, we know that J_1's deadline is no earlier than the original completion time of J_2 since J_2's deadline is earlier than J_1's. Therefore, J_1 also meets its deadline after this exchange of blocks.

We perform this interchange of blocks for every pair of blocks not following the EDF algorithm. The resulting schedule is an EDF schedule.   □

Another optimal, run-time scheduler is the *least-laxity-first* (LL or LLF) algorithm (also known as the *minimum-laxity-first* (MLF) algorithm or *least-slack-time-first*

(LST) algorithm). Let $c(i)$ denote the remaining computation time of a task at time i. At the arrival time of a task, $c(i)$ is the computation time of this task. Let $d(i)$ denote the deadline of a task relative to the current time i. Then the laxity (or slack) of a task at time i is $d(i) - c(i)$. Thus the laxity of a task is the maximum time the task can delay execution without missing its deadline in the future. The LL scheduler executes at every instant the ready task with the smallest laxity. If more than one task have the same laxity, LL randomly selects one for execution next.

For a uniprocessor, both EDF and LL schedulers are optimal for preemptable tasks with no precedence, resource, or mutual exclusion constraints. There is a simple necessary and sufficient condition for scheduling a set of independent, preemptable periodic tasks [Liu and Layland, 1973].

Schedulability Test 4: Let c_i denote the computation time of task J_i. For a set of n periodic tasks such that the relative deadline d_i of each task is equal to or greater than its respective period p_i ($d_i \geq p_i$), a necessary and sufficient condition for feasible scheduling of this task set on a uniprocessor is that the utilization of the tasks is less than or equal to 1:

$$U = \sum_{i=1}^{n} \frac{c_i}{p_i} \leq 1.$$

For a task set containing some tasks whose relative deadlines d_i are less than their respective periods, no easy schedulability test exists with a necessary and sufficient condition. However, a simple sufficient condition exists for EDF-scheduling of a set of tasks whose deadlines are equal to or shorter than their respective periods. This schedulability test generalizes the sufficient condition of Schedulability Test 4.

Schedulability Test 5: A sufficient condition for feasible scheduling of a set of independent, preemptable, and periodic tasks on a uniprocessor is

$$\sum_{i=1}^{n} \frac{c_i}{\min(d_i, p_i)} \leq 1.$$

The term $c_i / \min(d_i, p_i)$ is the *density* of task J_i. Note that if the deadline and the period of each task are equal ($d_i = p_i$), then Schedulability Test 5 is the same as Schedulability Test 4.

Since this is only a sufficient condition, a task set that does not satisfy this condition may or may not be EDF-schedulable. In general, we can use the following schedulability test to determine whether a task set is not EDF-schedulable.

Schedulability Test 6: Given a set of n independent, preemptable, and periodic tasks on a uniprocessor, let U be the utilization as defined in Schedulability Test 4

$(U = \sum_{i=1}^{n} \frac{c_i}{p_i})$, d_{max} be the maximum relative deadline among these tasks' deadlines, P be the least common multiple (LCM) of these tasks' periods, and $s(t)$ be the sum of the computation times of the tasks with absolute deadlines less than t. This task set is not EDF-schedulable iff either of the following conditions is true:

$$U > 1$$

$$\exists t < \min\left(P + d_{max}, \left(\frac{U}{1 - U}\right) \max_{1 \leq i \leq n} (p_i - d_i)\right)$$

such that $s(t) > t$.

A proof sketch for this test is in [Krishna and Shin, 1997].

Comparing Fixed and Dynamic-Priority Schedulers   The RM and DM algorithms are fixed-priority schedulers whereas the EDF and LL algorithms are dynamic-priority schedulers. A fixed-priority scheduler assigns the same priority to all instances of the same task, thus the priority of each task is fixed with respect to other tasks. However, a dynamic-priority scheduler may assign different priorities to different instances of the same task, thus the priority of each task may change with respect to other tasks as new task instances arrive and complete.

In general, no optimal fixed-priority scheduling algorithm exists since given any fixed-priority algorithm, we can always find a schedulable task set that cannot be scheduled by this algorithm. On the other hand, both EDF and LL algorithms are optimal dynamic-priority schedulers. Consider the following examples using the RM and EDF schedulers.

Example.   Two periodic tasks are given with the following arrival times, computation times, and periods (which are equal to their corresponding deadlines):

$$J_1: S_1 = 0, c_1 = 5, p_1 = 10 \text{ (also denoted (5,10))},$$

$$J_2: S_2 = 0, c_2 = 12, p_2 = 25 \text{ (also denoted (12,25))}.$$

Since $U = \frac{5}{10} + \frac{12}{25} = 0.98 \leq 1$, Schedulability Test 4 is satisfied, thus we can feasibly schedule these tasks with EDF, as shown in Figure 3.5.

We describe the schedule for an interval equal to the LCM(10,25) of the periods, which is 50. The absolute deadline is the relative deadline (here it is also the period)

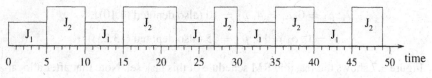

Figure 3.5   EDF schedule.

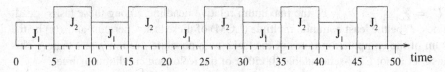

Figure 3.6   Infeasible RM schedule.

plus the arrival time. At time 0, both tasks are ready and the absolute deadline of J_1 (10) is less than that of J_2 (25) ($D_1 < D_2$), so J_1 has higher priority and thus begins execution, finishing at time 5. At this time, J_2 is the only ready task so it begins execution. At time 10, the second instance of J_1 arrives. Now the absolute deadlines are compared, $D_1 = 20 < D_2 = 25$, so J_1 has higher priority. J_2 is preempted and J_1 begins execution, finishing at time 15. At this time, J_1 is the only ready task so it resumes its execution.

At time 20, the third instance of J_1 arrives. The absolute deadlines are compared, $D_1 = 30 > D_2 = 25$, so now J_2 has higher priority and continues to run. At time 22, the first instance of J_2 finishes and the third instance of J_1 begins execution. At time 25, the second instance of J_2 arrives. The absolute deadlines are compared, $D_1 = 30 < D_2 = 50$, so J_1 has higher priority and continues to run. At time 27, the third instance of J_1 finishes and the second instance of J_2 begins execution. At time 30, the fourth instance of J_1 arrives. The absolute deadlines are compared, $D_1 = 40 < D_2 = 50$, so J_1 has higher priority. J_2 is preempted and the fourth instance of J_1 begins execution, finishing at time 35. At this time, the second instance of J_2 is the only ready task so it resumes its execution.

At time 40, the fifth instance of J_1 arrives. The absolute deadlines are compared, $D_1 = D_2 = 50$, so both tasks have the same priority. A task, here J_1, is selected to run. At time 45, the fifth instance of J_1 finishes and the second instance of J_2 resumes execution, finishing at time 49. Note that to reduce context switching, continuing to execute J_2 at time 45 until it finishes is better.

Attempting to schedule these two tasks using the RM scheduler yields an infeasible schedule, as shown in Figure 3.6. Since J_1 has a shorter period and thus a higher priority, it is always scheduled first. As a result, the first instance of J_2 is allocated only 10 time units before its deadline of 25 and so it finishes at time 27, causing it to miss its deadline after time 25.

Next we consider another example in which the two tasks are both RM- and EDF-schedulable.

Example. Two periodic tasks exist with the following arrival times, computation times, and periods:

$$J_1: S_1 = 0, c_1 = 4, p_1 = 10 \text{ (also denoted (4,10))},$$

$$J_2: S_2 = 0, c_2 = 13, p_2 = 25 \text{ (also denoted (13,25))}.$$

Figure 3.7 shows the feasible RM schedule of this task set. Note that after allocating processor time to task J_1, which has a shorter period and hence higher priority,

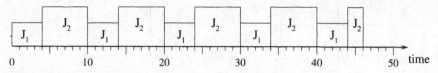

Figure 3.7   RM schedule.

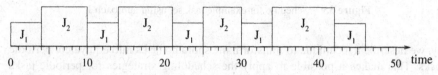

Figure 3.8   EDF schedule.

sufficient processor time is still left for J_2 during its first period. This is not the case in the previous example task set, causing J_1 to miss its deadline in the first period.

Since $U = \frac{4}{10} + \frac{13}{25} = 0.92$, we can feasibly schedule these tasks with EDF as shown in Figure 3.8. We describe the schedule for an interval equal to the LCM(10,25) of the periods, which is 50. The absolute deadline is the relative deadline (here it is also the period) plus the arrival time. At time 0, both tasks are ready and the absolute deadline of J_1 (10) is less than that of J_2 (25) ($D_1 < D_2$), so J_1 has higher priority and thus begins execution, finishing at time 4. At this time, J_2 is the only ready task so it begins execution. At time 10, the second instance of J_1 arrives. Now the absolute deadlines are compared, $D_1 = 20 < D_2 = 25$, so J_1 has higher priority. J_2 is preempted and J_1 begins execution, finishing at time 14. At this time, J_2 is the only ready task so it resumes its execution.

At time 20, the third instance of J_1 arrives. The absolute deadlines are compared, $D_1 = 30 > D_2 = 25$, so now J_2 has higher priority and continues to run. At time 21, the first instance of J_2 finishes and the third instance of J_1 begins execution and finishes at time 25. At this time, the second instance of J_2 arrives and is the only ready task so it starts execution. At time 30, the fourth instance of J_1 arrives and the absolute deadlines are compared, $D_1 = 40 < D_2 = 50$, so J_1 has higher priority and begins to run.

At time 34, the fourth instance of J_1 finishes and the second instance of J_2 resumes execution. At time 40, the fifth instance of J_1 arrives. The absolute deadlines are compared, $D_1 = D_2 = 50$, so both tasks have the same priority and thus one can be randomly chosen to run. To reduce context switching, the second instance of J_2 continues to execute until it finishes at time 42. At this time, the fifth instance of J_1 begins execution and finishes at time 46.

We next consider scheduling sporadic tasks together with periodic tasks.

Sporadic Tasks   Sporadic tasks may be released at any time instant but a *minimum separation* exists between releases of consecutive instances of the same sporadic task. To schedule preemptable sporadic tasks, we may attempt to develop a new strategy, or reuse a strategy we have presented. In the spirit of software reusabil-

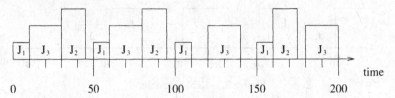

Figure 3.9 Schedule for example task set using approach 1.

ity, we describe a technique to transform the sporadic tasks into equivalent periodic tasks. This makes it possible to apply the scheduling strategies for periodic tasks introduced earlier.

A simple approach to schedule sporadic tasks is to treat them as periodic tasks with the minimum separation times as their periods. Then we schedule the periodic equivalents of these sporadic tasks using the scheduling algorithm described earlier. Unlike periodic tasks, sporadic tasks are released irregularly or may not be released at all. Therefore, even though the scheduler (say the RM algorithm) allocates a time slice to the periodic equivalent of a sporadic task, this sporadic task may not actually be released. The processor remains idle during this time slice if this sporadic task does not request service. When this sporadic task does request service, it immediately runs if its release time is within its corresponding scheduled time slice. Otherwise, it waits for the next scheduled time slice for running its periodic equivalent.

Example. Consider a system with two periodic tasks J_1 and J_2 both arriving at time 0, and one sporadic task J_3 with the following parameters. The minimum separation for two consecutive instances of J_3 is 60, which is treated as its period here.

$$J_1: c_1 = 10, \ p_1 = 50,$$

$$J_2: c_2 = 15, \ p_2 = 80, \ \text{and}$$

$$J_3: c_3 = 15, \ p_3 = 60.$$

An RM schedule is shown in Figure 3.9.

The second approach to schedule sporadic tasks is to treat them as one periodic task J_s with the highest priority and a period chosen to accommodate the minimum separations and computation requirements of this collection of sporadic tasks. Again, a scheduler is used to assign time slices on the processor to each task, including J_s. Any sporadic task may run within the time slices assigned to J_s while the other (periodic) tasks run outside of these time slices.

Example. Consider a system with periodic and sporadic tasks. We create a periodic task J_s for the collection of sporadic tasks with $c_s = 20$, $p_s = 60$. An RM schedule is shown in Figure 3.10.

The third approach to schedule sporadic tasks, called *deferred server* (DS) [Lehoczky, Sha, and Strosnider, 1987], is the same as the second approach with the following modification. The periodic task corresponding to the collection of

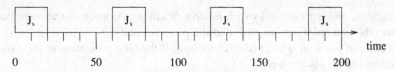

Figure 3.10   Schedule for example task set using approach 2.

sporadic tasks is the deferred server. When no sporadic task waits for service during a time slice assigned to sporadic tasks, the processor runs the other (periodic) tasks. If a sporadic task is released, then the processor preempts the currently running periodic tasks and runs the sporadic task for a time interval up to the total time slice assigned to sporadic tasks.

Example.   Consider a system with periodic and sporadic tasks. We create a periodic task J_s for the collection of sporadic tasks with $c_s = 20$, $p_s = 60$. Hence, we allocate 20 time units to sporadic tasks every 60 time units.

A sporadic task J_1 with $c_1 = 30$ arrives at time 20. Since 20 time units are available in the first period of 60 time units, it is immediately scheduled to run for 20 time units. At time 40, this task is preempted and other (periodic) tasks may run. Then at time 60, which is the start of the second period of 60 time units, J_1 is scheduled to run for 10 time units, fulfilling its computation requirement of 30 time units.

A sporadic task J_2 with $c_1 = 50$ arrives at time 100. Since 10 time units are still available in the second period of 60 time units, it is immediately scheduled to run for 10 time units. At time 110, this task is preempted and other (periodic) tasks may run. At time 120, which is the start of the third period of 60 time units, J_1 is scheduled to run for 20 time units and then it is preempted. Finally at time 180, which is the start of the fourth period of 60 time units, J_1 is scheduled to run for 20 time units, fulfilling its computation requirement of 50 time units. The schedule is shown in Figure 3.11.

For a deferred server with an arbitrary priority in a system of tasks scheduled using the RM algorithm, no schedulable utilization is known that guarantees a feasible scheduling of this system. However, for the special case in which the DS has the shortest period among all tasks (so the DS has the highest priority), a schedulable utilization exists [Lehoczky, Sha, and Strosnider, 1987; Strosnider, Lehoczky, and Sha, 1995].

Schedulability Test 7:   Let p_s and c_s be the period and allocated time for the deferred server. Let $U_s = c_i/p_s$ be the utilization of the server. A set of n independent,

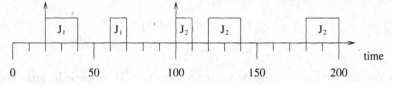

Figure 3.11   Schedule for example task set using approach 3: deferred server.

preemptable, and periodic tasks with relative deadlines the same as the correspond-ing periods on a uniprocessor such that the periods satisfy $p_s < p_1 < p_2 < \cdots < p_n < 2p_s$ and $p_n > p_s + c_s$ is RM-schedulable if the total utilization of this task set (including the DS) is at most

$$U(n) = (n - 1) \left[\left(\frac{U_s + 2}{U_s + 1} \right)^{\frac{1}{n-1}} - 1 \right].$$

3.2.2 Scheduling Nonpreemptable Tasks

So far we have assumed that tasks can be preempted at any integer time instants. In practice, tasks may contain critical sections that cannot be interrupted. These critical sections are needed to access and modify shared variables or to use shared resources such as disks. Now we consider the scheduling of nonpreemptable tasks and tasks with nonpreemptable subtasks. An important goal is to reduce task waiting time and context-switching time [Lee and Cheng, 1994]. Using fixed-priority schedulers for non-real-time tasks may potentially lead to the priority inversion problem [Sha, Raj-kumar, and Lehoczky, 1990], which occurs when a low-prioirty task with a critical section blocks a higher-priority task for an unbounded or long period of time.

The EDF and LL algorithms are no longer optimal if the tasks are not preempt-able. For instance, without preemption, we cannot transform a feasible non-EDF schedule into an EDF schedule by interchanging computation blocks of different tasks as described in the proof of EDF optimality. This means that the EDF algo-rithm may fail to meet a deadline of a task set even if another scheduler can produce a feasible schedule for this task set. In fact, no priority-based scheduling algorithm is optimal for nonpreemptable tasks with arbitrary start times, computations times, and deadlines, even on a uniprocessor [Mok, 1984].

Scheduling Nonpreemptable Sporadic Tasks As above, we apply the scheduling strategies for periodic tasks introduced earlier by first transforming the sporadic tasks into equivalent periodic tasks [Mok, 1984], yielding the following schedulability test.

Schedulability Test 8: Suppose we have a set M of tasks that is the union of a set M_p of periodic tasks and a set M_s of sporadic tasks. Let the nominal (or initial) laxity l_i of task T_i be $d_i - c_i$. Each sporadic task $T_i = (c_i, d_i, p_i)$ is replaced by an equivalent periodic task $T_i' = (c_i', d_i', p_i')$ as follows:

$$c_i' = c_i$$
$$p_i' = \min(p_i, l_i + 1)$$
$$d_i' = c_i.$$

If we can find a feasible schedule for the resulting set M' of periodic tasks (which includes the transformed sporadic tasks), we can schedule the original set M of tasks without knowing in advance the start (release or request) times of the sporadic tasks in M_s.

A sporadic task (c, d, p) can be transformed into and scheduled as a periodic task (c', d', p') if the following conditions hold: (1) $d \geq d' \geq c$, (2) $c' = c$, and (3) $p' \leq d - d' + 1$. A proof can be found in [Mok, 1984].

3.2.3   Nonpreemptable Tasks with Precedence Constraints

So far we have described scheduling strategies for independent and preemptable tasks. Now we introduce precedence and mutual exclusion (nonpreemption) constraints to the scheduling problem for single-instance tasks (tasks that are neither periodic nor sporadic) on a uniprocessor.

A *task precedence graph* (also called a *task graph* or *precedence graph*) shows the required order of execution of a set of tasks. A node represents a task (or subtask) and directed edges indicate the precedence relationships between tasks. The notation $T_i \rightarrow T_j$ means that T_i must complete execution before T_j can start to execute. For task T_i, incoming edges from predecessor tasks indicate all these predecessor tasks have to complete execution before T_i can start execution. Outgoing edges to successor tasks indicate that T_i must finish execution before the successor tasks can start execution. A topological ordering of the tasks in a precedence graph shows one allowable execution order of these tasks.

Suppose we have a set of n one-instance tasks with deadlines, all ready at time 0 and with precedence constraints described by a precedence graph. We can schedule this task set on a uniprocessor with the algorithm shown in Figure 3.12.

This algorithm executes a ready task whose predecessors have finished execution as soon as the processor is available.

Example.   Consider the following tasks with precedence constraints:

$$T_1 \rightarrow T_2$$
$$T_1 \rightarrow T_3$$
$$T_2 \rightarrow T_4$$
$$T_2 \rightarrow T_6$$

Algorithm:

1. Sort the tasks in the precedence graph in topological order (so that the task(s) with no in-edges are listed first). If two or more tasks can be listed next, select the one with the earliest deadline; ties are broken arbitrarily.
2. Execute tasks one at a time following this topological order.

Figure 3.12   Scheduling algorithm A for tasks with precedence constraints.

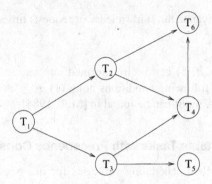

Figure 3.13 Precedence graph.

$$T_3 \rightarrow T_4$$
$$T_3 \rightarrow T_5$$
$$T_4 \rightarrow T_6.$$

The precedence graph is shown in Figure 3.13. The tasks have the following computation times and deadlines:

$$T_1: c_1 = 2, d_1 = 5,$$
$$T_2: c_2 = 3, d_2 = 7,$$
$$T_3: c_3 = 2, d_3 = 10,$$
$$T_4: c_4 = 8, d_4 = 18,$$
$$T_5: c_5 = 6, d_5 = 25, \text{ and}$$
$$T_6: c_6 = 4, d_6 = 28.$$

A variation of this algorithm, shown in Figure 3.14, is to lay out the schedule by considering the task with the latest deadline first and then shifting the entire schedule toward time 0.

Algorithm:

1. Sort the tasks according to their deadlines in non-decreasing order and label the tasks such that $d_1 \leq d_2 \leq \cdots \leq d_n$.
2. Schedule task T_n in the time interval $[d_n - c_n, d_n]$.
3. While there is a task to be scheduled do
   Suppose S is the set of all unscheduled tasks whose successors have been scheduled. Schedule as late as possible the task with the latest deadline in S.
4. Shift the tasks toward time 0 while maintaining the execution order indicated in step 3.

Figure 3.14 Scheduling algorithm B for tasks with precedence constraints.

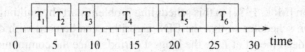

Figure 3.15 Schedule for tasks with precedence constraints.

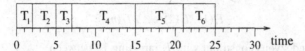

Figure 3.16 Schedule for tasks with precedence constraints after shifting tasks.

Step 1 of the algorithm A sorts the tasks in topological order: $T_1, T_2, T_3, T_4, T_5, T_6$. Note that tasks T_2 and T_3 are concurrent; so are pair T_4 and T_5 and pair T_5 and T_6. Step 2 of the algorithm produces the schedule shown in Figure 3.16.

Using scheduling algorithm B, we obtain the feasible schedule before shifting tasks, shown in Figure 3.15. Figure 3.16 shows the feasible schedule produced by the scheduler after shifting tasks toward time 0.

3.2.4 Communicating Periodic Tasks: Deterministic Rendezvous Model

Allowing tasks to communicate with each other complicates the scheduling problem. In fact, interprocess communication leads to precedence constraints not only between tasks but also between blocks within these tasks. For example, the Ada programming language provides the primitive *rendezvous* to allow one task to communicate with another at a specific point during the task execution. Ada is used in the implementation of a variety of embedded and real-time systems, including airplane avionics. If a task A wants to communicate with process B, task A executes *rendezvous*(B). Task A then waits until task B executes a corresponding *rendezvous*(A).

As a result, these pair of rendezvous impose a precedence constraint between the computations of tasks A and B by requiring that all the computations prior to the rendezvous primitive in each task be completed *before* the computations following the rendezvous primitive in the other task can start. To simplify our scheduling strategy, we assume here that the execution time of a rendezvous primitive is zero or that its execution time is included in the preceding computation block.

A one-instance task can rendezvous with another one-instance task. However, it is semantically incorrect to allow a periodic task and a sporadic task to rendezvous with each other since the sporadic task may not run at all, causing the periodic task to wait forever for the matching rendezvous. Two periodic tasks may rendezvous with each other, but there are constraints on the lengths of their periods to ensure correctness.

Two tasks are *compatible* if their periods are exact multiples of each other. To allow two (periodic) tasks to communicate in any form, they must be compatible. One attempt to schedule compatible and communicating tasks is to use the EDF scheduler to execute the ready task with the nearest deadline that is not blocked due to a rendezvous.

The solution [Mok, 1984] to this scheduling problem starts by building a database for the runtime scheduler so that the EDF algorithm can be used with dynamically assigned task deadlines. Let L be the longest period. Since the communicating tasks are compatible, L is the same as the LCM of these tasks' periods. We denote a chain of scheduling blocks generated in chronological order for task T_i in interval $[0, L]$ by

$$T_i(1), T_i(2), \ldots, T_i(m_i).$$

If there is a rendezvous constraint with T_i targeting T_j between

$$T_i(k) \text{ and } T_i(k + 1),$$
$$T_j(l) \text{ and } T_j(l + 1),$$

then the following precedence relations are specified:

$$T_i(k) \rightarrow T_j(l + 1),$$
$$T_j(l) \rightarrow T_i(k + 1).$$

Within each task, the precedence constraints are:

$$T_i(1) \rightarrow T_i(2) \rightarrow \ldots \rightarrow T_i(m_i).$$

After generating the precedence graph corresponding to these constraints, we use the algorithm shown in Figure 3.17 to revise the deadlines.

Example. Consider the following three periodic tasks:

$T_1: c_1 = 1, d_1 = p_1 = 12.$

$T_2: c_{2,1} = 1, c_{2,2} = 2, d_2 = 5, p_2 = 6.$

$T_3: c_{3,1} = 2, c_{3,2} = 3, d_3 = 12, p_3 = 12.$

T_2 must rendezvous with T_3 after the first scheduling block.

T_3 must rendezvous with T_2 after the first and second scheduling blocks.

Algorithm:

1. Sort the scheduling blocks in $[0, L]$ in reverse topological order, so the block with the latest deadline appears first.
2. Initialize the deadline of the kth instance of $T_{i,j}$ to $(k - 1)p_i + d_i$.
3. Let S and S' be scheduling blocks; the computation time and deadline of S are respectively denoted by c_S and d_S. Considering the scheduling blocks in reverse topological order, revise the corresponding deadlines by $d_S = \min(d_S, \{d'_S - c'_S : S \rightarrow S'\})$.
4. Use the EDF scheduler to schedule the blocks according to the revised deadlines.

Figure 3.17   Scheduling algorithm for tasks with rendezvous constraints.

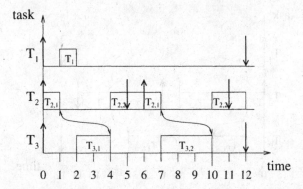

Figure 3.18 Infeasible EDF schedule for tasks with rendezvous constraints.

Here the longest period is 12, which is also the LCM of all three periods. Thus, we generate the following scheduling blocks:

$$T_1(1)$$
$$T_2(1), T_2(2), T_2(3), T_2(4)$$
$$T_3(1), T_3(2).$$

Now we specify the rendezvous constraints between blocks:

$$T_2(1) \rightarrow T_3(2),$$
$$T_3(1) \rightarrow T_2(2),$$
$$T_2(3) \rightarrow T_3(3), \text{ and}$$
$$T_3(2) \rightarrow T_2(4).$$

Without revising the deadlines, the EDF algorithm yields an infeasible schedule, as shown in Figure 3.18. Using the revised deadlines, the ED algorithm produces the schedule shown in Figure 3.19.

3.2.5 Periodic Tasks with Critical Sections: Kernelized Monitor Model

We now consider the problem of scheduling periodic tasks that contain critical sections. In general, the problem of scheduling a set of periodic tasks employing only semaphores to enforce critical sections is nondeterministic polynomial-time decidable (NP)-hard [Mok, 1984]. Here we present a solution for the case in which the length of a task's critical section is fixed [Mok, 1984]. A system satisfying this constraint is the kernelized monitor model, in which an ordinary task requests service from a monitor by attempting to rendezvous with the monitor. If two or more tasks request service from the monitor, the scheduler randomly selects one task to ren-

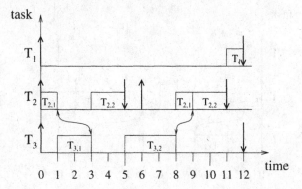

Figure 3.19 EDF schedule for tasks with rendezvous constraints, after revising deadlines.

dezvous with the monitor. Even though a monitor does not have an explicit timing constraint, it must meet the current deadline of the task for which it is performing a service.

Example. Consider the following two periodic tasks:

$$T_1: c_{1,1} = 4, c_{1,2} = 4, d_1 = 20, p_1 = 20,$$
$$T_2: c_2 = 4, d_2 = 4, p_2 = 10.$$

The second scheduling block of T_1 and the scheduling block of T_2 are critical sections.

If we use the EDF algorithm without considering the critical sections, the schedule produced will not meet all deadlines, as shown in Figure 3.20.

At time 8 after completing the second block of T_1, the second instance of T_2 has not arrived yet so the EDF algorithm executes the next ready task with the earliest deadline, which is the second block of T_1. When the second instance of T_2 arrives, T_1 is still executing its critical section (the second block), which cannot be preempted. At time 12, T_2 is scheduled and it misses its deadline at time 15.

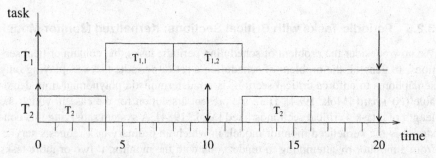

Figure 3.20 Infeasible EDF schedule for tasks with critical sections.

Algorithm:

1. Sort the scheduling blocks in $[0, L]$ in (forward) topological order, so the block with the earliest request times appears first.

2. Initialize the request times of the kth instance of each block $T_{i,j}$ in $[0, L]$ to $(k-1)p_i$.

3. Let S and S' be scheduling blocks in $[0, L]$; the computation time and deadline of S are respectively denoted by c_S and d_S. Considering the scheduling blocks in (forward) topological order, revise the corresponding request times by $r_S = \max(r_S, \{r_{S'} + q : S' \rightarrow S\})$.

4. Sort the scheduling blocks in $[0, L]$ in reverse topological order, so the block with the latest deadline appears first.

5. Initialize the deadline of the kth instance of each scheduling block of T_i to $(k-1)p_i + d_i$.

6. Let S and S' be scheduling blocks; the computation time and deadline of S are respectively denoted by c_S and d_S. Considering the scheduling blocks in reverse topological order, revise the corresponding deadlines by $d_S = \min(d_S, \{d'_S - q : S \rightarrow S'\})$.

7. Use the EDF scheduler to schedule the blocks according to the revised request times and deadlines. Do not schedule any block if the current time instant is within a forbidden region.

Figure 3.21   Scheduling algorithm for tasks with critical sections.

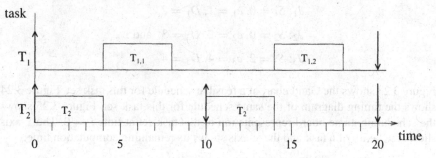

Figure 3.22   Schedule for tasks with critical sections.

Therefore, we must revise the request times as well as the deadlines, and designate certain time intervals as *forbidden regions* reserved for critical sections of tasks. For each request time r_s, the interval $(k_s, r_s), 0 \le r_s - k_s < q$, is a forbidden region if the scheduling of block S cannot be delayed beyond $k_s + q$. The scheduling algorithm is shown in Figure 3.21.

Example. This algorithm produces a feasible schedule, shown in Figure 3.22, for the above two-task system.

3.3   MULTIPROCESSOR SCHEDULING

Generalizing the scheduling problem from a uniprocessor to a multiprocessor system greatly increases the problem complexity since we now have to tackle the problem of assigning tasks to specific processors. In fact, for two or more processors, no scheduling algorithm can be optimal without a priori knowledge of the (1) deadlines, (2) computation times, and (3) start times of the tasks.

3.3.1   Schedule Representations

Besides representations of task schedules such as timing diagrams or Gantt charts, an elegant, dynamic representation of tasks exists in a multiprocessor system called the *scheduling game board* [Dertouzos and Mok, 1989]. This dynamic representation graphically shows the statuses (remaining computation time and laxity) of each task at a given instant.

Example.   Consider a two-processor system ($n = 2$) and three single-instance tasks with the following arrival times, computation times, and absolute deadlines:

$$J_1\colon S_1 = 0, c_1 = 1, D_1 = 2,$$
$$J_2\colon S_2 = 0, c_2 = 2, D_2 = 3, \text{ and}$$
$$J_3\colon S_3 = 2, c_3 = 4, D_3 = 4.$$

Figure 3.23 shows the Gantt chart of a feasible schedule for this task set. Figure 3.24 shows the timing diagram of the same schedule for this task set. Figure 3.25 shows the scheduling game board representation of this task set at time $i = 0$. The x-axis shows the laxity of a task and the y-axis shows its remaining computation time.

3.3.2   Scheduling Single-Instance Tasks

Given n identical processors and m tasks at time $i, m > n$, our objective is to ensure that all tasks complete their execution by their respective deadlines. If $m \leq n$ (the number of tasks does not exceed the number of processors), the problem is trivial since each task has its own processor.

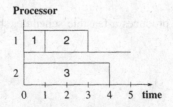

Figure 3.23   Gantt chart.

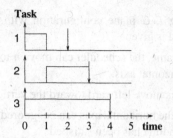

Figure 3.24   Timing diagram.

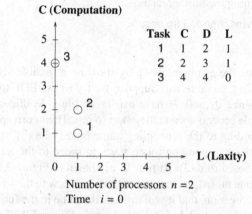

Figure 3.25   Scheduling game board.

Let $C(i)$ denote the remaining computation time of a task at time i, and let $L(i)$ denote the laxity (slack) of a task at time i. On the L-C plane of the scheduling game board, executing any n of the m tasks in parallel corresponds to moving at most n of the m tokens one division (time unit) downward and parallel to the C-axis. Thus, for tasks executed:

$$L(i + 1) = L(i),$$
$$C(i + 1) = C(i) - 1.$$

The tokens corresponding to the remaining tasks that are not executed move to the left toward the C-axis. Thus, for tasks not executed:

$$L(i + 1) = L(i) - 1,$$
$$C(i + 1) = C(i).$$

Rules for the Scheduling Game Board   Each configuration of tokens on the L-C plane represents the scheduling problem at a point in time. The rules for the scheduling game (corresponding to the scheduling problem) are:

1. Initially, the starting L-C plane configuration with tokens representing the tasks to be scheduled is given.

2. At each step of the game, the scheduler can move n tokens one division downward toward the horizontal axis.

3. The rest of the tokens move leftward toward the vertical axis.

4. Any token reaching the horizontal axis can be ignored, that is, it has completed execution and its deadline has been satisfied.

5. The scheduler fails if any token crosses the vertical axis into the second quadrant before reaching the horizontal axis.

6. The scheduler wins if no failure occurs.

Example. We continue the example above by showing a feasible schedule for the task set in the scheduling game board. Suppose we try to use EDF to schedule this task set. At time 0, since J_1 and J_2 have earlier absolute deadlines, they are assigned the two available processors and they start to run. Their corresponding tokens move downward according to the scheduling game board rule (2). At this time, J_3 is not scheduled so its corresponding token starts to move to the left according to the scheduling game board rule (3). At time 1, as shown in Figure 3.26, J_1 finishes execution and J_2 has one more time unit to run, but J_3 is now to the left of the C-axis with a negative laxity, meaning that it will miss its deadline in the future.

We now show a feasible schedule for this task set in Figure 3.27. Instead of using EDF, we try LL. At time 0, since J_3 has the smallest laxity, it is assigned an available processor and starts to run. Since J_1 and J_2 have the same laxity, one (J_1) is chosen randomly to execute in the remaining available processor. Their corresponding tokens move downward according to the scheduling game board rule (2). At this time, J_2 is not scheduled so its corresponding token starts to move to the left according to the scheduling game board rule (3).

At time 1, J_1 finishes execution. J_2 and J_3 are the only ready tasks so they are scheduled to run. Their corresponding tokens move downward according to the scheduling game board rule (2). J_2 finishes execution at time $i = 3$ and J_3 finishes execution at time $i = 4$.

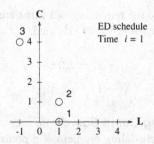

Figure 3.26 Game board showing deadline miss.

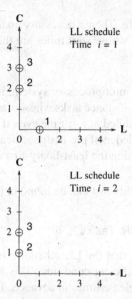

Figure 3.27   Game board showing a feasible schedule.

Sufficient Conditions for Conflict-Free Task Sets   For two or more processors, no deadline scheduling algorithm can be optimal without a priori knowledge
of the deadlines, computation times, and start times of the tasks. If no such a priori
knowledge is available, optimal scheduling is possible only if the set of tasks does not
have subsets that conflict with each another [Dertouzos and Mok, 1989]. A special
case is that in which all tasks have unit computation times. Then the EDF algorithm
is optimal even in the multiprocessor case.

To derive a sufficient condition for multiprocessor scheduling of single-instance
tasks, we first introduce the following notations, which divide the scheduling game
board into 3 regions:

$$R_1(k) = \{J_j : D_j \le k\},$$
$$R_2(k) = \{J_j : L_j \le k \wedge D_j > k\},$$
$$R_3(k) = \{J_j : L_j > k\}.$$

Then we define the following function [Dertouzos and Mok, 1989].

Surplus Computing Power Function: Define for every positive integer k,

$$F(k, i) = kn - \sum_{R_1} C_j - \sum_{R_2} (k - L_j).$$

This function provides a measure of the surplus computing power of the multiprocessor system in terms of available processor time units between a given time instant i

and k time units into the future. Then a necessary condition for scheduling to meet the deadlines of a set of tasks whose start times are the same (at time $i = 0$) is that for all $k > 0$, $F(k, 0) \geq 0$.

Schedulability Test 9: For a multiprocessor system, if a schedule exists that meets the deadlines of a set of single-instance tasks whose start times are the same, then the same set of tasks can be scheduled at run-time even if their start times are different and not known a priori. Knowledge of pre-assigned deadlines and computation times alone is enough to schedule using the least-laxity-first algorithm.

A proof for this schedulability test can be found in [Dertouzos and Mok, 1989].

3.3.3 Scheduling Periodic Tasks

The preceding section shows that the LL scheduler is optimal for a set of single-instance tasks satisfying a sufficient condition. This makes it possible to schedule tasks without knowing their release times in advance. This LL scheduler is no longer optimal for periodic tasks. Next, we present a simple sufficient condition for scheduling periodic tasks.

Simple Condition for Scheduling Periodic Tasks A simple sufficient condition is given in [Dertouzos and Mok, 1989] for feasible scheduling of a set of independent, preemptable, and periodic tasks on a multiprocessor system.

Schedulability Test 10: Given a set of k independent, preemptable (at discrete time instants), and periodic tasks on a multiprocessor system with n processors with

$$U = \sum_{i=1}^{k} \frac{c_i}{p_i} \leq n,$$

let

$$T = GCD(p_1, \ldots, p_k),$$

$$t = GCD\left(T, T\left(\frac{c_1}{p_1}\right), \ldots, T\left(\frac{c_k}{p_k}\right)\right).$$

A sufficient condition for feasible scheduling of this task set is t is integral.

If a task set satisfies Schedulability Test 10, it can be scheduled as follows. For each interval of T time units beginning at time 0, we schedule each task J_i, starting with task J_1, for $T(c_i/p_i)$ time units. Therefore, within one period of task J_i, this task executes

$$\left(\frac{p_i}{T}\right) T\left(\frac{c_i}{p_i}\right) = c_i$$

time units, which is the computation time of J_i. The length of each of these time slices p_i/T is an integer owing to the definition of T. We begin by assigning tasks to processor 1 and "fill it up" until we encounter a task that cannot be scheduled on this processor. Then we assign it to processor 2. If processor 1 still has available time, we check to see if we can assign the next task to it. We repeat this procedure for the remaining tasks and processors. We are ready to show an example.

Example. Consider the following set of periodic tasks (period = deadline):

$$\text{Task } J_1: c_1 = 32, \quad p_1 = 40,$$
$$\text{Task } J_2: c_2 = 3, \quad p_2 = 10,$$
$$\text{Task } J_3: c_3 = 4, \quad p_3 = 20, \text{ and}$$
$$\text{Task } J_4: c_4 = 7, \quad p_4 = 10.$$

Suppose two processors are available for executing these tasks. Is it possible to schedule these four tasks without missing a deadline?

Since the utilization of this task set is

$$U = \sum_{i=1}^{4} \frac{c_i}{p_i} = \frac{32}{40} + \frac{3}{10} + \frac{4}{20} + \frac{7}{10} = 2 \le n = 2,$$

the necessary condition for scheduling is satisfied. Then we use the sufficient condition in Schedulability Test 10 to check if the task set is schedulable.

$$T = GCD(40, 10, 20, 10) = 10,$$

so

$$t = GCD\left(10, 10\left(\frac{32}{40}\right), 10\left(\frac{3}{10}\right), 10\left(\frac{4}{20}\right), 10\left(\frac{7}{10}\right)\right)$$
$$= GCD(8, 3, 2, 7) = 1.$$

Therefore, since 1 is integral, a feasible schedule exists for this task set. One feasible schedule is shown in Figure 3.28.

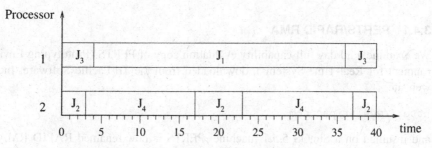

Figure 3.28   Schedule for four periodic tasks on two processors.

In [Lee and Cheng, 1994], we consider the cost of task migration between processors and show that $U \leq n$ is both a necessary and sufficient condition for feasible scheduling for this type of task set.

3.4 AVAILABLE SCHEDULING TOOLS

A variety of tools are available for scheduling and schedulability analysis of real-time tasks. Here we review three such tools and report on our experience using them to schedule tasks in the NASA/International Space Station X-38 Crew Return Vehicle avionics [Rice and Cheng, 1999]. Although the X-38 task scheduling paradigm is not the dynamic scheduling example best supported by commercial scheduling tools, and no sporadic or asynchronous events seem to be present, the requirements for a tool to represent timing relationships of the system, deadlines, and the need for "what-if" analysis and workload adjustment nevertheless exist. Thus, the following tools are briefly and subjectively evaluated against supporting this particular project model:

1. PERTS (now renamed RAPID RMA),
2. PerfoRMAx, and
3. TimeWiz.

We outline the criteria and requirements for the scheduling tool evaluation and present a summary of each tool evaluation against the criteria:

1. ability to represent/model system,
2. ability to perform "what-if" schedulability analysis for changing workloads and to visualize deadlines,
3. ability to provide hardcopy reports of timelines representing system,
4. cost,
5. ease of use, and
6. maturity.

In addition to these evaluation criteria, we also provide information on the product, company, and platform for each scheduling tool.

3.4.1 PERTS/RAPID RMA

We examine a 30-day full-capability evaluation copy of PERTS (Prototyping Environment for Real-Time Systems), downloaded from the Tri-Pacific Software, Inc. web site

http://www.tripac.com

and installed on a SunOS 5.5.1 machine. PERTS is now renamed RAPID RMA, which provides Common Object Request Broker Architecture (CORBA) mapping capabilities, and interfaces to ObjecTime and Wind River's WindView. PERTS provides a complete user documentation as well as a tutorial. The PERTS tool focuses on a task-resource model for the system, which is especially suited for the X-38 project, and provides a graphical means of depicting the system. The X-38's 50-Hz critical task loop is modeled with the PERTS tool. The CPU resources, the Instrumentation Control Processor (ICP) and the Flight Critical Processor (FCP), are first modeled using the PERTS resource editor. We input information such as resource type, processing rate, and preemptability into the tool. Next, the 50-Hz flight critical tasks, the 50-Hz non-flight critical tasks, and a sample 10-Hz flight critical 10 Hertz task are defined in the PERTS task editor.

Attributes such as task name, ready time, deadline, period, workload, and resource(s) utilized are defined for each task. Dependencies between tasks, even on different CPU resources, such as what is required to ensure proper sequencing for X-38 tasks, are easily and graphically represented. A robust set of scheduling, sporadic server, and resource sharing policies are provided in the tool, though only a fixed-priority periodic user-defined scheduling policy across two nodes is required to model the X-38 task system. Because of the deterministic task execution times required in this system, the full power of the scheduling algorithms provided is not utilized. Rather, to ensure a set task execution order, user-specified priorities as well as a phase-offset start time for each task are manually assigned.

PERTS provides the capability for single- and multi-node schedulability analysis across multiple resources, which is precisely what is needed for the X-38 system. The ability to schedule between each of the two processors, the ICP and the FCP, in a Flight Critical Chassis (FCC) and represent dependencies between tasks running on these different resources is required and is provided by the PERTS tool. Single-node analysis is performed running the task set as described above, and the tool graphically shows a 50% CPU utilization for the FCP, which is what is expected. After running a schedule, a display that combines all resources and tasks on a single timeline is produced.

Of all the tools evaluated, the task-resource model provided by this tool is especially useful for modeling the X-38 system. By increasing workloads or changing start times, it is verified that the PERTS tool meets the requirement for schedulability analysis. A task set that is not schedulable is clearly identified as such. The timeline display gives a clear block diagram but does not provide the timeline hardcopy/reporting capability necessary for team communication. Only a screen print is available for hardcopy output. In general, the tool is intuitive, is rich in analysis capability, and seems to have the greatest maturity of all tools evaluated, and taken as is, it best met our scheduler tool evaluation criteria listed above.

3.4.2 PerfoRMAx

We examine an evaluation copy of PerfoRMAx downloaded from the AONIX web site

http://www.aonix.com

and run on a Windows 95 machine. The evaluation copy does not provide a "save" capability, so the X-38 task system is not modeled; rather, we analyze example programs and a complete tutorial to assess the capabilities of this tool. Analogies between example projects provided with the tool and the X-38 are drawn to analyze how this tool might be used to represent the X-38 task structure. The tool provides a tabular, rather than graphical, interface for specifying the system, so the system being studied seems more difficult to visualize. PerfoRMAx utilizes an event-action-resource model for task scheduling. Because tasks in the X-38 system are not sporadic, but rather cyclic and based mainly on a minor frame time, the event-action model used by this tool is less intuitive than the task-resource model provided by PERTS. To use this tool, the user must first define the events, actions, and resources in the system, along with attributes for each. Events are triggers that start a particular action (task).

In the case of the X-38, there are no sporadic events, only timed events to start task execution. In order to model the X-38 system, a triggering event for each task either needs to be artificially defined, or one event that sets off an entire list of tasks, based on a timer, needs to be defined. If the first method is chosen in which each task is triggered by a different event, the tool provides no intuitive way to capture dependencies between events/tasks to ensure deterministic task sequencing. In the latter case, if one event is used to set off a chain of actions, the tool limits chained actions to a number smaller than this project requires. Since the tool produces a timeline based on events only, a single event triggering a number of tasks would show up on the timeline as one item.

We need the ability to view each task and their start/end times on a timeline. To model the system as a set of one or more chained actions seems to be a less intuitive representation for the project and appears to prohibit the per-action or per-task timing analysis needed by the system. The tool does not provide an easy representation of the order dependencies across multiple resources, so the requirement for schedulability analysis of the system is not satisfied. Because a particular task execution order is desired in the X-38 and no phasing information is allowed as input into the tool, it is quite difficult to predetermine task start times and end with the desired resultant schedule even if each task is represented as an event-action pair. A smaller set of scheduling algorithms and event-action specification attributes is provided, and task timing interrelationships are not as easily captured. Hardcopy output of the timeline display does not seem to be available above an entire screen capture. Robust online help and status messages are provided, and extensibility is advertised.

3.4.3 TimeWiz

We examine an evaluation copy of TimeWiz requested from TimeSys Corporation at:

`http://www.timesys.com`

and received and installed on a Windows 95 machine. The evaluation copy does not provide a "save" capability, so like the perfoRMAx tool, the X-38 system is not modeled. Instead, we analyze example programs, a complete tutorial, and robust online help to assess the capabilities of this tool. In addition, a representative from TimeSys has visited the NASA Johnson Space Center, where the X-38 is being designed, and provided an informative consultation on how to best model the X-38 system.

Similar to PerfoRMAx, TimeWiz utilizes an event-action resource model for task scheduling, which seems less intuitive a model for this project. TimeWiz provides a more extensive and robust user interface and some graphical representation capabilities, but the majority of information is entered and viewed tabularly. A rich set of single-node scheduling methodologies and resource sharing paradigms is provided, though only a simple user-defined priority scheduling algorithm is needed. Many object attributes are provided to record aspects of the system. Because, like PerfoRMAx, the timeline display depicts events rather than actions versus time, in order to produce the timeline display as required, each task needs to be artificially paired with a similarly named event. Unlike PerfoRMAx, however, this tool has begun to provide capabilities to capture dependencies and/or precedence relations between events, called "user defined internal events." However, since these dependencies are not yet integrated with the scheduling engine, the requirement to provide schedulability analysis for this system is not met.

Without a way to model dependencies between actions on the same and different resources, the scheduler can devise a valid schedule but have the actions out of the desired sequence. Starttimes (phases) and priorities can be manually entered, so it is possible to generate the desired deterministic schedule. A system timeline showing event start/stop times on all resources in the system is not provided, but is required by the X-38 project. The timeline display is on a per-resource basis, does not contain deadline/start time annotations, and shows events (triggers) rather than actions, and hardcopy capabilities for the timeline are currently limited. This product may be the most preliminary of those evaluated, but it is rapidly evolving to meet particular customer needs and seems extremely well supported. Other features of the tool include an Application Programming Interface (API) for extensibility and some integrated reporting capabilities.

3.5 AVAILABLE REAL-TIME OPERATING SYSTEMS

The goals of conventional, non-real-time operating systems are to provide a convenient interface between the user and the computer hardware while attempting to maximize average throughput, to minimize average waiting time for tasks, and to ensure the fair and correct sharing of resources. However, meeting task deadlines is not an essential objective in non-real-time operating systems since its scheduler usually does not consider the deadlines of individual tasks when making scheduling decisions.

For real-time applications in which task deadlines must be satisfied, a real-time operating system (RTOS) with an appropriate scheduler for scheduling tasks with timing constraints must be used. Since the late 1980s, several experimental as well as commercial RTOSs have been developed, most of which are extensions and modifications of existing operating systems such as UNIX. Most current RTOSs conform to the IEEE POSIX standard and its real-time extensions [Gallmeister and Lanier, 1991; Gallmeister, 1995; Posix]. Commercial RTOSs include LynxOS, RTMX O/S, VxWorks, and pSOSystem.

LynxOS is LynuxWorks's hard RTOS based on the Linux operating system. It is scalable, Linux-compatible, and highly deterministic, and is available from

http://www.lynx.com/

LynuxWorks also offers BlueCat Linux, an open-source Linux for fast embedded system development and deployment.

RTMX O/S has support for X11 and Motif on M68K, MIPS, SPARC and PowerPC processors, and is available from

http://www.rtmx.com/

VxWorks and pSOSystem are Wind River's RTOSs with a flexible, scalable, and reliable architecture, and are available for most CPU platforms. Details can be found in

http://www.windriver.com/products/html/os.html

3.6 HISTORICAL PERSPECTIVE AND RELATED WORK

Scheduling real-time tasks has been extensively studied. The fact that the deadline of every task must be satisfied distinguishes real-time scheduling from non-real-time-scheduling, in which the entire task set is treated as an aggregrate and an overall performance such as throughput is more important. One of the first fundamental works in the field of real-time scheduling is the seminal paper by Liu and Layland [Liu and Layland, 1973], which has laid the groundwork for uniprocessor scheduling using the RM algorithm as well as deadline-based techniques.

Lehoczky, Sha, and Ding give an exact characterization of the RM scheduler and present the necessary and sufficient conditions for RM schedulability in [Lehoczky, Sha, and Ding, 1989]. Lehoczky then provides in [Lehoczky, 1990] an approach for RM scheduling of periodic tasks whose deadlines do not equal their corresponding periods. Mok [Mok, 1984] presents the deterministic rendezvous model and the kernelized monitor model for scheduling periodic tasks.

Lehoczky, Sha, and Strosnider present the deferred server (DS) algorithm [Lehoczky, Sha, and Strosnider, 1987] for scheduling sporadic tasks in a system with periodic tasks. For the special case in which the DS has the shortest period among all tasks (so the DS has the highest priority), a schedulable utilization is presented in [Lehoczky, Sha, and Strosnider, 1987; Strosnider, Lehoczky, and Sha, 1995]. An approach for checking for EDF schedulability is given in [Baruah, Mok, and Rosier, 1990]. Xu and Parnas [Xu and Parnas, 1990] describe scheduling algorithms for tasks with precedence constraints. Sha et al. [Sha, Rajkumar, and Lehoczky, 1990] present a framework for solving the priority inversion problem.

Lin et al. [Lin, Liu, and Natarajan, 1987] propose the concept of imprecise computations that allows a task to trade the quality of the its produced output with the processor time allocated to this task. Wang and Cheng [Wang and Cheng, 2002] recently introduced a new schedulability test and compensation strategy for imprecise computation. Applications of this imprecise computation approach include the work on video transmission by Huang and Cheng [Huang and Cheng, 1995] and by Cheng and Rao [Cheng and Rao, 2002], and the work on TIFF image transmission in ATM networks by Wong and Cheng [Wong and Cheng, 1997].

Several general textbooks on real-time scheduling are available. Liu's book [Liu, 2000] describes many scheduling algorithms and presents real-time communication and operating systems issues. Krishna and Shin's book [Krishna and Shin, 1997] also discusses scheduling but is shorter and more tutorial. It also covers real-time programming languages, databases, fault tolerance, and reliability issues. Burns and Wellings' book [Burns and Wellings, 1990; Burns and Wellings, 1996] focuses on programming languages for real-time systems. Shaw's book [Shaw, 2001] describes real-time software design, operating systems, programming languages, and techniques for predicting execution time.

3.7 SUMMARY

Scheduling a set of tasks (processes) is to determine when to execute which task, thus determining the execution order of these tasks, and in the case of a multiprocessor or distributed system, to also determine an assignment of these tasks to specific processors. This task assignment is analogous to assigning tasks to a specific person in a team of people. Scheduling is a central activity of a computer system, usually performed by the operating system. Scheduling is also necessary in many non-computer systems such as assembly lines.

In non-real-time systems, the typical goal of scheduling is to maximize average throughput (number of tasks completed per unit time) and/or to minimize average waiting time of the tasks. In the case of real-time scheduling, the goal is to meet the deadline of every task by ensuring that each task can be completed by its specified deadline. This deadline is derived from environmental constraints imposed by the application.

Schedulability analysis is to determine whether a specific set of tasks or a set of tasks satisfying certain constraints can be successfully scheduled (completing execution of every task by its specified deadline). A *schedulability test* is used to validate that a given application can satisfy its specified deadlines when scheduled according to a specific scheduling algorithm. This schedulability test is often done at compile time, before the computer system and its tasks start their execution. If the test can be performed efficiently, then it can be done at run-time as an on-line test. A *schedulable utilization* is the maximum utilization allowed for a set of tasks that will guarantee a feasible scheduling of this task set.

A hard real-time system requires that every task or task instance completes its execution by its specified deadline, and failure to do so even for a single task or task instance may lead to catastrophic consequences. A soft real-time system allows some tasks or task instances to miss their deadlines, but a task or task instance that misses a deadline may yield a lower-quality output. Basically two types of schedulers exist: compile-time (static) and run-time (on-line or dynamic).

Optimal scheduler: An *optimal scheduler* is one that may fail to meet a deadline of a task only if no other scheduler can.

Note that optimal in real-time scheduling does not necessarily mean fastest average response time or smallest average waiting time. A task T_i is characterized by the following parameters:

   S: start, release, or arrival time,
   c: (maximum) computation time,
   d: relative deadline (deadline relative to the task's start time),
   D: absolute deadline (wall clock time deadline).

Mainly three types of tasks exist. A *single-instance* task executes only once. A *periodic* task has many instances or iterations, and a fixed period exists between two consecutive releases of the same task. A *sporadic* task has zero or more instances, and a minimum separation occurs between two consecutive releases of the same task. An *aperiodic* task is a sporadic task with either a soft deadline or no deadline. Therefore, if the task has more than one instance (sometimes called a job), we also have the following parameter:

   p: period (for periodic tasks); minimum separation (for sporadic tasks).

The following are additional constraints that may complicate scheduling:

1. Frequency of tasks requesting service periodically,
2. Precedence relations among tasks and subtasks,
3. Resources shared by tasks, and
4. Whether task preemption is allowed or not.

If tasks are preemptable, we assume that a task can be interrupted only at discrete (integer) time instants unless otherwise indicated.

The application and the environment in which the application is embedded are main factors determining the start (release) time, deadline, and period of a task. The computation (or execution) times of a task are dependent on its source code, object code, execution architecture, memory management policies, and actual number of page faults and I/O.

For real-time scheduling purposes, we use the worst-case execution (or computation) time (WCET) as C. This time is not simply an upper bound on the execution of the task code without interruption. This computation time has to include the time the CPU is executing non-task code, such as code for handling page fault caused by this task, as well as the time an I/O request spends in the disk queue for bringing in a missing page for this task.

Determining the computation time of a process is crucial to successfully scheduling it in a real-time system. An overly pessimistic estimate of the computation time would result in wasted CPU cycles, whereas an under-approximation could result in missed deadlines.

One way of approximating WCET is to perform testing and use the largest computation time seen during these tests. Another typical approach to determining a process's computation time is analyzing the source code [Harmon, Baker, and Whalley, 1994; Park, 1992; Park, 1993; Park and Shaw, 1990; Shaw, 1989; Puschner and Koza, 1989; Nielsen, 1987; Chapman, Burns, and Wellings, 1996; Lundqvist and Stenstrvm, 1999; Sun and Liu, 1996]. An alternative to the above methods is to use a probability model to model the WCET of a process as suggested by Burns and Edgar [Burns and Edgar, 2000]. The idea here is to model the distribution of the computation time and use it to compute a confidence level for any given computation time.

A popular real-time scheduling strategy is the *rate-monotonic* (RMS or RM) scheduler, which is a fixed (static)-priority scheduler using the task's (fixed) period as the task's priority. RMS executes at any time instant the instance of the ready task with the shortest period first. If two or more tasks have the same period, RMS randomly selects one for execution next. The RM scheduling algorithm is not optimal in general since schedulable task sets exist that are not RM-schedulable. However, there is a special class of period task sets for which the RM scheduler is optimal.

Schedulability Test 1: Given a set of n independent, preemptable, and periodic tasks on a uniprocessor such that their relative deadlines are equal to or larger than their respective periods and their periods are exact (integer) multiples of each other, let U be the total utilization of this task set. A necessary and sufficient condition for feasible scheduling of this task set is

$$U = \sum_{i=1}^{n} \frac{c_i}{p_i} \le 1.$$

Schedulability Test 2: Given a set of n independent, preemptable, and periodic tasks on a uniprocessor, let U be the total utilization of this task set. A sufficient condition for feasible scheduling of this task set is

$$U \le n(2^{1/n} - 1).$$

Schedulability Test 3: Let

$$w_i(t) = \sum_{k=1}^{i} c_k \left\lceil \frac{t}{p_k} \right\rceil, \quad 0 < t \le p_i.$$

The inequality

$$w_i(t) \leq t$$

holds for any time instant t chosen as follows,

$$t = kp_j, j = 1, \ldots, i, k = 1, \ldots, \left\lfloor \frac{p_i}{p_j} \right\rfloor$$

iff task J_i is RM-schedulable. If $d_i \neq p_i$, we replace p_i by $\min(d_i, p_i)$ in the above expression.

Another fixed-priority scheduler is the deadline-monotonic (DM) scheduling algorithm, which assigns higher priorities to tasks with shorter *relative* deadlines. If every task's period is the same as its deadline, the RM and DM scheduling algorithms are equivalent. In general, these two algorithms are equivalent if every task's deadline is the product of a constant k and this task's period, that is, $d_i = kp_i$.

An optimal, run-time scheduler is the *earliest-deadline-first* (also known as EDF or ED) algorithm, which, at every instant, first executes the ready task with the earliest (closest or nearest) absolute deadline. If more than one task have the same deadline, EDF randomly selects one for execution next. EDF is a dynamic-priority scheduler since task priorities may change at run-time depending on the nearness of their absolute deadlines. Some authors [Krishna and Shin, 1997] call EDF a DM scheduling algorithm whereas others [Liu, 2000] define the DM algorithm as a fixed-priority scheduler that assigns higher priorities to tasks with shorter *relative* deadlines.

Another optimal, run-time scheduler is the *least-laxity-first* (LL) algorithm. Let $c(i)$ denote the remaining computation time of a task at time i. At the arrival time of a task, $c(i)$ is the computation time of this task. Let $d(i)$ denote the deadline of a task relative to the current time i. Then the laxity (or slack) of a task at time i is $d(i) - c(i)$. Thus the laxity of a task is the maximum time the task can delay execution without missing its deadline in the future. The LL scheduler executes at every instant the ready task with the smallest laxity. If more than one task have the same laxity, LL randomly selects one for execution next.

For a uniprocessor, both ED and LL schedulers are optimal for preemptable tasks with no precedence, resource, or mutual exclusion constraints. A simple necessary and sufficient condition exists for scheduling a set of independent, preemptable periodic tasks [Liu and Layland, 1973].

Schedulability Test 4: Let c_i denote the computation time of task J_i. For a set of n periodic tasks such that relative deadline d_i of each task is equal to or greater than its respective period p_i $(d_i \geq p_i)$, a necessary and sufficient condition for feasible scheduling of this task set on a uniprocessor is that the utilization of the tasks is less than or equal to 1:

$$U = \sum_{i=1}^{n} \frac{c_i}{p_i} \leq 1.$$

Schedulability Test 5: A sufficient condition for feasible scheduling of a set of independent, preemptable, and periodic tasks on a uniprocessor is

$$\sum_{i=1}^{n} \frac{c_i}{\min(d_i, p_i)} \leq 1.$$

The term $c_i / \min(d_i, p_i)$ is the *density* of task J_i.

Schedulability Test 6: Given a set of n independent, preemptable, and periodic tasks on a uniprocessor, let U be the utilization as defined in Schedulability Test 4 ($U = \sum_{i=1}^{n} \frac{c_i}{p_i}$), d_{max} be the maximum relative deadline among these tasks' deadlines, P be the least common multiple (LCM) of these tasks' periods, and $s(t)$ be the sum of the computation times of the tasks with absolute deadlines less than t. This task set is not EDF-schedulable iff either of the following conditions is true:

$$U > 1$$

or

$$\exists t < \min\left(P + d_{max}, \left(\frac{U}{1 - U} \right) \max_{1 \leq i \leq n} (p_i - d_i) \right)$$

such that $s(t) > t$.

A fixed-priority scheduler assigns the same priority to all instances of the same task, thus the priority of each task is fixed with respect to other tasks. However, a dynamic-priority scheduler may assign different priorities to different instances of the same task, thus the priority of each task may change with respect to other tasks as new task instances arrive and complete.

In general, there is no optimal fixed-priority scheduling algorithm since given any fixed-priority algorithm, we can always find a schedulable task set that cannot be scheduled by this algorithm. On the other hand, both EDF and LL algorithms are optimal dynamic-priority schedulers.

Sporadic tasks may be released at any time instant but there is a *minimum separation* between releases of consecutive instances of the same sporadic task. To schedule preemptable sporadic tasks, we can transform the sporadic tasks into equivalent periodic tasks. This makes it possible to apply the scheduling strategies for periodic tasks introduced earlier.

A simple approach to schedule sporadic tasks is to treat them as periodic tasks with the minimum separation times as their periods. Then we schedule the periodic equivalents of these sporadic tasks using the scheduling algorithm described earlier.

Unlike periodic tasks, sporadic tasks are released irregularly or may not be released at all. Therefore, even though the scheduler (say the RM algorithm) allocates a time slice to the periodic equivalent of a sporadic task, this sporadic task may not actually be released. The processor remains idle during this time slice if this sporadic task does not request service. When this sporadic task does request service, it immediately runs if its release time is within its corresponding scheduled time slice. Otherwise, it waits for the next scheduled time slice for running its periodic equivalent.

The second approach to schedule sporadic tasks is to treat them as one periodic task J_s with the highest priority and a period chosen to accommodate the minimum separations and computation requirements of this collection of sporadic tasks. Again, a scheduler is used to assign time slices on the processor to each task, including J_s. Any sporadic task may run within the time slices assigned to J_s, whereas the other (periodic) tasks run outside of these time slices.

The third approach, called *deferred server* (DS) [Lehoczky, Sha, and Strosnider, 1987], to schedule sporadic tasks, is the same as the second approach with the following modification. The periodic task corresponding to the collection of sporadic tasks is the DS. When there is no sporadic task waiting for service during a time slice assigned to sporadic tasks, the processor runs the other (periodic) tasks. If a sporadic task is released, then the processor preempts the currently running periodic tasks and runs the sporadic task for a time interval up to the total time slice assigned to sporadic tasks.

For a deferred server with an arbitrary priority in a system of tasks scheduled using the RM algorithm, no known schedulable utilization guarantees a feasible scheduling of this system. However, for the special case in which the DS has the shortest period among all tasks (so the DS has the highest priority), there is a schedulable utilization [Lehoczky, Sha, and Strosnider, 1987; Strosnider, Lehoczky, and Sha, 1995].

Schedulability Test 7: Let p_s and c_s be the period and allocated time for the deferred server. Let $U_s = \frac{c_s}{p_s}$ be the utilization of the server. A set of n independent, preemptable, and periodic tasks with relative deadlines being the same as the corresponding periods on a uniprocessor such that the periods satisfy $p_s < p_1 < p_2 < \cdots < p_n < 2p_s$ and $p_n > p_s + c_s$ is RM-schedulable if the total utilization of this task set (including the DS) is at most

$$U(n) = (n - 1) \left[\left(\frac{U_s + 2}{U_s + 1} \right)^{\frac{1}{n-1}} - 1 \right].$$

Schedulability Test 8: Suppose we have a set M of tasks that is the union of a set M_p of periodic tasks and a set M_s of sporadic tasks. Let the nominal (or initial) laxity l_i of task T_i be $d_i - c_i$. Each sporadic task $T_i = (c_i, d_i, p_i)$ is replaced by an equivalent periodic task $T_i' = (c_i', d_i', p_i')$ as follows:

$$c_i' = c_i,$$

$$p_i' = \min(p_i, l_i + 1),$$
$$d_i' = c_i.$$

If we can find a feasible schedule for the resulting set M' of periodic tasks (which includes the transformed sporadic tasks), then we can schedule the original set M of tasks without knowing in advance the start (release or request) times of the sporadic tasks in M_s.

A sporadic task (c, d, p) can be transformed into and scheduled as a periodic task (c', d', p') if the following conditions hold: (1) $d \geq d' \geq c$, (2) $c' = c$, and (3) $p' \leq d - d' + 1$.

A task precedence graph (also called a task graph or precedence graph) shows the required order of execution of a set of tasks. A node represents a task and directed edges indicate the precedence relationships between tasks. The notation $T_i \rightarrow T_j$ means that T_i must complete execution before T_j can start to execute.

Schedulability Test 9: For a multiprocessor system, if a schedule exists which meets the deadlines of a set of single-instance tasks whose start times are the same, then the same set of tasks can be scheduled at run time even if their start times are different and not known a priori. Knowledge of pre-assigned deadlines and computation times alone is enough for scheduling using the LL algorithm.

EDF-based scheduling algorithms are available for communicating tasks using the deterministic rendezvous model and for periodic tasks with critical sections using kernelized monitor model.

Generalizing the scheduling problem from a uniprocessor to a multiprocessor system greatly increases the problem complexity since we now have to tackle the problem of assigning tasks to specific processors. In fact, for two or more processors, no scheduling algorithm can be optimal without a priori knowledge of the (1) deadlines, (2) computation times, and (3) start times of the tasks.

Schedulability Test 10: Given a set of k independent, preemptable (at discrete time instants), and periodic tasks on a multiprocessor system with n processors with

$$U = \sum_{i=1}^{k} \frac{c_i}{p_i} \leq n,$$

let

$$T = GCD(p_1, \ldots, p_k)$$
$$t = GCD\left(T, T\left(\frac{c_1}{p_1}\right), \ldots, T\left(\frac{c_k}{p_k}\right)\right).$$

A sufficient condition for feasible scheduling of this task set is that t is integral.

EXERCISES

1. Suppose a task consists of n subtasks J_i, each of which has computation time $c_i, i = 1, \ldots, n$. This task requests service at time k and has absolute deadline D. Give a formula to compute the latest deadline for completing each subtask such that the deadline of the entire task can be satisfied.

2. A scheduler is said to obey the stack discipline if whenever task A is preempted by task B, task A cannot resume execution before task B completes. A random scheduler is one that selects a task to execute every time unit by random choice. Does the random scheduler obey the stack discipline? Justify your answer clearly or give a counter-example.

3. The rate-monotonic scheduling algorithm is used to assign priority to the following task set. All tasks arrive at time 0.

```
task   period   computation time
A        30            1
B        10            1
C         6            1
D         5            1
E         2            1
```

   (a) Show a schedule. What is the maximum response time for each task? Show all your calculations.
   (b) If the periods of the tasks in a task set are all multiples of a base unit, say 4, is the static priority scheduler as good as the earliest deadline scheduler for this type of task set? Give a proof or show a counter-example.

4. Determine whether the following task set is RM-schedulable. If yes, show an RM schedule. All tasks arrive at time 0.

```
task   period   computation time
A        50            8
B        20            3
C        35           15
D        10            2
```

5. Schedule the task set in exercise 3 using the FIFO (FCFS) scheduler. Is the schedule feasible?

6. Schedule the task set in exercise 3 using the EDF scheduler.

7. Schedule the task set in exercise 3 using the LL scheduler.

8. Show three periodic tasks that do not satisfy the simple schedulable utilization (Schedulability Test 2) but can still be RM-scheduled.

9. Construct a set of periodic tasks (showing start times, computation times, and periods) that can be scheduled by the EDF algorithm but not by the RM algorithm.

10. Prove the optimality of the LL algorithm for a set of independent, preemptable tasks on a uniprocessor.

11. Under what condition(s) are the RM algorithm and the EDF algorithm equivalent?

12. There is an optimal priority-based scheduling algorithm for nonpreemptable tasks with arbitrary start times, computations times, and deadlines on a uniprocessor. Suppose the start times are 0 for all tasks in a task set. Is the EDF or LL algorithm optimal for this type of task set? Justify your answer.

13. Consider the following three periodic tasks:

$T_1: c_{1,1} = 1, c_{1,2} = 2, c_{1,3} = 3, d_1 = p_1 = 18.$

$T_2: c_{2,1} = 1, c_{2,2} = 2, d_2 = 5, p_2 = 6.$

$T_3: c_3 = 1, d_3 = p_3 = 18.$

T_1 must rendezvous with T_2 after the first, second, and third scheduling blocks.

T_2 must rendezvous with T_1 after the first scheduling block.

Construct a schedule for this task set.

14. Is it possible to find a set of n^3 tasks which can be scheduled on a multiprocessor systems with n processors. Justify your answer.

15. Graphically show on a scheduling game board the three regions $(R_1(k), R_2(k), R_3(k))$ of tasks defined in section 3.3.2. Describe the urgency of the tasks in each region.

16. The scheduling game board is a concise way of representing a scheduling problem at a particular instant of time. If tasks are not independent, that is, they have precedence constraints, then the existing game board representation and the execution rules as defined in the paper are not appropriate. Furthermore, the necessary and sufficient condition for scheduling tasks may no longer apply. Give an extension to the game board and the execution rules to handle precedence constraints, and suggest a technique and/or a new necessary and sufficient condition for scheduling.

17. Explain why there are "conflict sets" of tasks when we consider multiprocessor scheduling of independent tasks but there are no such conflict sets in uniprocessor scheduling.

18. Consider the sufficient condition for scheduling a set of periodic tasks: t must be integral. Is it still possible to schedule a set of periodic tasks if t is not integral but U (utilization) is less than n (number of processors). Justify your answer. If yes, show a task set and its schedule.

CHAPTER 4

MODEL CHECKING OF
FINITE-STATE SYSTEMS

One way to show that a program or system meets the designer's specification is to manually construct a proof using axioms and inference rules in a deductive system such as temporal logic, a first-order logic capable of expressing relative ordering of events. This traditional, manual approach to concurrent program verification is tedious and error-prone even for small programs. For finite-state concurrent systems and systems that can be represented as such, we can use model checking instead of proof construction to check their correctness relative to their specifications.

In the model checking approach, we represent the concurrent system as a finite-state graph, which can be viewed as a finite *Kripke structure*. The specification or safety assertion is expressed in propositional temporal logic formulas. We can then check whether the system meets its specification using an algorithm called a *model checker*. In other words, the model checker determines whether the Kripke structure is a model of the formula(s). Several model checkers are available and they vary in code and run-time complexity. Here we describe one of the first model checkers, proposed by [Clarke, Emerson, and Sistla, 1986], and a more efficient symbolic model checker, developed later by [Burch et al., 1990a].

In Clarke, Emerson, and Sistla's [1986] approach, the system to be checked is represented by a *labeled finite-state graph* and the specification is written in a propositional, branching-time temporal logic called *computation tree logic* (CTL). The use of linear-time temporal logic, which can express fairness properties, is ruled out since a model checker such as logic has high complexity. Instead, fairness requirements are moved into the semantics of CTL. In this chapter, we use the terms program and system interchangeably.

4.1   SYSTEM SPECIFICATION

To construct the finte-state graph corresponding to a given concurrent program, we have to thoroughly understand the program and determine the effect of each statement or action in the program. If a flow or control graph has been used in the design of the program, we can use it to determine the effect of each statement. One way to construct the finite-state graph is to begin with the initial state labeled with the initial values of all program variables or attributes, which are called *labels* here. Then for each possible next statement, we execute the statement and examine any change to one or more program variables. We construct a new state if it is different from any existing state. Note that sometimes we need to construct a new state even if its labels are the same as those in an existing state because the sequence of actions leading to the present state is different from that leading to the existing state. A directed edge is constructed from the state we are considering to the new state. We repeat this state and edge construction step for each new state until there are no states to consider. An example program and the corresponding finite-state graph in adjacency matrix form are shown in section 4.4.1.

For other systems that are not computer programs, we can perform a similar graph construction. First, we identify the state attributes that are relevant in the system to be specified in the CTL structure.

Example. In a railroad crossing scenario, the train has several possible positions: BEFORE-APPROACH means that the train has not been detected by the crossing sensor so it is far from the crossing, APPROACH means that the train has been detected by the crossing sensor and is approaching the crossing, BEFORE-CROSSING means that the train is near the crossing but is not on it yet, CROSSING means that the train is crossing and thus occupying the crossing intersection, and AFTER-CROSSING means that the train has left the crossing. Therefore, the state attribute train-position has one of the above five values at a given time or state here. Next, we simulate or actually execute the possible actions in the system and observe the changes in the state attributes in a way similar to that of executing statements in a program and observing the changes in the program variables. We can then construct the finite-state graph as described above and shown in Figure 4.1.

Note that given a particular system to be specified, we can model it with the level of details required by our goal. In the railroad crossing example, each position of the train can be further divided into more precise numerical coordinates. This of course requires more states and transitions in the CTL structure, which in turn makes the analysis more complex.

The state-graph construction is very important since the correctness of the model checking depends on correctly capturing the concurrent program to be checked in the state graph. This construction is not discussed in [Clarke, Emerson, and Sistla, 1986] but an algorithm for it can be easily implemented [Cheng et al., 1993; Zupan and Cheng, 1994b] (see chapters 10 and 12). We first formally define the CTL structure.

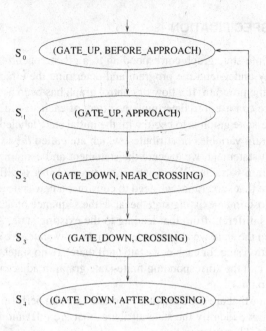

Figure 4.1 CTL structure for the railroad crossing system.

CTL Structure: Formally, the *CTL structure* (*state graph*) is a triple, $M = (S, R, P)$, where

1. S is a finite set of states,
2. R is a binary relation on S which gives the possible transitions between states, and
3. P assigns to each state the set of atomic propositions true in that state.

The next step is to specify the specification or safety assertion in CTL.

CTL consists of a set AP of atomic propositions, which can be attributes such as C1 (process 1 in critical section), program variable value C = 1 (variable C has value 1), or BEFORE-CROSSING in the railroad crossing scenario. Every atomic proposition is a CTL formula. More complex CTL formulas can be constructed using the operators NOT, AND, AX, EX, AU, and EU. The operators NOT and AND have their usual meanings. To define the remaining operators, we need to define a *path* as an infinite, directed sequence of states (some of which may be the same) in the CTL structure.

The symbol X is the *next-time operator*. The formula AX f_1 means that f_1 holds in every immediate successor of the current program state. Alternatively, the formula EX f_1 means that f_1 holds in some immediate successor of the current program state. The symbol U is the *until operator*. The formula A[f_1 U f_2] means that for every computation path there exists an initial prefix of the path such that f_2 holds at the last state of the prefix and f_1 holds at all other states along the prefix. Alternatively, the formula $E[f_1 \ U \ f_2]$ means that for some computation path there exists an initial prefix of the path such that f_2 holds at the last state of the prefix and f_1 holds at all other states along the prefix.

To simplify the specification, we use the following abbreviations. $AF(f)$ means $A[\text{True U } f]$: f holds in the future along every path from the initial state s_0, so f is inevitable. $EF(f)$ means $E[\text{True U } f]$: some path from the initial state s_0 exists that leads to a state at which f holds, so f potentially holds. $EG(f)$ means NOT $AF(\text{NOT } f)$: some path from the initial state s_0 exists on which f holds at every state. $AG(f)$ means NOT $EF(\text{NOT } f)$: f holds at every state on every path from the initial state s_0, so f holds globally.

Figure 4.1 shows the finite-state graph of our simple railroad crossing system. Each state consists of two variables (gate-position, train-position). The initial state is $s0$.

4.2 CLARKE–EMERSON–SISTLA MODEL CHECKER

The Clarke–Emerson–Sistla (CES) model checker can determine whether a formula f_0 written in CTL is true in a given CTL structure. It uses a compositional approach to analysis and hence operates in stages. The first stage checks all subformulas of length 1 in f_0, that is, all atomic propositions. These atomic propositions hold in states having labels that are identical to these propositions. The second stage checks all subformulas of length 2 in f_0 based on the results in stage 1, and labels each state with the subformulas that hold in that state, and so on. As a result, each state will be labeled with the set of subformulas of length less than or equal to i after the completion of the ith stage. At completion, the model checker will have checked the entire formula of length n.

The following data structures and functions [Clarke, Emerson, and Sistla, 1986] to access the labels associated with each state. The variables $arg1$ and $arg2$ refer to the first and second arguments of a binary temporal operator. The variable $labeled[s][f]$ is true if state s is labeled with formula numbered f, false otherwise. The function $addlabel(s, f, labeled)$ adds formula f to the current label of state s by modifying the array $labeled$.

To simplify the input of CTL formulas and internal processing, we use prefix notation to write the formulas. Now the length of a formula is equal to the total number of operands and operators in it. Suppose that formula f is assigned an integer i. If f is unary (e.g., $f = \text{NOT } f_1$), then we assign the integers $i+1$ through $i+\text{length}(f_1)$ to the subformulas of f_1. If f is binary (e.g., $f = \text{AU } f_1 f_2$), then we assign the integers $i+1$ through $i+\text{length}(f_1)$ to the subformulas of f_1 and $i+\text{length}(f_1)+1$ through $i+\text{length}(f_1)+\text{length}(f_2)$ to the subformulas of f_2. Using this assignment, in one pass through f, we can build two arrays, $nf[\text{length}(f)]$ and $sf[\text{length}(f)]$, where $nf[i]$ is the ith subformula of f in the above numbering and $sf[i]$ is the list of numbers assigned to the immediate subformulas of the ith formula. For example, if $f = (\text{AU (NOT CROSSING) GATE-DOWN})$, then nf and sf are

```
nf[1] (AU (NOT CROSSING) GATE-DOWN)              sf[1] (2 4)
nf[2] (NOT CROSSING)                             sf[2] (3)
nf[3] CROSSING                                   sf[3] nil
nf[4] GATE-DOWN                                  sf[4] nil.
```

Therefore, we can determine in constant time the operator of a formula f and the numbers assigned to its arguments given f's number. This enables us to efficiently implement the function *labelgraph*. Instead of using the function labeled as in [Clarke, Emerson, and Sistla, 1986], we use the array *labeled*[][] and the initial array *initlabeled*[][], making the access and update faster. *labeled*[s][a] is true if state s is labeled with formula number a.

To handle an arbitrary formula f, we apply the *labelgraph* function to each subformula of f, starting with the highest numbered (simplest) formula and working backwards. Note that the indices in the following C code start from 0 instead of 1 since arrays in C are indexed from 0.

```
for (fi=flength; fi >= 1; fi--)
    labelgraph(fi,s,&correct);
```

The following C function *labelgraph*(fi, s, b) determines whether fi holds in state s. Note that it can handle seven cases: fi is atomic or has one of the following operators (NOT, AND, AX, EX, AU, or EU).

```
/*==========================================================================*/
/*        function labelgraph                                               */
/*==========================================================================*/


/* procedure labelgraph (fi,s,b) */
labelgraph (fi,s,b)
short fi, s;
Boolean *b;
{
    short i;
    switch(nf[fi-1][0].opcode)
        {
        case atomic:
                atf(fi,s,b);
                break;
        case nt:
                ntf(fi,s,b);
                break;
        case ad:
                adf(fi,s,b);
                break;
        case ax:
                axf(fi,s,b);
                break;
        case ex:
                exf(fi,s,b);
                break;
```

```
        case au:
                for (i=0; i <= numstates; i++)
                    marked[i] = false;
                for (i=0; i <= numstates; i++)
                    if (!marked[i])
                        auf(fi,s,b);
                break;
        case eu:
                euf(fi,s,b);
                break;
    }
}
/*labelgraph*/
```

The following recursive C function *auf*(*f i*, *s*, *b*) determines whether the formula *f i* with an AU operator holds in state *s*. The code for initialization and for processing formulas with the other six operators is listed in section 4.5.

```
/*==========================================================================*/
/*      function auf                                                       */
/*      In : fi = input formula number                                     */
/*           s  = state of the transition graph at which f is to be proved */
/*      Out : b = true if formula f is true at state s                     */
/*      Description:                                                       */
/*      Use DFS to determine whether (au arg1 arg2) is true in state s     */
/*==========================================================================*/


/* procedure auf (fi,s,b) */
auf (fi,s,b)
short fi, s;
Boolean *b;
{
    short a1, a2, s1;
    Boolean b1;
    a1 = sf[fi-1].arg1;
    a2 = sf[fi-1].arg2;
    *b = true;
    /*
    #-------------------------------------------------------------------
    # If s is marked, check to see if s is labeled with fi; return true
    # if it is, else false.
    #-------------------------------------------------------------------
    */
    if (marked[s])
        {
            if (labeled[s][fi-1])
                *b = true;
            else *b = false;
        }
```

```
      else
            /*
            #------------------------------------------------------------------------
            # If the state has not been visited (marked), mark it and check to see
            # if it is labeled with the argument 2.
            #------------------------------------------------------------------------
            */ {
               marked[s] = true;
               if (labeled[s][a2-1] || initlabeled(s,nf[a2-1]))
                     {
                        addlabel(s,fi,labeled);
                        *b = true;
                     }
               else if (!(labeled[s][a1-1] || initlabeled(s,nf[a1-1])))
                     {
                        *b = false;
                     }
               else {
                     /*
                     #------------------------------------------------------------
                     # For all successor states of s, check to see if f is true.
                     #------------------------------------------------------------
                     */
                     s1 = 0;
                     while (*b && (s1 <= numstates))
                           {
                              if ((s != s1) && (e[s][s1] == 1))
                                    {
                                       auf(fi,s1,&b1);
                                       if (!b1)
                                          *b = false;
                                    }
                              s1 = s1 + 1;
                           }
                     if (*b)
                        addlabel(s,fi,labeled);
                  }
            }
}
/*auf*/
```

The function *auf* basically performs a depth-first search of the CTL structure starting from state *s*. It checks whether each path from *s* has a prefix with states labeled with the first argument of AU and eventually leading to a state labeled with the second argument of AU. It does so by labeling state *s* and the successor states of *s* that satisfy the formula *fi*, and then calling the function itself recursively to perform the same check. As soon as a state that is not labeled with the first argument is reached prior to reaching a state labeled with the second argument, the function returns false.

4.2.1 Analysis Complexity

If the states in the CTL structure are correctly labeled with $arg1$ and $arg2$ of f, function auf requires time O(number of states in CTL structure+number of transitions). Since each pass through the main loop takes time O(number of states in CTL structure + number of transitions), the entire model checker requires $O(\text{length}(f)^*,$ (number of states in CTL structure + number of transitions)).

4.3 EXTENSIONS TO CTL

Extensions to CTL are needed to handle the verification of correctness along *fair* execution sequences and to specify absolute time instead of relative ordering of events. Here, we discuss how to extend CTL to handle fairness properties. For example, with a real-time rule-based program, we would like to consider the execution paths (sequences of rule firings) in which enabled rules are equally likely to be selected for execution, that is, a fair scheduler is assumed. Similarly, with a collection of concurrent processes, we would like to consider only the computation paths in which each process is executed infinitely often. In general, a fairness condition asserts that requests for service are granted sufficiently often [Garbay et al., 1980]. Many definitions exist of "requests" and "sufficiently often." Here, we say a path is *fair* if enabled events in each state along the path are equally likely to happen.

CTL cannot express the correctness of fair executions. More precisely, the property that some proposition P should eventually hold on all fair executions cannot be specified in CTL. To handle fairness while maintaining an efficient model checking algorithm, we modify the semantics of CTL [Clarke, Emerson, and Sistla, 1986] to yield a new logic called CTL-F. It has the same syntax but a structure is now a 4-tuple (S, R, P, F), where S, R, P have the same meaning as described earlier and F is a collection of predicates on S. A path is F-fair iff for each $g \subseteq F$, infinitely many states on the path satisfy predicate g. In CTL-F, all path quantifiers range over fair paths but the semantics remain the same as in CTL. For any given finite structure $M = (S, R, P)$, collection $F = G_1, \ldots, G_n$ of subsets of S, and state $s_0 \in S$, there exists an F-fair path in M starting at s_0 iff there exists a strongly connected component C of the graph of M such that (1) a finite path exists from s_0 to a state $t \in C$ and (2) for each G_i a state $t_i \in C \cap G_i$ exists.

4.4 APPLICATIONS

One application of a model checker is to determine whether a program will terminate, that is, reach a fixed point, under all conditions. For instance, the module *mcf* in [Browne, Cheng, and Mok, 1988] (described in chapter 10) is a temporal logic model checker based on the Clarke–Emerson–Sistla algorithm for checking the satisfiability of temporal logic formulas written in CTL. Our model checker assumes that strong fairness is observed by the scheduler, that is, rules that are enabled infinitely often will eventually fire. Under this assumption, a cycle in the state space graph that has at least one edge exiting from it is sufficient to allow the program to reach a fixed point in a finite number of iterations. (The program will leave the states in the cycle because the rule associated with the exit edge must eventually fire.) However, the model checker will warn the designer that the program may require a finite but unbounded number of iterations to reach a fixed point.

4.4.1 Analysis Example

We now describe how a model checker can be applied to determine whether a rule-based program written in the EQL (equational logic) language (described in chapter 10) will always terminate. The purpose of the following program is to determine whether an object is detected at each monitor-decide cycle. The system consists of two processes and an external alarm clock which invokes the program by periodically setting the variable *wakeup* to true.

```
(* Example EQL Program *)
PROGRAM distributed;
CONST
false = 0;
true = 1;
a = 0;
b = 1;
VAR
synca,
syncb,
wakeup,
objectdetected : BOOLEAN;
arbiter : INTEGER;
INPUTVAR
sensora,
sensorb : INTEGER;
INIT
synca := true,
syncb := true,
wakeup := true,
objectdetected := false,
arbiter := a
RULES
(* process A *)
objectdetected := true ! synca := false
IF (sensora = 1) AND (arbiter = a) AND (synca = true)
    [] objectdetected := false ! synca := false
IF (sensora = 0) AND (arbiter = a) AND (synca = true)
    [] arbiter := b ! synca := true ! wakeup := false
IF (arbiter = a) AND (synca = false) AND (wakeup = true)

(* process B *)
    [] objectdetected := true ! syncb := false
IF (sensorb = 1) AND (arbiter = b) AND (syncb = true)
```

```
AND (wakeup = true)
        [] objectdetected := false ! syncb := false
IF (sensorb = 0) AND (arbiter = b) AND (syncb = true)
AND (wakeup = true)
        [] arbiter := a ! syncb := true ! wakeup := false
IF (arbiter = b) AND (syncb = false) AND (wakeup = true)

TRACE objectdetected
PRINT synca, syncb, wakeup, objectdetected, arbiter, sensora,
sensorb
END.
```

In this example, the input variables are *sensora* and *sensorb* and the program variables are *objectdetected*, *synca*, *syncb*, *arbiter*, and *wakeup*. The symbol [] is a rule separator and the symbol ! separates parallel assignments within the same rule.

Each process runs independently of the other. An alarm clock external to the program is used to invoke the processes after some specified period of time. A rule is fired by executing the assignment statement when the enabling condition becomes true. In this example, the shared variable *arbiter* is used as a control-synchronization variable which enforces mutually exclusive access to shared variables such as *object-detected* by different processes. The variables *synca* and *syncb* are used as control-synchronization variables within process A and process B, respectively. Note that for each process, at most two rules will be fired before control is transferred to the other process. Initially, process A is given mutually exclusive access to variables *objectdetected* and *synca*.

The EQL program with the initial input values can be represented by a finite state–space graph. An automatic graph generator for this purpose is available [Cheng et al., 1993].

```
Finite State Space Graph Corresponding to Input Program:
-----------------------------------------------------------

state next states
-----------------


rule # 1 2 3 4 5 6
0:      1 0 0 0 0 0
1:      1 1 2 1 1 1
2:      2 2 2 2 2 2

State Labels:
-------------

state (synca, syncb, wakeup, objectdetected, arbiter, sensora, sensorb)

0       1 1 1 0 0 1 0
1       0 1 1 1 0 1 0
2       1 1 0 1 1 1 0
```

Next, we write the CTL temporal logic formula for checking whether this program will reach a fixed point in finite time from the initial state corresponding to the initial input and program variable values. This formula, together with the representation of the labeled state–space graph, is the input to the model checker and the timing analyzer.

```
3
1 1 0
0 1 1
0 0 1
0 n1 ;
1 n1 ;
2 f1 ;
(au n1 f1)
0
```

The temporal logic model checker can now be used to determine whether a fixed point is always reachable in a finite number of iterations by analyzing this finite state–space graph with the given initial state. To verify that the program will reach a fixed point from any initial state, the reachability graph of every initial state must be analyzed by the model checker. The complete state–space graph of the example EQL program, which consists of eight separate finite reachability graphs, one for each distinct initial state, is shown in Figure 10.5 in Chapter 10. For example, the graph with initial state $(t, t, t, -, a, 0, 1)$, corresponding to the combination of input values and initial program values, is one of $2^3 = 8$ possible graphs that must be checked by the model checker.

In general, for a finite-domain EQL program with n input variables and m program variables, the total number of reachability graphs that have to be checked in the worst case (i.e., all combinations of the values of the input and program variables are possible) is $\prod_{i=1}^{n} |X_i| \prod_{j=1}^{m} |S_j|$, where $|X_i|$, $|S_j|$ are respectively the size of the domains of the ith input and jth program variable. If all variables are binary, then this number is 2^{n+m}. In practice, the number of reachability graphs that must be checked is substantially less because many combinations of input and program variable values do not constitute initial states.

4.5 COMPLETE CTL MODEL CHECKER IN C

```
/*===============================================================================*/
/*                                                                               */
/*      Program Model Checker                    Albert Mo Kim Cheng             */
/*                                                                               */
/*      Description of the Program:                                              */
/*                                                                               */
/*             This program implements the Clarke-Emerson-Sistla algorithm       */
/*      for verifying finite-state concurrent systems using temporal logic       */
/*      specifications.                                                          */
/*                                                                               */
/*-------------------------------------------------------------------------------*/
```

```
/*                                                                          */
/*       Input:                                                             */
/*               1. global state transition graph e                        */
/*               2. initial labels flabel                                  */
/*               3. temporal logic formula to be proved                    */
/*               4. state at which formula is to be proved                 */
/*                                                                          */
/*       Output:                                                           */
/*               1. labeled global state transition graph                  */
/*               2. formula proved to be true or false                     */
/*                                                                          */
/*--------------------------------------------------------------------------*/
/*                                                                          */
/*       Functions:                                                        */
/* 1. typeoperator - returns type of operator when given a code */
/* 2. empty - true if the stack is empty       */
/* 3. initlabeled - true if state s is initially labeled with f */
/*                                                                          */
/*       Procedures:                                                       */
/* 1.  readgraph - read in the global state transition graph   */
/* 2.  push - push item into stack          */
/* 3.  pop - pop item from stack          */
/* 4.  readf - reads temporal logic formula     */
/* 5.  buildnfsf - builds arrays nf and sf      */
/* 6.  addlabel - adds label to state s          */
/* 7.  initsystem - initializes the proof system     */
/* 8.  initlabeled - true if s is initially labeled with f     */
/* 9.  atf - procedure for processing atomic proposition     */
/* 10. ntf - procedure for processing NOT operator     */
/* 11. adf - procedure for processing AND operator     */
/* 12. axf - procedure for processing AX operator     */
/* 13. exf - procedure for processing EX operator     */
/* 14. auf - procedure for processing AU operator     */
/* 15. euf - procedure for processing EU operator     */
/* 16. labelgraph - labels the state transition graph     */
/* 17. readlabel - reads in the initial labels of the graph     */
/* 18. printheading - prints program heading     */
/* 19. printoutput - prints labeled graph and proof result     */
/*                                                                          */
/*==========================================================================*/


/* program modelchecker */

#include <stdio.h>
#include <local/ptc.h>


#define maxstates 100 /* maximum number of states in the global */
/* state transition graph  */
#define maxflength 100 /* maximum length of the input formula  */

/*--------------------------------------------------------------------------*/
```

```
#define atomic 0
#define nt 1
#define ad 2
#define ax 3
#define ex 4
#define au 5
#define eu 6
typedef byte operatortype;
typedef struct item *itemptr;
struct item
     {
         short ip;
         itemptr next;
     };
typedef char codetype[2];
struct optype
     {
         short p;
         operatortype opcode;
         codetype op;
     };
typedef byte graphtype[maxstates+1][maxstates+1];
typedef struct optype ftype[maxflength];
typedef codetype fcode[maxflength+1];
typedef fcode flabeltype[maxstates+1];
typedef Boolean labeltype[maxflength][maxstates+1];
struct flist
     {
         short arg1, arg2;
     };
typedef ftype nftype[maxflength];
typedef struct flist sftype[maxflength];
typedef Boolean marktype[maxstates+1];

/*-------------------------------------------------------------------------*/

graphtype e; /* global state transition graph */
labeltype labeled; /* indicates which formulas are */
/* labeled in each state */
nftype nf; /* array of subformulas numbered */
/* in the order they appear in   */
/* the original formula */
sftype sf; /* gives the list of arguments, if */
/* any, of each subformula operator*/
short fi,  /* number corresponding to a subformula */
      s,   /* state at which formula is to be */
   /* proved true or false     */
         numstates,  /* number of states in the graph */
         flength; /* length of the input formula */
ftype formula; /* input formula to be proved */
marktype marked; /* indicates which states in the */
/* state transition graph have been */
/* visited in procedure labelgraph */
```

```
Boolean correct; /* true if formula is true at state s */
flabeltype flabel; /* set of initial labels in character */
/* form        */


/*============================================================================*/
/* function typeoperator      */
/* In : op = two letter code representing an operator or variable       */
/* Out : typeoperator = type of operator       */
/*============================================================================*/


/* function typeoperator (op) */
operatortype typeoperator (_op)
codetype _op;
{
   codetype op;
   operatortype _typeoperator;
   ARRAYcopy(_op,op,sizeof(op));

   if ((op[0] != 'a') && (op[0] != 'e') && (op[0] != 'n'))
       _typeoperator = atomic;
   else {
           switch(op[0])
               {
               case 'a':
                       if ((op[1] != 'd') && (op[1] != 'u') && (op[1] != 'x'))
                           _typeoperator = atomic;
                       else {
                               switch(op[1])
                                   {
                                   case 'd':
                                           _typeoperator = ad;
                                           break;
                                   case 'u':
                                           _typeoperator = au;
                                           break;
                                   case 'x':
                                           _typeoperator = ax;
                                           break;
                                   }
                           }
                       break;
               /*
               #------------------------------------------------------------
               */ case 'e':
                       if (op[1] == 'u')
                           _typeoperator = eu;
                       else if (op[1] == 'x')
                           _typeoperator = ex;
                       else _typeoperator = atomic;
                       break;
               /*
               #------------------------------------------------------------
```

```
                        */ case 'n':
                            if (op[1] == 't')
                                _typeoperator = nt;
                            else _typeoperator = atomic;
                            break;
                    }
            }
        return(_typeoperator);
}
/*typeoperator*/


/*=========================================================================*/
/* procedure readgraph        */
/* Out : e   = graph          */
/*       numstates = number of states in the graph        */
/*=========================================================================*/


/* procedure readgraph (e,numstates) */
readgraph (e,numstates)
graphtype e;
short *numstates;
{
    short i, j;
    fprintf(stdout," Please enter the number of states in the graph:");
    writeln(stdout);
    writeln(stdout);
    fscanf(stdin,"%d",numstates);
    readln(stdin);
    *numstates = *numstates - 1;
    fprintf(stdout," Please enter graph in adjacency matrix form:");
    writeln(stdout);
    writeln(stdout);
    for (i=0; i <= maxstates; i++)
        for (j=0; j <= maxstates; j++)
            e[i][j] = 0;
    for (i=0; i <= *numstates; i++)
        {
            for (j=0; j <= *numstates; j++)
                fscanf(stdin,"%d",&e[i][j]);
            readln(stdin);
        }
    fprintf(stdout,"   ");
    for (i=0; i <= *numstates; i++)
        fprintf(stdout,"%3d",i);
    writeln(stdout);
    for (i=0; i <= *numstates; i++)
        {
            fprintf(stdout,"%3d",i);
            for (j=0; j <= *numstates; j++)
                fprintf(stdout,"%3d",e[i][j]);
            writeln(stdout);
```

```
      }
   writeln(stdout);
}
/*readgraph*/


/*==============================================================================*/
/* procedure readlabel        */
/* Out : flabel    = initial labels of the graph        */
/*==============================================================================*/


/* procedure readlabel (flabel) */
readlabel (flabel)
flabeltype flabel;
{
   char symbol;
   short i, j, s;
   fprintf(stdout," Please enter the initial labels in the following form: ");
   writeln(stdout);
   fprintf(stdout," state number      label1 label2 ... labeln ; ");
   writeln(stdout);
   writeln(stdout);
   /*
   #----------------------------------------------------------------------------
   # Read in the initial labels for each state.
   #----------------------------------------------------------------------------
   */
   for (s=0; s <= numstates; s++)
      {
          fscanf(stdin,"%d",&i);
          symbol = getc(stdin);
          j = 1;
          while (symbol != ';')
                 {
                     if (symbol != ' ')
                        {
                            flabel[s][j][0] = symbol;
                            flabel[s][j][1] = getc(stdin);
                            j = j + 1;
                        }
                     symbol = getc(stdin);
                 }
          readln(stdin);
          writeln(stdout);
          fprintf(stdout,"%3d ",s);
          j = 1;
          while (flabel[s][j][0] != ' ')
                 {
                     putc(flabel[s][j][0],stdout);
                     fprintf(stdout,"%c ",flabel[s][j][1]);
                     j = j + 1;
                 }
```

```
      }
   writeln(stdout);
   writeln(stdout);
}
/*readlabel*/


/*=============================================================================*/
/* procedure printheading       */
/*=============================================================================*/


/* procedure printheading */
printheading ()
{
   fprintf(stdout," Program Model Checker by Albert Mo Kim Cheng");
   writeln(stdout);
   fprintf(stdout,"-----------------------------------------------------------");
   writeln(stdout);
   writeln(stdout);

}
/*printheading*/


/*=============================================================================*/
/* procedure printoutput        */
/*=============================================================================*/


/* procedure printoutput */
printoutput ()
{
   short i, j;
   /*
   #----------------------------------------------------------------------
   # First, print out the numbered input formula.
   #----------------------------------------------------------------------
   */
   writeln(stdout);
   fprintf(stdout,"-----------------------------------------------------------");
   writeln(stdout);
   writeln(stdout);
   fprintf(stdout," Temporal Logic Formula: ");
   writeln(stdout);
   fprintf(stdout,"-------------------------");
   writeln(stdout);
   writeln(stdout);
   for (i=1; i <= flength; i++)
      fprintf(stdout,"%3d",i);
   writeln(stdout);
   putc(' ',stdout);
   for (i=1; i <= flength; i++)
```

```
    {
        putc(formula[i-1].op[0],stdout);
        fprintf(stdout,"%c ",formula[i-1].op[1]);
    }
writeln(stdout);
writeln(stdout);
/*
#-----------------------------------------------------------------------------
# Now, rint the labeled transition graph.
#-----------------------------------------------------------------------------
*/
fprintf(stdout," Labeled State Transition Graph: ");
writeln(stdout);
fprintf(stdout,"----------------------------------");
writeln(stdout);
writeln(stdout);
fprintf(stdout," State      Labels ");
writeln(stdout);
fprintf(stdout," -----      ------ ");
writeln(stdout);
for (i=0; i <= numstates; i++)
    {
        fprintf(stdout,"%4d      ",i);
        for (j=1; j <= flength; j++)
            if (labeled[i][j-1])
                fprintf(stdout,"%3d",j);
        writeln(stdout);
    }
writeln(stdout);
fprintf(stdout,"---------------------------------------------------------");
writeln(stdout);
writeln(stdout);
if (correct)
    {
        fprintf(stdout," The formula is proved to be true. ");
        writeln(stdout);
    }
else {
        fprintf(stdout," The formula is proved to be false. ");
        writeln(stdout);
    }
}
/*printoutput*/


/*============================================================================*/
/* procedure push     */
/* In : p = integer       */
/*      top = top of stack     */
/* Out : top = top of stack       */
/*============================================================================*/
```

```
/* procedure push (p,top) */
push (p,top)
short p;
itemptr *top;
{
    itemptr node;
    node = (itemptr)malloc(sizeof(struct item));
    node->ip = p;
    node->next = *top;
    *top = node;
}
/*push*/



/*=========================================================================*/
/* procedure pop       */
/* In : top = top of the stack      */
/* Out : p = integer      */
/*       top = top of the stack      */
/*=========================================================================*/


/* procedure pop (p,top) */
pop (p,top)
short *p;
itemptr *top;
{
    itemptr temp;
    *p = (*top)->ip;
    temp = *top;
    *top = (*top)->next;
    free(temp);
}
/*pop*/



/*=========================================================================*/
/* function empty      */
/* In : top = top of the stack      */
/* Out : empty = true if the stack top points to is empty      */
/*=========================================================================*/


/* function empty (top) */
Boolean empty (top)
itemptr top;
{
    Boolean _empty;

    if (top == (itemptr)(NULL))
        _empty = true;
    else _empty = false;
```

```
      return(_empty);
}
/*empty*/


/*==========================================================================*/
/* procedure readf        */
/* Out : f  = formula         */
/*        flength = length of the formula        */
/*==========================================================================*/


/* procedure readf (f,flength,s) */
readf (f,flength,s)
ftype f;
short *flength, *s;
{
    itemptr ptop; /* top of the stack of numbers corresponding */
     /* to parentheses found in the input formula */
    short i, j, ip, lp; /* number of left parentheses read */
    char lastsymbol, symbol; /* the input character */
    fprintf(stdout," Please enter the formula to be in proved in prefix form:");
    writeln(stdout);
    writeln(stdout);
    ptop = (itemptr)(NULL);
    for (i=1; i <= maxflength; i++)
        {
            f[i-1].p = 0;
            f[i-1].opcode = atomic;
            for (j=1; j <= 2; j++)
                f[i-1].op[j-1] = ' ';
        }
    i = 1;
    symbol = getc(stdin);
    /*
    #----------------------------------------------------------------------
    # If the formula is not atomic, then the following code insures that
    # all subformulas will be read properly.
    #----------------------------------------------------------------------
    */
    if (symbol == '(')
          {
              lp = 1;
              f[i-1].p = lp;
              push(lp,&ptop);
              while (!empty(ptop))
                      {
                          if (symbol != ' ')
                              lastsymbol = symbol;
                          symbol = getc(stdin);
                          if (symbol == '(')
                                {
                                    lp = lp + 1;
                                    f[i-1].p = lp;
```

```
                                    push(lp,&ptop);
                            }
                    else if (symbol == ')')
                            {
                                if (lastsymbol != ')')
                                    i = i - 1;
                                pop(&ip,&ptop);
                                f[i-1].p = ip;
                            }
                    else if (symbol != ' ')
                          {
                            f[i-1].op[0] = symbol;
                            symbol = getc(stdin);
                            if (((symbol >= 'a')&&(symbol <= 'z'))||((symbol >=
                                '0')&&(symbol <= '9')))
                                f[i-1].op[1] = symbol;
                            f[i-1].opcode = typeoperator(f[i-1].op);
                            i = i + 1;
                          }
                }
            *flength = i;
        }
    else
        /*
        #-------------------------------------------------------------------
        # If the formula is atomic, indicate that its length is one.
        #-------------------------------------------------------------------
        */ {
            f[i-1].op[0] = symbol;
            symbol = getc(stdin);
            if (((symbol >= 'a') && (symbol <= 'z')) || ((symbol >= '0') &&
                (symbol <= '9')))
                f[i-1].op[1] = symbol;
            *flength = 1;
        }
    readln(stdin);
    fprintf(stdout," Please enter the state at which the formula is to be
      proved:");
    writeln(stdout);
    writeln(stdout);
    fscanf(stdin,"%d",s);
    readln(stdin);
    for (i=1; i <= *flength; i++)
        {
            putc(f[i-1].op[0],stdout);
            fprintf(stdout,"%c ",f[i-1].op[1]);
        }
    writeln(stdout);
    fprintf(stdout,"state = %d",*s);
    writeln(stdout);
    writeln(stdout);
}
/*readf*/
```

```
/*==============================================================================*/
/* procedure buildnfsf        */
/* In : f = input formula         */
/*      fl = length of input formula        */
/* Out : nf = list of numbered subformulas        */
/*       sf = list of arguments for each subformula operator        */
/*==============================================================================*/

/* procedure buildnfsf (f,fl,nf,sf) */
buildnfsf (_f,fl,nf,sf)
ftype _f;
short fl;
nftype nf;
sftype sf;
{
    ftype f;
    short fi, lp, i, j;
    ARRAYcopy(_f,f,sizeof(f));

    for (fi=1; fi <= maxflength; fi++)
       {
          for (i=1; i <= maxflength; i++)
             {
                nf[fi-1][i-1].op[0] = ' ';
                nf[fi-1][i-1].op[1] = ' ';
                nf[fi-1][i-1].p = 0;
                nf[fi-1][i-1].opcode = atomic;
             }
          sf[fi-1].arg1 = 0;
          sf[fi-1].arg2 = 0;
       }
    /*
    #----------------------------------------------------------------------
    # In one pass, compute all values for arrays nf and sf using markers
    # in f[i].p (parentheses help us determine the span of a formula).
    #----------------------------------------------------------------------
    */

    for (fi=1; fi <= fl; fi++)
       {
          nf[fi-1][0].op[0] = f[fi-1].op[0];
          nf[fi-1][0].op[1] = f[fi-1].op[1];
          nf[fi-1][0].opcode = f[fi-1].opcode;
          nf[fi-1][0].p = f[fi-1].p;
          lp = f[fi-1].p;
          i = fi;
          j = 1;
          /*
          #----------------------------------------------------------------------
          # If the operator opcode is not atomic, meaning that it is an
          # operator, then we must find the end of the operand subformulas
          # that this opcode is operating on by searching for the matching
          # number corresponding to the matching parenthesis.
          #----------------------------------------------------------------------
```

```
                    */
                    if (f[fi-1].opcode != atomic)
                       {
                         do {
                             j = j + 1;
                             i = i + 1;
                             nf[fi-1][j-1].op[0] = f[i-1].op[0];
                             nf[fi-1][j-1].op[1] = f[i-1].op[1];
                             nf[fi-1][j-1].opcode = f[i-1].opcode;
                             nf[fi-1][j-1].p = f[i-1].p;
                         } while (!(f[i-1].p <= lp));
                         /*
                         #----------------------------------------------------------------
                         # Now compute the values of array sf - the number(s)
                         # corresponding to the argument(s) of operator f[fi].opcode. If
                         # the opcode is unary -- nt, ax, and ex, then only one argument
                         # number is determined.
                         #----------------------------------------------------------------
                         */
                         i = fi + 1;
                         sf[fi-1].arg1 = i;
                         if ((f[fi-1].opcode != nt) && (f[fi-1].opcode != ax) &&
                            (f[fi-1].opcode != ex))
                            {
                              if (f[i-1].opcode == atomic)
                                  sf[fi-1].arg2 = i + 1;
                              else {
                                    lp = f[i-1].p;
                                    do {
                                        i = i + 1;
                                    } while (!(f[i-1].p <= lp));
                                    sf[fi-1].arg2 = i + 1;
                              }
                            }
                       }
                 }
      /*do*/
      writeln(stdout);
      fprintf(stdout," Array sf:");
      writeln(stdout);
      for (i=1; i <= fl; i++)
         {
           fprintf(stdout,"%3d %4d %4d",i,sf[i-1].arg1,sf[i-1].arg2);
           writeln(stdout);
         }
      writeln(stdout);
}
/*buildnfsf*/
```

```
/*===============================================================================*/
/* function initlabeled      */
/* In : s = state of the transition graph      */
/*      f = subformula      */
/* Out : initlabeled = true if state s is initially labeled with f      */
/* Description:      */
/* Determine if state s is labeled with subformula f.      */
/*===============================================================================*/


/* function initlabeled (s,f) */
Boolean ihitlabeled (s,_f)
short s;
ftype _f;
{
    ftype f;
    Boolean _initlabeled;
    short i;
    Boolean b;
    ARRAYcopy(_f,f,sizeof(f));

    /*
    #-------------------------------------------------------------------------
    # If the opcode is atomic, meaning that it is a single atomic
    # proposition, then we only need to find it in state s by looking
    # at the flabel (array of initial labels in character form).
    # If found, b is set to true, else false.
    #-------------------------------------------------------------------------
    */
    if (f[0].opcode == atomic)
        {
            b = false;
            i = 0;
            while ((!b) && (flabel[s][i][0] != ' '))
                {
                    if ((flabel[s][i][0] == f[0].op[0]) && (flabel[s][i][1] ==
                    f[0].op[1]))
                        b = true;
                    i = i + 1;
                }
        }
    /*
    #-------------------------------------------------------------------------
    # If the opcode is nt (not), then we have to search the whole array
    # flabel to see if the input label is there.  If it is found, then
    # b is set to false, else true.
    #-------------------------------------------------------------------------
    */ else if (f[0].opcode == nt)
        {
            b = true;
            i = 0;
            while (b && (flabel[s][i][0] != ' '))
```

```
                  {
                     if ((flabel[s][i][0] == f[0].op[0]) && (flabel[s][i][1] ==
                        f[0].op[1]))
                        b = false;
                     i = i + 1;
                  }
         }
   else b = false;
   return(b);
}
/*initlabeled*/



/*===========================================================================*/
/* procedure addlabel     */
/* In : s = state of the transition graph      */
/*      fi = number corresponding to a subformula      */
/* Out : label = state s is labeled with nf[fi]     */
/* Description:      */
/* Label state s with label nf[fi] by setting the boolean      */
/* value labeled[s,fi] to true.      */
/*===========================================================================*/


/* procedure addlabel (s,fi,labeled) */
addlabel (s,fi,labeled)
short s, fi;
labeltype labeled;
{
   labeled[s][fi-1] = true;
}



/*===========================================================================*/
/* procedure initsystem     */
/* Description:      */
/* Initialize the proof system: the initial labels and bit      */
/* array labeled.      */
/*===========================================================================*/


/* procedure initsystem */
initsystem ()
{
   short i, s;
   for (s=0; s <= maxstates; s++)
      {
         /*
         #-----------------------------------------------------------------
         # Assign label t (true) to every state since t is true everywhere.
         #-----------------------------------------------------------------
         */
         flabel[s][0][0] = 't';
         flabel[s][0][1] = ' ';
```

```
        for (i=1; i <= maxflength; i++)
          {
              labeled[s][i-1] = false;
              flabel[s][i][0] = ' ';
              flabel[s][i][1] = ' ';
          }
      }
}
/*initsystem*/



/*==============================================================================*/
/* procedure atf        */
/* In : fi = input formula number          */
/*      s = state of the transition graph at which f is to be proved      */
/* Out : b = true if formula f is true at state s        */
/* Description:        */
/* If state s is labeled with nf[fi], then return true, else      */
/* false.        */
/*==============================================================================*/


/* procedure atf (fi,s,b) */
atf (fi,s,b)
short fi, s;
Boolean *b;
{
   short s1;
   for (s1=0; s1 <= numstates; s1++)
     if (labeled[s1][fi-1] || initlabeled(s1,nf[fi-1]))
        if (!labeled[s1][fi-1])
           addlabel(s1,fi,labeled);
   if (labeled[s][fi-1])
      *b = true;
   else *b = false;
}
/*atf*/

/*==============================================================================*/
/* procedure ntf        */
/* In : fi = input formula number          */
/*      s = state of the transition graph at which f is to be proved      */
/* Out : b = true if formula f is true at state s        */
/* Description:        */
/* If state s is not labeled with arg1, then label state s      */
/* (nt arg1) and return true, else false.        */
/*==============================================================================*/


/* procedure ntf (fi,s,b) */
ntf (fi,s,b)
short fi, s;
Boolean *b;
```

```
{
   short s1, a1;
   a1 = sf[fi-1].arg1;
   for (s1=0; s1 <= numstates; s1++)
      if (!(labeled[s1][a1-1]) || initlabeled(s1,nf[a1-1]))
         addlabel(s1,fi,labeled);
   if (labeled[s][fi-1])
      *b = true;
   else *b = false;
}
/*ntf*/
```

```
/*==============================================================================*/
/* procedure adf        */
/* In : fi = input formula number          */
/*      s = state of the transition graph at which f is to be proved    */
/* Out : b = true if formula f is true at state s        */
/* Description:        */
/* If both arguments are labeled in state s, then label       */
/* state s (ad arg1 arg2) and return true, else false.        */
/*==============================================================================*/
```

```
/* procedure adf (fi,s,b) */
adf (fi,s,b)
short fi, s;
Boolean *b;
{
   short s1, a1, a2;
   a1 = sf[fi-1].arg1;
   a2 = sf[fi-1].arg2;
   for (s1=0; s1 <= numstates; s1++)
      if (labeled[s1][a1-1] || initlabeled(s1,nf[a1-1]))
         if (labeled[s1][a2-1] || initlabeled(s1,nf[a2-1]))
            addlabel(s1,fi,labeled);
   if (labeled[s][fi-1])
      *b = true;
   else *b = false;
}
/*adf*/
```

```
/*==============================================================================*/
/* procedure axf        */
/* In : fi = input formula number          */
/*      s = state of the transition graph at which f is to be proved    */
/* Out : b = true if formula f is true at state s        */
/* Description:        */
/* If all successor states of state s are labeled with arg1,      */
/* then label state s with (ax arg1) and return true, else false.        */
/*==============================================================================*/
```

```
/* procedure axf (fi,s,b) */
axf (fi,s,b)
short fi, s;
Boolean *b;
{
   Boolean b1;
   short s1, s2, a1;
   a1 = sf[fi-1].arg1;
   for (s1=0; s1 <= numstates; s1++)
      {
         b1 = true;
         s2 = 0;
         while (b1 && (s2 <= numstates))
               {
                  if ((s1 != s2) && (e[s1][s2] == 1))
                     if (!(labeled[s2][a1-1] || initlabeled(s2,nf[a1-1])))
                        *b = false;
                  s2 = s2 + 1;
               }
         if (b1)
            addlabel(s1,fi,labeled);
      }
   if (labeled[s][fi-1])
      *b = true;
   else *b = false;
}
/*axf*/


/*=============================================================================*/
/* procedure exf      */
/* In : fi = input formula number         */
/*      s = state of the transition graph at which f is to be proved    */
/* Out : b = true if formula f is true at state s     */
/* Description:      */
/* If at least one successor state of state s are labeled with  */
/* arg1, then label state s with (ex arg1) and return true, else false. */
/*=============================================================================*/


/* procedure exf (fi,s,b) */
exf (fi,s,b)
short fi, s;
Boolean *b;
{
   Boolean b1;
   short s1, s2, a1;
   a1 = sf[fi-1].arg1;
   for (s1=0; s1 <= numstates; s1++)
      {
         b1 = false;
         s2 = 0;
         while ((!b1) && (s2 <= numstates))
```

```
                {
                    if ((s1 != s2) && (e[s1][s2] == 1))
                        if (labeled[s][a1-1] || initlabeled(s,nf[a1-1]))
                            {
                                b1 = true;
                                addlabel(s2,fi,labeled);
                            }
                    s2 = s2 + 1;
                }
        }
    if (labeled[s][fi-1])
        *b = true;
    else *b = false;
}
/*exf*/


/*-----------------------------------------------------------------------------*/
/* procedure dfs        */
/* Description:         */
/* First label the given state s2 with (eu arg1 arg2); then      */
/* for all immediate predecessors of s2 which are labeled with arg1,     */
/* perform a DFS.  When this procedure terminates, all states in paths   */
/* in which the prefix is arg1 (all consecutive states are labeled with  */
/* arg1 and the end state is labeled with arg2) are labeled with         */
/* (eu arg1 arg2).       */
/*-----------------------------------------------------------------------------*/


/* procedure dfs (s2,f1) */
dfs (s2,f1)
short s2, f1;
{
    short s1;
    addlabel(s2,fi,labeled);
    for (s1=0; s1 <= numstates; s1++)
        if ((s1 != s2) && (e[s1][s2] == 1))
            if (labeled[s1][a1-1] || initlabeled(s1,nf[a1-1]))
                if (!labeled[s1][fi-1])
                    dfs(s1);
}
/*dfs*/


/*=============================================================================*/
/* procedure euf        */
/* In : fi = input formula number        */
/*      s = state of the transition graph at which f is to be proved     */
/* Out : b = true if formula f is true at state s        */
/* Description:         */
/* Use DFS to label all states at which (eu arg1 arg2) is        */
/* true.  euf returns b = true if state s is labeled (eu arg1 arg2).     */
/*=============================================================================*/
```

```
/* procedure euf (fi,s,b) */
euf (fi,s,b)
short fi, s;
Boolean *b;
{
   short s2, a1, a2;
   /*
   #--------------------------------------------------------------------
   # For all states which are labeled with arg2, perform a depth first
   # search to label all states in paths which have prefix arg1 and end
   # state labeled with arg2.  If state s is labeled with (eu arg1 arg2),
   # then return b = true, else false.
   #--------------------------------------------------------------------
   */
   a1 = sf[fi-1].arg1;
   a2 = sf[fi-1].arg2;
   for (s2=0; s2 <= numstates; s2++)
      if (labeled[s2][a2-1] || initlabeled(s2,nf[a2-1]))
         dfs(s2,fi);
   if (labeled[s][fi-1])
      *b = true;
   else *b = false;
}
/*euf*/


/*==========================================================================*/
/* procedure auf - shown above                                          */
/*==========================================================================*/


/*==========================================================================*/
/* procedure labelgraph - shown above                                   */
/*==========================================================================*/


/*==========================================================================*/
/* Main program     */
/* */
/* First, initialize the system and print out a pretty heading.         */
/* Then, read in the global state transition graph, the set of          */
/* initial labels of the graph, and the formula to be proved.           */
/* Next, construct the arrays nf and sf as described in Clarke           */
/* et al. paper.  Finally, for each subformula, label the state          */
/* transition graph and determine whether the input formula is true      */
/* or not.     */
/*==========================================================================*/


main(argc, argv)
int argc;
char **argv;
{
   printheading();
   initsystem();
```

```
    readgraph(e,&numstates);
    readlabel(flabel);
    readf(formula,&flength,&s);
    buildnfsf(formula,flength,nf,sf);
    for (fi=flength; fi >= 1; fi--)
        labelgraph(fi,s,&correct);
    printoutput();
}
/*modelchecker*/
```

4.6 SYMBOLIC MODEL CHECKING

The CES model checker and other early model checkers are explicit-state model
checkers. They represent a finite state graph using adjacency lists and explicitly list
all states in the graph. Since many models have an exponential number of states,
explicit-state model checkers suffer from the state explosion problem and are not
practical for the verification of many realistic systems. To alleviate this problem, this
section introduces symbolic model checking [Burch et al., 1990a], which represents
states and transitions as Boolean formulas to reduce redundancy in the graph. These
Boolean formulas are then represented by even more compact binary decision diagrams [Lee, 1959; Akers, 1978], which can then be manipulated by very efficient
algorithms [Bryant, 1986]. As a result, symbol model checking makes it practical to
verify much larger systems than those analyzable by explicit-state model checking.

4.6.1 Binary Decision Diagrams

Binary decision diagrams (BDDs) are concise graphical representations of Boolean
logic formulas. Boolean logic formulas can be represented by truth tables, Karnaugh
maps, or canonical sum-of-products form but these representations contain redundant
information in different places, leading to an exponential number of entries or states.

As a first attempt to reduce this redundancy, we represent a Boolean formula by a
binary decision tree. Nodes represent variables and the two outdoing edges of each
node indicate that the values of the variable are false (0) or true (1), respectively. The
leaves are labeled with 0 or 1 corresponding to the truth value of the formula given
an assignment of values to the variables.

By traversing a given tree (corresponding to a formula) from the root to a leaf,
the value of the formula can be determined given an assignment of values to the
variables. Starting from the root labeled with a variable, if the value assigned is 0,
we follow the edge labeled with 0 to another node. If the value assigned is 1, we
follow the edge labeled with 1 to another node. If the next node is a leaf, then its
label is the truth value of the formula. Otherwise, we repeat this step from this node
until a leaf is reached.

Note that the binary decision tree has many identical subtrees. By removing subtrees with redundant information, BDDs can be derived. The resulting structure
is a directed acyclic graph where each node (except the leaves) has at most two
incoming edges and at most two outgoing edges. Leaf nodes may have more than

two incoming edges. The nodes in a BDD are also traversed in sequence from the root to a leaf, but the BDD enforces a total ordering of the variables in the sequence. Therefore, BDDs are also called ordered BDDs to emphasize this ordering feature. Bryant [Bryant, 1986] added further restrictions on variable ordering in BDDs to allow for efficient manipulation algorithms. We now formally define Bryant's ordered BDDs.

Ordered Binary Decision Diagrams: A Boolean formula can be represented by a function graph (ordered BDD), which is a rooted, directed, acyclic graph with two types of vertices. A nonterminal vertex v has an $index(v)$ from the set $\{1, \ldots, n\}$ and two children $low(v)$ and $high(v)$. A terminal vertex (leaf) has a $value(v)$ of 0 or 1. If $low(v)$ is a nonterminal vertex, then $index(v) < index(low(v))$. Similarly, if $high(v)$ is a nonterminal vertex, then $index(v) < index(high(v))$.

Example. The formula $(p \wedge q) \vee (r \wedge s) \vee (t \wedge u)$ is represented by the BDD in Figure 4.2. The acyclic directed graph clearly imposes a total ordering of the variables in the sequence from the root to a leaf: $index(p) < index(q) < index(r) < index(s) < index(t) < index(u)$, or more informally, $p < q < r < s < t < u$.

Example. The formula $(p \vee q) \wedge (r \vee s) \wedge (t \vee u)$ is represented by the BDD in Figure 4.3. Again, the acyclic directed graph imposes a total ordering of the variables in the sequence from the root to a leaf: $index(p) < index(q) < index(r) < index(s) < index(t) < index(u)$, or more informally, $p < q < r < s < t < u$. .

Besides being much more compact than other representations, ordered BDDs are *canonical representations* of Boolean formulas. This property means that each Boolean formula with a specific variable ordering has a unique and minimal BDD rep-

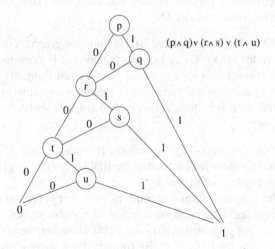

Figure 4.2 BDD for formula $(p \wedge q) \vee (r \wedge s) \vee (t \wedge u)$.

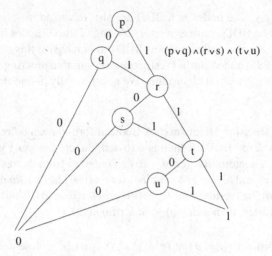

Figure 4.3   BDD for formula $(p \vee q) \wedge (r \vee s) \wedge (t \vee u)$.

resentation. (In fact, BDDs can be viewed as deterministic finite automata (DFA) discussed in chapter 2.) Therefore, we can check that two Boolean formulas are equivalent by checking if they have isomorphic representations, that is, their BDDs exactly match in both structure and attributes. Also, determining the satisfiability of a formula only requires comparing its BDD with that of the constant function *false*(0).

From now on, when we say BDDs, we refer to minimal BDDs. The size of a BDD is very dependent on the selected variable ordering, and is exponential in the number of variables in the worst case. However, for many practical Boolean formulas, a good variable ordering exists (often determined by a human domain expert) that yields BDDs whose size is linear. Note that determining an optimal variable ordering is itself a nondeterministic polynomial-time decidable (NP)-complete problem. We now formally define isomorphic BDDs.

Isomorphic BDDs: Given two ordered BDDs (function graphs) G_1 with vertex set V_1 and G_2 with vertex set V_2. G_1 and G_2 are isomorphic if a one-to-one function h from V_1 to V_2 exists such that for any vertex $v_1 \in V_1$ satisfying $h(v_1) = v_2 (\in V_2)$, either (1) v_1 and v_2 are terminal vertices and $value(v_1) = value(v_2)$ or (2) v_1 and v_2 are nonterminal vertices with $index(v_1) = index(v_2)$, $h(low(v_1)) = low(v_2)$, and $h(high(v)) = high(v_2)$.

Given the BDDs corresponding to Boolean formulas f and g, [Bryant, 1986] presents efficient algorithms for computing the BDDs of $\neg f$, $f \wedge g$, and the restriction of f with a variable x set to 0 or 1.

The model checking algorithm also requires two other operations: quantification over Boolean variables (QBF) and substitution of variable names. Algorithms for these operations are not presented in [Bryant, 1986]. However, we can use the restriction algorithm to derive the BDD of a QBF formula. First, we describe the restriction notation.

Algorithm Restrict:
Input: BDD representing Boolean formula f, variable x, value b (either 0 or 1).
Output: BDD with the above restriction.
while (not visited(v)) do
    if $v = x$ then
      if $b = 0$
        then change pointer to v to point to $low(v)$
        else change pointer to v to point to $high(v)$
    reduce BDD and assign unique identifiers to the vertices
End Restrict

Figure 4.4   Algorithm restrict.

Restriction: The notation $f|_{x=0}$ means the restriction of Boolean formula f with variable x set to 0. Similarly, the notation $f|_{x=1}$ means the restriction of Boolean formula f with variable x set to 1.

The restriction algorithm (Figure 4.4) converts the BDD of a Boolean function f into one representing f for a specific variable set to a specific value.

The quantification algorithms are based on the following definitions.

Existentially Quantified Boolean Formula: Given a Boolean formula f and a Boolean variable x, $\exists x[f] = f|_{x=0} \vee f|_{x=1}$.

Universally Quantified Boolean Formula: Given a Boolean formula f and a Boolean variable x, $\forall x[f] = \neg\exists x[\neg f]$.

For quantification of more than one variable, the following notations are used.

General Quantified Boolean Formula: Given a vector of Boolean variables $x = \langle x_1, \ldots, x_n \rangle$, the notation $Q\bar{x}[f]$, where Q is either $\exists$ or $\forall$, denotes $Qx_1[\ldots Qx_n[f] \ldots]$.

Now the substitution of variable names can be done using the quantification algorithm above.

Substitution of Variable Names: The substitution of a variable x by a variable y in a formula f, assuming that the variable y is not free in f is $f\langle x \leftarrow y \rangle = \exists x[(x \leftrightarrow y) \wedge f]$.

Since the symbolic model checker very frequently executes these operations, more efficient algorithms are used in the implemented verification tool [Burch et al., 1990a].

Symbolic Model Checking Algorithm:

Input: model M represented by BDDs and CTL formula f.

Output: whether f is satisfied.

Let $f\langle s \rangle$ denote the value of formula f in state s.

If formula f is:

  atomic proposition P: return the BDD for P.

  $\neg f_1$ or $f_1 \wedge f_2$: execute Bryant's algorithms [Bryant, 1986] for Boolean connectives.

  EX f: return $f\langle s \rangle = true$ iff there is a successor state s' such that $f\langle s' \rangle = true$,
    that is, $\exists s'[f\langle s' \rangle \wedge N(s, s')]$.

  E[f_1 U f_2]: construct the BDD (representing the states in which f holds) by iterating
    E[f_1 U f_2] = $f_2 \vee (f_1 \wedge$ EX E[f_1 U f_2]).

  EG f: construct the BDD by finding the greatest fixed point EG f and iterating
    EG $f = f \wedge$ EX EG f.

All other CTL operators can be stated using the above operators.

Figure 4.5   Symbolic model checking algorithm.

4.6.2   Symbolic Model Checker

Instead of explicitly enumerating all states in the model, which is a labeled state transition system or Kripke structure, we symbolically represent it as BDDs, hence the name symbolic model checker (SMC) [Burch et al., 1990a]. We have to find a way to translate the model into BDDs. Suppose that the current state of the system is represented by a vector of Boolean variables $S = \{s_0, \ldots, s_{n-1}\}$ and the next state of the system is represented by a vector of Boolean variables $S' = \{s'_0, \ldots, s'_{n-1}\}$. Using S and S', the transition relation between the values of the variables in the current and the next states can be stated as a Boolean formula $N(s_0, \ldots, s_{n-1}, s'_0, \ldots, s'_{n-1})$. Note that a finite-domain non-Boolean variable can be easily converted into a vector of Boolean variables. We give an example of this conversion in chapter 12 (section 12.3.1).

Each transition in this transition graph models the time passage of one time unit. Without further extensions, non-unit as well as nondeterministic transition time can be modeled by a sequence of unit transitions. Later, we will see that it is easy to extend this transition graph into a more powerful model called the *timed transition graph* [Campos et al., 1994].

The symbolic model checker, shown in Figure 4.5, takes as input the model M represented by BDDs and the formula f to be verified (in the initial states of M). For every atomic proposition in S, it outputs a BDD with one Boolean variable such that the BDD is true in a state iff the formula f is true in that state.

4.7   REAL-TIME CTL

CTL can specify the relative ordering of events or actions in a finite state system, but it cannot directly express when these events or actions occur. An awkward way of specifying that some event will occur in the future in at most a fixed number of time units is by nesting EX or AX operators. Real-time systems impose bounds on the response time of events and actions. To handle properties with these quantitative constraints, CTL has been extended in a number of ways. Here we describe one extension [Emerson et al., 1990] that adds time intervals to CTL temporal operators and introduces the bounded until operator $U[x, y]$.

The formula $E[f_1 \ U[x, y] \ f_2]$ at a given state means that a path exists beginning at this state and leading to a future state where f_2 holds, f_1 holds at every state between the beginning state and this future state, and the distance between the beginning state and this future state is within the interval $[x, y]$. This definition is now formalized.

Existentially Bounded Until Operator: The formula $E[f_1 \ U[x, y] \ f_2]$ at state s_0 means that a path exists beginning at s_0 and some i such that $x \le i \le y$ and f_2 holds at state s_i and $\forall j < i$, f_1 holds at state s_j.

Example. Let f_1 denote that the wireless telephone's battery power is in the "low" position. Let f_2 denote that the wireless telephone is "off." Then $E[f_1 \ U \ [5, 18] \ f_2]$ states that there is an execution path in which the telephone will turn "off" within a time interval between 5 and 18 time units of the telephone's battery power indicating the "low" position, and before this "off" state the telephone's battery power is in the "low" position.

The formula $EG[x, y]f$ at state s_0 means that there exists a path beginning at s_0 and $\forall i, x \le i \le y$, f holds at state s_i.

4.7.1 Minimum and Maximum Delays

Now we describe algorithms [Campos et al., 1994] for finding the minimum and maximum delays between two events. These are known as *quantitative algorithms* since they compute numerical timing information about events rather than just relative ordering of events in a system. Given a real-time system, they are used to verify that given timing constraints are satisfied and also to predict the system's performance, telling how well the system performs relative to the given timing constraints. These algorithms start from states satisfying the first event, explore all possible execution paths, and terminate when a state satisfying the second event is reached.

The minimum delay algorithm (Figure 4.6) takes as input the *start_set* and the *final_set* of states satisfying the first event and the second event, respectively. If a state in *final_set* is reachable from a state in *start_set*, it returns the length in terms of the number of edges in a shortest path from a state in *start_set* to a state in *final_set*. If none of the states in *final_set* is reachable, then the algorithm returns infinity. For example, the first event can be a request to use a non-sharable resource by a real-time process and the second event can be the allocation of this resource to this process, so the minimum delay algorithm finds the minimum waiting time for this process to obtain the resource.

The function *successors_set(S)* returns the set of successor states of state S and is defined as *successors_set(S)* $= \{s' | N(s, s')$ is true for some $s \in S\}$. This func-

---

procedure *min_delay(start_set, final_set)*
$i := 0$;
$R := start\_set$;
$R' := successors\_set(R) \cup R$;
while $R' \neq R \wedge R' \cap final\_set = \emptyset$ do
    $i := i + 1$;
    $R := R'$;
    $R' := successors\_set(R') \cup R'$;
if $R \cap final\_set \neq \emptyset$
    then return i;
    else return ∞;

Figure 4.6   Minimum delay algorithm.

tion, the sets R and R' of states, and the intersection and union operations are all implemented using BDDs.

Next we describe the maximum delay algorithm (Figure 4.7), which also takes as input the *start_set* and the *final_set* of states satisfying the first event and the second event, respectively. If a state in *final_set* is reachable from a state in *start_set*, it returns the length in terms of the number of edges in a longest path from a state in *start_set* to a state in *final_set*. If an infinite path exists from a state in *start_set* that never reaches a state in *final_set*, then the algorithm returns infinity. Again, for example, the first event can be a request to use a non-sharable resource by a real-time process and the second event can be the allocation of this resource to this process, so the maximum delay algorithm finds the maximum waiting time for this process to obtain the resource. If we impose a deadline (relative to the resource request time by this process) for the allocation of this resource to this process, then the maximum delay algorithm tells us whether this deadline can be satisfied or not.

The set *not_final_set* represents the set of states which are not in the set *final_set*. The function *predecessors_set(S')* returns the set of predecessor states of state S and is defined as *predecessors_set*$(S') = \{s | N(s, s')$ is true for some $s' \in S'\}$. As in the minimum delay algorithm, this predecessor function, the sets R and R' of states,

---

procedure *max_delay(start_set, final_set)*
$i := 0$;
$R := true$;
$R' := not\_final\_set$;
while $R' \neq R \wedge R' \cap start\_set \neq \emptyset$ do
    $i := i + 1$;
    $R := R'$;
    $R' := predecessors\_set(R') \cup not\_final\_set$;
if $R = R'$
    then return ∞;
    else return i;

Figure 4.7   Maximum delay algorithm.

and the intersection operations are all implemented using BDDs. Here, a backward search is needed to identify a longest path.

Two reasons exist for the efficiency of these quantitative algorithms. First, Boolean formulas are used to represent the sets of states satisfying certain events, and these formulas are represented by BDDs in the implementation. Since sets are represented by BDDs, the operations on these sets are implemented as efficient operations on the BDDs described earlier. Second, these operations are applied to sets of many states instead of individual states, thus significantly reducing computation time for exhaustive state space exploration.

4.7.2 Minimum and Maximum Number of Condition Occurrences

Often we are interested in knowing the number of states satisfying a given condition along a path, for example, how many times a train arrives and passes a railroad crossing. Here, we describe two condition counting algorithms [Campos et al., 1994] that compute the minimum and maximum number of states satisfying a given condition over all finite paths from a state in the *start_set* to a state in the *final_set*, thus telling the minimum and maximum number of occurrences of this condition over all finite paths between these states.

Similar to the minimum and maximum delay algorithms, these quantitative algorithms start from states satisfying the first event, explore all possible execution paths and count the number of states satisfying a given condition, and terminate when a state satisfying the second event is reached. Before running either condition counting algorithm, we have to first check that a finite path is present in the transition graph from a state in the *start_set* to a state in the *final_set* using the maximum delay algorithm described above.

We need to introduce a counter variable in each state to remember the number of states satisfying the given condition along the path traversed so far. To do this systematically, a new state transition system is introduced in which each state is a pair of the original state and the positive integer counter [Campos et al., 1994]. Let N be the set of natural numbers. The state set is $S_a = S \times N$.

Augmented Transition Relation: Given an original state-transition graph with transition relation $N \subseteq S \times S$, the corresponding augmented transition relation $N_a \subseteq S_a \times S_a$ is defined as

$$N_a(\langle s, k \rangle, \langle s', k' \rangle) = N(s, s') \wedge (s' \in \text{condition} \wedge k' = k + 1 \vee$$
$$s' \notin \text{condition} \wedge k' = k).$$

This means that in the augmented transition relation N_a, there is a transition from $\langle s, k \rangle$ to $\langle s', k' \rangle$ iff there is a transition from state s to state s' in the original transition relation N and either s' belongs to the condition and the counter k' is $k + 1$ or s' does not belong to the condition and k' is the same as k. Therefore, the condition counter k for state s is incremented only if state s satisfies this condition.

Let $T \subseteq S_a$. Again, the function $successors\_set(T)$ returns the set of predecessor states of state S and is defined as $successors\_set(T) = \{t' | N(t, t')$ is true for some $t \in T\}$. We now outline the minimum counting algorithm.

Procedure min_count ($start\_set, condition, final\_set$)
$current\_min := \infty$;
$R = \{\langle s, 1\rangle | s \in start\_set \cap condition\} \cup \{\langle s, 0\rangle | s \in start\_set \cap \overline{condition}\}$;
loop
$\quad$ $reached\_final\_set := R \cap final\_set$;
$\quad$ if $reached\_final\_set \neq \emptyset$ then
$\quad$ begin
$\quad\quad$ $m := \max\{k | \langle s, k\rangle \in reached\_final\_set\}$;
$\quad\quad$ if $m < current\_min$ then $current\_min := m$
$\quad$ end;
$\quad$ $R' := R \cap not\_final\_set$;
$\quad$ if $R' = \emptyset$ then return $current\_min$;
$\quad$ $R := successors\_set(R')$
endloop;

Figure 4.8 Minimum condition-counting algorithm.

In the algorithm (Figure 4.8), variable $current\_min$ gives the minimum count for all previous iterations. The set R is the set of states in S_a reached in the current iteration of the loop. The algorithm checks the endpoints of paths with i states during the ith iteration. If the states are in $final\_set$ (meaning they are the terminal states of paths), the counter values are used to compute the minimum count for these paths and the current minimum is updated. If the states are not in $final\_set$ (meaning they are not terminal states of paths), the loop continues after deriving the successors of these non-terminal states. The algorithm returns the current minimum as the minimum count when all reached states are in $final\_set$.

Procedure max_count ($start\_set, condition, final\_set$)
$current\_max := -\infty$;
$R = \{\langle s, 1\rangle | s \in start\_set \cap condition\} \cup \{\langle s, 0\rangle | s \in start\_set \cap \overline{condition}\}$;
loop
$\quad$ $reached\_final\_set := R \cap final\_set$;
$\quad$ if $reached\_final\_set \neq \emptyset$ then
$\quad$ begin
$\quad\quad$ $m := \max\{k | \langle s, k\rangle \in reached\_final\_set\}$;
$\quad\quad$ if $m > current\_max$ then $current\_max := m$
$\quad$ end;
$\quad$ $R' := R \cap not\_final\_set$;
$\quad$ if $R' = \emptyset$ then return $current\_max$;
$\quad$ $R := successors\_set(R')$
endloop;

Figure 4.9 Maximum condition-counting algorithm.

We derive the maximum condition counting algorithm by reversing the inequalities and by replacing min by max, as shown in Figure 4.9.

4.7.3 Non-Unit Transition Time

Events in a real-time system may take different lenghts of time to occur, leading to non-unit transition time between two states in the state transition system modeling this real-time system. Also, transition time between two specific states may also change for different instances of the same event. However, the state transition system presented earlier assumes that every transition takes one time unit. One way to handle non-unit transition time is to extend the *unit-time state transition graph* into a *timed transition graph* [Campos and Clarke, 1993].

Timed Transition Graph (TTG): A *timed transition graph (TTG) model* attaches a discrete time interval of a pair of natural numbers [*lower_bound, upper_bound*] to each transition in a finite-state transition graph.

The notation $N(s, lower\_bound, upper\_bound, s')$ means that the transition from state s to state s' may nondeterministically take any number of time units between *lower_bound* and *upper_bound*. Using the same approach as in the augmented state transition graph model for the condition counting algorithms, here we add a time counter to each state to indicate the number of time units to transition out of this state.

Timed Transition Relation (TTR): Given an original state-transition graph with transition relation $N \subseteq S \times S$, the corresponding augmented transition relation $N_a \subseteq S_a \times S_a$ is defined as

$$N_a(\langle s, t \rangle, \langle s', t' \rangle) = N(s, \delta, s') \wedge t' = t + \delta.$$

This means that in the augmented transition relation N_a, a transition exists from $\langle s, t \rangle$ to $\langle s', t' \rangle$ iff a transition exists from state s to state s' in the original transition relation N that may take δ time units, $t' = t + \delta$, and $lower\_bound \leq \delta \leq upper\_bound$.

Now we consider how to determine quantitative properties of a real-time system specified in a TTG model. To compute the minimum and maximum delays between two sets of states satisfying two events, we can use the same minimum and maximum delay algorithms described earlier with the extra steps described below (Figure 4.10).

We can also apply the condition counting algorithms without modification to TTGs by first extending the augmented transition relation in the unit-time transition system described earlier into the augmented *timed* transition relation.

Augmented Timed Transition Relation (ATTR): Given an original state-transition graph with transition relation $N \subseteq S \times S$, the corresponding augmented timed transition relation $N_a \subseteq S_a \times S_a$ is defined as

$$N_a(\langle s, t \rangle, \langle s', t' \rangle) = N(s, \delta, s') \wedge (s \in condition \wedge t' = t + \delta \vee$$

$$s \notin condition \wedge t' = t).$$

---

procedure *TTG_min_delay(start_set, final_set)*
time_counter := 0 for every $\langle s, time\_counter \rangle \in start\_set$;
reachable_set := set of states $\langle s, t \rangle$ reachable from *start_set* in t time units;
min_delay(start_set, final_set);

Figure 4.10   TTG minimum delay algorithm.

This means that in the augmented transition relation N_a, there is a transition from $\langle s, t \rangle$ to $\langle s', t' \rangle$ iff there is a transition from state s to state s' in the original transition relation N, and either s belongs to the condition and the counter t' is $t + d$ or s does not belongs to the condition and t' is the same as t. This transition relation increments the time counter only when the state s belongs to the condition. Therefore, a path exists with t time units spent in states belonging to *condition* along this path from a state in *start_set* to state s if an augmented state $\langle s, t \rangle$ is reachable from *start_set*.

4.8   AVAILABLE TOOLS

Several versions of SMV (symbolic model verifier) are available, two of which are from the Carnegie Mellon University (CMU) Model Checking group and Cadence Berkeley Laboratories. TCMU's SMV is the first model checker based on BDDs. Their respective URLs are

```
http://www.cs.cmu.edu/~modelcheck/smv.html
http://www-cad.eecs.berkeley.edu/~kenmcmil/smv/
```

CMU's SMV takes as input a specification (called a program) consisting of several modules. A module is a description that may be instantiated several times within the model. Every SMV specification has a module called main with no formal parameters, which form the root of the model hierarchy. The main module is the starting point for building the finite-state model for a given description. A declaration

$$\text{MODULE process}(p1, \ldots, pn)$$

defines *process* as a module with n formal parameters.

Local variables may be declared in a module. The type of variable may be Boolean, an enumeration type or an integer subrange. For example, the values of the following local variable *state1* can be *gate_up* or *gate_down*:

$$\text{VAR state1: gate\_up, gate\_down;}$$

Modules are also instantiated using variable declarations. A module may contain instances of other modules, allowing a structural hierarchy to be built. For example, the module main declares the variable p0 as an instance of proc

$$\text{VAR p0: proc(s0, s1, turn, 0);}$$

The *init* and *next* functions define the values of the variables in each state, as shown in the following example showing a partial description of the automatic climate control system in Figure 2.13 in chapter 2:

```
init(state0) := comfort;
next(state0) := case
  (state0 = comfort): {cold, hot, comfort};
  (state0 = cold) : turn_on_heater;
  (state0 = hot) : turn_on_ac;
  ...
esac;
```

The code above defines the initial value of *state0* to be *comfort*, and the value of that variable in the next state as a function of the value of the variables in the current state. If *state0* is *comfort*, then in the next state its value could be *cold*, *hot*, or *comfort*, and the choice is made nondeterministically. If *state0* is *cold*, then in the next state its value is *turn_on_heater*. If *state0* is *hot*, then in the next state its value is *turn_on_ac*. The operators & (AND) and | (OR) can be used to express more complex conditions on state values.

SyMP (symbolic model prover) is a new tool combining model checking and theorem proving to facilitate verification. More details about SyMP can be found in

```
http://www.cs.cmu.edu/~modelcheck/symp.html
```

Recently, a new symbolic model checker called NuSMV has been developed as a joint project between the Formal Methods group in the Automated Reasoning System division at Italy's ITC-IRST and the Model Checking group at Carnegie Mellon University. NuSMV is a reimplementation and extension of SMV, and can be found at

```
http://nusmv.irst.itc.it/
```

The open architecture of NuSMV for model checking makes it a reliable core for developing custom verification tools, verifying industrial designs, and serving as a testbed for formal verification techniques.

4.9   HISTORICAL PERSPECTIVE AND RELATED WORK

Clarke and Emerson first developed analysis algorithms called temporal logic model checkers to verify desirable properties of untimed systems specified as finite state machines [Clarke and Emerson, 1981; Clarke, Emerson, and Sistla, 1986]. To reduce the run time for model checking, Burch et al. [Burch et al., 1990a] and McMillan [McMillan, 1992] invented symbolic model checking algorithms in which the transition relation is represented by a binary decision diagram (BDD) [Lee, 1959; Akers, 1978; Bryant, 1986] so that states are not explicitly enumerated, thus significantly reducing verification time. BDDs were first invented by Lee [Lee, 1959] and later refined by Akers [Akers, 1978]. To further combat the problem of checking large specifications, Sokolsky and Smolka recently proposed incremental model checking [Sokolsky and Smolka, 1994] and local model checking [Sokolsky and Smolka, 1995]. These model checkers explore only the portion of the state space responsible in determining the outcome of the verification. Recently, Amla, Emerson, Kurshan, and Namjoshi [Amla and Emerson, 2001] presented a front-end called RTDT for the efficient model checking of synchronous timing diagrams.

Burch models timing constraints with trace theory [Burch, 1989a], and adds timing specification capability to CTL by combining CTL, trace theory, and timing models [Burch, 1989b]. Burch et al. apply symbolic model checking to sequential circuit verification [Burch et al., 1990a; Burch et al., 1994], and to problems with large state spaces [Burch et al., 1990a]. McMillan [McMillan, 1992] uses the SMV to check several industrial specifications, including the IEEE Futurebus+ cache coherence protocol [Clarke et al., 1993]. Cleaveland and others implement an integrated toolset called the Concurrency Factory [Cleaveland et al., 1994] to specify and verify concurrent systems. This toolset is based on their earlier toolset called the Concurrency Workbench [Cleaveland, Parrow, and Steffen, 1993].

To further tackle the state explosion problem, [Henzinger, Kupferman, and Vardi, 1996] present an automata-theoretic approach to TCTL (a real-time extension of CTL) model checking that combines on-the-fly and space-efficient model checking methods. Their approach yields a PSPACE on-the-fly model-checking algorithm for TCTL. On-the-fly model checking explores only the portion of the state space that is essential for determining the satisfaction of the specification. Space-efficient model checking uses extra time to reconstruct information rather than using extra space to store it.

[Campos et al., 1994] apply symbolic model checking to real-time systems by introducing quantitative algorithms for computing minimum and maximum delays between two events and for calculating the minimum and maximum number of times a given condition holds between two events or sets of states. The length of a path is in terms of the number of transitions in it. To demonstrate the capability of these techniques, they apply them to verify timing properties of aircraft control. They generalize this definition in their timed transition graphs [Campos and Clarke, 1993] to allow a transition to model the passage of more than one unit of time. Furthermore, the time taken by a transition may be different for different executions of the same modeled system.

[Iversen et al., 2000] use model-checking to verify real-time control programs. [Closse, et al., 2001] provide a tool called TAXYS for the development and verification of real-time embedded systems. [Havelund, Lowry, and Penix, 2001] present a formal analysis of a spacecraft controller using the tool SPIN.

Recently, [Kupferman and Vardi, 2000] proposed an automata-theoretic approach to modular model checking and dealt with assume-guarantee specifications with the guarantee specified by branching temporal formulas. The specification of a module in modular verification, also called the assume-guarantee paradigm, consists of describing the guaranteed behavior of the module and the assumed behavior of the system in which the module is interacting. They consider two approaches, one in which the assumption is specified by branching temporal formulas and the other in which the assumption is specified by linear temporal logic. Guarantees are specified in CTL, and CTL*.

[Browne, Cheng, and Mok, 1988; Cheng and Wang, 1990; Cheng et al., 1993] incorporated a modified model checker in the analysis tool Estella (described in chapter 10) for determining whether a real-time rule-based system has bounded response time. This modified model checker also computes the worst-case response time of a rule-based system by finding the longest path in terms of the number of edges from a start state to a fixed point. If the response time of the rule-base system is bounded, Estella also finds its worst-case response time. The implemented model checker also makes use of on-the-fly and space-efficient techniques. Estella employs semantics-based analysis and avoids model checking if the rule-based system being checked satisfies certain constraints, thus dramatically reducing the analysis time.

4.10   SUMMARY

For finite-state concurrent systems, we can use model checking instead of proof construction to check their correctness relative to their specifications. In the model checking approach, we represent the concurrent system as a finite-state graph, which can be viewed as a finite Kripke structure. The specification or safety assertion is expressed in propositional temporal logic formulas. We can then check whether the system meets its specification using an algorithm called a *model checker*. In other words, the model checker determines whether the Kripke structure is a model of the formula(s). Several model checkers are available and they vary in code and run-time complexity. Here we describe one of the first model checkers proposed by [Clarke, Emerson, and Sistla, 1986], and a more efficient symbolic model checker developed later by [Burch et al., 1990a].

In Clarke, Emerson, and Sistla's approach, the system to be checked is represented by a labeled finite-state graph and the specification is written in a propositional, branching-time temporal logic called computation tree logic (CTL). The use of linear-time temporal logic, which can express fairness properties, is ruled out since a model checker for such logic has high complexity. Instead, fairness requirements are moved into the semantics of CTL.

One way to construct the finite-state graph corresponding to a given concurrent program is to begin with the initial state labeled with the initial values of all program variables or attributes, which are called labels here. Then for each possible next statement, we execute the statement and examine if any change occurs to one or more program variables. We construct a new state if it is different from any existing state. Note that sometimes we need to construct a new state even if its labels are the same as those in an existing state because the sequence of actions leading to the present state is different from that leading to the existing state. A directed edge is constructed from the state we are considering to the new state. We repeat this state and edge construction step for each new state until there are no more states to consider.

For other systems that are not computer programs, we can perform a similar graph construction. First, we identify the state attributes that are relevant in the system to be specified in the CTL structure.

The Clarke–Emerson–Sistla (CES) model checker can determine whether a formula f_0 written in CTL is true in a given CTL structure. It uses a compositional approach to analysis and hence operates in stages. The first stage checks all subformulas of length 1 in f_0, that is, all atomic propositions. These atomic propositions hold in states having labels that are identical to these propositions. The second stage checks all subformulas of length 2 in f_0 based on the results in stage 1 and labels each state with the subformulas that hold in that state, and so on. As a result, each state will be labeled with the set of subformulas of length less than or equal to i after the completion of the ith stage. At completion, the model checker will have checked the entire formula of length n.

The CES model checker and other early model checkers are *explicit-state model checkers*. They represent a finite-state graph using adjacency lists and explicitly list all states in the graph. Since many models have an exponential number of states, explicit-state model checkers suffer from the state explosion problem and are not practical for the verification of many realistic systems. To alleviate this problem, *symbolic model checking* [Burch et al., 1990a] is introduced, which represents states and transitions as Boolean formulas in order to reduce redundancy in the graph. These Boolean formulas are then represented by even more compact *binary decision diagrams* (BDDs) [Lee, 1959; Akers, 1978], which can then be manipulated by very efficient algorithms [Bryant, 1986]. As a result, symbol model checking makes it practical to verify much larger systems than those analyzable by explicit-state model checking.

BDDs are concise graphical representations of Boolean formulas. Boolean logic formulas can be represented by truth tables, Karnaugh maps, or canonical sum-of-products forms, but these representations contain redundant information in different places, leading to an exponential number of entries or states.

A Boolean formula can be represented by a function graph (ordered BDD), which is a rooted, directed, acyclic graph with two types of vertices. A nonterminal vertex v has an *index(v)* from the set $\{1, \ldots, n\}$ and two children *low(v)* and *high(v)*. A terminal vertex (leaf) has a *value(v)* of 0 or 1. If *low(v)* is a nonterminal vertex, then $index(v) < index(low(v))$. Similarly, if *high(v)* is a nonterminal vertex, then $index(v) < index(high(v))$.

Besides being much more compact that other representations, ordered BDDs are canonical representations of Boolean formulas. This property means that each Boolean formula with a specific variable ordering has a unique and minimal BDD representation. In fact, BDDs can be viewed as deterministic finite automata (DFA), discussed in chapter 2. Therefore, we can check that two Boolean formulas are equivalent by checking if they have isomorphic representations, that is, their BDDs match exactly in both structure and attributes. Also, determining the satisfiability of a formula only requires comparing its BDD with that of the constant function *false* (0).

Instead of explicitly enumerating all states in the model, which is a labeled state transition system or Kripke structure, we symbolically represent it as BDDs, hence the name symbolic model checker (SMC) [Burch et al., 1990a]. We have to find a way to translate the model into BDDs. Suppose that the current state of the system is represented by a vector of Boolean variables $S = \{s_0, \ldots, s_{n-1}\}$ and the next state of the system is represented by a vector of Boolean variables $S' = \{s'_0, \ldots, s'_{n-1}\}$. Using S and S', the transition relation between the values of the variables in the current and the next states can be stated as a Boolean formula $N(s_0, \ldots, s_{n-1}, s'_0, \ldots, s'_{n-1})$. Note a finite-domain non-Boolean variable can be easily converted into a vector of Boolean variables.

Each transition in this transition graph models the passage of one time unit. Without further extensions, non-unit as well as nondeterministic transition time can be modeled by a sequence of unit transitions. It is easy to extend this transition graph into a more powerful model called the timed transition graph (TTG) [Campos et al., 1994].

The symbolic model checker takes as input the model M represented by BDDs and the formula f to be verified (in the initial states of M). For every atomic proposition in S, it outputs a BDD with one Boolean variable such that the BDD is true in a state iff the formula f is true in that state.

CTL can specify the relative ordering of events or actions in a finite state system, but it cannot directly express when these events or actions occur. An awkward way of specifying that some event will occur in the future in at most a fixed number of time units is by nesting EX or AX operators. Real-time systems impose bounds on the response time of events and actions. To handle properties with these quantitative constraints, CTL has been extended in a number of ways. One extension [Emerson et al., 1990] adds time intervals to CTL temporal operators and introduces the bounded until operator $U[x, y]$. Quantitative algorithms exist for computing the following values between two events: (1) the minimum and maximum delays and (2) minimum and maximum number of condition occurrences. Also, extensions of these algorithms are available for handling non-unit transition time.

EXERCISES

1. Express the following safety assertion in CTL: In the hospital intensive care unit, once the pulse/blood pressure monitor pad, blood oxygen sensor, and respiration sensor are properly attached to the patient's arm, index finger, and nose, respectively, and the alarm is enabled, the alarm sounds if any of the following conditions becomes true and remains sounding until a nurse or doctor arrives and disables the alarm: pulse rate is above 120 beats per minute, systolic blood pressure is above 180 mmHg, blood oxygen count is below 80%, or respiration rate is above 35 times per minute.

2. Consider the CES model checker for CTL. If we are going to model the execution of a program with n Boolean variables and m integer variables, each of

which ranges from 0 to 10 (inclusive), what is the maximal number of states in the state graph.

3. Consider a simple algorithm for solving the mutual exclusion problem for two processes. Construct the state transition diagram for this algorithm. Prove or disprove the following properties by first expressing them in CTL formulas and then by following as much as possible the labeling technique in the CES model checker.

   (a) Only one of the two processes can be in the critical section at any one time.

   (b) The two processes will not deadlock.

4. Specify the state graph in exercise 2 as a description for CMU's symbolic model verifier (SMV).

5. Construct the state graph of the following mobile telephone/entertainment system: While the mobile telephone/entertainment system is turned on, if the telephone subsystem receives an incoming call while the radio, CD, or cassette player is on, then the telephone subsystem will ring after the radio/CD/cassette player is temporarily turned off. The radio/CD/cassette player resumes playing after either: the telephone rings 12 times without a user pressing the "send" button, or the "send" button is pressed within the 12 rings and the conversation is ended by the user pressing the "end" button.

   The telephone subsystem does not ring on receiving an incoming call while the mobile telephone/entertainment system is turned off; in this case, the phone-mail subsystem is activated to record incoming messages.

6. The goal of this problem is to apply the CES model-checking algorithm to the verification of a timing-based mutual algorithm by Attiya and Lynch, described in detail in [Attiya and Lynch, 1989]. For this problem, assume there are only two operators (processes). Construct the state transition diagram for this algorithm. Prove or disprove the following properties by first expressing them in CTL formulas and then by following as much as possible the labeling technique in [Clarke, Emerson, and Sistla, 1986].

   (a) Only one process can be in the critical section at any one time.

   (b) The processes will not deadlock.

7. Represent the following Boolean formulas as binary decision diagrams (BDDs):

   (a) $a \wedge (b \vee c)$.

   (b) $a \vee (b \wedge (c \vee d))$.

   (c) $(a \wedge b) \vee (c \wedge d)$.

8. Compare the space requirements for representing a Boolean formula using

   (a) a truth table (described in chapter 2) and

   (b) a BDD.

9. Explain how the following three types of finite-state graphs together with the temporal logic CTL model transitions with time constraints:

   (a) graph with untimed transition,

    (b) graph with unit transition time, and

    (c) graph with non-unit transition time.

10. Determine the run-time complexity of the minimum and maximum delay algorithms as well as the minimum and maximum condition-counting algorithms.

11. Consider a smart airbag deployment system in an automobile. A sensor is attached to the driver's seat that detects the distance between the driver and the steering wheel. This distance depends on the shape and size of the driver and on the position of the steering wheel. Based on this distance, the airbag computer determines how fast the airbag should be fully inflated. The airbag will deploy when a collision impact with a speed exceeding 30 mph occurs; otherwise, it will not deploy. If the distance is far (> 1.5 ft), the airbag will be fully deployed within 50 ms. If the distance is average (between 1.0 ft and 1.5 ft), the airbag will be fully deployed within 40 ms. If the distance is near (< 1.0 ft), the airbag will be fully deployed within 30 ms. Specify this system as a timed transition graph (TTG).

CHAPTER 5

VISUAL FORMALISM, STATECHARTS, AND STATEMATE

Finite-state machines (FSMs) have been used extensively in the specification and analysis of many computer-based as well as non-computer-based systems, ranging from electronic circuits to econometric models. They can model in detail the behavior of a system, and several algorithms exist to perform the analysis. Unfortunately, classical state machines such as those employed in the standard, explicit-state CTL model-checking approach [Clarke, Emerson, and Sistla, 1986] lack support for modularity and suffer from exponential-state explosion. The first problem often arises when FSMs are used to model complex systems that contain similar subsystems. The second problem is evident in systems in which the addition of a few variables or components can substantially increase the number of states and transitions, and hence the size of the FSM. Furthermore, the inability to specify absolute time and time intervals limits the usability of classical FSMs for the specification of real-time systems.

To tackle the first two problems, we can introduce modular and hierarchical features to classical FSMs. [Harel et al., 1987] developed a visual formalism called Statecharts to solve these two problems as well as the problem of specifying *reactive systems*. Reactive systems are complex control-driven mechanisms that interact with discrete occurrences in the environment in which they are embedded. They include real-time computer systems, communication devices, control plants, VLSI circuits, and airplane avionics. The reactive behavior of these systems cannot be captured by specifying the corresponding outputs resulting from every possible set of inputs. Instead, this behavior has to be described by specifying the relationship of inputs, outputs, and system state over time under a set of system- and environment-dependent timing and communication constraints.

The Statecharts language provides graphic features (labeled boxes) to denote states (or sets of states) and transitions between states. A transition from one state

134

to another state takes place when the associated event(s) and condition(s) are enabled. A state can be decomposed into lower-level states via *refinement*, and a set of states can be combined into a higher-level state via *clustering*. This hierarchical specification approach makes it possible for the specifier to zoom-in and zoom-out of a section of the Statecharts specification, thus partially remedying the exponential-state explosion problem in classical FSMs. Furthermore, AND and OR clustering relations, together with the notions of *state exclusivity* and *orthogonality*, can readily support concurrency and independence in system specification. As we will see in this chapter, these features dramatically reduce the state-explosion problem by not considering all states in a classical FSM at once.

To develop a comprehensive tool capable not only of system specification, [Harel et al., 1990b] extended the work on Statecharts, which is capable also of behavioral description, to derive high-level languages for structural and functional specifications. The language *module-charts* is used to describe a structural view with a graphical display of the components of the system. The language *activity-charts* is used to describe a functional view with a graphical display of the functions of the system. They also added mechanisms that provide a friendly user interface, simulated system executions, dynamic analysis, code generation, and rapid prototyping. The entire specification and development environment is known as STATEMATE.

5.1 STATECHARTS

Statecharts [Harel, 1987] is an extension of classical finite-state machines and their visual counterparts, state-transition diagrams. This visual language is better than classical FSMs for specifying the behavior of reactive systems. It supports the AND or OR decomposition of states into substates with an instantaneous broadcast communication between states at different levels. Statecharts thus combines the concepts of state diagrams, depth, orthogonality, and broadcast communication into one specification language.

5.1.1 Basic Statecharts Features

In Statecharts, labeled boxes are used to denote states and directed edges indicate the transitions between states. A transition takes place when the associated event(s) occur(s) and condition(s) is/are satisfied. More precisely, an expression labeling a transition is of the form

$$event[condition]/action$$

where *event* is the event enabling the transition, *condition* is the condition which must hold for *event* to enable transition, and *action* is the action that is executed at precisely the time when the transition is taken. Usually, events and conditions can be treated as inputs and actions as outputs, as in traditional FSMs. However, these three parts of the transition label are optional. A selected list of special events, conditions,

state S	entered(S) exited(S)	in(S)	
activity A	started(A) stopped(A)	active(A) hanging(A)	start(A) stop(A) suspend(A) resume(A)
data items D1,D2 condition C	read(D1) written(D1) true(C) false(C)	D1 = D2 D1 < D2 D1 > D2 $\cdots$	D1 := expression make_true(C) make_false(C)
event E action A n time units	timeout(E,n)		schedule(A,n)

Figure 5.1   Special events, conditions, and actions.

and actions is shown in Figure 5.1. Extensions to FSMs include the use of variables in the label of a transition, logical comparisons in conditions, and assignnment statements in actions.

Example. The following label for a transition indicates that when the system is in the *countdown* state, the *emergency* state is not active, and the triggering event "started(*ignition*) occurs," then both the action "start(*launch*)" and the two assignments ("a := b + c + 1" and "d := a + 2") are executed in parallel:

started(*ignition*)[in(*countdown*) and not active(*emergency*)]/start(*launch*);

a := b + c + 1; d := a + 2

Note that the expressions to the right of the assign operator ":=" must be side-effect free. The parallel execution of these assignments consists of the evaluation of all these expressions using the values of the variables prior to the assignments, followed by updating the variables to the left of the assign operator with the values of the corresponding expressions. Suppose a = 1, b = 2, c = 3. Then after the transition is taken: a = 6, d = 3. Chapter 10 describes additional details of parallel assignments in the context of real-time rule-based systems.

Actions can also be associated with the entrance to and an exit from a state at any level.

Before we proceed to describe more details of the syntax and semantics of Statecharts, we illustrate several basic concepts of Statecharts with an automotive example.

Example. Figure 5.2 shows two Statecharts of specifications of the behavior of the pedals of an automobile. Here, the specified parts of the automobile is the *specified system*. Both specifications show that the automobile can be in one of three states:

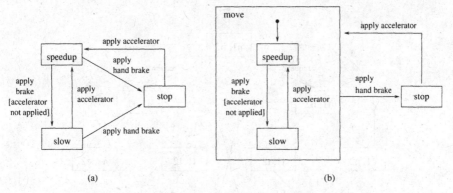

Figure 5.2   Two Statecharts of the behavior of a car's pedals.

stop, *move*, and *slow*. Figure 5.2(a) shows that (1) the transition from the state "stop" to the state "speedup" occurs when the accelerator is applied; (2) the transition from the state "speedup" to the state "slow" occurs when the brake is applied provided that the condition within the bracket is true (accelerator is not applied); (3) the transition from the state "slow" to the state "speedup" occurs when the accelerator is applied; and (4) the transitions from the states "speedup" and "slow" to the state "stop" occur when the hand brake is applied.

OR-Decomposition   By clustering the states "speedup" and "slow" into a new state "move," we obtain an equivalent specification in Figure 5.2(b). Now, saying that the automobile (specified system) is in state "move" means that it is either in state "speedup" OR state "slow." The transition labeled "apply hand brake" leaving state "move" is a high-level interrupt and denotes an exit from "move." Whether the system is in state "speedup" OR "slow" does not matter; this transition takes the system from either state to state "stop." Note that the transition labeled "apply accelerator" from state "stop" to the outside of state "move" seems to be ambiguous. However, the internal default arrow attached to state "speedup" means the system enters state "speedup" if the transition labeled "apply accelerator" is taken. When the system designer works with the higher control levels of the automobile, there is no need to view the details within state "move." Thus the specification and analysis complexity can be simplified with OR-decomposition through clustering.

AND-Decomposition   Another way to reduce the number of states is to use AND-decomposition, as shown in the following example.

Example.   Figures 5.3 and 5.4 show two equivalent Statecharts of specifications of a solution to the two-process mutual exclusion problem. In any correct solution, only one process is allowed in the critical section (c1 or c2) at any given time. The first Statechart specification, in Figure 5.3, resembles a classical FSM, whereas the second Statechart specification, in Figure 5.4, applies AND-decomposition to reduce

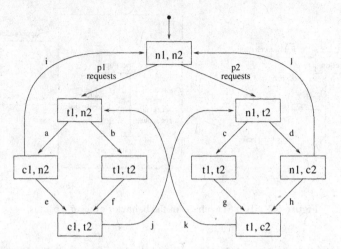

Figure 5.3 Statechart A of a solution to the mutual exclusion problem.

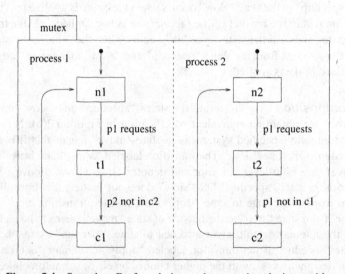

Figure 5.4 Statechart B of a solution to the mutual exclusion problem.

the number of states. In the second specification, if the system is in state "mutex," then it must be in both states "process 1" (p1) and "process 2" (p2). In the first specification, the initial entrance is to state "n1,n2," whereas in the second specification, the unspecified entrance to "mutex" is resolved by the default arrows to enter the pair {n1,n2}.

Transitions in "process 1" and "process 2" take place concurrently as governed by the transition labels. Therefore, if "p1 requests" is true, then the system will be in state pair {t1,n2}. If "p2 requests" is true simultaneously, then the system will be in pair {t1,t2}. Here, "process 1" and "process 2" are called *orthogonal* state components obtained by AND-decomposition. AND-decomposition can be applied at any level of states and is more convenient than single-level communicating FSMs. As seen in this example, this orthogonality feature can reduce the state-explosion problem.

Next we describe selected features of Statecharts.

Delays and Timeouts   The event expression *timeout(event, number)* represents the event that happens right after the specified *number* of time units have passed since the occurrence of the specified *event*. In a real-time system, it is often required to specify that the system stays in a particular state for a certain period of time. This can be done graphically by a box (representing the state) with a squiggle (a resistor-like notation), and a numerical bound is specified next to it. Both lower and upper bounds can be specified. In the case of a state with a lower bound and an exit, events do not apply in this state prior to the lower bound. After the system stays in this state for the specified period of time, it moves to another state.

In the specification of real-time systems, a need exists to specify an upper bound or a lower bound on the time spent in a state. A box with a squiggle along with a time upper bound (or lower bound) represents a state with a duration. The syntax for the duration specification is $\Delta t_1 < \Delta t_2$, where either Δt_i may be omitted. A generic event stands for *timeout(entered state, bound)*, where *state* is the source of the transition and *bound* is the specified bound.

Condition and Selection Entrances   To reduce the number of line drawings in a complicated entrance to substates of a superstate, Statecharts employs two connectives represented by a circle. The *conditional* connective C replaces two or more arrows from outside a state to this state's substates. This is done by drawing one arrow from outside the state to the C-connective (a circle with a C in it) and then drawing arrows from the connective to their respective substates. The user has the option of separately specifying the arrows from the C-connective to their corresponding states.

The *selection* connective S also replaces two or more arrows from outside a state to this state's substates. Here, the state to be entered is selected by the value of a generic event and this value is one of the values labeling the substates. For example, a robotic arm operator can move the robot arm "up," "down," "left," "right," "forward," or "backward" by pressing one of the corresponding six buttons. These six events can be modeled by six substates within a "move" state. There is an arrow enters the "move" state from outside this state to the S-connective (a circle with an 'S' in it), but no arrows need to be drawn from this connective to the six states.

Unclustering   If the Statechart description is large, we can uncluster it by keeping the parts of interest large. This is done by drawing parts of the Statechart outside of their natural boundaries. This technique is useful for describing a large system. However, unclustering should not be used often since it can create a tree-like structure.

5.1.2 Semantics

At the time of its development, Statecharts was purely a specification language with no underlying basis for formal analysis or verification. It was not associated with any logics or algebras, and hence was often regarded as a semi-formal specification language. More recently, [Harel and Naamad, 1996] presented a semantics for Statecharts.

The behavior of a Statechart can be defined by a simulation of the sequence of steps allowed. The start of a step can be triggered by one or more events. Given the current state, we select a maximal set of compound transitions to fire from the currently enabled set of transitions. A compound transition is a sequence of enabled and thus executable transitions. All the executions of a step or transition are performed in parallel. Statecharts uses the instantaneous broadcasting of events as the communication mechanism among states at any level.

5.2 ACTIVITY-CHARTS

The language activity-charts describes the functional decomposition of a system. It is a conceptual modeling language which graphically shows activities or functions with rectilinear shapes. Solid arrows indicate the flow of data items whereas dashed arrows represent the flow of control items. Basic (or atomic) activities cannot be decomposed into lower-level activities and may be described as code in a programming language such as C. The details within a higher-level activity are specified by its lower-level activities. An activity takes in input items and produces output items while it is active.

Data-stores represent buffers where databases or data structures can be stored in an activity. Control activities appear as empty boxes in an activity chart and show the behavioral view of the system. A control activity can control other related activities by sensing their statuses and giving commands to them. The language of Statecharts is used to describe the contents of these control activities.

5.3 MODULE-CHARTS

The language module-charts describes the system modules (the physical components), the environment modules (external to the system), and the flow of data and control signals among these modules. Therefore, module-charts provides a structural view of the system. Rectilinear shapes denote modules and rectangles with dashed lines signify storage modules. Environment modules are also represented by rectangles with dashed lines but they are outside the specified system. As in the states in Statecharts, submodules in module-charts may appear inside a module and several levels of encapsulation may exist. Labeled arrows and hyperarrows represent the flow of information between modules.

Figure 5.5 shows the module-chart of a simplified car. CAR is the main component, which is decomposed into several submodules, two of which are brake-system

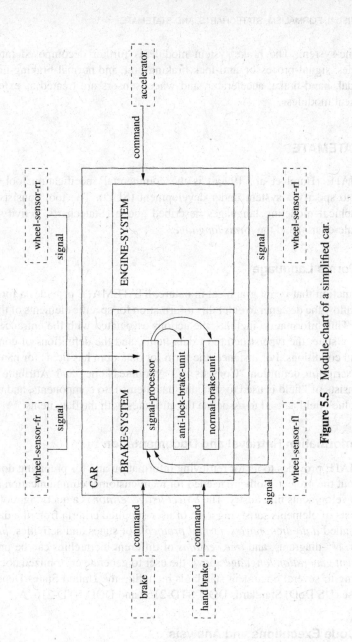

Figure 5.5 Module-chart of a simplified car.

and engine-system. The brake-system module is further decomposed into three submodules: signal-processor, anti-lock-braking-unit, and normal-braking-unit. The brake-pedal, hand-brake, accelerator, and wheel-sensors are treated as external or environment modules.

5.4   STATEMATE

STATEMATE [Harel et al., 1990a] is the commercial specification tool for the designer to specify a system under development (SUD). The tool consists of the three graphical modeling languages described above (Statecharts, activity-charts, and module-charts) and the *forms language*.

5.4.1   Forms Language

For information that is not graphical in nature, STATEMATE provides a forms language to allow the designer to enter this information for specific elements of the specification. This information includes the actions associated with the entrance to and exit from a state, the type/structure of data items, and the definitions of compound events and conditions. For instance, the form for data item has fields for name, synonym, description, definition, "Consists of," "Attribute Name," and "Attribute Value." The "Consists of" field is used to structure data items into components, and the "Attribute Value" field is used to associate the attributes with the data items.

5.4.2   Information Retrieval and Documentation

STATEMATE provides tools for retrieving information and for preparing documentation about the project. Both are needed for team/customer communication in large project developments in industry. The *object list generator* is a querying tool for accessing lists of elements satisfying a set of user-supplied criteria from the database. Reports called *data dictionaries*, *textual protocols* of states and activities, *interface diagrams*, N^2-diagrams, and *tree versions* of different hierarchies can be prepared. A *document generation language* allows the user to generate customized documents conforming to several document standards including the United States Department of Defense (US DoD) Standards DOD-STD-2167 and DOD-STD-2167A.

5.4.3   Code Executions and Analysis

Statecharts was first developed as a standard specification language to facilitate communication between customers, managers, engineers, and programmers in a design and development team. In 1987, the first version of STATEMATE incorporating the Statecharts language was completed and released by AD CAD. STATEMATE can execute a single step of the behavior of the specified system from the initial system state or any given system state. This is done by algorithmic procedures that follow the semantics of Statecharts, module-charts, and activity-charts. This stepwise execution is similar to the stepwise execution of a program by a typical program debugger. Therefore, this execution ability serves as a debugging mechanism for detecting errors or inconsistencies in the specified system.

It is often not practical to execute interactively the steps of interest, so STATE-MATE provides a *simulation control language* (SCL) to specify programmed executions, that is, the user can specify the sequence of steps to take. Breakpoints can be specified so that the tool can stop after executing specified steps and wait for further instructions from the user. It is possible to restrict the *scope* of the simulated executions so that it is not necessary for the entire system to be completely specified before we can simulate steps in a specified part of the system. Results of the simulated executions are recorded in a trace database, and a number of simulation reports can be generated.

By carefully writing an SCL program, we can test parts of the specified program that may contain errors or inconsistencies. We can attach a watchdog statechart to the system being tested so that this watchdog statechart will enter a special state when a specified situation occurs. This is useful in finding states in which a specified condition is true. However, testing all scenarios is not practical even for small systems due to the state explosion problem, as noted by STATEMATE implementors. In fact, doing so would be equivalent to generating the entire FSM or reachability graph of the specified system, which is what Statecharts wants to avoid in the first place. Also, such exhaustive testing cannot be applied to a system with an infinite number of states. STATEMATE developers plan to provide the capability of verifying specification against a temporal logic formula, but so far the tool by itself does not have this formal analysis ability.

STATEMATE can automatically translate a specification into an Ada or C prototype code. If testing of the generated code detects errors, the corresponding specification can be revised and the code regenerated. This facility can move the prototype code closer to the final software by iterating through several of these *model revision-code generation* steps. This procedure is known as *incremental substitution*.

5.5 AVAILABLE TOOLS

As a commercial product, STATEMATE (and hence Statecharts) has been used for more applications than experimental specification and analysis tools. One of the first and the most notable and widely publicized application is probably the mission-specific avionics system for the Israel Aircraft Industries' Lavi fighter aircraft. Part of the avionics system is specified in Statecharts. Other published applications include cruise control, processing modeling, and communication protocols.

STATEMATE is a well-designed specification tool and has a convenient user interface. It is acceptable in small projects for testing and limited reachability analysis. It is better than less formal or semi-formal approaches but lacks the formal analysis and verification capabilities of newer approaches such as logic- and algebra-based tools. This weakness limits STATEMATE's usability as a specification tool in the early stages of system specification and design, for unambiguous communication between customers and developers about the system to be designed. However, new versions of the tool allow an interface between the Statecharts specification facility and temporal-logic-based model checkers. The tool is also useful in detecting inconsistencies or conflicts in the specification. More details about STATEMATE can be found at

http://www.ilogix.com

The current version of STATEMATE from I-Logix is called Statemate MAGNUM. It is a comprehensive graphical modeling and simulation tool for the rapid development of complex embedded systems. Using this tool, the user can create a complete specification, thus serving as a formal step between system requirements and system implementation. This specification may be executed or graphically simulated for exploring "what if" scenarios to determine if the behavior and the interactions between system elements are correct. Therefore, the user can detect and then correct errors resulting from ambiguous requirements early in the design process.

Another tool available from I-Logix is Rhapsody, an enterprise-wide visual programming environment incorporating a Statechart and activity-chart/diagram specification facility for designing and implementing real-time embedded systems and software applications. It is based on the Unified Modeling Language and is available in several language platforms, including C, C++, and J. Rhapsody thus combines both functional decomposition and object methods, allowing the graphic design of the behavior of objects. This environment provides real-time behavioral semantics, software packages, target real-time operating system support, model/code associativity, design-level debugging and validation, and production quality customized code generation. Therefore, Rhapsody helps the designer produce a model that is also the resulting application code with complete documentation. Rhapsody integrates the analysis, design, implementation, and test phases of the software design process. Its architecture is open and configurable to allow for future enhancements. Rhapsody comes with interfaces to commercial configuration management tools, requirement traceability tools, integrated development environments, testing tools, and human machine interface tools. Rhapsody shifts the focus of work from coding and debugging to design. Other Rhapsody features include model/code associativity, team-based development, system requirements through use cases, component collaboration and scenario analysis with sequence diagrams, architectural modeling with object modeling, and system-wide management and viewing.

With Rhapsody, the designer can develop and modify target application code as often as needed while completing and validating performance and behavioral characteristics of the graphical model, using the same diagrams for designing the model to debug the application at the desgin level. This is possible since the code is the real code written in one of the supported programming languages rather than a simulated model of the application. The tool allows the linking of design documentation and implementation throughout the design process.

5.6 HISTORICAL PERSPECTIVE AND RELATED WORK

Statecharts generalizes classical FSMs, and Mealy [Mealy, 1955] and Moore [Moore, 1956] finite automata. The semantics of Statecharts is identical to that proposed in a survey paper by Green [Green, 1982] on flowchart drawing techniques from a psychological viewpoint. In this paper, Green showed a state machine with high-level states where transitions can exit a state at any level. Similarly in Statecharts, an event is an interrupt from all low-level states.

[Ward and Mellor, 1985] used data flow diagrams to specify real-time systems. Alan Shaw introduced another formalism for specifying real-time systems called communicating real-time state machines (CRSMs) [Shaw, 1992]. CRSMs are also based on finite-state machines and borrow some concepts from Statecharts though CRSMs are more restricted. Unlike Statecharts, which uses the broadcasting of events as the communication mechanism among states, CRSMs employ a distributed model of concurrency in which communication is achieved via synchronous one-to-one message-passing between components.

A CRSM is a finte-state machine whose transitions are labeled with guarded commands of the form

$$guard \rightarrow command[timing\ constraint]$$

A *guard* is a Boolean expression over the variables of the CRSM. If it is omitted, the constant *true* is assumed. A *command* can be either an internal command or an input/output command. An internal command may be a computation specified in some programming language or an occurrence of some physical event. The I/O notation and semantics are borrowed from Hoare's Communicating Sequential Processes (CSP) [Hoare, 1978; Hoare, 1985], described in chapter 9.

The Modechart graphical specification language (described in chapter 6) introduced by Mok et al. [Jahanian and Stuart, 1988; Jahanian and Mok, 1994] is another alternative to Statecharts/STATEMATE. Furthermore, Modechart claims to remedy the weaknesses (especially in the initial versions) of the Statecharts language in handling absolute timing specifications.

As discussed earlier, finite-state machines or state transition diagrams can be used to specify systems, but their size and complexity can be prohibitive for practical systems. The developers of Statecharts point out that FSMs cannot be easily translated into code for prototyping, testing, or execution. However, recent developments in program optimization and synthesis provide automated tools for converting an FSM into corresponding high-level code. The optimizing tool developed by Zupan and Cheng [Zupan and Cheng, 1994b; Zupan and Cheng, 1998] can automatically synthesize a rule-based program from a state-transition diagram. This tool is described in chapter 12.

5.7 SUMMARY

Many computer-based as well as non-computer-based systems can be specified by finite-state machines (FSMs). FSMs can model in detail the behavior of a system, and several algorithms exist to perform the analysis. Unfortunately, classical-state machines such as those employed in the standard, explicit-state CTL model-checking approach [Clarke, Emerson, and Sistla, 1986] lack support for modularity and suffer from exponential-state explosion. The first problem often arises when FSMs are used to model complex systems that contain similar subsystems. The second problem is evident in systems where the addition of a few variables or components can substantially increase the number of states and transitions, and hence the size of the FSM. Furthermore, the inability to specify absolute time and time intervals limits the usability of classical FSMs for the specification of real-time systems.

To tackle the first two problems, we can introduce modular and hierarchical features to classical FSMs. [Harel, 1987] developed a visual formalism called Statecharts to solve these two problems as well as the problem of specifying reactive systems. Reactive systems are complex control-driven mechanisms that interact with discrete occurrences in the environment in which they are embedded.

The reactive behavior of these systems cannot be captured by specifying the corresponding outputs resulting from every possible set of inputs. Instead, this behavior has to be described by specifying the relationship. However, new versions of the tool allow an interface between the Statecharts specification facility and temporal-logic-based model checkers of inputs, outputs, and system state over time under a set of system- and environment-dependent timing and communication constraints.

The Statecharts language provides graphic features (labeled boxes) to denote states (or sets of states) and transitions between states. A transition from one state to another takes place when the associated event(s) and condition(s) are enabled. A state can be decomposed into lower-level states via *refinement*, and a set of states can be combined into a higher-level state via *clustering*. This hierarchical specification approach makes it possible for the specifier to zoom-in and zoom-out of a section of the Statecharts specification, thus partially remedying the exponential-state-explosion problem in classical FSMs. Furthermore, AND and OR clustering relations, together with the notions of *state exclusivity* and *orthogonality*, can readily support concurrency and independence in system specification. These features dramatically reduce the state-explosion problem by not considering all states in a classical FSM at once.

To develop a comprehensive tool capable not only of system specification, [Harel et al., 1990a] extended the work on Statecharts, which is capable also of behavioral description, to derive high-level languages for structural and functional specifications. The language module-charts is used to describe a structural view with a graphical display of the components of the system. The language activity-charts is used to describe a functional view with a graphical display of the functions of the system. They also added mechanisms that provide a friendly user interface, simulated system executions, dynamic analysis, code generation, and rapid prototyping. The entire specification and development environment is known as STATEMATE.

Other hierarchical FSM-based specification tools include communicating real-time state machines (CRSMs) and Modechart.

EXERCISES

1. Describe the advantages of Statecharts over classical finite-state transition systems.
2. Describe the usage of Statecharts, activity-charts, and module-charts. Which one can describe the lowest-level details in a specified system?
3. What are the advantages of OR-decomposition and AND-decomposition? In what scenarios would their use be appropriate?
4. What is the purpose of the SCL? How does it help in the development of correct application code?
5. Consider the Statecharts for a solution to the two-task mutual exclusion problem in Figures 5.3 and 5.4. Statechart A is basically a classical finite-state machine whereas Statechart B takes advantage of Statecharts' features. Show the two corresponding Statecharts for a system with three tasks. Describe how Statechart B (for both the two-task and three-task systems) avoids the state-explosion problem found in Statechart A.
6. Construct the Statechart of the behavior of any electronic digital watch. An example is shown in [Harel, 1987].
7. Specify the smart airbag deployment system described in chapter 4 (exercise 6) as a Statechart. Compare the expressiveness and space requirement for the Statechart model and the timed transition graph model.
8. Consider the following high-level specification of the NASA 2001 Mars Odyssey Orbiter [Cass, 2001]. Before and during launch, the orbiter is folded into a protective housing. After launch, the solar panel extends to convert solar energy into electric energy for navigational use. When the orbiter approaches Mars, its engine fires and the orbiter inserts into Mars' orbit. After braking, the orbiter deploys its high-gain antenna. At any time after launch, if an emergency occurs (expected steps are not executed as observed by a specialized monitoring computer), the orbiter skips the above steps and enters a safe mode and lets mission controllers take over control of the orbiter. Represent the behavior of the orbiter using a Statechart.

CHAPTER 6

REAL-TIME LOGIC, GRAPH-THEORETIC ANALYSIS, AND MODECHART

A real-time system can be specified in one of two ways. The first is to structurally and functionally describe the system by specifying its mechanical, electrical, and electronic components. This type of specification shows how the components of the system work as well as their functions and operations. The second is to describe the behavior of the system in response to actions and events. Here, the specification tells sequences of events allowed by the system. For instance, a structural-functional specification of the real-time anti-lock braking system in an automobile describes the braking system components and sensors, how they are interconnected, and how the actions of each component affects the other. This specification shows, for example, how to connect the wheel sensors to the central decision-making computer that controls the brake mechanism.

On the other hand, a behavioral specification shows only the response of each braking system component in response to an internal or external event, but does not describe how one can build such a system. For instance, this specification shows that when the wheel sensors detect wet road conditions, the decision-making computer will instruct the brake mechanism to pump the brakes at a higher frequency within 100 ms. Since we are interested in the timing properties of the system, a behavioral specification without the complexity of the structural specification often suffices for verifying the satisfaction of many timing constraints. Furthermore, to reduce specification and analysis complexity, we restrict the specification language to handle only timing relations. This is a departure from techniques that employ specification languages capable of describing logical as well as timing relations, such as real-time CTL.

148

6.1 SPECIFICATION AND SAFETY ASSERTIONS

To show that a system or program meets certain safety properties, we can relate the specification of the system to the safety assertion representing the desired safety properties. This assumes that the actual implementation of the system is faithful to the specification. Note that even though a behavioral specification does not show how one can build the specified system, one can certainly show that the implemented system, built from the structural-functional specification, satisfies the behavioral specification.

One of the following three cases may result from the analysis relating the specification and the safety assertion:

1. The safety assertion is a theorem derivable from the specification, thus the system is safe with respect to the behavior denoted by the safety assertion.
2. The safety assertion is unsatisfiable with respect to the specification, so the system is inherently unsafe since the specification will cause the safety assertion to be violated.
3. The negation of the safety assertion is satisfiable under certain conditions, meaning that additional constraints must be added to the system to ensure its safety.

The specification and the safety assertion can be written in one of several real-time specification languages. The choice of language would in turn determine the algorithms that can be used for the analysis and verification. We begin the study with the event-action model and a first-order logic called real-time logic (RTL) [Jahanian and Mok, 1986].

6.2 EVENT-ACTION MODEL

The event-action model [Heninger, 1980; Jahanian and Mok, 1986] captures the data dependency and temporal ordering of computational actions that must be taken in response to events in a real-time application. There are four basic concepts.

1. An *action* is a schedulable unit of work and can be primitive or composite. A *primitive* action is atomic in that it cannot or does not need to be broken into subactions for the purpose of analysis. It consumes a bounded amount of time. A *composite* action is a partial ordering of primitive actions or other composite actions. The same action may appear more than once in a composite action. Recursive actions and circular chains of actions where an action is a subaction of its predecessor in the chain are not allowed.

   The notation A;B indicates that the sequential execution of action A is followed by action B. For example, TRAIN-APPROACH;DOWN-GATE means that the train first approaches the railroad crossing sensor, then the gate moves down. The notation A∥B indicates the parallel execution of action A and action B. For example, DOWN-GATE∥RING-BELL means that the moving-down of the gate and the ringing of the alerting bell happen simultaneously.

2. A *state predicate* is an assertion about the state of the specified system. For example, GATE-IS-DOWN is true if the gate is in the down position.

3. An *event* is a temporal marker for indicating a point in time that is significant in describing the system behavior. There are four classes of events:

    (a) An *external* event is caused by actions outside the specified system. For example, APPLY-BRAKE is an external event which means the pressing of the brake pedal by the drive or operator.

    (b) A *start* event marks the beginning of an action, for example, the start of the DOWN-GATE action.

    (c) A *stop* event marks the end of an action, for example, the end of the DOWN-GATE action.

    (d) A *transition* event marks the change in a certain attribute of the system state. For example, GATE-IS-DOWN becomes true when the gate is moved to the down position.

4. A *timing constraint* is an assertion about the absolute timing of system events.

6.3   REAL-TIME LOGIC

The motivation for introducing real-time logic [Jahanian and Mok, 1986] is that the specifications written in the event-action model cannot be easily to manipulated by a computer. RTL is a first-order logic with special features to capture the timing requirements of the specified system while making the specification easy to manipulate mechanically. RTL was especially attractive because at the time of its introduction, temporal logic was able to express relative ordering of events or actions [Heninger, 1980; Bernstein and Harter, 1981], but temporal logic has not yet been extended with the capability of expressing absolute timing characteristics.

For example, conventional temporal logic can specify that an action B follows another action A such as TRAIN-APPROACH followed by DOWN-GATE, but cannot specify that DOWN-GATE will occur within a certain time period (say 5 s) after the occurrence of TRAIN-APPROACH. Furthermore, temporal logic uses an interleaving model of computation to specify concurrency in computer systems, but this model cannot express true parallelism. For example, temporal logic models two parallel actions as if one is followed by the other or vice versa, so that from an initial state s_0 there are two paths, corresponding to the two orderings of these actions, leading to state s_1.

A scheduler is often an integral part of a real-time system. The correctness of a real-time system depends on the correctness of its scheduler. Temporal logic, however, usually assumes the fair scheduling of the specified system's resources and events. This is appropriate for non-time-critical systems but certainly is not sufficient for the analysis of real-time systems.

RTL is based on the event-action model, augmented with several features such as the occurrence function @, which assigns time values to event occurrences. $@(TrainApproach, i) = x$ means that the ith occurrence of the train approach occurs at time x. There are three types of RTL constants: actions, events, and integers. Action constants are as defined in the event-action model and capital letters are used to denote them to distinguish them from variables. A subaction B_i of a composite action A is denoted as $A.B_i$. Event constants serve as temporal markers and are classified into: (1) start events indicating the beginning of actions, preceded by $\uparrow$; (2) stop events indicating the end of actions, preceded by $\downarrow$; (3) transition events indicating the change in certain attributes of the system state; and (4) external events, preceded by Ω.

Example. We now use RTL to specify a simple railroad crossing with one train rail. From the field measurements and the knowledge about the mechanical characteristics of the train, train sensor, gate controller, and gate, we obtain the following specifications. The goal of the gate controller is to ensure that when the train is crossing the intersection of the road with the rail, no car is on the intersection. In this simplified · version, this is achieved by having the gate in the down position when the train is crossing.

Specification in English: When the train approaches the train sensor and is detected by the sensor, a signal is sent to the gate controller to initiate the lowering of the gate at the railroad crossing.

The gate will be moved to the down position within 30 s from the time when the train approach is detected by the sensor.

The gate needs at least 15 s to lower itself to the down position.

Safety Assertion in English: If the train needs at least 45 s to travel from the sensor position to the railroad crossing, and the train crossing is completed within 60 s from the time the train is detected by the sensor, then we are assured that at the start of the train crossing the gate has moved to the down position and that the train leaves the railroad crossing within 45 s from the time the gate has completed moving to the down position.

We now show the specification and the safety assertion in RTL.

Specification in RTL:

$$\forall x \, @(TrainApproach, x) \leq @(\uparrow Downgate, x) \land$$

$$@(\downarrow Downgate, x) \leq @(TrainApproach, x) + 30$$

$$\forall y \, @(\uparrow Downgate, y) + 15 \leq @(\downarrow Downgate, y)$$

Safety Assertion in RTL:

$$\forall t \forall u \, @(TrainApproach, t) + 45 \le @(Crossing, u) \, \wedge$$

$$@(Crossing, u) < @(TrainApproach, t) + 60 \rightarrow$$

$$@(\downarrow Downgate, t) \le @(Crossing, u) \, \wedge$$

$$@(Crossing, u) \le @(\downarrow Downgate, t) + 45$$

To use existing theorem proving methods [Chang and Lee, 1973] to prove that the safety assertion (SA) is a theorem derivable from the specification (SP), we further translate the above into Presburger arithmetic formulas. The following Presburger arithmetic formulas with uninterpreted functions correspond to the RTL formulas describing the SP and SA.

Specification in Presburger Arithmetic Formulas:

$$\forall x f(x) \le g_1(x) \wedge g_2(x) \le f(x) + 30$$

$$\forall y g_1(y) + 15 \le g_2(y)$$

Safety Assertion in Presburger Arithmetic Formulas:

$$\forall t \forall u f(t) + 45 \le h(u) \wedge h(u) < f(t) + 60 \rightarrow$$

$$g_2(t) \le h(u) \wedge h(u) \le g_2(t) + 45$$

In these formulas, t, u, x, and y are variables, f, g_1, g_2, and h are uninterpreted integer functions. f corresponds to the occurrence function for event TrainApproach. g_1 corresponds to the occurrence function for the start of action Downgate. g_2 corresponds to the occurrence function for the end of action Downgate. h corresponds to the occurrence function for event Crossing.

The problem of determining whether SA follows from SP is in general undecidable for the full set of RTL formulas, so not all analysis problems of this type can be solved. For the subclass of RTL formulas that are decidable, the solutions still require exponential run time.

Several ways are available to improve the efficiency of the analysis. First, we can use approximations to yield a simpler set of specification and safety assertions for analysis. Second, we can focus the analysis on the part of the specification that is relevant to the validity of the given safety assertions. Third, we can restrict the specification language so that less general but more efficient analysis procedures can be applied. Here we consider the third approach.

6.4 RESTRICTED RTL FORMULAS

One restricted class of RTL formulas [Jahanian and Mok, 1987] is motivated by the fact that in the specification of many real-time systems:

1. the RTL formulas consist of arithmetic inequalities involving two terms and an integer constant in which a term is either a variable or a function; and
2. the RTL formulas do not contain arithmetic expressions that have a function taking an instance of itself as an argument.

Such a restricted RTL class would allow the potential use of a graph-theoretic approach for analysis. For instance, we can use a single-source shortest-paths algorithm for the simple integer programming problem where each inequality is of the form $x_i - x_j \leq \pm a_{ij}$ where x_i and x_j are variables and a_{ij} is an integer constant. We can also use a constraint graph to represent the set of inequalities. Each variable is presented by a node in the graph, and an inequality $x_i \pm a_{ij} \leq x_j$ is represented by a directed edge with weight $\pm a_{ij}$ connecting x_i to x_j. Then, a set of inequalities represented by such a graph is unsatisfiable iff a cycle is present in the graph with a positive total weight on it.

As a result of these observations, we restrict the RTL formulas to consist of arithmetic inequalities of the following form:

occurrence function $\pm$ integer constant $\leq$ occurrence function.

Note that $@(E_1, i) \pm I < @(E_2, j)$ can be rewritten as $@(E_1, i) \pm I + 1 \leq @(E_2, j)$. Also, $\neg(@(E_1, i) \pm I \leq @(E_2, j))$ can be rewritten as $@(E_2, j) \pm I + 1 \leq @(E_1, i)$.

All formulas in the preceding railroad crossing example satisfy this restriction and thus are in this RTL subclass. However, the formula

$$\forall t \exists u \, @(TrainApproach, t) + u \leq @(Crossing, t),$$

which is not found in the example, is not in the restricted RTL subclass since the first argument of $\leq$ is the sum of a function and a variable.

To facilitate the analysis, we first transform the RTL formula F into the corresponding Presburger arithmetic formula F'. Each occurrence function $@(e, i)$ is replaced by a function $f_e(i)$ where e is an event and i is an integer or a variable. Next, we express F' in clausal form F'' in preparation for the analysis. F'' is a formula of the form

$$C_1 \wedge C_2 \wedge \cdots \wedge C_n.$$

Each C_i is a disjunctive clause

$$L_1 \vee L_2 \vee \cdots \vee L_n$$

and each L_j is a literal of the form

$$v_1 \pm I \leq v_2$$

where v_1 and v_2 are uninterpreted integer functions corresponding to the occurrence functions and I is an integer constant.

Given a system specification SP and a safety assertion SA expressed in the restricted RTL subclass, the goal is to show that SA is a theorem derivable from SP, that is, SP $\rightarrow$ SA. This is equivalent to showing that the negation of SP $\rightarrow$ SA, that is, $\neg$(SP $\rightarrow$ SA), is unsatisfiable. Since SP $\rightarrow$ SA can be rewritten as $\neg$SP $\vee$ SA, our analysis is to prove that the formula SP $\wedge \neg$SA is unsatisfiable. The following example shows the clausal form of the specification and the negation of the safety assertion of the preceding example.

Example. Consider SP and $\neg$SA in clausal form. T and U are Skolem constants corresponding to variables t and u, respectively.

Specification in Clausal Form:

$$f(x) \leq g_1(x)$$
$$g_2(x) \leq f(x) + 30$$
$$g_1(y) + 15 \leq g_2(y)$$

Rewriting the formula yields the following three clauses:

$$(x) \leq g_1(x)$$
$$g_2(x) - 30 \leq f(x)$$
$$g_1(y) + 15 \leq g_2(y)$$

Negation of Safety Assertion in Clausal Form:

$$\neg(\forall t \forall u f(t) + 45 \leq h(u) \wedge h(u) < f(t) + 60 \ \rightarrow \ g_2(t)$$
$$\leq h(u) \wedge h(u) \leq g_2(t) + 45)$$

is equivalent to

$$\neg(\forall t \forall u \ \neg(f(t) + 45 \leq h(u) \wedge h(u) < f(t) + 60) \vee (g_2(t)$$
$$\leq h(u) \wedge h(u) \leq g_2(t) + 45))$$

is equivalent to

$$\exists t \exists u \ (f(t) + 45 \leq h(u) \wedge h(u) < f(t) + 60) \wedge ((h(u) < g_2(t) \vee g_2(t) + 45 < h(u))$$

is equivalent to

$$\exists t \exists u \ (f(t) + 45 \leq h(u) \wedge h(u) < f(t) + 60) \wedge ((h(u) + 1$$
$$\leq g_2(t) \vee g_2(t) + 46 \leq h(u)).$$

Rewriting the formula in clausal form yields the following three clauses:

$$f(T) + 45 \leq h(U)$$

$$h(U) - 59 \leq f(T) \text{ (which is equivalent to } h(U) < f(T) + 60)$$

$$h(U) + 1 \leq g_2(T) \quad \vee \quad g_2(T) + 46 \leq h(U)$$

Next we construct the constraint graph corresponding to the formulas in clausal form.

6.4.1   Graph Construction

For each literal $v_1 \pm I \leq v_2$, we construct a node labeled v_1, a node labeled v_2, and an edge $\langle v_1, v_2 \rangle$ with weight $\pm I$ from node v_1 to node v_2. The outline of the algorithm [Jahanian and Mok, 1987] to construct the constraint graph is as follows.

Algorithm Build Graph: Initially, the graph G is empty.
For each clause C_i, for each literal in C_i: $v_1 \pm I \leq v_2$:

1. Find the cluster with the function symbol of term v_1. If not found, create a new cluster.
2. Search the cluster found or created in step 1 for a node labeled v_i. If not found, add the node labeled v_1 to the cluster. (Note that if the cluster has just been created in step 1, the search is not necessary as the cluster is empty.)
3. Repeat steps 1 and 2 for the term v_2.
4. Create a directed edge $\langle v_1, v_2 \rangle$ with weight $\pm I$ from node v_1 to node v_2.

Figure 6.1 shows the construction of the constraint graph corresponding to the above example specification and negation of the safety assertion.

6.5   CHECKING FOR UNSATISFIABILITY

We can use the constructed constraint graph G representing F'' to determine whether F'' is unsatisfiable by identifying cycles with positive weights in G. To do so, we first define unification and then redefine the concepts of a path and a cycle for this type of graph.

Unification: We say there is a unification of v_i and v'_i if a substitution S (which replaces a term by another term) exists such that $v_i S = v'_i S$ where $v_i S$ and $v'_i S$ denote the terms after applying S to v_i and v'_i, respectively.

Chapter 2 contains a discussion of unification as well as related concepts, and provides examples.

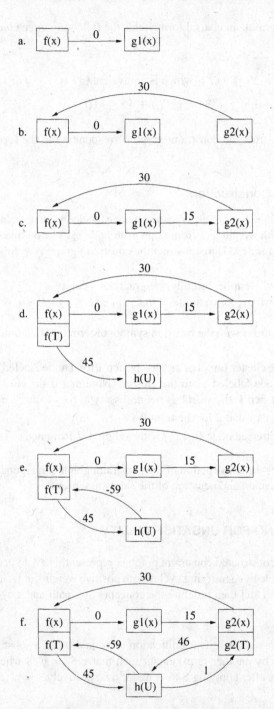

Figure 6.1 Constructing the constraint graph corresponding to example.

Path: We say there is a path from node v_0 to node v_n in a graph G if there is a sequence of edges $\langle v_0, v_1 \rangle$, $\langle v'_1, v_2 \rangle$, $\langle v'_2, v_3 \rangle$, ..., $\langle v'_{n-2}, v_{n-1} \rangle$, $\langle v'_{n-1}, v_n \rangle$ and a substitution S such that there is pairwise unification of v_i and v'_i for all $1 \leq i < n$. Note that each pair of v_i and v'_i, $1 \leq i < n - 1$, must be either the same or in the same cluster.

Cycle: A cycle exists in a graph G if there is a sequence of edges $\langle v_0, v_1 \rangle$, $\langle v'_1, v_2 \rangle$, $\langle v'_2, v_3 \rangle$, ..., $\langle v'_{n-2}, v_{n-1} \rangle$, $\langle v'_{n-1}, v_n \rangle$ and a substitution S such that there is a path from v_0 to v_n, and v_0 and v_n can be unified with the substitution S. Again, note that v_0 and v_n must be either the same or in the same cluster. The weight of a path or cycle is defined as the sum of the weights of the edges in the path or cycle.

Now we are ready to show that if there is a cycle with positive weight in the graph G corresponding to formula F'', then the formula consisting of the conjunction of literals (inequalities) corresponding to the edges in the cycle is unsatisfiable. We apply the substitution S to each inequality L_i in the cycle.

$$v_0 S + I_0 \leq v_1 S \wedge$$
$$v'_1 S + I_1 \leq v_2 S \wedge$$
$$v'_2 S + I_2 \leq v_3 S \wedge$$
$$\vdots$$
$$v'_{n-1} S + I_{n-1} \leq v_n S$$

Then we add these inequalities, yielding

$$I_0 + I_1 + \cdots + I_{n-1} \leq 0,$$

which is clearly unsatisfiable, meaning that the original RTL inequalities corresponding to these edges are unsatisfiable.

6.6 EFFICIENT UNSATISFIABILITY CHECK

We have shown that if every edge in a positive cycle corresponds to a literal that belongs to a unit clause, then the formula F'' must be unsatisfiable, and hence the safety assertion SA is derivable from the specification SP. However, if an edge in the cycle corresponds to a literal that belongs to a non-unit clause, then we have to show that each of the remaining literals in this clause corresponds to an edge in a different positive cycle. The intuitive reason behind this is that the clause is disjunctive. Therefore, to show that the entire clause is unsatisfiable (false), each of its disjuncts must be shown to be unsatisfiable (false). In our example, the negation of the safety assertion contains the clause

$$h(U) + 1 \leq g_2(T) \ \lor \ g_2(T) + 46 \leq h(U).$$

If an edge in a positive cycle that corresponds to $h(U) + 1 \leq g_2(T)$ is identified, then we also have to show that another positive cycle exists with an edge corresponding to the second literal $g_2(T) + 46 \leq h(U)$.

Obviously, as the number of edges in positive cycles that correspond to literals belonging to non-unit clauses increases, the number of different positive cycles that must be identified increases combinatorially. In fact, the problem of determining the unsatisfiability of F'' is NP-complete. Considering the difficulty of the problem, a more efficient, but still exponential-run-time, algorithm is developed in [Jahanian and Mok, 1987] to check for unsatisfiability.

The algorithm makes use of the following observations. Recall that the formula F'' is a conjunction of n clauses

$$C_1 \land C_2 \land \cdots \land C_n,$$

where each C_k is a disjunctive clause

$$L_{k,1} \lor L_{k,2} \lor \cdots \lor L_{k,m_k}.$$

Note that the literals in different clauses need not be distinct. We use the following notations to denote the inequalities corresponding to the edges in the ith positive cycle found:

$$X_{i,1}, X_{i,2}, \ldots, X_{i,n_i},$$

where $X_{i,j}$ is the literal corresponding to the jth edge in the ith positive cycle found, and each $X_{i,j}$ is in at least one of the C_ks. Suppose

$$P_i = X_{i,1} \land X_{i,2} \land \cdots \land X_{i,n_i}.$$

We know from the above discussion that P_i is unsatisfiable. Therefore, F'' is satisfiable iff $F'' \land \neg P_i$ is satisfiable. As a result, the existence of the positive cycle is equivalent to adding the clause

$$\neg P_i = \neg X_{i,1} \lor \neg X_{i,2} \lor \cdots \lor \neg X_{i,n_i}$$

to F'', making it possible to use $\neg P_i$ to show that F'' is unsatisfiable.

Example. We use capital letters to denote the literals in the set S_1 of clauses of F'':

$$A = f(x) \leq g_1(x)$$

$$B = g_2(x) - 30 \leq f(x)$$

$$C = g_1(y) + 15 \leq g_2(y)$$

$$D = f(T) + 45 \leq h(U)$$

$$E = h(U) - 59 \leq f(T)$$

$$F \vee G = h(U) + 1 \leq g_2(T) \vee g_2(T) + 46 \leq h(U).$$

Each clause in the following set S_2 of clauses corresponds to a positive cycle found:

$$\neg F \vee \neg G$$

$$\neg B \vee \neg D \vee \neg F$$

$$\neg A \vee \neg C \vee \neg G \vee \neg E.$$

The unsatisfiability check algorithm builds a search tree using the clauses in set S_2, and while doing so, determines the unsatisfiability of the clauses in sets S_1 and S_2. Each new level in the tree is the result of examining a new clause in S_2 corresponding to a new positive cycle found. Each node in the tree is either one literal in a clause of S_2 or the conjunction of literals in different clauses of S_2. In our example, the nodes in the first level correspond to literals in the first clause of S_2, that

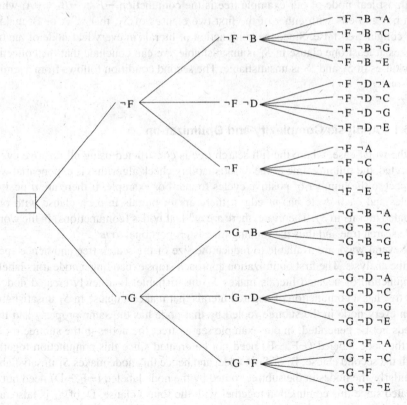

Figure 6.2   Worst-case search tree for example.

is, literals $\neg F$ and $\neg G$. To build the second level, the algorithm adds the literals in the second clause of S_2, that is, literals $\neg B$, $\neg D$, and $\neg F$, to each subtree rooted by literals $\neg F$ and $\neg G$. Similarly, the algorithm constructs the remaining levels in the tree. Figure 6.2 shows the worst-case search tree for the set S_2. A worst-case tree is one in which all conjunctions of literals are explored. However, in practice, a large number of nodes need not be constructed (1) by checking for unsatisfiability as soon as the algorithm creates a new node or (2) by rearranging the order of the clauses in S_2 according to certain heuristics to reduce the size of the tree.

To prove that the conjunction of clauses in S_1 and S_2 is unsatisfiable, we need to show that each leaf node in the tree satisfies one of the following two conditions: (1) the conjunction of literals in the leaf node and at least one clause in S_1 is false, or (2) the conjunction of literals in the leaf node is by itself unsatisfiable.

The first condition follows from basic logic: $C_k \wedge \neg C_k$ where C_k is a clause in set S_1 and $\neg C_k$ is the conjunction of literals in a leaf node; that is,

$$(L_{k,1} \vee L_{k,2} \vee \cdots \vee L_{k,m_k}) \wedge (\neg L_{k,1} \wedge \neg L_{k,2} \wedge \cdots \wedge \neg L_{k,m_k})$$

is always false, making the collection of clauses in S_1 and S_2 unsatisfiable. The leftmost leaf node of our example tree is the conjunction $\neg F \wedge \neg B \wedge \neg A$, which can be "and-ed" with either of the first two clauses of S_1, that is, A or B, making the conjunction false. Since the conjunction of literals in every leaf node of the tree makes at least one clause in S_1 is unsatisfiable, we can conclude that the collection of clauses in S_1 and S_2 is unsatisfiable. The second condition follows from a similar reasoning.

6.6.1 Analysis Complexity and Optimization

In the worst case, where the full search tree is constructed using all positive cycles detected, the running time of the unsatisfiability check algorithm is exponential with respect to the number of positive cycles found. For example, if there are n positive cycles and each cycle has m edges, there are m literals in each clause with only negated literals in S_2. Therefore, there are m^n leaf nodes (conjunctions) in the worst-case search tree and thus the running time is proportional to m^n.

Several ways are available to reduce the size of the search tree and hence speed up the analysis. The first optimization approach stops expanding a node if its labeled conjunction of negated literals makes S_1 unsatisfiable. If a newly created node in the tree has a conjunction of negated literals that makes a clause in S_1 unsatisfiable, then every node in the subtree rooted by that node has the same property and thus needs not be generated. In our example search tree, the nodes in the subtree rooted by the node labeled $(\neg F, \neg B)$ need not be created since this conjunction together with the second clause, B, of S_1 is false, and hence this node makes S_1 unsatisfiable. Similarly, the nodes in the subtree rooted by the node labeled $(\neg F, \neg D)$ need not be created since this conjunction together with the fourth clause, D, of S_1 is false, and hence this node makes S_1 unsatisfiable.

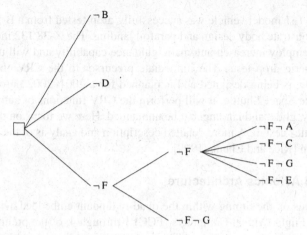

Figure 6.3   Rearranging positive cycles to trim the search tree.

The second optimization approach rearranges the order of the clauses in S_2 (corresponding to the positive cycles found) so that the first approach can be applied as soon as possible, that is, closer to the root of the search tree. This may require backtracking by undoing the generation of a tree node. In our example search tree, the node labeled ($\neg$F, $\neg$B) makes S_1 unsatisfiable because $\neg$B "and-ed" with the second clause, B, is false. Note that the first negated literal $\neg$F does not contribute to the unsatisfiability of S_1. We can reject the first positive cycle by rearranging the first and second clauses, corresponding to the first and second positive cycles found, so that the second clause appears first. This makes it possible to declare unsatisfiability of S_1 for two nodes $\neg$B and $\neg$D at the first level of the tree. This approach may trim the tree under many conditions, as shown in Figure 6.3.

The third optimization approach, which is not pointed out in [Jahanian and Mok, 1987], reuses the unsatisfiability of previously generated nodes to declare that a newly generated node v makes S_1 unsatisfiable if the labels of v have been generated earlier. In our example, note that the labels of the last node ($\neg$F, $\neg$G) are the same as those of a previous leaf node.

6.7   INDUSTRIAL EXAMPLE: NASA X-38 CREW RETURN VEHICLE

Now we use RTL to specify and analyze the timing properties of the avionics of the X-38, a family of vehicles built as incremental development prototypes for the Crew Return Vehicle (CRV) of the International Space Station (ISS). The CRV, planned for a 2003 launch on board the Space Shuttle, will be attached to the ISS and will have the capability to automatically and safely bring to earth a crew of seven passengers in the event of an emergency ISS evacuation. The CRV will be designed to autonomously perform all guidance, navigation, and control functions, the deorbit burn, a parafoil-assisted glide through the atmosphere, and will be designed to land horizontally at one of several predetermined landing sites.

The X-38 131 model vehicle was successfully drop-tested from a B-52 in March 1998 to demonstrate body design and parafoil landing. The X-38 132 model will incrementally employ increased automatic guidance capability and will undergo several atmospheric drop tests. The immediate precursor to the CRV, the X-38 281 model vehicle, is being designed and is planned for a 2001–2002 on-orbit deployment from the Space Shuttle. It will perform the CRV functions of automatic guidance, re-entry, glide, and landing, but be unmanned. Here we focus on the X-38 201 vehicle avionics design. A more detailed description and analysis of the X-38 avionics is found in [Rice and Cheng, 1999].

6.7.1   X-38 Avionics Architecture

Here, we focus on the timing within the quad-redundant embedded avionic control units, called Flight Critical Computers (FCC) 1 through 4, of the preliminary X-38 201 vehicle data system architecture. These units receive all sensor input values, provide all embedded guidance and application processing, and control actuation. Each FCC is a unit comprised of two PowerPC processors, Input/Output cards, and several other devices in a Versa Module Europa (VME) bus chassis. The first processor, called the Flight Critical Processor (FCP), houses all application software, such as guidance, navigation, and control. The second processor, the Instrumentation Control Processor (ICP), is responsible for assembling inputs from all other sensors and sending the data over the VME backplane to the FCP for processing. Both processors run the VxWorks real-time operating system as well as specially developed system services.

6.7.2   Timing Properties

For safety and verifiability reasons, all X-38 avionics design efforts have focused on designing a system that is highly deterministic. The quad-redundant design of the four FCCs relies on Byzantine agreement (a voting and message-passing protocol) to tolerate a single Byzantine fault [Pease, Shostak, and Lamport, 1980; Lamport, Shostak, and Pease, 1982]. Because of this design, tasks are required to run at the same time in all processors, with results of their processing being voted every 20-ms "minor" frame. The ICP and FCP processors are thus synchronized to the same 20-ms processing frame. Another example of similar real-time fault-tolerant avionics is the quad-redundant fly-by-wire flight control of the Lockheed F-117A stealth fighter aircraft. Other examples of fault-tolerant avionics include the Boeing 777 Integrated Airplane Information Management System [Yeh, 1998] and the Airbus 340 Flight Warning System.

We consider a snapshot of the anticipated task timing relationships for the X-38 vehicle. The most critical control loop begins 18 ms into the processing frame where the ICP inputs all 50 Hz (cycles per second) sensor data. These data are passed to the FCP, which reads the sensor data, processes them, and provides output actuator commands back to the ICP. The ICP then reads and issues those commands to affected actuators. To effect safe guidance of the vehicle, this whole processing loop must be completed within 10 ms. To ensure this type of deterministic processing, tasks are generally assigned fixed priorities based upon the Rate-Monotonic Scheduling algorithm presented in chapter 3, and scheduling is partially accomplished with the aid of a cyclic executive.

6.7.3 Timing and Safety Analysis Using RTL

To analyze and verify system timing properties, we use RTL, described in this chapter, to specify the safety-critical aspects of the X-38 system. As we have seen, RTL allows timing and safety analysis which may flexibly be used for what-if scenarios as well as life-cycle system verification, and may be extensible to represent broader aspects of the X-38 avionic system. The two X-38 flight-critical control loops, as well as one non-flight critical control loop and the associated safety assertion, are modeled. After converting the RTL representation into a Presburger arithmetic format and ultimately a constraint graph, cycle analysis verifies safety assertion satisfaction.

6.7.4 RTL Specification

This section presents the RTL specification for a representative set of X-38 tasks. The tasks listed under "workload and event definitions" contain the workloads in milliseconds (ms) for each task modeled. Nomenclature of the task names are that the first three characters define the processor; the next character designates either I(input), P(process), or O(output); the number identifies the speed of the process in Hertz or cycles per second, next is the criticality such as FC(flight-critical) or NFC(non-flight-critical); and last is any other necessary information such as data type. The variable i represents the loop count or iteration number. For example, the set of tasks in the flight critical 50-Hz control loop are the first five listed and are shown below.

> ; $50HzFCworkloads$
>
> $\forall i @(\uparrow ICP\_I50FC\_SENSOR, i) + 2 \geq @(\downarrow ICP\_I50FCSENSOR, i)$
>
> $\forall i @(\uparrow FCP\_I50FC, i) + 1 \geq @(\downarrow FCP\_I50FC, i)$
>
> $\forall i @(\uparrow FCP\_P50FC, i) + 5 \geq @(\downarrow FCP\_P50FC, i)$
>
> $\forall i @(\uparrow FCP\_O50FC, i) + 1 \geq @(\downarrow FCP\_O50FC, i)$
>
> $\forall i @(\uparrow ICP\_I50FC\_CMDS, i) + 1 \geq @(\downarrow ICP\_I50FC\_CMDS, i)$

The workload for the first task, designated "Instrumentation Control Processor (ICP) Input (I) of 50 Hz Flight Critical (FC) Sensor Data," is a maximum of 2 ms. The above group of tasks are representative of the ICP reading all 50-Hz flight-critical sensors, such as flap, rudder positions, and Global Positioning System data; passing that data to the FCP as input; having the guidance application process that data and formulate command output; passing that output to the ICP; and having the ICP actuate the command. This list is the first of two flight-critical timing loops, requiring completion within 10 ms for safe vehicle control. The 10-Hz flight-critical control loop is similar, but a loop completion time of 50 ms, rather than 10 ms, is required. This completion requirement is represented in the safety assertion section. The non-flight-critical tasks only receive sensor input, produce no command output, and are included as a representation of the many non-flight-critical tasks that run in the background but whose execution is not considered safety-critical. The precedence-relations section depicts the order in which the tasks must execute. For example, to properly specify system behavior, it must be stated that the end of any task must not occur before its beginning.

$$\forall i \, @(\uparrow ICP\_I50FC\_SENSOR, i) \leq @(\downarrow ICP\_I50FC\_SENSOR, i)$$

Furthermore, the beginning of the next task to execute must not occur before the end of its predecessor. In this case, the FCP's input of flight critical data must happen after the ICP's 50 Hz sensor scan.

; 50 Hz FC precedence relations

$$\forall i \, @(\downarrow ICP\_I50FC\_SENSOR, i) \leq @(\uparrow FCP\_I50FC, i)$$

A precedence relationship between the end of the successor task and the initiation of the predecessor task must also be represented. In this case, the FCP's input of flight-critical data should happen at or before the completion of the ICP's sensor scan predecessor task workload. In reality, we want the FCP_I50FC task to happen precisely after the completion of the ICP_I50FC_SENSOR task, but this truth is captured by the clauses cited above in addition to the workload definition.

$$\forall i \, @(\uparrow FCP\_I50FC, i) - 2 \leq @(\uparrow ICP\_I50FC\_SENSOR, i)$$

The priority assertions loosely mimic a rate-monotonic scheduling paradigm in which the higher rate tasks have priority over lower rate tasks. For example, the following formula states that the flight-critical 50-Hz task has precedence over the flight-critical 10-Hz task.

$$\forall i \, @(\downarrow FCP\_I50FC, i) \leq @(\uparrow FCP\_I10FC, i)$$

; 50 Hz FC higher priority than 10 Hz FC

$$\forall i \, @(\downarrow FCP\_I50FC, i) \leq @(\uparrow FCP\_I50NFC, i)$$

; 50 Hz FC higher priority than 50 Hz NFC

The periodicity section simply defines the rates at which the tasks execute, in ms, and in this case they are to run precisely every 20 or 100 ms, so they are found in pairs as follows.

$$\forall i \, @(\uparrow ICP\_I50FC\_SENSOR, i) + 20 \leq @(\uparrow ICP\_I50FC\_SENSOR, i + 1)$$

$$\forall i \, @(\uparrow ICP\_I50FC\_SENSOR, i + 1) - 20 \leq @(\uparrow ICP\_I50FC\_SENSOR, i)$$

Finally, the safety assertion, shown below, states that each of the flight-critical control loops, the 50-Hz and the 10-Hz, from initial sensor read through command actuation, must execute within 10 and 50 ms, respectively.

$$\forall i\, @((\downarrow ICP\_I50FC\_CMDS, i) \leq @(\uparrow ICP\_I50FC\_SENSOR, i) + 10 \wedge$$

$$(\downarrow ICP\_I10FC\_CMDS, i) \leq @(\uparrow ICP\_I10FC\_SENSOR, i) + 50)$$

The negation of the safety assertion is ultimately used to verify safety-critical system performance through constraint graph analysis.

RTL System Specification Representation:

Workload and event definitions:
; 50 Hz FC workloads

$$\forall i\, @(\uparrow ICP\_I50FC\_SENSOR, i) + 2 \geq @(\downarrow ICP\_I50FCSENSOR, i)$$

$$\forall i\, @(\uparrow FCP\_I50FC, i) + 1 \geq @(\downarrow FCP\_I50FC, i)$$

$$\forall i\, @(\uparrow FCP\_P50FC, i) + 5 \geq @(\downarrow FCP\_P50FC, i)$$

$$\forall i\, @(\uparrow FCP\_O50FC, i) + 1 \geq @(\downarrow FCP\_O50FC, i)$$

$$\forall i\, @(\uparrow ICP\_I50FC\_CMDS, i) + 1 \geq @(\downarrow ICP\_I50FC\_CMDS, i)$$

; 10 Hz FC workloads

$$\forall i\, @(\uparrow ICP\_I10FC\_SENSOR, i) + 2 \geq @(\downarrow ICP\_I10FCSENSOR, i)$$

$$\forall i\, @(\uparrow FCP\_I10FC, i) + 1 \geq @(\downarrow FCP\_I10FC, i)$$

$$\forall i\, @(\uparrow FCP\_P10FC, i) + 40 \geq @(\downarrow FCP\_P10FC, i)$$

$$\forall i\, @(\uparrow FCP\_O10FC, i) + 1 \geq @(\downarrow FCP\_O10FC, i)$$

$$\forall i\, @(\uparrow ICP\_I10FC\_CMDS, i) + 1 \geq @(\downarrow ICP\_I10FC\_CMDS, i)$$

; 50 Hz NFC workloads

$$\forall i\, @(\uparrow ICP\_I50NFC\_SENSOR, i) + 5 \geq @(\downarrow ICP\_I50NFCSENSOR, i)$$

$$\forall i\, @(\uparrow FCP\_I50NFC, i) + 1 \geq @(\downarrow FCP\_I50NFC, i)$$

Precedence relations:
; precedence between start and stop events

$$\forall i\, @(\uparrow ICP\_I50FC\_SENSOR, i) \leq @(\downarrow CP\_I50FCSENSOR, i)$$

$$\forall i\, @(\uparrow FCP\_I50FC, i) \leq @(\downarrow FCP\_I50FC, i)$$

$$\forall i\, @(\uparrow FCP\_P50FC, i) \leq @(\downarrow FCP\_P50FC, i)$$

$$\forall i\, @(\uparrow FCP\_O50FC, i) \leq @(\downarrow FCP\_O50FC, i)$$

$$\forall i\, @(\uparrow ICP\_I50FC\_CMDS, i) \leq @(\downarrow ICP\_I50FC\_CMDS, i)$$

$$\forall i\, @(\uparrow ICP\_I10FC\_SENSOR, i) \leq @(\downarrow ICP\_I10FCSENSOR, i)$$

$\forall i \, @(\uparrow FCP\_I10FC, i) \leq @(\downarrow FCP\_I10FC, i)$

$\forall i \, @(\uparrow FCP\_P10FC, i) \leq @(\downarrow FCP\_P10FC, i)$

$\forall i \, @(\uparrow FCP\_O10FC, i) \leq @(\downarrow FCP\_O10FC, i)$

$\forall i \, @(\uparrow ICP\_I10FC\_CMDS, i) \leq @(\downarrow ICP\_I10FC\_CMDS, i)$

$\forall i \, @(\uparrow ICP\_I50NFC\_SENSOR, i) \leq @(ICP\_I50NFCSENSOR, i)$

$\forall i \, @(\uparrow FCP\_I50NFC, i) \leq @(FCP\_I50NFC, i)$

$\forall i \, @(\uparrow FCP\_P50NFC, i) \leq @(FCP\_P50NFC, i)$

; precedence between end of first task and beginning of next
; 50 Hz FC precedence relations

$\forall i \, @(ICP\_I50FC\_SENSOR, i) \leq @(\uparrow FCP\_I50FC, i)$

$foralli \, @(FCP\_I50FC, i) \leq @(\uparrow FCP\_P50FC, i)$

$\forall i \, @(FCP\_P50FC, i) \leq @(\uparrow FCP\_O50FC, i)$

$\forall i \, @(FCP\_O50FC, i) \leq @(\uparrow ICP\_I50FC\_CMDS, i)$

; 10 Hz FC precedence relations

$\forall i \, @(\downarrow ICP\_I10FC\_SENSOR, i) \leq @(\uparrow FCP\_I10FC, i)$

$\forall i \, @(\downarrow FCP\_I10FC, i) \leq @(\uparrow FCP\_P10FC, i)$

$\forall i \, @(\downarrow FCP\_P10FC, i) \leq @(\uparrow FCP\_O10FC, i)$

$\forall i \, @(\downarrow FCP\_O10FC, i) \leq @(\uparrow ICP\_I10FC\_CMDS, i)$

; 50 Hz NFC precedence relations

$\forall i \, @(\downarrow ICP\_I50NFC\_SENSOR, i) \leq @(\uparrow FCP\_I50NFC, i)$

$\forall i \, @(\downarrow FCP\_I50NFC, i) \leq @(\uparrow FCP\_P50NFC, i)$

; precedence between beginning of prior task and beginning of next

$\forall i \, @(\uparrow FCP\_I50FC, i) - 2 \leq @(\uparrow ICP\_I50FC\_SENSOR, i)$

$\forall i \, @(\uparrow FCP\_P50FC, i) - 1 \leq @(\uparrow FCP\_I50FC, i)$

$\forall i \, @(\uparrow FCP\_O50FC, i) - 5 \leq @(\uparrow FCP\_P50FC, i)$

$\forall i \, @(\uparrow ICP\_I50FC\_CMDS, i) - 1 \leq @(\uparrow FCP\_O50FC, i)$

$\forall i \, @(\uparrow FCP\_I10FC, i) - 2 \leq @(\uparrow ICP\_I10FC\_SENSOR, i)$

$\forall i \, @(\uparrow FCP\_P10FC, i) - 1 \leq @(\uparrow FCP\_I10FC, i)$

$\forall i \, @(\uparrow FCP\_O10FC, i) - 40 \leq @(\uparrow FCP\_P10FC, i)$

$\forall i \, @(\uparrow ICP\_I10FC\_CMDS, i) - 1 \leq @(\uparrow FCP\_O10FC, i)$

$\forall i \, @(\uparrow FCP\_I50NFC, i) - 5 \leq @(\uparrow ICP\_I50NFC\_SENSOR, i)$

$\forall i \, @(\uparrow FCP\_P50NFC, i) - 1 \leq @(\uparrow FCP\_I50NFC, i)$

Priority assertions:

; 50 Hz FC higher priority than 10 Hz FC

$\forall i \, @(FCP\_I50FC, i) \leq @(\uparrow FCP\_I10FC, i)$

; 50 Hz FC higher priority than 50 Hz NFC

$\forall i \, @(FCP\_I50FC, i) \leq @(\uparrow FCP\_I50NFC, i)$

Periodicity:

; 50 Hz FC tasks, p = 20

$\forall i \, @(\uparrow ICP\_I50FC\_SENSOR, i) + 20 \leq @(\uparrow ICP\_I50FC\_SENSOR, i + 1)$

$\forall i \, @(\uparrow FCP\_I50FC, i) + 20 \leq @(\uparrow FCP\_I50FC, i + 1)$

$\forall i \, @(\uparrow FCP\_P50FC, i) + 20 \leq @(\uparrow FCP\_P50FC, i + 1)$

$\forall i \, @(\uparrow FCP\_O50FC, i) + 20 \leq @(\uparrow FCP\_O50FC, i + 1)$

$\forall i \, @(\uparrow ICP\_I50FC\_CMDS, i) + 20 \leq @(\uparrow ICP\_I50FC\_CMDS, i + 1)$

$\forall i \, @(\uparrow ICP\_I50FC\_SENSOR, i + 1) - 20 \leq @(\uparrow ICP\_I50FC\_SENSOR, i)$

$\forall i \, @(\uparrow FCP\_I50FC, i + 1) - 20 \leq @(\uparrow FCP\_I50FC, i)$

$\forall i \, @(\uparrow FCP\_P50FC, i + 1) - 20 \leq @(\uparrow FCP\_P50FC, i)$

$\forall i \, @(\uparrow FCP\_O50FC, i + 1) - 20 \leq @(\uparrow FCP\_O50FC, i)$

$\forall i \, @(\uparrow ICP\_I50FC\_CMDS, i + 1) - 20 \leq @(\uparrow ICP\_I50FC\_CMDS, i)$

; 10 Hz FC tasks, p = 100

$\forall i \, @(\uparrow ICP\_I10FC\_SENSOR, i) + 100 \leq @(\uparrow ICP\_I10FC\_SENSOR, i + 1)$

$\forall i \, @(\uparrow FCP\_I10FC, i) + 100 \leq @(\uparrow FCP\_I10FC, i + 1)$

$\forall i \, @(\uparrow FCP\_P10FC, i) + 100 \leq @(\uparrow FCP\_P10FC, i + 1)$

$\forall i \, @(\uparrow FCP\_O10FC, i) + 100 \leq @(\uparrow FCP\_O10FC, i + 1)$

$\forall i \, @(\uparrow ICP\_I10FC\_CMDS, i) + 100 \leq @(\uparrow ICP\_I10FC\_CMDS, i + 1)$

$\forall i \, @(\uparrow ICP\_I10FC\_SENSOR, i + 1) - 100 \leq @(\uparrow ICP\_I10FC\_SENSOR, i)$

$\forall i \, @(\uparrow FCP\_I10FC, i + 1) - 100 \leq @(\uparrow FCP\_I10FC, i)$

$\forall i \, @(\uparrow FCP\_P10FC, i + 1) - 100 \leq @(\uparrow FCP\_P10FC, i)$

$\forall i \, @(\uparrow FCP\_O10FC, i + 1) - 100 \leq @(\uparrow FCP\_O10FC, i)$

$\forall i \, @(\uparrow ICP\_I10FC\_CMDS, i + 1) - 100 \leq @(\uparrow ICP\_I10FC\_CMDS, i)$

; 50 Hz NFC tasks

$\forall i \, @(\uparrow ICP\_I50NFC\_SENSOR, i) + 20 \leq @(\uparrow ICP\_I50NFC\_SENSOR, i + 1)$

$\forall i \, @(\uparrow FCP\_I50NFC, i) + 20 \leq @(\uparrow FCP\_I50NFC, i + 1)$

$\forall i \, @(\uparrow FCP\_P50NFC, i) + 20 \leq @(\uparrow FCP\_P50NFC, i + 1)$

$$\forall i @ (\uparrow ICP\_I50NFC\_SENSOR, i + 1) - 20 \leq @ (\uparrow ICP\_I50NFC\_SENSOR, i)$$

$$\forall i @ (\uparrow FCP\_I50NFC, i + 1) - 20 \leq @ (\uparrow FCP\_I50NFC, i)$$

$$\forall i @ (\uparrow FCP\_P50NFC, i + 1) - 20 \leq @ (\uparrow FCP\_P50NFC, i)$$

Safety assertion:

$$\forall i @ ((\downarrow ICP\_I50FC\_CMDS, i) \leq @ (\uparrow ICP\_I50FC\_SENSOR, i) + 10 \wedge$$

$$(\downarrow ICP\_I10FC\_CMDS, i) \leq @ (\uparrow ICP\_I10FC\_SENSOR, i) + 50)$$

; 50 Hz and 10 Hz loops must maintain a maximum 10 ms and 50 ms
; "transport lag," respectively, between sensor input and
; effector output
Negation of safety assertion in RTL:

$$\exists i @ ((\uparrow ICP\_I50FC\_SENSOR, i) + 10 < @ (\downarrow ICP\_I50FC\_CMDS, i) \vee$$

$$(\uparrow ICP\_I10FC\_SENSOR, i) + 50 < @ (\downarrow ICP\_I10FC\_CMDS, i))$$

6.7.5 RTL Representation Converted to Presburger Arithmetic

We now convert the RTL formulas into the Presburger arithmetic format to aid in subsequent graphing. The notation convention is to use an "S_" or an "E_" to represent the start or end task events, respectively.

Presburger Arithmetic Representation:

Workloads:
; 50 Hz FC workloads

$$E\_ICP\_I50FC\_SENSOR(i) - 2 \leq S\_ICP\_I50FC\_SENSOR(i)$$

$$E\_FCP\_I50FC(i) - 1 \leq S\_FCP\_I50FC(i)$$

$$E\_FCP\_P50FC(i) - 5 \leq S\_FCP\_P50FC(i)$$

$$E\_FCP\_O50FC(i) - 1 \leq S\_FCP\_O50FC(i)$$

$$E\_ICP\_I50FC\_CMDS(i) - 1 \leq S\_ICP\_I50FC\_CMDS(i)$$

; 10 Hz FC workloads

$$E\_ICP\_I10FC\_SENSOR(i) - 2 \leq S\_ICP\_I10FC\_SENSOR(i)$$

$$E\_FCP\_I10FC(i) - 1 \leq S\_FCP\_I10FC(i)$$

$$E\_FCP\_P10FC(i) - 40 \leq S\_FCP\_P10FC(i)$$

$$E\_FCP\_O10FC(i) - 1 \leq S\_FCP\_O10FC(i)$$

$$E\_ICP\_I10FC\_CMDS(i) - 1 \leq S\_ICP\_I10FC\_CMDS(i)$$

; 50 Hz NFC workloads

$$E\_ICP\_I50NFC\_SENSOR(i) - 5 \leq S\_ICP\_I50NFC\_SENSOR(i)$$

$$E\_FCP\_I50NFC(i) - 1 \leq S\_FCP\_I50NFC(i)$$

$$E\_FCP\_P50NFC(i) - 2 \leq S\_FCP\_P50NFC(i)$$

precedence:
; precedence between start and stop events
; 50 Hz FC workloads

$$S\_ICP\_I50FC\_SENSOR(i) \leq E\_ICP\_I50FC\_SENSOR(i)$$

$$S\_FCP\_I50FC(i) \leq E\_FCP\_I50FC(i)$$

$$S\_FCP\_P50FC(i) \leq E\_FCP\_P50FC(i)$$

$$S\_FCP\_O50FC(i) \leq E\_FCP\_O50FC(i)$$

$$S\_ICP\_I50FC\_CMDS(i) \leq E\_ICP\_I50FC\_CMDS(i)$$

; 10 Hz FC workloads

$$S\_ICP\_I10FC\_SENSOR(i) \leq E\_ICP\_I10FC\_SENSOR(i)$$

$$S\_FCP\_I10FC(i) \leq E\_FCP\_I10FC(i)$$

$$S\_FCP\_P10FC(i) \leq E\_FCP\_P10FC(i)$$

$$S\_FCP\_O10FC(i) \leq E\_FCP\_O10FC(i)$$

$$S\_ICP\_I10FC\_CMDS(i) \leq E\_ICP\_I10FC\_CMDS(i)$$

; 50 Hz NFC workloads

$$S\_ICP\_I50NFC\_SENSOR(i) \leq E\_ICP\_I50NFC\_SENSOR(i)$$

$$S\_FCP\_I50NFC(i) \leq E\_FCP\_I50NFC(i)$$

$$S\_FCP\_P50NFC(i) \leq E\_FCP\_P50NFC(i)$$

; precedence between end of first task and beginning of next task
; 50 Hz FC precedence relations

$$E\_ICP\_I50FC\_SENSOR(i) \leq S\_FCP\_I50FC(i)$$

$$E\_FCP\_I50FC(i) \leq S\_FCP\_P50FC(i)$$

$$E\_FCP\_P50FC(i) \leq S\_FCP\_O50FC(i)$$

$$E\_FCP\_O50FC(i) \leq S\_ICP\_I50FC\_CMDS(i)$$

; 10 Hz FC precedence relations

$$E\_ICP\_I10FC\_SENSOR(i) \leq S\_FCP\_I10FC(i)$$

$$E\_FCP\_I10FC(i) \leq S\_FCP\_P10FC(i)$$

$$E\_FCP\_P10FC(i) \leq S\_FCP\_O10FC(i)$$

$$E\_FCP\_O10FC(i) \leq S\_ICP\_I10FC\_CMDS(i)$$

; 50 Hz NFC precedence relations

$$E\_ICP\_I50NFC\_SENSOR(i) \leq S\_FCP\_I50NFC(i)$$

$$E\_FCP\_I50NFC(i) \leq S\_FCP\_P50NFC(i)$$

; precedence between beginning of prior task and beginning of next task

$$S\_FCP\_I50FC(i) - 2 \leq S\_ICP\_I50FC\_SENSOR(i)$$

$$S\_FCP\_P50FC(i) - 1 \leq S\_FCP\_I50FC(i)$$

$$S\_FCP\_O50FC(i) - 5 \leq S\_FCP\_P50FC(i)$$

$$S\_ICP\_I50FC\_CMDS(i) - 1 \leq S\_FCP\_O50FC(i)$$

$$S\_FCP\_I10FC(i) - 2 \leq S\_ICP\_I10FC\_SENSOR(i)$$

$$S\_FCP\_P10FC(i) - 1 \leq S\_FCP\_I10FC(i)$$

$$S\_FCP\_O10FC(i) - 40 \leq S\_FCP\_P10FC(i)$$

$$S\_ICP\_I10FC\_CMDS(i) - 1 \leq S\_FCP\_O10FC(i)$$

$$S\_FCP\_I50NFC(i) - 5 \leq S\_ICP\_I50NFC\_SENSOR(i)$$

$$S\_FCP\_P50NFC(i) - 1 \leq S\_FCP\_I50NFC(i)$$

periodicity:
; 50 Hz FC tasks, p = 20

$$S\_ICP\_I50FC\_SENSOR(i) + 20 \leq S\_ICP\_I50FC\_SENSOR(i + 1)$$

$$S\_FCP\_I50FC(i) + 20 \leq S\_FCP\_I50FC(i + 1)$$

$$S\_FCP\_P50FC(i) + 20 \leq S\_FCP\_P50FC(i + 1)$$

$$S\_FCP\_O50FC(i) + 20 \leq S\_FCP\_O50FC(i + 1)$$

$$S\_ICP\_I50FC\_CMDS(i) + 20 \leq S\_ICP\_I50FC\_CMDS(i + 1)$$

$$S\_ICP\_I50FC\_SENSOR(i + 1) - 20 \leq S\_ICP\_I50FC\_SENSOR(i)$$

$$S\_FCP\_I50FC(i + 1) - 20 \leq S\_FCP\_I50FC(i)$$

$$S\_FCP\_P50FC(i + 1) - 20 \leq S\_FCP\_P50FC(i)$$

$$S\_FCP\_O50FC(i + 1) - 20 \leq S\_FCP\_O50FC(i)$$

$$S\_ICP\_I50FC\_CMDS(i + 1) - 20 \leq S\_ICP\_I50FC\_CMDS(i)$$

; 10 Hz FC tasks, p = 100

$$S\_ICP\_I10FC\_SENSOR(i) + 100 \leq S\_ICP\_I10FC\_SENSOR(i + 1)$$

$$S\_FCP\_I10FC(i) + 100 \leq S\_FCP\_I10FC(i + 1)$$

$$S\_FCP\_P10FC(i) + 100 \leq S\_FCP\_P10FC(i + 1)$$

$$S\_FCP\_O10FC(i) + 100 \leq S\_FCP\_O10FC(i + 1)$$

$$S\_ICP\_I10FC\_CMDS(i) + 100 \leq S\_ICP\_I10FC\_CMDS(i + 1)$$

$$S\_ICP\_I10FC\_SENSOR(i + 1) - 100 \leq S\_ICP\_I10FC\_SENSOR(i)$$

$$S\_FCP\_I10FC(i + 1) - 100 \leq S\_FCP\_I10FC(i)$$

$$S\_FCP\_P10FC(i + 1) - 100 \leq S\_FCP\_P10FC(i)$$

$$S\_FCP\_O10FC(i + 1) - 100 \leq S\_FCP\_O10FC(i)$$

$$S\_ICP\_I10FC\_CMDS(i + 1) - 100 \leq S\_ICP\_I10FC\_CMDS(i)$$

; 50 Hz NFC tasks

$$S\_ICP\_I50NFC\_SENSOR(i) + 20 \leq S\_ICP\_I50NFC\_SENSOR(i + 1)$$

$$S\_FCP\_I50NFC(i) + 20 \leq S\_FCP\_I50NFC(i + 1)$$

$$S\_FCP\_P50NFC(i) + 20 \leq S\_FCP\_P50NFC(i + 1)$$

$$S\_ICP\_I50NFC\_SENSOR(i + 1) - 20 \leq S\_ICP\_I50NFC\_SENSOR(i)$$

$$S\_FCP\_I50NFC(i + 1) - 20 \leq S\_FCP\_I50NFC(i)$$

$$S\_FCP\_P50NFC(i + 1) - 20 \leq S\_FCP\_P50NFC(i)$$

Priority assertions:

$$E\_FCP\_I50FC(i) \leq S\_FCP\_I10FC(i)$$

; 50 Hz FC higher priority than 10 Hz FC

$$E\_FCP\_I50FC(i) \leq S\_FCP\_I50NFC(i)$$

; 50 Hz FC higher priority than 50 Hz NFC
Negation of safety assertion:

$$S\_ICP\_I50FC\_SENSOR(I) + 11 \leq E\_ICP\_I50FC\_CMDS(I) \vee$$

$$S\_ICP\_I10FC\_SENSOR(I) + 51 \leq E\_ICP\_I10FC\_CMDS(I)$$

6.7.6 Constraint Graph Analysis

To verify the satisfaction of the safety assertion, the Presburger formulas are represented in a constraint graph shown in [Rice and Cheng, 1999]. The system specification alone produces a graph with no positive cycles. Negation of the safety assertion, however, yields edges that produce positive cycles between clusters, thus it verifies critical system performance. For example, a positive cycle with vertices *S_ICP_I50FC_SENSOR*, *E_ICP_I50FC_CMDS*, *S_ICP_I50FC_CMDS*, *S_FCP_O50FC*, *S_FCP_P50FC*, *S_FCP_I50FC*, and back to *S_ICP_I50FC_SENSOR*, yields a cycle with weight 1.

6.8 MODECHART SPECIFICATION LANGUAGE

Although the RTL language is very capable specifying timing properties of real-time systems, using it to specify practical systems can be tedious and error-prone due to its textual nature. To remedy this problem, a hierarchical graphical specification language called Modechart is introduced, in [Jahanian and Mok, 1994]. The semantics of Modechart are given in terms of RTL, allowing a translation of a Modechart specification into corresponding RTL formulas. Since Modechart is hierarchical, the resulting RTL formulas after the translation are also hierarchically organized.

A Modechart specification represents a real-time system as a collection of *modes* (drawn as boxes) and transitions (drawn as edges between modes). The collection of modes represents the (control) state of the specified system and transitions represent the control flow of the specified system [Stuart et al., 2001]. A Modechart specification is also called a *modechart*. Earlier definitions of Modechart [Jahanian and Stuart, 1988] treat modes as control information imposing structure to the operations of the specified system.

The model of computation used by Modechart considers a computation as a sequence (partial ordering) of sets of time-stamped event occurrences. All event occurrences in the same set happen simultaneously. Earlier definitions of Modechart [Jahanian and Stuart, 1988] emphasize that in this model of computation, no notion of a state exists despite the graph-orientation of the language, and hence no concept exists of an invariant satisfying a set of states. Two modecharts are shown in Figures 6.4 and 6.5.

6.8.1 Modes

A mode is drawn as a box and is considered *active* from the time it is entered to the time just before it is exited. Also, a mode is both active and inactive at the time

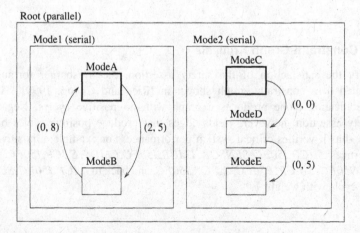

Figure 6.4 Modechart 1.

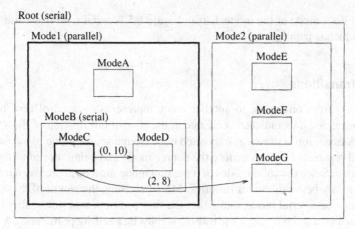

Figure 6.5 Modechart 2.

instant when the mode is exited or entered. There are three types of modes: atomic, serial, and parallel.

An *atomic* mode has no internal structure and represents a primitive control state of the system. Atomic modes are basic building blocks of a Modechart specification. In Figure 6.4, the atomic modes are ModeA, ModeB, ModeC, ModeD, and ModeE. In Figure 6.5, the atomic modes are ModeA, ModeC, ModeD, ModeE, ModeF, and ModeG.

A *serial* mode contains one or more child modes connected sequentially by transitions, and these child modes are said to be in series. Therefore, a serial mode is a sequential composition of its child modes. In Figure 6.4, the serial modes are Mode1 and Mode2. In Figure 6.5, the serial modes are Root and ModeB. One of the child modes in a serial mode must be active at any time when the serial mode is active. One of these child modes is labeled as the initial mode, and this is the mode that is entered when the serial mode itself is entered. The initial mode is represented by a box with bold lines. In Figure 6.4, the initial mode of Mode1 is ModeA. In Figure 6.5, the initial mode of Mode2 is ModeC. However, if the transition leading to this serial mode points to another child mode M that is different from the initial mode, then mode M is entered instead when the serial mode itself is entered.

A *parallel* mode contains zero or more unconnected child modes, and these child modes are said to be in parallel. Therefore, a parallel mode is a parallel composition of its child modes. In Figure 6.4, the parallel mode is Root. In Figure 6.5, the parallel modes are Mode1 and Mode2. All of the child modes in a parallel mode must be active at any time when the parallel mode is active. A parallel mode with no child modes is equivalent to an atomic mode.

In a Modechart specification, the *root* mode is the outermost mode with no parent. A computation begins by entering the root mode at time 0. Note that a root mode can be one of the following: atomic, serial, or parallel. The Root mode of the modechart in Figure 6.4 is parallel with two child modes, each of which is serial. On the other hand, the Root mode of the modechart in Figure 6.5 is serial with two child modes, each of which is parallel.

6.8.2 Transitions

A transition from one mode to another mode represents the control flow between these modes, and thus indicates a change in the control information of the specified system. A transition is drawn as a directed edge from a source mode to a destination mode and represents control exiting the source mode and being moved to the destination mode. Since the child modes of a parallel mode must be all active, a transition can occur only between modes in series. More precisely, the parent of these pair of modes must be a serial mode, and either the first common ancestor of these pair of modes must be a serial mode or the transition must be a self-loop. In Figure 6.4, there are transitions from ModeA to ModeB, from ModeC to ModeD, and from ModeD to ModeE. In Figure 6.5, there are transitions from ModeC to ModeD and from ModeC to ModeG.

A mode transition is an event that happens instantaneously (takes zero time units), just like an RTL transition event, and is denoted $M_s \rightarrow M_d$, where M_s is the source mode and M_d is the destination mode. An earlier notation [Jahanian and Mok, 1994] for a transition event is $M_s - M_d$. The event of entering a mode M is denoted $\rightarrow M$, and the event of exiting a mode M is denoted $M \rightarrow$, both of which happen instantaneously. Note that "a mode is active" is not an event since by definition an event occurs at an instant of time taking zero time units.

Since the model of computation used by Modechart considers a computation as a sequence of sets of event occurrences, every computation is a sequence of sets of mode entry events, mode exit events, and/or transition events. Each transition is labeled with a condition, and when this condition is satisfied, this transition occurs. A condition is expressed in disjunctive normal form $c_1 \vee \cdots \vee c_k$ and each disjunct c_i is either a *triggering condition* or a *timing condition*.

A triggering condition is expressed in conjunctive normal form $e_1 \wedge \cdots \wedge e_n$ and each conjunct is either an *event* or a *predicate*. For a triggering condition to be satisfied, all events in it must occur and all predicates in it must hold at the same time. More precisely, each conjunct is chosen from one of the following:

1. Event $\rightarrow M$ is satisfied when mode M is entered.
2. Event $M \rightarrow$ is satisfied when mode M is exited.
3. Event $M1 \rightarrow M2$ is satisfied when the transition $M1 \rightarrow M2$ occurs.
4. Predicate $M == true$ is satisfied if mode M is active.
5. Predicate $M == false$ is satisfied if mode M is not active.
6. Mode list predicate $\{(M1, \ldots, MN)\}$ is satisfied if any of the list's modes are active.
7. Before list predicate $\{(< M1, \ldots, MN)\}$ is satisfied if any of the list's modes are active and have been active for at least one time unit.

A timing condition is a delay and deadline pair of the form (r, d), where $r \leq d$ and both values are non-negative integers. This timing condition is also known as a lower/upper bound condition. The notation *(delay r)* means (r, ∞). *(deadline d)* means $(0, d)$. *(alarm r)* means (r, r). In Figure 6.4, the transition with triggering condition (a timing condition) (2,5) from ModeA to ModeB indicates that this transition can occur 2 times units after ModeA is entered and within 5 time units after this mode is entered. In Figure 6.5, the transition with triggering condition (0,10) from ModeC to ModeD indicates that this transition can occur immediately after ModeC is entered and within 10 time units after this mode is entered. The transition with triggering condition (2,8) from ModeC to ModeG indicates that this transition can occur 2 time units after ModeC is entered and within 8 time units after this mode is entered.

6.9 VERIFYING TIMING PROPERTIES OF MODECHART SPECIFICATIONS

To verify timing properties in a Modechart specification, we first generate a *computation graph* [Jahanian and Stuart, 1988] from the specification. This computation graph represents all behaviors allowed by the Modechart specification. Then we apply specialized decision procedures [Jahanian and Stuart, 1988] or more general model-checking algorithms [Clarke, Emerson, and Sistla, 1986] to the computation graph to determine if a given timing property is satisfiable. To apply either of these approaches, the computation is viewed as the model of the specified system and the timing property to be checked is given as an RTL formula. Then the decision procedure or model checker decides whether the computation graph satisfies this property.

We first describe the computations of a specified system and how these are represented by an infinite computation tree. Then we show how this computation tree can be converted into a finite computation graph for analysis and verification.

6.9.1 System Computations

Given a Modechart specification, we can generate a *computation tree* showing all possible behaviors of the system, that is, all possible sequences of sets of event occurrences. The computation tree is a rooted directed tree, possibly of infinite size, with nodes labeled with events and with edges indicating causality. This is similar to the computation tree corresponding to a state transition graph representing a specified system for model checking in chapter 4. However, a node in the computation tree here is a *point* in time when events occur, and it does not assign values to variables in a predicate.

Therefore, here we refer to a node in the computation tree as a point, and a point P pointed to by an edge represents the event occurrence caused by the events along the path from the root to P. A point may be labeled with more than one event if the events occur at the same time. Since there are timing constraints on transitions between modes in the Modechart specification, the corresponding computation tree is augmented with lower/upper bound requirements on time separation (distance) between two points along a path starting from the root.

A computation of a system is an assignment of time values, consistent with the lower/upper bound requirements, to the events along a path starting from the root of the tree. Given a pair of points P_a and P_b, with $a < b$, along a path (so P_a appears earlier than P_b on the path), we represent the lower bound separation requirement as $P_a + I \leq P_b$ and the upper bound separation requirement as $P_b \leq P_a + I$, where I is a non-negative integer.

We can use a weighted directed graph, called a *separation graph*, to represent the set of time bound separations on a path in a computation tree. In this graph, the nodes are the points in the corresponding path, and the weights associated with the edges indicate the time separation between the nodes.

6.9.2 Computation Graph

Since the above computation tree augmented with lower/upper bound requirements is usually infinite, a need exists to generate a finite *computation graph* that represents the computations of the system [Jahanian and Stuart, 1988] so that model checking or similar verification techniques can be applied to it. To derive a finite computation graph from an infinite computation tree, we use a point P_a that is already generated instead of generating a new one P_b (as in the case of the computation tree) if P_a is equivalent to P_b except for their time stamps. In other words, an infinite number of equivalent points are grouped together into an equivalence class. Since a finite number of equivalence classes exist in the point space of a Modechart specification, we can obtain a finite computation graph by generating at most one point from each equivalence class.

The computation graph construction algorithm starts by generating the root point of the computation graph. Then it checks every transition from the active modes in the root point to if see it can be taken. As discussed before, a transition can occur if it satisfies its associated triggering or timing condition. If a transition can be taken, the algorithm generates a new point (successor to the root point) if it is not in the same equivalence class as the root point, and this transition and this new point are added to the computation graph. The above steps are repeated in a breadth-first exploration for every new point until no new points can be included in the computation graph. Note the similarity of this construction and the generation of a finite-state graph to a program described in chapter 4.

6.9.3 Timing Properties

We now describe two practical classes of timing properties expressed in RTL for which simple verification procedures are available to check their satisfiability in a computation graph [Jahanian and Stuart, 1988]. The following definitions are needed to specify these properties.

Endpoint: Given an event E, an integer variable i, and a non-negative integer constant k, an *endpoint* is an application of an occurrence function of the form $@(E, i \pm k)$.

Note that in this form, the expression $i \pm k$ is the occurrence index of this occurrence function application.

Related Endpoints: If the integer variables appearing in the occurrence indices of a pair of endpoints' occurrence function applications are the same, then these two endpoints are *related*.

For example, $@(E_1, x)$ and $@(E_2, x + 8)$ are related endpoints.

Interval: Given two events E_1 and E_2, two non-negative integer constants k_1 and k_2, and an integer variable i, an *interval* is a pair of related endpoints of the form $@(E_1, i \pm k_1)$ and $@(E_2, i \pm k_2)$.

Recall that a computation graph uses one point to represent an equivalence class of an infinite number of points, and the events happening in these points are usually different instances of the same event. Therefore, if a cycle exists whose points are labeled with the same number of events E_1 and E_2 in the computation graph, then by marking an E_1-labeled point as its ith occurrence, we can traverse this cycle forward or backward a constant number of times to locate the point representing the ith occurrence of event E_2, depending on whether this occurrence of E_2 follows or precedes, respectively, the ith occurrence of event E_1.

Preservation of Related Endpoints: Given a computation graph G and a pair of related endpoints with events E_1 and E_2, a cycle *preserves* this pair of endpoints if in this cycle the number of E_1-labeled points is equal to the number of E_2-labeled points.

Preservation of an RTL Formula: If every cycle in a computation graph preserves every pair of related endpoints in an RTL formula, then this graph *preserves* this formula.

We can check in polynomial time whether two endpoints are preserved by a computation graph, but the following cases can be checked by inspection. A computation preserves a pair of endpoints containing events E_1 and E_2 if one of the following cases is true:

1. $E_1 = E_2$, that is, they are the same event.
2. $E_1 = \rightarrow M$ and $E_2 = M \rightarrow$, that is, these events are the entry and exit events of the same mode.
3. $E_1 = (S := true)$ and $E_2 = (S := false)$, that is, these events are transition events of the same state variable.

4. $E_1 = \uparrow A$ and $E_2 = \downarrow A$, that is, these events are the start and stop events of the same action.

Next we describe two classes of RTL formulas that are preserved by a computation graph. Simple procedures are available for determining whether a computation graph satisfies a property in one of these classes.

6.9.4   Minimum and Maximum Distance Between Endpoints

This class of timing properties specifies the relative and absolute ordering as well as the time distance between related endpoints. Given two related endpoints e_1 and e_2 and a non-negative integer time distance k, the RTL formulas expressing these timing properties are of the form $\exists x F$ or $\forall x F$, where F is a quantifier-free formula with each inequality of the form

$$e_1 \pm k \leq e_2.$$

Each inequality can be rewritten as one of the following to specify:

1. The minimum time distance k between two endpoints: $k \leq e_2 - e_1$.
2. The maximum time distance k between two endpoints: $e_1 - e_2 \leq k$.

We now present the minimum and maximum distance algorithms for two related endpoints. Their functions and operations are similar to the minimum and maximum delay algorithms [Campos et al., 1994] presented in chapter 4, but *cycle unrolling* is required here since a point may correspond to an equivalence class of points representing different time-stamped occurrences of the same event.

Let G be the computation graph and F be the RTL formula specifying minimum distances between endpoints. The following algorithm (Figure 6.6) determines if every computation in G satisfies the minimum-distance timing property specified in F.

The following algorithm (Figure 6.7) determines if every computation in G satisfies the maximum-distance timing property specified in F.

If the formula F is universally quantified, then we run the appropriate algorithm above for every E_j-labeled point in the graph G, and each run must return *true* for G to satisfy F. Otherwise, if the formula F is existentially quantified, then at least one

---

procedure *check_min_distance*(e_1, e_2, k, G, F)
find a point P labeled with E_j, where $1 \leq j \leq n$;
find all corresponding endpoints in F by unrolling each cycle a constant
    number of times;
$d :=$ shortest distance between e_1 and e_2 in unrolled G;
if $k \leq d$ then return *true* else return *false*;

Figure 6.6   Algorithm for checking minimum distance.

procedure *check_max_distance*(e_1, e_2, k, G, F)
find a point P labeled with E_j, where $1 \leq j \leq n$;
find all corresponding endpoints in F by unrolling each cycle a constant
    number of times;
$d :=$ longest distance between e_1 and e_2 in unrolled G;
if $d \leq k$ then return *true* else return *false*;

Figure 6.7   Algorithm for checking maximum distance.

run of the appropriate algorithm above for an E_j-labeled point in the graph G must return *true* for G to satisfy F.

6.9.5   Exclusion and Inclusion of Endpoint and Interval

This class of timing properties specifies the exclusion or inclusion of an endpoint or an interval within another interval. Here we add an integer offset to an endpoint: $@(E, i \pm k) \pm c$.

Given an interval I_1 with endpoints e_1 and e_2 and an interval I_2 with endpoints e_3 and e_4, the RTL formulas expressing the timing properties in this class are in one of the two forms.

Let Q_a and Q_b be quantifiers on the interval occurrence index variables. The first form describes that an interval includes another:

$$Q_a Q_b e_1 \leq e_3 \wedge e_4 \leq e_2.$$

For example, this RTL formula states that while mode *PASSED* is active, an execution of the action *Upgate* begins after entering this mode 10 s or later:

$$\forall x \exists y @(\rightarrow PASSED, x) + 10 \leq @(\uparrow Upgate, y) \wedge @(\downarrow Upgate, y)$$

$$\leq @(M \rightarrow, x).$$

The second form describes that an interval excludes another:

$$Q_a Q_b e_4 \leq e_1 \vee e_2 \leq e_3.$$

For example, this RTL formula states that actions *Upgate* and *Downgate* are mutually exclusive:

$$\forall x \forall y @(\downarrow Downgate, y) \leq @(\uparrow Upgate, x) \vee @(\downarrow Upgate, x)$$

$$\leq @(\uparrow Downgate, y).$$

The algorithm to determine whether a computation graph satisfies a given RTL formula specifying a timing property in this class depends on the combination of quantifiers in Q_a and Q_b as well as on whether it is an inclusion or exclusion property. For example, suppose we like to check whether some instance of an interval I_1 contains an instance of an interval I_2. First, we find in the graph an instance of interval I_2. Then we check if an instance of interval I_1 contains within it interval I_2, and the algorithm returns true if this is the case. If we like to check whether every instance of an interval I_1 contains an instance of an interval I_2, we need to repeat the above steps for every appearance of I_2. Other cases and combinations of quantifiers can be checked similarly.

6.10   AVAILABLE TOOLS

Modechart Toolset (MT) [Clements et al., 1993b] is a set of tools using the Mode-chart language for the specification, modeling, and analysis of real-time embedded systems. It supports the creation, modification, and storage of Modechart specifi-cations and allows the analysis of Modechart specifications using a consistency and completeness checker, a simulator, and a verifier. A user manual for MT can be found in [Rose, Perez, and Clements, 1994].

XSVT [Stuart et al., 2001] is a new prototype tool built as part of MT that com-bines simulation and verification techniques to analyze Modechart specifications.

6.11   HISTORICAL PERSPECTIVE AND RELATED WORK

[Jahanian and Mok, 1986] developed RTL as a concise, first-order logic language to formally specify real-time systems and their absolute timing properties. They pro-posed an analysis framework relating the system specification and the desired safety assertion(s). The Bledsoe-Hines decision procedure was suggested as a means to check and verify the satisfaction of the safety assertion(s) given a system specifica-tion. However, for RTL, this analysis problem is in general undecidable, and requires exponential time to solve for decidable cases. Other real-time logics include the In-terval Logic developed recently by [Mattolini and Nesi, 2001].

To derive a more efficient analysis algorithm, [Jahanian and Mok, 1987] define a subclass of RTL formulas that is a class of practical real-time systems. This graph-theoretic approach is based on inequalities and graph analysis, and does not require the use of logic decision procedures.

The Modechart graphical specification language was introduced by Mok et al. [Jahanian and Stuart, 1988; Jahanian and Mok, 1994] to facilitate the specification of real-time systems and as an alternative to Statecharts and STATEMATE. Fur-thermore, Modechart claims to remedy the weaknesses of Statechart in handling absolute-timing specifications. To combat the state-explosion problem, [Stuart et al., 2001] combine simulation and verification techniques to make it easier to understand specifications and to speed up verification of properties expressed in CTL-like forms. [Brockmeyer et al., 2000] provide a flexible and extensible simulation environment for testing real-time specifications.

Recently, [Rice and Cheng, 1999] used RTL and the constraint graph approach described here to specify and verify part of the X-38 Space Station Crew Return Vehicle Avionics. Part of the analysis is shown in this chapter.

6.12 SUMMARY

A real-time system can be specified in one of two ways. The first is to structurally and functionally describe the system by specifying its mechanical, electrical, and electronic components. This type of specification shows how the components of the system work and shows their functions and operations. The second is to describe the behavior of the system in response to actions and events. Here, the specification tells sequences of events allowed by the system.

To show that a system or program meets certain safety properties, we can relate the *specification* of the system to the *safety assertion* representing the desired safety properties. This assumes that the actual implementation of the system is faithful to the specification. Note that even though a behavioral specification does not show how one can build the specified system, one can certainly show that the implemented system, built from the structural-functional specification, satisfies the behavioral specification.

One of the following three cases may result from the analysis relating the specification and the safety assertion. (1) The safety assertion is a theorem derivable from the specification, thus the system is safe with respect to the behavior denoted by the safety assertion. (2) The safety assertion is unsatisfiable with respect to the specification, so the system is inherently unsafe since the specification will cause the safety assertion to be violated. (3) The negation of the safety assertion is satisfiable under certain conditions, meaning that additional constraints must be added to the system to ensure its safety.

The *event-action model* [Heninger, 1980; Jahanian and Mok, 1986] captures the data dependency and temporal ordering of computational actions that must be taken in response to events in a real-time application. There are four basic concepts.

1. An *action* is a schedulable unit of work and can be primitive or composite. A *primitive* action is atomic in that it cannot or does not need to be broken into subactions for the purpose of analysis. It consumes a bounded amount of time. A *composite* action is a partial ordering of primitive actions or other composite actions.

2. A *state predicate* is an assertion about the state of the specified system.

3. An *event* is a temporal marker for indicating a point in time that is significant in describing the system behavior. There are four classes of events:

    (a) An *external* event is caused by actions outside the specified system.

    (b) A *start* event marks the beginning of an action, for example, the start of the DOWN-GATE action.

    (c) A *stop* event marks the end of an action, for example, the end of the DOWN-GATE action.

    (d) A *transition* event marks the change in certain attributes of the system state.

4. A *timing constraint* is an assertion about the absolute timing of system events.

The motivation for introducing the real-time logic (RTL) [Jahanian and Mok, 1986] is that the specifications written in the event-action model cannot be easily manipulated by a computer. RTL is a first-order logic with special features to capture the timing requirements of the specified system while making the specification easy to manipulate mechanically. RTL was especially attractive because at the time of its introduction, temporal logic was able to express the relative ordering of events or actions [Heninger, 1980; Bernstein and Harter, 1981], but temporal logic has not yet been extended with the capability of expressing absolute timing characteristics. Furthermore, temporal logic uses an interleaving model of computation to specify concurrency in computer systems, but this model cannot express true parallelism. For instance, temporal logic models two parallel actions as if one is followed by the other or vice versa, so that from an initial state s_0 there are two paths, corresponding to the two orderings of these actions, leading to state s_1.

A scheduler is often an integral part of a real-time system. The correctness of a real-time system depends on the correctness of its scheduler. Temporal logic, however, usually assumes the fair scheduling of the specified system's resources and events. This is appropriate for non-time-critical systems but certainly is not sufficient for the analysis of real-time systems.

RTL is based on the event-action model, augmented with several features such as the occurrence function @, which assigns time values to event occurrences.

There are three types of RTL constants: *actions, events*, and *integers*. Action constants are as defined in the event-action model and capital letters are used to denote them to distinguish them from variables. A subaction B_i of a composite action A is denoted as $A.B_i$. Event constants serve as temporal markers and are classified into: (1) start events indicating the beginning of actions, preceded by $\uparrow$; (2) stop events indicating the end of actions, preceded by $\downarrow$; (3) transition events indicating the change in certain attributes of the system state; and (4) external events, preceded by Ω.

One restricted class of RTL formulas [Jahanian and Mok, 1987] is motivated by the fact that in the specification of many real-time systems:

1. the RTL formulas consist of arithmetic inequalities involving two terms and an integer constant in which a term is either a variable or a function; and
2. the RTL formulas do not contain arithmetic expressions that have a function taking an instance of itself as an argument.

Such a restricted RTL class allows the use of a graph-theoretic approach for analysis. For example, we can use a single-source shortest-paths algorithm for the simple integer programming problem where each inequality is of the form $x_i - x_j \leq \pm a_{ij}$, where x_i and x_j are variables and a is an integer constant. We can also use a constraint graph to represent the set of inequalities. Each variable is presented by a node in the graph, and an inequality $x_i \pm a_{ij} \leq x_j$ is represented by a directed edge with weight $\pm a_{ij}$ connecting x_i to x_j. Then, a set of inequalities represented by such a graph is unsatisfiable iff there is cycle in the graph with a positive total weight.

The class of RTL formulas consists of arithmetic inequalities of the following form:

$$\text{occurrence function} \pm \text{integer constant} \leq \text{occurrence function.}$$

To show the practicality of RTL specification and the constraint graph analysis approach, we use RTL to specify and analyze the timing properties of the avionics of the X-38, a family of vehicles built as incremental development prototypes for the Crew Return Vehicle of the International Space Station.

Modechart specifications allow a graphical interface between the user and the analysis tool. To verify timing properties in a Modechart specification, we first generate a computation graph from the specification. This computation graph represents all behaviors allowed by the Modehcart specification. Then we apply specialized decision procedures [Jahanian and Stuart, 1988] or more general model-checking algorithms [Clarke, Emerson, and Sistla, 1986] to the computation graph to determine if a given timing property is satisfiable. To apply either of these approaches, the computation is viewed as the model of the specified system and the timing property to be checked is given as an RTL formula. Then the decision procedure or model checker decides whether the computation graph satisfies this property.

The computations of a specified system are represented by an infinite computation tree. Then this computation tree can be converted into a finite computation graph for analysis and verification.

Two classes of RTL formulas are preserved by a computation graph: (1) minimum and maximum distance between endpoints and (2) exclusion and inclusion of endpoint and interval.

EXERCISES

1. Express the following safety assertion in RTL: If the brake actuator is activated (ACTIVATED) within 30 time units of the completion of action TRANSMIT (which transmits the signal from the brake to the brake actuator), we are assured that within 100 time units of pressing the brake (BRAKE), the brake actuator is activated, and within 120 time units of pressing the brake but at least 40 time units after pressing the brake, the braking mechanism will be applied (STOP).

2. Express the following safety assertion in RTL: In the hospital intensive care unit, once the pulse/blood pressure monitor pad, blood oxygen sensor, and respiration sensor are properly attached to the patient's arm, index finger, and nose, respectively, and the alarm is enabled, the alarm sounds if any of the following conditions becomes true and remains sounding until a nurse or doctor arrives and disables the alarm: pulse rate is above 120 beats per minute for 20 s, systolic blood pressure is above 180 mmHg for 60 s, blood oxygen count is below 80% for 15 s, or respiration rate is above 35 times per minute for 30 s.

3. Compare the timing specification features of Statechart/STATEMATE (described in chapter 5) and Modechart.

4. If all edges involved in a positive cycle in a constraint graph G correspond to literals that belong to unit clauses, F'' (SP $\wedge \neg$SA in clausal form) must be unsatisfiable. If an edge corresponds to a literal that belongs to non-unit disjunctive clause C_i, then it must be shown that each of the remaining literals in C_i is also involved in a different positive cycle. Explain why this is necessary.

5. Consider the following set of inequalities.
   1. $t_1 : C \leq A$
   2. $t_2 : A - 15 \leq B$
   3. $t_3 : B + 15 \leq C$
   4. $t_4 \vee t_6 : C - 10 \leq D \vee B + 10 \leq D$
   5. $t_5 \vee t_7 : D + 15 \leq C \vee D + 15 \leq B$
   6. $t_7 \vee t_8 : D + 15 \leq B \vee D + 5 \leq D$

   (a) Construct the constraint graph for these inequalities.
   (b) List the positive cycles.
   (c) Using these positive cycles, construct a tree to find out if this set of inequalities is unsatisfiable. You might have to check that the inequalities in a leaf node are by themselves not satisfiable.

6. Consider the generation of the search tree in the graph-theoretic analysis technique. This technique requires a re-ordering of the clauses under certain circumstances to reduce the size of the search tree. Does this re-ordering always reduces the size of the search tree? Explain. If not, give a counter-example.

7. The goal of this problem is to apply formal techniques based on RTL to the specification and verification of a timing-based mutual algorithm by [Attiya and Lynch, 1989]. For this problem, assume there are only two operators (processes). Construct a set of RTL formulas that specify the actions of the processes executing this algorithm. Prove the safeness and verify the response time of the mutual-exclusion algorithm claimed in their paper by using the graph-theoretic technique.

8. Give two decidable classes of timing properties for the modechart/computation graph approach. Then give two classes of timing properties for which the modechart/computation graph approach cannot provide a solution.

9. Consider again the specification of the NASA 2001 Mars Odyssey Orbiter [Cass, 2001] described in chapter 5 (exercise 8), but now with timing constraints on the different events and actions.

   The orbiter is in the ready mode before launch. Before and during launch, the orbiter is folded into a protective housing. The execution time for the launch is 60 s. The start of the launch occurs after a delay of 30 s but within 90 s of the time the orbiter becomes ready.

   After launch, the solar panel extends within 120 s to convert solar energy into electric energy for navigational use. When the orbiter approaches Mars after 18 months, its engine fires within 20 s and the orbiter inserts into Mars' orbit.

Braking starts 50 s after the start of engine firing, and braking takes 20 s. After braking, the orbiter deploys its high-gain antenna within 100 s. At any time after launch, if an emergency occurs (expected steps are not executed as observed by a specialized monitoring computer), the orbiter skips the above steps and enters a safe mode within 10 s and lets mission controllers take over control of the orbiter. Represent the behavior of the orbiter using

(a) RTL

(b) Modechart.

10. Use Modechart to specify a smart traffic light controller for the intersection of two roads, one running North-South (NS), and the other running East-West (EW). Both EW and NS are four-lane roads. Each of the roads has a sensor, which once every T seconds informs the signal controller whether any cars are approaching the intersection along that road or are waiting at the intersection for the light to change. If the light along the road is green, the sensor also indicates the speed (in m/s) of the cars on each of the four lanes (0 if no car is approaching on a lane). The speeds are measured D feet away from the intersection. For this problem assume that $T = 1/2$ and $D = 300$. Each sensor writes its output to a buffer. It may overwrite a value in the buffer. Every write to a buffer is time-stamped automatically and raises a (maskable) interrupt in the controller. The signal controller must abide by the following constraints:

1. It starts with the NS light green and the EW light red and runs in normal mode. The other modes are power off mode, degraded mode, and automatic mode, but you need to only specify the normal mode described below.

2. Normal mode: If the light has just changed to green along either EW or NS, the controller ignores inputs from the sensors for the next 40 s. After that, it checks the time-stamps on the buffers. If both times-tamps are no more than $T/2$ s old, it proceeds to step 3. If either of them is no more than $T/2$ s old, it proceeds to step 2a. Otherwise, it unmasks the sensors' interrupts and waits for sensor input for at most $T/2$ s, and proceeds to step 2a on receiving an input. If it does not receive a value within $T/2$ s, it enters and runs in automatic mode.

2a. The controller unmasks the sensors' interrupts and awaits an input from the other sensor for at most $T/2$ s. It goes to step 3 on receiving the input; if it does not receive an input, it enters and runs in automatic mode.

3. The controller first masks interrupts that the sensors may raise. If neither sensor has detected a car approaching or halted, the controller does nothing. Otherwise, if exactly one sensor has detected a car, the controller changes the light in the other direction to red (without going through the intermediate yellow) and then changes the light in that sensor's direction to green. If both sensors have detected cars, let us, for convenience, assume that the NS light was green and EW was red. The controller computes the time since the NS sensor input—call this X. It then calculates the distance the fastest car in NS would have advanced in $X + C$ s (where C is the time in seconds for the

controller to do these calculations), and checks that the remaining distance is enough for the car to come safely to a halt (using a table lookup). If it is judged to be safe, the controller returns to step 2. Otherwise, it changes the green light to yellow (for a period read from a table—this time is dependent on the speed of the car), then to red. It then changes the red light on EW to green and returns to step 2.

CHAPTER 7

VERIFICATION USING TIMED AUTOMATA

Finite automata and temporal logics have been used extensively to formally verify qualitative properties of concurrent systems. The properties include deadlock- or livelock-freedom, the eventual occurrence of an event, and the satisfaction of a predicate. The need to reason with absolute time is unnecessary in these applications, whose correctness depends only on the relative ordering of the associated events and actions. These automata-theoretic and temporal logic techniques using finite-state graphs are practical in a variety of verification problems in network protocols, electronic circuits, and concurrent programs. More recently, several researchers have extended these techniques to timed or real-time systems while retaining many of the desirable features of their untimed counterparts.

In this chapter, we present two automata-theoretic techniques based on timed automata. The Lynch–Vaandrager approach [Lynch and Vaandrager, 1991; Heitmeyer and Lynch, 1994] is more general and can handle finite and infinite state systems, but it lacks an automatic verification mechanism. Its specification can be difficult to write and understand, even for relatively small systems. The Alur–Dill approach [Alur, Fix, and Henzinger, 1994] is less ambitious and is based on finite automata, but it offers an automated tool for verification of desirable properties. Its *dense-time* model can handle time values selected from the set of real numbers, whereas *discrete-time* models such as those in Statecharts and Modecharts use only integer time values.

7.1 LYNCH–VAANDRAGER AUTOMATA-THEORETIC APPROACH

[Heitmeyer and Lynch, 1994] advocate the use of three specifications to formally describe a real-time system. A specification consists of the description of one or more timed automata. First, an *axiomatic* specification specifies the system in a descriptive, axiomatic style without showing how it operates. Then, an *operational* specification describes the operation of the system. A formal proof is required to show that the operational specification *implements* the axiomatic specification.

There are several ways to construct this proof. [Lynch and Attiya, 1992; Lynch and Vaandrager, 1991] have used assertional techniques for untimed, concurrent, and distributed systems, and thus propose adapting these techniques to verify timing properties of real-time systems. In particular, the method of simulations is used to establish the relationships (such as implementation) between two specifications described by two corresponding timed automata. Here, the concept of simulations includes special cases such as *refinement mappings*, *backward and forward simulations*, and *history and prophecy mapping*.

Several definitions exist for a general timed automaton. One variation proposed by Lynch and Vaandrager is as follows [Lynch and Vaandrager, 1991].

Timed Automaton: Formally, a timed automaton A is a general labeled transition system with four components:

states(A) is a set of states.

start(A) is a nonempty set of start states.

acts(A) is a set of actions. Actions can be internal or external. Internal actions are within the system. External actions include visible actions (which can be input or output actions) and special time-passage actions $v(t)$, where t is a positive real number.

steps(A) is a set of steps (usually known as transitions in other definitions of automata).

The number of states can be finite or infinite. To improve readability, the notation $s \xrightarrow{\pi} _A s'$ is used instead of $(s, \pi, s') \in steps(A)$, where A is a timed automaton. The subscript A is often omitted when no ambiguity exists.

7.1.1 Timed Executions

Having defined the concept of a timed automaton, we next consider its behavior by observing its execution from one point in time to another. A timed execution is a sequence of internal, visible, and time-passage actions, connected by their intervening states, and augmented with the notion of trajectories for each time-passage action. A *trajectory* indicates the state changes during time-passage steps. To formally define a time execution, we first define the notion of a timed execution fragment.

Timed Execution: A *timed execution fragment* is a finite or infinite alternating sequence

$$\alpha = \omega_0 \pi_1 \omega_1 \pi_2 \omega_2 \ldots,$$

where (1) each ω_i is a trajectory and each π_i is a non-time-passage action, and (2) each π_{i+1} connects the final state s of the preceding trajectory ω_i with the initial state s' of the succeeding trajectory ω_{i+1}, that is, $s \xrightarrow{\pi_{i+1}} s'$.

If the first state of the first trajectory, ω_0, of a timed execution fragment is a start state, then this fragment is a *timed execution*.

A state of a timed automaton A is *reachable* if it is the final state of the final trajectory in some finite-timed execution of A. A *time of occurrence* is associated with each instance of a state or action in a timed execution. This is done by summing all the preceding time-passage values. Note that this notion of time of occurrence is similar to that of the occurrence in real-time logic (RTL).

Given a timed automaton A, of practical interest is the set *atexecs*(A) of *admissible* timed executions in which the total amount of time passage is ∞. Next, we define timed traces to represent the visible behavior of timed automata for solving verification problems.

7.1.2 Timed Traces

A timed trace of any timed execution is the sequence of visible events that occur in the timed execution, paired with their times of occurrence. This sequence has the form

$$(\pi_1, t_1), (\pi_2, t_2), (\pi_3, t_3), \dots,$$

where the πs are non-time-passage actions and the ts are non-negative real-valued times.

The notation *ttrace*(α) denotes the timed trace of the timed execution α. The timed traces obtained from all the admissible timed executions of a timed automaton A constitute the set *attraces*(A) of *admissible timed traces* of A.

Example. Consider a traffic semaphore with three light signals. Initially, there is no light when the system is off. Once it is turned on at time 0, the event *turn_green* makes the green light turn on. Next, the event *turn_yellow*, occurring 20 s later, turns the green light off and then the yellow light on. Next, the *turn_red* event occurring 5 s later turns the yellow light off and then the red light on. Next, the event *turn_green*, occurring 15 s later, turns the red light off and then the green light on. This sequence is repeated infinitely often. The timed trace of this timed execution is

$$(turn\_green, 0), (turn\_yellow, 20), (turn\_red, 25), (turn\_green, 40), \dots.$$

Operations on automata exist that allow the definitions of complex automata by combining simpler automata. These operations include projection and parallel composition.

7.1.3 Composition of Timed Automata

To model a complex system, we need to combine several automata representing different parts of the system through composition. Two timed automata A and B are *compatible* iff they have no common output actions and the internal actions of A are different from those of B. Then the *composition* of A and B, written as $A \times B$, is the timed automaton with:

$$states(A \times B) = states(A) \times states(B)$$

$$start(A \times B) = start(A) \times start(B)$$

$$acts(A \times B) = acts(A) \cup acts(B).$$

Step $(s_A, s_B) \xrightarrow{\pi}_{A \times B} (s'_A, s'_B)$ exists iff $s_A \xrightarrow{\pi}_A s'_A$ if $\pi \in acts(A)$, else $s_A = s'_A$, and $s_B \xrightarrow{\pi}_B s'_B$ if $\pi \in acts(B)$, else $s_B = s'_B$.

This means that A and B can execute jointly on a common input or time-passage action, or on an output of one that is an input of the other.

7.1.4 MMT Automata

The above definition of a timed automaton is very general. To allow more efficient verification via simulations, a more specialized automaton is introduced. A Merritt–Modugno–Tuttle (MMT) automaton [Merritt, Modugno, and Tuttle, 1991] is an I/O automaton augmented with upper and lower bounds on time between specific actions. The MMT automaton model can be used to represent many types of timed automata. An I/O automaton is a labeled transition system for representing an untimed asynchronous system. Its internal and output actions are grouped into tasks.

I/O Automaton: An I/O automaton A has the following components:

states(A) is a set of states.

start(A) is a nonempty subset of start states.

acts(A) is a set of actions. Actions can be internal or external. External actions can be input or output actions.

steps(A) is a set of steps (usually known as transitions in other publications). This is a subset of $states(A) \times acts(A) \times statesA)$.

part(A) is a partition of the locally controlled (internal and output) actions into at most countably many equivalence classes.

Note that the definition of a basic timed automaton is basically that of an I/O automaton extended with the notion of time for *steps(A)*. To define an MMT automaton, [Lynch and Attiya, 1992; Lynch and Vaandrager, 1991] extend the I/O automaton model with lower and upper time bound information. More precisely, an MMT automaton is an I/O automaton with only finitely many partition classes; and for each class C, lower and upper time bounds are defined and denoted *lower(C)*

and $upper(C)$, where $0 \leq lower(C) < \infty$ and $0 < upper(C) \leq \infty$. In other words, the lower bounds cannot be infinite and the upper bounds cannot be 0.

Since an MMT automaton can represent the time differences between certain actions in the modeled system or its component, the execution of the MMT automaton shows the behavior of the modeled system over time. A timed execution of an MMT automaton is an alternating sequence of the form $s_0, (\pi_1, t_1), s_1, \ldots$, where the πs can be input, output, or external actions. For each i, $s_i \xrightarrow{\pi_{j+1}} s_{j+1}$ must hold such that the successive times are nondecreasing and are required to satisfy the specified *lower* and *upper* time bound requirements.

The points at which the bounds for a class C begin to be measured are called *initial indices*. Index i is defined as an initial index for a class C enabled in state s_i, and one of the following must hold: $i = 0$, C is not enabled in s_{j-1}, or $\pi_i \in C$. With this definition, the following conditions must hold for every initial index i for a class C:

1. If *upper* $\neq \infty$, there exists $k > i$, $t_k \leq t_i + upper(C)$, such that either $\pi_k \in C$ or C is not enabled in state s_k.

2. There does not exist $k > i$, $t_k < t_i + lower(C)$, and $\pi_k \in C$.

Condition (1) is the upper bound requirement; an upper bound of ∞ means that actions in the corresponding class may never occur. Condition (2) is the lower bound requirement. The condition of *admissibility* must also hold; that is, if the sequence is infinite, then the times of actions approach ∞.

7.1.5 Verification Techniques

A problem P can be formulated as a set of finite or infinite sequences of actions with corresponding times. Then a timed automaton A is said to *solve* P if all its admissible timed traces are in P. Since we can express P as the set of admissible timed traces of another timed automaton B, the concept of admissible timed traces induces a preorder on timed automata. The notation $A \leq B$ means that the set of admissible timed traces of A is a subset of the set of admissible timed traces of B.

Example. The following MMT automaton describes the behavior of the pedals of a simplified automobile, which has been specified in Statecharts in chapter 4. The automobile can be in one of three states: stop, move, or slow. The inputs are *apply_accelerator*, *apply_brake*, and *apply_hand_brake*. The nontrivial time bounds are *speed up*: $[0, t_{speedup}]$, *slow*: $[0, t_{speedup}]$, and *stop*: $[0, t_{speedup}]$, where $t_{speedup}$, t_{slow}, and t_{stop} are the upper bounds on the time for the car to speed up, slow, and stop, respectively. The state components *now*, *latest(speedup)*, *latest(slow)*, and *latest(stop)* are also needed to add timing specifications to each state.

As in the Statecharts specification, the MMT automaton shows that (1) the transition from the state "stop" to the state "speed up" occurs when the accelerator is applied; (2) the transition from the state "speedup" to the state "slow" occurs when the brake is applied; (3) the transition from the state "slow" to the state "speedup" occurs when the accelerator is applied; and (4) the transitions from the states "speedup" and "slow" to the state "stop" occur when the hand brake is applied.

Automaton C: car's pedals system
States:
    $status \in stop, slow, speedup$, initially $stop$
    now, a non-negative real, initially 0

Transitions:

apply_accelerator
Precondition:
    $s.status \in stop, slow$
Effect:
    $s'.status = to\_speedup$
    $s'.latest(speedup) = now + t_{speedup}$
    $s'.latest(stop) = \infty$
    $s'.latest(slow) = \infty$

apply_brake
Precondition:
    $s.status = speedup$
Effect:
    $s'.status = to_{slow}$
    $s'.latest(slow) = now + t_{slow}$
    $s'.latest(speedup) = \infty$
    $s'.latest(stop) = \infty$

apply_hand_brake
Precondition:
    $s.status \in speedup, slow$
Effect:
    $s'.status = stop$
    $s'.latest(stop) = now + t_{stop}$
    $s'.latest(speedup) = \infty$
    $s'.latest(slow) = \infty$

speedup
Precondition:
    $s.status = speeding\_up$
Effect:
    $s'.status = speedup$
    $s'.latest(speedup) = \infty$

slow
Precondition:
   s.status = slowing
Effect:
   s'.status = slow
   $s'.latest(slow) = \infty$

stop
Precondition:
   s.status = stopping
Effect:
   s'.status = stop
   $s'.latest(stop) = \infty$

7.1.6 Proving Time Bounds with Simulations

By including lower and upper time bounds on classes of the specification automaton, the Larch Prover [Garland and Guttag, 1991] has been used to perform simple simulation proofs for verifying timing properties of real-time and distributed systems.

7.2 ALUR–DILL AUTOMATA-THEORETIC APPROACH

To verify that an implementation of a system satisfies the specification of the system, we first represent or encode the specification as a Buchi automaton A_S and the implementation as a Buchi automaton A_I. Then we check that the implementation meets the specification iff $L(A_I) \subseteq L(A_S)$, or check for the emptiness of $L(A_I) \cap L(A_S)^C$; that is, the intersection of the languages accepted by the implementation and the languages accepted by the complement of the specification (negation of the specification) is empty.

Alur and Dill extend timed automata with a finite set of real-valued clocks to express timing constraints on non-clock variables. Clocks are like timers (or stopwatches) and thus can be reset (set to time 0). Clock values increase uniformly with time; that is, at any instant the value of a clock is equal to the time elapsed since the last time it was reset. Each transition in a timed automaton is labeled, in addition to the input symbol, with either a clock value assignment or a clock constraint. A transition with a clock constraint is enabled only if the current values of the clocks satisfy this timing constraint. We begin the discussion by reviewing untimed traces and then extend these to timed traces.

7.2.1 Untimed Traces

A *trace* is a linear sequence of the observable events of a process. In general, each process has a set of observable events and the behavior of this process can be modeled by the set of its traces. For example, a traffic light turning green is an event in a traffic light system, as is the opening of a valve in a fuel system. A trace is a linear sequence of *sets* of events in the Alur–Dill model. A trace and a process are defined formally as follows.

Untimed Trace: Given a set E of events, an untimed trace or simply a trace $\overline{\rho} = \rho_1\rho_2\rho_3 \cdots$ is an infinite word over the set of nonempty subsets of E.

A word is also known as a *string* in descriptions of automata and languages (chapter 2).

Untimed Process: An untimed process is a pair (E, S) where E is the set of the observable events of the process and S is the set of the possible traces of the process.

Example. Consider a traffic semaphore with three light signals. Initially the *green* light is on. Next, the *green* light turns off and then the *yellow* light turns on. Next, the *yellow* light turns off and then the *red* light turns on. Next, the *red* light turns off and then the *green* light turns on. This sequence is repeated infinitely often. By treating *green*, *yellow*, and *red* as events, the only possible trace is:

$$\overline{\rho}_P = \{green\}, \{yellow\}, \{red\}, \{green\}, \{yellow\}, \{red\}, \ldots.$$

Keeping the notations simple by removing the set symbols, { }, this infinite sequence is denoted as

$$green\ yellow\ red\ green\ yellow\ red \cdots = (green\ yellow\ red)^{\omega}.$$

Process P is denoted by $(\{green, yellow, red\}, (green\ yellow\ red)^{\omega})$.

Operations on processes exist that allow the definitions of complex processes by combining simpler processes. These operations include projection and parallel composition.

7.2.2 Timed Traces

In the Alur–Dill model, a real-valued time is associated with each symbol in a word to form a *timed word*.

Time Sequence: A *time sequence* $\overline{\tau} = \tau_1, \tau_2, \tau_3 \ldots$, where τ_i is a positive real number, is an infinite sequence of time values such that (1) the sequence increases strictly monotonically and (2) for every real number, there is a τ_j with a larger value.

Note that condition 2 prevents an infinite number of events to occur within a finite period of time.

Timed Word: A timed word over an alphabet Σ is a pair $(\overline{\rho}, \overline{\tau})$ where $\overline{\rho}$ is an infinite word and $\overline{\tau}$ is a time sequence.

Timed Language: A timed language over an alphabet Σ is a set of timed words over Σ.

Using these definitions, if each symbol ρ_i denotes the occurrence of an event, the corresponding time value τ_i indicates the time of occurrence of this event.

Example. *A timed language:* Given an alphabet with two events, {*ok, timeout*}, define a timed language L consisting of all timed words $(\overline{\rho}, \overline{\tau})$ such that there is no *ok* after time 10.5; that is, the event *timeout* definitely becomes true at time 10.5 but may be true earlier. Formally, the language is:

$$L = \{(\overline{\rho}, \overline{\tau}) \mid \forall i((\tau_i > 10.5) \rightarrow (\rho_i = timeout))\}.$$

This concept of a time value associated to an event occurrence is similar to the time value given by the occurrence function in real-time logic (chapter 6) and the chronos variable in time ER nets (chapter 8). An occurrence function assigns a time to the occurrence of an instance of an event. A variable chronos assigns a time-stamp to the production of a token in a Petri net.

The following *Untime* operation is a projection of a timed trace $(\overline{\rho}, \overline{\tau})$ on the first component, the sequence of event occurrences $\overline{\rho}$. This operation effectively deletes the time values corresponding to the event occurrence symbols and is useful when we do not need the absolute time values.

Untime Operation: Given a timed language L over an alphabet Σ, $Untime(L)$ is the ω-language with words $\overline{\rho}$ such that $(\overline{\rho}, \overline{\tau}) \in L$ for some time sequence $\overline{\tau}$.

Example. We apply the *Untime* operation to the above language L:

$Untime(L) = \omega$-language with words containing only finitely many *oks*.

Timed Trace: A *time trace* over a set E of events is a pair $(\overline{\rho}, \overline{\tau})$ where $\overline{\rho}$ is a (untimed) trace over the set E and $\overline{\tau}$ is a time sequence.

Timed Process: A timed process is a pair (E, L) where E is a (finite) set of events and L is a set of timed traces over the set E.

Example. *A timed process:* Consider the climate control system example shown in Figure 2.13 (chapter 2). To simply this example, we focus on the events in the heater section. Assume that the initial instances of the events occur at fixed times and that subsequent instances of the corresponding events occur at fixed time intervals. The event *turn_on_heater* happens 10 s after the event *cold* occurs, followed by the event *comfort* 5 s later, followed by the event *turn_off_heater* 5 s later, followed by the event *cold* 30 s later. Suppose the event *cold* first occurs at time 0. This process is represented by a timed process:

$$P^T = (\{cold, turn\_on\_heater, comfort, turn\_off\_heater\}, \{\rho_P\})$$

and it has a single time trace

$$\rho_P = (cold, 0), (turn\_on\_heater, 10), (comfort, 15), (turn\_off\_heater, 20),$$
$$(cold, 50), (turn\_on\_heater, 60), (comfort, 65), (turn\_off\_heater, 70),$$
$$(cold, 100) \ldots$$

Again, the *Untime* operation can be used to delete the time values corresponding to events.

Untime Operation for a Process: Given a timed process $P = (E, L)$, *Untime* $[(E, L)]$ is the untimed process where E is the event set and the trace set with traces $\overline{\rho}$ such that for some sequence $\overline{\rho}$, $(\overline{\rho}, \overline{\tau}) \in L$.

Example. Automaton α_1: Consider again the example of the automatic air conditioning and heating system (Figure 2.13) in chapter 2, which specifies the operations of a climate control system according to changes to a room temperature. The automaton representing this system can only specify relative ordering of the events but cannot specify when these events should occur. Hence, it cannot be used to verify a timing-dependent climate control system. Now we introduce timing constraints to the transitions of this automaton, yielding the timed automaton shown in Figure 7.1.

Two clocks (clock variables) are present in the transition table, c_1 and c_2. Suppose the automaton starts in state s_0 and reads the input symbol *cold*, then it takes the transition (indicating that the room temperature falls below 68°F) and moves to state s_4. The clock c_1 is reset (set to 0 by the assignment $c_1 := 0$) along this transition. In

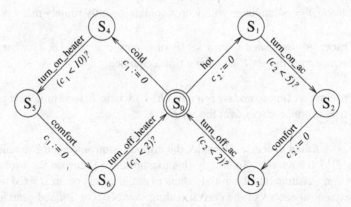

Figure 7.1   Automaton α_1 for automatic air conditioning and heating system.

state s_4, clock c_1 shows the time passed since the reading of the input symbol *cold* (the occurrence of the event *cold*).

The automaton can move from state s_4 to state s_5 only if this clock value is less than 10 (seconds). In other words, this transition is enabled only if c_1 is less than 10 (indicated by $(c_1 < 10)$? along the transition). This timing constraint can be considered as the maximum delay for the *turn_on_heater* event to happen after detecting the *cold* event. This is the same as saying the deadline for the occurrence of the *turn_on_heater* event is less than 10 since the *cold* event is detected.

In state s_5, if the automaton reads the input symbol *comfort*, then it takes the transition (indicating that the room temperature is at least $68°F$) and moves to state s_6. The clock c_1 is again reset (set to 0 by the assignment $c_1 := 0$) along this transition. In state s_6, clock c_1 shows the time passed since the reading of the input symbol *comfort* (the occurrence of the event *comfort*).

The automaton can move from state s_6 back to state s_0 only if this clock value is less than 2 (seconds). In other words, this transition is enabled only if c_1 is less than 2 (indicated by $(c_1 < 2)$? along the transition). As before, this timing constraint can be considered as the maximum delay for the *turn_off_heater* event to happen after detecting the *comfort* event. This is the same as saying the deadline for the occurrence of the *turn_off_heater* event is less than 2 since the *comfort* event is detected.

The behavior of the automaton starting from the initial state s_0 if the input symbol *hot* (indicating that the room temperature is above $78°F$) is read is similar except that the air conditioner will be turned on and the deadlines are different. Note that different clocks can be reset or restarted at different times and they are independent (need not be synchronized). In this example, we can use a single clock to impose the timing constraints since either the heater or the air conditioner can be activated but not both at the same time. This automaton accepts the language:

$$L_1 = \{((cold\ turn\_on\_heater\ comfort\ turn\_off\_heater$$

$$\cup\ hot\ turn\_on\_ac\ comfort\ turn\_off\_ac)^{\omega}, \overline{\tau})$$

$$|\forall x((\tau_{4x+5} < \tau_{4x+4} + 10)(\tau_{4x+7} < \tau_{4x+6} + 2)$$

$$(\tau_{4x+2} < \tau_{4x+1} + 5)(\tau_{4x+4} < \tau_{4x+3} + 2))\}.$$

Example.   Automaton α_2: Consider the timed transition table of the example automaton (Figure 7.2) representing the receiving of two messages (*msg1* and *msg2*) and their corresponding acknowledgments (*ack1* and *ack2*). *ack1* must be sent 2 s after receiving *msg1*, and *ack2* must be sent within 5 s of receiving *msg2*. *ack1* must be sent before sending *ack2*. This last condition effectively requires that *ack1* must be sent 2 s after receiving *msg1* and within 5 s of receiving *msg2* so that *ack2* can be sent within 5 s of receiving *msg2*. This automaton has two clocks and accepts the language:

$$L_2 = \{((msg1\ msg2\ ack1\ ack2)^{\omega}, \overline{\tau})|\forall x((\tau_{4x+3} > \tau_{4x+1} + 2)(\tau_{4x+4} < \tau_{4x+2} + 5))\}.$$

Having described two examples, we now define the types of comparisons allowed in specifying a clock constraint.

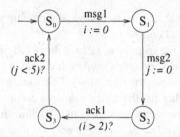

Figure 7.2 Automaton α_2 for message sending and acknowledgment.

Clock Constraints: An *atomic constraint* is of the form c *operator* t, where c is a clock variable, t is a time constant (a nonnegative rational number), and *operator* is either $<$ or $\leq$. A clock constraint is an atomic constraint or a conjunction of atomic constraints.

Next we define an assignment of values to clocks, called a clock interpretation.

Clock Interpretation: A *clock interpretation* for a set of clocks is an assignment of a positive real value to each clock. A clock constraint may contain one or more clocks. A clock interpretation v for a set C of clocks is said to satisfy a clock constraint δ over C iff the assignment of the values in v to these clocks makes δ true. Given a positive real t, the expression $v + t$ is a clock interpretation that assigns the value $v(c) + t$ to every clock c.

We are now ready to define a state extended with a clock interpretation.

Extended State: Given a timed transition table, an extended state $\langle s, v \rangle$ is a state $s \in S$ extended with a clock interpretation v for C.

7.2.3 Alur–Dill Timed Automata

Alur and Dill extend the ω-automata to accept timed words, yielding a theory of timed regular languages. The definition of a timed Buchi automaton is based on a Buchi automaton extended with a finite set of clocks and clock constraints.

Timed Transition Table: A *timed transition table* A is a 5-tuple $\langle \Sigma, S, S_0, C, E \rangle$, where Σ is a finite alphabet, S is a finite set of states, $S_0 \subseteq S$ is a set of start states, C is a finite set of clocks, and E is a set of transitions. A transition on input symbol α $\langle s, s', \alpha, \lambda, \delta \rangle$ is represented by an edge from state s to state s'. λ is the finite set of clocks to be reset with this transition. δ is a clock constraint over C.

The corresponding *region automaton* $R(A)$ for a timed transition table $A = \langle \Sigma, S, S_0, C, E \rangle$ is a transition table over the alphabet Σ.

The states of $R(A)$ are pairs $\langle s, \alpha \rangle$ where $s \in S$ and α is a clock region. The initial states of $R(A)$ are pairs $\langle s_0, [v_0] \rangle$ where $s_0 \in S_0$ and $v_0(x) = 0$ for all $x \in C$. An edge $\langle \langle s, \alpha \rangle, \langle s', \alpha' \rangle, a \rangle$ exists in $R(A)$ iff $\langle s, v \rangle \xrightarrow{a} \langle s', v' \rangle$ for some $v \in \alpha$ and some $v' \in \alpha'$.

Now we define a *run of a timed transition table*, which is an execution path with events and their corresponding occurrence times.

Run of a Timed Transition Table: A run $r = (\overline{s}, \overline{v})$ of a timed transition table (as defined above) over a timed word $(\overline{\rho}, \overline{\tau})$ is an infinite sequence

$$r : \langle s_0, v_0 \rangle \xrightarrow{\rho_1, \tau_1} \langle s_1, v_1 \rangle \xrightarrow{\rho_2, \tau_2} \langle s_2, v_2 \rangle \xrightarrow{\rho_3, \tau_3} \cdots$$

where $s_i \in S$ for all $i \geq 0$ and v_i is a clock interpretation for C such that

1. $s_0 \in S_0$ and for all $t \in C$, $v_0(t) = 0$; and
2. an edge in $E \langle s_{i-1}, s_i, \rho_i, \lambda_i, \delta_i \rangle$ exists for all $i \geq 1$ such that $(v_{i-1} + \tau_i - \tau_{i-1})$ satisfies δ_i and $v_i = [\lambda_i \rightarrow 0](v_{I-1} + \tau_i - \tau_{I-1})$.

Example. *A run of a timed transition table:* Consider again the timed transition table of the example automaton above representing the receiving of two messages (*msg*1 and *msg*2) and their corresponding acknowledgments (*ack*1 and *ack*2). *ack*1 must be sent 2 s after receiving *msg*1, and *ack*2 must be sent within 5 s of receiving *msg*2. Suppose we have the word

$$(msg1, 1), (msg2, 2.6), (ack1, 4), (ack2, 5.8), \ldots .$$

Note that the occurrence time values for the events satisfy the clock constraints. With a clock interpretation given by the values $[i, j]$, the initial part of the run is:

$$r : \langle s_0, [0, 0] \rangle \xrightarrow{msg1, 1} \langle s_1, [0, 1] \rangle \xrightarrow{msg2, 2.6} \langle s_2, [1.6, 0] \rangle$$
$$\xrightarrow{ack1, 4} \langle s_3, [3, 1.4] \rangle \xrightarrow{ack2, 5.8} \langle s_4, [4.8, 3.2] \rangle \cdots .$$

Initially, all the clocks have value 0. Starting from state s_0, the automaton takes the transition on reading *msg*1 at time 1 and moves to state s_1. The clock assignment along this transition resets clock i to 0 whereas clock j advances to 1, hence the clock interpretation in state s_1 is $[0, 1]$.

Then, on reading *msg*2 at time 2.6, the automaton moves to state s_2. The clock assignment along this transition resets clock j to 0 whereas clock i advances to 1.6 since absolute time has advanced 1.6 s (the time interval between the receipt of *msg*1 and the receipt of *msg*2), hence the clock interpretation in state s_2 is $[1.6, 0]$.

Next on reading *ack*1 at time 4, the automaton moves to state s_3. Absolute time has advanced 1.4 s since reading *msg*2, so both clocks advance 1.4 s, hence the clock interpretation in state s_3 is [3, 1.4]. Note that this transition is taken more than 2 s after receiving $msg1$.

Finally, on reading $ack2$ at time 5.8, the automaton moves to state s_4. Absolute time has advanced 1.8 s since reading $ack1$, so both clocks advance 1.8 s, hence the clock interpretation in state s_4 is [4.8, 3.2]. Note that this transition is taken within 5 s of receiving $msg2$.

Now we are ready to define timed languages and timed Buchi automata by combining time transition tables and acceptance criteria. We need to define the *inf* set first. $inf(r)$ is a set of states in $s \in S$ where $s = s_i$ for infinitely many $i \geq 0$.

Timed Buchi Automaton: A timed Buchi automaton (TBA) is a 6-tuple $\langle \Sigma, S, S_0, E, C, F \rangle$, where the first five components of the tuple form a timed transition table and the last component, F, is a set of accepting states.

Accepting Run: A run $r = (\overline{s}, \overline{v})$ of a TBA over a timed word $(\overline{\rho}, \overline{\tau})$ is an accepting run iff $F \cap inf(r) \neq \emptyset$.

Let $L(\alpha)$ be the language of timed words accepted by the TBA α. Then $L(\alpha)$ is the set $\{(\overline{\rho}, \overline{\tau}) \mid \alpha$ has an accepting run over $(\overline{\rho}, \overline{\tau})\}$.

$L(\alpha)$ belongs to a class of languages called timed regular languages.

Timed Regular Language: A *timed language* L is a *timed regular language* iff for some TBA α, $L = L(\alpha)$.

We are getting close to developing a strategy for verification using timed automata. In the case of an untimed deterministic finite automaton, there is a single initial state, and the state in which the automaton is in together with the next input symbol read determine the unique next state. Here, we can define a deterministic timed automaton in a similar way. The current state together with the next input symbol and its occurrence time uniquely determine the next state. Unlike untimed DFA, a timed DFA may have more than one outgoing transition with the same input symbol from a given state. This is allowed if the time constraints along these transitions are mutually exclusive, that is, these time constraints cannot be true at the same time.

Deterministic Timed Automaton: A deterministic timed automaton (DTA or DTFA) is a timed automaton with a deterministic timed transition table. A timed transition table $\langle \Sigma, S, S_0, E, C \rangle$ is deterministic iff

1. it has a single initial state, and
2. the clock constraints δ_1 and δ_2 are mutually exclusive (cannot be true at the same time) for all $s \in S$, for all $a \in \Sigma$, and for every pair of edges $\langle s, -, a, -, \delta_1 \rangle$ and $\langle s, -, a, -, \delta_2 \rangle$.

The motivation for using a DTA is that it can be easily complemented since at most one run exists over a given timed word. Complementation is needed when we verify that the implementation A_I meets the specification A_S by checking for the emptiness of $L(A_I) \cap L(A_S)^C$, that is, the intersection of the languages accepted by the implementation and the languages accepted by the complement of the specification (negation of the specification) is empty.

7.3 ALUR–DILL REGION AUTOMATON AND VERIFICATION

To prove that the language accepted by an automaton is nonempty, we need to show that there is an infinite accepting path in the automaton's transition table. For a timed automaton, the timing constraints disallow certain paths in the transition table. Alur and Dill [Alur, 1991; Alur and Dill, 1994] show that given a timed automaton, a Buchi automaton can be constructed such that the set of untimed words accepted by the Buchi automaton is the same as the one obtained by the *Untime* operation on the timed words accepted by the timed automaton. They provide an algorithm for checking emptiness for timed automata with clock constraints containing only integer constants.

Clock constraints containing rational numbers can be converted into integers by multiplying each constant by the least common multiple (LCM) of the denominators of all the constants in the clock constraints of an automaton. Note that this does not change the untimed language.

7.3.1 Clock Regions

Since the number of clock interpretations is infinite, the number of extended states is infinite and uncountable. This makes it impossible to construct an automaton with extended states given an automaton with no clock interpretations. However, to verify that two automata are equivalent, for example, that an implementation of a system (represented by an automaton) satisfies the specification of the system (represented by another automaton), we have to find a way to build the corresponding finite automata.

One approach used in other analysis and verification techniques is to aggregate an infinite set of extended states into one state or a finite set of states. Here, this is achieved by grouping infinite sets of states into a finite number of clock regions, and then by showing that runs (or execution paths) from the same states in both automata are similar if their clock values agree.

Suppose the non-clock components of two extended states from these two automata are the same. If these states agree on the integral parts of their clock values as well as on the ordering of the fractional parts of their clock values, then the runs beginning from these extended states are similar. Note that the values of the integral parts of clocks can be unbounded. However, we are only interested in those values that are less than or equal to the largest integer c appearing in clock constraints since these bounded values satisfy these clock constraints and determine allowed execution paths. We now formalize these ideas.

A positive real number t can be expressed as $\lfloor t \rfloor + fract(t)$ and hence has two parts: the integral part $\lfloor t \rfloor$ and the fractional part $fract(t)$. Suppose for each $i \in C$, c_i is the largest integer that i is compared to in some clock constraint. We first define an equivalence relation called *time-abstract bisimulation*.

Time-Abstract Bisimulation: The equivalence relation "$\sim$," also known as the *time-abstract bisimulation*, over the set of clock interpretations for C is defined as follows. $v \sim v'$ iff all three of these conditions hold:

1. For all $i \in C$, either $\lfloor v(i) \rfloor = \lfloor v'(i) \rfloor$ or $v(i) > c_i$ and $v'(i) > c_i$.
2. For all $i, j \in C$ where $v(i) \leq c_i$ and $v(j) \leq c_j$, $fract(v(i)) \leq fract(v(j))$ iff $fract(v'(i)) \leq fract(v'(j))$.
3. For all $i \in C$ where $v(i) \leq c_i$, $fract(v(i)) = 0$ iff $fract(v'(i)) = 0$.

Clock Region: A *clock region* for automaton α is an equivalence class of clock interpretations induced by $\sim$.

We can define each clock region by specifying:

1. a clock constraint from the set for every clock i: $\{i = c | c = 0, \ldots, c_i\} \cup \{c - 1 < i < c | c = 1, \ldots, c_i\} \cup \{i > c_i\}$, and
2. whether $fract(i)$ is $<, =,$ or $> fract(j)$ for every pair of clocks i and j where $c - 1 < i < c$ and $d - 1 < j < d$ appear in the clock constraint in (1) for some c and d.

The number of these clock regions as specified above is bounded but is exponential in the encoding of the clock constraints. A clock region R is said to *satisfy* a clock constraint δ iff every clock interpretation v in R satisfies δ.

Recall that v is a clock interpretation for a finite set C of clocks. The notation $[v]$ indicates the clock region containing v; that is, v belongs to the clock region $[v]$. Furthermore, we uniquely characterize each clock region by specifying a finite set of clock constraints that the region satisfies.

Example. A clock region: Suppose there are two clocks (i and j) in a timed transition table, $c_i = 1$ and $c_j = 2$. There are 8 clock regions, as shown in Figure 7.3.

The notion of region equivalence is very important in grouping related clock interpretations together into a single clock region, thus making analysis manageable, as we will see later. The following time-abstract transition relation over the (time) extended states helps illustrate the usefulness of the concept of region equivalence.

Time-Abstract Transition Relation over Extended States: Given an alphabet symbol a, for two extended states $\langle s, v \rangle$ and $\langle s', v' \rangle$, $\langle s, v \rangle \overset{a}{\rightarrow} \langle s', v' \rangle$ iff there is an edge $\langle s, s', a, \lambda, \delta \rangle$ and a time increment t (a positive real number) such that $v + t$ satisfies δ and $v' = [\lambda \rightarrow 0](v + t)$.

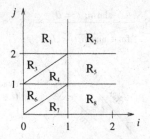

Figure 7.3   Clock regions for two clocks, $c_i = 1$ and $c_j = 2$.

Property of Time-Abstract Bisimulation (Equivalence Relation $\sim$): If $v_i \sim v_j$ and $\langle s, v_i \rangle \xrightarrow{a} \langle s', v_i' \rangle$, then a clock interpretation v_j' exists such that $v_i' \sim v_j'$ and $\langle s, v_j \rangle \xrightarrow{a} \langle s', v_j' \rangle$.

Given an automaton with a clock constraint δ, if two clock interpretations are equivalent ($v \sim v'$), then v satisfies δ iff v' satisfies δ.

7.3.2   Region Automaton

Having defined a clock region as an equivalence class of potentially infinite clock interpretations, we now aggregate every group of equivalent (time) extended states into a single region-state. This leads to the definition of a *region automaton $R(A)$* where A is the original timed automaton. Each state $\langle s, p \rangle$ in the region automaton consists of the state $s \in S$ of the corresponding timed automaton and the clock region p, which is the equivalence class of the current clock values.

The region automaton simulates the corresponding timed automaton by following these rules. If the extended state of A is $\langle s, v \rangle$, then the corresponding state of $R(A)$ is $\langle s, [v] \rangle$. A transition exists in $R(A)$ from state $\langle s, p \rangle$ to state $\langle s', p' \rangle$ labeled with a iff in A a transition exists from state $\langle s, v \rangle$ with $v \in p$ to state $\langle s', v' \rangle$ labeled with a for some $v' \in p'$.

Projection: The projection $[r] = (\bar{s}, [\bar{v}])$ of a run $r = (\bar{s}, \bar{v})$ of automaton A of the form

$$r : \langle s_0, v_0 \rangle \xrightarrow{\rho_1, \tau_1} \langle s_1, v_1 \rangle \xrightarrow{\rho_2, \tau_2} \langle s_2, v_2 \rangle \xrightarrow{\rho_3, \tau_3} \cdots$$

is the sequence

$$[r] : \langle s_0, [v_0] \rangle \xrightarrow{\rho_1} \langle s_1, [v_1] \rangle \xrightarrow{\rho_2} \langle s_2, [v_2] \rangle \xrightarrow{\rho_3} \cdots .$$

Progressive Run: Given a region automaton $R(A)$, a run $r = (\bar{s}, \bar{p})$ is *progressive* iff there is an infinite number of is ($i \geq 0$) for each clock $j \in C$ such that p_i satisfies $[(j = 0) \vee (j > c_j)]$.

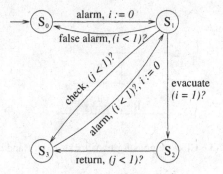

Figure 7.4 Automaton α_3.

Example. Figure 7.4 shows a timed automaton α_3 with the alphabet

$$\{alarm,\ false\ alarm,\ check,\ evacuate,\ return\}.$$

The construction of the corresponding region automaton $R(\alpha_3)$ is left as an exercise.

7.3.3 Verification Algorithm

Now we are ready to describe the Alur–Dill verification approach. A great deal of theory and definitions have been presented so far, but the main idea is as follows. Untimed automata are extended with clock variables and timing constraints on transitions to yield timed Buchi automata (TBAs), which can represent timed regular processes. Then to allow the analysis of TBAs with an infinite number of extended states, corresponding region automata are introduced.

The verification algorithm to be described can verify the correctness of finite-state real-time systems. TBAs model finite-state real-time systems. The objective is to check that the implementation of a real-time system meets the specification of this system. Both the implementation and the specification are first represented by TBAs. Then we prove that the desired inclusion, that the language accepted by the implementation automaton, is a subset of the language accepted by the specification automaton.

Given a timed process (A, L) where L is a language over the alphabet $P(A)$, if L is a timed regular language, then this is a timed regular process representable by a timed automaton. Usually, an implementation is represented by a TBA A_I that is a composition of n components with each component described by a timed regular process $P_i = (A_i, L(A_i))$. The system specification is represented by a timed regular language S over the alphabet $P(A)$, where $A = A_1 \cup \cdots \cup A_n$. The system is said to be correct iff the following inclusion is satisfied: $L(A_I) \subseteq S$. The verification algorithm is shown in Figure 7.5.

Algorithm Verify:
Given: n implementation TBAs $A_i = \langle P(A_i), S_i, S_{i_0}, E_i, C_i, F_i \rangle$ and
  specification deterministic TBA $A_S = \langle P(A), S_0, S_{0_0}, E_0, C_0, F_0 \rangle$
Construct the transition table of $R(A)$ of the product A of the timed
  transition tables of A_i with A_S.
Set of clocks $C = C_1 \cup \cdots \cup C_n$.
State $\langle s_0, \ldots, s_n \rangle$ where $s_i \in S_i$.
Initial states each of the form $\langle s_0, \ldots, s_n \rangle$ where $s_i \in S_{i_0}$.
Transition is coupling of the transitions of individual automata labeled
  with consistent event sets.
The system is correct iff no cycle in the region automaton
  satisfies all the following conditions:
  1. The cycle is reachable from an initial state of $R(A)$.
  2. The cycle has one (or more) region(s) satisfying $[(j = 0) \vee (j > c_j)]$
     for each clock $j \in C$ (the progressiveness condition).
  3. The cycle has a transition from automaton A_i for each $i = 1, \ldots, n$.
  4. The cycle has a state with an ith component belonging to the
     accepting set F_i (the fairness requirements of all
     implementation automata are satisfied).
  5. The cycle has no state with the 0th component belonging to the
     accepting set F_0 (the fairness requirement of the
     specification automaton is not satisfied).

Figure 7.5 Verification algorithm.

7.4 AVAILABLE TOOLS

[Heitmeyer and Lynch, 1994] use the Larch Prover (LP) [Garland and Guttag, 1991] to perform simple simulations proof for verifying timing properties of real-time and distributed systems specified as MMT automata.

LP is an interactive theorem-proving system developed at MIT by Stephen J. Garland and John V. Guttag for multisorted first-order logic. It is used to reason about concurrent algorithms, circuit designs, hardware, and software. LP is intended to assist users in finding and correcting flaws in conjectures during the early stages of the design process. This is in contrast to most other theorem provers, which attempt to find automatically proofs for correctly stated conjectures. LP has a convenient user interface, handles large problems efficiently, and can be used without training. LP is available at

http://nms.lcs.mit.edu/Larch/LP/overview.html

Useful information about the Larch language can be found at

http://www.sds.lcs.mit.edu/spd/larch/
http://www.research.compaq.com/SRC/larch/larch-home.html

Several tools are available that allow the specification of real-time systems as finite-timed automata and perform verification.

COSPAN (COordinated SPecification ANalysis) [Courcoubetis et al., 1992a; Alur, Henzinger, and Ho, 1996] is a verifier that supports automata-theoretic verification of coordinating processes with timing constraints. It incorporates several heuristics to speed up its performance. Experimental results of using the tool for several benchmark problems are presented in [Alur, Henzinger, and Ho, 1996]. More details about the commercial tool called Formal Check, based on COSPAN, can be found in

http://www.cadence.com/datasheets/formalcheck.html

VIS (Verification Interacting with Synthesis) [VIS, 1996] is a tool that integrates the verification, simulation, and synthesis of finite-state hardware systems. It provides a Verilog front end and supports fair CTL model checking (described in chapter 4), language-emptiness checking, combinational and sequential equivalence checking, cycle-based simulation, and hierarchical synthesis. More details about VIS can be found at

http://www-cad.eecs.berkeley.edu/Respep/Research/vis/

HSIS [Aziz et al., 1994] is a binary decision tree (BDD)-based environment for formal verification of hardware systems. It has an open language design by using a compact and expressive intermediate format, BLIF-MV, and supports a synthesis subset of Verilog. It uses efficient BDD-based algorithms (described in chapter 4) and supports model checking and language containment in a single unified environment using expressive fairness constraints as well as state minimization using bisimulation and similar techniques. It provides a debugging environment for both language containment and model checking, and automatic algorithms for the early quantification problem. More details about HSIS can be found at

http://www-cad.eecs.berkeley.edu/Respep/Research/hsis/

Kronos [Yovine, 1997] is a tool for modeling the components of real-time systems using timed automata. The correctness requirements are specified in the real-time temporal logic TCTL. TCTL extends the CTL temporal logic (described in chapter 4) to provide quantitative temporal reasoning over dense time. The tool uses a model-checking algorithm that allows a symbolic representation of the infinite-state space by sets of linear constraints. More details about Kronos can be found at

http://www-verimag.imag.fr/TEMPORISE/kronos/

HyTech (HYbrid TECHnology Tool) [Alur, Henzinger, and Ho, 1996; Henzinger, Ho, and Wong-Toi, 1995; Henzinger, Ho, and Wong-Toi, 1997] is a tool for the analysis of embedded systems with continuous variables other than clocks, such as air pressure and temperature. The model of timed automata is extended to the model of hybrid automata with continuous variables so that discrete controllers embedded in an environment with continuous variables can be modeled. This tool can derive the condition under which a linear hybrid system satisfies a temporal requirement. It allows the specification of these hybrid systems as collections of automata with discrete and continuous components and then verifies using symbolic model checking the given temporal requirements. More details about HyTech can be found at

http://www-cad.eecs.berkeley.edu/~tah/HyTech/

7.5 HISTORICAL PERSPECTIVE AND RELATED WORK

[Mealy, 1955] and [Moore, 1956] were among the first to publish work on finite automata for use in modeling electronic circuits.

[Heitmeyer, Jeffords, and Labaw, 1993] present the generalized railroad crossing (GRC) problem as a benchmark for checking the practicality and efficiency of different approaches for specifying and verifying real-time systems. Lynch and Vaandrager use their timed automaton model [Lynch and Vaandrager, 1991] together with invariants and simulation mapping techniques to solve the GRC problem. A complete discussion on this solution is presented in [Heitmeyer and Lynch, 1994]. Several researchers study the issues of decomposing a large problem into smaller subproblems for analysis. A sample of these results includes [Abadi and Lamport, 1991; Lynch and Vaandrager, 1992; Shaw, 1992].

The Lynch–Vaandrager automata-theoretic approach [Lynch and Vaandrager, 1991; Heitmeyer and Lynch, 1994] is very general and can handle finite- and infinite-state systems, but it lacks an automatic verification mechanism. The Alur–Dill approach [Alur, Fix, and Henzinger, 1994] and is based on finite automata, but it offers an automated tool for verification of desirable properties. To model continuous variables other than clocks, such as speed and pressure, [Alur et al., 1995a] recently extended the timed automata model to the model of hybrid automata [Grossman et al., 1993], which can model discrete controllers and monitors embedded in a continuously changing environment.

[Henzinger et al., 1995] studied the decidable classes of problems using hybrid automata. [Henzinger, Ho, and Wong-Toi, 1997] developed a model checker for hybrid systems called HyTech. Henzinger and Majumdar [Henzinger and Majumdar, 2000] applied symbolic model checking to rectangular hybrid systems [Puri and Varaiya, 1994]. Other work on hybrid automata includes [Alur et al., 1995a; Grossman et al., 1993; Halbwachs, Raymond, and Proy, 1994; Henzinger and Ho, 1995; Ho, 1995; Kesten, Manna, and Pnueli, 1996; Manna and Pnueli, 1993; Maler, Manna, and Pnueli, 1992; Nicollin, Sifakis, and Yovine, 1993; Olivero, Sifakis, and Yovine, 1994; Vestal, 2000; Zhou, Hoare, and Hansen, 1993].

[Abdeddaim and Maler, 2001] used timed automata for job-shop scheduling. Recently, [Larsen et al., 2001] studied efficient cost-optimal reachability analysis for priced timed automata. [Dang, 2001] investigated the binary reachability analysis of pushdown timed automata with dense clocks.

7.6 SUMMARY

Qualitative properties of concurrent systems can be formally verified using finite automata and temporal logics. These properties include deadlock- or livelock-freedom, the eventual occurrence of an event, and the satisfaction of a predicate. The need to reason with absolute time is unnecessary in these applications, whose correctness depends only on the relative ordering of the associated events and actions. These automata-theoretic and temporal logic techniques using finite-state graphs are practical in a variety of verification problems in network protocols, electronic circuits, and concurrent programs. More recently, several researchers have extended these techniques to timed or real-time systems while retaining many of the desirable features of their untimed counterparts.

In this chapter, we present two automata-theoretic techniques based on timed automata. The Lynch–Vaandrager approach [Lynch and Vaandrager, 1991; Heitmeyer and Lynch, 1994] is more general and can handle finite and infinite state systems, but it lacks an automatic verification mechanism. Its specification can be difficult to write and understand even for relatively small systems. The Alur–Dill approach [Alur, Fix, and Henzinger, 1994] is less ambitious and is based on finite automata, but it offers an automated tool for verification of desirable properties. Its *dense-time* model can handle time values selected from the set of real numbers, whereas *discrete-time* models such as those in Statecharts and Modecharts use only integer time values.

[Heitmeyer and Lynch, 1994] advocate the use of three specifications to formally describe a real-time system. A specification consists of the description of one or more timed automata. First, an *axiomatic* specification specifies the system in a descriptive, axiomatic style without showing how it operates. Then, an *operational* specification describes the operation of the system. A formal proof is required to show that the operational specification *implements* the axiomatic specification. The Larch Prover (LP) can be used to perform simple simulations proofs.

Several ways are available to construct this proof. [Lynch and Attiya, 1992; Lynch and Vaandrager, 1991] have used assertional techniques for untimed, concurrent, and distributed systems, and thus propose adapting these techniques to verify timing properties in real-time systems. In particular, the method of simulations is used to establish the relationships (such as implementation) between two specifications described by two corresponding timed automata. Here, simulations include special cases such as refinement mappings, backward and forward simulations, and history and prophecy mapping.

Several definitions exist for a general timed automaton. One variation proposed by [Lynch and Vaandrager, 1991] is defined as follows.

Timed Automaton: A timed automaton A is a general labeled transition system with four components:

states(A) is a set of states.

start(A) is a nonempty set of start states.

acts(A) is a set of actions. Actions can be internal or external. Internal actions are within the system. External actions include visible actions (which can be input or output actions) and special time-passage actions $v(t)$, where t is a positive real number.

steps(A) is a set of steps (also known as transitions).

The number of states can be finite or infinite. To improve readability, the notation $s \xrightarrow{\pi} {}_A s'$ is used instead of $(s, \pi, s') \in steps(A)$, where A is a timed automaton. The subscript A is often omitted when there is no ambiguity.

We consider the behavior of a timed automaton by observing its execution from one point in time to another. A *timed execution* is a sequence of internal, visible, and time-passage actions, connected by their intervening states and augmented with the notion of trajectories for each time-passage action.

Given a timed automaton A, of practical interest is the set $atexecs(A)$ of *admissible* timed executions in which the total amount of time passage is ∞. *Time traces* represent the visible behavior of timed automata for solving verification problems.

To model a complex system, we need to combine several automata representing different parts of the system through composition. Two timed automata A and B are *compatible* iff they have no common output actions and the internal actions of A are different from those of B.

To allow more efficient verification via simulations, the Merritt–Modugno–Tuttle (MMT) automaton [Merritt, Modugno, and Tuttle, 1991] is introduced. It is an I/O automaton augmented with upper and lower bounds on time between specific actions. The MMT automaton model can be used to represent many types of timed automata. An I/O automaton is a labeled transition system for representing an untimed asynchronous system. Its internal and output actions are grouped into tasks.

In the Alur–Dill automata-theoretic approach, to verify that an implementation of a system satisfies the specification of the system, we first represent or encode the specification as a Buchi automaton A_S and the implementation as a Buchi automaton A_I. Then we check that the implementation meets the specification iff $L(A_I) \subseteq L(A_S)$, or check for the emptiness of $L(A_I) \cap L(A_S)^C$; that is, the intersection of the languages accepted by the implementation and the languages accepted by the complement of the specification (negation of the specification) is empty.

Alur and Dill extend timed automata with a finite set of real-valued clocks to express timing constraints on non-clock variables. Clocks are like timers (or stopwatches) and thus can be reset (set to time 0). Clock values increase uniformly with time; that is, at any instant the value of a clock is equal to the time elapsed since the last time it was reset. Each transition in a timed automaton is labeled, in addition to the input symbol, with either a clock value assignment or a clock constraint. A transition with a clock constraint is enabled only if the current values of the clocks satisfy this timing constraint.

Alur and Dill extended the ω-automata to accept timed words, yielding a theory of *timed regular languages*.

Timed Transition Table: A *timed transition table* A is a 5-tuple $\langle \Sigma, S, S_0, C, E \rangle$, where Σ is a finite alphabet, S is a finite set of states, $S_0 \subseteq S$ is a set of start states, C is a finite set of clocks, and E is a set of transitions. A transition on input symbol α $\langle s, s', \alpha, \lambda, \delta \rangle$ is represented by an edge from state s to state s'. λ is the finite set of clocks to be reset with this transition. δ is a clock constraint over C.

The corresponding *region automaton* $R(A)$ for a timed transition table $A = \langle \Sigma, S, S_0, C, E \rangle$ is a transition table over the alphabet Σ.

To prove that the language accepted by an automaton is nonempty, we need to show that an infinite accepting path exists in the automaton's transition table. For a timed automaton, the timing constraints disallow certain paths in the transition table. [Alur and Dill, 1994] show that given a timed automaton, a Buchi automaton can be constructed such that the set of untimed words accepted by the Buchi automaton is the same as the one obtained by the *Untime* operation on the timed words accepted by the timed automaton. They provide an algorithm for checking emptiness for timed automata with clock constraints containing only integer constants.

Untimed automata are extended with clock variables and timing constraints on transitions to yield *timed Buchi automata* (TBAs), which can represent time regular processes. Then to allow the analysis of TBAs with infinite extended states, corresponding region automata are introduced.

The verification algorithm can verify the correctness of finite-state real-time systems. TBAs model finite-state real-time systems. The objective is to check that the implementation of a real-time system meets the specification of this system. Both the implementation and the specification are first represented by timed automata. Then we prove the desired inclusion, that the language accepted by the implementation automaton is a subset of the language accepted by the specification automaton.

Given a timed process (A, L) where L is a language over the alphabet $P(A)$, if L is a timed regular language, then this is a timed regular process representable by a timed automaton. Usually, an implementation is represented by a TBA A_I that is a composition of n components with each component described by a timed regular process $P_i = (A_i, L(A_i))$. The system specification is represented by a timed regular language S over the alphabet $P(A)$, where $A = A_1 \cup \cdots \cup A_n$. The system is said to be correct iff the following inclusion is satisfied: $L(A_I) \subseteq S$.

EXERCISES

1. Use an MMT automaton to specify the simple railroad crossing with one train rail, described and specified using RTL in chapter 6.

2. Using the notations in the Lynch–Vaandrager approach, show a timed trace of a timed execution of the automaton in exercise 1.

3. Explain the differences between the Lynch–Vaandrager timed automaton and the MMT automaton.

4. Use a single clock to respecify the example climate control system in Figure 7.1.

5. Show a run of the timed transition table for the automaton in exercise 2.

6. Suppose there are two clocks (i and j) in a timed transition table, $c_i = 2$ and $c_j = 3$. Show all clock regions.

7. How does a region automaton make it possible to represent an infinite number of time-extended states in a finite representation?

8. Construct the region automaton for automaton α_3 in Figure 7.4.

9. Specify the hospital intensive care unit monitoring subsystem in chapter 6 (exercise 2) as an Alur–Dill timed automaton.

10. Specify the smart airbag deployment system described in chapter 4 (exercise 6) as an Alur–Dill timed automaton. Compare the expressiveness and space requirement for the timed automaton model and the timed transition graph model.

CHAPTER 8

TIMED PETRI NETS

Petri nets were developed as an operational formalism for specifying untimed concurrent systems. They can show concurrent activities by depicting control and data flows in different parts of the modeled system. As an operational formalism, a Petri net gives a dynamic representation of the state of a system through the use of moving tokens. The original, classical, untimed Petri nets have been used successfully to model a variety of industrial systems. More recently, time extensions of Petri nets have been developed to model and analyze time-dependent or real-time systems. The fact that Petri nets can show the different active components of the modeled system at different stages of execution or at different instants of time makes this formalism especially attractive for modeling embedded systems that interact with the external environment.

8.1 UNTIMED PETRI NETS

A Petri net, or place-transition net, consists of four basic components: places, transitions, directed arcs, and tokens. A place is a state the specified system (or part of it) may be in. The arcs connect transitions to places and places to transitions. If an arc goes from a place to a transition, the place is an input for that transition and the arc is an input arc to that transition. If an arc goes from a transition to a place, the place is an output for that transition and the arc is an output arc from that transition. More than one arc may exist from a place to a transition, indicating the input place's multiplicity. A place may be empty, or may contain one or more tokens. The state of a Petri net is defined by the number of tokens in each place, known as the marking and represented by a marking vector M. $M[i]$ is the number of tokens in place i.

Graphically, circles denote places, bars represent transitions, arrows denote arcs, and heavy dots represent tokens.

As an operational formalism, a Petri net shows a particular state of the system and evolves to the next state according to the following rules. Given a marking, a transition is enabled if the number of tokens in each of its input places is at least the number of arcs, n_i, from the place to the transition. We select n_i tokens as enabling tokens.

An enabled transition may fire by removing all enabling tokens from its input places and by putting in each of its output places one token for each arc from the transition to that place. If the number of input arcs and output arcs differs, the tokens will not be conserved. If two or more transitions are enabled, any transition may fire. The choice of the next-firing transition is nondeterministic. Each firing of a transition changes the marking and thus produces a new system state. Note that an enabled transition may fire, but is not forced (required) to fire.

Example.   Three-process mutual exclusion problem: Figure 8.1 shows the Petri net of the solution to a three-process mutual exclusion problem. There are 10 places in this net, three for each of the three tasks, and one "shared" among the three tasks.

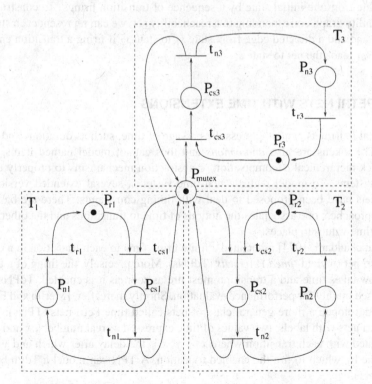

Figure 8.1   Petri net of a three-process mutual exclusion algorithm.

A dot in place P_{ni} means that task T_i is in the non-critical region. A dot in place P_{ri} means that task T_i is in the requesting (trying) region. A dot in place P_{csi} means that task T_i is in the critical section. There are nine transitions in this net, three for each of the three tasks. The figure illustrates the state of the Petri net in which all three tasks are requesting to enter the critical section. This is indicated by dots in P_{r1}, P_{r2}, and P_{r3}.

There are three enabled transitions in this net, t_{cs1}, t_{cs2}, and t_{cs3}, since the input places of each transition contain tokens. The dot in place P_{mutex} indicates that one token (privilege) is available to grant to one task to enter and execute the critical section. The task to obtain this privilege is selected nondeterministically. Suppose task T_1 is selected, then the transition t_{cs1} fires by removing the tokens from both of its input places and then putting a token in its output place P_{cs1}, indicating that task T_1 is executing the critical section. Note that transitions t_{cs2} and t_{cs3} are now disabled since the token in P_{mutex} has been removed by the firing of t_{cs1}.

After task T_1 finishes executing its critical section, it goes back to its non-critical region. This is modeled by firing transition t_{n1}, which removes the token in input place P_{cs1}, and then putting a token in its output place P_{n1} and a token in its output place P_{mutex}. Now either T_2 and T_3 may be selected to enter the critical section since transitions t_{cs2} and t_{cs3} become enabled.

Given an initial state, the *reachability set* of a Petri net is the set of all states reachable from the initial state by a sequence of transition firings. To construct the reachability graph corresponding to a reachability set, we can represent each state by a node and add a directed edge from state s_1 to state s_2 if firing a transition enabled in state s_1 leads the net to state s_2.

8.2 PETRI NETS WITH TIME EXTENSIONS

Classical Petri nets cannot express the passage of time, such as durations and time-outs. The tokens are also *anonymous* and thus cannot model named items. They also lack hierarchical decomposition or abstraction mechanisms to properly model large systems. To model realistic real-time systems, several extended versions of Petri nets have been proposed to deal with timing constraints. There are basically two approaches: one associates the notions of time to transitions and the other associates time values to places.

[Ramchandani, 1974] associated a finite firing time to each transition in a classical Petri net to yield *timed Petri nets* (TdPNs). More precisely, the firing of a transition now takes time and a transition must fire as soon as it is enabled. TdPNs have been used mainly for performance evaluation. Shortly thereafter, [Merlin and Farber, 1976] developed a more general class of nets called time Petri nets (TPNs). These are Petri nets with labels: two values of time expressed as real numbers, x and y, are associated with each transition where $x < y$. x is the delay after which and y is the deadline by which to fire the enabled transition. A TPN can model a TdPn but not vice versa.

8.2.1 Timed Petri Nets

A TdPN is formally defined as a tuple (P, T, F, V, M_0, D) where

P is a finite set of places;

T is a finite, ordered set of transitions $t_1, \ldots, t_m$;

B is the backward incidence function $B : T \times P \rightarrow N$, where N is tghe set of nonnegative integers;

$V : F \rightarrow (P, T, F)$ is the arc multiplicity;

$D : T \rightarrow N$ assigns to every transition t_I a nonnegative real number N indicating the duration of the firing of t_I; and

M_0 is the initial marking.

A TdPN follows the following *earliest firing schedule* transition rule: An enabled transition at a time k must fire at this time if there is no conflict. Transitions with no firing durations $(D(t) = 0)$ fire first. When a transition starts firing at time t it removes the corresponding number of tokens from its input places at time t and adds the corresponding number of tokens to its output places at time $k + D(t)$. At any time, a maximal set of concurrently enabled transitions (maximal step) is fired.

8.2.2 Time Petri Nets

A TPN is formally defined as a tuple (P, T, B, F, M_0, S) where

P is a finite set of places;

T is a finite, ordered set of transitions $t_1, t_2, \ldots, t_m$;

B is the backward incidence function $B : T \times P \rightarrow N$, where N is the set of nonnegative integers;

F is the forward incidence function $F : T \times P \rightarrow N$;

M_0 is the initial marking function $M_0 : P \rightarrow N$;

S is the static interval mapping
$S : T \rightarrow Q^* \times (Q^* \cup \infty)$, where Q^* is the set of positive rational numbers.

[Merlin and Farber, 1976] specifies timing constraints on a transition t_i using constrained static rational values as follows.

Static Firing Interval: Suppose $\alpha_i{}^S$ and $\beta_i{}^S$ are rational numbers, then

$$S(t_i) = (\alpha_i{}^S, \beta_i{}^S),$$

where $0 \leq \alpha^S < \infty, 0 \leq \beta^S \leq \infty$, and $\alpha^S \leq \beta^S$ if $\beta^S \neq \infty$ or $\alpha^S < \beta^S$ if $\beta^S = \infty$.

The interval $(\alpha_i{}^S, \beta_i{}^S)$ is the static firing interval for transition t_i, indicated by the superscript S, where $\alpha_i{}^S$ is the static earliest firing time (EFT) and β^S is the static latest firing time (LFT). In general, for states other than the initial state, the firing intervals in the firing domain will be different from the static intervals. These dynamic lower and upper bounds are denoted α_i and β_i, respectively, and are called simply EFT and LFT, respectively.

Both the static and dynamic lower and upper bounds are relative to the instant at which t_i is enabled. If t_i is enabled at time θ, then while t_i is continuously enabled, it must fire only in the time interval between $\theta + \alpha_i^S$ (or $\theta + \alpha_i$) and $\theta + \beta_i^S$ (or $\theta + \beta_i$).

For modeling real-time systems, EFT corresponds to the delay before a transition can be fired, and LFT is the deadline by which a transition must fire. In Merlin's model, time can be either discrete or dense. Also, the firing of a transition happens instantaneously; that is, firing a transition takes no time.

If there is no time interval associated with a transition, this transition is a classical Petri net transition and the time interval can be defined as $\alpha_i^S = 0, \beta_i^S = \infty$. This indicates that an enabled transition may fire, but is not forced (required) to fire. Therefore, TPNs are timed restrictions of Petri nets.

TPN States: A state S of a TPN is a pair (M, I) where M is a marking, and I is a firing interval set which is a vector of possible firing times.

For each transition enabled by marking M, a corresponding entry exists of the form (EFT,LFT) in I. Since the number of transitions enabled by a marking varies, the number of entries in I also varies as the Petri net runs. If the enabled transitions are ordered (numbered) in I, then entry i in I is the ith transition in the set of transitions enabled by M.

Example. For the example Petri net in Figure 8.1, $M = P_{r1}(1), P_{r2}(1), P_{r3}(1),$ $P_{mutex}(1)$. Four places are marked, each containing one token. There are three enabled transitions: $t_{cs1}, t_{cs2},$ and t_{cs3}. Suppose I has the following three time interval entries: $(1, 6)$ $(2, 7)$ $(3, 8)$. Transition t_{cs1} may fire at any time between 1 and 6. Transition t_{cs2} may fire at any time between 2 and 7. Transition t_{cs3} may fire at any time between 3 and 8. Note that as soon as one transition fires, the other two become disabled.

Conditions for Firing Enabled Transitions   Again, assuming the current TPN state $S = (M, I)$, a subset of the set of all enabled transitions may fire owing to the EFT and LFT timing restrictions on these transitions. Formally, a transition t_i is firable from state S at time $\theta + \delta$ iff both of the following conditions hold:

1. t_i is enabled by marking M at time θ under the usual enabling condition of classical Petri nets; that is, $\forall p(M(p) \geq B(t_i, p))$; and
2. δ is at least EFT of t_i and at most the minimum of the LFTs of all transitions enabled by M; that is, EFT of $t_i \leq \delta \leq \min(\text{LFTs of } t_k \text{ enabled by } M)$.

The reason for condition (2) is as follows. Suppose t_j is the transition with the smallest LFT among all enabled transitions. Then t_j must fire at time $\delta = \text{LFT}_j$ if no other enabled transition has fired, modifying the marking and thus the state of the TPN.

The firing of a transition t_i at relative time δ leads the TPN to a new state $S' = (M', I')$, which can be derived as follows:

1. The new marking M' is derived with the usual Petri nets rule: $\forall p M'(p) = M'(p) - B(t_i, p) + F(t_i, p)$.
2. To derive the new set of time intervals I', we first remove from I the intervals associated with the transitions that are disabled after firing t_i. Note that t_i is also diabled after its firing. Then we shift the remaining time intervals by δ towards the origin of times, truncating them if necessary to obtain nonnegative values. This corresponds to incrementing time by δ. Finally, we add to I the static intervals of the newly enabled transitions, yielding I'. Thus the domain of the new state is the product of the time intervals of the remaining enabled transitions and those of the newly enabled transitions.

We use the following notation to denote that transition t_i is firable from state S at time δ and its firing leads to state S':

$$S \xrightarrow{(t_i, \delta)} S'.$$

Firing Schedule: A *firing schedule* is a sequence of pairs $(t_i, \delta_1)(t_2, \delta_2) \cdots (t_n, \delta_n)$. This schedule is feasible from state S iff states exist such that

$$S \xrightarrow{(t_1, \delta_1)} S_1 \xrightarrow{(t_2, \delta_2)} S_2 \cdots \longrightarrow S_{n-1} \xrightarrow{(t_n, \delta_n)} S_n.$$

With this definition, we can construct the reachability graph to characterize the behavior of a TPN. However, as in other state space graphs, this reachability graph may have an infinite number of states and hence cannot be constructed in practice. Some simulation techniques that do not require the construction of the entire reachability graph have been proposed but are not appropriate for the analysis of safety-critical real-time systems. Later in this chapter we describe an efficient exhaustive analysis technique for a class of TPNs.

Example. For the example Petri net in Figure 8.1,

$$M_0 = P_{r1}(1), P_{r2}(1), P_{r3}(1), P_{mutex}(1).$$

$$I_0 = (1, 8)(2, 7)(3, 6).$$

Therefore, any one of the three transitions $t_{cs1}, t_{cs2}, t_{cs3}$ may fire according to the following timing restrictions. Transition t_{cs1} may fire in the period between relative time 1 (the EFT of (1,8)) and relative time 6 (the minimum of the LFTs (6,7,8) of the intervals for the three enabled transitions). Similarly, transition t_{cs2} may fire in the period between relative time 2 (the EFT of $(2, 7)$) and relative time 6; and transition t_{cs3} may fire in the period between relative time 3 (the EFT of $(3, 6)$) and relative time 6. The choice of which transition to fire is nondeterministic.

Thus at any time δ_1 within the infinite number of real values in interval $(1, 6)$, firing t_{cs1} leads to state $S_1 = (M_1, I_1)$:

$$M_1 = p_{cs1}(1), \ p_{r2}(1), \ p_{r3}(1) \quad \text{and}$$

$$I_1 = (1, 2).$$

Notice transitions t_{cs2} and t_{cs3} have been disabled by the firing of t_{cs1} and thus their associated time intervals are removed from I. Also, transition t_{cs1} is disabled after its own firing. Transition t_{n1} has enabled t_{cs1} and so the associated time interval $(1, 2)$ is added to I.

Next, there is only one enabled transition to fire. Firing t_{n1} leads to state $S_2 = (M_2, I_2)$:

$$M_1 = p_{n1}(1), \ p_{r2}(1), \ p_{r3}(1) \quad \text{and}$$

$$I_1 = (2, 4).$$

8.2.3 High-Level Timed Petri Nets

High-level timed Petri nets (HLTPNs), or time environment/relationship nets (TERNs) [Ghezzi et al., 1991], integrate functional and temporal descriptions in the same model. In particular, HLTPNs provide features that can precisely model the identities of a system's components as well as their logical and timing properties and relationships. A HLTPN is a classical Petri net augmented with the following features.

For each place, a restriction exists on the type of tokens that can mark it; for example, each place has one or more types. If any type of token can mark a place, then this place has the same meaning as in a classical Petri net. Each token has a time-stamp indicating its creation time (or birth date) and a data structure for storing its associated data.

Each transition has a predicate that determines when and how the transition is enabled. This is similar to a transition in TPNs but is more elaborate. In HLTPNs, this predicate expresses constraints based on the values of the data structures and time-stamps of the tokens in the input places. A transition also has an action that specifies the values of the data to be associated with the tokens produced by the transition firing. This action depends on the data and time-stamps of the tokens removed by the firing. Finally, a transition has a time function that specifies the minimum and maximum firing times. This function depends also on the data and time-stamps of the tokens removed by the firing. Graphically, a transition is represented by a box or rectangle.

Environment/Relationship Nets We first more formally describe environment/relationship (ER) nets without timing extensions. Tokens in ER nets are environments, functions that associate values to variables. Each transition has an associated action that specifies the types of tokens for enabling the transitions and the types of tokens produced by the firing. More precisely, in an ER net:

1. Tokens are environments or possibly partial functions on ID and $V: ID \rightarrow V$, where I is a set of identifiers and V is a set of values. $\text{ENV} = V^{ID}$ is the set of all environments.

2. Each transition t has an associated action, which is a relationship: $\alpha(t) \subseteq \text{ENV}^{k(t)} \times \text{ENV}^{h(t)}$, where $k(t)$ and $h(t)$ are the cardinalities of the preset and postset of transition t, respectively. The weight of each arc is 1. Also, $h(t) > 0$ for all t. The predicate of transition t, denoted $\pi(t)$, is the projection of $\alpha(t)$ on $\text{ENV}^{k(t)}$.

3. A marking M is an assignment of multisets of environments to places.

4. In a marking M, a transition t is enabled iff for every input place p_i of t, at least one token env_i exists such that the enabling tuple $\langle env_1, \ldots, env_{k(t)} \rangle \in \pi(t)$. More than one enabling tuple may exist for transition t, and a token may appear in more than one enabling tuple.

5. A firing is a triple $x = \langle \text{enab}, t, \text{prod} \rangle$, where enab is the input tuple, prod is the output tuple, and $\langle \text{enab}, \text{prod} \rangle \in \alpha(t)$.

6. In a marking M, the firing $\langle \text{enab}, t, \text{prod} \rangle$ occurs by removing the enabling tuple enab from the input places of transition T and storing the tuple prod in the output places of transition T, thus producing a new marking, M'.

7. A firing sequence starting from marking M_0 is a finite sequence of firings,

$$\langle \langle \text{enab}_1, t_1, \text{prod}_1 \rangle, \cdots, \langle \text{enab}_n, t_n, \text{prod}_n \rangle \rangle,$$

where t_1 is enabled in M_0 by enab_1; each $t_i, i = 2, \ldots, n$, is enabled in M_{i-1} by the firing $\langle \text{enab}_{i-1}, t_{i-1}, \text{prod}_{i-1} \rangle$ and its firing produces M_i.

Example. Figure 8.2 shows a sample ER net, which consists of three places and one transition with an action:

$$token_1 = \{\langle x, -1 \rangle, \langle y, 2 \rangle\}$$

$$token_2 = \{\langle x, 2 \rangle, \langle y, 2 \rangle\}$$

$$token_3 = \{\langle x, 1 \rangle, \langle y, 2 \rangle\}$$

$$act = \{\langle \langle p_1, p_2 \rangle, p_3 \rangle | p_1.x < p_2.x \wedge p_1.y = p_2.y \wedge$$

$$p_3.x = p_1.x + p_2.x \wedge p_3.y = p_1.y\}$$

Only tokens $token_1$ and $token_3$ satisfy the predicate in the action act associated with the transition t since $-1 < 1$ and $2 = 2$. Hence only these two tokens form an

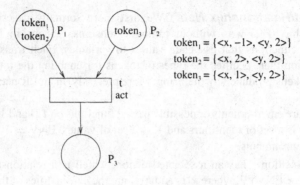

Figure 8.2 Sample ER net.

enabling tuple for transition t. Firing t produces an environment in place p_3 where $p_3.x = -1 + 1 = 0$ and $p_3.y = 2$.

In the next section, we describe in detail time ER nets, the most recent of the three time-extended Petri nets introduced here.

8.3 TIME ER NETS

To extend ER nets to specify the notions of time, a variable *chronos* is introduced [Ghezzi et al., 1991] to represent the time-stamp of the token in each environment. This time-stamp gives the time when the token is produced. The time-stamps of the tokens put in output places are produced by the actions associated with the transitions and are based on the selected input enabling a tuple's environments' values.

The variable *chronos* can take on nonnegative real numbers when used in a continuous time model, or nonnegative integers when used in a discrete time model. This concept of a time-stamp assigned to a token when it is produced is similar to the time value given by the occurrence function in real-time logic and the time value τ indicating the time of the corresponding event occurrence in timed languages and automata. An occurrence function assigns a time to the occurrence of an instance of an event. τ denotes the occurrence time of an event ρ in the pair (ρ, τ).

To enforce time restrictions on *chronos*, we need the following axioms.

Local Monotonicity Axiom: Let c_1 be the value of chronos in the environments removed by (before) any firing, and let c_2 be the value of chronos in the environments produced by (after) this firing. Then, $c_1 \leq c_2$.

Constraint on Time-Stamps Axiom: The values of all elements of the tuple prod in any firing $x = \langle \text{enab}, t, \text{prod} \rangle$ are equal to chronos. This *time of the firing* is denoted as $\text{time}(x)$.

Firing Sequence Monotonicity Axiom: The times of the firings are monotonically nondecreasing with respect to their occurrence in any firing sequence.

Equivalent Firing Sequences: Given an initial marking M_0, two firing sequences s and s' are equivalent iff s is a permutation of s'.

Time-Ordered Firing Sequence: A firing sequence $\langle t_1, \ldots, t_n \rangle$ is time-ordered in an ER net satisfying the constraint on time-stamps axiom iff for every $i, j, i < j \rightarrow time(t_i) \le time(t_j)$.

For each firing sequence s with an initial marking M_0 in an ER net satisfying the local monotonicity axiom and the constraint on time-stamps axiom, a time-ordered firing sequence s' exists equivalent to s.

Time ER Net (TERN): An ER net satisfying both the local monotonicity axiom and the constraint on time-stamps axiom, and with a variable chronos in every environment, is a TERN.

Example. Figure 8.3 shows a partial TERN for a smart traffic light system at an intersection. The traffic light for cars turns green when a car arrives at the intersection.

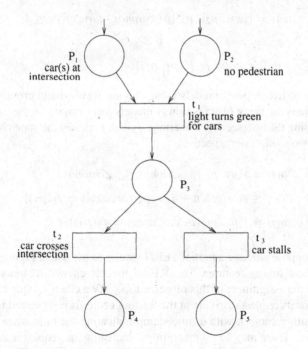

Figure 8.3   Partial TERN for a smart traffic light system.

A car arriving at the intersection is represented by a token in place p_1 (car(s) at intersection), with a time-stamp indicating the time when this car arrives and stops at the intersection. There may be no token in p_1, indicating no car is at the intersection, of there may be one or more tokens in p_1, indicating one or more cars present at the intersection. Each token contains a variable indicating the position of the car at the intersection. This is useful in determining which token (car) to be selected for making the next move, whether or not to cross the intersection. The second choice models a car stalling (staying in the same position) due to mechanical problems or the driver falling asleep.

A token in place p_2 (no-pedestrian) means that no pedestrians crossing the intersection. At most one token can be in this place.

The firing of transition t_1 models the car traffic light turning green. If the light is already green, then this transition keeps the light green. This transition removes one token from place p_1 when fired to indicate the car selected for crossing the intersection. This car must be at the front of the queue of cars waiting at the intersection (indicated by the variable position of the car token), and the time interval between the time when the light turns green and the current time cannot exceed δ_1 (so that the right of way is not monopolized by cars traveling on one street). δ_1 can be a constant or a function dependent on how busy the intersection is and the time of day. Function f_1 indicates how the status of the car changes when the light turns green and the car is selected for further action (the driver gets ready to release the brake and press the accelerator):

$$act_1 = \{\langle\langle p_1, p_2\rangle, p_3\rangle | p_3.chronos \text{ - } turn\_green \leq \delta_1$$

$$\wedge p_3.car = p_1.car$$

$$\wedge p_3.car\_status = f_1(p_1, p_2)\}.$$

The firing of transition t_2 models a car moving forward and crossing the intersection, whereas the firing of transition t_3 models a car staying in the same position without crossing the intersection. Functions f_2 and f_3 model the state changes of the car in these two scenarios, respectively:

$$act_2 = \{\langle p_3, p_4\rangle | p_3.chronos \leq p_4.chronos$$

$$\leq turn\_green + \delta_1 \wedge p_4.car\_status = f_2(p_3)\}$$

$$act_3 = \{\langle p_3, p_5\rangle | p_5.car\_status = f_3(p_3)\}.$$

Example. Suppose we have a partial TERN similar to the one in Figure 8.3 but with the use of more timing features. This TERN models clients' requests for using a resource and the assignment of this resource to satisfy a client's request.

A client (or its request) arriving at the waiting center is represented by a token in place p_1 (waiting_center), with a time-stamp indicating the time when this client's request arrives. There may be no token in p_1, indicating no request is at the waiting center, or one or more tokens in p_1, indicating one or more requests at the waiting center. Each token contains a variable *deadline*, indicating the deadline by which to complete serving the request, and a variable *valid_interval*, indicating the validity interval of the data in this request. The variable *deadline* indicates the time instant after which the service of the request is no longer useful. The variable *valid_interval* indicates the time interval within which the data is current; the data become obsolete after this validity interval. The second endpoint of this validity interval is the data's expiration time. The values of these variables determine which token (request) will be selected for making the next move, whether or not to be assigned the resource. The second choice may model the resource controller not allocating the resource to this request due to unforeseen problems.

A token in place p_2 (resource_center) means that the single resource is available for allocation. At most one token can be in this place.

The firing of transition t_1 models the resource controller ready to allocate the resource to a request. This transition, when fired, removes one token from place p_1 to indicate the request selected for using the resource. The deadline of this selected request must be less than the current time and the current time must still be within the validity interval of the request's data (the current time cannot be greater than the data's expiration time):

$$act_1 = \{\langle\langle p_1, p_2\rangle, p_3\rangle | p_3.chronos < p_1.deadline \land p_3.chronos$$

$$\leq p_1.expiration\_time - p_1.chronos \land p_3.request$$

$$= p_1.request \land p_3.resource\_center\_status = f_1(p_1, p_2)\}.$$

The firing of transition t_2 models the resource controller, assigning the usage of the resource to the selected request, whereas the firing of transition t_3 models the resource controller not allocating the resource to the request due to unforeseen problems. The assignment and usage of the resource must happen before the deadline and the expiration time of the selected request. Also, due to buffering restrictions for a request, this resource assignment must occur within δ time units after the request is selected for resource assignment:

$$act_2 = \{\langle p_3, p_4\rangle | p_4.chronos < p_3.deadline \land p_4.chronos$$

$$\leq p_3.expiration\_time - p_3.chronos \land p_4.request\_status = f_2(p_3)\}$$

$$act_3 = \{\langle p_3, p_5\rangle | p_5.request\_status = f_3(p_3)\}.$$

8.3.1 Strong and Weak Time Models

In untimed Petri nets, whether or not a transition is enabled depends on its input places. An enabled transition may or may not fire; it is not required to always fire. Hence, firing decisions are made locally. The same is true for TERNs. However, situations occur in which we have to specify that certain transitions must fire when enabled and within a certain period, especially in real-time systems. To handle these cases, the Milano's group [Ghezzi et al., 1991; Ghezzi, Morasca, and Pezze, 1994] introduces the *strong time model*, where enabled transitions must fire. To define strong TERNs, we need the following definitions.

Set of Possible Firing Times: Given a tuple i of input tokens and a transition t in a TERN, the set of firing times for i and t is

$$f\_time(t, i) = \{x \mid \langle i, o \rangle \in \alpha(t) x = o.\text{chronos}\}.$$

The following definition of strong firing sequence says that an enabling tuple must fire by a due time and there exists no other firing that would prevent it from firing later.

Strong Firing Sequence: Suppose M_0 is the initial marking of a TERN, $s = \langle s_1, \ldots, s_n \rangle$ is a firing sequence, and M_i is a marking produced by the ith firing of this sequence. s is *strong* iff it is time-ordered and for every marking $M_i, i = 0, \ldots, n - 1$ and for every transition t', there is no tuple enab' enabling t' in M_i such that $\text{time}(s_{i+1}) > \text{Sup}(f\_time(\text{enab}', t))$.

Strong Firing Sequences Axiom: All firing sequences are strong.

Strong Time ER Nets (STERNs): A STERN is a TERN satisfying the local monotonicity axiom, the constraint on time-stamps axiom, and the strong firing sequences axiom.

In fact, STERNs are a proper subset of TERNs. TERNs, which do not represent strong time models, are appropriate to represent *weak time models*. If we do not specify that a TERN is strong, it is understood that it represents a weak time model without stating that it is a weak TERN. Weak TERNs do not satisfy the strong firing sequences axiom.

It is possible to construct a strong TERN from any given TERN. One way to do this that preserves the topology of the original TERN is to add to it a new place Arbiter (ARB), which is a member of the preset and postset of every transition. The ARB environment records the global state of the net and the actions (associated with the transitions dependent on the ARB environment) are augmented to satisfy the strong firing sequences axiom. Basically, an added constraint is present in each action such that its associated transition may fire before or at a time that is the minimum of the maximum times of the possible firings of the original TERN.

To avoid increasing the visual complexity of a TERN by making it a strong TERN, we can simply interpret it as a strong TERN without introducing the new place ARB and adding the above constraint to every action.

8.4 PROPERTIES OF HIGH-LEVEL PETRI NETS

We now introduce several properties of high-level Petri nets (ER nets) and comment on how difficult it is to determine these properties. These properties apply also to TPNs and TERNs. Let M_0 be the initial marking.

Reachability Property: A marking M_k is *reachable* from a marking M_0 iff either these two markings are the same ($M_k = M_0$) or there is at least one firing sequence $\langle\langle enab_1, t_1, prod_1\rangle, \cdots, \langle enab_k, t_k, prod_k\rangle\rangle$ where $k > 0$, $enab_i$ is enabled in the marking M_{i-1}, and the firing of $enab_i$ yields the marking M_i for $1 \leq i \leq k$.

Using this reachability property, we can specify a desirable configuration that the net should enter, and using an appropriate analysis strategy similar to state-graph reachability analysis, we can check if this property is satisfied. Similarly, we may want to specify an undesirable configuration that the net should never enter, and check that this is true.

Boundedness Property: A high-level Petri net is *S-bounded* iff the number of tokens in each marking reachable from M_0 and in each place is at most S. The net is *bounded* iff a nonnegative integer S exists such that the net is S-bounded.

Using this boundedness property, we can express that the number of tokens in a place is bounded or not. Since tokens may represent instances of resources or processes, this property is very useful in specifying termination and finiteness requirements. For instance, in the smart traffic light system example, we can specify that the number of cars at the intersection is at most S.

Weak Boundedness Property: A high-level Petri net is S–weakly bounded iff the number of tokens that are part of an enabling tuple in each marking reachable from M_0 and in each place is at most S. The net is weakly bounded iff a nonnegative integer S exists such that the net is S–weakly bounded.

Since tokens in a place may have valid time intervals after which they expire, they cannot participate in enabling transitions after these expiration times. Hence, it is possible for these *dead tokens* to accumulate in a place in a particular application without an upper bound on their number. The tokens with no validity time intervals or within their valid time intervals are *live tokens* and can participate in enabling transitions. In many applications, as long as the number of these live tokens is bounded in each place in the net, the modeled application is correct even if the total number of tokens may be unbounded in a place. This scenario is captured by the weak boundedness property.

If a net is weakly bounded, each transition has a bounded number of enabling tuples. Note that boundedness implies weak boundedness, but not vice versa. For instance, tokens may represent sensor information that trigger a system response only when this information is current. Thus, sensor information that is not current can be represented by dead tokens and thus do not trigger a system response.

Transition Liveness: An ER net is *transition live* iff for each transition t and for each marking M reachable from M_0, a marking M' is reachable from M and t is enabled in M'.

This property specifies that every transition from any marking leads to another reachable marking.

Token Liveness: An ER net is *token live* iff for each token q in any marking M reachable from M_0, a marking M' is reachable from M and q is in an enabling tuple in M'.

This property means that every token in a place is live.

Net Liveness Property: An ER net is *net live* iff at least one enabled transition exists in every marking reachable from M_0.

This property indicates that there is at least one firable transition in the net.

Static-Conflict Free Net: An ER net is *static-conflict free* iff for any two different transitions t_1 and t_2, $\dot{t}_1 \cap \dot{t}_2 = \emptyset$.

Dynamic-Conflict Free Net: An ER net is *dynamic-conflict free* iff for any reachable marking M a different pair does not exist in M $\langle enab_1, t_1 \rangle$, $\langle enab_2, t_2 \rangle$ such that $enab_1$ enables t_1, $enab_2$ enables t_2, and the firing of t_1 using tuple $enab_1$ disables the firing of t_2 using tuple $enab_2$.

To determine whether a net is static-conflict free, we can check the net topology. To determine whether a net is dynamic-conflict free, we have to know the values while the net runs.

Only one general proven relationship exists among these properties: An ER net that is transition live implies that it is net live. In general, determining whether the above properties hold is undecidable. However, if we make the HLTPN or TERN specifications less precise, we are able to check some of the above properties.

8.5   BERTHOMIEU–DIAZ ANALYSIS ALGORITHM FOR TPNS

Determining state reachability is a fundamental problem in the analysis of Petri nets. The same is true for the analysis of time Petri nets. Even for classical Petri nets, the rechability problem is undecidable. [Berthomieu and Diaz, 1991] invented an efficient enumerative method to analyze time Petri nets. They restrict the static EFTs and LFTs for transitions to use only rational numbers. Furthermore, related states are grouped into a *state class* to reduce the state exploration time.

State class: A state class is a pair $C = (M, D)$ where M is a marking such that all states in the class have the same marking and D is the firing domain of the class, that is, the union of the firing domains of all the states in the class.

D can be expressed as the solution set of a system of inequalities such that a distinct variable exists for each transition enabled by marking M:

$$D = t \mid A \cdot t \geq b,$$

where A is a matrix, b is a vector of constants, and t is a vector of variables corresponding to the enabled transitions.

A state class contains all possible firing times that may happen from a given reachable marking. With this definition of a state class, we can compactly express the firing domain of the initial state class. The initial class contains the initial state and shows the initial marking as well as the initial static intervals. Whereas expressions of intervals for states are simple, expressions of domains for state classes represent complex relationships between the firing times of several transitions.

8.5.1 Determining Fireability of Transitions from Classes

Since a state class is an aggregate of many related states, we need to define new conditions for firing transitions from a class. Again assume that transition $t(i)$ is the ith transition enabled by marking M, then $t(i)$ is fireable from class $C = (M, D)$ iff the following two conditions hold:

1. $t(i)$ is enabled by marking M, that is, $\forall p(M(p) \geq B(t(i), p))$.
2. The firing interval corresponding to $t(i)$ must satisfy the following augmented system of inequalities:

$$A \cdot t \geq b$$
$$t(i) \leq t(j) \quad \text{for all } j, \ j \neq i$$

where $t(j)$ is also the firing interval related to the jth component of vector t.

Thus the firing of $t(i)$ must occur before the minimum of all LFTs corresponding to all enabled transitions. A system of inequalities is needed to express these complex relationships since using only the EFTs and LFTs of the transitions cannot adequately express condition (2).

Example. For the example Petri net in Figure 8.1, the initial class C_0 is:

$$M_0 = P_{r1}, P_{r2}, P_{r3}, P_{mutex},$$
$$D_0 = (all\ solutions\ to)1 \leq \delta_{cs1} \leq 8, 2 \leq \delta_{cs2} \leq 7, 3 \leq \delta_{cs3} \leq 6.$$

Furthermore, the following inequalities must be satisfied to fire t_{cs1}:

$$\delta_{cs1} \leq \delta_{cs2}, \delta_{cs1} \leq \delta_{cs3}.$$

Similarly, t_{cs2} can fire if

$$\delta_{cs2} \leq \delta_{cs1}, \delta_{cs2} \leq \delta_{cs3}$$

and t_{cs3} can fire if

$$\delta_{cs3} \leq \delta_{cs1}, \delta_{cs3} \leq \delta_{cs2}.$$

Suppose transition t_{cs1} fires, then the next class C_1 is

$$M_1 = P_{cs1}, P_{r2}, P_{r3},$$
$$D_1 = 1 \leq \delta_{n1} \leq 2.$$

We can determine all possible firing times for transitions, including those that remain enabled after a firing, by changing the variables resulting from the translation in the augmented system, as follows. Suppose t_{cs2} fires at relative time δ_{cs1F}. After firing t_{cs1}, the other two enabled transitions t_{cs2} and t_{cs3} are disabled. To illustrate this complex scenario, suppose t_{cs2} and t_{cs3} remain enabled. This is possible if P_{mutex} originally has, say, three tokens. Then t_{cs2} and t_{cs3} stay enabled after relative time δ_{cs1F} has elapsed. Thus the new time values δ'_{cs2} and δ'_{cs3} can be calculated by using $\delta_i = \delta'_i + \delta_{cs1F}$. Therefore, after firing t_{cs1}, we have:

$$2 \leq \delta'_{cs2} + \delta_{cs1F} \leq 7 \tag{1}$$

$$3 \leq \delta'_{cs3} + \delta_{cs1F} \leq 6 \tag{2}$$

or

$$2 - \delta_{cs1F} \leq \delta'_{cs2} \leq 7 - \delta_{cs1F} \tag{3}$$

$$3 - \delta_{cs1F} \leq \delta'_{cs3} \leq 6 - \delta_{cs1F} \tag{4}$$

where

$$1 \leq \delta_{cs1F} \leq 3. \tag{5}$$

Inequalities can be rewritten as:

$$2 - \delta'_{cs2} \leq \delta_{cs1F} \leq 7 - \delta'_{cs2} \tag{6}$$

$$3 - \delta'_{cs3} \leq \delta_{cs1F} \leq 6 - \delta'_{cs3}. \tag{7}$$

To derive the firing times of the next state class and show the relationships between the firing times of t_{cs2} and t_{cs3}, we eliminate δ_{cs1F} from inequalities (6) and (7):

$$0 \leq \delta'_{cs2} \leq 6 \qquad \text{from (3) and (5)}$$
$$0 \leq \delta'_{cs3} \leq 5 \qquad \text{from (4) and (5)}$$
$$\delta'_{cs3} - \delta'_{cs2} \leq 1 \qquad \text{from (6) and (7)}$$
$$\delta'_{cs2} - \delta'_{cs3} \leq 1 \qquad \text{from (6) and (7).}$$

8.5.2 Deriving Reachable Classes

To construct the reachability graph of classes rather than simple states for a Petri net, we first describe the rules for deriving the next class reachable from a given class by firing a transition.

Given a domain D, the following procedure derives domain D'.

1. Add the fireability conditions for transition $t(f)$ to the system of inequalities defining domain D, that is, $A \cdot t \geq b$, yielding the following augmented system:

$$A \cdot t \geq b$$

$$t(f) \leq t(j) \quad \text{for all } j, \; j \neq f.$$

   Then express all times related to variables $t(f)$, $j \neq f$, as the sum of the time of the fired transitions $t(f)$ and of a new variable $t''(j)$ defined as

$$t''(j) = t(j) - t(f) \quad \text{for all } j, \; j \neq f,$$

   and remove variable $t(f)$ from the system by deriving new firing intervals and the corresponding constraint relationships as shown earlier. This change of variables yields the following system:

$$A'' \cdot t'' \geq b''$$

$$0 \leq t''.$$

   Variables A'' and b'' are derived from A and b, respectively, the equations defining the new variables. Fourier's method is then used to eliminate variable $t(f)$.

2. Remove all variables corresponding to the transitions disabled by the firing of $t(f)$ while maintaining the relationships they imply using a similar technique as in (1). These transitions are enabled by M but not enabled by $M(\cdot) - B(t(f), \cdot)$ before computing the new marking.

3. Augment the system of inequalities with new variables such that there is one for each newly enabled transition. These variables are defined to belong to their static firing intervals. These newly enabled transitions are enabled by $M - B(t(f), \cdot)$ and enabled by M'. The final system of inequalities is

$$A' \cdot t' \geq b'.$$

A variable for each transition is enabled by marking M', and the solution set of this system defines D'.

8.6 MILANO GROUP'S APPROACH TO HLTPN ANALYSIS

The Politecnico di Milano group, headed by Ghezzi (with original members Mandrioli, Morasca, and Pezze, and later Morzenti, San Pietro, and Silva), sought to develop comprehensive tools to specify and validate large systems using HLTPNs and more recently a logic called TRIO.

Initially, [Ghezzi et al., 1991] do not introduce new analysis techniques, but rather state that HLTPNs/TERNs can be readily analyzed by executing specifications. As with non-timed Petri nets, this is done by first providing an initial marking and then executing a given HLTPN specification to explore the nets' behaviors. However, this is specification testing and can only uncover potential errors, but cannot guarantee the absence of errors if all possible execution paths are not checked. Furthermore, the number of states to be explored increases drastically with the introduction of time and may be infinite.

Ghezzi et al. also suggest analyzing specifications by first defining general properties of nets which state desirable (or undesirable) behaviors of the specified system, and then employing the specification to prove (or disprove) these properties as theorems. However, most of these properties are undecidable.

More recently, the Milano group developed a tool called Cabernet to support the specification and validation of real-time systems based on HLTPNs. While the underlying analysis mechanism is still mainly based on executing specifications, Cabernet is a more integrated tool compared to others in that it supports the specification of control, data, functionality, and time using HLTPNs. Designers can edit, execute, and analyze HLTPNs using Cabernet's kernel engine.

Cabernet can perform timed reachability analysis by exploring a time reachability tree. To avoid the problem of exploring a potentially infinite-state reachability tree, it restricts the exploration up to a specified time deadline. Using the axiom stating that time eventually increases, and a suit of symbolic execution techniques, makes the set of states in the timed reachability tree finite. This is practical in proving safety and liveness properties limited to a finite time interval in real-time systems.

To make the analysis more efficient, Cabernet can focus on a specific firing model that may ignore one or more features such as data, functionality, and time. Statecharts/STATEMATE also offers a similar capability in specifying and analyzing state systems. Thus the designer can readily customize Cabernet for a given application. Another feature of Cabernet is that it provides net decomposition, which allows the designer to refine a high-level specification to a detailed one via property-preserving transformation. The correctness of these transformations can be verified by the tool in constant time.

8.6.1 Facilitating Analysis with TRIO

Since verifying even basic properties of time ER nets is undecidable, the Milano group [Ghezzi, Mandrioli, and Morzenti, 1990] introduced a logic called TRIO to facilitate the analysis. TRIO is a first-order logic extended with a temporal domain allowing basic arithmetic and the temporal operator *Dist*. In this regard, TRIO is similar to Jahanian and Mok's RTL, which is also a first-order logic augmented with the occurrence function to assign time to occurrences of events and actions.

Given a formula F, $Dist(F, t)$ means that F holds at a time instant t time units from the current time (when this sentence is stated). If the *Dist* operator is not used in a formula, the current time is assumed. We can define other derived temporal operators based on the *Dist* operator. The following is a selected list of derived temporal operators:

$Futr(F, d) = d \geq 0 \wedge Dist(F, d)$ future

$Past(F, d) = d \geq 0 \wedge Dist(F, -d)$ past

$Lasts(F, d) = \forall d'(0 < d' < d \rightarrow Dist(F, d'))F$ holds over a period of length d

$Lasted(F, d) = \forall d'(0 < d' < d \rightarrow Dist(F, -d'))F$ held over a period of length d

$Until(A1, A2) = \exists(t > 0 \wedge Futr(A2, t) \wedge Lasts(A1, t))A1$ holds until $A2$ becomes true

$Alw(F) = \forall d Dist(F, d)F$ always holds

$AlwF(F) = \forall d(d > 0 \rightarrow Dist(F, d))F$ will always hold in the future

$AlwP(F) = \forall d(d < 0 \rightarrow Dist(F, d))F$ always held in the past

$SomP(F) = \exists d(d < 0 \wedge Dist(F, d))$ F held sometimes in the past

$Som(F) = \exists d\ Dist(F, d)$ Sometimes F held or will hold

$UpToNow(F) = \exists d(d > 0 \wedge Past(F, d) \wedge Lasted(F, d))$ F held for a nonzero time interval that ended at the current instant

$Becomes(F) = F \wedge UpToNow(\neg F)$ F holds at the current instant but it did not hold for a nonzero interval that preceded the current instant

$LastTime(F, t) = Past(F, t) \wedge (Lasted(\neg F, t))$ F occurred for the last time t units ago

The Milano group proposed the dual-language approach to specification and verification using TRIO as a descriptive formalism and Petri nets as an operational formalism. The basic idea is to first *axiomatize* (or perform an *axiomatization* of) the operational formalism (the Petri net), that is, to state a formal correspondence between the syntax and semantics of these two formalisms. Then this axiomatization is used to prove that the system modeled by the operational formalism has the descriptive formalism's properties.

8.7 PRACTICALITY: AVAILABLE TOOLS

The TRIO toolset is a facility for the specification, design, and validation of real-time systems, based on temporal logic. It is used to make the analysis of real-time systems specified as Petri nets more efficient. Ongoing work includes defining a family of languages for the specification of complex, highly structured systems, together with defining a toolset for writing specifications, validating them by means of analysis and simulation, and planning the verification of the implementation via test case generation. The TRIO research group also plans to identify classes of formulas of the language that are decidable algorithmically. Improvement in the user interface includes the implementation of a history checker, a history semiautomatic generator, a graphic editor for histories, and a model generator.

More details about the TRIO toolset can be found at

http://www.elet.polimi.it/section/compeng/se/TRIO/

8.8 HISTORICAL PERSPECTIVE AND RELATED WORK

Petri invented Petri nets to model concurrent systems, and an excellent introduction can be found in [Peterson, 1981]. Peterson also presented a tutorial on Petri nets in [Peterson, 1977].

Ramachandani [Ramchandani, 1974] was the first to introduce timing extensions to classical Petri nets to yield TdPNs. A fixed firing duration is associated with each transition. Merlin [Merlin and Farber, 1976] then invented TPNs with static and dynamic firing intervals. Merlin's TPNs are more general than TdPNs, so a TdPN can be modeled by a TPN but not vice versa.

[Leveson and Stolzy, 1987] used Petri nets to perform safety analysis of a simple railroad crossing system. In their study, the functional behavior of the system can be modeled by Petri nets, but the absolute timing aspects cannot be adequately modeled.

Jensen proposed colored Petri nets [Jensen, 1987] and Genrich invented predicate/transition nets [Genrich, 1987] to allow tokens to hold values so that items modeled by these tokens can be individually identified. However, these nets are unable to specify timing aspects.

[Ghezzi et al., 1991] developed HLTPNs or ER nets to model time-critical systems. HLTPNs provide a unified framework integrating both functional and timing descriptions. His group [Felder, Mandrioli, and Morzenti, 1994] also proposed the use of both logic and Petri net models to prove properties of real-time systems. [Mandrioli, Morasca, and Morzenti, 1995] presented techniques for automatically generating functional test cases from formal specifications of real-time systems written in the logic language TRIO.

[Bucci and Vicario, 1995] proposed the use of communicating timed Petri nets in a compositional approach to validate time-critical systems. Recently, [Vicario, 2001] presented an enumerative technique to support the reachability and timeliness analysis of dense time–dependent models. Equivalence classes are used for discrete and compact enumeration of the state space. This technique recovers timed reachability properties among states by analyzing the timing constraints embedded within equivalence classes.

[Jones, Landweber, and Lien, 1977] directly proved that the reachability and boundedness problems for Petri nets are undecidable. [Berthomieu and Diaz, 1991] developed an efficient procedure for verifying properties specified in a TPN. More recently, [Hulgaard and Burns, 1995] proposed the use of algebraic techniques to perform efficient timing analysis of a class of Petri nets. [Yoneda et al., 1991] showed how to speed up timing verification using TPNs.

[Holliday and Vernon, 1987] were among the first to propose a generalized timed Petri net model for performance analysis. More recently, [Balaji et al., 1992] employed a Petri-net-based model for evaluating the performance of real-time scheduling algorithms. [Tsai, Yang, and Chang, 1995] proposed the use of timing constraints Petri nets to perform schedulability analysis of specifications of real-time systems.

8.9 SUMMARY

A Petri net is an operational formalism for specifying untimed concurrent systems. They can show concurrent activities by depicting control and data flows in different parts of the modeled system. As an operational formalism, a Petri net gives a dynamic representation of the state of a system through the use of moving tokens. The original, classical, untimed Petri nets have been used successfully to model a variety of industrial systems. More recently, time extensions of Petri nets have been developed to model and analyze time-dependent or real-time systems.

A Petri net, or place-transition net, consists of four basic components: *places*, *transitions*, *directed arcs*, and *tokens*. A *place* is a state in which the specified system (or part of it) may be. The *arcs* connect transitions to places and places to transitions. If an arc goes from a place to a transition, the place is an input for that transition and the arc is an input arc to that transition. If an arc goes from a transition to a place, the place is an output for that transition and the arc is an output arc from that transition. More than one arc may exist from a place to a transition, indicating the input place's multiplicity. A place may be empty or may contain one or more *tokens*. The *state* of a Petri net is defined by the number of tokens in each place, known as the marking and represented by a marking vector M. $M[i]$ is the number of tokens in place i.

Graphically, circles denote places, bars represent transitions, arrows denote arcs, and heavy dots represent tokens.

A Petri net shows a particular state of the system and evolves to the next state according to the following rules:

1. Given a marking, a transition is enabled if the number of tokens in each of its input places is at least the number of arcs, n_i, from the place to the transition. n_i tokens are selected as enabling tokens.
2. An enabled transition may fire by removing all enabling tokens from its input places and by putting in each of its output places one token for each arc from the transition to that place.
3. If the number of input arcs and output arcs differs, the tokens will not be conserved.
4. If two or more transitions are enabled, any transition may fire. The choice of the next-firing transition is nondeterministic.
5. Each firing of a transition changes the marking and thus produces a new system state.
6. An enabled transition may fire, but is not forced (required) to fire.

Given an initial state, the *reachability set* of a Petri net is the set of all states reachable from the initial state by a sequence of transition firings. To construct the reachability graph corresponding to a reachability set, we can represent each state by a node and add a directed edge from state s_1 to state s_2 if firing a transition enabled in state s_1 leads the net to state s_2.

Classical Petri nets cannot express the passage of time, such as durations and timeouts. The tokens are also anonymous and thus cannot model named items. They also lack hierarchical decomposition or abstraction mechanisms to properly model large systems. To model realistic real-time systems, several extended versions of Petri nets have been proposed to deal with timing constraints. There are basically two approaches. One associates the notions of time to transitions, and the other associates time values to places.

[Ramchandani, 1974] associated a finite firing time to each transition in a classical Petri net to yield *timed Petri nets* (TdPNs). More precisely, the firing of a transition now takes time and a transition must fire as soon as it is enabled. TdPNs have been used mainly for performance evaluation. Shortly after, [Merlin and Farber, 1976] developed a more general class of nets called time Petri nets (TPNs). These are Petri nets with labels: two values of time expressed as real numbers, x and y, are associated with each transition where $x < y$. x is the delay after which and y is the deadline by which to fire the enabled transition. A TPN can model a TdPN but not vice versa.

A TdPN is formally defined as a tuple (P, T, F, V, M_0, D) where

P is a finite set of places,

T is a finite, ordered set of transitions $t_1, \ldots, t_m$,

$V : F \rightarrow (P, T, F)$ is the arc multiplicity;

$D : T \rightarrow N$ assigns to every transition t_I a nonnegative real number N indicating the duration of the firing of t_I; and

M_0 is the initial marking.

A TdPN follows the *earliest firing schedule* transition rule: An enabled transition at a time k must fire at this time if there is no conflict. Transitions with no firing durations ($D(t) = 0$) fire first. When a transition starts firing at time t it removes the corresponding number of tokens from its input places at time t and adds the corresponding number of tokens to its output places at time $k + D(t)$. At any time a maximal set of concurrently enabled transitions (maximal step) is fired.

A TPN is formally defined as a tuple (P, T, B, F, M_0, S) where

P is a finite set of places,

T is a finite, ordered set of transitions $t_1, t_2, \ldots, t_m$,

B is the backward incidence function $B : T \times P \rightarrow N$, where N is the set of nonnegative integers,

F is the forward incidence function $F : T \times P \rightarrow N$,

M_0 is the initial marking function $M_0 : P \rightarrow N$, and

S is the static interval mapping $S : T \rightarrow Q^* \times (Q^* \cup \infty)$, where Q^* is the set of positive rational numbers.

Merlin specified timing constraints on a transition t_i using constrained static rational values as follows. Suppose $\alpha_i{}^S$ and $\beta_i{}^S$ are rational numbers. Then

$$S(t_i) = (\alpha_i{}^S, \beta_i{}^S),$$

where $0 \leq \alpha^S < \infty, 0 \leq \beta^S \leq \infty$, and $\alpha^S \leq \beta^S$ if $\beta^S \neq \infty$ or $\alpha^S < \beta^S$ if $\beta^S = \infty$.

The interval $(\alpha_i{}^S, \beta_i{}^S)$ is the static firing interval for transition t_i, indicated by the superscript S, where $\alpha_i{}^S$ is the static earliest firing time (EFT) and β^S is the static latest firing time (LFT). In general, for states other than the initial state, the firing intervals in the firing domain will be different from the static intervals. These dynamic lower and upper bounds are denoted α_i and β_i, respectively, and are called simply EFT and LFT, respectively.

Both the static and dynamic lower and upper bounds are relative to the instant at which t_i is enabled. If t_i is enabled at time θ, then while t_i is continuously enabled, it must fire only in the time interval between $\theta + \alpha_i{}^S$ (or $\theta + \alpha_i$) and $\theta + \beta_i{}^S$ (or $\theta + \beta_i$).

For modeling real-time systems, EFT corresponds to the delay before a transition can be fired, and LFT is the deadline by which a transition must fire. In Merlin's model, time can be either discrete or dense. Also, the firing of a transition happens instantaneously; that is, firing a transition takes no time. If no time interval is associated with a transition, this transition is a classical Petri net transition and the time interval can be defined as: $(\alpha_i^S = 0, \beta_i{}^S = \infty)$. Therefore, TPNs are timed restrictions of Petri nets.

High-level timed Petri nets (HLTPNs), or time environment/relationship nets (TERNs) [Ghezzi et al., 1991], integrate functional and temporal descriptions in the same model. In particular, HLTPNs provide features that can precisely model the identities of a system's components as well as their logical and timing properties and relationships. A HLTPN is a classical Petri net augmented with the following features.

For each place, a restriction exists on the type of tokens that can mark it; for example, each place has one or more types. If any type of token can mark a place, then this place has the same meaning as in a classical Petri net. Each token has a time-stamp indicating its creation time (or birth date) and a data structure for storing its associated data.

Each transition has a predicate that determines when and how the transition is enabled. This predicate expresses constraints based on the values of the data structures and time-stamps of the tokens in the input places. A transition also has an action that specifies the values of the data to be associated with the tokens produced by the transition firing. This action depends on the data and time-stamps of the tokens removed by the firing. Finally, a transition has a time function that specifies the minimum and maximum firing times. This function also depends on the data and time-stamps of the tokens removed by the firing.

Tokens in environment/relationship (ER) nets are environments, functions that associate values to variables. Each transition has an associated action that specifies the types of tokens for enabling the transitions and the types of tokens produced by the firing.

To extend ER nets to specify the notions of time, a variable *chronos* is used to represent the time-stamp of the token in each environment. This time-stamp gives the time when the token is produced. The time-stamps of the tokens put in output places are produced by the actions associated with the transitions and are based on the values of the environments of the selected input enabling tuple.

EXERCISES

1. Explain the difference between an untimed Petri net and a timed/time Petri net.

2. Consider the Petri net in Figure 8.1 modeling three tasks competing to execute the critical section. There are 10 places, one shared by all three tasks, and three places for each task. If we need to model an additional task, we need to add only three more places to model the internal events in this new task. Thus the size of the net is linearly proportional to the number of tasks. However, if we model this mutual-exclusion solution as a state-transition graph or Kripke structure (chapter 4), the number of states in this state graph grows exponentially as the number of modeled tasks increases. Explain why this is the case. On the other hand, a Statechart specification avoids this state explosion in its modeling of this mutual-exclusion problem (chapter 5). Explain why this is the case.

3. Explain the differences between strong and weak time ER nets. Under what conditions should

   (a) a strong time ER net be used?

   (b) a weak time ER net be used?

4. Consider the ER net in Figure 8.2. Specify an alternate action with a predicate satisfying:

   (a) $token_2$ and $token_3$.

   (b) all 3 tokens.

5. Specify the car pedals system described as an MMT automaton using a time ER net.

6. Specify the hospital intensive care unit monitoring subsystem in chapter 6 (exercise 2) as a time ER net.

7. Construct a TERN corresponding to the example of the resource center with client requests (section 8.3).

8. Specify the smart airbag deployment system described in chapter 4 (exercise 6) as a TERN. Compare the expressiveness and space requirement for the TERN model and the timed transition graph model.

9. What is the run-time and space complexity of the Berthomieu–Diaz analysis algorithm?

CHAPTER 9

PROCESS ALGEBRA

A computer process is a program or section of a program (such as a function) in execution. It may be in one of the following states: ready, running, waiting, or terminated. A process algebra is a concise language for describing the possible execution steps of computer processes. It has a set of operators and syntactic rules for specifying a process using simple, atomic components. It is usually not a logic-based language.

Central to process algebras is the notion of *equivalence*, which is used to show that two processes have the same behavior. Well-established process algebras such as Hoare's Communicating Sequential Processes (CSP) [Hoare, 1978; Hoare, 1985], Milner's Calculus of Communicating Systems (CCS) [Milner, 1980; Milner, 1989], and Bergstra and Klop's Algebra of Communicating Processes (ACP) [Bergstra and Klop, 1985] have been used to specify and analyze concurrent processes with interprocess communication. These are untimed algebras since they allow one to only reason about the relative ordering of the execution steps and events.

To use a process algebra or a process-algebraic approach to specify and analyze a system, we write the requirements specification of the system as an *abstract process* and the design specification as a *detailed process*. We then show that these two processes are equivalent, thus showing the design specification is correct with respect to the requirements specification. Here, the requirements specification may include the desired safety properties.

9.1 UNTIMED PROCESS ALGEBRAS

A process algebra has four basic components: (1) a *concise language* to specify a system as a process or set of processes, (2) an *unambiguous semantics* to provide precise meanings for the behavior of the specified processes, showing the possible execution steps of these processes, (3) an *equivalence* or *preorder relation* to compare the behavior of the processes, and (4) a *set of algebraic laws* to syntactically manipulate the process specifications. There are several notions of equivalence. In general, two processes are *equivalent* if every execution step of one process is also the same execution of the other process and vice versa. If the set of execution steps or behavior of a process is a subset of another process, a *preorder* exists between these two processes.

A typical process algebra has the following set of operators for composing processes or atomic components to specify complex systems. A *prefix* operator specifies the ordering of actions and events. A *choice* (or *summation*) operator selects one option among several possible choices. A *parallel* (or *composition*) operator indicates that two processes execute simultaneously. A *hiding and restriction* operator abstracts lower-level details such as communicating steps to reduce analysis complexity. A *recursion* operator describes a list of possibly infinite processes. Note that similar operators are used in David Parnas' event-action model language described in chapter 6. In this chapter, we describe the untimed process algebra CCS and the timed process algebra called Algebra of Communicating Shared Resources (ACSR). We show how ACSR can be used to specify real-time systems, which can then be analyzed using syntactic and semantic techniques.

9.2 MILNER'S CALCULUS OF COMMUNICATING SYSTEMS

Inspired by Dana Scott's theory of computation, [Milner, 1980] developed a process algebra called the Calculus of Communicating Systems (CCS) to specify the behavior of untimed, concurrent, and communicating systems. He proposes the concept of *observation equivalence* of programs, and thus a *congruence relation*.

Observation Equivalence and Congruence: Two programs are *observation equivalent* if and only if they are indistinguishable by observation. Then, two programs are *observation congruent* if and only if they are observation equivalent.

Since an *observation congruence class* is considered a behavior, CCS is thus an algebra of behaviors in which each program stands for its congruence class. The syntax of CCS consists of (1) value expressions; (2) labels, sorts, and relabeling; (3) behavior identifiers; and (4) behavior expressions.

Value Expressions: *Value expressions* are constructed from simple variables, constant symbols, and function symbols signifying known total functions over values. *Labels* are $\Lambda = \Delta \cup \overline{\Delta}$, and τ. A *sort* L is a subset of Λ and a sort $L(B)$ is assigned to each behavior expression B. Given that P and Q are sorts, $S : P \rightarrow Q$ is a *relabeling* from P to Q if (1) it is a bijection and (2) it respects complements; that is, $\overline{S(a)} = S(\overline{a})$ for $a, \overline{a} \in L$.

Each behavior identifier has a preassigned arity $n(b)$ which indicates the number of value parameters, and a sort $L(b)$.

Behavior Expressions: *Behavior expressions* are constructed with six types of *behavior operators*, by parameterizing behavior identifiers and by conditionals. The *behavior operators* are: inaction, summation, action, composition, restriction, and relabeling.

The *inaction* operator NIL (null) produces no atomic actions. The *summation* operator "+" in $A + B$ adds the atomic actions of A and B, yielding a sum of A and B's actions. The *action* operator "." is used to express axioms. The *composition* operator "|" in $A \mid B$ signifies that an action of A or B in the composition produces an action of the composite in which the other component is unaffected. The *restriction* operator "\" in $A \backslash b$ indicates that B is restricted so that there are no b or $\overline{b}$ actions. An identifier can be parameterized as in $b(E_1, \ldots, E_{n(b)})$. A conditional is of the form *if E then B else B'*. The definition operator " $\overset{def}{=}$ " in $X \overset{def}{=} P$ defines process X as a more complex process expression P.

Example. Consider a system of two processes. Let N_i be the non-critical sections of process i, T_i be its section requesting to enter its critical section, and C_i be its critical section. The following CCS statement specifies that action P is the summation of three actions, each of which is a composition of two actions:

$$P \overset{def}{=} N_1|N_2 + T_1|N_2 + N_1|T_2.$$

More precisely, one choice is for the system's two processes to stay in the non-critical sections. The second choice is for process 1 to request to enter its critical section while process 2 remains in the non-critical section. The third choice is for process 2 to request to enter its critical section while process 1 remains in the non-critical section.

The following CCS statement specifies that action Q has a choice of executing the critical section of process 1 or executing the critical section of process 2. Also, while executing C_1, C_2 is not allowed. Similarly, while executing C_2, C_1 is not allowed.

$$Q \overset{def}{=} C_1 \backslash \{C_2\} + C_2 \backslash \{C_1\}.$$

9.2.1 Direct Equivalence of Behavior Programs

Behavior programs having the same semantic derivations can be considered equivalent. In fact, these programs yield an equivalent relation or congruence, thus any program can be replaced by an equivalent one in any context without changing the behavior of the entire system. For example, the programs $A + A'$ and $A' + A$ are different but obviously interchangeable. Other example rules include: $A + (B + C) = (A + B) + C$; $A + NIL = A$; and $A + A = A$.

Summation Sum $\equiv$	$A + NIL = A$
	$A + A = A$
	$A + B = B + A$
	$A + (B + C) = (A + B) + C$
Action Act $\equiv$	$\alpha\overline{x}.A = \alpha\overline{y}.A\{\overline{y}/\overline{x}\}$
	where $\overline{y}$ is a vector of distinct variables not in A
Composition Com $\sim$	$A\|B = B\|A$
	$A\|(B\|C) = (A\|B)\|C$
	$A\|NIL = A$
Restriction Res $\equiv$	$NIL\backslash\alpha = NIL$
	$(A + B)\backslash\alpha = A\backslash\alpha + B\backslash\alpha$
	$(g.A)\backslash\alpha = NIL \, if \, \alpha = name(g)$
	$else, \, = g.(A\backslash\alpha)$
Relabeling Rel $\equiv$	$NIL[S] = NIL$
	$(A + B)[S] = A[S] + B[S]$
	$(g.B)[S] = S(g).(B[S])$
Rel $\sim$	$A[I] = A, \, I : L \rightarrow L$ is the identity mapping
	$A[S] = A[S']$
	$A[S][S'] = A[S'oS]$
	$A[S]\backslash\beta = A\backslash\alpha[S], \beta = name(S(\alpha))$
	$(A\|B)[S] = A[S]\|B[S]$
Conditional	$if \, true \, then \, A \, else \, B = A$
	$if \, false \, then \, A \, else \, B = B$
Unobservable action τ	$g.\tau.A = g.A$
	$A + \tau.A = \tau.A$
	$g.(A + \tau.B) + g.B = g.(A + \tau.B)$
	$A + \tau.(A + B) = \tau.(A + B)$
Observation equivalence	$A \approx \tau.A$
	$\neg(P \wedge Q) = (\neg P \vee \neg Q)$

Figure 9.1 CCS laws.

Direct Equivalence: Two behavior programs are *directly equivalent* iff for every input, both programs produce the same behavior, that is, same results.

Given a specification written in CCS, we can use equational laws to rewrite it in a form we desire. To show that two specifications are equivalent, we can use these laws to rewrite them to establish equivalence. We summarize selected CCS laws for easy reference in Figure 9.1.

9.2.2 Congruence of Behavior Programs

The results of the actions of directly equivalent programs must be identical. To generalize the direct equivalence relation, a congruence relation that requires only the results be equivalent is introduced. Using this congruence relation, equivalence between programs is also preserved by the substitution of equivalent programs.

9.2.3   Equivalence Relations: Bisimulation

The concept of bisimulation is used to establish the equivalence between two processes. Bisimulation compares the execution trees of these two processes. Two common types of bisimulation exist: strong bisimulation and weak bisimulation [Milner, 1989].

Strong Bisimulation: A binary relation r is a strong bisimulation for a given transition "$\rightarrow$" if, for $(P, Q) \in r$ and for any action or event a,

1. if $P \xrightarrow{a} P'$, then $\exists Q', Q \xrightarrow{a} Q'$ and $(P', Q') \in r$, and
2. if $Q \xrightarrow{a} Q'$, then $\exists P', P \xrightarrow{a} P'$ and $(P', Q') \in r$.

This basically means that if P (or Q) can execute one step on event a, then Q (or P) should be able to execute one step on event a such that both of the next states are also bisimilar.

Weak Bisimulation: A binary relation r is a weak bisimulation for a given transition "$\rightarrow$" if, for $(P, Q) \in r$ and for any action or event $a \in D$,

1. if $P \xrightarrow{a} P'$, then $\exists Q', Q \overset{\hat{a}}{\Longrightarrow} Q'$ and $(P', Q') \in r$, and
2. if $Q \xrightarrow{a} Q'$, then $\exists P', P \overset{\hat{a}}{\Longrightarrow} P'$ and $(P', Q') \in r$.

9.3   TIMED PROCESS ALGEBRAS

Introducing the notion of time to untimed process algebras makes them applicable to specify and verify real-time systems while maintaining their modular verification capabilities as well as their single-language specification advantage. Dual-language specifications include model checking and the time ER net/TRIO approach. For instance, in model checking, the modeled system is specified as a state-transition graph and the property to be checked is specified in temporal logic.

The time extension is done by adding timed operators to the original set of untimed operators. Several timed process algebras exist as a result of these timed extensions. These real-time process algebras can specify process synchronization delays and upperbounds in terms of absolute timing intervals but vary in the way they model the resources used by processes.

On one end of the spectrum is the assumption that each type of resource is unlimited so that a ready process (not blocked by communication constraints, as discussed in chapter 3) can start execution without delay. On the other end of the spectrum is the assumption that a single processor exists so that all process executions are interleaved. Between these two extreme assumptions are real-time process algebras that assume a limited number of resources. One popular timed process algebra that assumes a limited number of n resources capable of executing n actions is the ACSR [Lee, Bremond-Gregoire, and Gerber, 1994].

9.4 ALGEBRA OF COMMUNICATING SHARED RESOURCES

The ACSR language is a discrete real-time process algebra based on CCS (described earlier) that provides several operators to handle timing properties. These operators can be used to *bound* the execution time of a sequence of actions, to *delay* the sequence's execution by a number of time units, and to *timeout* while waiting for specific actions to occur. The *exception* operator can be inserted into any place within a process and allows an exception to be raised, immediately handled by an external exception-handling process, just like in an exception-handling mechanism of a real computer process. The *interrupt* operator allows the specification of responses or reactions to asynchronous actions or events. The ACSR computation model views a real-time system as a collection of communicating processes competing for shared resources. Every execution step is either an *action* or an *event*.

Action: An *action* is set of consumptions of resources $\{r_1, \ldots, r_n\}$ at corresponding non-negative priority levels $p_1, \ldots, p_n$ for one time unit. A resource consumption is denoted by a pair (r_i, p_i).

The execution of an action is constrained by the availability of the the specified resources and the priorities of competing actions. For example, the action $\{(cpu1, 2)\}$ means the use of the resource $cpu1$ at priority level 2 for one time unit, and the action $\{(cpu1, 2), (disk2, 1)\}$ means the use of the resource $cpu1$ at priority level 2 and the use of the resource $disk2$ at priority level 1 for one time unit. The action $\emptyset$ indicates idling for one time unit, that is, the non-consumption of any resource for one time unit.

An *event* serves as a synchronization or communication mechanism between processes, or as an observation or monitoring step by an entity external to the specified system.

Event: Each event e_i has a corresponding priority p_i and is denoted by a pair (e_i, p_i).

The execution of an event is instantaneous and does not consume any resource. As for actions, priorities are used to determine which event to execute if there is more than one ready event. Unless synchronization constraints exist between matching events in two processes, they execute their events asynchronously.

Timed Behavior: A *timed behavior* is a possibly infinite sequence of execution steps. More precisely, this behavior is a sequence of actions in which a sequence of zero or more events may appear between any two consecutive actions.

9.4.1 Syntax of ACSR

We next describe in detail the syntax and semantics of the different types of ACSR processes. NIL is a process that performs no action and is always deadlocked. This is the same as CCS's *inaction* operator NIL, which produces no atomic actions. The action prefix operator ":" in $A : P$ indicates that the resource-consuming action A executes at the first time unit, and then process P runs. The event prefix operator "." in $(a, n).P$ indicates that the event (a, n) executes (occurs) instantly with no time passage, and then process P runs. In CCS, "." is the *action* operator used to express axioms.

The choice operator "+" in $P + Q$ is basically an "or," signifying a choice is available between processes P and Q. The effect is that this composed process may behave like either P or Q. In CCS, "+" is the *summation* operator, so $A + B$ adds the atomic actions of A and B, yielding a sum of A and B's actions. The parallel operator "$\parallel$" in $P \parallel Q$ indicates that processes P and Q can execute in parallel. This is similar to CCS's composition operator "$|$".

The close operator "[ ]" in $[P]_I$ creates a process that only uses resources in the set I. The restriction operator "\" in $P \backslash F$ indicates that while process P is executing, events with labels in F cannot execute. This similar to CCS's *restriction* operator "\" as in $A \backslash b$, which indicates that B is restricted so that there are no b or $\bar{b}$ actions. The hiding operator "\\" in $P \backslash\backslash H$ hides the identity of the resources in the set H from process P. The notation $recX.P$ signifies process P is recursive so that the described behavior of P is infinite.

The following operator allows ACSR to specify absolute timing properties. The notation $P \Delta^\alpha_t (Q, R, S)$ indicates that a temporal scope binds the process P and is called the *scope construct*. t is a non-negative integer time bound. If P ends successfully before t by executing the event α, control is transferred to Q, called the *success-handler*. Otherwise, if P does not end successfully before t, control is transferred to R, called the *timeout exception-handler*. S may interrupt P before t time units and break the binding of P to this temporal scope, that is, cause P to exit this temporal scope.

The definition operator "$\overset{def}{=}$" in $X \overset{def}{=} P$ allows one to use the process name X instead of its longer and more complex process expression P. As usual, subscripts are used to indicate indexed processes and events as in P_2 and $(e_1, k).P$. The notation P^n means that P executes or occurs n times, that is, $P : P : \dots : P$, in which there are n Ps. This is similar to the notation used in regular expressions described in chapter 2.

Note that operators such as "." have implicit timing specifications. Many notations (operators) borrow from logic operators.

9.4.2 Semantics of ACSR: Operational Rules

A labeled transition system (represented by a state space graph) is used to describe and define the executions of a process. The labeled transition system of a process is a labeled directed graph $G = (V, E)$. V is a set of states of a process. E is a set of edges, each of which denotes an execution step or action e_i such that an edge (P_i, P_j) connects state P_i to state P_j iff there is a step e_i that is enabled at state P_i, and executing e_i will modify the state of the process to have the same values as the tuple at state P_j. An invocation of a process can be thought of as tracing a path in the labeled transition system.

The states are described by a concrete syntax (a process) in process algebra. We use a finite set of transition rules to infer the execution steps of the behavior of a process. Two transition systems are available for defining the semantics of ACSR: *unconstrained* and *prioritized*.

Unconstrained Transition System: In the unconstrained transition system, $P \xrightarrow{e} P'$ denotes a transition, and no indication is given of a priority for pruning impossible execution steps.

Prioritized Transition System: In the prioritized transition system, $P \xrightarrow{e}_\pi P'$ denotes a transition, and priority information is used to ignore impossible execution steps.

Operational rules are used to define the semantics of the ACSR operators. An operational rule defines an execution step corresponding to a transition in the labeled transition system. It describes a particular behavior of a process. Two ACSR axioms exist for action prefix and event prefix. These are similar to CCS's prefix operator.

Axiom
    The following axiom is for action prefix:
    ActT

$$\frac{-}{A : P \xrightarrow{A} P}$$

Example. Consider the process $C_{1,j} \overset{def}{=} \emptyset : C_{1,j} + \{(cpu1, 1)\} : C_{1,j+1} + \{(cpu2, 1)\} : C_{1,j+1}, 0 \leq j < c_1$. The last branch $\{(cpu2, 1)\} : C_{1,j+1}, 0 \leq j < c_1$ means that this process can use the resource *cpu2* at priority level 1 for one time unit and go to process $C_{1,j+1}$.

Axiom
    The following axiom is for event prefix:
    ActI

$$\frac{-}{A : (a, n).P \xrightarrow{(a,n)} P}$$

Example. The process $T_1 \overset{def}{=} (s_1, 1).C_{1,0}$ can execute event $(s_1, 1)$ and go to process $C_{1,0}$.

The choice rules allow the selection of one option between two possible choices and are the same for actions and events. The choice operator is the same as CCS's summation operator Sum.

Choice
ChoiceL

$$\frac{P \xrightarrow{e} P'}{P + Q \xrightarrow{e} P'}$$

ChoiceR

$$\frac{Q \xrightarrow{e} Q'}{P + Q \xrightarrow{e} Q'}$$

Example. The process $C_{1,j} \stackrel{def}{=} \emptyset : C_{1,j} + \{(cpu1, 1)\} : C_{1,j+1} + \{(cpu2, 1)\} : C_{1,j+1}, 0 \le j < c_1$ may choose one of three execution steps: idling for one time unit, using resource $cpu1$, or using resource $cpu2$.

The parallel operator Par is used to specify communication and concurrency. In CCS, the parallel operator Par is called the composition operator Com. The ParT rule applies to two synchronous time-consuming transitions. The ParIL, ParIR, and ParCom rules apply to event transitions, which may be asynchronous.

Parallel Composition
ParT

$$\frac{P \xrightarrow{A_1} P', Q \xrightarrow{A_2} Q'}{P \parallel Q \xrightarrow{A_1 \cup A_2} P' \parallel Q'}$$

with $(s(A_1) \cap s(A_2) = \emptyset)$, where $s(A_1)$ and $s(A_2)$ are the sets of resources used by actions A_1 and A_2, respectively. This constraint indicates that only one process may use a specific resource during a time step.
ParIL

$$\frac{P \xrightarrow{(a,n)} P'}{P \parallel Q \xrightarrow{(a,n)} P' \parallel Q}$$

ParIR

$$\frac{Q \xrightarrow{(a,n)} Q'}{P \parallel Q \xrightarrow{(a,n)} P \parallel Q'}$$

ParCom

$$\frac{P \xrightarrow{(a,n)} P', \; Q \xrightarrow{(\overline{a},m)} Q'}{P \parallel Q \xrightarrow{(\rho,n+m)} P' \parallel Q'}$$

Example. The following shows the parallel composition of five processes:

$$Radar \overset{def}{=} [(Scheduler \parallel T_1 \parallel T_2 \parallel T_3 \parallel T_4) \setminus \{s_1, s_2, s_3, s_4\}]_{\{cpu1, cpu2\}}.$$

The scope operator is used to specify behaviors induced by a temporal scope. The ScopeCT and ScopeCI rules mean that while $t > 0$ and P does not execute an event $\overline{b}$, P's executions continue. The "end" ScopeE rule means that P can exit the temporal scope by executing an event $\overline{b}$. This label $\overline{b}$ becomes the identity label ρ on exit. The timeout ScopeT rule means that when $t = 0$, indicating timeout from the scope, control is transferred to the timeout exception-handler R. The ScopeI rule means that while the scope is active, process S may kill (interrupt) process P.

Scope
ScopeCT

$$\frac{P \xrightarrow{A} P'}{P \Delta^b{}_t(Q, R, S) \xrightarrow{A} P' \Delta^b{}_{t-1}(Q, R, S)}$$

where $t > 0$.
ScopeCI

$$\frac{P \xrightarrow{(a,n)} P'}{P \Delta^b{}_t(Q, R, S) \xrightarrow{(a,n)} P' \Delta^b{}_t(Q, R, S)}$$

where $\overline{a} \neq b, t > 0$).
ScopeE

$$\frac{P \xrightarrow{(\overline{b},n)} P'}{P \Delta^b{}_t(Q, R, S) \xrightarrow{(\rho,n)} Q}$$

where $t > 0$.
ScopeT

$$\frac{R \xrightarrow{e} R'}{P \Delta^b{}_t(Q, R, S) \xrightarrow{e} R'}$$

where $t = 0$.

ScopeI

$$\frac{S \xrightarrow{e} S'}{P \Delta^b{}_t(Q, R, S) \xrightarrow{e} S'}$$

where $t > 0$.

The restriction operator Res is used to specify a subset of events, indicated by labels, that are not allowed in the behavior of the system. Actions are not affected. Therefore, we can allow only those execution steps not involving these excluded events as specified by the given labels. This operator is the same as CCS's restriction operator.

Restriction
ResT

$$\frac{P \xrightarrow{A} P'}{P \backslash F \xrightarrow{A} P' \backslash F}$$

ResI

$$\frac{P \xrightarrow{(a,n)} P'}{P \backslash F \xrightarrow{(a,n)} P' \backslash F}$$

where $a, \bar{a} \notin F$.

Example. The following process illustrates the restriction operator:

$$Radar \overset{def}{=} [(Scheduler \parallel T_1 \parallel T_2 \parallel T_3 \parallel T_4) \backslash \{s_1, s_2, s_3, s_4\}]_{\{cpu1, cpu2\}}.$$

The set of events $\{s_1, s_2, s_3, s_4\}$ are excluded from the behavior of the above five parallel processes.

The hiding operator Hide is used to hide information about resource usage from the external environment. Events are not affected.

Hiding
HideT

$$\frac{P \xrightarrow{A} P'}{P \backslash\backslash H \xrightarrow{A'} P' \backslash\backslash H}$$

where $A' = \{(r, n) \in A | r \notin H\}$.
HideI

$$\frac{P \xrightarrow{(a,n)} P'}{P \backslash H \xrightarrow{(a,n)} P' \backslash H}$$

The close operator is used to assign private resources to a process.

Close
CloseT

$$\frac{P \xrightarrow{A_1} P'}{[P]_I \xrightarrow{A_1 \cup A_2} [P']_I}$$

where $A_2 = \{(r, 0) | r \in I - s(A_1)\}$.
CloseI

$$\frac{P \xrightarrow{(a,n)} P'}{[P]_I \xrightarrow{(a,n)} [P']_I}$$

The recursion operator Rec is used to specify infinite behaviors via recursion.

Recursion
Rec

$$\frac{P[recX.P/X] \xrightarrow{e} P'}{recX.P \xrightarrow{e} P'}$$

The operator $recX.P$ indicates recursion, and $P[recX.P/X]$ means the substitution of $recX.P$ for every free occurrence of X in P. This operator is used to specify infinite behaviors such as a system are always idle or a system never deadlocks.

Example. The second part of following statement specifies that the system is forever idle.

$$Radar \setminus \setminus \{cpu1, cpu2\} \approx_\pi recX.\emptyset : X$$

9.4.3   Example Airport Radar System

An airport radar and signal processing system is a hard real-time system. Here, we use ACSR to specify and analyze a simplified radar system. At any given time, four airplanes are approaching the airport runway and hence are detected and tracked by the airport radar. These airplanes are said to be within the approach range of the radar. Planes that have landed leave the radar tracking range. For each plane detected in the approach range, signal processing must be performed to compute vital data such as altitude and speed of the plane, and to display its graphical representation on the radar screen.

The signal processing for each tracked plane is done by a corresponding process. Obviously, a plane that is closer to the airport must be checked more often to guarantee a safe landing since there is usually more air traffic. Therefore, a process handling a closer plane must be executed more often than one handling a plane that is farther away. This means first process has a shorter period than the second process. Hence, we assign a higher priority to the process associated with a closer plane and a lower priority to the process associated with a plane that is farther away.

This scheduling strategy follows that of rate-monotonic policy (described in chapter 3), which assigns a static priority to a process; this priority is inversely proportional to the period of the process, that is, a process with a shorter period has a higher priority. In a more realistic radar system, the periods of the signal processing processes should be dynamic and decrease as their corresponding tracked planes get closer to the airport runway. However, for simplicity, let us assume that these periods are fixed. In fact, the latest version of ACSR cannot yet handle dynamic priorities. In this specification, we also assume that context-switching due to preemption of processes takes no time and an instance of a process is ready at the start of its period. We are now ready to show the ACSR specification of this radar system.

$$Radar \stackrel{def}{=} [(Scheduler \parallel T_1 \parallel T_2 \parallel T_3 \parallel T_4) \setminus \{s_1, s_2, s_3, s_4\}]_{\{cpu1, cpu2\}}$$

$$Scheduler \stackrel{def}{=} S_1 \parallel S_2 \parallel S_3 \parallel S_4$$

$$S_1 \stackrel{def}{=} (\overline{s_1}, 1).\emptyset^{p_1} : S_1$$

$$S_2 \stackrel{def}{=} (\overline{s_2}, 1).\emptyset^{p_2} : S_2$$

$$S_3 \stackrel{def}{=} (\overline{s_3}, 1).\emptyset^{p_3} : S_3$$

$$S_4 \stackrel{def}{=} (\overline{s_4}, 1).\emptyset^{p_4} : S_4$$

$$T_1 \stackrel{def}{=} (s_1, 1).C_{1,0}$$

$$T_2 \stackrel{def}{=} (s_2, 2).C_{2,0}$$

$$T_3 \stackrel{def}{=} (s_3, 3).C_{3,0}$$

$$T_4 \stackrel{def}{=} (s_4, 4).C_{4,0}$$

$$C_{1,j} \stackrel{def}{=} \emptyset : C_{1,j} + \{(cpu1, 1)\} : C_{1,j+1} + \{(cpu2, 1)\} : C_{1,j+1}, \quad 0 \le j < c_1$$

$$C_{1,c_1} \stackrel{def}{=} \emptyset : C_{1,c_1} + T_1$$

$$C_{2,j} \stackrel{def}{=} \emptyset : C_{2,j} + \{(cpu1, 2)\} : C_{2,j+1} + \{(cpu2, 3)\} : C_{2,j+1}, \quad 0 \le j < c_2$$

$$C_{2,c_2} \stackrel{def}{=} \emptyset : C_{2,c_2} + T_2$$

$$C_{3,j} \stackrel{def}{=} \emptyset : C_{3,j} + \{(cpu1, 3)\} : C_{3,j+1} + \{(cpu2, 3)\} : C_{3,j+1}, \quad 0 \le j < c_3$$

$$C_{3,c_3} \stackrel{def}{=} \emptyset : C_{3,c_3} + T_3$$

$$C_{4,j} \stackrel{def}{=} \emptyset : C_{4,j} + \{(cpu1, 4)\} : C_{4,j+1} + \{(cpu2, 4)\} : C_{4,j+1}, \quad 0 \le j < c_4$$

$$C_{4,c_4} \stackrel{def}{=} \emptyset : C_{4,c_4} + T_4$$

The first line (*Radar*) specifies that the scheduler and signal-processing processes (*Scheduler*, T_1, T_2, T_3, T_4) use only resources in $\{cpu1, cpu2\}$, that is, $cpu1$ and $cpu2$. It also says that the behavior of *Scheduler* and the four processes are limited by the events in $\{s_1, s_2, s_3, s_4\}$. The next five lines (pertaining to *Scheduler*) specify the instantiations of these four signal-processing processes. More precisely, *Scheduler* periodically instantiates a process T_i as follows. First, process S_i signals process T_i to start (become ready) by sending the event $\overline{s_i}$. Then S_i stays idle for the period p_i of the process before sending $\overline{s_i}$ again. The next four lines specify the priorities of the four processes in using a cpu according to the rate-monotonic algorithm. For other types of scheduling algorithms, we can easily change these priorities, which are associated with actions. As soon as signaled to start, each process T_i attempts to execute for c_i time units using either cpu resource $cpu1$ or $cpu2$.

The next eight lines show that a process may remain idle (no cpu usage) or may use either $cpu1$ or $cpu2$. In the first case, process T_i idles by executing the process $\emptyset : C_{i,j}$, which also means that T_i is preempted since it has lower priority. In the second case, the processes $C_{i,j}$ update the computation times used by process T_i in each cpu. Each process C_{i,c_i} specifies that after process T_i finishes its execution, it stays idle waiting for the next periodic instantiation.

The key point here is that if T_i is not allocated a cpu resource for c_i time units within its period p_i, it will not be able to synchronize with *Scheduler*, which sends the starting event $\overline{s_i}$ once in every period p_i. This will cause process S_i of *Scheduler* to deadlock, leading the whole *Radar* system to deadlock. Therefore, a deadlock in this system means the failure to successfully schedule a given set of signal-processing processes. This example illustrates that in order to determine schedulability or other feasibility conditions, we have to first specify the system in a way that the failure to satisfy the condition is equivalent to a deadlock, which can be readily checked using either syntactic or semantic analysis techniques.

9.5   ANALYSIS AND VERIFICATION

To verify that a design specification is correct with respect to a requirements specification using a process-algebraic approach, we show that the two processes representing respectively these two specifications are equivalent. Two ways exist to establish this equivalence: *syntax-based* and *semantics-based* techniques. The syntax-based technique uses a suite of equational laws to manipulate the textual representations of two processes to show that they are equivalent or not equivalent. These equational laws are similar to those used in mathematics to show that two expressions are equivalent. On the other hand, the semantics-based technique compares the two prioritized labeled transition systems representing all possible behaviors of these processes and determines whether they are equivalent. Here, semantics refers to the behaviors of the processes.

The laws in a large subset of ACSR laws are the same as those in CCS. The ACSR-specific laws include three new laws for the choice operator, one new law for the parallel (composition) operator Par (Com), six new laws for the scope rule, one

Choice(5)	$[P + Q]_I = [P]_I + [Q]_I$
Choice(6)	$(a_1, n_1).P_1 + (a_2, n_2).P2 = (a_2, n_2).P2$ if $(a_1, n_1) < (a_2, n_2)$
Choice(7)	$A : P + (\tau, n).Q = (\tau, n).Q$ if $n > 0$

Par(3)	$(\sum_{i \in I} A_i : P_i + \sum_{j \in J} (a_j, m_j).Q_j) \parallel (\sum_{k \in K} B_k : R_k + \sum_{l \in L} (b_l, n_l).S_l)$
	$= \sum_{i \in I, k \in K, \rho(A_i) \cap \rho(B_k) = \emptyset} (A_i \cup B_k) : (P_i \parallel R_k) +$
	$\sum_{j \in J} (a_j, m_j).(Q_j \parallel (\sum_{k \in K} B_k : R_k + \sum_{l \in L} (b_l, n_l).S_l)) +$
	$\sum_{l \in L} (b_l, n_l).((\sum_{i \in I} A_i : P_i + \sum_{j \in J} (a_j, m_j).Q_j) \parallel S_l +$
	$\sum_{j \in J, l \in L, a_j = b_l} (\tau, m_j + n_l).(Q_j \parallel S_l)$

Scope(1)	$A : P \Delta^b_t(Q, R, S) = A : P \Delta^b_{t-1}(Q, R, S) + S$ if $t > 0$
Scope(2)	$(a, n).P \Delta^b_t(Q, R, S) = (a, n).(P \Delta^b_t(Q, R, S) + S$ if $t > 0 \wedge \overline{a} \neq b$
Scope(3)	$(a, n).P \Delta^b_t(Q, R, S) = (\tau, n).Q + S$ if $t > 0 \wedge \overline{a} = b$
Scope(4)	$P \Delta^b_0(Q, R, S) = R$
Scope(5)	$(P_1 + P_2) \Delta^b_t(Q, R, S) = P_1 \Delta^b_t(Q, R, S) + P_2 \Delta^b_t(Q, R, S)$
Scope(6)	$(NIL) \Delta^b_t(Q, R, S) = S$ if $t > 0$

Restriction Res	$(A : P) \backslash F = A : (P \backslash F)$

Close(1)	$[NIL]_I = NIL$
Close(2)	$[P + Q]_I = [P]_I + [Q]_I$
Close(3)	$[A : P]_I = (A \cup B) : [P]_I$ where $B = \{(r, 0) \vert r \in I - \rho(A)\}$
Close(4)	$[(a, n).P]_I = (a, n).[P]_I$

Rec(1)	$recX.P = P[recX.P/X]$

Figure 9.2 ACSR-specific laws.

new law for the restriction operator Res, and four new laws for the close rule. These laws are given in Figure 9.2. The Rec operator is similar to CCS's action operator Act, but Rec uses slightly different notations, so the ACSR law pertinent to Rec is also listed in Figure 9.2. The law Par(3) for the parallel operator uses the summation symbol, $\sum$ (or sum, "+") to indicate the choice of zero or more processes.

These two analysis techniques are based on two equivalence or bisimulation relations [Park, 1981]. Bisimulation compares the execution trees of two processes to determine whether these processes are equivalent. It is also used to show that two automata are equivalent (described in chapter 2) or that two timed automata are equivalent (described in chapter 7). Two common types of bisimulation exist: strong bisimulation and weak bisimulation [Milner, 1989], as presented in the description of CCS.

There is a largest bisimulation "$\sim$" over "$\longrightarrow$." There is a largest strong bisimulation "$\sim_\pi$" over "$\longrightarrow_\pi$." $\sim_\pi$ is a prioritized strong equivalence, or simply strong equivalence.

As we have seen in the description of CCS, and unlike other state transition models, a small set of equational laws can be used to prove strong equivalence between processes. The equality sign, $=$, is used to indicate that two processes are strongly equivalent. As in conventional mathematics these equational laws can be applied many times for processes or instances of processes that satisfy their forms.

Using semantics-based analysis to determine whether two processes are bisimilar, we first construct the two labeled transition systems corresponding to these processes. Then, we combine these two transition systems. Finally, we derive the *largest bisimulation relation* for the combined labeled transition system [Clements, 1993]. To reduce the complexity of the ACSR requirements specification when trying to prove timing properties, we can ignore the identity of the resources and the absolute priorities of matching events and actions. The relative ordering of these events and actions suffices.

9.5.1 Analysis Example

We now apply the analysis technique to determine whether a given set of processes is schedulable in the airport radar system example. The maximal computation times of the four processes are: $c_1 = 32$, $c_2 = 4$, $c_3 = 7$, $c_4 = 3$. Their corresponding periods are: $p_1 = 40$, $p_2 = 20$, $p_3 = 10$, $p_4 = 10$.

Since we are reasoning with processes or their representations, the radar system represented as an ACSR specification will deadlock if a process misses its deadline. Therefore, to check whether a set of processes is schedulable, we need to show that the system never deadlocks. Since the ACSR specification also states how the resources are used and how the processes synchronize, we can simplify the analysis by ignoring (or hiding) this information about resource usage and synchronization. Thus, the processes are schedulable if the system is forever idle. Therefore, determining the schedulability means verifying that

$$Radar \setminus \{cpu1, cpu2\} \approx_\pi recX.\emptyset : X.$$

Since a feasible schedule, if one exists, repeats after each time interval of length that is equal to the least common multiple of all the periods (chapter 3), it is sufficient to prove that

$$Radar \setminus \{cpu1, cpu2\} \approx_\pi \emptyset^4 0 : (Radar \setminus \{cpu1, cpu2\}).$$

Substituting the given numerical values, *Radar* becomes:

$$Radar \stackrel{def}{=} [(Scheduler \parallel T_1 \parallel T_2$$

$$\parallel T_3 \parallel T_4)$$

$$\setminus \{s_1, s_2, s_3, s_4\}]_{\{cpu1, cpu2\}}$$

$$\stackrel{def}{=} [((\overline{s_1}, 1).\emptyset^{40} : (\overline{s_1}, 1).S_1 \parallel (\overline{s_2}, 1).\emptyset^{20} : (\overline{s_2}, 1).S_2 \parallel$$

$$(\overline{s_3}, 1).\emptyset^{10} : (\overline{s_3}, 1).S_3 \parallel (\overline{s_4}, 1).\emptyset^{10} : (\overline{s_4}, 1).S_4 \parallel$$

$$(s_1, 1).C_{1,0} \parallel (s_2, 2).C_{2,0} \parallel (s_3, 3).C_{3,0}, \parallel (s_4, 4).C_{4,0}$$

$$\setminus \{s_1, s_2, s_3, s_4\}]_{\{cpu1, cpu2\}}.$$

Next, we apply several ACSR laws to repeatedly rewrite the process *Radar* until

$$Radar \setminus \setminus \{cpu1, cpu2\} \approx_\pi \emptyset^{40} : (Radar \setminus \setminus \{cpu1, cpu2\})$$

is proved. This statement indicates that the system never deadlocks and thus establishes

$$Radar \setminus \setminus \{cpu1, cpu2\} \approx_\pi recX.\emptyset : X.$$

Deciding which laws to apply is difficult and requires a great deal of practice. The tool kit VERSA [Clarke, Lee, and Xie, 1995] rewrites the process specification only after the user directs it to do so with a specific, predefined ACSR law specified by the user. It does not automatically construct a proof. The VERSA equivalence tester can automatically convert an ACSR process specification into a labeled transition system, but the user has to assist the tool by pruning transitions that are unreachable due to the semantics of the transition system. This pruning is crucial in reducing the analysis time when checking for deadlocks or equivalence.

9.5.2 Using VERSA

The Verification Execution and Rewrite System for ACSR (VERSA) system [Clarke, Lee, and Xie, 1995] maintains as much as possible the syntax of ACSR while using ASCII keyboard-typable notations for special ACSR characters and subscripted or superscripted variables. Similar techniques are used in other analysis tools, such as the model checker for CTL [Clarke, Emerson, and Sistla, 1986]. VERSA also adds syntactic conventions from mathematics and programming languages as well as features for facilitating the specification of large systems. We summarize the differences between ACSR and VERSA in Figure 9.3.

Syntactic conventions used in *Mathematica* (http://www.wolfram.com) are employed in VERSA to define indexed process variables, resource names, and event labels. Specifications may be divided into logical components and recombined using file inclusion. We can define symbolic constants and macros using a #define notation,

ACSR:	VERSA:
$\alpha, \overline{\alpha}, \alpha', \alpha_i$	a, 'a, a', a[i]
τ	t or tau
NIL	NIL
$\|$	$\|$ *or* $|$
$P\Delta^\alpha_t(Q, R, S)$	scope(P,a,t,Q,R,S)
∞	inf or infinite or infinity
$[P]_I$	[P]I
$\emptyset$	{} or idle

Figure 9.3 Differences between ACSR and VERSA.

as in the C programming language. VERSA also provides indexed composition and set construction operators for operating on sets of indexed names.

VERSA has a query facility for the user to inquire about identifiers and the binding of process variables, as well as for comparing actions and for comparing processes for equality. For example, the query

$$T[1] == T[2]?$$

compares processes T_1 and T_2 for equality. One often-used notion of equivalence is that of prioritized strong equivalence. Here, VERSA converts the algebraic process descriptions bound to these processes to state machines and then employs a state minimization algorithm to preserve strong bisimulation to these two machines simultaneously. The original machines are strongly bisimilar if the corresponding minimal state machine contains a state with the start state of both original machines. Since this construction of the state machine from its corresponding algebraic expression requires space exponential in the length of the expression, checking for prioritized strong equivalence is restricted for algebraic expressions with small state machines.

VERSA and its graphical user interface version, X-VERSA, are implemented in C++. It is made more portable with the use of the LEDA class library, and the libg++ and X/Motif libraries. The input and output interface is built with the Lex and Yacc compiler construction tools. To make the analysis more efficient, the tool kit makes use of a low-level programming language and the latest state space construction and bisimulation testing algorithms. Indexed names are not supported in X-VERSA.

9.5.3 Practicality

Originally, the lack of a graphical input-output interface makes ACSR and its corresponding tool kit VERSA more difficult to use than other tools with a graphical user interface. Recently, a graphical language [Ben-Abdallah, Lee, and Choi, 1995; Ben-Abdallah, 1996; Ben-Abdallah and Lee, 1998] was introduced to provide a better user interface. Even when compared to several other techniques, such as RTL, writing and understanding the system specification in ACSR or other process algebras seem to be more difficult since there is an extra level of process abstraction. Also, some of the notations are cumbersome. However, the fact that several practical timing constraints are already expressed by the timing operators of ACSR makes it attractive to specify systems more compactly, whereas in other specification languages such timing constraints must be explicitly written. Since process algebras were originally designed to specify processes, their timed extensions are especially appropriate for describing resource-sharing processes with timing constraints.

9.6 RELATIONSHIPS TO OTHER APPROACHES

In the context of the Jahanian and Mok's RTL approach [Jahanian and Mok, 1986], the abstract process loosely corresponds to the safety assertion and the detailed process corresponds to the system specification. Determining equivalence of these processes is analogous to finding the relationship between the specification and the safety assertion. In the context of whether an actual system implementation exactly follows the system specification, or whether a specification is a faithful representation of an implemented system, the abstract process corresponds to the specification and the detailed process represents the implementation.

To perform semantic analysis for determining equivalence of two processes in ACSR, the process behaviors are first described as (translated into) a prioritized labeled transition system. This transition system is basically a state space graph used in other approaches such as untimed automata (chapter 2), model-checking (chapter 4), Statecharts (chapter 5), RTL (chapter 6), and timed automata (chapter 7), and thus also suffers from the state-explosion problem. However, this transition system is usually smaller since it describes only behaviors of interest to the analysis, such as deadlock-freedom. The process-algebraic method constructs a specification of a system with encoded constraints such that whenever certain safety or timing properties are violated, the specified process enters an exception state. The analysis consists of finding the set of reachable states and then checking whether the exception state is in this set.

9.7 AVAILABLE TOOLS

VERSA is a toolset with the following analysis functions:

1. derivation of system properties from ACSR specifications using rewriting rules;
2. generation and analysis of the state space to verify safety properties, and testing of equivalence of different process formulations;
3. interactive execution of the process specification to study specific system behaviors.

The basic version of VERSA has a command-oriented interface for inputting process descriptions, binding them to identifiers, and operating on them. The graphics-oriented version of VERSA provides an X/Motif user interface, known as X-VERSA, with a point-and-click interface. This significantly improves the usability of the algebraic term rewriting facility. VERSA extends the basic ACSR syntax with a number of notational conventions borrowed from programming languages. VERSA is available at

http://www.cis.upenn.edu/~lee/duncan/versa.html

9.8 HISTORICAL PERSPECTIVE AND RELATED WORK

Process algebras were first developed to specify and analyze concurrent processes in distributed systems without absolute timing characteristics. These algebras include Hoare's CSP [Hoare, 1978; Hoare, 1985], Milner's CCS [Milner, 1980; Milner, 1989], and Bergstra and Klop's ACP [Bergstra and Klop, 1985].

Because of their capabilities in specifying systems and manipulating their specifications in compact forms, process algebras have been extended recently by several researchers to handle the notion of real time. Reed and Roscoe proposed a timed version of CSP called Timed CSP [Reed and Roscoe, 1987]. The ISO specification standard LOTOS [Bolognesi and Brinksma, 1987] is based on CSP, and a timed version of LOTOS called Timed LOTOS has been used to specify and analyze a number of industrial systems. Baeten and Bergstra extended ACP to produce a timed version of ACP [Baeten and Bergstra, 1991]. [Aceto and Murphy, 1993] also considered adding the notion of time to process algebras. [Moller and Tofts, 1990] extended CCS to yield a Temporal Calculus of Communicating Systems (TCCS). [Nicollin and Sifakis, 1991] introduced the Algebra of Timed Processes (ATP) and show its applications. [Yi, 1991] added the notion of time to CCS and proposed an interleaving model for specifying and verifying real-time systems.

Lee's group's first proposal to add the notion of time to process algebras produced a real-time algebra without the notions of resources and priorities [Zwarico, 1988]. Later, [Gerber and Lee, 1989; Gerber and Lee, 1990] extended CCS to yield a Calculus of Communicating Shared Resources (CCSR), the first timed process algebra to support the notions of both resources and priorities. More recently, Lee's group added instantaneous synchronization events to CCSR to yield ACSR [Bremond-Gregoire, 1994; Lee, Bremond-Gregoire, and Gerber, 1994]. To improve the user interface, [Ben-Abdallah, Lee, and Choi, 1995; Ben-Abdallah, 1996; Ben-Abdallah and Lee, 1998] introduced a graphical language called GCSR together with a formal semantics specifying and analyzing real-time systems. [Ben-Abdallah et al., 1998] and [Choi, Lee, and Xie, 1995] also applied the process-algebraic approach to analyze the schedulability of real-time systems.

9.9 SUMMARY

A process algebra is a concise language (usually not logic-based) for describing the possible execution steps of computer processes. It has a set of operators and syntactic rules for specifying a process using simple, atomic components. Process algebras use the notion of *equivalence* to show that two processes have the same behavior. Well-established process algebras such as Hoare's Communicating Sequential Processes (CSP) [Hoare, 1978; Hoare, 1985], Milner's Calculus of Communicating Systems (CCS) [Milner, 1980; Milner, 1989], and Bergstra and Klop's Algebra of Communicating Processes (ACP) [Bergstra and Klop, 1985] have been used to specify and analyze concurrent processes with interprocess communication. These are untimed algebras since they allow one to only reason about the relative ordering of execution steps and events.

To use a process algebra or a process-algebraic approach to specify and analyze a system, we write the requirements specification of the system as an *abstract process* and the design specification as a *detailed process*. We then show that these two processes are equivalent, thus showing the design specification is correct with respect to the requirements specification. Here, the requirements specification may include the desired safety properties.

A process algebra has four basic components: (1) a *concise language* to specify a system as a process or set of processes, (2) an *unambiguous semantics* to provide precise meanings for the behavior of the specified processes, showing the possible execution steps of these processes, (3) an *equivalence* or *preorder relation* to compare the behavior of the processes, and (4) a *set of algebraic laws* to syntactically manipulate the process specifications.

To specify and verify real-time systems while maintaining their modular verification capabilities as well as their single-language specification advantage, untimed process algebras have been extended with the notion of time by adding timed operators to the original set of untimed operators. Several timed process algebras exist as a result of these timed extensions. These real-time process algebras can specify process synchronization delays and upperbounds in terms of absolute timing intervals but vary in the way they model the resources used by processes.

On one end of the spectrum is the assumption that each type of resources is unlimited so that a ready process (not blocked by communication constraints, as discussed in chapter 3) can start execution without delay. On the other end of the spectrum is the assumption that a single processor exists so that all process executions are interleaved. Between these two extreme assumptions, real-time process algebras assume a limited number of resources. One popular timed process algebra that assumes a limited number of n resources capable of executing n actions is the Algebra of Communicating Shared Resources (ACSR) [Lee, Bremond-Gregoire, and Gerber, 1994].

The ACSR language is a discrete real-time process algebra based on CCS (described earlier) that provides several operators to handle timing properties. Two ways are available to establish equivalence: *syntax-based* and *semantics-based* techniques. The VERSA system [Clarke, Lee, and Xie, 1995] maintains as much as possible the syntax of ACSR while using ASCII keyboard-typable notations for special ACSR characters and subscripted or superscripted variables. Here, VERSA converts the algebraic-process descriptions bound to these processes to state machines and then employs a state minimization algorithm to preserve strong bisimulation simultaneously to these two machines. The original machines are strongly bisimilar if the corresponding minimal state machine contains a state with the start state of both original machines. Since this construction of the state machine from its corresponding algebraic expression requires space exponential in the length of the expression, checking for prioritized strong equivalence is restricted for algebraic expressions with small state machines.

EXERCISES

1. How do process-algebraic techniques such as those based on CCS and ACSR verify that two system specifications have the same behavior without exploring their state representations (such as finite-state machines)?

2. Use CCS laws to determine whether the following two statements are equivalent:

   (a) $((P + (Q + R))|(S + (T + V)))|(X + Y)$
   (b) $((Y + X)|((V + S) + T))|((P + Q) + R)$.

3. Use CCS to specify the solution to the two-process mutual-exclusion problem.

4. Use the definition operator to specify a recursive process without using the *rec* operator.

5. How does ACSR extend CCS to allow the specification of real-time systems? Describe the timing-related operator.

6. The radar system specified using ACSR employs a rate-monotonic scheduler to assign priorities to its signal-processing tasks. It also has two resources, *cpu*1 and *cpu*2.

   (a) Suppose the least-laxity scheduler is used instead to assign task priorities. Rewrite the ACSR specification.

   (b) Suppose one resource *cpu* and one resource *disk* are available. A signal-processing task must use *cpu* for a certain amount of time and then use *disk* for a certain amount of time. Rewrite the ACSR specification.

7. Explain the difference between syntactic analysis and semantic analysis. Is it possible to find two processes that cannot be shown to be equivalent using syntactic analysis but can be proved to be equivalent using semantic analysis?

8. Specify the mobile telephone/entertainment system described in chapter 4 (exercise 5) as an ACSR process.

9. Specify the smart airbag deployment system described in chapter 4 (exercise 6) as an ACSR process. Compare the expressiveness and space requirement for the ACSR model and the timed transition graph model.

CHAPTER 10

DESIGN AND ANALYSIS OF PROPOSITIONAL-LOGIC RULE-BASED SYSTEMS

Real-time decision systems are computer-controlled systems that must react to events in the external environment by making decisions based on sensor inputs and state information sufficiently fast to meet environment-imposed timing constraints. They are used in applications that would require human expertise if such decision systems were not available. Human beings tend to be overwhelmed by a transient information overload resulting from an emergency situation, thus expert systems are increasingly used under many circumstances to assist human operators. As the complexity of tools and machineries increases, it is obvious that more intelligent and thus more complex embedded decision systems are expected to be developed and installed to monitor and control the environments in which they are embedded.

Since the solutions to many of these decision problems are often nondeterministic or cannot be easily expressed in algorithmic form, these applications increasingly employ rule-based (or knowledge-based) expert systems. In recent years, such systems are also increasingly used to monitor and control the operations of complex safety-critical real-time systems. This chapter gives an introduction to real-time expert systems by describing a class of these systems in which decisions are computed by propositional-logic rule-based programs implemented in the *equational logic language EQL*.

We begin by describing EQL and we present several examples. The notion of the state space of an equational rule-based program is then introduced. Next, we demonstrate the use of a set of analysis tools that have been implemented to perform timing and safety analyses of real-time equational rule-based programs. The theoretical formulation and solution strategies of the relevant analysis and synthesis problems are then given. Complexity issues of the various analysis and synthesis problems are also discussed. Next, we present the specification language Estella for customizing the analysis tool. Finally, we describe quantitative algorithms for predicting the timing performance of rule-based systems.

To show that the analysis tools are practical enough to verify realistic real-time decision systems, we have used them to analyze several rule-based systems, including a subset of the Cryogenic Hydrogen Pressure Malfunction Procedure in the Pressure Control System of the Space Shuttle Vehicle [Helly, 1984]. This malfunction procedure is used to warn Shuttle pilots and operators of possible malfunctions of the pressure control system and to give helpful advice for correcting possible malfunctions.

10.1   REAL-TIME DECISION SYSTEMS

A real-time decision system interacts with the external environment by taking sensor readings and computing control decisions based on these readings and stored state information. We can characterize a real-time decision system by the following model with seven components:

1. a sensor vector $\bar{x} \in X$,
2. a decision vector $\bar{y} \in Y$,
3. a system state vector $\bar{s} \in S$,
4. a set of environmental constraints A,
5. a decision map D, $D : S \times X \to S \times Y$,
6. a set of timing constraints T, and
7. a set of integrity constraints I.

In this model, X is the space of sensor input values, Y is the space of decision values, and S is the space of system state values. (We shall use $\bar{x}(t)$ to denote the value of the sensor input $\bar{x}$ at time t, etc.)

The environmental constraints A are relations over X, Y, S and are assertions about the effect of a control decision on the external world which in turn affect future sensor input values. Environmental constraints are usually imposed by the physical environment in which the real-time decision system functions.

The decision map D relates $\bar{y}(t + 1), \bar{s}(t + 1)$ to $\bar{x}(t), \bar{s}(t)$; that is, given the current system state and sensor input, D determines the next decisions and system state values. For our purpose, decision maps are implemented by equational rule-based programs.

The decisions specified by D must conform to a set of integrity constraints I. Integrity constraints are relations over X, S, Y and are assertions that the decision map D must satisfy to ensure safe operation of the physical system under control. The implementation of the decision map D is subject to a set of timing constraints T which are assertions about how fast the map D has to be performed. Figure 10.1 illustrates the model of a real-time decision system.

Let us consider a simple example of a real-time decision system. Suppose we want to automate a toy race car so that it will drive itself around a track as fast as

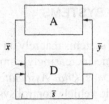

- Environment constraints:
  A relates $\bar{x}(t+1)$ with $\bar{y}(t)$
- Decision system:
  D relates $\bar{y}(t+1), \bar{s}(t+1)$ with $\bar{x}(t), \bar{s}(t)$
- D is subject to:
  - integrity constraints I: assertions over $\bar{s}, \bar{y}$
  - timing constraints T

Figure 10.1   A real-time decision system.

possible. The sensor vector consists of variables denoting the position of the car and the distance to the next obstacle ahead. The decision vector consists of two variables: one to indicate whether to accelerate, decelerate, or maintain the same speed, and another to indicate whether to turn left, turn right, or keep the same heading. The system state vector consists of variables denoting the current speed and heading of the car. The set of environmental constraints consists of assertions that express the physical laws governing where the next position of the car will be, given its current position, velocity, and acceleration. The integrity constraints are assertions restricting the acceleration and heading of the car so that it will stay on the race track and not run into an obstacle. The decision map may be implemented by some equational rule-based program. The input and decision variables of this program are respectively the sensor vector and decision vectors. The timing constraint consists of a bound on the length of the *monitor-decide cycle* of the program, that is, the maximum number of rule firings before a fixed point is reached.

There are two practical problems of interest with respect to this model:

1. Analysis problem: Does a given equational rule-based program satisfy the integrity and timing constraints of the real-time decision system?

2. Synthesis problem: Given an equational rule-based program that satisfies the integrity constraints but is not fast enough to meet the timing constraints, can we transform the given program into one that meets both the integrity and the timing constraints?

To investigate these problems, we first describe what real-time expert systems are and the EQL language. Then we formulate these problems in terms of a state-space representation of equational rule-based programs, in the next section.

10.2   REAL-TIME EXPERT SYSTEMS

The operations and functions of systems that rely on the computer for real-time monitoring and control have become increasingly complex. These *embedded systems* include airplane avionics (e.g., the *Pilot Associate*-driven aircraft and navigation systems [Bretz, 2002], automatic vehicle control systems [Bretz, 2001; Hamilton et al., 2001; Gavrila et al., 2001; Jones, 2002], *fly-by-wire* Airbus 330/340/380 and Boeing 777 [Yeh, 1998]), smart robots (e.g., the Autonomous Land Vehicle and the Boeing X-45A Unmanned Combat Air Vehicle), space vehicles (e.g., unmanned spacecrafts [Cass, 2001], the NASA Space Shuttle and satellites [Paulson, 2001], and the International Space Station), electric and communication grid monitoring centers, portable wireless devices [Smailagic, Siewiorek, and Reilly, 2001; Want and Schilit, 2001], and hospital patient-monitoring devices [Moore, 2002].

In addition to verifying functional/logical correctness requirements, a problem that has been more thoroughly studied with non-time-critical software systems, it is equally important to verify that these systems satisfy stringent response-time requirements. Based on input sensor values, the embedded expert system must make decisions within bounded time to respond to the changing external environment; the result of missing a deadline may inflict serious damage to the real-time system and may result in the loss of life and property. Therefore, it is essential to accurately determine an upper bound on the execution time of the embedded expert system before it is put into use.

The added complexity of timing requirements makes the design and maintenance of these systems particularly difficult. Few attempts have been made to formalize the question of whether rule-based systems can deliver adequate performance in *bounded time*. In this chapter, we provide a formal framework for answering this important question. We shall also describe a set of software tools that have been designed to ensure that programs for computing complex decisions in real time can indeed meet their specified timing constraints.

The class of real-time programs that are investigated herein are called *equational rule-based* (EQL) *programs*. An EQL program has a set of rules for updating variables that denote the state of the physical system under control. The firing of a rule computes a new value for one or more state variables to reflect changes in the external environment as detected by sensors. Sensor readings are sampled periodically. Every time sensor readings are taken, the state variables are recomputed iteratively by a number of rule firings until no further change in the variables can result from the firing of a rule. The EQL program is then said to have reached a *fixed point*. Intuitively, rules in an EQL program are used to express the constraints on a system and also the goals of the controller. If a fixed point is reached, the state variables have settled down to a set of values that are consistent with the constraints and goals as expressed by the rules.

EQL differs from the popular *expert system* languages such as OPS5 in some important ways. These differences reflect the goal of our work, which is not to invent yet another *expert system shell* but to investigate whether and how performance objectives can be met when rule-based programs are used to perform safety-critical functions in real time. Whereas the interpretation of a language like OPS5 is defined by the *recognize-act cycle* [Forgy, 1981], the basic interpretation cycle of EQL is defined by fixed-point convergence. The fixed-point semantics of EQL follow closely that of the language Unity developed by Chandy and Misra. It is our belief that the time it takes to converge to a fixed point is a more pertinent measure of the response time of a rule-based program than the length of the *recognize-act cycle*. More importantly, we do not require the firing of rules that lead to a fixed point to be implemented sequentially; rules can be fired in parallel if they do not interfere with one another. The definition of response time in terms of fixed-point convergence is architecture-independent and is therefore more robust.

In view of the safety-critical functions that computers are beginning to be relied upon to perform in real time, it is incumbent upon us to ensure that some acceptable performance level can be provided by a rule-based program, subject to reasonable assumptions about the quality of the input.

10.3 PROPOSITIONAL-LOGIC RULE-BASED PROGRAMS: THE EQL LANGUAGE

An EQL program is organized like the following model:

PROGRAM name;
CONST declaration;
VAR declaration;
INPUTVAR declaration;
INIT

          statement,
          statement,
             ⋮
             ⋮
          statement
INPUT
          READ variable_list
RULES
            rule
         [] rule
             ⋮
             ⋮
         [] rule
TRACE variable_list
PRINT variable_list
END.

An EQL program is composed of four major distinct sections: the declaration section, the initialization section, the rule section, and the output section. The syntax of EQL follows closely that of the language Pascal. EQL programs are an entirely free format, with no restrictions on columns or spacing. A comment can be indicated by enclosing it within the character pairs (* *).

Identifiers are used in the program to name variables, constants, and the program name. The rules for forming an identifier are as follows. All alphabetic characters used are lowercase. The first character must be a lowercase alphabetic character: 'a'...'z'. All succeeding characters must be alphabetic, numeric, or the underscore character '_'. No special characters or punctuation marks are allowed, and no embedded blanks are allowed. Identifiers may be as long as desired, subject to the restrictions of the system in which EQL is implemented.

10.3.1   The Declaration Section

The declaration of an EQL program consists of three different types of declaration: CONST, VAR, and INPUTVAR. Each type of declaration must appear at most once and in the order indicated above.

10.3.2   The CONST Declaration

The CONST declaration assigns a name to a scalar constant. No predefined constants exist in EQL and thus all constants used in the program must be declared, including the values of the Boolean constants *true* and *false*. For example, the following declaration declares four constants.

```
CONST
        false    = 0 ;
        true     = 1 ;
        bad      = 2 ;
        good     = 3 ;
```

10.3.3   The VAR Declaration

All variables used in the program except input variables must be declared in the VAR section. Input variables are those that do not appear on the left-hand-side of any assignment statement. They are used to store the values read from sensors attached to the external environment. For example, the following VAR declaration declares three variables of type BOOLEAN.

```
VAR
        sensor_a_status, sensor_b_status, object_detected : BOOLEAN ;
```

10.3.4   The INPUTVAR Declaration

All input variables used in the program must be declared in the INPUTVAR section. For example, the following INPUTVAR declaration declares three input variables of type INTEGER.

INPUTVAR
  sensor_a, sensor_b, sensor_c : INTEGER ;

10.3.5 The Initialization Section INIT and INPUT

All non-input variables are assigned initial or default values in the initialization section INIT before the start of the firing of the rules in the RULES section of the program. For example, the following statements initialize the variables: *sensor_a_status, sensor_b_status,* and *object_detected.*

INIT

  sensor_a_status := good,
  sensor_b_status := good,
  object_detected := false

At the beginning of each execution of an EQL program, input values are read into the input variables listed in the READ statement.

INPUT

  READ sensor_a, sensor_b

10.3.6 The RULES Section

The RULES section is composed of a finite set of rules, each of which is of the form:

$$a_1 := b_1 \,!\, a_2 := b_2 \,!\ldots! \, a_m := b_m \text{ IF } enabling \; condition$$

A rule has three parts:

  VAR = set of variables on left-hand side of the assignment, i.e., the a_is,

  VAL = expressions on right-hand side of assignment, i.e., the b_is, and

  EC = enabling condition.

A *subrule* of rule y with m VAR variables is of the form:

$$c_1 := d_1 \,!\, c_2 := d_2 \,!\ldots! \, c_p := d_p \text{ IF } enabling \; condition$$

where each c_i is a VAR variable in rule y, d_i is the expression to be assigned to variable c_i in the original rule, and $p \leq m$. A *single-assignment subrule* of rule y is then of the form:

$$c := d \text{ IF } enabling \; condition$$

where c is a VAR variable in rule y and d is the expression to be assigned to variable c in the original rule.

An enabling condition is a predicate on the variables in the program. A rule is enabled if its enabling condition becomes true. A rule firing is the execution of the multiple assignment statement. A rule is *fireable* only when it is enabled and if by firing it will change the value of some variable in VAR. A multiple assignment statement assigns values to one or more variables in parallel. The VAL expressions must be side-effect free. The execution of a multiple assignment statement consists of the evaluation of all the VAL expressions, followed by updating the VAR variables with the values of the corresponding expressions. For ease of discussion, we define three sets of variables for an EQL program:

$$L = \{v \mid v \text{ is a variable appearing in VAR}\}$$

$$R = \{v \mid v \text{ is a variable appearing in VAL}\}$$

$$T = \{v \mid v \text{ is a variable appearing in EC}\}$$

An invocation of an EQL program is a sequence of rule firings (execution of multiple assignment statements whose enabling conditions are true). When two or more rules are enabled, the selection of which rule to fire is nondeterministic or up to the run-time scheduler.

An EQL program is said to have reached a *fixed point* when none of its rules is fireable. An EQL program is said to always reach a fixed point in *bounded time* if and only if the number of rule firings needed to take the program from an initial state to a fixed point is always bounded by a fixed upper bound. This bound is imposed by performance constraints. It is possible that a program can reach different fixed points starting from the same initial state, depending on which rules and how the rules are fired. This may suggest that the correctness of the program is violated, whereas for some applications this is acceptable. Our concern in this chapter is, however, on the verification of timing requirements of rule-based programs.

EQL is an equational rule-based language which we have implemented to run under BSD UNIX.[1] The current system includes a translator **eqtc** which translates an EQL program into an equivalent C program for compilation and execution in a UNIX-based machine. The module **eqtc** and other system modules are implemented in C. An example of an EQL program is shown below.

Example 1.   RULES *section of a simple object-detection program:*

```
(* 1 *)          object_detected := true IF sensor_a = 1 AND sensor_a_status = good
(* 2 *)     []   object_detected := true IF sensor_b = 1 AND sensor_b_status = good
(* 3 *)     []   object_detected := false IF sensor_a = 0 AND sensor_a_status = good
(* 4 *)     []   object_detected := false IF sensor_b = 0 AND sensor_b_status = good
```

If sensor_a and sensor_b read in values 1 and 0, respectively, then the above program will never reach a fixed point since the variable object_detected will be set to *true* and *false* alternatively by rules 1 and 4. Recall that a rule is enabled if its enabling

---

[1] UNIX is a registered trademark of AT&T Bell Laboratories.

condition is true, and that a rule can fire when it is enabled and if by firing it will change the value of at least one VAR variable. Thus a rule can fire more than once as long as it remains fireable. Rule 1 and rule 4 are said to be not compatible. Similarly, if sensor_a and sensor_b read in values 0 and 1, respectively, then the above program will never reach a fixed point since the variable object_detected will be set to *true* and *false* alternatively by rules 2 and 3. Rule 2 and rule 3 are not compatible.

In a real-time system, the goal is to have the decision program converge to a fixed point within a bounded number of rule firings. To ensure that the above decision system will converge to a fixed point given any set of sensor input values, some additional information may be needed to settle the conflicting sensor readings. For example, the following rules may be added to the above program:

5. [] *sensor_a_status* := bad IF *sensor_a* $\neq$ *sensor_c* AND *sensor_b_status* = good
6. [] *sensor_b_status* := bad IF *sensor_b* $\neq$ *sensor_c* AND *sensor_a_status* = good

where *sensor_c* is an additional input variable. If one of the above two rules is fired, then two of the tests (either tests 1 and 3 or tests 2 and 4) in rules 1–4 will be falsified, thus permanently disabling two of those four rules. The variable *object_detected* will then have a stable value since rules 1 and 4 or rules 2 and 3 can no longer fire alternatively. Since the default scheduler of EQL will eventually fire an enabled rule, all the variables in the above program will converge to stable values after a finite (but unbounded) number of iterations. In section 10.8, we show how this program can be made to converge to stable values in bounded time.

The above example is sufficiently simple that with a little thought one can understand its behavior, and in particular, whether a fixed point can be reached or not. In general, it is non-trivial to determine the behavior of rule-based programs because there is no obvious flow of control. Even small rule-based programs can take quite a bit of work to understand, as the following example illustrates. In a real-time system, the goal is to have the rule-based program converge to a fixed point within a bounded number of rule firings. We would therefore like to determine whether or not the rule-based program will reach a fixed point in a bounded number of rule firings. For a program of this size, the answer is obvious. However, the problem is not trivial for larger programs. In general, the analysis problem to determine whether a rule-based program will reach a fixed point is undecidable if the program variables can have infinite domains, that is, there is no general procedure for answering all instances of the decision problem [Browne, Cheng, and Mok, 1988].

10.3.7 The Output Section

The TRACE statement prints the values of the specified variables following the firing of a rule in each cycle. For example, the following TRACE statement prints the values of the variables *sensor_a_status, sensor_b_status*, and *object_detected* following the firing of any rule:

TRACE sensor_a_status, sensor_b_status, object_detected

The PRINT statement prints the values of the specified variables only after the entire program has reached a fixed point. For example, the following PRINT statement prints the values of the same variables after the program has reached a fixed point.

PRINT sensor_a_status, sensor_b_status, object_detected

We now show a larger sample EQL program, a distributed program for determining whether an object is detected at each *monitor-decide cycle*. The system consists of two processes and an external alarm clock which invokes the program by setting the variable *wake_up* to *true* periodically.

Example 2.   Object detection:

```
(* Example EQL Program *)
PROGRAM example2;
CONST
        false  = 0;
        true   = 1;
        a      = 0;
        b      = 1;
VAR
        sync_a,
        sync_b,
        wake_up,
        object_detected : BOOLEAN;
        arbiter         : INTEGER;
INPUTVAR
        sensor_a,
        sensor_b        : INTEGER;
INIT
        sync_a := true,
        sync_b := true,
        wake_up := true,
        object_detected := false,
        arbiter := a
INPUT
        READ sensor_a, sensor_b
RULES
(* process A *)
          object_detected := true ! sync_a := false
                IF (sensor_a = 1) AND (arbiter = a) AND (sync_a = true)
      [] object_detected := false ! sync_a := false
                IF (sensor_a = 0) AND (arbiter = a) AND (sync_a = true)
      [] arbiter := b ! sync_a := true ! wake_up := false
                IF (arbiter = a) AND (sync_a = false) AND (wake_up = true)
```

```
(* process B *)
      [] object_detected := true ! sync_b := false
                 IF (sensor_b = 1) AND (arbiter = b) AND (sync_b = true)
                    AND (wake_up = true)
      [] object_detected := false ! sync_b := false
IF (sensor_b = 0) AND (arbiter = b) AND (sync_b = true)
                 AND (wake_up = true)
      [] arbiter := a ! sync_b := true ! wake_up := false
                 IF (arbiter = b) AND (sync_b = false) AND (wake_up = true)

TRACE object_detected
PRINT sync_a, sync_b, wake_up, object_detected, arbiter, sensor_a, sensor_b
END.
```

In this example, the input variables are *sensor_a* and *sensor_b*, and the program variables are *object_detected, sync_a, sync_b, arbiter*, and *wake_up*. The three sets of variables L, R, T are:

$$L = \{\text{object\_detected, sync\_a, sync\_b, arbiter, wake\_up}\},$$

$$R = \phi,$$

$$T = \{\text{sensor\_a, sensor\_b, arbiter, sync\_a, sync\_b, wake\_up}\}.$$

Each process runs independently of the other. An alarm clock external to the program is used to invoke the processes after some specified period of time. A rule is fired in the same way as in the non-distributed case, namely, the assignment statement is executed when the enabling condition becomes true. In this example, the shared variable *arbiter* is used as a control/synchronization variable that enforces mutually exclusive access to shared variables, such as *object_detected*, by different processes. The variables *sync_a* and *sync_b* are used as control/synchronization variables within process A and process B, respectively. Note that for each process, at most two rules will be fired before control is transferred to the other process. Initially, process A is given the mutually exclusive access to variables *object_detected* and *sync_a*.

The reader who finds the above example difficult to understand need not be discouraged inasmuch as the point of the example is to impress upon the reader the need for computer-aided tools to design this class of programs. We shall discuss in later sections a set of computer-aided design tools that have been implemented for this purpose. But first, we need to be more precise about the class of systems to which our equational rule-based programs are applied. Then we can formulate the relevant technical questions in terms of a state-space representation.

10.4 STATE-SPACE REPRESENTATION

The state-space graph of an equational rule-based program is a labeled directed graph $G = (V, E)$. V is a set of vertices, each of which is labeled by a tuple: $(x_1, \ldots, x_n, s_1, \ldots, s_p)$, where x_i is a value in the domain of the ith input sensor variable and s_j is a value in the domain of the jth program variable. We say that a rule is *enabled* at vertex i iff its test is satisfied by the tuple of variable values at vertex i. E is a set of edges, each of which denotes the firing of a rule such that an edge (i, j) connects vertex i to vertex j iff there is a rule R that is enabled at vertex i and firing R will modify the program variables to have the same values as the tuple at vertex j. Whenever no confusion exists, we shall use the terms state and vertex interchangeably. Obviously, if the domains of all the variables in a program are finite, the corresponding state-space graph must be finite. We note that the state-space graph of a program need not be connected.

A *path* in the state-space graph is a sequence of vertices $v_1, \ldots, v_i, v_{i+1}, \ldots,$ such that an edge connects v_i to v_{i+1} for each i. Paths can be finite or infinite. The length of a finite path $v_1, \ldots, v_k$ is $k - 1$. A *simple path* is a path in which no vertex appears more than once. A *cycle* in the state-space graph is a path $v_1, \ldots, v_k$ such that $v_1 = v_k$. A path corresponds to the sequence of states generated by a sequence of rule firings of the corresponding program.

A vertex in a state-space graph is said to be a *fixed point* if it does not have any out-edges or if all of its out-edges are self-loops (i.e., cycles of length 1). Obviously, if the execution of a program has reached a fixed point, every rule is either not enabled or its firing will not modify any of the variables.

An invocation of an equational rule-based program can be thought of as tracing a path in the state-space graph. A *monitor-decide* cycle starts with the update of input sensor variables, and this puts the program in a new state. A number of rule firings will modify the program variables until the program reaches a fixed point. Depending on the starting state, a monitor-decide cycle may take an arbitrarily long time to converge to a fixed point if at all. We say that a state in the state-space graph is *stable* if all paths starting from it will lead to a fixed point. A state is *unstable* if none of the paths from it will lead to a fixed point. A state is *potentially unstable* if there is a path from it that does not lead to a fixed point. By definition, a fixed point is a stable state. It is easy to see that a state s is stable iff any path from s is simple until it ends in a fixed point. A state is potentially unstable iff a cycle is reachable from it or if there is an infinite simple path leading from it.

Figure 10.2 illustrates these concepts. If the current state of the program is A, then the program can reach the fixed point $FP2$ in four rule firings by taking the path $(A, D, F, H, FP2)$. If the path $(A, D, E, \ldots, FP1)$ is taken, the fixed point $FP1$ will be reached after a finite number of rule firings. State A is stable because all

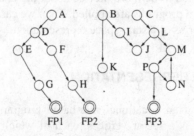

Figure 10.2   State-space graph of a real-time decision program.

paths from A will lead to a fixed point. If the current state of the program is B, the program will iterate forever without reaching a fixed point. All the states $\{B, I, J, K\}$ in the cycle (B, I, J, K, B) are unstable. Note that no out-edge is present from any of the states in this cycle. Once the program enters one of these states, it will iterate forever. If the current state of the program is C, the program may enter and stay in a cycle if the path $(C, L, J, \ldots)$ is followed. If the path $(C, L, M, \ldots)$ is taken, the cycle (M, P, N, M) may be encountered. The program may eventually reach the fixed point $FP3$ if at some time the scheduler fires the rule corresponding to the edge from P to $FP3$ when the program is in state P. To ensure this, however, the scheduler must observe a *strong fairness* criterion: if a rule is enabled infinitely often, it must be fired eventually. In this case, paths from state C to $FP3$ are finite but their lengths are unbounded. C is a potentially unstable state.

In designing real-time decision systems, we should never allow an equational rule-based program to be invoked from an unstable state. Potentially unstable states can be allowed only if an appropriate scheduler is used to always select a sufficiently short path to a fixed point whenever the program is invoked from such a state. We say that a fixed point is an *end-point* of a state s if that fixed point is reachable from s. It should be noted that not every tuple that is some combination of sensor input and program variable values can be a state from which a program may be invoked. After a program reaches a fixed point, it will remain there until the sensor input variables are updated, and the program will then be invoked again in this new state. The states in which a program is invoked are called *launch states*. Formally, we define a launch state[2] as follows:

1. The initial state of a program is a launch state.
2. A tuple obtained from an end point (which is a tuple of input and program variables) of a launch state by replacing the input variable components with any combination of input variable values is a launch state.
3. A state is a launch state iff it can be derived from rules (1) and (2).

In this chapter, the timing constraint of interest is a deadline that must be met by every monitor-decide cycle of an equational rule-based program. In terms of the state-space representation, the timing constraint imposes an upper bound on the length of paths from a launch state to a fixed point. Integrity constraints are assertions that must hold at the end points of launch states. Given a program that meets the integrity constraints but violates the timing constraint, the synthesis problem is to transform this program into one that also meets the timing constraint. This can be done by program transformation techniques and/or by customizing the scheduler to

---

[2]The above definition of a launch state is conservative in the sense that not all combinations of input variables need to be considered in the construction of launch states because future sensor readings are restricted by the environmental constraints. However, since environmental constraints are necessarily approximations of the external world, it seems prudent not to include them in the definition of a launch state. We emphasize that it is possible to take advantage of environmental constraints in cutting down the number of launch states for analysis purposes.

fire the rules selectively so that an invocation always fires the rules corresponding to the shortest path from the launch state to an end point.

In the next section, we shall describe some of the tools that we have implemented to mechanize the analysis problem, that is, to determine if the upper bound on the monitor-decide cycle can indeed be met in the worst case. Some of the theoretical issues related to the analysis and synthesis problems will be discussed in sections 10.6 and 10.8.

10.5 COMPUTER-AIDED DESIGN TOOLS

The complexity and size of real-time decision systems often necessitate the use of computer-aided design tools. This chapter reports on a suite of analysis tools that have been implemented to ensure that equational rule-based programs written in the language EQL can indeed meet their specified timing and integrity constraints. In particular, the tools are used to perform a pre-run-time analysis on an EQL program to verify that the variables in the program will always converge to stable values in bounded time at each invocation.

As in the design of most complex software systems, we envision the development of real-time rule-based systems to be an iterative process. Our goal is to speed up this iterative process by automating it as much as possible. Figure 10.3 shows the interaction of a designer with the tools. In each design cycle, the equational rule-based program is analyzed by the analysis tools for compliance with the timing and integrity constraints. Violations are passed to the designer who can then modify the program with the help of the synthesis tools until the program meets all the constraints. It should be emphasized, however, that the purpose of the design tools is not to encourage people to write sloppy programs and rely on the tools to fix them. Design tools are particularly necessary for rule-based programs because the addition and/or deletion of just one rule may drastically change the behavior of a program,

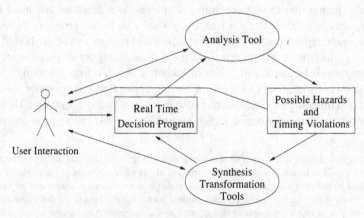

Figure 10.3 Development of real-time decision systems.

and it is essential to guard against unintended interference in the work of individual members of a design team.

In this chapter, our main focus is on a suite of analysis tools that have been implemented for the equational rule-based language EQL. For efficient execution, a translator of EQL programs into C code exists. We selected C as the target language since it is widely available and has efficient compilers. Since EQL has nondeterministic constructs, our translator generates the appropriate C code to simulate nondeterminism and parallelism on a sequential machine.

Our software tools provide:

1. a translator for transforming an EQL program into its corresponding state-space graph as described in the previous section. The state-space graph serves as an intermediate form of the program under development and is used for mechanical analysis and synthesis.

2. a temporal-logic verifier for checking integrity assertions about EQL programs. (In the current implementation, these assertions can be expressed in the temporal logic called computation tree logic [Clarke, Emerson, and Sistla, 1986] described in chapter 4.) Specifically, the verifier determines, given any launch state, whether some fixed points are always reachable in a finite number of iterations and whether the reachable fixed points are safe, that is, satisfy the specified integrity constraints. If the given EQL program cannot reach a fixed point from a particular launch state, the temporal-logic verifier will warn the designer of the existence of a cycle that does not have a path exiting from it.

3. a timing analyzer for determining the maximum number of iterations to reach a safe fixed point, and the sequence of states traversed (along with the sequence of rules fired) from the launch state to the fixed point. This helps the designer pinpoint the sets of rules that may constitute a performance bottleneck so that optimization efforts can be concentrated on them. The timing analyzer can also be used to investigate the performance of customized schedulers that are used to deterministically select a rule to fire when two or more rules are enabled.

A suite of practical prototyping tools has been implemented on a Sun Microsystems[3] workstation running under UNIX BSD 4.2 to perform timing and safety analysis of real-time equational rule-based programs. Although these are the first versions of the analysis tools, they are nonetheless sufficiently practical for analyzing realistic real-time decision systems. To demontrate their usefulness, we have used these tools to verify that a subset of the Cryogenic Hydrogen Pressure Malfunction Procedure of the Space Shuttle Vehicle Pressure Control System will reach a safe fixed point in a finite number of iterations from any launch state.

Figure 10.4 illustrates the dependency among the modules in our tool system. The names of the modules and descriptions of their functions follow:

1. **eqtc** – EQL to C translator
2. **ptf** – EQL to finite state-space graph translator for a launch state

---

[3]SUN is a registered trademark of SUN Microsystems Inc.

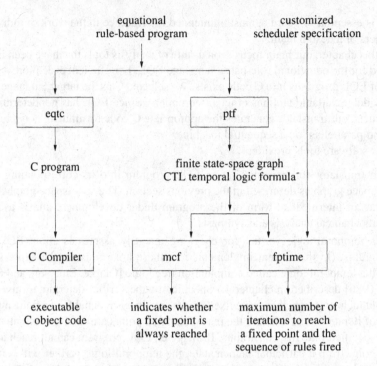

Figure 10.4   Computer-aided design tools for real-time decision systems.

3. **ptaf** – EQL to finite state-space graphs translator for all launch states
4. **mcf** – CTL model checker (extended to cover fairness)
5. **fptime** – Timing analyzer on state-space graphs

The module **eqtc** translates a program written in the equational rule-based language EQL into a C program suitable for compilation using the **cc** compiler under UNIX, as described earlier. EQL is a Unity-based language with nondeterministically scheduled rules and parallel assignment statements.

The module **ptf** translates an EQL program with finite domains (all variables have finite ranges) into a finite state-space graph that contains all the states reachable from the launch state corresponding to the initial values of the variables given in the program. It also generates the appropriate temporal-logic formula for checking whether the program will reach a fixed point. **ptf** produces a file named *mc.in* which will be read by the fairness-extended model checker **mcf** and the timing analyzer module **fptime**. The file *mc.in* contains the internal representation of the state-space graph of the corresponding EQL program.

The module **ptaf** is similar to **ptf**, but it automatically generates the complete state-space graph (i.e., it generates all the states reachable from every launch state). **ptaf** invokes the model checker and the timing analyzer to determine whether the program will reach a fixed point in a finite number of iterations, starting from any launch state. If the EQL program indeed reaches a fixed point in a finite number of iterations starting from any launch state, **ptaf** informs the designer accordingly. Otherwise, **ptaf** stops at the first launch state for which the program may not reach a fixed point in a finite number of iterations and informs the designer about the unstable launch state.

The module **mcf** is a temporal-logic model checker based on the Clarke–Emerson–Sistla algorithm for checking the satisfiability of temporal-logic formulas written in CTL [Clarke, Emerson, and Sistla, 1986]. Our model checker assumes that strong fairness is observed by the scheduler; that is, rules that are enabled infinitely often will eventually fire. Under this assumption, a cycle in the state-space graph that has at least one edge exiting from it is not sufficient to cause the program not to reach a fixed point in a finite number of iterations. (The program will leave the states in the cycle because the rule associated with the exit edge must eventually fire.) However, the model checker will warn the designer that the program may require a finite but unbounded number of iterations to reach a fixed point. The default scheduler used to schedule the next enabled rule to fire is fair and is based on a linear-congruential pseudo–random number generator.

The module **fptime** is a timing analyzer that computes the maximum number of iterations for a given program to reach a fixed point if at least one reachable fixed point exists. In addition, it provides the sequence of rule firings leading from the launch state to this fixed point. It can also compute the number of iterations to any other fixed point and the corresponding sequence of rule firings if the designer so desires. **fptime** has been designed so that a designer will be able to specify restrictions on the scheduler if it is desired to determine how the specified scheduling restrictions may affect the number of rule firings. This is useful for investigating the performance of customized schedulers.

10.5.1 Analysis Example

We now describe how our tools can be applied to the distributed EQL program of example 2. With the EQL-to-C translator **eqtc**, we can translate the equational rule-based program in example 2 into a C program by invoking the command

$$\text{eqtc} < \text{example2} > \text{example2.c.}$$

This program can be compiled using a C compiler (the **cc** command in UNIX) and then executed to obtain the stable output values if a fixed point is reachable in a finite number of iterations. The current version of **eqtc** simulates the reading of external sensors by initializing the input variables before any rule is fired. The C program generated by the **eqtc** translator is shown below.

```
#include <stdio.h>
#include "scheduler.c"
#define maxseq 24
#define false 0
#define true 1
#define a 0
```

```
#define b 1
int znext,
    randseq[maxseq],
    counter;

main() {
    extern int znext,
                randseq[maxseq],
                counter;
    int i;

    int sync_a, sync_b, wake_up, object_detected;
    int arbiter;
    int sensor_a, sensor_b;

            sync_a = true;
            sync_b = true;
            wake_up = true;
            arbiter = a;
            sensor_a = 1;
            sensor_b = 0;

    init_random_seq(randseq, &znext, z0, &counter);
    while (!fixed_point())
    { i = schedule(randseq, &znext, 6);
        switch(i) {
            case 1:
                if ((sensor_a == 1) && (arbiter == a) && (sync_a == true) &&
                (wake_up == true)) {
                    object_detected = true;
                    sync_a = false;
                }
                break;
            case 2:
                if ((sensor_a == 0) && (arbiter == a) && (sync_a == true) &&
                (wake_up == true)) {
                    object_detected = false;
                    sync_a = false;
                }
                break;
            case 3:
                if ((arbiter == a) && (sync_a == false) && (wake_up == true)) {
                    arbiter = b;
                    sync_a = true;
                    wake_up = false;
                }
                break;
            case 4:
                if ((sensor_b == 1) && (arbiter == b) && (sync_b == true) &&
                (wake_up == true)) {
                    object_detected = true;
                    sync_b = false;
                }
                break;
```

```
      case 5:
        if ((sensor_b == 0) && (arbiter == b) && (sync_b == true) &&
        (wake_up == true)) {
          object_detected = false;
          sync_b = false;
        }
        break;
      case 6:
        if ((arbiter == b) && (sync_b == false) && (wake_up == true)) {
          arbiter = a;
          sync_b = true;
          wake_up = false;
        }
        break;
    }
    printf(" object_detected = %d\\n", object_detected);
  }
  printf(" object_detected = %d\\n", object_detected);
}
```

The EQL program with the initial input values can be translated into a finite state-space graph by using the **ptf** translator with the command:

$$\text{\textbf{ptf}} < \text{example2}.$$

ptf generates the following output for user reference:

```
Finite State Space Graph Corresponding to Input Program:
-----------------------------------------------------------

state    next states
-----    -----------

rule #   1 2 3 4 5 6
0:       1 0 0 0 0 0
1:       1 1 2 1 1 1
2:       2 2 2 2 2 2

State Labels:
-------------

state   (sync_a, sync_b, wake_up, object_detected, arbiter, sensor_a, sensor_b)

0        1 1 1 0 0 1 0
1        0 1 1 1 0 1 0
2        1 1 0 1 1 1 0
```

ptf also generates a CTL temporal-logic formula for checking whether this program will reach a fixed point in finite time from the launch state corresponding to the initial input and program variable values. This formula is stored in the file *mc.in*, which is generated as input to the model checker and the timing analyzer. *mc.in* contains the adjacency matrix representation of the labeled state-space graph.

```
3
1 1 0
0 1 1
0 0 1
0 n1 ;
1 n1 ;
2 f1 ;
(au n1 f1)
0
```

The temporal-logic model checker **mcf** can then be used to determine whether a fixed point is always reachable in a finite number of iterations by analyzing this finite state-space graph with the given launch state:

$$\mathbf{mcf} < mc.in.$$

To verify that the program will reach a fixed point from any launch state, the (finite) reachability graph of every launch state must be analyzed by the model checker. The complete state-space graph of the example EQL program, which consists of eight separate finite reachability graphs, one for each distinct launch state, is shown in Figure 10.5. The graph with launch state (3,0), corresponding to the combination of input values and initial program values specified in the C program, is one of $2^3 = 8$ possible graphs that must be checked by the model checker.

In general, for a finite-domain EQL program with n input variables and m program variables, the total number of reachability graphs that have to be checked in the worst case (i.e., all combinations of the values of the input and program variables are possible) is

$$\left(\prod_{i=1}^{i=n} |X_i| \cdot \prod_{j=1}^{j=m} |S_j| \right)$$

where $|X_i|$, $|S_j|$ are respectively the size of the domains of the ith input and jth program variable. If all variables are binary, this number is 2^{n+m}. In practice, the number of reachability graphs that must be checked is substantially less because many combinations of input and program variable values do not constitute launch states. Other techniques are also available that do not require examination of the entire state-space graph. They will be discussed in the next section.

Finally, the timing analyzer **fptime** can be invoked to determine the longest sequence of rule firings leading to a fixed point, if at least one exists, by the command:

$$\mathbf{fptime} < mc.in.$$

The following is the partial output of the **fptime** module corresponding to the reachability graph with launch state (3, 0):

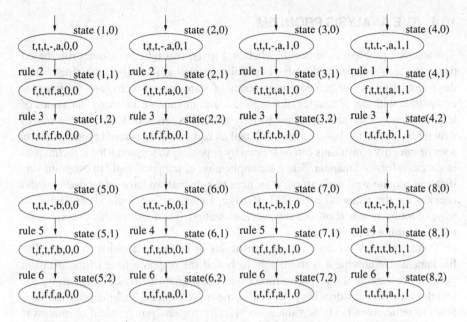

state = (*sync_a, sync_b, wake_up, object_detected, arbiter, sensor_a, sensor_b*)
t = TRUE, f = FALSE, a = name of process A, b = name of process B, - = don't care

Figure 10.5 Complete finite state-space graph representing the program example2.

```
> initial state:        0
> fixed-point state(s):
> 2
> initial state: 0      fixed-point state: 2
> maximum number of iterations: 2
> path:        0      1      2
```

The module **ptaf** performs the above translation and analysis on the complete state-space graph of the example EQL program automatically. The command:

$$\textbf{ptaf} < \text{example2}$$

produces the following messages:

```
> The program always reaches a fixed point in finite time.
> The maximum number of iterations to reach a fixed point is 2.
> 8 FSMs checked.
```

In the next two sections, we shall discuss the complexity of the analysis and synthesis problems of real-time equational rule-based programs. In the appendix, we shall illustrate the practicality of our tools by analyzing a "real-life" real-time decision system: the Cryogenic Hydrogen Pressure Malfunction Procedure of the Space Shuttle Vehicle Pressure Control System [Helly, 1984].

10.6 THE ANALYSIS PROBLEM

The analysis problem is to decide whether a given real-time equational rule-based program meets the specified timing constraints as well as integrity constraints. Since the formulation of our problem is in terms of state-space graphs, our approach is compatible with the semantics of temporal logic: in spite of the many variations of temporal logic, their semantics are usually defined in terms of Kripke (state space) structures. Hence, the issue of verifying that an equational rule-based program meets a set of integrity constraints can be treated by appealing to temporal-logic techniques in a straightforward manner. Since the application of temporal logic to program verification is quite well understood, it suffices to note that we have integrated a model checker for the temporal-logic CTL [Clarke, Emerson, and Sistla, 1986] into our suite of tools, as was shown in the previous section. The focus of this chapter is on meeting timing constraints.

There are many types of timing constraints in real-time decision systems. The fundamental requirement is to be able to bound the response time of the decision system. We capture the response time of an equational rule-based program by the length of the monitor-decide cycle, that is, the time it takes for all the program variables to settle down to stable values. Technically, the analysis problem of interest is to decide whether a fixed point can always be reached from a launch state on any sufficiently long but finite path. In general, the analysis problem is undecidable if the program variables can have infinite domains, that is, no general procedure exists for answering all instances of the decision problem.

The undecidability result follows from the observation that any two-counter machine can be encoded by an equational rule-based program that uses only "+" and "−" as operations on integer variables and ">" and "=" as atomic predicates such that a two-counter machine accepts an input if and only if the corresponding equational rule-based program can reach a fixed point from an initial condition determined by the input to the two-counter machine. Since two-counter machines can simulate arbitrary Turing machines, our analysis problem is equivalent to the Turing machine halting problem. The formal proof of this result is straightforward but tedious and is omitted here. We illustrate the idea of the proof by exhibiting a two-counter machine (Figure 10.6) and the corresponding equational rule-based program. This two-counter machine accepts the integer input in its first register iff it is odd. The same input integer is used to initialize the variable c_1 in the program below. The variables s and f are used to keep track of respectively the current state of the two-counter machine and whether the two-counter machine has entered an accepting state. Notice that the program below reaches a fixed point iff only rule 5 is enabled.

Equational rule-based program for simulating the two-counter machine of Figure 10.6.

initially: $s = 1, c_1 = $ INPUT, $c_2 = 0, f = 0$

1. $s := 2\,!\,c_1 := c_1 - 1\,!\,f := f + 1$ IF $s = 1$ AND $c_1 > 0$
2.   [] $s := 3\,!\,c_1 := c_1\,!\,f := f + 1$ IF $s = 1$ AND $c_1 = 0$

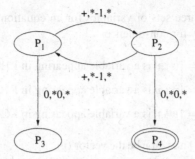

Figure 10.6   A two-counter machine for testing odd input.

3. [] $s := 3 ! c_1 := c_1 ! f := f + 1$ IF $s = 3$
4. [] $s := 4 ! c_1 := c_1 ! f := f + 1$ IF $s = 2$ AND $c_1 = 0$
5. [] $s := 4 ! c_1 := c_1 ! f := f$ IF $s = 4$
6. [] $s := 1 ! c_1 := c_1 - 1 ! f := f + 1$ IF $s = 2$ AND $c_1 > 0$

10.6.1   Finite Domains

Even though the analysis problem is undecidable in general, it is trivially true that the analysis problem is decidable if all the variables of an equational rule-based program range over finite domains. In this case, the state-space graph of the program must be finite and can thus be analyzed by an algorithm that performs an exhaustive check on the finite graph. In section 10.5, we described a suite of tools for analyzing equational rule-based programs. The default approach is to generate the reachability graph from the initial (launch) state and use the model checker to determine whether a fixed point is always reachable on any path from the initial state. (Fixed points are expressed by an atomic predicate on a state that is true if and only if out-edges from the state are self-loops.) This approach is viable if the state-space graph is reasonably small, but in the worst case may require exponential computation time as a function of the number of variables in the program. More precisely, it can be shown that the computational complexity of the analysis problem restricted to finite graphs is PSPACE-complete.

It should be emphasized that in practice, it is often not necessary to check the complete state space to solve the analysis problem. Under appropriate conditions, efficient procedures exist that can be applied to reduce the size of the state space by a simple textual analysis of the program. In particular, rules of certain forms are always guaranteed to reach a fixed point in a finite number of iterations. As an example, one of these special forms[4] which is especially useful, will be given below. First, some definitions are in order.

---

[4] It is unnecessary for all the rules of a program to be in a special form in order to be able to reduce the state space. Techniques exist that can be applied recursively to fragments of a program and the result can be used to transform the whole program into a simpler one.

We defined earlier three sets of variables for an equational rule-based program. They are repeated below for convenience.

$$L = \{v \mid v \text{ is a variable appearing in LHS}\}$$

$$R = \{v \mid v \text{ is a variable appearing in RHS}\}$$

$$T = \{v \mid v \text{ is a variable appearing in EC}\}$$

Let $T = \{v_1, v_2, \ldots, v_n\}$ and let $\bar{v}$ be the vector $\langle v_1, v_2, \ldots, v_n \rangle$. With this definition, each test (enabling condition) in a program can be viewed as a function $f(\bar{v})$ from the space of $\bar{v}$ to the set $\{true, false\}$. Let f_a be the function corresponding to the test a and let V_a be the subset of the space of $\bar{v}$ for which the function f_a maps to *true*. We say that two tests a and b are *mutually exclusive* iff the subsets V_a and V_b of the corresponding functions f_a and f_b are disjoint. Obviously, if two tests are mutually exclusive, only one of the corresponding rules can be enabled at a time.

For some rules, it is straightforward to determine if two tests are mutually exclusive. For example, consider tests of the form:

$$C_1 \quad AND \quad C_2 \quad AND \quad \cdots \quad AND \quad C_m,$$

where each C_i is a predicate of the form

$$\langle variable \rangle \langle relational\ operator \rangle \langle constant \rangle$$

For a test a of this form, it is easy to see that the subset V_a of the space of $\bar{v}$ for which f_a maps to *true* can be expressed as the cross product:

$$V_{a,1} \times V_{a,2} \times \cdots \times V_{a,n}$$

such that $f_a(\bar{v})$ maps to *true* iff the ith component of $\bar{v}$ is in $V_{a,i}$, for $i = 1, \ldots, n$. Note that if the variable v_k does not appear in test a, then $V_{a,k}$ is the entire domain of v_k. To verify that two tests a and b are mutually exclusive, it suffices to find at least one variable v_i for which $V_{a,i} \cap V_{b,i} = \emptyset$. If no such v_i is found, the two tests are not mutually exclusive.

Let L_x denote the set of variables appearing in the left-hand-side (LHS) of rule x. Two rules a and b are said to be *compatible* iff at least one of the following conditions holds:

(CR1) Test a and test b are mutually exclusive

(CR2) $L_a \cap L_b = \emptyset$

(CR3) Suppose $L_a \cap L_b \neq \emptyset$. Then for every variable v in $L_a \cap L_b$, the same expression must be assigned to v in both rule a and rule b.

We are now ready to give a special form of rules for which the analysis problem can be solved efficiently.

10.6.2 Special Form: Compatible Assignment to Constants, *L* and *T* Disjoint

A set of rules are said to be in special form if all three of the following conditions hold.

1. Constant terms are assigned to all the variables in L, that is, $R = \emptyset$.
2. All of the rules are compatible pairwise.
3. $L \cap T = \emptyset$.

We claim that an equational rule-based program whose rules are in special form will always reach a fixed point in a finite number of iterations. The fact that L and T are disjoint means that the logical value of every test will remain constant throughout an invocation once all sensor readings have been taken and assigned to the input variables. Thus condition (3) implies that a rule is either enabled or disabled throughout an invocation of the program. So we need only to focus on the set of rules that are enabled. If condition CR1 holds for every pair of rules, then at most one of the rules is enabled at any invocation, and since assignments are always to constants, the program will reach a fixed point in one iteration. If condition CR2 holds, then every variable appears at most once in LHS of the enabled rules. Hence, one constant at most can be assigned to any particular variable, and the program must reach a fixed point after all the enabled rules have been fired. If two or more enabled rules can be fired that assign to the same variable, condition CR3 guarantees that they will assign the same value to the variable, and again the program must reach a fixed point after all the rules have been fired. Obviously, the number of iterations before reaching a fixed point is bounded by the number of rules in the program. (This assumes that the scheduler must not execute a rule more than once if no variable will be changed by executing the rule.) Tighter bounds are possible by taking into account rules whose tests are mutually exclusive.

To illustrate the application of the special form, consider the programs in examples 3–5 below. In example 3, even though the two tests in this program are not mutually exclusive because ($b = c = true$) is true in both test 1 and test 2, the fact that all LHS variables are distinct makes the rules compatible (condition CR2 is satisfied) and thus is sufficient to guarantee that this program will reach a fixed point in a finite number of iterations.

In example 4, test 1 and test 3 are not mutually exclusive. However, rule 1 and rule 3 are compatible by condition CR2. Rule 2 and rule 3 are compatible because their tests are mutually exclusive, and so are rule 1 and rule 2. Thus, this program will reach a fixed point in finite time.

Finally, consider example 5. Note that the same value (the constant *true*) is assigned to the variable $a1$ that appears in the LHS of both rules 1 and 2. Hence, condition CR3 is satisfied and thus the rules are compatible; hence, this program is guaranteed to reach a fixed point in finite time.

Example 3.   This program satisfies condition CR1:

  input: read(b, c)

1. $a1$:= true IF b = true
2. [] $a2$:= false IF c = true

Example 4.   This program satisfies condition CR2:

  input: read(b, c)

1. $a1$:= true IF b = true AND c = true
2. [] $a1$:= true IF b = true AND c = false
3. [] $a2$:= false IF c = true

Example 5.   This program satisfies condition CR3:

  input: read(b, c)

1. $a1$:= true IF b = true
2. [] $a1$:= true IF c = true

The utility of the special form above might seem quite limited since the three conditions of the special form must be satisfied by the *complete* set of rules in a program. However, the main use of the special form in our analysis tools is not to identify special-case programs. The leverage of the special form comes about when we can apply it to a subset of rules and conclude that at least some of the variables must attain stable values in finite time. The exploitation of the special form in a general strategy will be explained in the next section.

10.6.3   The General Analysis Strategy

Our general strategy for tackling the analysis problem is best understood by an example.

Example 6

  input: read(b, c)

1. $a1$:= true IF b = true AND c = true
2. [] $a1$:= true IF b = true AND c = false
3. [] $a2$:= false IF c = true
4. [] $a3$:= true IF $a1$ = true AND $a2$ = false
5. [] $a4$:= true IF $a1$ = false AND $a2$ = false
6. [] $a4$:= false IF $a1$ = false AND $a2$ = true

For this program, $L \cap T \neq \emptyset$ and thus the rules are not of the special form described in the preceding section. However, observe that rules 1, 2, and 3 by themselves are of the special form and that all the variables in these rules do not appear in LHS of the rest of the rules of the program, and thus will not be modified by them. (Rules 1, 2, and 3 are actually the rules in the program of example 4.) We can readily conclude that the variables $a1$ and $a2$ must attain stable values in finite time, and these two variables can be considered as *constants* for rules 4, 5, and 6 of the program. We can take advantage of this observation and *rewrite* the program into a simpler one, as shown below.

input: read($a1, a2$)

4. [] $a3 := $ true IF $a1 = $ true AND $a2 = $ false
5. [] $a4 := $ true IF $a1 = $ false AND $a2 = $ false
6. [] $a4 := $ false IF $a1 = $ false AND $a2 = $ true

Note that $a1$ and $a2$ are now treated as input variables. This reduced program is of the special form since all assignments are to constants, L and T are disjoint, and all tests are mutually exclusive. Hence this program is always guaranteed to reach a fixed point in finite time. This guarantees that the original program must reach a fixed point in finite time.

In fact, more special forms can be exploited in the above fashion. Our general strategy for tackling the analysis problem is as follows.

1. Identify some subset of the rules that is of a special form (determined by looking up a catalog of special forms) and that can be treated independently. Rewrite the program to take advantage of the fact that some variables can be treated as constants because of the special form.
2. If none of the special forms applies, identify an independent subset of the rules and check the state space for that subset to determine if a fixed point can always be reached. Rewrite the program as in (1) to yield simpler programs (with fewer rules) if possible.
3. Perform an analysis on each of the programs resulting from (1) or (2).

In the appendix, we present an analysis of the Cryogenic Hydrogen Pressure Malfunction Procedure of the Space Shuttle Vehicle Pressure Control System. By performing a simple transformation (rewriting) on the subset of this program, we can actually obtain an equivalent program that is of the special form. The transformation consists of replacing those test variables that also appear in the LHS by their corresponding test expressions as long as the tests do not contain any LHS variables. (The replacement for some test variables may involve more than one level of substitution of variables. Both the original version and the transformed version of the program appear in the appendix.) As a result, the transformed program satisfies special form condition (3), whereas the original version does not. All rules in the transformed program are compatible and the program is always guaranteed to reach a fixed point in a finite number of iterations.

We are incorporating more powerful textual analysis procedures into our suite of design tools as they are discovered. A more comprehensive treatment of special forms that guarantee that an EQL program will always reach a fixed point in finite time, together with formal proofs of correctness, will be given later in this chapter.

10.7 INDUSTRIAL EXAMPLE: ANALYSIS OF THE CRYOGENIC HYDROGEN PRESSURE MALFUNCTION PROCEDURE OF THE SPACE SHUTTLE VEHICLE PRESSURE CONTROL SYSTEM

In this section, we analyze a "real-life" real-time decision system using our analysis tools. The real-time decision system is called the Cryogenic Hydrogen Pressure Malfunction Procedure of the Space Shuttle Vehicle Pressure Control System. It is invoked in every monitor-decide cycle to diagnose the condition of the Cryogenic Hydrogen Pressure Control System and to give advice for correcting the diagnosed malfunctions. The complete EQL program for this malfunction procedure consists of 36 rules, 31 sensor input variables, and 32 program variables. We have verified, using our analysis tools, that a large subset of this decision system is guaranteed to reach a safe fixed point in a finite number of iterations. The EQL program for this subset, given below, consists of 23 rules, 20 sensor input variables, and 23 program variables. Understanding the meaning of most of these sensor input and program variables requires specialized knowledge of the pressure control system, but this is not essential for understanding this example.

Define the following sensor input variables:

v63a1a	sensor H2 P Normal.
v63a1b	sensor H2 P High.
v63a1c	sensor H2 P Low.
v63a3	sensor Press in all tks < 153 psia.
v63a5	sensor Both P and TK P of affected tk low.
v63a8	sensor Received O2 PRESS Alarm and/or S68 CRYO H2 PRES and
	S68 CRYO 2 PRES msg lines.
v63a11	sensor TK3 and/or TK4 the affected tk.
v63a12	sensor TK3 and TK4 depleted, QTY < 10%.
v63a13	sensor a13.
v63a16	sensor CNTLR cb of affected tk on Pnl ML868 open.
v63a17	sensor TK3 and TK4 Htrs cycle on when press in both tks = 217–223 psia.
v63a22	sensor a22.
v63a23	sensor TK3 and/or TK4 the affected tk.
v63a26	sensor TK3 and TK4 htrs were deactivated (all htrs switches
	in OFF when the problem occurred).
v63a29	sensor Press in both TK3 and TK4 > 293.8 psia.
v63a31	sensor Both P and TK P of affected tk high.

v63a32	sensor MANF Ps agree with P and TK P of affected TK.
v63a34a	sensor P high.
v63a34b	sensor TK P high.
v63b7	sensor b7.

Define the following program variables:

v63a2	diagnosis: C/W failure.
v63a4	diagnosis: System leak. Execute ECLS SSR-1(7).
v63a6	diagnosis: Leak between affected TK and check valve. Leak cannot be isolated.
v63a7	action: Deactivate htrs in affected tk.
v63a9	recovery: Reconfigure htrs per BUS LOSS SSR.
v63a10	temporary variable.
v63a14	if true, then CNTLR cb of affected tk (TK1 and/or TKS) on Pnl 013 is open.
	if false, then CNTLR cb of affected tk (TK1 and/or TK2) on Pnl 013 is closed.
v63a15	diagnosis: Possible electrical problem. Do not attempt to reset circuit breaker.
v63a18	diagnosis: P 63axduce failed low. Continue to operate TK3 and TK4 in AUTO.
v63a19	diagnosis: Possible electrical problem. Do not attempt to reset circuit breaker.
v63a20	diagnosis: PWR failure in affected HTR CNTLR.
v63a21	action: deactivate htrs in affected tk(s).
v63a24	diagnosis: P Xducer failed low. Continue to operate TK1 and TK2 in AUTO.
v63a25	diagnosis: PWR failure in affected htr cntlr.
v63a27	diagnosis: Instrumentation failure. No action required.
v63a28	action: Operate TK1 and TK2 htrs in manual mode.
v63a30	diagnosis: Auto pressure control failure.
v63a33	diagnosis: Line blockage in tk reading high.
v63a35	diagnosis: Auto pressure control or RPC failure.
v63a36	diagnosis: Instrumentation failure.
v63a37	action: Leave affected htrs deactivated until MCC develops consumables management plan.
v63a38	diagnosis: Instrumentation failure.
v63a39	action: Activate htrs.

The syntax of EQL is similar to Pascal with declarations of constants and variables. Input variables are declared in the INPUTVAR section. The INIT part initializes the program variables as well as the input variables. As indicated previously, since EQL is used for the design and analysis of real-time decision systems, the current version simulates the reading of external sensors by initializing the input variables before any rule is fired in the invocation. In an actual implementation of the real-time decision system, the EQL program should read in the input values from sensors attached to the external environment before each invocation of the set of rules. The RULES part specifies the set of rules of the program. The TRACE statement instructs the program to print out the values of the specified variables after every rule firing, and the PRINT statement prints out the values of the specified variables after the program reaches a fixed point. The EQL program for the subset of the malfunction procedure is:

PROGRAM cryov63a;
CONST
        true = 1;
        false = 0;
VAR
        v63a2, v63a4, v63a6, v63a7, v63a9, v63a10, v63a14, v63a15, v63a18, v63a19, v63a20,
        v63a21, v63a24, v63a25, v63a27, v63a28, v63a30, v63a33, v63a35, v63a36, v63a37,
        v63a38, v63a39 : BOOLEAN;
INPUTVAR
        v63a1a, v63a1b, v63a1c, v63a3, v63a5, v63a8, v63a11, v63a12, v63a13, v63a16,
        v63a17, v63a22, v63a23, v63a26, v63a29, v63a31, v63a32, v63a34a, v63a34b,
        v63b7 : BOOLEAN;
INIT
        v63a2 := false, v63a4 := false, v63a6 := false, v63a7 := false, v63a9 := false,
        v63a14 := false, v63a15 := false, v63a18 := false, v63a19 := false, v63a20 := false,
        v63a21 := false, v63a10 := false, v63a24 := false, v63a25 := false, v63a27 := false,
        v63a28 := false, v63a30 := false, v63a33 := false, v63a35 := false, v63a36 := false,
        v63a37 := false, v63a38 := false, v63a39 := false,

        v63a1a := true, v63a1b := true, v63a1c := true, v63a3 := true, v63a5 := true,
        v63a8 := true, v63a11 := true, v63a12 := true, v63a13 := true, v63a16 := true,
        v63a17 := true, v63a22 := true, v63a23 := false, v63a26 := true, v63a29 := false,
        v63a31 := true, v63a32 := false, v63a34a := true, v63a34b := true, v63b7 := true
RULES
        v63a2 := true IF (v63a1a = true)
        []v63a4 := true IF (v63a1c = true) AND (v63a3 = true)
        []v63a6 := true IF (v63a1c = true) AND (v63a3 = false) AND (v63a5 = true)
        []v63a7 := true IF (v63a6 = true)
        []v63a9 := true IF (v63a1c = true) AND (v63a3 = false) AND (v63a5 = false) AND
                        (v63a8 = true)
        []v63a10 := true IF (v63a9 = true)
        []v63a14 := true IF (v63a12 = true) OR ((v63a12 = false) AND (v63a13 = true))
        []v63a15 := true IF (v63a1c = true) AND (v63a3 = false) AND (v63a5 = false) AND
                        (v63a8 = false) AND (v63a11 = false) AND
                        (v63a12 = true) AND (v63a14 = true)
        []v63a18 := true IF (v63a1c = true) AND (v63a3 = false) AND (v63a5 = false) AND
                        (v63a8 = false) AND (v63a11 = true) AND
                        (v63a16 = true) AND (v63a17 = true)
        []v63a19 := true IF (v63a1c = true) AND (v63a3 = false) AND (v63a5 = false) AND
                        (v63a8 = false) AND (v63a11 = true) AND (v63a16 = true)
        []v63a20 := true IF (v63a1c = true) AND (v63a3 = false) AND (v63a5 = false) AND
                        (v63a8 = false) AND (v63a11 = true) AND
                        (v63a16 = true) AND (v63a17 = false)
        []v63a21 := true IF (v63a19 = true) OR (v63a20 = true)
        []v63a24 := true IF (v63a22 = true) AND (v63a14 = false) AND (v63a12 = true) AND
                        (v63a11 = false) AND (v63a8 = false) AND (v63a5 = false) AND
                        (v63a3 = false) AND (v63a1c = true)

[]v63a25 := true IF (v63a22 = false) AND (v63a14 = false) AND (v63a12 = true) AND
        (v63a11 = false) AND (v63a8 = false) AND (v63a5 = false) AND
        (v63a3 = false) AND (v63a1c = true)

[]v63a27 := true IF (v63a26 = true) AND (((v63a23 = true) AND (v63a1b = true)) OR
        (v63b7 = true))

[]v63a28 := true IF (v63a25 = true) OR (v63a15 = true)

[]v63a30 := true IF (((v63a1b = true) AND (v63a23 = true)) OR (v63b7 = true)) AND
        (v63a26 = false) AND (v63a29 = true)

[]v63a33 := true IF (v63a32 = false) AND (v63a31 = true) AND (v63a29 = false) AND
        (v63a26 = false) AND (v63a23 = true) AND (v63a1b = true)

[]v63a35 := true IF (v63a32 = true) AND (v63a31 = true) AND (v63a29 = true) AND
        (v63a26 = false) AND (v63a23 = true) AND (v63a1b = true)

[]v63a36 := true IF (v63a34b = true) AND (v63a31 = false) AND
        (v63a29 = false) AND (v63a26 = false) AND (v63a23 = true) AND
        (v63a1b = true)

[]v63a37 := true IF (v63a30 = true) AND (v63a33 = false) AND
        (v63a35 = false) AND (v63a38 = true)

[]v63a38 := true IF (v63a34a = true) AND (v63a31 = false) AND
        (v63a29 = false) AND (v63a26 = false) AND (v63a23 = true) AND
        (v63a1b = true)

[]v63a39 := true IF (v63a36 = true)

TRACE
    v63a2, v63a4, v63a6, v63a7, v63a9, v63a10, v63a14, v63a15, v63a18, v63a19, v63a20,
    v63a21, v63a24, v63a25, v63a27, v63a28, v63a30, v63a33, v63a35, v63a36, v63a37,
    v63a38, v63a39
PRINT
    v63a2, v63a4, v63a6, v63a7, v63a9, v63a10, v63a14, v63a15, v63a18, v63a19, v63a20,
    v63a21, v63a24, v63a25, v63a27, v63a28, v63a30, v63a33, v63a35, v63a36, v63a37,
    v63a38, v63a39
END.

To execute the EQL program on the Sun 3 workstation for a particular set of sensor input values given in the INIT section of the program, we translate it into a C program using the **eqtc** translator: **eqtc** ⟨example⟩ example.c. This program can be compiled using the **cc** compiler and then executed to obtain the stable output values if a fixed point exists. Note that a scheduler is used to determine the next enabled rule to fire, and the program will continue execution as long as the fixed point has not been reached. Due to space limitations, we omit the listing of the generated C program, which is similar to the one given in section 10.5.

To analyze the performance of the program given a particular combination of sensor input values, the EQL program with the given input is transformed into a finite state–space graph using the **ptf** translator by using the command: **ptf** ⟨example⟩ example.fsg. It also generates a CTL temporal-logic formula for checking whether this program will reach a fixed point in bounded time using the given input. The file *mc.in* is generated as input to the model checker and the timing analyzer.

```
Finite State Space Graph Corresponding to Input Program:
-----------------------------------------------------------

state    next states
-----    -----------

rule #  1 2 3 4 5 6 7 8 9 10 11 12 13 14 15 16 17 18 19 20 21 22 23
0:      1 2 0 0 0 0 3 0 0 0  0  0  0  0  4  0  0  0  0  0  0  0  0
1:      1 5 1 1 1 1 6 1 1 1  1  1  1  1  7  1  1  1  1  1  1  1  1
2:      5 2 2 2 2 2 8 2 2 2  2  2  2  2  9  2  2  2  2  2  2  2  2
3:      6 8 3 3 3 3 3 3 3 3  3  3  3  3 10  3  3  3  3  3  3  3  3
4:      7 9 4 4 4 4 10 4 4 4  4  4  4  4  4  4  4  4  4  4  4  4  4
5:      5 5 5 5 5 5 11 5 5 5  5  5  5  5 12  5  5  5  5  5  5  5  5
6:      6 11 6 6 6 6 6 6 6 6  6  6  6  6 13  6  6  6  6  6  6  6  6
7:      7 12 7 7 7 7 13 7 7 7  7  7  7  7  7  7  7  7  7  7  7  7  7
8:      11 8 8 8 8 8 8 8 8 8  8  8  8  8 14  8  8  8  8  8  8  8  8
9:      12 9 9 9 9 9 14 9 9 9  9  9  9  9  9  9  9  9  9  9  9  9  9
10:     13 14 10 10 10 10 10 10 10 10 10 10 10 10 10 10 10 10 10 10 10 10 10
11:     11 11 11 11 11 11 11 11 11 11 11 11 11 11 15 11 11 11 11 11 11 11 11
12:     12 12 12 12 12 12 15 12 12 12 12 12 12 12 12 12 12 12 12 12 12 12 12
13:     13 15 13 13 13 13 13 13 13 13 13 13 13 13 13 13 13 13 13 13 13 13 13
14:     15 14 14 14 14 14 14 14 14 14 14 14 14 14 14 14 14 14 14 14 14 14 14
15:     15 15 15 15 15 15 15 15 15 15 15 15 15 15 15 15 15 15 15 15 15 15 15

State Labels:
-------------

state  (v63a2, v63a4, v63a6, v63a7, v63a9, v63a10, v63a14, v63a15, v63a18,
        v63a19, v63a20, v63a21, v63a24, v63a25, v63a27, v63a28, v63a30,
        v63a33, v63a35, v63a36, v63a37, v63a38, v63a39, v63a1a, v63a1b,
        v63a1c, v63a3, v63a5, v63a8, v63a11, v63a12, v63a13, v63a16, v63a17,
        v63a22, v63a23, v63a26, v63a29, v63a31, v63a32, v63a34a, v63a34b,
        v63b7)

0      0 0 0 0 0 0 0 0 0 0 0 0 0 0 0 0 0 0 0 0 0 0 0 0 1 1 1 1 1 1 1 1 1 1
       0 1 0 1 0 1 1 1
1      1 0 0 0 0 0 0 0 0 0 0 0 0 0 0 0 0 0 0 0 0 0 0 0 1 1 1 1 1 1 1 1 1 1
       0 1 0 1 0 1 1 1
2      0 1 0 0 0 0 0 0 0 0 0 0 0 0 0 0 0 0 0 0 0 0 0 0 1 1 1 1 1 1 1 1 1 1
       0 1 0 1 0 1 1 1
3      0 0 0 0 0 0 1 0 0 0 0 0 0 0 0 0 0 0 0 0 0 0 0 0 1 1 1 1 1 1 1 1 1 1
       0 1 0 1 0 1 1 1
4      0 0 0 0 0 0 0 0 0 0 0 0 0 0 1 0 0 0 0 0 0 0 0 0 1 1 1 1 1 1 1 1 1 1
       0 1 0 1 0 1 1 1
5      1 1 0 0 0 0 0 0 0 0 0 0 0 0 0 0 0 0 0 0 0 0 0 0 1 1 1 1 1 1 1 1 1 1
       0 1 0 1 0 1 1 1
6      1 0 0 0 0 0 1 0 0 0 0 0 0 0 0 0 0 0 0 0 0 0 0 0 1 1 1 1 1 1 1 1 1 1
       0 1 0 1 0 1 1 1
7      1 0 0 0 0 0 0 0 0 0 0 0 0 0 1 0 0 0 0 0 0 0 0 0 1 1 1 1 1 1 1 1 1 1
       0 1 0 1 0 1 1 1
8      0 1 0 0 0 0 1 0 0 0 0 0 0 0 0 0 0 0 0 0 0 0 0 0 1 1 1 1 1 1 1 1 1 1
       0 1 0 1 0 1 1 1
9      0 1 0 0 0 0 0 0 0 0 0 0 0 0 1 0 0 0 0 0 0 0 0 0 1 1 1 1 1 1 1 1 1 1
       0 1 0 1 0 1 1 1
```

```
10      0 0 0 0 0 0 1 0 0 0 0 0 0 0 1 0 0 0 0 0 0 0 0 1 1 1 1 1 1 1 1 1 1 1
        0 1 0 1 0 1 1 1
11      1 1 0 0 0 0 1 0 0 0 0 0 0 0 0 0 0 0 0 0 0 0 0 0 1 1 1 1 1 1 1 1 1 1
        0 1 0 1 0 1 1 1
12      1 1 0 0 0 0 0 0 0 0 0 0 0 0 1 0 0 0 0 0 0 0 0 0 1 1 1 1 1 1 1 1 1 1
        0 1 0 1 0 1 1 1
13      1 0 0 0 0 0 1 0 0 0 0 0 0 0 1 0 0 0 0 0 0 0 0 0 1 1 1 1 1 1 1 1 1 1
        0 1 0 1 0 1 1 1
14      0 1 0 0 0 0 1 0 0 0 0 0 0 0 1 0 0 0 0 0 0 0 0 0 1 1 1 1 1 1 1 1 1 1
        0 1 0 1 0 1 1 1
15      1 1 0 0 0 0 1 0 0 0 0 0 0 0 1 0 0 0 0 0 0 0 0 0 1 1 1 1 1 1 1 1 1 1
        0 1 0 1 0 1 1 1
```

The file *mc.in* contains the adjacency matrix representation of the labeled finite state-space graph and a CTL formula for checking the reachability of a fixed point.

```
16
1 1 1 1 1 0 0 0 0 0 0 0 0 0 0 0
0 1 0 0 0 1 1 1 0 0 0 0 0 0 0 0
0 0 1 0 0 1 0 0 1 1 0 0 0 0 0 0
0 0 0 1 0 0 1 0 1 0 1 0 0 0 0 0
0 0 0 0 1 0 0 1 0 1 1 0 0 0 0 0
0 0 0 0 0 1 0 0 0 0 1 1 0 0 0 0
0 0 0 0 0 0 1 0 0 0 0 1 0 1 0 0
0 0 0 0 0 0 0 1 0 0 0 0 1 0 0 0
0 0 0 0 0 0 0 0 1 0 0 1 0 0 1 0
0 0 0 0 0 0 0 0 0 1 0 0 1 0 1 0
0 0 0 0 0 0 0 0 0 0 1 0 0 1 1 0
0 0 0 0 0 0 0 0 0 0 0 1 0 0 0 1
0 0 0 0 0 0 0 0 0 0 0 0 1 0 0 1
0 0 0 0 0 0 0 0 0 0 0 0 0 1 0 1
0 0 0 0 0 0 0 0 0 0 0 0 0 0 1 1
0 0 0 0 0 0 0 0 0 0 0 0 0 0 0 1
0 n1 ;
1 n1 ;
2 n1 ;
3 n1 ;
4 n1 ;
5 n1 ;
6 n1 ;
7 n1 ;
8 n1 ;
9 n1 ;
10 n1 ;
11 n1 ;
12 n1 ;
13 n1 ;
14 n1 ;
15 f1 ;
(au n1 f1)
0
```

The temporal-logic model checker **mcf** is then used to determine whether a fixed point is reachable in a bounded number of iterations by analyzing this finite state-space graph with the specified launch state: **mcf** < *mc.in*. To verify that the program is guaranteed to reach a fixed point given any legal combination of input values, all finite state-space graphs, each with a different launch state must be analyzed by the model checker. Therefore, the above graph is one of 2^{20} possible graphs that must be checked using the model checker if all combinations of the 20 input values are allowed. The tool **ptaf** automatically performs the above translation and analysis on all state-space graphs corresponding to the EQL program.

Finally, the timing analyzer **fptime** is invoked to determine, for the particular set of input values, the number of rule firings and the sequence of rule firings leading to a fixed point, if at least one exists: **fptime** < *mc.in*. The following is a partial output from **fptime**:

```
> initial state:     0
> fixed-point state(s):
> 15
> initial state: 0    fixed-point state: 15
> maximum number of iterations: 4
> path:      0    1    5    11    15
```

Using the completely automated tool **ptaf**, we obtain the following messages:

```
> The program always reaches a fixed point in finite time.
> The maximum number of iterations to reach a fixed point is 6.
```

Applying the transformation described earlier to the above program, we obtain the following equivalent program, which falls into a subclass of EQL programs for which the question of bounded-time fixed-point reachability can be easily answered by performing a simple textual analysis and without generating the corresponding state-space graph. This equivalent program is of the special form described earlier. Notice that all LHS variables are distinct. Hence, all rules in this program are compatible and thus the program is always guaranteed to reach a fixed point in a bounded number of iterations.

```
PROGRAM cryov63a;
CONST
     true = 1;
     false = 0;
VAR
     v63a2, v63a4, v63a6, v63a7, v63a9, v63a10, v63a14, v63a15, v63a18, v63a19, v63a20,
     v63a21, v63a24, v63a25, v63a27, v63a28, v63a30, v63a33, v63a35, v63a36, v63a37,
     v63a38, v63a39 : BOOLEAN;
INPUTVAR
     v63a1a, v63a1b, v63a1c, v63a3, v63a5, v63a8, v63a11, v63a12, v63a13, v63a16,
     v63a17, v63a22, v63a23, v63a26, v63a29, v63a31, v63a32, v63a34a, v63a34b,
     v63b7 : BOOLEAN;
```

INIT
        v63a2 := false, v63a4 := false, v63a6 := false, v63a7 := false, v63a9 := false,
        v63a14 := false, v63a15 := false, v63a18 := false, v63a19 := false, v63a20 := false,
        v63a21 := false, v63a10 := false, v63a24 := false, v63a25 := false, v63a27 := false,
        v63a28 := false, v63a30 := false, v63a33 := false, v63a35 := false, v63a36 := false,
        v63a37 := false, v63a38 := false, v63a39 := false,

        v63a1a := true, v63a1b := true, v63a1c := true, v63a3 := true, v63a5 := true,
        v63a8 := true, v63a11 := true, v63a12 := true, v63a13 := true, v63a16 := true,
        v63a17 := true, v63a22 := true, v63a23 := false, v63a26 := true, v63a29 := false,
        v63a31 := true, v63a32 := false, v63a34a := true, v63a34b := true, v63b7 := true

RULES
        v63a2 := true IF (v63a1a = true)
        []v63a4 := true IF (v63a1c = true) AND (v63a3 = true)
        []v63a6 := true IF (v63a1c = true) AND (v63a3 = false) AND (v63a5 = true)
        []v63a7 := true IF (v63a1c = true) AND (v63a3 = false) AND (v63a5 = true)
        []v63a9 := true IF (v63a1c = true) AND (v63a3 = false) AND (v63a5 = false) AND
                        (v63a8 = true)
        []v63a10 := true IF (v63a1c = true) AND (v63a3 = false) AND (v63a5 = false) AND
                        (v63a8 = true)
        []v63a14 := true IF (v63a12 = true) OR ((v63a12 = false) AND (v63a13 = true))
        []v63a15 := true IF (v63a1c = true) AND (v63a3 = false) AND (v63a5 = false) AND
                        (v63a8 = false) AND (v63a11 = false) AND (v63a12 = true) AND
                        ((v63a12 = true) OR ((v63a12 = false) AND (v63a13 = true)))
        []v63a18 := true IF (v63a1c = true) AND (v63a3 = false) AND (v63a5 = false) AND
                        (v63a8 = false) AND (v63a11 = true) AND (v63a16 = true) AND
                        (v63a17 = true)
        []v63a19 := true IF (v63a1c = true) AND (v63a3 = false) AND (v63a5 = false) AND
                        (v63a8 = false) AND (v63a11 = true) AND (v63a16 = true)
        []v63a20 := true IF (v63a1c = true) AND (v63a3 = false) AND (v63a5 = false) AND
                        (v63a8 = false) AND (v63a11 = true) AND (v63a16 = true) AND
                        (v63a17 = false)
        []v63a21 := true IF ((v63a1c = true) AND (v63a3 = false) AND (v63a5 = false) AND
                        (v63a8 = false) AND (v63a11 = true) AND (v63a16 = true)) OR
                        ((v63a1c = true) AND (v63a3 = false) AND (v63a5 = false) AND
                        (v63a8 = false) AND (v63a11 = true) AND (v63a16 = true) AND
                        (v63a17 = false))
        []v63a24 := true IF (v63a22 = true) AND
                        ((v63a12 = true) OR ((v63a12 = false) AND (v63a13 = true))) AND
                        (v63a12 = true) AND (v63a11 = false) AND (v63a8 = false) AND
                        (v63a5 = false) AND (v63a3 = false) AND (v63a1c = true)
        []v63a25 := true IF (v63a22 = false) AND
                        (v63a12 = true) OR ((v63a12 = false) AND (v63a13 = true)) AND
                        (v63a12 = true) AND (v63a11 = false) AND (v63a8 = false) AND
                        (v63a5 = false) AND (v63a3 = false) AND (v63a1c = true)
        []v63a27 := true IF (v63a26 = true) AND (((v63a23 = true) AND (v63a1b = true)) OR
                        (v63b7 = true))

[]v63a28 := true IF ((v63a22 = false) AND
(v63a12 = true) OR ((v63a12 = false) AND (v63a13 = true)) AND
(v63a12 = true) AND (v63a11 = false) AND (v63a8 = false) AND
(v63a5 = false) AND (v63a3 = false) AND (v63a1c = true)) OR
((v63a26 = true) AND (((v63a23 = true) AND (v63a1b = true)) OR
(v63b7 = true)))

[]v63a30 := true IF ((((v63a1b = true) AND (v63a23 = true)) OR (v63b7 = true)) AND
(v63a26 = false) AND (v63a29 = true)

[]v63a33 := true IF (v63a32 = false) AND (v63a31 = true) AND (v63a29 = false) AND
(v63a26 = false) AND (v63a23 = true) AND (v63a1b = true)

[]v63a35 := true IF (v63a32 = true) AND (v63a31 = true) AND (v63a29 = true) AND
(v63a26 = false) AND (v63a23 = true) AND (v63a1b = true)

[]v63a36 := true IF (v63a34b = true) AND (v63a31 = false) AND
(v63a29 = false) AND (v63a26 = false) AND (v63a23 = true) AND
(v63a1b = true)

[]v63a37 := true IF ((((v63a1b = true) AND (v63a23 = true)) OR (v63b7 = true)) AND
(v63a26 = false) AND (v63a29 = true)) AND
((v63a32 = false) AND (v63a31 = true) AND (v63a29 = false) AND
(v63a26 = false) AND (v63a23 = true) AND (v63a1b = true)) AND
((v63a32 = true) AND (v63a31 = true) AND (v63a29 = true) AND
(v63a26 = false) AND (v63a23 = true) AND (v63a1b = true)) AND
((v63a34a = true) AND (v63a31 = false) AND (v63a29 = false) AND
(v63a26 = false) AND (v63a23 = true) AND (v63a1b = true))

[]v63a38 := true IF ((v63a34a = true) AND (v63a31 = false) AND
(v63a29 = false) AND (v63a26 = false) AND (v63a23 = true) AND
(v63a1b = true))

[]v63a39 := true IF (v63a34b = true) AND (v63a31 = false) AND
(v63a29 = false) AND (v63a26 = false) AND (v63a23 = true) AND
(v63a1b = true)

TRACE
v63a2, v63a4, v63a6, v63a7, v63a9, v63a10, v63a14, v63a15, v63a18, v63a19, v63a20,
v63a21, v63a24, v63a25, v63a27, v63a28, v63a30, v63a33, v63a35, v63a36, v63a37,
v63a38, v63a39
PRINT
v63a2, v63a4, v63a6, v63a7, v63a9, v63a10, v63a14, v63a15, v63a18, v63a19, v63a20,
v63a21, v63a24, v63a25, v63a27, v63a28, v63a30, v63a33, v63a35, v63a36, v63a37,
v63a38, v63a39
END.

10.8 THE SYNTHESIS PROBLEM

The following definition is needed to formalize the synthesis problem. We say that an equational rule-based program P_2 is an *extension* of a program P_1 iff the following conditions hold: (1) The variables of P_1 are a subset of those of P_2; (2) P_1 has the same launch states as the projection of the state space of P_2 onto that of P_1; that is, if P_2 has more variables than P_1, we consider only those variables in P_2 that are also in P_1; (3) The launch states of P_1 and the corresponding ones in P_2 have the same end points. Notice that we do not require the state-space graph of P_1 to be the same as the corresponding graph of P_2; for example, the paths from launch states to their end points may be shorter in P_2. The synthesis problem is: Given an equational rule-based program P that always reaches a safe fixed point in finite time but is not fast enough to meet the timing constraints under a fair scheduler, determine whether an extension of P exists that meets both the timing and integrity constraints under some scheduler.

For programs in which all variables have finite domains, we can in principle compute all the end points for each launch state since the state-space graph is finite. We can create a new program from the given program as follows. The new program has the same variables as the given program. Suppose s is a launch state and s' is an end point of s. We create a rule r that is enabled iff the program is in s and firing r will result in the program being in s'; i.e., the enabling condition of r is to match the values of the variables in s, and the multiple assignment statement of r assigns to the variables the corresponding values of those in s'. By this construction, the new program will always reach a fixed point in one iteration. Thus in theory, a solution always exists for the synthesis problem in the case of finite variables. This solution is very expensive in terms of memory since there are at least as many rules as there are launch states, even though some optimization can be performed to minimize the number of rules by exploiting techniques similar to those used in programmable logic array optimization. However, we still have to compute the end points for each launch state, and this can be computationally expensive.

We would like to find solutions to the synthesis problem without having to check the entire state space of a program. Two general approaches have been identified:

1. transforming the given equational rule-based program by adding, deleting, and/or modifying rules, and
2. optimizing the scheduler to select the rules to fire such that a fixed point is always reached within the response-time constraint. This assumes that at least one sufficiently short path exists from a launch state to every one of its end points.

We shall illustrate both approaches with the program in example 1, which is reproduced below.

Example 7

initially: *object_detected* = false, *sensor_a_status*, *sensor_b_status* = good
input: read(*sensor_a*, *sensor_b*, *sensor_c*)

1.   *object_detected* := true IF *sensor_a* = 1 AND *sensor_a_status* = good
2. [] *object_detected* := true IF *sensor_b* = 1 AND *sensor_b_status* = good
3. [] *object_detected* := false IF *sensor_a* = 0 AND *sensor_a_status* = good
4. [] *object_detected* := false IF *sensor_b* = 0 AND *sensor_b_status* = good

5. []   *sensor_a_status* := bad IF *sensor_a* ≠ *sensor_c* AND *sensor_b_status* = good
6. []   *sensor_b_status* := bad IF *sensor_b* ≠ *sensor_c* AND *sensor_a_status* = good

In this program, the variables *sensor_a_status* and *sensor_b_status* are initially set to *good*, and the variable *object_detected* is initially set to *false*. At the beginning of each invocation, the sensor values are read into the variables *sensor_a*, *sensor_b*, *sensor_c*. Note that if *sensor_a* and *sensor_b* read in values 1 and 0, respectively, rule 1 and rule 4 may fire alternatively for an unbounded number of times before either rule 5 or rule 6 is fired. Similarly, if *sensor_a* and *sensor_b* read in values 0 and 1, respectively, rule 2 and rule 3 may fire alternatively for an unbounded number of times before either rule 5 or rule 6 is fired. In this case, *sensor_c* can be used to arbitrate between rules 1 and 4, or rules 2 and 3 by firing rule 5 or 6. (However, notice that only one of rules 5 and 6 may fire in each invocation; we do not want *sensor_c* to override both *sensor_a* and *sensor_b*.) This program will reach a fixed point in finite time since fairness guarantees that rule 5 or rule 6 will eventually be fired.

In approach (1), we ensure that this program will reach a fixed point in a bounded number of iterations starting from any launch state by performing the appropriate program transformation. First, we detect those rules that may constitute a cyclic firing sequence. In this program, the alternate firings of rule 1 and rule 4, or rule 2 and rule 3, may constitute a cyclic firing sequence. Noting that the firing of either rule 5 or rule 6 may disable two of rules 1–4, we add a rule (rule 7) and some additional conditions to enforce the firing of either rule 5 or rule 6 first if a conflict exists between the values read into *sensor_a* and *sensor_b*, thus breaking the cycle. The transformed program, which is always guaranteed to reach a fixed point in a bounded number of iterations, is shown below.

> initially: *object_detected* = false, *sensor_a_status, sensor_b_status* = good
> invoke: *conflict* := true
> input: read(*sensor_a, sensor_b, sensor_c*)

1.   *object_detected* := true IF *sensor_a* = 1 AND *sensor_a_status* = good AND
                    conflict = false
2. []   *object_detected* := true IF *sensor_b* = 1 AND *sensor_b_status* = good AND
                    conflict = false
3. []   *object_detected* := false IF *sensor_a* = 0 AND *sensor_a_status* = good AND
                    conflict = false
4. []   *object_detected* := false IF *sensor_b* = 0 AND *sensor_b_status* = good AND
                    conflict = false
5. []   *sensor_a_status* := bad IF *sensor_a* ≠ *sensor_c* AND *sensor_b_status* = good
6. []   *sensor_b_status* := bad IF *sensor_b* ≠ *sensor_c* AND *sensor_a_status* = good
7. []   *conflict* := false IF *sensor_a* = *sensor_b* OR *sensor_a_status* = bad OR
                    sensor_b_status = bad

In this program, the variable *conflict* is always set to *true* by the *invoke* command of EQL, which is executed at the beginning of each invocation.

In approach (2), we customize an optimal scheduler that always selects the shortest path to any end point from a launch state. For the program in the example, this can be achieved by a fixed-priority scheduler which assigns a higher priority to rules 5 and 6; that is, if rule 5 or rule 6 is enabled, it is always fired before rules 1–4.

It should be emphasized that the two approaches for solving the synthesis problem are not in general polynomial time. Determining whether a scheduler exists that meets a response-time constraint is NP-hard, as we shall show in the next section.

10.8.1 Time Complexity of Scheduling Equational Rule-Based Programs

Consider the following equational rule-based program:

initially: $R = 0, t_1 = t_2 = \cdots = t_n = 0$

input: read (C)

1. $\quad R := R + q_1(\bar{t})!t_1 := t_1 + 1$ IF $R < C$
2. [] $\quad R := R + q_2(\bar{t})!t_2 := t_2 + 1$ IF $R < C$

.

.

$n.$ [] $\quad R := R + q_n(\bar{t})!t_n := t_n + 1$ IF $R < C$

In the above program, $\bar{t}$ is the vector $\langle t_1, t_2, \ldots, t_n \rangle$. We can think of the variable R, which is initially 0, as the accumulated reward for firing the rules, and t_i as the number of times rule i has been fired, which is initially 0 for all n rules. The function $q_i(\bar{t})$ gives the additional reward that can be obtained by firing rule i one more time. All the $q_i(\bar{t})$s are monotonically nondecreasing functions of $\bar{t}$, so the program may reach a fixed point in finite time, assuming that some q_is return positive values.

The *time-budgeting problem* is to decide whether the above program can increase R from 0 to $\geq C$ in T iterations, for some given T. The time-budgeting problem arises when an output must be computed within a response-time constraint of T by a real-time decision system that is composed of n subsystems. To compute the output, the decision system must invoke a number of subsystems $S_i, i = 1, \ldots, n$, each of which computes a partial output. The quality q_i of each partial output is dependent on the time t_i allocated to the subsystem S_i, and the overall quality of the output depends on some function of the quality of the partial outputs. Given a fixed time period T, the objective of the time-budgeting problem is to maximize the overall quality $R = q_1 + \cdots + q_n$ by determining an optimal partition of T into n time slices, where each time slice $t_i, i = 1, \ldots, n$ corresponds to the time allocated to subsystem S_i.

Referring to the EQL program above, it is obvious that the time-budgeting problem is in NP since a nondeterministic algorithm can guess the number of times each of the n rules should be fired and can check in polynomial time whether $t_1 + t_2 + \cdots + t_n \leq T$ and $R \geq C$. This time-budgeting problem can be shown to be NP-complete by an easy reduction from the NP-complete *knapsack problem*. The knapsack problem consists of a finite set U, a size $s(u)$, and a value $v(u)$ for each $u \in U$, a size constraint T, and a value objective C. All values $s(u)$, $v(u)$, T, and C are positive integers. The issue is to determine whether a subset $U_1 \in U$ exists such that the sum of the sizes $s(u) \in U_1 \leq T$ and the sum of the values $v(u) \in U_1 \geq C$. To transform the knapsack problem into the time-budgeting problem, let each item $u_i \in U$ correspond to a unique rule i such that

$$q_i(\bar{t}) = \begin{cases} 0 & \text{if} \quad t_i < s(u_i) \\ v(u_i) & \text{if} \quad t_i \geq s(u_i) \end{cases}.$$

Obviously, the knapsack problem has a solution iff it is possible to schedule a subset of the rules to fire a total of T times so that $R \geq C$.

The time-budgeting problem captures the property of an important class of real-time applications in which the precision and/or certainty of a computational result can be traded for computation time. Solution methods to this problem are therefore of practical interest. For the case in which the total reward is the sum of the value functions of the subsystems, the problem can be solved by a well known pseudo-polynomial time algorithm based on the dynamic programming solution to the knapsack problem. Since this computation is done off-line, computation time is usually not critical. However, if the total reward is a more complex function than the sum, the dynamic programming approach may not apply. We shall propose another approach that is suboptimal but can handle complex total reward functions. The idea is to use a continuous function to interpolate and bound each reward function and then apply the method of Lagrange multipliers to maximize the total reward, subject to the given timing constraint. This approach will be explored in the next section.

10.8.2   The Method of Lagrange Multipliers for Solving the Time-Budgeting Problem

Given that the reward for firing the ith rule t_i times is $q_i(t_i)$, and T is the maximum number of iterations allowed, the time-budgeting problem can be formulated as a combinatorial optimization problem whose objective is to maximize R subject to the constraint: $t_1 + \cdots + t_n - T = 0$. For the above program, $R(\bar{t}) = q_1(t_1) + \cdots + q_n(t_n)$. Other than the requirement that the t_is must be integral, this problem is in a form that can be solved by the method of Lagrange multipliers. To maximize (or minimize) a reward function $f(\bar{t})$ subject to the side condition $g(\bar{t}) = 0$ (i.e., response time constraint in our case), we solve for $\bar{t}$ in $\nabla H(\bar{t}, \lambda) = 0$, where λ is the Lagrange multiplier and

$$H(\bar{t}, \lambda) = f(\bar{t}) - \lambda \cdot g(\bar{t}).$$

Example 8. Consider the following EQL program, which is an instance of the time-budgeting problem with two rules.

initially: $R = 0, t_1 = t_2 = 0$
input: read(C)

1. $R, t_1 := R + q_1(\hat{t}), t_1 + 1$ IF $R < C$
2. [] $R, t_2 := R + q_2(\hat{t}), t_2 + 1$ IF $R < C$

Let $T = 10$. The reward functions, q_1 and q_2, for these two rules are given below.

Discrete reward function q_1									
t_1	1	2	3	4	5	6	7	8	9	10
q_1	4	5	7	8	9	9	10	11	12	12

Discrete reward function q_2									
t_1	1	2	3	4	5	6	7	8	9	10
q_1	6	8	9	9	10	10	10	10	10	10

The Lagrange multipliers method can be applied as follows. First, we interpolate and bound the two sets of data points with two continuous and differentiable functions f_1 and f_2, obtaining $f_1(t_1) = 4 \cdot t_1^{1/2}$, $f_2(t_2) = 10 \cdot (1 - e^{-t_2})$. The graph below (Figure 10.7) shows the plots of the two discrete reward functions and their

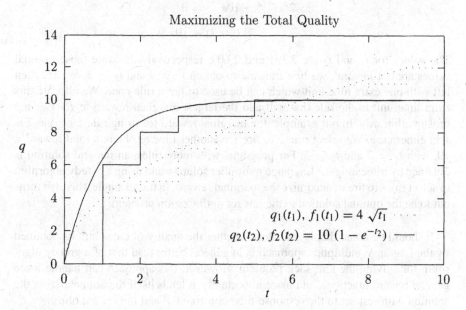

Figure 10.7   Continuous functions f_1 and f_2 approximating the discrete functions q_1 and q_2.

respective approximate continuous functions. The discrete reward function q_1 and its corresponding approximate function f_1 are plotted in dotted lines. The discrete reward function q_2 and its corresponding approximate function f_2 are plotted in solid lines.

The side constraint of this problem is $t_1 + t_2 = T = 10$. Both t_1 and t_2 must be non-negative because a rule cannot fire a negative number of times. We have:

$$H(t_1, t_2, \lambda) = f(\bar{t}) - \lambda \cdot g(\bar{t})$$
$$= f_1(t_1) + f_2(t_2) - \lambda \cdot (t_1 + t_2 - T)$$
$$= 4\,t_1^{1/2} + 10\,(1 - e^{-t_2}) - \lambda\,(t_1 + t_2 - 10).$$

Differentiating $H(t_1, t_2, \lambda)$ with respect to t_1, t_2, and λ, and then setting each derivative equal to 0, we obtain the following three equations:

$$\frac{\partial H}{\partial t_1} = 2\,t_1^{-1/2} - \lambda = 0, \tag{1}$$

$$\frac{\partial H}{\partial t_2} = 10\,e^{-t_2} - \lambda = 0, \tag{2}$$

$$\frac{\partial H}{\partial \lambda} = -(t_1 + t_2) + 10 = 0. \tag{3}$$

Combining the first two equations, we obtain two equations with two unknowns. Solving for t_1 and t_2, we get

$$2t_1^{-1/2} - 10e^{-t_2} = 0$$

$$t_1 + t_2 = 10.$$

The values for t_1 and t_2 are 7.391 and 2.609, respectively. Because these optimal values are not integral, we first truncate to obtain $t_1 = 7$ and $t_2 = 2$. We are then left with one extra time unit which can be used to fire a rule once. We allocate this extra time unit to the rule that will add the largest marginal reward to R. Ties are broken arbitrarily. In our example, the marginal reward for firing rule 1 or rule 2 is 1 in either case. We select rule 2 to fire for another time to obtain a total reward = 19, with $t_1 = 7$ and $t_2 = 3$. For programs with more rules, an integral solution is obtained by truncating the Lagrange multiplier solution and using a greedy algorithm to select rules to fire to maximize the marginal reward. In this example, this also turns out to be the optimal solution to the integer optimization problem.

It should be noted that it is unclear whether the quality of the solutions obtained by the Lagrange multiplier approach is in general better than that of a greedy algorithm for solving the knapsack problem. However, this approach can handle more general reward functions, and more importantly, it lends itself to parameterizing the solution with respect to the response-time constraint T and the reward objective C. For example, we may use a quadratic B-spline interpolation algorithm to interpolate and bound each set of discrete reward values to obtain n quadratic functions. After taking the partial derivatives, as required by the Lagrange multiplier method, we have $n + 1$ linear equations. Given the values of T and C at run time, these equations can be efficiently solved, for example, by the Gaussian elimination algorithm. The use of a continuous function to bound the rewards also gives us a better handle on guaranteeing that an equational rule-based program can meet some minimum performance index in bounded time than *ad hoc* greedy algorithms, which must be analyzed for individual reward functions. Such guarantees are of great importance for safety-critical applications.

10.9 SPECIFYING TERMINATION CONDITIONS IN ESTELLA

So far we have introduced the basic features of real-time expert systems and a framework for analysis. Now we describe a comprehensive analysis approach and a language for specifying termination conditions of rule-based systems. We have seen that determining how fast an expert system can respond under all possible situations is a difficult and, in general, an undecidable problem [Browne, Cheng, and Mok, 1988].

The focus here is on determining whether a rule-based EQL program has bounded response time. The verification of whether a rule-based program satisfies the specification, that is, checking logical correctness, has been studied extensively by non-real-time system researchers and developers. Earlier, we described an efficient analysis methodology for analyzing a large class of rule-based EQL programs to determine whether a program in this class has bounded response time. In particular, we identified several sets of primitive behavioral constraint assertions called "special forms" of rules with the following property: an EQL program that satisfies all constraints in one of these sets of constraint assertions is guaranteed to have bounded response time. Once a rule set is found to have bounded response time, efficient algorithms reported in [Cheng, 1992b] can be used to compute tight response-time bounds for this rule set.

Since the verification of these constraint assertions is based on static analysis of the EQL rules and does not require checking the state-space graph corresponding to all execution sequences of these rules, our analysis methodology makes the analysis of programs with a large number of rules and variables feasible. A suite of computer-aided software engineering tools based on this analysis approach has been implemented and has been used successfully to analyze several real-time expert systems developed by Mitre and NASA for the Space Shuttle and the planned Space Station.

Unlike the design and analysis of non-time-critical systems and software, the design and analysis of real-time systems and software often require specialized knowledge about the application under consideration. General techniques applicable to all or even to a large class of real-time systems and software incur a large penalty in either performance or works for very small systems. Here, we enhance the applicability of our analysis technique by introducing a new facility with which the rule-based programmer can specify application-specific knowledge to determine the performance of an even wider range of programs. The idea is to provide the rule-based programmer a new language called Estella that has been designed for specifying behavioral constraint assertions about rule-based EQL programs. These application-specific assertions capture the requirements for achieving certain performance levels for a rule-based program in a particular application, and are used by the general analyzer to determine whether an EQL program has bounded response time. These assertions represent information about the program that is too difficult to be detected mechanically by the analysis tools.

We first review our analysis methodology and explain the motivation for using Estella to specify behavioral constraint assertions that guarantee any program satisfying these constraints will have bounded response time. Next, we introduce the Estella language and show how it can be used in conjunction with the *General Analysis Tool* (GAT) to analyze EQL programs and to facilitate the development of EQL systems with guaranteed response time. We then demonstrate the practicality of the Estella-GAT facility by analyzing two industrial rule-based systems developed by Mitre and NASA for the planned Space Station. We also discuss efficient algorithms for implementing the Estella-GAT facility.

10.9.1 Overview of the Analysis Methodology

The following definitions are needed to describe the analysis algorithm. A *special form* is a set of behavioral constraint assertions on a set of rules. A set of rules satisfying all assertions of a special form is always guaranteed to reach a fixed point in bounded time. The *state-space graph* of a rule-based program is a labeled directed graph $G = (V, E)$. V is a set of vertices, each of which is labeled by a tuple: $(x_1, \ldots, x_n, y_1, \ldots, y_m)$, where x_i is a value in the domain of the ith input sensor variable and s_j is a value in the domain of the jth non-input variable. A rule is said to be *enabled* at vertex i if and only if its enabling condition is satisfied by the tuple of variable values at vertex i. E is a set of edges, each of which denotes the firing of a rule such that an edge (i, j) connects vertex i to vertex j if and only if there is a rule R which is enabled at vertex i, and firing R will modify the non-input variables to have the same values as the tuple at vertex j. We sketch the main steps of the general analysis algorithm below. Details on its implementation will be presented later.

1. Identify some subset of the rules that is of a special form (determined by looking up a catalog of special forms) and that can be treated independently. We call a subset of rules *independent* if and only if its fixed-point convergence can be determined without considering the behavior of the rest of the rules in the program.
2. Rewrite the program to take advantage of the fact that some variables can be treated as constants because of the special form.

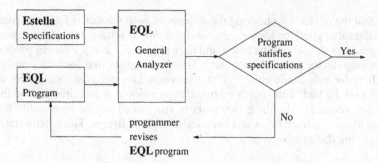

Figure 10.8 Overview of the analysis methodology.

If none of the special forms applies, identify an independent subset of the rules and check the state-space graph for that subset to determine if a fixed point can always be reached. Rewrite the program as in (1) to yield simpler programs, if possible.

Perform an analysis on each of the programs resulting from (1) or (2). If the analyzer detects that the EQL program may not always have bounded response time, it will report a list of rules that may cause the timing violations in the program. If after examining the rules in question the programmer concludes that those rules that are involved in the apparent timing violations are actually acceptable (for instance, the scheduler knows about these cycles), he/she can interactively specify additional behavioral constraint assertions (BCAs) as input to the analyzer and then re-analyze the EQL program. Thus the Estella facility allows the programmer to tailor the analysis tools to application-specific rule-based programs. Figure 10.8 shows the Estella-GAT facility for analyzing EQL programs. We later describe in detail the components of the Estella facility.

Estella is a new language for specifying behavioral constraint assertions about EQL programs. These assertions characterize rules that satisfy certain syntactic and/or semantic structures. The structures are used to capture the requirements for achieving certain performance levels for a rule-based program in a particular application. Once these application-specific BCAs are entered as input to the Estella compiler and an EQL program is read into the GAT analyzer, the analyzer will make use of the general analysis algorithm described above, the primitive BCAs, and the programmer-defined application-specific BCAs to determine whether the rules in the EQL program will always reach a fixed point in bounded time. The theoretical foundation of the general analysis algorithm is discussed in [Browne, Cheng, and Mok, 1988].

The following example demonstrates the utility of the Estella facility for specifying behavioral constraint assertions on rule-based systems.

Example 1'. Specifying compatibility criteria for rules in the simple object-detection program: As explained earlier, two pairs of rules are not compatible: rule 1 and rule 4, rule 2 and rule 3. Let the variables *sensor_a* and *sensor_b* contain respectively the values as detected by radar sensor *a* and by radar sensor *b*, both of which scan the same region of the sky. Now suppose the rule-based programmer knows that the device for checking the statuses of both sensors is fail-safe; that is, it returns the value good for *sensor_x_status* if and only if *sensor_x* is working properly, where $x = a$ or b, and returns bad if and only if *sensor_x* is not working properly or the checking device has malfunctioned. This fact implies that for rule 1 and rule 4 (as well as for rule 2 and rule 3), if the sensor values disagree, one of the sensor statuses must be bad. Thus only one rule can be enabled at one time and no infinite firings can occur. Hence, these two pairs of rules need not be compatible for this program to reach a fixed point in a bounded number of firings. The Estella statement for specifying this condition is

```
COMPATIBLE_SET = ({1,4}, {2,3})
```

This statement states that the pair of rules 1 and 4 and the pair of rules 2 and 3 are specified to be compatible even though they do not satisfy the predefined conditions of compatibility. This Estella compatibility condition can be used to assist the analysis tool to identify this program as one that is guaranteed to reach a fixed point in bounded time. Therefore, Estella allows the programmer to specify knowledge about the rules that is too difficult or impossible to be detected by the analysis tools. The specification of assertions such as the above compatibility condition relies on the knowledge of the programmer about the domain of the rule-based program being developed. This is reasonable and as we shall see in the following sections, the programmer focuses, by use of the analysis tool, on the sets of rules that potentially cause the timing violations so that he/she can apply application-specific knowledge to further analyze the rule-based program.

10.9.2   Facility for Specifying Behavioral Constraint Assertions

The facility for specifying BCAs on EQL rules and for analyzing EQL programs consists of the following major components:

1. the BCA special form recognition procedure generator,
2. the EQL program information extractor, and
3. the general analyzer.

These three components are depicted in Figure 10.9. The BCA recognition procedure generator serves as a compiler to the BCA specification written in Estella and generates the corresponding procedure for recognizing the specified BCAs of rules with bounded response times.

The EQL program information extractor is a collection of procedures that extract relevant information from the EQL program to be analyzed. These procedures provide information in the form of objects that can be used in the Estella specification. For example, the ER graph constructor builds the ER graph from the EQL program and provides objects such as ER cycles or ER edges which can be named by Estella primitives. The information extractor is designed to be expandable so that it can easily accommodate new procedures for extracting information as the need arises and for providing objects previously not available.

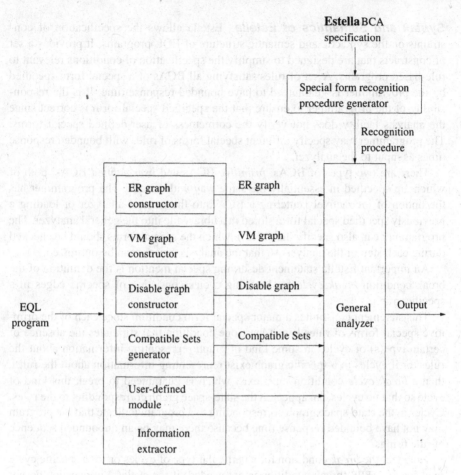

Figure 10.9 The Estella-General Analysis Tool.

The general analyzer takes as input the information provided by the information extractor and the recognition procedures generated by the BCA recognition procedure generator and stores the procedures in its knowledge base. Then, given an EQL program, the general analyzer determines whether the program can reach a fixed point in bounded time. We shall see that when potential timing violations are detected, the general analyzer identifies the subset(s) of rules on which the programmer needs to focus his/her attention. This is very helpful for debugging the timing violations of the program as the analyzer isolates the relevant rules from a much larger set of rules.

Estella is primarily designed for specifying behavioral constraint assertions abou rules written in the EQL language. It is expressive enough to allow for the specification of a wide range of BCAs about EQL rules, and it does not require the rule-based programmer to possess knowledge of the implementation details of the Estella compiler or the recognition procedures.

Syntax and Semantics of Estella   Estella allows the specification of constraints on the syntactic and semantic structure of EQL programs. It provides a set of constructs that are designed to simplify the specification of conditions relevant to rule-based programs. A set of rules satisfying all BCAs of a special form specified by the programmer is guaranteed to have bounded response time. It is the responsibility of the programmer to ensure that the specified special form is correct since the analysis facility does not verify the correctness of user-defined special forms. The programmer may specify different special forms of rules with bounded response times as input to the analyzer.

There are two types of BCAs, *primitive* BCAs and *user-defined* BCAs, both of which are specified in essentially the same way with Estella. The programmer has the option of interactively entering a BCA into the general analyzer or loading a previously specified special form stored in a library file into the general analyzer. The programmer can also specify the order in which the special forms should be checked during each step of the analysis so that the analysis process can be optimized.

An important Estella statement deserving special mention is the definition of the break condition *break_cycle* for breaking cycles consisting of specific edges in a specific graph.

This statement constitutes a major special form condition since each of the primitive special forms of rules has at least one condition that stipulates the absence of certain type(s) of cycles in some kind of graph representing information about the rules, or if cycles in a specific graph exist representing information about the rules, then a *break_cycle* condition must exist which is guaranteed to break this kind of cycle so that no cycles can appear in the state-space graph corresponding to the rules. Cycles in the state-space graph corresponding to a program indicate that the program may not have bounded response time because there may be an unbounded sequence of rule firings.

Note that the *break* condition for a particular type of cycles or for a specific cycle may specify TRUE (break condition is not needed) if the cycle(s) in question do not cause a cycle in the state-space graph corresponding to the program.

We first provide an informal description of Estella to highlight its features. A formal specification of Estella in the YACC grammar is given in Appendix A. The following definitions are needed to describe the language constructs of Estella. The mutual exclusion relation defined below is used to determine whether two rules can be enabled at the same time.

Mutual Exclusion: Let $T = \{v_1, v_2, \ldots, v_n\}$ and let $\bar{v}$ be the vector $\langle v_1, v_2, \ldots, v_n \rangle$. With this definition, each enabling condition in a program can be viewed as a function $f(\bar{v})$ from the space of $\bar{v}$ to the set $\{true, false\}$. Let f_a be the function corresponding to the enabling condition a and let V_a be the subset of the space of $\bar{v}$ for which the function f_a maps to *true*. Let $V_{a,i}$ be the subset of the values of v_i for which the function f_a may map to *true*; that is, if the value of the variable v_i is in the subset $V_{a,i}$, then an assignment of values to the variables in the set $T - \{v_i\}$ exists such that the function f_a maps to *true*. Note that if the variable v_k does not appear in the enabling condition a, then $V_{a,k}$ is the entire domain of v_k. We say that two enabling conditions a and b are *mutually exclusive* if and only if the subsets V_a and V_b of the corresponding functions f_a and f_b are disjoint. Obviously, if two enabling conditions are mutually exclusive, only one of the corresponding rules can be enabled at a time.

The following definition is used to determine whether the firing of a rule can cause another rule to become enabled.

Potentially Enable Relation: Rule a is said to *potentially enable* rule b if and only if there exist at least one reachable state in the state-space graph of the program where (1) rule b is disabled and (2) firing rule a enables rule b.

The following definition is used to determine whether the firing of a rule can cause another rule to become disabled.

Disable Relation: Rule a is said to *disable* rule b if for all reachable program states where rule a and rule b are both enabled, firing rule a disables rule b.

The enable-rule graph shows the potential enable relationships among rules in a program. It is used to determine whether infinite rule firings can occur as a result of a set of rules that are mutually enabling.

Enable Rule Graph: The *enable-rule* (ER) graph of a set of rules is a labeled directed graph $G = (V, E)$. V is a set of vertices such that a vertex exists for each rule. E is a set of edges such that an edge connects vertex a to vertex b if and only if rule a potentially enables rule b.

The variable modification graph shows whether the firing of a rule can modify a VAL variable in another rule. Recall that a rule is fireable only when it is enabled and if by firing it will change the value of some variable in VAR. Thus the variable-modification graph can be used to determine which set of rules can fire again as a result of a change (by the firing of another rule not in this set) to the content of at least one of their VAL variables.

Variable Modification Graph: The *variable-modification* (VM) graph of a set of rules is a labeled directed graph $G = (V, E)$. V is a set of vertices, each of which is labeled by a tuple (i, j) corresponding to a distinct single-assignment subrule, where i is the rule number and j is the single-assignment subrule number within rule i (counting from left to right). E is a set of edges, each of which denotes the interaction between a pair of single-assignment subrules such that an edge connects vertex m to vertex n if and only if $L_m \cap R_n \neq \emptyset$.

The disable edge is used to represent the disable relation.

Disable Edge: A *disable* edge connects vertex r to vertex s if and only if the firing of rule r always disables the enabling condition of rule s.

The disable graph shows the disable relationships among rules in a program, and it is defined as follows.

Disable Graph: The *disable* graph of a set of rules is a labeled directed graph $G = (V, E)$. V is a set of vertices such that a vertex exists for each rule. E is a set of disable edges.

We are now ready to describe the language constructs of Estella, which provides the following predefined constants:

$$\{\} = \text{empty set.}$$

Estella provides the following predefined set variables:

$$L = \{v \mid v \text{ is a variable appearing in VAR}\}$$

$$R = \{v \mid v \text{ is a variable appearing in VAL}\}$$

$$T = \{v \mid v \text{ is a variable appearing in EC}\}$$

$$L[i] = \{v \mid v \text{ is a variable appearing in VAR of rule } i\}$$

$$L[i.j] = \{v \mid v \text{ is a variable appearing in VAR of rule } i, \text{ subrule } j\}$$

$$R[i] = \{v \mid v \text{ is a variable appearing in VAL of rule } i\}$$

$$R[i.j] = \{v \mid v \text{ is a variable appearing in VAL of rule } i, \text{ subrule } j\}$$

$$T[i] = \{v \mid v \text{ is a variable appearing in EC of rule } i\}$$

Estella provides the following predefined expression variables which are used to refer to the actual expression or the EQL variable in the location indicated by the indices of the variables:

$$\text{LEXP}[i.j] = \text{VAR variable of rule } i, \text{ subrule } j.$$

$$\text{REXP}[i.j] = \text{VAL expression of rule } i, \text{ subrule } j.$$

$$\text{TEXP}[i] = \text{EC of rule } i.$$

Estella provides the following predefined functions:

INTERSECT(A, B): intersection of set A and set B, where A and B are set variables or elements enclosed by "{" and "}."

UNION(A, B): union of set A and set B, where A and B are set variables or elements enclosed by "{" and "}."

RELATIVE_COMPLEMENT(A, B): relative complement = set A − set B, where A and B are set variables or elements enclosed by "{" and "}."

Estella provides the following predefined predicates:

MEMBER(a, B): a is a member of set B, where a is an EQL variable, and B is a set variable or elements enclosed by "{" and "}."

IN_CYCLE(EDGE(*edge_type*, a, b)): edge (a, b) of type *edge_type* is in the cycle found. This predicate is used only as a condition within the predicate BREAK_CYCLE and the cycle referred to is the one referred to by BREAK_CYCLE.

EQUAL(a, b): a is equal to b, where a and b can be set variables, expression variables, or values.

COMPATIBLE(a, b): rule a and rule b are compatible (defined earlier)

MUTEX(a, b): enabling condition of rule a and enabling condition of rule b are mutually exclusive.

COMPATIBLE_SET = (compatible_sets): This predicate specifies set of compatible sets of rules. All pairs of rules in each of these compatible sets are considered compatible by the rule-based programmer even though they do not satisfy the predefined requirements of compatibility. This predicate allows the programmer to relax the compatibility condition for some pairs of rules when he/she knows that this would not cause the rules to fire infinitely often without reaching a fixed point.

BREAK_CYCLE(*graph_type*, *cycles_list*) = *break_condition*: *graph_type* is the type of graph, *cycles_list* is an optional argument listing specific cycles in the graph of *graph_type*, and *break_condition* is a condition for breaking a cycle in the graph of *graph_type*. This predicate specifies a condition for breaking all cycles or specific cycles (when the second argument, *cycles_list*, is specified). Thus programs with cycles (as specified in conditions of the primitive special forms) that satisfy the *break_condition* so specified will not cause unbounded rule firings.

Estella provides the following primitive objects:

VERTEX: vertex in a graph(ER, VM, or *disable*).

EDGE(ENABLE_RULE, a, b): edge from vertex a to vertex b in the enable-rule graph.

EDGE(DISABLE, a, b): edge (a, b) in the disable graph.

EDGE(VARIABLE_MODIFICATION, a, b): edge (a, b) in the variable-modification graph.

CYCLE(ENABLE_RULE): a cycle in the enable-rule graph.

CYCLE(VARIABLE_MODIFICATION): a cycle in the variable-modification graph.

Estella provides the following primitive constructs:

specification: a well-formed formula as defined below.

Terms are defined recursively as follows.

1. A constant is a term.
2. A variable is a term.
3. If f is a function symbol with n parameters, and $x_1, \ldots, x_n$ are terms, then $f(x_1, \ldots, x_n)$ is a term.

All terms are generated by applying rules (1), (2), and (3).

If p is a predicate symbol with n parameters, and $x_1, \ldots, x_n$ are terms, then $p(x_1, \ldots, x_n)$ is an atomic formula.

A well-formed specification is defined recursively as follows.

1. An atomic formula is a specification.
2. If F and G are specifications, then not(F), (F OR G), (F AND G), ($F \rightarrow G$), and ($F \leftrightarrow G$) are specifications.
3. If F is a specification and x_list is a list of free variables in F, then FORALL x_list (F) and EXIST x_list (F) are specifications.

Specifications are generated only by a finite number of applications of rule (1), rule (2), and rule (3).

$\{P\}R\{Q\}$

Assertion: P and Q are predicates on the variables of an EQL program, and R is a sequence of one or more rules. This construct states that if the program is at a state in which the predicate P is true, then following the execution of the rules in R, the program reaches a state in which the predicate Q is true. Note that an assertion in Estella, like other constructs, is a constraint specified by the programmer, and this condition must be satisfied by a program in order to guarantee that the program has bounded response time. The analyzer performs the following: given the initial state in which the predicate P is satisfied, execute the rules in R (note that it is possible that none of the rules are enabled and thus no rule is fired) and determine whether the program reaches a state in which the predicate Q is satisfied.

Specifying Special Forms with Estella   In this section, we show how Estella is used to define three primitive special forms for ensuring that EQL programs satisfying these special forms will always have bounded response time. A set of rules in a primitive special form has a response-time bound associated with that special form. To compute a numerical upper bound on the number of rule firings once a rule set is found to be in a special form, efficient algorithms reported in [Cheng, 1992b] can be used to compute a tight response-time bound for this rule set. This two-step analysis method is employed to make the analysis more efficient by postponing the more computation-intensive second step, that of determining a tight upper bound on execution time, until after a rule set is found to be in a special form. If the rule set is not in a special form, the second step need not be performed.

Definition of the Predicate: *compatible*: Let L_x denote the set of variables appearing in VAR of rule x. Two rules a and b are said to be *compatible* if and only if at least one of the following conditions holds:

1. Enabling condition a and enabling condition b are mutually exclusive.
2. $L_a \cap L_b = \emptyset$.
3. Suppose $L_a \cap L_b \neq \emptyset$. Then for every variable v in $L_a \cap L_b$, the same expression must be assigned to v in both rules a and b.

Estella Specification of COMPATIBLE(a,b):

```
   MUTEX(a,b)
or EQUAL(INTERSECT(L[a],L[b]), { })
or FORALL v (FORALL a.p, b.q ((((MEMBER(v,intersect(L[a],L[b]))
      AND EQUAL(v,LEXP[a.p]))
      AND EQUAL(v,LEXP[b.q]))
      -$>$ EQUAL(REXP[a.p],REXP[b.q])))
```

compatible is a predefined predicate in Estella. Note that the compatibility condition can be considered as a break condition since it is used to break a possibly cyclic sequence of rule firings.

Definition of Special Form A: Constant terms are assigned to all the variables in L.

All of the rules are compatible pairwise.

$L \cap T = \emptyset$.

Estella Specification of Special Form A:

```
SPECIAL_FORM a:
    EQUAL(R,{ });
    FORALL i,j (COMPATIBLE(i,j));
    EQUAL(INTERSECT(L,T), { })
END.
```

Definition of Special Form B: A set of rules is said to be in special form B if the following five conditions hold:

1. Constant terms are assigned to all the variables in L, that is, $R =$ empty.
2. All of the rules are compatible pairwise.
3. $L \cap T \neq \emptyset$.

4. For each cycle in the ER graph corresponding to this set of rules, no two rules in the cycle assign different expressions to the same variable.
5. Rules in disjoint simple cycles (with at least two vertices) in the ER graph do not assign different expressions to a common variable appearing in their VAR.

Estella Specification of Special Form Conditions B1–B4:

```
SPECIAL_FORM b:
    EQUAL(R,{ });
    FORALL i,j (COMPATIBLE(i,j));
    NOT(EQUAL(INTERSECT(L,T),{ }));
    BREAK_CYCLE(ENABLE_RULE) =
        (NOT(EXIST i,j
                ( ( NOT(EQUAL(i,j)) AND
                    ( IN_CYCLE(EDGE(ENABLE_RULE,i,j)) AND
                      EXIST i.p, j.q
                        ( (EQUAL(LEXP[i.p],LEXP[j.q]) AND
                            NOT(EQUAL(REXP[i.p],REXP[j.q]))) ) )
                )
            )
        )
    )
END.
```

Definition of Special Form C: A set of rules is said to be in special form C if the following four conditions hold:

1. Variable terms are assigned to the variables in L, that is, $R \neq \emptyset$.
2. All of the rules are pairwise compatible.
3. $L \cap T = \emptyset$.
4. For each cycle in the variable-modification graph corresponding to this set of rules, at least a pair of rules (subrules) is in the cycle that are compatible by condition CR1 (mutual exclusion).

Estella Specification of Special Form C:

```
SPECIAL_FORM c:
    NOT(EQUAL(R,{ }));
    FORALL i,j (COMPATIBLE(i,j));
    EQUAL(INTERSECT(L,T), { });
    BREAK_CYCLE(VARIABLE_MODIFICATION) =
        (EXIST i, j (EXIST i.k, j.l
            ((IN_CYCLE(EDGE(VARIABLE_MODIFICATION,i.k,j.l)) AND
             MUTEX(i,j))))
        )
END.
```

10.9.3   Context-Free Grammar for Estella

The top-level commands of the analyzer are:

```
check_command     | 'rp' /* read program */
                  | 'ls' /* load special form */
                  | 'sf' /* new special form */
                  | 'ps' /* print special forms */
                  | 'ds' /* delete special form */
                  | 'vm' /* verbose mode? */
                  | 'cs' /* compatible set */
                  | 'bc' /* break condition */
                  | 'an' /* analyze */
                  | 'ex' /* exit */
                  ;
```

The context-free grammar for Estella is specified in the YACC language.

```
estella_command   : special_form
                  | exception
                  ;

special_form      : special_form_name special_form_body end_mark
                  ;

special_form_name : 'special_form' IDENTIFIER ':'
                  ;

special_form_body : conditions
                  ;

end_mark          : 'end' '.'
                  ;

conditions : condition
           | conditions ';' condition
           ;

condition  : specification
           | break_condition
           ;

exception  : compatible_set
           | break_condition
           ;

term       : var_set
           | variable
           | function_name '(' term arg2')'
           ;

elements_list: element
             | elements_list ',' element
             ;
```

```
element        : IDENTIFIER
               | var_set
               ;


arg2           :
               | ',' term
               ;


atom_formula : predicate_name '(' term arg2 ')'
               ;


specification : atom_formula
               | 'NOT' '(' specification ')'
               | '(' specification connective specification ')'
               | quantifier rule_list '(' specification ')'
               | quantifier subrule_list '(' specification ')'
               ;


connective     : 'OR'
               | 'AND'
               | '->'
               | '<->'
               ;


quantifier     : 'FORALL'
               | 'EXIST'
               ;


set_variable : 'L'
               | 'R'
               | 'T'
               | 'L' '[' irule_number ']'
               | 'L' '[' irule_number '.' isubrule_number ']'
               | 'R' '[' irule_number ']'
               | 'R' '[' irule_number '.' isubrule_number ']'
               | 'T' '[' irule_number ']'
               ;


exp_variable : 'l' '[' irule_number '.' isubrule_number ']'
               | 'r' '[' irule_number '.' isubrule_number ']'
               | 't' '[' irule_number ']'
               ;


irule_number : inumber
               ;


isubrule_number : inumber
                ;


inumber        : NUMBER
               | IDENTIFIER
               ;
```

```
graph_variable : 'edge' '(' graph_type ',' pvertex ',' pvertex ')'
               | 'cycle' '(' graph_type ')'
               ;


pvertex        : vertex
               | vmvertex
               ;


graph_type     : 'ENABLE_RULE'
               | 'DISABLE'
               | 'VARIABLE_MODIFICATION'
               ;


sets           : set
               | sets ',' set
               ;


set            : '{' list '}'
               | '{' '}'
               ;


list           : set_rule_list
               ;


set_rule_list: rule_number
               | set_rule_list ',' rule_number
               ;


rule_list      : rule
               | rule_list ',' rule
               ;


rule           : rule_number
               ;


subrule_list   : subrule
               | subrule_list ',' subrule
               ;


subrule        : IDENTIFIER '.' subrule_number
               | NUMBER '.' subrule_number
               ;


compatible_set : 'COMPATIBLE_SET' '=' '(' sets ')'
               ;


break_condition : 'BREAK_CYCLE' '(' graph_type ')' '=' break_cond
                | 'BREAK_CYCLE' '(' graph_type ',' cycles_list ')'
                  '=' break_cond
                ;


break_cond      : specification
                | simple_pascal_expression
                ;
```

```
cycles_list      : '{' cycles '}'
                 ;

cycles           : cycle
                 | cycles ',' cycle
                 ;

cycle            : '(' vertex_list ')'
                 | '(' vmvertex_list ')'
                 ;

vertex_list      : vertex
                 | vertex_list ',' vertex
                 ;

vertex           : irule_number
                 ;

vmvertex_list    : vmvertex
                 | vmvertex_list ',' vmvertex
                 ;

vmvertex         : irule_number '.' isubrule_number
                 ;

rule_number      : IDENTIFIER
                 ;

subrule_number   : IDENTIFIER
                 ;

variable         : IDENTIFIER
                 | graph_variable
                 | set_variable
                 | exp_variable
                 ;

function_name    : 'INTERSECT'
                 | 'UNION'
                 | 'RELATIVE_COMPLEMENT'
                 | 'VALUE'
                 ;

predicate_name   : 'MEMBER'
                 | 'IN_CYCLE'
                 | 'EQUAL'
                 | 'COMPATIBLE'
                 | 'MUTEX'
                 ;

pascal_expression    : disjunctive_expr
                     | pascal_expression 'OR' disjunctive_expr
                     ;
```

```
disjunctive_expr           : conjunctive_expr
                           | disjunctive_expr  'AND'  conjunctive_expr
                           ;

conjunctive_expr           : simple_expression
                           | conjunctive_expr  '='   simple_expression
                           | conjunctive_expr  '<>'  simple_expression
                           | conjunctive_expr  '<='  simple_expression
                           | conjunctive_expr  '>='  simple_expression
                           | conjunctive_expr  '<'   simple_expression
                           | conjunctive_expr  '>'   simple_expression
                           ;

simple_expression          : term1
                           | simple_expression '+' term1
                           | simple_expression '-' term1
                           ;

term1                      : factor
                           | term1 '*' factor
                           | term1 'DIV' factor
                           | term1 'MOD' factor
                           ;

factor                     : variable
                           | NUMBER
                           | '(' pascal_expression ')'
                           | 'NOT' factor
                           | '+' term1
                           | '-' term1
                           ;

simple_pascal_expression : '(' simple_exp ')'
                           ;

simple_exp : exp
           | simple_exp 'AND' exp
           ;

exp        : IDENTIFIER '=' value
           ;

value      : IDENTIFIER
           | NUMBER
           ;
```

10.10 TWO INDUSTRIAL EXAMPLES

To demonstrate the applicability of the Estella-GAT, we use it to analyze two expert systems from Mitre and NASA.

10.10.1   Specifying Cycles and Break Conditions for Analyzing the ISA Expert System

The purpose of the Integrated Status Assessment (ISA) Expert System is to determine the faulty components in a network. This is a real-time expert system developed by Mitre for the planned NASA Space Station. A component can be either an *entity* (node) or a *relationship* (link). A relationship is a directed edge connecting two entities. Components are in one of three states: nominal, suspect, or failed. A failed entity can be replaced by an available backup entity. This expert system makes use of simple strategies to trace failed components in a network. The EQL version of the ISA Expert System consists of 35 rules, 46 variables (29 of which are input variables), and 12 constants.

After reading in the ISA program, the analyzer checks the rules to determine if every rule pair satisfies the compatibility condition. Two pairs of rules have been identified as being not compatible: rule 8 and rule 32, and rule 9 and rule 33. At this point, the rule-based programmer can take one of the following actions:

1. revise the ISA program to make the above rule pairs compatible,
2. employ a special form that does not require the above rules to be compatible to perform further analysis, or
3. specify the above rules as compatible by using the COMPATIBLE_SET predicate if he/she considers these rules to be compatible in his/her application domain.

Suppose the programmer selects the third action, then the command "cs" (compatible set) can be used to specify compatible sets of rules.

```
command > cs

compatible set specification >
    COMPATIBLE\_SET = ({8,32}, {9,33})
compatible sets entered
```

Now we load two predefined special forms (stored in files sfA and sfB) into the analyzer using the "ls" (load special form) command:

```
command > ls

special form file name > sfA
special form file sfA entered

command > ls

special form file name > sfB
special form file sfB entered
```

Special forms can also be specified interactively using the "sf" (new special form) command. During the first iteration of the general analysis, a bad cycle in the ER graph corresponding to the ISA Expert System has been identified: (10,18,34).

```
Step 1:
    9 strongly connected components in dependency graph.
    Bad cycle: 34->10->18

Independent special form subset is empty.

Analysis stops.
```

This indicates that the program, when started in at least one of the initial states, may not reach a fixed point. The rules involved in this ER cycle and another ER cycle (10,18,35) are given below.

```
(* 10 *)
[] state3 := failed IF find_bad_things = true AND
state3 = suspect AND
NOT (rel1_state = suspect AND rel1_mode = on AND
rel1_type = direct) AND
NOT (rel2_state = suspect AND rel2_mode = on AND
rel2_type = direct)

(* 18 *)
[] state3 := nominal ! reconfig3 := true
IF state3 = failed AND mode3 <> off AND config3 = bad

(* 34 *)
[] sensor3 := bad ! state3 := suspect IF state1 = suspect AND
rel1_mode = on AND rel1_type = direct AND
state3 = nominal AND rel3_mode = on AND
rel3_type = direct AND state4 = suspect AND
find_bad_things = true

(* 35 *)
[] sensor3 := bad ! state3 := suspect IF state2 = suspect AND
rel2_mode = on AND rel2_type = direct AND
state3 = nominal AND rel3_mode = on AND
rel3_type = direct AND state4 = suspect AND
find_bad_things = true
```

Now suppose the programmer knows that these rules will never fire infinitely because of the use of a scheduler that prevents these rules from firing forever. The general break condition for cycles in the enable-rule graph in special form B needs to be relaxed for these rules. We do not actually modify this general break condition; we make use of the exception command "bc" (break cycle condition) to define an application-specific assertion. To indicate that the above three rules will not fire infinitely often, the following Estella statement is used to specify that the break condition for the cycle (10,18,34) in the enable rule graph of the program is TRUE, and thus this ER cycle will not cause unbounded rule firings. The general analyzer would then ignore this cycle when checking to see whether the set of rules containing these three rules are in a special form. We specify this break condition in the Estella facility as follows:

```
command > bc

with respect to special form > b

break condition specification >
    BREAK_CYCLE(ENABLE_RULE, {(10,18,34)}) = TRUE
```

10.10.2   Specifying Assertions for Analyzing the FCE Expert System

The purpose of the Fuel Cell (FCE) Expert System is to determine the statuses of the different components of the fuel cell system based on current sensor readings and previous system state values. Then it displays the corresponding diagnostics according to the evaluation of the statuses of the different components of the system. The EQL version of this expert system contains 101 rules, 56 program variables, 130 input variables, and 78 constants.

The FCE program is organized into three main sections: (1) the meta rule section (testFCE1.eql), (2) 12 ordinary rule classes (testFCE2.*.eql), and (3) the output section (testFCE3.eql).

Meta Rules of the Fuel Cell Expert System

```
(* 1 *)
    work_rule_base := fc_exit_t7_3d
    IF NOT (tce = last_tce AND cool_rtn_t = last_cool_rtn_t AND
    koh_in_conc = last_koh_in_conc AND
    koh_out_conc = last_koh_out_conc AND
    prd_h20_lnt = last_prd_h20_lnt)
(* 2 *)
[] work_rule_base := fc_stack_t7_1b
    IF NOT (cool_rtn_t1 = last_cool_rtn_t1 AND
    cool_rtn_t2 = last_cool_rtn_t2 AND
    cool_rtn_t3 = last_cool_rtn_t3 AND
    fc_mn_dv = last_fc_mn_dv AND
    mn_bus = last_mn_bus AND
    fc_mn_conn = last_fc_mn_conn AND
    status = last_status AND
    su_atr = last_su_atr AND
    voltage = last_voltage AND
    voltage1 = last_voltage1 AND
    voltage2 = last_voltage2 AND
    voltage3 = last_voltage3 AND
```

```
      stk_t_status = last_stk_t_status AND
      stk_t_status2 = last_stk_t_status2 AND
      stk_t_status3 = last_stk_t_status3 AND
      stack_t = last_stack_t AND
      delta_v = last_delta_v AND
      stk_t_rate = last_stk_t_rate AND
      cool_rtn_t = last_cool_rtn_t AND
      stk_t_disconn2 = last_stk_t_disconn2 AND
      stk_t_disconn3 = last_stk_t_disconn3 AND
      amps1 = last_amps1 AND
      amps2 = last_amps2 AND
      amps3 = last_amps3)
(* 3 *)
[] work_rule_base := cool_pump7_1a
      IF NOT (cntlr_pwr = last_cntlr_pwr AND
      cool_pump_dp = last_cool_pump_dp AND
      fc_rdy_for_ld = last_fc_rdy_for_ld AND
      status = last_status AND
      tce = last_tce)
(* 4 *)
[] work_rule_base := fc_amps7_3c
      IF NOT (status = last_status AND
      mn_bus = last_mn_bus AND
      load_status = last_load_status AND
      voltage = last_voltage AND
      amps = last_amps AND
      fc_mn_conn = last_fc_mn_conn)
(* 5 *)
[] work_rule_base := fc_delta_v7_4_1_4
      IF NOT (ss1_dv = last_ss1_dv AND
      ss2_dv = last_ss2_dv AND
      ss3_dv = last_ss3_dv AND
      ss1_dv_rate = last_ss1_dv_rate AND
      ss2_dv_rate = last_ss2_dv_rate AND
      ss3_dv_rate = last_ss3_dv_rate)
(* 6 *)
[] work_rule_base := fc_ech7_3_1_2
      IF NOT (fc_rdy_for_ld = last_fc_rdy_for_ld AND
      end_cell_htr1 = last_end_cell_htr1 AND
      end_cell_htr2 = last_end_cell_htr2 AND
      fc_mn_conn = last_fc_mn_conn AND
      fc_ess_conn = last_fc_ess_conn)
(* 7 *)
[] work_rule_base := fc_purge7_2
      IF NOT (purge_vlv_sw_pos = last_purge_vlv_sw_pos AND
      auto_purge_seq = last_auto_purge_seq AND
      h2_flow_rate = last_h2_flow_rate AND
      o2_flow_rate = last_o2_flow_rate AND
      purge_htr_sw_pos = last_purge_htr_sw_pos AND
      fc_purge_alarm = last_fc_purge_alarm AND
      fc_purge_seq_alarm = last_fc_purge_seq_alarm AND
      fc_purge_t_alarm = last_fc_purge_t_alarm)
```

```
(* 8 *)
[] work_rule_base := fc_cool_p7_3e
   IF NOT (cool_p = last_cool_p AND
   cool_p_rate = last_cool_p_rate AND
   h2_flow_rate = last_h2_flow_rate AND
   o2_flow_rate = last_o2_flow_rate AND
   cool_pump_dp = last_cool_pump_dp AND
   purge_vlv_sw_pos = last_purge_vlv_sw_pos AND
   auto_purge_seq = last_auto_purge_seq AND
   o2_reac_vlv = last_o2_reac_vlv AND
   h2_reac_vlv = last_h2_reac_vlv AND
   fc_mn_conn = last_fc_mn_conn AND
   bus_tie_status = last_bus_tie_status AND
   delta_v = last_delta_v AND
   status = last_status AND
   cool_ph20_p = last_cool_ph20_p)
(* 9 *)
[] work_rule_base := fc_h20_vlvt7_3g
   IF NOT (h20_rlf_vlv_t = last_h20_rlf_vlv_t AND
   h20_rlf_t_msg = last_h20_rlf_t_msg AND
   h20_rlf_sw_pos = last_h20_rlf_sw_pos AND
   h20_rlf_timer = last_h20_rlf_timer AND
   h20_vlv_t_rate = last_h20_vlv_t_rate)
(* 10 *)
[] work_rule_base := prd_h20_lnt7_3f
   IF NOT (prt_h20_lnt = last_prt_h20_lnt AND
   prd_h20_sw_pos = last_prd_h20_sw_pos AND
   fc_mn_conn = last_fc_mn_conn AND
   amps = last_amps)
(* 11 *)
[] work_rule_base := fc_reacs7_1_1_1
   IF NOT (fc_rdy_for_ld = last_fc_rdy_for_ld AND
   o2_reac_vlv = last_o2_reac_vlv AND
   h2_reac_vlv = last_h2_reac_vlv AND
   o2_flow_rate = last_o2_flow_rate AND
   h2_flow_rate = last_h2_flow_rate AND
   cool_p = last_cool_p)
(* 12 *)
[] work_rule_base := fc_general
           IF NOT (cool_p = last_cool_p AND
                   cool_pump_dp = last_cool_pump_dp AND
                   h2_reac_vlv = last_h2_reac_vlv AND
                   o2_reac_vlv = last_o2_reac_vlv AND
                   fc_rdy_for_ld = last_fc_rdy_for_ld AND
                   fc_mn_conn = last_fc_mn_conn AND
                   fc_ess_conn = last_fc_ess_conn AND
                   status = last_status AND
                   cntlr_pwr = last_cntlr_pwr)
(* 13 *)
       [] work_rule_base := fc_volts7_3b
           IF NOT (status = last_status AND
                   delta_v = last_delta_v AND
                   fc_mn_conn = last_fc_mn_conn AND
```

```
                    fc_pripl_conn = last_fc_pripl_conn AND
                    mn_pripl_conn = last_mn_pripl_conn AND
                    bus_tie_status = last_bus_tie_status AND
                    amps = last_amps AND
                    voltage = last_voltage AND
                    load_status = last_load_status AND
                    cntlr_pwr = last_cntlr_pwr AND
                    mna_voltage = last_mna_voltage AND
                    mnb_voltage = last_mnb_voltage AND
                    mnc_voltage = last_mnc_voltage)
```

After reading in the FCE program, the analyzer checks the rules to determine if every rule pair satisfies the compatibility condition. The following pairs of rules have been identified as being not compatible:

```
Incompatible rule pairs: (R1,R2) (R1,R3) (R1,R4) (R1,R5) (R1,R6) (R1,R7)
 (R1,R8) (R1,R9) (R1,R10) (R1,R11) (R1,R12) (R1,R13) (R2,R3) (R2,R4) (R2,R5)
 (R2,R6) (R2,R7) (R2,R8) (R2,R9) (R2,R10) (R2,R11) (R2,R12) (R2,R13) (R3,R4)
 (R3,R5) (R3,R6) (R3,R7) (R3,R8) (R3,R9) (R3,R10) (R3,R11) (R3,R12) (R3,R13)
 (R4,R5) (R4,R6) (R4,R7) (R4,R8) (R4,R9) (R4,R10) (R4,R11) (R4,R12) (R4,R13)
 (R5,R6) (R5,R7) (R5,R8) (R5,R9) (R5,R10) (R5,R11) (R5,R12) (R5,R13) (R6,R7)
 (R6,R8) (R6,R9) (R6,R10) (R6,R11) (R6,R12) (R6,R13) (R7,R8) (R7,R9) (R7,R10)
 (R7,R11) (R7,R12) (R7,R13) (R8,R9) (R8,R10) (R8,R11) (R8,R12) (R8,R13)
 (R9,R10) (R9,R11) (R9,R12) (R9,R13) (R10,R11) (R10,R12) (R10,R13) (R11,R12)
 (R11,R13) (R12,R13) (R18,R26) (R18,R47) (R18,R48) (R18,R49) (R18,R50)
 (R18,R51) (R30,R31) (R43,R44) (R43,R45) (R43,R46) (R44,R45) (R44,R46)
 (R45,R46) (R47,R49) (R48,R49) (R57,R63) (R63,R66) (R63,R67)
```

The meta rule section contains high-level control rules used to determine which ordinary rule classes should be enabled. The meta rules are shown in Appendix B. From the documentation accompanying the FCE Expert System, it is evident that each meta rule fires at most once and thus a fixed point will be reached in bounded time even though the rules are not compatible. The following Estella statement captures this application-specific assertion:

$$\text{COMPATIBLE\_SET} = (\{1,2,3,4,5,6,7,8,9,10,11,12,13\})$$

This statement states that all 13 rules in the meta rule section are compatible pairwise even though they do not satisfy the predefined requirements of compatibility. We specify this compatibility condition in the Estella facility as follows:

```
command > cs

compatible set specification >
    COMPATIBLE\_SET = ({1,2,3,4,5,6,7,8,9,10,11,12,13})
compatible sets entered
```

Now we load two predefined special forms into the analyzer using the "ls" (load special form) command, as explained earlier. We then analyze the rules in the meta rule section:

```
command > an
Select the rules to be analyzed:
  1. the whole program
  2. a continuous segment of program
  3. separated rules
Enter your choice: 2

Enter the first rule number:1
Enter the last rule number:13

Step 1:
  S.C.C.: R13 R12 R11 R10 R9 R8 R7 R6 R5 R4 R3 R2 R1
  1 strongly connected components in dependency graph.
  independent subset: 1 2 3 4 5 6 7 8 9 10 11 12 13
  13 rules in special form a.

0 rules remaining to be analyzed:

Textual analysis is completed.
The program always reaches a fixed point in bounded time.
```

After revising the FCE program to make the remaining incompatible non-meta rules compatible, the analyzer reports that the entire program is always guaranteed to reach a fixed point in bounded time. Empirical analysis of larger programs is under way. Readers interested in experimenting with the Estella-GAT system may contact the author for the latest version.

10.11   THE ESTELLA-GENERAL ANALYSIS TOOL

In this section, we describe efficient algorithms for implementing the Estella-GAT.

10.11.1   General Analysis Algorithm

The general analysis tool allows the rule-based programmer to select a subset of the rules in a program for analysis. The subset may contain either a contiguous list of rules or separated rules. This provision reduces analysis time by directing the analyzer to focus on checking trouble spots which the rule-based programmer considers as possible sources of timing violations. In the following section, we show how the analyzer uses decomposition techniques to break the program into independent sets so that it does not have to analyze the entire program at once.

Algorithm GA_Estella_Compiler

Input: A complete EQL program or a set of EQL rules; a list of special forms and exceptions, if any, specified in Estella.

Output: If the program will always reach a fixed point in bounded time, output "yes." If the program may not always reach a fixed point in bounded time according to the analysis, output "no" and the rules involved in the possible timing violations.

1. Parse the special form specifications and exceptions; then generate the corresponding BCA recognition procedures.
2. Construct the high-level dependency graph corresponding to the EQL program.
3. WHILE there are more rules for analysis DO:

    Identify forward-independent sets of rules that are in special forms. If at least one rule set in special form is found and there are more rules to be analyzed, then mark those forward-independent sets identified as checked (which effectively removes those rules from further analysis), rewrite the remaining rules to take advantage of the fact that some variables can be treated as constants because of the special form, and repeat this step. If no more rules exist for analysis, output "yes" (the EQL rules have bounded response time) and exit WHILE loop. If no independent set of rules is in a special form catalogue but the variables in some rule set have finite domains, check whether this rule set can always reach a fixed point in bounded time by using a state-based model-checking algorithm [Clarke, Emerson, and Sistla, 1986], described in chapter 4. If it is determined that the rule set will always reach a fixed point in bounded time, repeat this step. If the rule set is unable to always reach a fixed point in bounded time, report the rules involved in the timing violations.

    Prompt the user for new special forms or exceptions. If no new special forms or exceptions are entered, output "no" (the EQL rules do not have bounded response time) and exit WHILE loop. End WHILE.

A set of rules in a primitive special form has a response-time bound associated with that special form. To compute more precise bounds after the general analyzer has determined that a program has bounded response time, the analysis tool invokes specialized algorithms to compute tight response-time bounds for the program. Owing to space limitations, these algorithms are reported in [Cheng, 1992b].

10.11.2   Selecting Independent Rule Sets

To determine whether a set of rules is independent from another set of rules, the selection algorithm makes use of the following theorem.

Theorem 1   (Sufficient conditions for independence). Let S and Q be two disjoint sets of rules. S is *independent* from Q (but Q may not be independent from S) if the following conditions hold:

1. $L_S \cap L_Q = \emptyset$.
2. The rules in Q do not potentially enable rules in S.
3. $R_S \cap L_Q = \emptyset$.

Proof of Theorem 1. Condition (1) guarantees that the firing of any rule in set Q will not change the content of any variable in L_S that has already settled down to stable value. This is so because the set of variables L_S and the set of variables L_Q are disjoint.

Condition (2) guarantees that the firing of any rule in set Q will not enable any rule in set S.

Condition (3) guarantees that the firing of any rule in set Q will not change the value of any expression containing variables that are assigned to variables in the set L_S. Condition (1) guarantees that once the rules in S have reached a fixed point, the contents of the variables in L_S will not change. At this point, a rule in S would not fire again unless at least one expression in R of that rule has changed its value since the last firing of that rule. However, $R_S \cap L_Q = \emptyset$, so the values of the expression in R_S will not change despite the presence of Q.

To determine whether rule a potentially enables rule b, the implementation makes use of the approximately enable checking function. This function returns true if rule a potentially enables rule b or if there is insufficient information (some expressions in the enabling condition part cannot be evaluated unless the whole state space of the program is checked). It returns false otherwise.   □

Approximately Potentially Enable Relation: Given are two distinct rules a and b. Let $x_i, i = 1, \ldots, n$ be variables in the set $L_a \cap T_b$. Rule a is said to *approximately potentially enable* rule b if rule a assigns the value m_i to variable x_i such that $m_i \in V_{b,i}, i = 1, \ldots, n$, and $n \geq 1$.

Note that the potentially enable relation definition implies this definition. The approximately potentially enable relation can be easily checked in polynomial time whereas the checking of the potentially enable relation may require an exhaustive state-space search. This approximation does not affect the validity of any of the special forms described because the approximately potentially enable relation is a superset of the potentially enable relation. Thus the ER graph (used in special form B) constructed using this approximation may contain more edges than the ER graph constructed using the "real" potentially enable relation. This is acceptable since the additional edges may cause more ER cycles, which in turn may lead the analyzer to reject some programs with bounded response time but *not* to conclude erroneously that a program with unbounded response time is one that has bounded response time.

Constructing and Checking the Dependency Graph   Before checking to determine if a subset of the rules is in a special form, the analysis algorithm first constructs a high-level dependency graph based on the above conditions for establishing independence of one set of rules from another set. Every rule in an EQL program is

identified by its rule number, which is assigned according to the position of the rule in the program.

Algorithm Construct_HLD_Graph High-level dependency graph construction.

Input: An EQL program.

Output: A high-level dependency graph corresponding to the input EQL program.

1. For every rule in the EQL program, create a vertex labeled with the rule number.
2. Let S contain rule i and let Q contain rule j, $i \neq j$. If one of the conditions (1), (2), or (3) is not satisfied, create a directed edge from vertex i to vertex j.
3. Find every strongly connected component in the dependency graph $G(V, E)$ constructed by step (1) and step (2).
4. Let $C_1, C_2, \ldots, C_m$ be the strongly connected components of the graph $G(V, E)$. Define $\bar{G}(\bar{V}, \bar{E})$ as follows:

$$\bar{V} = \{C_1, C_2, \ldots, C_m\}$$

$$\bar{E} = \{(C_i, C_j) | i \neq j, (x, y) \in E, x \in C_i \text{ and } y \in C_j\}$$

We call $\bar{G}$ the *high-level dependency graph* of the input EQL program. Each of the vertices C_i in this high-level dependency graph is called a *forward-independent set*.

A high-level dependency graph is shown in Figure 10.10.

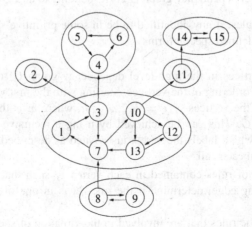

Figure 10.10 A high-level dependency graph and its strongly connected components.

Theorem 2. The high-level dependency graph of any EQL program is a directed acyclic graph.

Proof of Theorem 2. Assume that $\bar{G}$ is not an acyclic graph. Then $\bar{G}$ has a directed circuit. However, all strongly connected components on it should have been one strongly connected component.   □

Timing and Space Requirements   All graphs used in the algorithms presented in this chapter are represented as adjacency lists. Let n be the number of vertices (or rules) and let e be the number of edges in G as constructed by step (1) and step (2). Step (1) can be performed in O(n)-time. Step (2) can be done in $O(n^2)$-time since every pair of rules must be checked. The checking of each of the three conditions can be done efficiently. Step (3) can be achieved in $O(MAX(n, e))$-time using the depth-first search strongly connected components algorithm of Tarjan [Tarjan, 1972]. The creation of edges for $\bar{G}$ in step (4) can be done in $O(e)$-time since in the worst case, all edges in G may have to be examined.

In the next section, we describe an algorithm for identifying special form sets in the high-level dependency graph.

Identifying Special Form Sets   The brute-force approach to identify sets of rules in a special form would be to generate all combinations of the rules in a program and then check the rules in each combination to see if they are in one of the special forms catalogued. However, this approach does not take into account the syntactic and semantic structure of an EQL program and it has exponential time complexity. We present an algorithm for identifying special form sets by checking the high-level dependency graph constructed by algorithm Construct_HLD_Graph.

Algorithm Identify_SF_Set. Identification of special form sets.

Input: A high-level dependency graph $\bar{G}$ corresponding to an EQL program.

Output: Sets of rules, if any, identified to be in some primitive special forms or in some user-defined special forms.

1. Sort the vertices in the high-level dependency graph $\bar{G}$ to obtain a reverse topological ordering of the vertices. Starting with the first vertex with no out-edge, label the vertices $v_i, i = 1, 2, \ldots, m$, where m is the total number of vertices in $\bar{G}$. This can be achieved by using a recursive depth-first search algorithm, which labels the vertex just visited as described above just before exiting from each cell.

2. For the set of rules contained in each vertex v_i such that v_i does not have any outgoing edge, determine if the rule set is in one of the special forms catalogued.

   Report the rules that are involved in the violation of specific special form conditions.

Timing Requirements   Step (1) can clearly be achieved in $O(MAX(n, e))$-time using a standard recursive depth-first search algorithm [Aho, Hopcroft, and Ullman, 1974]. The timing and space requirements for step (2) depend on the order in which the special forms are checked as well as on the complexity of the recognition algorithms used for each individual special form.

Theorem 3. All rules in a forward-independent set, v_i, are always guaranteed to reach a fixed point in bounded time if

1. all rules in v_i by themselves can always reach a fixed point in bounded time and
2. for every forward-independent set v_j such that there is an edge (v_i, v_j) in $\bar{G}$, all rules in v_j are always guaranteed to reach a fixed point in bounded time.

Proof of Theorem 3.   There are two cases to consider:

If v_i does not have any out-edge, then v_i is independent of any v_j, $i \neq j$. v_i is certainly guaranteed to always reach a fixed point in bounded time if the rules in it are always guaranteed to reach a fixed point in bounded time.

If v_i has outgoing edges, then v_i is not independent from other vertices. Let $v_j, j = 1, 2, \ldots, p$ be these vertices such that for each v_j, there is an edge (v_i, v_j) in $\bar{G}$. Assume that rules in v_i may not reach a fixed point in bounded time. Then there must be at least one variable v_1 in L of v_i whose value is changed infinitely often. However, it is assumed that rules in v_i are always able to reach a fixed point in bounded time. Thus there must be another vertex v_k such that v_i is not independent from v_k and rules in v_k cannot reach a fixed point in bounded time. However, this violates our assumption that every v_j is always guaranteed to reach a fixed point in bounded time. Hence, rules in v_i are always guaranteed to reach a fixed point if both conditions (1) and (2) are satisfied.   □

Theorem 4. Let $v_j, j = 1, 2, \ldots, p$ be a list of p mutually independent sets of rules. Suppose v is not independent from any v_js. If v is always guaranteed to reach a fixed point in bounded time, and each of the v_js is always guaranteed to reach a fixed point in bounded time, then all rules in $v \cup v_1 \cup v_2 \cup \ldots \cup v_p$ are always guaranteed to reach a fixed point in bounded time.

Proof of Theorem 4.   Consider two different rule sets, v_a and v_b, taken from the list of v_js. Since v_a and v_b are mutually independent, the firing of rules in v_a does not enable rules in v_b. Thus the rules in v_b will reach a fixed point in bounded time despite the presence of v_a. The same argument applies to v_a. Extending this reasoning to more than two sets in the list of v_js, we can conclude that rules in $v_1 \cup \cdots \cup v_p$ are guaranteed to reach a fixed point in bounded time.

Let $K = v_1 \cup \cdots \cup v_p$. Since v is not independent from each set in the list of v_js, it is not independent of rules in K. However, rules in K are independent from rules in v. Therefore, the firing of rules in v does not enable rules in K. Consequently, rules in K will reach a fixed point in bounded time despite the presence of v. After the rules in K have reach a fixed point, the variables in K will no longer change their contents and thus these variables will not enable or disable rules in v. At this point, only rules in v may fire. Since v is guaranteed to reach a fixed point in bounded time, it can be concluded that the rules in $v \cup v_1 \cup \cdots \cup v_p$ are also always guaranteed to reach a fixed point in bounded time. □

10.11.3   Checking Compatibility Conditions

Checking whether the second condition (CR2) or the third condition (CR3) for compatibility is satisfied by a pair of rules is a straightforward exercise in comparing sets and expressions. We shall therefore discuss the checking of the first condition: mutual exclusion.

The Boolean function $mutex(e_1, e_2)$ determines whether two Boolean expressions, e_1 and e_2, are mutually exclusive. The goal of $mutex$ is not to conquer the general mutual exclusion problem. Instead, it tries to efficiently detect as much mutual exclusion as possible. When it returns true, it means that the two expressions are mutually exclusive. However, when it returns false, it means that either they are not mutually exclusive or there is insufficient information (without executing the rules and without a priori knowledge of the input values) to determine the mutual exclusion. Therefore, the two expressions may still be mutually exclusive even when $mutex$ returns false.

This approximation does not affect the validity of any of the special forms (all of which use the mutual exclusion check in the compatibility condition) described because the approximate mutual exclusion relation is a subset of the mutual exclusion relation. Thus certain pairs of enabling conditions which are mutually exclusive may not be recognized as such using this approximate mutual exclusion check. This is acceptable since every pair of enabling conditions that are recognized by the approximate mutual exclusion check are guaranteed to be mutually exclusive. Therefore, the analyzer never concludes erroneously that a program with unbounded response time is one that has bounded response time, though some programs which have bounded response time may be rejected because the mutual exclusion relation between at least one pair of rules may not be recognized using this approximation.

$mutex$ makes use of a divide-and-conquer strategy inspired by the following observations. Let e_1, e_2, e_3 be arbitrary Boolean expressions. For (e_1 AND e_2) and e_3 to be mutually exclusive, either e_1 or e_2 (or both) must be mutually exclusive with e_3. For (e_1 OR e_2) and e_3 to be mutually exclusive, both e_1 and e_2 must be mutually exclusive with e_3. Therefore we can continuously divide the problem into subproblems until both Boolean expressions are simple expressions.

A subtle problem arises when NOT operators appear in expressions. For example, to decide whether the expressions (NOT e_1) and e_2 are mutually exclusive, we cannot simply negate the answer returned from $mutex(e_1, e_2)$, because errors may occur when $mutex(e_1, e_2)$ returns false, meaning e_1 and e_2 may or may not be mutually exclusive. Let us assume that these expressions are properly parenthesized. We define the *level* of an operator as the number of open parentheses within the scope of this operator. Thus an operator whose scope has no parenthesis is at level 0. Then this problem can be solved by applying DeMorgan's laws (chapter 2, Figure 2.3) to the expressions to move the occurrence of NOT operators to the lowest level.

In the implementation, we do not explicitly rewrite the expressions before calling *mutex*. Instead, a flag to indicate whether special NOT processing is needed is associated with each expression in *mutex* to keep track of the net effect of NOT operators down to the level at which this NOT appears. If $mutex(e_1, e_2)$ returns true, then (NOT e_1) and e_2 are not mutually exclusive; thus the flag is initialized to false to indicate that no special negation processing is needed. Otherwise, if $mutex(e_1, e_2)$ returns false, then whether (NOT e_1) and e_2 are mutually exclusive or cannot be determined without additional information. We assume that these two expressions are mutually exclusive and set the flag to true to indicate that special negation processing is needed later. If a NOT operator is encountered at another level, this flag is negated. This procedure is repeated as often as needed while this flag is passed down to the subroutines in charge of the subexpressions. After all NOTs have been processed and if the flag is false, we can conclude that (NOT e_1) and e_2 are not mutually exclusive. Otherwise, if the flag is true, no such conclusion can be warranted.

The detection of mutual exclusion between two simple expressions s_1 and s_2 is handled by function $smutex(s_1, s_2)$. A simple expression can be

a Boolean variable, for example, sensor_a_good;

a constant, e.g., FALSE; or

a relational test, whose operator can be one of =, $\langle \rangle$, >, <, >=, <=, and whose operands can be either variables or arithmetic expressions.

Although tedious, *smutex* handles the examination case by case. It also invokes function *eval(e)*, which, given an expression e, determines whether it can be evaluated. If it can be evaluated, *eval* also returns the result of evaluation.

It should be noted that compatibility is independent of any special form. When the analyzer determines that rule a and rule b are compatible or when the user specifies this fact, these two rules are considered compatible under any context (when checked by any special form recognition procedures).

Timing Requirements The complexity of *eval* is linearly proportional to the length, in terms of the number of operators, of the expression to be evaluated. Although the general problem of mutual-exclusion detection is of exponential complexity, *mutex* has been implemented to give answers in quadratic time.

10.11.4 Checking Cycle-Breaking Conditions

Cycle-breaking conditions are kept in a list, with the latest specified break condition placed at the head and the earliest specified break condition, which is the one in the special form part, placed at the tail. Later specified break conditions are checked first and therefore are treated as exceptions. Since conditions in a special form may specify different types of graphs, one list exists for each type of graph. We define any cycle found in a graph representing some information about a program to be *acceptable* if it does not cause a cycle in the state-space graph of the program. A cycle is *not acceptable* if it may cause a cycle in the state-space graph of the program. An arbitrary cycle-breaking condition is evaluated as follows:

Algorithm Eval_CB_Conditions Evaluating general cycle-breaking conditions.

When a cycle is found in the graph of type graph_type:
    initially, assume the cycle is acceptable;
  if (cycles_list is not specified **or**
      the cycle is found in the specified cycles_list)
  then if (break_condition is evaluated to FALSE)
    then the cycle is not acceptable
    else the cycle is acceptable
  else if (cycles_list is specified but the cycle is not found in it)
    then check the next break_condition in the list of break conditions for this
        graph_type, if any
    else the cycle is acceptable

To allow for the checking of arbitrary break conditions for each cycle in an arbitrary graph representing the syntactic and/or semantic structure of a program, the checking algorithm may be required to perform an exhaustive search on the arbitrary graph. The brute-force approach would have to determine every cycle in the graph and then check whether the break condition is satisfied for each cycle found. If $|E| \ll |V|$, where $|E|$ and $|V|$ are, respectively, the number of edges and the number of vertices in a graph (e.g., ER graph, VM graph) corresponding to a program, then this approach is still practical. The selection algorithm construct_HLD_graph (section 10.11.2) described earlier decomposes the program into forward-independent modules which can be analyzed independently. This effectively breaks a large graph (corresponding to the entire program) into a set of smaller graphs (corresponding to independent modules of rules), each of which is more amenable to efficient analysis. It should be noted that an arbitrary graph corresponding to the rules in a forward-independent set may be different from the dependency graph (a strongly connected component) corresponding to these rules. Thus the arbitrary graph may be further decomposed into smaller components for analysis.

Furthermore, it should be noted that the types of graphs used for static analysis are much smaller in size than the state-space graph corresponding to a program. For instance, each vertex in an ER graph corresponds to a distinct rule in a program. If a program has n rules, there are n vertices and at most $n(n-1)/2$ edges in the corresponding ER graph. In contrast, each of the vertices in a state-space graph represents a distinct vector of all variables in a program. For instance, for a finite-domain program with m variables, the total number of states in the corresponding state-space graph in the worst case (i.e., all combinations of the values of the variables are possible) is

$$\prod_{i=1}^{i=m} |X_i|$$

where $|X_i|$ is the size of the domain of the ith variable. If all variables are binary, this number is 2^m. Hence, our static analysis technique is a significant improvement over those based primarily on conventional finite-state-based checking [Emerson et al., 1990].

To further improve the efficiency of checking cycle-breaking conditions, we have developed the following strategies that are applicable to some classes of break conditions and cycles. As in most strategies for attacking NP-complete graph problems, our strategies take advantage of special characteristics of a graph type and of the particular form of break conditions. Any attempt to find checking algorithms which are efficient for arbitrary graphs and arbitrary break conditions would not seem promising.

For a class of break conditions that expresses relationships between two rules in a cycle, we can first determine those pairs of rules that violate the break condition being checked. Then for each pair of these rules, we check to see whether the pair of vertices corresponding to this pair of rules lie in a cycle. If the answer is yes, we can immediately conclude that the cycle detected is not broken by the break condition.

For certain classes of graphs and a class of break conditions, it is possible to first prune the acceptable cycles in the graph without actually finding all vertices in a cycle, and then apply a general cycle-checking algorithm. This would greatly reduce the number of cycles that have to be checked.

10.12 QUANTITATIVE TIMING ANALYSIS ALGORITHMS

We now present quantitative algorithms for determining the worst-case execution times (WCETs) of EQL programs. As defined earlier, given a program p, the *response time analysis problem* is to determine the response time of p. This problem consists of (1) determining whether or not the execution of p always terminates in bounded time and (2) computing the maximal execution time of p.

We have shown that the response-time analysis problem is undecidable if the program variables have infinite domains and is PSPACE-hard in the case where all of the variables have finite domains. However, we have observed that the use of a simple syntactic and semantic check of programs coupled with other techniques such as state-space graph checks can dramatically reduce the time needed in the analysis. Sets of syntactic and semantic constraint assertions exist such that if the set S of rules satisfies any of them, then the execution of S always terminates in bounded time. Each of these sets of syntactic and semantic constraint assertions is called a special form.

The focus of the remainder of this chapter is to formally prove the correctness of two special forms and to determine tight response-time upper bounds of EQL rule-based programs. For each known special form, an algorithm used to calculate the maximal response time of programs satisfying this special form is presented. Additionally, to enhance the applicability of the proposed algorithms, we show how the General Analysis Algorithm can be used with these algorithms.

10.12.1 Overview

We have described a set of preliminary tools for analyzing EQL programs that was reported in [Browne, Cheng, and Mok, 1988]. The function of this set of tools is to check whether or not the execution of a given EQL program always terminates in a bounded number of rule firings. Several real-life real-time rule-based programs have been rewritten in EQL and analyzed by this set of tools (e.g., the Cryogenic Hydrogen Pressure Malfunction Procedure of the Space Shuttle Vehicle Pressure Control System [Helly, 1984], the Integrated Status Assessment Expert System [Marsh, 1988], the Fuel Cell Expert System).

To avoid exhaustive state and path exploration when determining the response-time upper bounds for the programs in which we are interested, we have introduced sets of syntactic and semantic constraint assertions such that if the EQL program p satisfies any of them, then the execution of p always terminates in bounded time. Each of these sets is called a special form. A facility called Estella with which the programmer can specify special forms and application-specific knowledge has been developed and integrated into analysis tools [Cheng and Wang, 1990; Cheng et al., 1993]. Cheng and Chen [Cheng, 1992b] report a response-time bound analysis based on the concept of special form.

Here, we prove the existence of two special forms and present algorithms for determining the response-time upper bounds of EQL programs satisfying a known special form. We employ a static method that performs an a priori syntactic and semantic check to see if the imposed timing constraints are met. We describe two quantitative algorithms, Algorithm_A and Algorithm_D, used to calculate the maximal response time of EQL programs satisfying a known special form.

To enhance the applicability of the presented algorithms and further reduce the time needed in analyzing EQL programs, the *general analysis algorithm* [Cheng and Wang, 1990] is used to partition this program such that only a small part of the given program is checked at one time. The general analysis algorithm partitions a program p into a hierarchy of sets of rules and takes advantage of the fact that the execution of a higher-level set is *independent* of that of a lower-level set. Hence, the execution of the program p can be regarded as the sequential execution of a series of subsets of rules of p. For each subset S, a syntactic and semantic check on S is conducted to see if S is in a known special form. If S is in a known special form, the corresponding algorithm is used to determine an upper bound on the number of rule firings by S during the execution of p; otherwise, the aforementioned temporal-logic model checker and timing analyzer are used to conduct an exhaustive check on the state-space graph of S to obtain an upper bound on the number of rule firings by S. If S does not have a finite upper bound on the number of rule firings, neither does p. Then, the general analysis algorithm will report this situation and stop at this point. If p is found not to have a finite upper bound on the number of rule firings, an optimization method reported in [Zupan and Cheng, 1994b; Zupan and Cheng, 1998] can be applied to transform p into a program with a bounded response time.

Since our method in most cases does not require checking the entire state-space graph of the system at hand, it makes the analysis of systems with a large number of rules and variables feasible. A suite of computer-aided software engineering tools based on this analysis approach has been implemented. It has been successfully used to analyze the aforementioned real-time rule-based expert systems developed by Mitre and NASA for the Space Shuttle and the planned Space Station [Cheng and Wang, 1990; Cheng et al., 1993]. These analysis tools show a dramatic improvement in terms of time and space over the other suite of tools that primarily relies on exhaustive state-space graph checks, as evidenced by the two seconds of time the former took in comparison with the two weeks of time the latter took when these two suites of tools were separately applied to analyze the aforementioned Cryogenic Hydrogen Pressure Malfunction Procedure of the Space Shuttle Vehicle Pressure Control System [Browne, Cheng, and Mok, 1988].

We briefly review the syntax and semantics of EQL and the concept of special forms. Then we prove the existence of two special forms. Two algorithms used to obtain response-time upper bounds for programs satisfying these special forms are presented. We discuss how the general analysis algorithm can be used to enhance the applicability of the presented algorithms.

10.12.2 The Equational Logic Language

An EQL program has a set of rules for updating variables that denote the state of the physical system under control. The firing of a rule assigns a new value to at least one variable to reflect changes in the external environment as detected by sensors. Sensor readings are sampled periodically. Every time sensor readings are taken, the variables are recomputed iteratively by a number of rule firings until no further change in the variables can result from the firing of a rule. The EQL program is then said to have reached a *fixed point*. Intuitively, the rules in an EQL program are used to express the constraints on and the goals of the system. If a fixed point is reached, the variables have settled down to a set of values that are consistent with the constraints and goals as expressed by the rules.

Let p denote an EQL program. p consists of a finite set of rules and a finite set of variables denoting the *state* of the system. The set of variables is called the *state variable*, ξ, which consists of two parts: the input variables and the non-input variables. That is,

$$\xi = [X, Y]$$
$$= [x_1, x_2, \ldots, x_n, y_1, y_2, \ldots, y_m],$$

where for each i, x_i is the ith input variable, and for each j, y_j is the jth non-input variable. The values of input variables are obtained through sensor readings sampled periodically and cannot be changed throughout the execution of p, whereas the non-input variables may be changed as the system progresses.

The set of rules is used to modify the state variable to reflect the progress of the system. For each rule r in p, r, consisting of a set of *assignments* and an *enabling condition*, is of this form

$$e_1 \mid \cdots \mid e_d \text{ IF } EC,$$

where $d \geq 1$ and the symbol $\mid$ stands for parallel AND, which means these assignments are simultaneously carried out. For each i, $1 \leq i \leq d$, e_i denotes an assignment of this form: $a_i := b_i$. a_i is a non-input variable that is assigned the value of the arithmetic/Boolean expression b_i if the rule r is fired. EC is a predicate on the variables in the program and is called the *enabling condition*, which can be viewed as a mapping from V to $\{true, false\}$, where V denotes the set of possible values of the state variable. There is a subset $V_r \subset V$ such that, for each $s \in V_r$, the value of the EC of r is true with respect to s. Also, for each variable x, a set $V_{r,x}$ exists such that the number z is contained in $V_{r,x}$ if and only if an $s \in V_r$ exists whose x-component is equal to the value of z.

r is a *single-assignment rule* if it contains only one assignment expression; otherwise, it is a *multiple-assignment rule*. To facilitate the explanation later, the rule r is referred to by:

- LHS: the left-hand side(s) of the assignment expression(s),
- RHS: the right-hand side(s) of the assignment expression(s), and
- EC: the enabling condition.

The variables appearing in r are usually classified into three sets (similar definitions are used to define L_p, R_p, and T_p for the program p):

- $L_r = \{v \mid v$ appears in the LHS of $r\}$,
- $R_r = \{v \mid v$ appears in the RHS of $r\}$, and
- $T_r = \{v \mid v$ appears in the EC of $r\}$.

The rule r is *enabled* if and only if its enabling condition is evaluated to be true; otherwise, it is *disabled*. r is *fireable* if and only if (1) it is enabled and (2) the firing of r changes the value of a variable in L_r. If r is selected (scheduled) to be executed, then it is *fired*. The firing of r consists of evaluating all of the RHS expressions of r in a parallel manner, followed by updating the LHS variables of r in a parallel manner with the values of corresponding RHS expressions. Note that the fact that r is fireable does not mean that r must be fired during the execution. It may be that the firing of another rule disables r before r is selected to be fired. Furthermore, a rule could be fired multiple times during execution.

The ith subrule of r, denoted r_i of this form: $a_i := b_i$ IF EC, is a single-assignment rule consisting of the ith assignment expression and the enabling condition of r. Hence, the rule r can be regarded as being composed of one or more subrules with the same enabling condition. For each subrule r_i, if a new value is assigned to the variable in L_{r_i} when r is fired, we say that r_i is fired. There may be more than one subrule being fired when r is fired.

10.12.3 Mutual Exclusiveness and Compatibility

If r and r' cannot be enabled simultaneously, then they are *mutually exclusive* (in terms of enabledness) to each other. The mutual exclusion graph is used to demonstrate the property of mutual exclusiveness among rules.

Mutual-Exclusion Graph: Let S denote a set of rules. The *mutual-exclusion* (ME) graph $G_S^{ME} = (V, E)$ is a labeled graph. V is a set of vertices representing rules such that there is a vertex labeled r in V if and only if there is a rule r in S. E is a set of edges representing the property of mutual exclusiveness such that E contains the edge (r, r') connecting the vertex r and the vertex r' if and only if the rule r and the rule r' are mutually exclusive to each other.

r and r' are *compatible* in terms of modifying the variables if and only if at least one of the following conditions holds (in the remainder of this chapter, two rules being compatible refers to two rules being compatible in terms of modifying the variables):

CR1. r and r' are mutually exclusive (in terms of enabledness) to each other.

CR2. $L_r \cap L_{r'} = \emptyset$.

CR3. For each variable x in $L_r \cap L_{r'}$, r and r' agree on the expression assigned to x.

To check the property of compatibility among a set of n rules, it takes $O(n^2)$-time for checking (CR2) and (CR3), and, in the worst case, exponential time for checking (CR1) (and constructing the ME graph). In our analysis tools, this mutual-exclusion-checking procedure is implemented by using an approximation algorithm that takes quadratic time for checking (CR1). It produces correct results for all of our test programs. The section on Estella provides details.

10.12.4 High-Level Dependency Graph

The high-level dependency (HLD) graph of a program shows the dependencies among subsets of rules in this program and is used as the basis to assign priorities to rules. Each of the vertices in the HLD graph represents a subset of rules and is called a *forward-independent set*.

The fireability of r (and the result of the firing of r) is *not affected* by the firing of r', if $L_{r'} \cap T_r = \emptyset$ and $L_{r'} \cap (L_r \cup R_r) = \emptyset$. The first condition ensures that the firing of r' has nothing to do with the enabledness of r, whereas the other means that, for each variable $x \in L_r$, the firing of r' has nothing to do with the value of x. If the fireability of r (and the result of the firing of r) is not affected by the firing of r' during the execution of p, we say r is *independent* of r'.

Assume S and S' are two sets of rules. If, for each pair of rules $r \in S$ and $r' \in S'$, r is independent of r', we say the set S is *independent* of the set S'. Hence, the set S is independent of the set S' if $L_{S'} \cap (T_S \cup L_S \cup R_S) = \emptyset$ [Cheng et al., 1993], which

Input A set, p, of EQL rules.

Output The high-level dependency graph $\overline{G}_p$.

1. For each rule $r \in p$, create a vertex labeled r.

2. Let S contain rule i and let S' contain rule j, $i \neq j$. If the condition $L_{S'} \cap (T_S \cup L_S \cup R_S) = \emptyset$ is not satisfied, create a directed edge from the vertex i to the vertex j.

3. Find every strongly connected component in the dependency graph $G(V, E)$ constructed by step 1 and step 2. Let $C_1, C_2, \ldots, C_m$ be the strongly connected components of $G(V, E)$.

4. Define $\overline{G}_p(\overline{V}, \overline{E})$ as follows:
   $\overline{V} = \{C_1, C_2, \ldots, C_m\}$
   $\overline{E} = \{(C_i, C_j) \mid i \neq j, (x, y) \in E, x \in C_i, \text{ and } y \in C_j\}$

Figure 10.11   The high-level dependency graph construction procedure.

constitutes a sufficient but not necessary condition for independence. If S and S' do not satisfy the above condition for independence, the corresponding HLD graph contains a directed edge from the vertex representing S to the vertex representing S', and the rules in S are assigned lower priorities than the rules in S'. Rules in the same forward-independent set are assigned the same priority.

[Cheng et al., 1993] report an HLD graph construction procedure, shown in Figure 10.11. This procedure requires $O(n^2)$-time to construct the HLD graph for an n-rule program. For more details about the HLD graph, the reader is referred to [Cheng et al., 1993].

Example 9. The following is a sample EQL program, where the symbol [] serves as a delimiter between two rules.

```
PROGRAM Program_1
VAR
    c, d, e, f, g, h : integer;
    x, y, z : boolean;
INPUTVAR
    a, b : integer;
INIT
    c := 0, d := 0, e := 0, f := 0, g := 0, h := 0,
    x := true, y := true, z := true
INPUT
    read(a, b)
RULES
    (*1*)   c := 1 IF a > 0 and b > 0
    (*2*) [] c := 2 IF a > 0 and b ≤ 0
    (*3*) [] d := 2 IF a ≤ 0
```

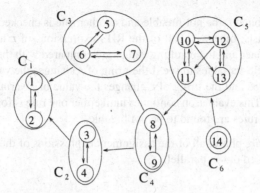

Figure 10.12 The HLD graph of Program_1.

(*4*) [] $d := c$ IF $a > 0$
(*5*) [] $e := c + 1$ IF $c \leq 1$ and $b > 0$
(*6*) [] $f := c + 1 \mid e := c - 1$ IF $c \leq 1$ and $b \leq 0$
(*7*) [] $f := c - 1$ IF $c \geq 0$
(*8*) [] $g := 1 \mid h := 1$ IF $f > 1$ and $d > 1$
(*9*) [] $g := 2 \mid h := 2$ IF $f \leq 1$ and $e > 1$
(*10*) [] $x := true$ IF $g = 2$ and $y = true$
(*11*) [] $x := false$ IF $g = 1$
(*12*) [] $y := true$ IF $h = 2$ and $x = false$
(*13*) [] $y := false$ IF $h = 1$
(*14*) [] $z := true$ IF $x = true$ and $y = true$
END.

Applying the HLD graph construction procedure to Program_1, the resulting HLD graph $G_{Program\_1}$ is shown in Figure 10.12. Rule 1 and rule 2 are assigned higher priorities than rule 3 and rule 4, which in turn are assigned higher priorities than rule 8 and rule 9, and so on. Note that rule 3 and rule 4 are assigned the same priority as rule 5, rule 6, and rule 7.

10.12.5 Program Execution and Response Time

The *execution* of the n-rule program p is a sequence of *recognize–act* cycles. Each recognize–act cycle consists of two phases: *match* and *fire*.

- During the *match* phase, a sequence of evaluations are conducted such that rules of p are evaluated in order of their priorities to determine a highest-priority fireable rule. The order of evaluating rules sharing the same priority is non-deterministic or up to the run-time scheduler. Suppose r is checked next. The enabling condition of r is evaluated first to see if r is enabled. If r is not enabled, r is found to be not fireable and another rule is checked if an unchecked rule still exists; otherwise, all of the RHS expressions of r are evaluated in a parallel manner and the resulting values are compared with the values of corresponding LHS variables to see if the firing of r changes the value of a variable. If r is enabled and the firing of r changes the value of a variable, r is found to be fireable. This evaluation continues until either one rule is found to be fireable or all of the rules are found to be not fireable.

- During the *fire* phase, all of the assignment expressions of the selected fireable rule are carried out in parallel.

The recognize–act cycle continues until none of the rules is fireable. p reaches a *fixed point* if none of its rules is fireable. The execution of p terminates when p reaches a fixed point.

Since all rules may not have the same number of assignment expressions and the same size of enabling conditions, evaluating and firing different rules may take different amounts of time. However, for each rule $r \in p$, it takes only up to a fixed amount of time to evaluate the enabling condition of r, since the size of the enabling condition of r is finite. In addition, the time needed for selecting a rule to evaluate is also finite since only a finite number of rules exist from which to choose. Assume the maximal amount of time needed to select and evaluate a rule is x units of time. Since there are n rules in p, the match phase needs at most $n * x$ units of time.

Furthermore, since there are only up to a fixed number, say m, of assignment expressions in each rule, it also takes only up to a fixed amount of time to conduct the fire phase. Assume the maximal amount of time needed to carry out an assignment expression is y units of time. The fire phase needs at most $m * y$ units of time. Hence, the time spent during each cycle is at most $n * x + m * y$ units of time. If the execution takes at most l recognize–act cycles to reach a fixed point, the response time is at most $l * (n * x + m * y)$ units of time. That is, the response time (i.e., execution time) of p is proportional to the number of recognize–act cycles (and thus the number of rule firings) during the execution of p. If we know the maximal amount of *actual* time needed to select and evaluate a rule and the maximal amount of *actual* time needed to carry out an assignment expression, then the response time of p can be easily calculated. Since these quantities are machine-dependent, the response time of p in this chapter is measured in terms of the number of rule firings during the execution of p. The program p has *a bounded response time* if and only if the number of rule firings during the execution of p is bounded by a fixed number.

The *exact upper bound* on the number of rule firings during the execution of p is the integer i representing the maximal number of rule firings that can possibly happen during the execution of p. An *upper bound* on the number of rule firings during the execution of p is an integer j, $j \geq i$. In the remainder of this chapter, an *upper bound for the program* p refers to an upper bound on the number of rule firings during the execution of p, unless otherwise stated. Let T^p represent an upper bound for the program p.

10.12.6   State-Space Graph

The execution of p can be modeled by the *state-space graph* of p. This graph is similar to the *execution graph* used by [Aiken, Widom, and Hellerstein, 1992]. The paths in the graph represent all of the possible rule firing sequences during the execution of p.

State-Space Graph: The state-space graph of p is a labeled directed graph $G_p = (V, E)$. V is a set of distinct vertices representing states such that V contains a vertex labeled v if and only if v is a possible value of the state variable. Note that each label v is an $(n+m)$-tuple, where n is the number of input variables and m is the number of non-input variables. E is a set of edges representing rule firings such that E contains the edge $\langle i, j \rangle$ from the vertex i to the vertex j if and only if (1) there is a rule r that is enabled at i and (2) the firing of r at i results in the state variable having the same value as j.

A rule is enabled at the vertex (state) i if and only if its enabling condition is evaluated to be *true* with respect to the label value of i; otherwise, it is disabled at i. For each vertex v in the state-space graph G_p, the label v corresponds to a value of the state variable, which consists of two parts: v^i of the set of input variables X and v^o of the set of non-input variables Y. The vertex v is a *launch state* if (1) the content of the label v is equal to the initial value of the state variable, or (2) v^i is a potential value of the set of input variables and v^o is a potential value of the set of non-input variables as a result of execution. On the other hand, v is a *final state* (i.e., *fixed point*) if it does not have an outgoing edge to another vertex. For each rule $r \in p$, r is not fireable when p reaches a final state.

The rule r is said to *potentially enable* the rule r' if a state s exists, at which r' is disabled, and firing r at s makes the value of the enabling condition of r' *true*. On the other hand, r is said to *disable* r' if, for each state s where r and r' are both enabled, firing r at s makes the value of the enabling condition of r' *false*.

10.12.7   Response-Time Analysis Problem and Special Form

Given a program p, the *response-time analysis problem* is to determine the response time of p. This problem consists of two parts: (1) checking whether or not the execution of p always terminates in a bounded number of rule firings and (2) if it does, obtaining an upper bound on the number of rule firings during the execution of p. Note that, if the execution of p does not always terminate in bounded time, the maximal response time of p is *infinite*.

p is *analyzable* by the algorithm α if α can determine whether or not the execution of p always terminates in a bounded number of rule firings. In general, the analysis problem is *undecidable* if the program variables have infinite domains and is PSPACE-hard in the case where all of the variables have finite domains [Browne, Cheng, and Mok, 1988]. Hence, even in the case where all of the variables have finite domains, the amount of time needed to analyze a system is usually very large.

However, it has been observed by the authors that sets of syntactic and semantic constraint assertions exist such that if the set of rules S satisfies any of them, the execution of S always terminates in bounded time. A *special form* is a set of syntactic and semantic constraint assertions on a set of rules. A set of rules satisfying all assertions of special form $\mathcal{F}$ is said to be *in* special form $\mathcal{F}$ and is guaranteed to always reach a fixed point in bounded time. Two special forms have been observed and, for each of them, we have developed an algorithm used to calculate response-time upper bounds for programs satisfying it. Hence, if a program (or part of a program) is determined to be in a known special form, the corresponding response-time upper-bound algorithm can be used such that the use of expensive exhaustive state-space graph checks can be avoided (or at least minimized).

10.12.8   Special Form A and Algorithm_A

The first set of syntactic and semantic constraint assertions is called *Special Form A*, which allows only constant expressions to be assigned to non-input variables. In addition, for each rule r in a Special Form A program p, r can be fired at most once during the execution of p.

10.12.9   Special Form A

Special Form A: Let S denote a set of rules. S is in *Special Form A* if the following conditions hold.

A1. $R_S = \emptyset$.
A2. For each pair of distinct rules r and r' in S, r and r' are compatible.
A3. $L_S \cap T_S = \emptyset$.

To check if a set of n rules is in Special Form A, the recognition procedure requires $O(n)$-time for checking the satisfiability of (A1) and $O(k^2)$-time for checking the satisfiability of (A3), where k is the number of variables in this set of rules. In addition, it takes quadratic time to check the satisfiability of (A2).

Theorem 5. If p is in Special Form A, then the execution of p always terminates in n rule firings, where n is the number of rules in p.

Proof of Theorem 5. The proof can be found in section 10.12.12.   □

Algorithm_A We now improve the upper bound above by exploiting the property of mutual exclusiveness among rules. If r and r' are compatible by mutual exclusiveness, then at least one of them, say r, is disabled at any moment during the execution of p. Hence, the rule r cannot be fired throughout the execution of p. This means that the value 1 can be subtracted from the value of n obtained by applying the theorem above to get a tighter (and better) upper bound for p. If a set of m rules exists in which each pair of distinct rules are compatible by mutual exclusiveness, the argument above applies to each pair of rules in this set (i.e., at most one rule in this set can possibly be enabled and fired). This means that the value $m - 1$ can be subtracted from the value n to get a better upper bound.

Let G_1 and G_2 be *complete* subgraphs of the ME graph G_p^{ME}. We say that G_1 and G_2 are *independent* of each other if and only if $V(G_1) \cap V(G_2) = \emptyset$. Both G_1 and G_2 can contribute in deriving a better response-time upper bound. For each independent complete ME subgraph G_i, if G_i consists of m_i vertices, then the value of $m_i - 1$ can be subtracted from the value of n.

Assume k is the number of independent complete ME subgraphs and m_i is the number of rules in the ith subgraph. As mentioned earlier, there is at most *one* rule firing by each set of rules corresponding to an independent complete ME subgraph during the execution of p. Hence, the smaller the value of k, the smaller the number of possible firings. For the purpose of deriving a tighter upper bound on the number of rule firings, we are interested in finding the *minimal* number of k. That is,

$$
\begin{aligned}
T^p &= n - \sum_{i=1\ldots k} (m_i - 1) \\
&= n - \sum_{i=1\ldots k} m_i + \sum_{i=1\ldots k} 1 \\
&= n - n + k \\
&= k
\end{aligned}
\tag{10.1}
$$

Figure 10.13 shows Algorithm_A, which results by applying the above strategy. Algorithm_A requires, as mentioned earlier, quadratic time to perform step (1), to construct the ME graph. For step (2), the problem of finding the minimal number of independent complete subgraphs can easily be proved to be a transformation from the problem of partitioning a graph into cliques, which is an NP-complete problem [Garey and Johnson, 1979]. Hence, we use an approximation method that checks the existence of each edge at most once to partition the ME graph into a set of independent complete subgraphs. Since there are only at most $n(n - 1)/2$ edges in the ME graph, where n is the number of rules, step (2) also requires, at most, quadratic time. Step (3) requires a constant time to output the value of k.

Input A Special Form A program p.

Output An integer representing the upper bound found.

1. Construct the ME graph G_p^{ME}.
2. Find the minimal number, k, of independent complete subgraphs of G_p^{ME}.
3. Output(k).

Figure 10.13 Algorithm_A.

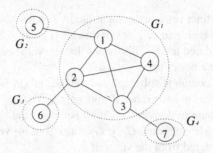

Figure 10.14   The ME graph of Program_2.

Example 10. The following is a sample Special Form A program.

PROGRAM Program_2
VAR
   c, d, e, f, g, h : *integer*;
   x, y, z : *boolean*;
INPUTVAR
   a, b : *integer* ;
INIT
   $c := 0, d := 0, e := 0, f := 0, g := 0, h := 0,$
   $x :=$ *true*, $y :=$ *true*, $z :=$ *true*
INPUT
   read(a, b)
RULES
   (*1*) $c := 1$ IF $a > 0$ and $b > 0$
   (*2*) [] $c := 2$ IF $a > 0$ and $b \le 0$
   (*3*) [] $c := 3$ IF $a \le 0$ and $b > 0$
   (*4*) [] $c := 4$ IF $a \le 0$ and $b \le 0$
   (*5*) [] $e := 1 \mid f := 1$ IF $a \le 0$ or $b \le 0$
   (*6*) [] $d := 1 \mid f := 1$ IF $a \le 0$ or $b > 0$
   (*7*) [] $d := 1 \mid e := 1$ IF $a > 0$ or $b > 0$
END.

Applying Algorithm_A to Program_2, step 1 constructs the ME graph $G^{ME}_{Program\_2}$ that can be divided into four subgraphs in step 2: G_1 contains four vertices (rules), G_2, G_3, and G_4 each contains only one vertex, as shown in Figure 10.14. Hence, step 3 determines that there are at most four rule firings during the execution of Program_2.

10.12.10   Special Form D and Algorithm_D

Special Form D is a relaxed version of Special Form A since it allows variables in L_p to appear in T_p and R_p, where p is a Special Form D program. For each rule

r in p, r may be dynamically enabled and disabled throughout the execution of p. This means that r may be fired more than once before p reaches a fixed point. On the other hand, the fact that r is enabled does not necessarily mean that r will be fired before p reaches a fixed point. It may be the case that the firings of other rules disable r before r gets an opportunity to be fired.

Rule-Dependency Graph The firing of r may result in the firing of r', if (1) r potentially enables r' or (2) $L_r \cap R_{r'} \neq \emptyset$. Each of these two conditions represents one potential firing sequence consisting of the firing of r followed by the firing of r'. The former results from the dependency between the LHS of r and the EC of r', whereas the latter results from the dependency between the LHS of r and the RHS of r'. The rule-dependency graphs are used to demonstrate potential firing sequences of EQL programs.

Rule-Dependency Graph: Let S denote a set of rules. The *rule-dependency* (RD) graph $G_S^{RD} = (V, M, N)$ is a labeled directed graph. V is a set of vertices representing subrules such that V contains a vertex labeled r_i if and only if there is a subrule r_i in S. M is a set of directed edges, called *ER edges*, such that M contains the edge $\langle r_i, r'_j \rangle$ if and only if r_i potentially enables r'_j. N is a set of directed edges, called *VM edges*, such that N contains the edge $\langle r_i, r'_j \rangle$ if and only if

1. $L_{r_i} \cap R_{r'_j} \neq \emptyset$, and
2. r_i does not disable r'_j if r_i and r'_j do not mutually exclude each other, or r_i potentially enables r'_j if r_i and r'_j mutually exclude each other.

A cycle C in G_S^{RD} is classified as

- an *ER cycle* if it contains only ER edges, or
- a *VM cycle* if it contains only VM edges, or
- an *EV cycle* if it contains both kinds of edges.

It is possible that a variable $x_i \in (L_{r_i} \cap T_{r'_j})$ exists such that it cannot be decided textually whether the value assigned to x_i by r_i is in $V_{r'_j, x_i}$. If this is the case, we assume the value assigned to x_i is in $V_{r'_j, x_i}$, thus indicating that the ER edge $\langle r_i, r'_j \rangle$ exists from the vertex r_i to the vertex r'_j in the actual implementation of the RD graph. In addition, in the worst case, the construction procedure requires exponential time as a function of the number of subrules to construct the RD graph, due to the checks for the property of mutual exclusiveness and enabledness/disabledness.

Note that although the existence of the ER edge $\langle r_i, r'_j \rangle$ in G_S^{RD} does not necessarily mean that the subrule r'_j will be enabled as a result of the firing of the subrule r_i, it does mean that r'_j *may* be enabled (and hence fired) as a result of the firing of r_i. On the other hand, if the VM edge $\langle r_i, r'_j \rangle$ exists in G_S^{RD}, then r_i assigns a value to a variable $x \in R_{r'_j}$ such that the value of the RHS of r'_j may change as a result of the firing of r_i. Hence, the firing of r_i *may* result in the firing of r'_j, too. If there is a path $\langle r_i, r'_j, \ldots, w_k, b_m, d_l \rangle$ in G^{RD}_S, then the firing of r_i may eventually result in the firing of d_l. In addition, if there is a cycle $C = \langle r_i, u_j, \ldots, w_k, b_m, d_l, r_i \rangle$ in G^{RD}_S, then the subrules in C *may* be repeatedly fired one after another an unlimited number of times such that S does not reach a fixed point in any bounded time.

Now, let r_i and r'_j be two subrules in S of the form

$$x = f_1(y) \text{ IF } E_1$$

and

$$y = f_2(x) \text{ IF } E_2,$$

respectively. G^{RD}_S contains a VM cycle C consisting of *only* r_i and r'_j. The equality assertion $x == f_1(y)$ must be true immediately after the firing of r_i, and the equality assertion $y == f_2(x)$ must be true immediately after the firing of r'_j. If these two equality assertions can be rewritten in such a way that they are identical, then there can be at most one subrule firing among r_i and r'_j if no other subrule is fired. For example, assume $f_1(y) = y + 1$ and $f_2(x) = x - 1$. The firing of either subrule, say r_i, prevents the other, r'_j, from being fired, since the firing of r'_j immediately after the firing of r_i does not change the value of a variable. Therefore, it is not possible for r_i and r'_j to be alternately fired for an unlimited number of times such that S does not reach a fixed point in bounded time. If this is the case, then C is called a *convergent cycle*. Note that *a convergent cycle is a VM cycle consisting of only two subrules (vertices)*, belonging to two different rules.

Special Form D   The first condition of Special Form D ensures that each pair of rules cannot alternately change the value of a variable for an unlimited number of time, while the other conditions ensure that rules cannot be cyclically fired.

Special Form D: Let S denote a set of rules. S is in Special Form D if the following conditions hold.

D1. For each pair of distinct rules r and r' in S, r and r' are compatible.

D2. The rule-dependency graph G^{RD}_S does not contain an EV cycle.

D3. For each ER cycle in G^{RD}_S, there does *not* exist a pair of subrules r_i and r'_j that disagree on the expression assigned to a variable $x \in (L_{r_i} \cap L_{r'_j})$.

D4. There does not exist a pair of subrules $r_i \in C^1$ and $r'_j \in C^2$, where C^1 and C^2 are distinct simple ER cycles in G^{RD}_S, such that r_i and r'_j disagree on the expression assigned to a variable $x \in (L_{r_i} \cap L_{r'_j})$.

D5. For each simple VM cycle C in G^{RD}_S, C is a convergent cycle, or the subrules (vertices) contained in C cannot all be enabled at the same time (i.e., $\cap_{r \in C} V_r = \emptyset$).

To check if a set of rules is in Special Form D, the recognition procedure requires exponential time in the worst case since it requires exponential time to determine all directed cycles in a directed graph [Garey and Johnson, 1979]. However, the RD graph is usually sparse, so the time required to check the satisfaction of Special Form D conditions is just a small fraction of what is required to conduct the state-space graph check.

Assume p is a Special Form D program. By the definition of Special Form D, p does not contain a rule that includes an assignment expression of the form $x := f(x)$; otherwise, a one-vertex VM cycle C in G_p^{RD} would exist, violating (D5) since C contains only one vertex. Also, a cycle C in G_p^{RD} does not exist such that all of the subrules (vertices) in C belong to the same rule in p. If such a C did exist, (D5) would be violated since all of these subrules would have the same enabling condition.

Theorem 6. If p is in Special Form D, then the execution of p always terminates in a bounded number of rule firings.

Proof of Theorem 6. The proof can be found in section 10.12.12. □

Algorithm_D Assume p is an n-rule Special Form D program. To find an upper bound on the number of rule firings during the execution of p, the *Divide-and-Conquer* strategy is employed here. For each rule $r \in p$, r can be fireable (and hence fired) because (1) the launch state makes r fireable or (2) the firings of other rules make r fireable. According to the definition of program execution, the execution of p is a sequence of rule firings. From the view point of counting the number of rule firings, this sequence of rule firings can be regarded as being composed of interleaving *subsequences*, each of which starts with the firing of some rule which is fireable at the launch state (i.e., we say this rule initiates a subsequence of rule firings during the execution of p). Note that it is possible that a rule can initiate a subsequence of rule firings and be initiated by the firing(s) of other rules during the same execution.

Since there are n rules in p, at most n subsequences of rule firings exist during the execution of p. The number of rule firings during the execution of p is equal to the sum of the numbers of rule firings in individual subsequences. According to Theorem 6, the execution of p always terminates in a bounded number of rule firings. This means that each subsequence consists of up to a bounded number of rule firings, and hence there is a finite upper bound on the number of rule firings in each subsequence. Let NI_r denote an upper bound on the number of rule firings in the subsequence initiated by r. The sum of NI_rs, one for each rule $r \in p$, is thus an upper bound on the number of rule firings during the execution of p. That is,

$$T^p = \sum_{r \in p} NI_r \tag{10.2}$$

To obtain NI_r, the divide-and-conquer strategy is employed again. Since each subrule may have an influence on other rules and hence result in the firings of other rules, directly or indirectly, each subrule r_i of r may initiate a *sub-subsequence* of rule firings. Let NI_{r_i} denote an upper bound on the number of rule firings in the sub-subsequence initiated by the firing of r_i. The sum of NI_{r_i}s, one for each subrule r_i of r, is thus an upper bound on the number of rule firings in the subsequence initiated by the firing of r. That is,

$$NI_r = \sum_{r_i \in r} NI_{r_i} \tag{10.3}$$

By the definition of rule firing and subrule firing, the sum of the numbers of times that the subrules of the rule g are fired (as a result of the firing of r_i) is not less than the number of times that g is fired (as a result of the firing of r_i). An upper bound on the former is thus also an upper bound on the latter. Let $NI_{r_i}^{g_j}$ denote an upper bound on the number of times that g_j is fired as a result of the firing of r_i. The sum of $NI_{r_i}^{g_j}$s, one for each subrule g_j of g, is an upper bound on the number of times that g is fired as a result of the firing of r_i. Let $NI_{r_i}^g$ denote this upper bound. The sum of all $NI_{r_i}^g$s, one for each rule $g \in p$, is thus an upper bound on the number of rule firings in the sub-subsequence initiated by the firings of r_i. That is,

$$NI_{r_i} = \sum_{g \in p} NI_{r_i}^g$$

$$= \sum_{g_j \in p} NI_{r_i}^{g_j} \tag{10.4}$$

We now show how to compute the value of $\sum_{g_j \in p} NI_{r_i}^{g_j}$. From now on, to simplify the notations used, for all i, let r_i denote a subrule of some rule of p. Furthermore, r_i and r_j do not have to be subrules of the same rule. As mentioned earlier, if the edge $\langle r_1, r_2 \rangle$ in G_p^{RD} exists, the firing of r_1 may result in the firing of r_2 since r_1 either assigns a new value to a variable in R_{r_2} (thus changes the RHS value of r_2) or potentially enables r_2. If there is a path $\langle r_1, r_2, \ldots, r_k \rangle$ in G_p^{RD}, the firing of r_1 may eventually result in the firing of r_k. Hence, any vertex (subrule) in G_p^{RD} reachable by r_1 can possibly be fired as a result of the firing of r_1 (i.e., it can possibly be in the sub-subsequence initiated by the firing of r_1). Furthermore, if more than one path from the vertex r_1 to the vertex r_k in G_p^{RD} exist, r_k may be fired more than once due to the firing of r_1, and the number of paths between r_1 and r_k is the number of possible firings of r_k as a result of the firing of r_1. That is due to the fact that r_k may be invoked by r_1 along each of these paths.

Now, assume $C = \langle r_1, r_2, \ldots, r_{k-1}, r_k, r_1 \rangle$ is a cycle in G_p^{RD}. Since G_p^{RD} does not contain an EV cycle (i.e., (D2)), C must be either an ER cycle or a VM cycle.

- C is an ER cycle. For each i, $1 \leq i \leq k - 1$, r_{i+1} may be *enabled* due to the firing of r_i. It is possible that, starting with r_1, the subrules in C are fired one after another in order of their positions in C. Due to (D3), none of the variables in C is assigned distinct values by distinct subrules in C. Hence, after a sequence of firings along the path $\langle r_1, r_2, \ldots, r_k \rangle$, the variable in L_{r_1} will not be assigned a new value by a second firing of r_1 since it is not assigned a distinct value by other subrules in C. This means the firing of r_1 cannot cause another firing of r_1.

- C is a VM cycle. Along the path of C, for each i, $1 \leq i \leq k - 1$, r_{i+1} may be *fireable* due to the fact that the firing of r_i changes the value of the variable in $R_{r_{i+1}}$. However, due to (D5), C contains at least one subrule, say r_j, which is disabled when r_1 is enabled. In addition, r_j cannot be enabled as a result of the firing of any subrule in C; otherwise, an EV cycle would exist, violating (D2). Hence, the firing of r_1 cannot result in the firing of r_j along the path of C. This also means the firing of r_1 cannot cause another firing of r_1.

Furthermore, assume there is a subrule r_i of the form $x := f$ If EC such that r_i potentially enables r_j and $x \in R_{r_j}$. Not only does an ER edge $\langle r_i, r_j \rangle$ exist, but also a VM edge $\langle r_i, r_j \rangle$ exists in G_p^{RD}. However, the effect of the firing of r_i on r_j via these two edges happens simultaneously. These two edges together should be treated as a single edge in terms of potential firing sequence. Hence, we first transform the RD graph into a *simplified* RD (SRD) graph, G_p^{SRD}, by combining edges connecting the same pair of vertices into one edge.

Based on the fact described above, we use a variation of the standard Depth-First-Search algorithm given in [Aho, Hopcroft, and Ullman, 1974] to traverse the simplified RD graph and obtain the maximal number of subrule firings as a result of the firing of the source vertex. Figure 10.15 outlines this modified algorithm.

Assume r_i is the source vertex. A global variable, *counter*, initialized to 0, is used to record the number of times that vertices are visited, representing the number of possible subrule firings as a result of the firing of r_i. This algorithm starts the process of search from r_i. Each time a vertex is visited, a new path from r_i to this vertex has been found. In general, suppose x is the most recently visited vertex. The search continues by selecting some unexplored edge $\langle x, v \rangle$. If v is *not* an "ancestor" of x, then v will be visited next, the variable *counter* will be increased by 1, and a new search starting from v will begin; otherwise, another unexplored out-going edge from

---

Procedure DFS(v);

Begin

        counter := *counter* + 1;

        For each edge $\langle v, w \rangle \in G_p^{SRD}$ Do

            If w is not an ancestor of v, then

                Begin

                    DFS(w);

                End;

End ;

Figure 10.15 Modified depth-first-search algorithm.

x will be selected. This process continues until all of the out-going edges from x are explored. When the traversal is finished, the value of *counter* stands for the maximal number of possible subrule (and thus rule) firings as a result of the firing of r_i (i.e., $NI_{r_i} = counter$).

Once we obtain all of the NI_{r_i}s of the subrules in p, we can obtain an upper bound on the number of rule firings during the execution of p by applying equations (10.2) and (10.3). However, we can tighten this upper bound by exploiting the property of mutual exclusiveness among rules, as we do in the case of Algorithm_A.

If a rule is disabled at the launch state of an execution, it cannot initiate a subsequence of rule firings during this particular execution. If r and r' are compatible by the property of mutual exclusiveness, then at least one of them, say r, is disabled at the launch state. This means that r cannot initiate a subsequence of rule firings during the execution of p. Hence, NI_r should not be counted in computing the upper bound for p. If a set of m rules exists in which each pair of distinct rules is compatible by the property of mutual exclusiveness, the argument above applies to each pair of rules in this set (i.e., at most one rule in this set can possibly initiate a subsequence of rule firings). This means that only one of the NI_rs corresponding to the rules in this set should be counted.

Hence, for the purpose of obtaining a tighter upper bound, the ME graph is partitioned into a minimal number of independent complete subgraphs such that the least number of NI_rs needs to be counted. Assume k is the minimal number of independent complete subgraphs of G_p^{ME} and p_i is the set of rules corresponding to the ith independent complete ME subgraph. For each p_i, $1 \leq i \leq k$, there is at most *one* rule that can initiate a subsequence of rule firings during the execution of p. Although we do not know in advance which rule in p_i can initiate a subsequence of rule firings, we know that the number of rule firings initiated by that rule cannot be greater than $\max_{r \in p_i}(NI_r)$. Hence, we obtain the following upper bound for p:

$$T^p = \sum_{p_i, 1 \leq i \leq k} \max_{r \in p_i}(NI_r). \qquad (10.5)$$

Input A Special Form D program p.

Output An integer representing an upper bound for p.

1. For each subrule $r_i \in G_p^{SRD}$, apply depth-first-search algorithm to r_i to obtain NI_{r_i}.

2. For each rule r, obtain $NI_r = \sum_{r_i \in r} NI_{r_i}$.

3. Partition G_p^{ME} into a minimal number, k, of independent complete subgraphs.

4. Output($\sum_{p_i, 1 \leq i \leq k} \max_{r \in p_i}(NI_r)$).

Figure 10.16   Algorithm_D.

Figure 10.16 shows the resulting algorithm by applying the strategies described above. Step 1 requires $O(\prod_i m_i)$-time in the worst case, where each m_i is the number of edges in the ith layer during the depth-first search. From our experience, the SRD graph is usually sparse and thus the value of m_i is usually small. Step 2 and step 4 require linear time to perform the summation and output operations. Step 3 requires quadratic time, as in the case of Algorithm_A.

Example 11. The following is a sample Special Form D program.

```
PROGRAM Program_3
VAR
    w, x, y, z, t, v : integer;
INPUTVAR
    g, h, i : integer;
INIT
    w := 1, x := 1, y := 1, z := 1, t := 1, v := 1
INPUT
    read(g, h, i)
RULES
    (*1*)   x := 1 | w := y IF g = 0 and y = 1
    (*2*) [] x := 0 | w := y IF g = 1
    (*3*) [] y := 1 | t := x IF h = 0 and x = 1
    (*4*) [] z := 2 * t IF t > 0
    (*5*) [] v := 0 IF x = 0 and i = 0
    (*6*) [] v := 1 IF x = 0 and i = 1
    (*7*) [] v := 1 IF x = 1 and i = 1
END.
```

The RD graph and the simplified RD graph of Program_3 are shown in Figures 10.17(a) and (b), respectively. Applying Algorithm_D, for each subrule r_i, step 1 finds all of the possible firing sequences starting from the firing of r_i. Figure 10.18 shows the subrules that are reachable by the subrule 1_1 (and hence can possibly be fired as a result of the firing of 1_1). That is, step 1 determines that $NI_{1_1} = 7$. Simi-

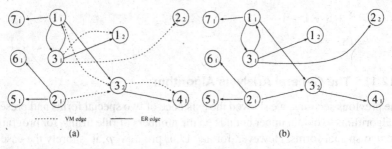

(a)   (b)

Figure 10.17   (a) The RD graph of Program_3. (b) The SRD graph of Program_3.

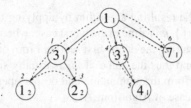

Figure 10.18 Traversing orders by the subrule 1_1.

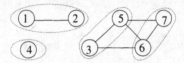

Figure 10.19 The ME graph of Program_3.

larly, $NI_{1_2} = 1$, $NI_{2_1} = 5$, $NI_{2_2} = 1$, $NI_{3_1} = 7$, $NI_{3_2} = 2$, $NI_{4_1} = 1$, $NI_{5_1} = 1$, $NI_{6_1} = 1$, and $NI_{7_1} = 1$.

Step 2 results in

$$NI_1 = NI_{1_1} + NI_{1_2} = 7 + 1 = 8,$$

$$NI_2 = NI_{2_1} + NI_{2_2} = 5 + 1 = 6,$$

$$NI_3 = NI_{3_1} + NI_{3_2} = 7 + 1 = 8,$$

$$NI_4 = NI_{4_1} = 1,$$

$$NI_5 = NI_{5_1} = 1,$$

$$NI_6 = NI_{6_1} = 1, \text{ and}$$

$$NI_7 = NI_{7_1} = 1.$$

The ME graph of Program_3 is then partitioned into four subgraphs by step 3, as shown in Figure 10.19. Finally, step 4 finds that

$$T_p = \max(NI_1, NI_2) + \max(NI_3, NI_5) + \max(NI_4) + \max(NI_6, NI_7)$$

$$= 8 + 8 + 1 + 1$$

$$= 18.$$

10.12.11 The General Analysis Algorithm

In the previous sections, we showed the existence of two special forms and presented two algorithms to obtain upper bounds on the numbers of rule firings for programs in these two special forms. However, for any EQL program p, it is rarely the case that p as a whole is in a known special form. Instead, it is frequently found that p can be partitioned into a hierarchy of sets of rules such that some of these sets are in a known special form. To exploit this property and to enhance the applicability of the two algorithms presented, the *general analysis algorithm* (GAA) has been developed and is reported in [Cheng and Wang, 1990].

Assume the program p can be partitioned into two sets, S and $S' = p - S$, such that S is independent of S'. Let t_S denote the number of rule firings during the execution of S under the circumstances that S is regarded as an independent program. Similarly, let $t_{S'}$ denote the number of rule firings during the execution of S' under the circumstances that S' is regarded as an independent program. According to the underlying execution model, the execution of the program p can be regarded as the execution of S, followed by the execution of S'. Hence, the number of times that the rules in S are fired during the execution of p is equal to t_S, and the number of times that the rules in S' are fired during the same period of time is equal to $t_{S'}$. The number of rule firings during the execution of p is thus equal to the value of $t_S + t_{S'}$. Hence, the value of an upper bound on t_S plus the value of an upper bound on $t_{S'}$ is an upper bound on the number of rule firings during the execution of p. If both t_S and $t_{S'}$ have finite upper bounds, a finite upper bound exists on the number of rule firings during the execution of p. On the other hand, if either t_S or $t_{S'}$ does not have a finite upper bound, a finite upper bound does not exist on the number of rule firings during the execution of p. Hence, p has a bounded response time if and only if both S and S' have bounded response times. The GAA [Cheng et al., 1991], shown in Figure 10.20, exploits the above arguments and makes use of the HLD graph.

Suppose p is the program to be analyzed. First, the HLD graph $\overline{G}_p$ is constructed. During the process of analysis, p and $\overline{G}_p$ are modified to reflect the progress of analysis. In general, suppose p is the set of rules remaining to be analyzed at a point during analysis and $\overline{G}_p$ is the corresponding HLD graph. In each iteration, GAA selects (and deletes) from p a subset of rules, S, corresponding to a vertex without an out-going edge in $\overline{G}_p$ (and modifies $\overline{G}_p$ accordingly), since the rules in this subset have the highest priorities among the remaining rules and the execution of this subset is not affected by the execution of other subsets.

S is then checked against known special forms to see if S is in a known special form. If it is, the corresponding response time algorithm is used to obtain an upper bound of S; otherwise, the aforementioned temporal-logic model checker and timing

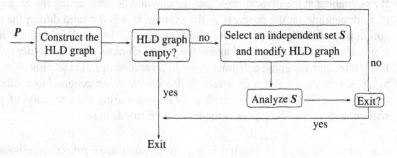

Figure 10.20 The general analysis algorithm.

analyzer are used to conduct an exhaustive check on the state-space graph of S to obtain the upper bound. If S does not have a finite upper bound on the number of rule firings, neither does p; otherwise, the obtained upper bound is accumulated into a register. The analysis process is repeatedly applied to p until there is no rule left or one subset is found not to have a finite upper bound.

Although the GAA still needs to conduct exhaustive state-space graph checks in some cases, the sizes of state-space graphs checked in most cases have been effectively reduced with the help of special forms, resulting in an obvious reduction in the time spent in analyzing real-time rule-based systems. By using the GAA, we have successfully reduced the time needed to analyze the aforementioned real-life real-time rule-based systems. For example, the complete EQL program for the Cryogenic Hydrogen Pressure Malfunction Procedure of the Space Shuttle Vehicle Pressure Control System consists of 36 rules, 31 sensor input variables, and 32 non-input variables. It took two weeks for a set of tools relying mainly on an exhaustive state-space graph check to complete the analysis. However, GAA verified that this program can be partitioned into forward-independent subsets such that each of these subsets is in Special Form A. This fact contributes to the huge reduction in time needed—from two weeks to two seconds—for a set of tools employing GAA (equipped with Special Form A only) to complete the analysis.

Another advantage of GAA, in case the analyzed program is found not to have a finite upper bound, is that the subset that results in this property is isolated from the remaining rules, since GAA stops analyzing once it finds a subset without a finite upper bound.

10.12.12 Proofs

Proof of Theorem 5. Assume p is in Special Form A and r is a rule in p. Due to (A3) (i.e., $L_p \cap T_p = \emptyset$), the value of the enabling condition of r remains unchanged throughout the execution of p. Hence, r remains enabled/disabled throughout the execution of p if it is enabled/disabled at the invocation of p.

- If r is disabled at the invocation of p, it will not be fired during the execution of p. Hence, it will contribute 0 with respect to the number of rule firings.

- If r is enabled at the invocation, it may or may not be fired during the execution of p, depending on the progress of the system. If it is not fired during the execution of p, it will still contribute 0 with respect to the number of rule firings. If it is fired, it will not be fired again due to (A1), unless there is another rule r' firing later and assigning a distinct value to a variable in $L_r \cap L_{r'}$. However, due to (A2), r' is disabled if it disagrees with r on the value assigned to a variable in $L_r \cap L_{r'}$. Hence, r will be fired at most once during the execution of p. It will contribute 1 with respect to the number of rule firings.

The above argument applies to each rule in p. Since there are n rules in p, obviously there are at most n rule firings during the execution of p. That is, $T^p = n$. $\qquad\square$

Proof of Theorem 6. Assume p is in Special Form D and does not always reach a fixed point in a bounded number of rule firings. This means that an execution of p exists that does not terminate in any bounded number of rule firings. Since only a finite number of rules in p exist, a rule r^1 must be firing infinitely often during this execution. According to the underlying execution model, r^1 can be fired only if its firing changes the value of one variable in p. Since only a finite number of variables in L_{r^1} exist, a variable $x_1 \in L_{r^1}$ must be assigned a new value by a subrule r_i^1 infinitely often.

Based on the values of $R_p \cap L_p$ and $T_p \cap L_p$, we divide the proof into four parts. To simplify the notations used next, the notation r_*^i is used to stand for the specific subrule of the rule r^i that assigns a value to a variable involved in the reasoning, unless otherwise stated. For example, without ambiguity, the subrule r_i^1 will be referred to as r_*^1. $\qquad\square$

1. $R_p \cap L_p = \emptyset$ and $T_p \cap L_p = \emptyset$. p is also a Special Form A program. According to Theorem 5, p always reaches a fixed point in a bounded number of rule firings.

2. $R_p \cap L_p = \emptyset$ and $T_p \cap L_p \neq \emptyset$. Due to $R_p \cap L_p = \emptyset$, r_*^1 always assigns the constant value m^1 to x_1. r_*^1 alone can change the value of x_1 at most once if another subrule does not exist that assigns a different value to x_1. Hence, there must be a rule $r^{1'}$ with a subrule $r_*^{1'}$ that assigns a distinct value $m^{1'}$ to x_1 and is fired infinitely often.

   Due to (D1), r_*^1 and $r_*^{1'}$ mutually exclude each other. There must be a variable x_2 whose value changes infinitely often and determines the enabledness of r_*^1 and $r_*^{1'}$. Now the argument applied to x_1 also applies to x_2. This means there is a pair of subrules, r_*^2 and $r_*^{2'}$, assigning distinct values to x_2 infinitely often. One of them, say r_*^2, potentially enables r_*^1, while the other potentially enables $r_*^{1'}$. Hence, there exist the edges $\langle r_*^2, r_*^1 \rangle$ and $\langle r_*^{2'}, r_*^{1'} \rangle$ in the RD graph G_p^{RD}. In addition, the argument applied to the pair of r_*^1 and $r_*^{1'}$ also applies to the pair of r_*^2 and $r_*^{2'}$. We continue to apply the same arguments to the variables and rules encountered.

   Two paths, $S = \langle r_*^k, r_*^{k-1}, \ldots, r_*^2, r_*^1 \rangle$ and $S' = \langle r_*^{k'}, r_*^{(k-1)'}, \ldots, r_*^{2'}, r_*^{1'} \rangle$, will be found. However, since there are only a finite number of rules (and thus subrules) in p, eventually, for some k, both r_*^k and $r_*^{k'}$ will turn out to be subrules already encountered previously. One of three situations will happen:

   (a) $r_*^k \in \{ r_*^{k-1}, r_*^{k-2}, \ldots, r_*^2, r_*^1 \}$ and $r_*^{k'} \in \{ r_*^{(k-1)'}, r_*^{(k-2)'}, \ldots, r_*^{2'}, r_*^{1'} \}$. Assume $r_*^k = r_*^i$ and $r_*^{k'} = r_*^{j'}$. Then $\langle r_*^k = r_*^i, r_*^{k-1}, \ldots, r_*^{i+1}, r_*^i \rangle$ forms a cycle and $\langle r_*^{k'_*} = r_*^{j'}, r_*^{(k-1)'}, \ldots, r_*^{(j+1)'}, r_*^{j'} \rangle$ forms another cycle, as shown in Figure 10.21(a). Obviously, r_*^k and $r_*^{k'}$ are respectively contained in disjoint simple cycles and assign distinct values to x_k, contradicting (D4).

   (b) Both r_*^k and $r_*^{k'}$ belong to $\{ r_*^{k-1}, r_*^{k-2}, \ldots, r_*^2, r_*^1 \}$. There are two cases to consider:

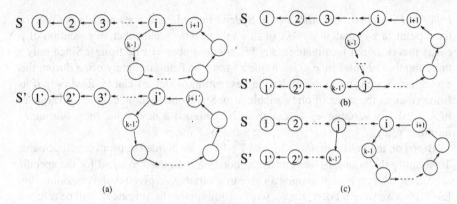

Figure 10.21 Rule enabling patterns.

- $r_*^k = r_*^i$ and $r_*^{k'} = r_*^j$, where $j > i$. In this case, $\langle r_*^k = r_*^i, r_*^{k-1}, \ldots, r_*^j = r_*^{k'}, \ldots, r_*^i \rangle$ forms a cycle C, as shown in Figure 10.21(b). Hence, r_*^k and $r_*^{k'}$ are contained in C and respectively assign distinct values to x_k, contradicting (D3).

- $r_*^k = r_*^i$ and $r_*^{k'} = r_*^j$, where $j < i$. In this case, $\langle r_*^k = r_*^i, r_*^{k-1}, \ldots, r_*^{i+1}, r_*^i \rangle$ forms a cycle C, as shown in Figure 10.21(c). r_*^i and r_*^j respectively assign distinct values to x_k. Now the argument applied to the pair r_*^1 and $r_*^{1'}$ also applies to the pair r_*^i and r_*^j. In addition, we know at this time that there is a path from r_*^i to r_*^j. Hence, starting from r_*^i and r_*^j, we conduct a new sequence of reasoning, resulting in another new sequence of reasoning.

  We continue to apply the same argument to pairs of subrules encountered. A sequence of paths, each of which connects a pair of subrules disagreeing on the expression assigned to a variable, will be found. Eventually, since only a finite number of rules in p exist, a rule previously encountered will be encountered again. A cycle containing rules disagreeing on the expression assigned to a variable will be found, contradicting (D3).

(c) Both r_*^k and $r_*^{k'}$ belong to $\{r_*^{(k-1)'}, r_*^{(k-2)'}, \ldots, r_*^{2'}, r_*^{1'}\}$. With $\{r_*^{(k-1)'}, r_*^{(k-2)'}, \ldots, r_*^{2'}, r_*^{1'}\}$ replacing $\{r_*^{k-1}, r_*^{k-2}, \ldots, r_*^2, r_*^1\}$, the argument in the previous situation also applies to this situation. Hence, this situation will not happen, either.

Since none of the three situations can possibly happen, it is not possible for p not to reach a fixed point in a bounded number of rule firings if $R_p \cap L_p = \emptyset$ and $T_p \cap L_p \neq \emptyset$.

3. $R_p \cap L_p \neq \emptyset$ and $T_p \cap L_p = \emptyset$. Assume r^1 is of the form $x := f \mid \cdots$ IF EC. Due to (D1) and $T_p \cap L_p = \emptyset$, any rule disagreeing with r^1 on the expression

assigned to x remains disabled throughout this execution of p. The fact that r^1 assigns a new value to x infinitely often means that f changes its value infinitely often. Hence, f must be a function in at least one variable such that it can change its value, otherwise it is a constant expression and cannot change its value. Only two possible situations exist for f to be a function in variables. We now discuss both situations and prove they cannot occur.

(a) f is a function in x (i.e., r is of the form $x := f(x) \mid \cdots$ IF EC). However, this means that a one-vertex cycle C would exist in G_p^{RD}, if such an r did exist. It is not possible to have a pair of subrules in C such that they are compatible by mutual exclusiveness, since C contains only one vertex. This would violate (D5). Hence, this situation cannot occur.

(b) f is a function in a variable y that is different from the variable x (i.e., r is of the form $x := f(y) \mid \cdots$ IF EC). There is a subrule r_*^1 of the form $x := f(y)$ IF EC, and y (and thus $f(y)$) changes its value infinitely often. There must be a rule r^2 (and a subrule r_*^2) assigning a value to y and firing infinitely often. Now, the argument applied to r^1 also applies to r^2. We continue to apply the same argument to each rule encountered. Eventually, since there are only a finite number of rules in p, the subrules encountered form a cycle C in G_p^{RD}. Since the subrules in C can be fired one after another infinitely often, C is not a convergency cycle and all of the subrules in C are enabled at the same time, violating (D5). Hence, this situation cannot occur either.

Since neither of the two situations can possibly happen, it is not possible for p not to reach a fixed point in a bounded number of rule firings if $R_p \cap L_p \neq \emptyset$ and $T_p \cap L_p = \emptyset$.

4. $R_p \cap L_p \neq \emptyset$ and $T_p \cap L_p \neq \emptyset$. Assume r^1 is of the form $\cdots \mid x_1 := f_1 \mid \cdots$ IF EC, where f_1 is an expression. The firing of r^1 changes the value of x_1 only if (1) the value of f_1 has changed such that it is not equal to the old value of x_1 or (2) a new value has been assigned to x_1 by another rule, say $r^{1'}$, such that the new value of x_1 is not equal to the value of f_1. There are two cases involving the value of f_1: constant or not constant.

- f_1 is a constant expression. This means r^1 can change the value of x_1 at most once if another rule does not exist assigning a distinct value to x_1. Since r^1 assigns a new value to x_1 infinitely often, there must be another rule $r^{1'}$ assigning a distinct value to x_1 infinitely often. r^1 and $r^{1'}$ mutually exclude each other, due to (D1). Hence, a variable x_2 exists whose value changes infinitely often and determines the enabledness of r^1 and $r^{1'}$. That, in turn, means there is a rule r^2 that assigns a new value to x_2 infinitely often and potentially enables r^1. Hence, the ER edge $\langle r^2, r^1 \rangle$ exists in G_p^{RD}. Now, the argument applied to the pair of x_1 and r^1 also applies to the pair of x_2 and r^2.

- f_1 is not a constant expression. f_1 must be a variable expression either in x_1 or not x_1.

    i. f_1 is an expression in x_1 (i.e., r^1 is of the form $\cdots \mid x_1 :=$ $f(x_1) \mid \cdots$ IF EC). However, this means that there would be a one-vertex VM cycle in G_p^{RD}, if such an r did exist. As mentioned earlier, this would violate (D5). Hence, this situation will not occur.

    ii. f_1 is not an expression in x_1. f_1 must be an expression in a variable different from x_1, say x_2, (i.e., r^1 is of the form $\cdots \mid x_1 := f(x_2) \mid \cdots$ IF EC). Hence, there is a subrule r_*^1 of the form $\underline{x_1 := f(x_2)\ \text{IF}\ EC}$, and the value of x_2 (and thus $f(x_2)$) changes infinitely often. A rule r^2 may exist that assigns a new value to x_2 and fires infinitely often. Hence, there is a VM edge $\langle r^2, r^1 \rangle$ in G_p^{RD}. Now, the argument applied to the pair of r^1 and x_1 also applies to the pair of r^2 and x_2.

We continue to apply the argument above to each rule and variable pair encountered. A path of ER edges or VM edges or both will be found. Eventually, since only a finite number of rules exist in p, a rule and variable pair that has been encountered previously will be encountered again. Hence, a cycle C will be found. One of three situations will happen (to simplify the explanation, if a variable x is assigned a value by a subrule in C, we say x is in C):

  (a) C is an EV cycle. However, the existence of an EV cycle would violate (D2). Thus, this situation will not occur.

  (b) C is an ER cycle. For each pair of r_*^i and x_i in C, the value of f_i assigned to x_i by r_*^i is a constant. This means that x_i is also assigned a distinct value infinitely often by another rule $r_*^{i'}$ that enables $r_*^{(i-1)'}$. Hence, the ER edge $\langle r_*^{i'}, r_*^{(i-1)'} \rangle$ also exists in G_p^{RD}. A path consisting of $\langle r_*^{i'}, r_*^{(i-1)'}, \ldots, r_*^{2'}, r_*^{1'} \rangle$ in G_p^{RD} shall also exist. Since there are only a finite number of rules in p, eventually we will end up with the same situation as we did in part (2) of this proof. That means this situation will not occur either.

  (c) C is a VM cycle. For each variable x_i in C, x_i gets a new value because the expression $f(x_{i+1})$ assigned to x_i by r_*^i changes infinitely often. Since the subrules in C can be fired one after another in the order they appear in C for an unlimited number of times, it is obvious that C is not a convergent cycle. In addition, for each subrule r_*^i in C, r_*^i must be enabled at the time when it is r_*^i's turn to be fired. If all of the subrules in C can be enabled at the same time, then (D5) is violated. On the other hand, if all of the subrules (vertices) contained in C cannot be enabled at the same time, there must be at least one disabled rule at any moment. Assume r_*^k is disabled at some moment during the execution considered. Hence, there must be a subrule, say g_*^1, whose firing will enable r_*^k. There are two cases to consider:

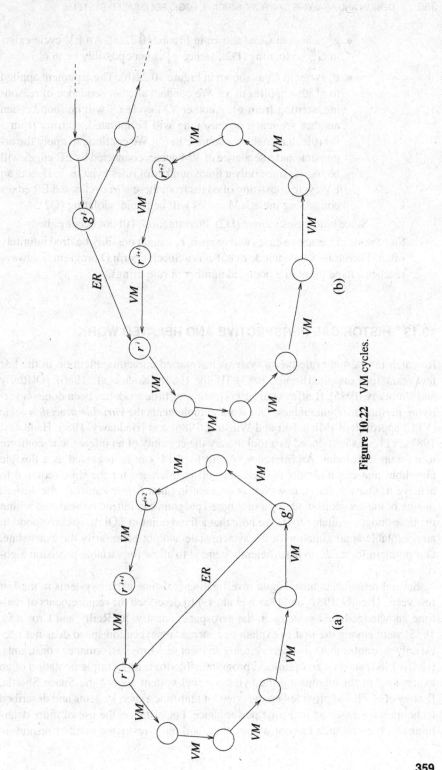

Figure 10.22 VM cycles.

- g_*^1 is also in C, as shown in Figure 10.22(a). An EV cycle exists in G_p^{RD}, violating (D2). Hence g_*^1 cannot possibly be in C.

- g_*^1 is not in C, as shown in Figure 10.22(b). The argument applied to r^1 also applies to g^1. We conduct another sequence of reasoning, starting from g^1. Another VM cycle C_2 will be found. Then another sequence of reasoning will be initiated, starting from a subrule that enables a subrule in C_2. We continue to apply the argument, and a sequence of VM cycles connected by ER edges will be found, since only a finite number of rules exist in p. Hence, an EV cycle consisting of edges from these VM cycles and ER edges connecting these VM cycles will be found, violating (D2).

Since both cases violate (D2), this situation will not occur either.

Since none of the above cases will happen, r_1 cannot possibly be fired infinitely often. Therefore, we conclude that if p is a Special Form D program, p always reaches a fixed point in a bounded number of rule firings.

10.13   HISTORICAL PERSPECTIVE AND RELATED WORK

Research in real-time rule-based systems has started attracting attention in the last few years, for example, [Benda, 1987], [Helly, 1984], [Koch et al., 1986], [O'Reilly and Cromarty, 1985], [Laffey et al., 1988], but very little work has been done on verifying performance guarantees. Our work complements the *variable precision logic* (VPL) approach of [Michalski and Winston, 1986] and [Haddawy, 1986; Haddawy, 1987]. VPL was introduced as a tool to vary the certainty of an inference to conform to a timing constraint. An inference system for VPL can be regarded as a flexible algorithm that can trade off the certainty of an inference for the time required to achieve it. Our emphasis, however, is on ensuring that *before run-time* the desired quality of the decisions made by a rule-based program can indeed be achieved within the time budget available to it. We note that a fixed point in EQL may correspond to an acceptable approximation of the system state and not necessarily the exact state. Our problem formulation is sufficiently general to allow for variable precision algorithms.

Several researchers have begun investigating real-time expert systems in the last few years. [Benda, 1987] and [Koch et al., 1986] described the requirements of real-time knowledge-based systems in the aerospace industry. [O'Reilly and Cromarty, 1985] were among the first to explain that increasing execution speed does not necessarily guarantee that an expert system can meet real-time performance constraints. [Helly, 1984] showed an optimized programmable-logic array implementation of an expert system for monitoring the hydrogen fuel system aboard the Space Shuttle. [Laffey et al., 1988] provided an overview of real-time expert systems and described techniques for ensuring real-time performance. For instance, the use of more deterministic controls, such as control variables, and more restricted conflict resolution strategies is proposed as a way to reduce the variability in the actual execution time of expert systems. [Payton and Bihari, 1991] argued that different levels (planning, knowledge-base access, computation, sensing) of an intelligent control system must closely cooperate in order to achieve real-time performance and adaptivity.

Many researchers also study the impact of parallelism in optimizing the performance of expert systems but usually do not consider the satisfaction of hard real-time constraints. For instance, [Ishida, 1991] proposed a parallel OPS5 rule-firing model consisting of three components: an inference analysis tool for detecting cases in which parallel rule firing yields results different from sequential firing, a parallel firing algorithm for firing rules in parallel in a multiprocessor architecture, and a parallel programming environment for providing language facilities to enable programmers to exploit parallelism. [Gupta, 1987] presented a parallel Rete algorithm which exploits parallelism at a very fine grain to reduce variations in the processing cost of productions affected in each recognize–act cycle, and described a hardware task scheduler for scheduling fine-grained tasks. [Oshisanwo and Dasiewicz, 1987] argued that not all the effects of parallelism can be determined at compile time, and thus on-line techniques must be applied to extract a higher degree of parallelism from the production system at run-time. Simple checks are developed for run-time detection of interference due to parallel rule firings. [Schmolze, 1991] described techniques for guaranteeing serializable results in synchronous parallel production systems. [Cheng, 1993b] introduced techniques for the automated extraction of rule-level parallelism from rule-based programs based on the analysis methodology reported in this chapter.

[Wang, Mok, and Emerson, 1992] claimed that few attempts have been made to formally address the response-time analysis problem. [Lark et al., 1990] considered the design and implementation issues in the development of Lockheed Pilot's Associate system. They advocated using experimentation and analysis to guarantee timeliness by requiring the application programmer to set an upper bound on process duration by extensive experimentation but did not show how to verify that the system will satisfy this upper bound. [Aiken, Widom, and Hellerstein, 1992] presented a static analysis method for determining whether arbitrary sets of database production rules satisfy certain properties, including termination. A directed graph demonstrating the triggering relationship among rules is checked to see if the execution of the corresponding set of rules is guaranteed to terminate. Some conditions that guarantee the property of termination are introduced. However, they do not provide an algorithm for obtaining an execution time (or execution time upper bound) for a set of rules that is found to have the property of termination. [Abiteboul and Simon, 1991] discussed, among other properties, the property of termination in the context of Datalog and its extensions and showed that this property is in general undecidable. Although they addressed the issue of whether a given language possesses the property of termination, the issue of determining whether an arbitrary program possesses the property of termination was not addressed.

Instead of addressing the response-time analysis problem, a great deal of effort has been focused on improving the speed of execution. [Ceri and Widom, 1991] developed a method to automatically derive efficient view-maintenance production rules exploiting the technique of incremental maintenance in the context of database systems. [Brant et al., 1991] studied the effects of the size of state space on the performance of the inference mechanism of a rule system. They claimed that it is possible to eliminate some states while improving performance by using lazy matching algorithms instead of evaluating all active rules.

Furthermore, extensive discussion has taken place on the exploitation of parallelism, and several parallel processing techniques have been proposed and applied to enhance the performance of rule-based systems [Ishida, 1991; Ishida and S. Stolfo, 1985; Kuo and Moldovan, 1991; Schmolze, 1991; Stoyenko, Hamacher, and Holt, 1991]. For example, [Ishida, 1991] proposed a parallel OPS5 rule firing model in which techniques based on a data dependency analysis for detecting interference among multiple rule firings are given. A parallel firing algorithm for firing rules in parallel in a multiprocessor architecture is also given. [Stoyenko, Hamacher, and Holt, 1991] proposed a parallel rule-based language, PARULEL, which is based on an inherently parallel execution semantics. They argued that sequential rule languages "hide" much of the parallelism inherent in the task to be solved by the rule program. [Kuo and Moldovan, 1991] identified the compatibility problem, caused by interfering rules, and the convergency problem, caused by violation of the problem-solving strategy, associated with a multiple rule firing system. They claimed that, to resolve these problems, it is not sufficient to just view a program as a collection of rules and concurrently fire compatible rules. It is also necessary to consider the effect of multiple rule firings on the problem-solving strategy.

However, rather than fast execution, the most important property of a real-time system should be the fulfillment of timing constraints. Fast execution helps to meet stringent timing constraints, but fast execution alone does not guarantee the fulfillment of timing constraints.

In this chapter, the time a rule-based program takes to converge to a fixed point is measured in terms of the number of rules fired. A more accurate measure would take into account the actual execution of each rule fired and the actual evaluation (match) time to determine which rule(s) can be fired next. We addressed some of these issues and proposed an efficient match algorithm in [Wang, Mok, and Cheng, 1990]. This new match algorithm lends itself to compile-time analysis of time bounds for the match part of expert-system execution, and it is more amenable to a number of optimization techniques on space-versus-time tradeoff. To further control the response of an expert system, we limit the size of the working memory by setting some criteria for accepting new working memory elements. This can be accomplished by means of a filter which may be dynamically adjusted to keep the size of the working memory manageable by throwing out less reliable data from a noisy sensor.

[Cheng et al., 1991] first proposed the Estella language for specifying special forms and application-specific knowledge. Estella is then refined and an analysis facility is described in [Cheng et al., 1993]. [Zupan, Cheng, and Bohanec, 1995a; Zupan, Cheng, and Bohanec, 1995b] described a static stability analysis method for fuzzy rule-chaining real-time systems.

10.14 SUMMARY

The main focus of this chapter is to address the question of whether a real-time decision system is sufficiently fast to meet stringent response-time requirements. We have provided a formal framework for investigating this question for propositional-logic rule-based programs. Our formulation makes use of the state-space representation of rule-based programs and relates the response time of a system to the length of paths to fixed points in the state-space graph. The analysis problem is to determine if a given program can always reach a fixed point within a bounded number of rule firings. The synthesis problem is how to make programs that are not fast enough meet response-time constraints.

The analysis problem is in general undecidable and is PSPACE-complete for programs with finite domains. We have developed a general strategy for tackling the analysis problem which combines exhaustive state-space search and the recognition of special forms of subsets of rules by textual analysis. The synthesis problem is in general NP-hard and is related to the time-budgeting problem. We have proposed a novel approach for solving the synthesis problem, using the method of Lagrange multipliers.

To support the development of real-time decision systems with stringent timing and integrity constraints, we have developed a suite of tools for prototyping programs for an equational rule-based language called EQL. Implementation of tools has been completed for (1) translating an EQL program into a C program, (2) transforming an EQL program into its state-space graph, (3) verifying assertions stated in temporal logic (Computation Tree Logic) about the EQL program, and (4) determining the maximum number of iterations and the sequence of rules that must be fired for an EQL program to reach a safe fixed point. We have used these tools to analyze a large subset of the Cryogenic Hydrogen Pressure Malfunction Procedure in the Pressure Control System of the Space Shuttle Vehicle. Chapter 12 describes algorithms to synthesize programs from ones that do not meet their response-time constraints.

Then we describe a specification facility called Estella, for specifying behavioral constraint assertions about real-time EQL programs. This facility allows customization of the analysis tools so that they can be applied to the analysis of application-specific rule-based systems. The Estella facility allows the programmer to specify information about the rule-based program that is too hard to be detected by the general analyzer. The development of the Estella–General Analysis Tool as a computer-aided software engineering tool is a significant step for aiding the rapid prototyping and development of expert systems with guaranteed response time. In particular, the programmer uses the analysis tool to focus on the sets of rules that potentially cause the timing violations so that he/she can apply application-specific knowledge to further analyze the rule-based program. Considering the complexity and unpredictability of rule-based programs, this tool is extremely useful in aiding the debugging of the detected timing violations. The techniques proposed and implemented in this chapter constitute an important contribution to the timing analysis of real-time rule-based systems, given the fact that fully automated analysis and synthesis of such systems are notoriously difficult to develop.

Up to this point, the time a rule-based program takes to converge to a fixed point is measured in terms of the number of rules fired. A more accurate measure would take into account the actual execution time of each rule fired and the actual evaluation (match) time to determine which rule(s) can be fired next. We address some of these issues and propose an efficient match algorithm in [Wang, Mok, and Cheng, 1990]. This new match algorithm lends itself to compile-time analysis of time bounds for the match part of expert system execution, and it is more amenable to a number of optimization techniques on space versus time tradeoff.

Traditionally, real-time rule-based systems have been designed and built using ad hoc techniques, resulting in tremendous difficulties in formally verifying the response times of resulting systems. Formal analysis of timing requirements is often ignored. Instead, a lot of research has focused on improving the response time of systems. However, it is true that fast computing alone is not enough for real-time systems. The fulfillment of imposed timing constraints should be the most important goal in designing real-time rule-based systems.

The emphasis of this chapter is on determining response-time upper bounds for real-time rule-based systems. A static method employing a priori syntactic and semantic checks is proposed.

Although some classes of real-time decision systems do exist whose response times are predictable, the amount of time needed to analyze these systems to predict their response time is usually large. However, the authors have observed that the use of simple syntactic and semantic checks of programs, coupled with other techniques such as state-space graph checks, can dramatically reduce the time needed to analyze these systems. It has been found that sets of syntactic and semantic constraint assertions exist such that if p satisfies any of them, the execution of p always terminates in bounded time. Each set of syntactic and semantic constraint assertions is called a special form. The set of programs satisfying a particular special form is thus a subclass of the class of all programs.

The existence of two special forms, namely Special Form A and Special Form D, for EQL programs has been proved. For each of these two special forms, an algorithm has been developed to obtain response-time upper bounds for programs satisfying the special form. Each algorithm takes advantage of the characteristics of the subclass for which it is intended to be used. Hence, although the subclass of programs in Special Form A is actually a subset of the subclass of programs in Special Form D, the former is isolated as a subclass to be handled by Algorithm A so that better upper bounds can be obtained. Another advantage of having Special Form A is that a program with acyclic variable dependency can be checked to determine whether it has a bounded response time without using exhaustive state-space graph checks [Cheng, 1993b].

To enhance the applicability of the proposed algorithms, the general analysis algorithm is employed so that the proposed algorithms can be collectively used to analyze a program that as a whole is not in a known special form. Although the general analysis algorithm uses an exhaustive state-space graph check in some cases, the sizes of state-space graphs checked in most cases have been effectively reduced, resulting in an obvious reduction in the time spent in analyzing real-time rule-based systems.

Applying our approach to the three systems (i.e., the SSV program, the ISA program, and the FCE program), we found that the programs can be partitioned into subsets, most of which are in known special forms. The subset of rules not in special form actually contains rules which lead to unbounded rule firings. So far, we do not have statistical data to show the percentage of programs that can be analyzed by the special form approach. However, from the limited experience we have, it is our view that this is a feasible approach to reducing the time needed to conduct analysis.

Chapter 11 describes the time analysis of more expressive, predicate-logic rule-based languages such as OPS5 [Forgy, 1981] and MRL [Wang, 1990a], both of which allow the use of structured variables.

EXERCISES

1. Why is the timing analysis of rule-based systems more difficult than that of sequential programs?

2. Describe the system represented by the rule-based program in example 2 (object detection) in terms of the real-time decision system model shown in Figure 10.1.

3. Construct the state-space graph corresponding to the rule-based program in example 2.

4. How can a model-checking algorithm such as the one for the computation tree logic be used to analyze the response time of EQL rule-based systems with finite-domain variables?

5. Consider the following EQL program:

```
      arbiter := b ! wake_up = false  IF (error = a)
[] object_detected := true
          IF (sensor_a = 1) AND (arbiter = a) AND (wake_up = true)
[] object_detected := false
          IF (sensor_a = 0) AND (arbiter = a) AND (wake_up = true)
[] arbiter := a ! wake_up = false  IF (error = b)
[] object_detected := true
          IF (sensor_b = 1) AND (arbiter = b) AND (wake_up = true)
[] object_detected := false
          IF (sensor_b = 0) AND (arbiter = b) AND (wake_up = true)
```

Use the general analysis strategy to analyze this program and report the analysis results.

6. Construct the enable-rule graph for the following rules and identify the simple cycles, if any.

```
            state3 := failed IF find_bad_things = true AND
                                 state3 = suspect AND
                                 NOT (rel1_state = suspect AND rel1_mode = on AND
                                      rel1_type = direct)
[]      state4 := nominal ! reconfig4 := true
                          IF state4 = failed AND mode4 <> off AND config4 = bad
[]      state3 := nominal ! reconfig3 := true
                          IF state3 = failed AND mode3 <> off AND config3 = bad
[]      sensor3 := bad ! state3 := suspect IF state1 = suspect AND
                          rel1_mode = on AND rel1_type = direct AND
                          state3 = nominal AND rel3_mode = on AND
                          rel3_type = direct AND state4 = suspect AND
                          find_bad_things = true
```

7. Specify Special Form D in the Estella specification language.

8. Explain the difficulty in checking whether two enabling conditions are mutually exclusive. Describe how the approximation algorithm presented tackles this analysis complexity.

9. Why is the response-time analysis of EQL programs that assign expressions containing variables to left-side variables much more difficult than those with only constant assignments?

10. Determine an upper bound on the execution time in terms of the number of rule firings for the following EQL program:

```
PROGRAM Example 1
INPUTVAR
      a,b : INTEGER;
VAR
      c,d,e,f,g,h:INTEGER;
INIT
      c:=0,d:=0,e:=0,f:=0,g:=0,h:=0
RULES
      (*r1*)    c:=1 IF a>0 and b>0
      (*r2*)[]  c:=2 IF a>0 and b<=0
      (*r3*)[]  d:=2 IF a<=0
      (*r4*)[]  d:=c IF a>0
      (*r5*)[]  e:=c+1 IF c<=1 and b>0
      (*r6*)[]  f:=c+1!e:=c-1 IF c<=1 and b<=0
      (*r7*)[]  f:=c-1 IF c>=0
      (*r8*)[]  g:=1!h:=1 IF f>1 and d>1
      (*r9*)[]  g:=2!h:=2 IF f<=1 and e>1
END.
```

CHAPTER 11

TIMING ANALYSIS
OF PREDICATE-LOGIC
RULE-BASED SYSTEMS

As rule-based expert systems become widely adopted in new application domains such as real-time systems, ensuring that they meet stringent timing constraints in these safety-critical and time-critical environments emerges as a challenging problem. As described in detail in chapter 10, in these systems, a change in the environment may trigger a number of rule firings to compute an appropriate response. If the computation takes too long, the expert system may not have sufficient time to respond to the ongoing changes in the environment, making the result of the computation useless or even harmful to the system being monitored or controlled. To evaluate and control the performance of a real-time expert system, it is necessary to relate the quality of a response computed by the expert system to the time available to compute it.

Even in a case where response time is not a major concern or a deadline is not imposed, the predictability is still a desired quality which may improve the resource utilization or the user productivity. For example, if the programmer has a tool to measure an upper bound on the maximal program response time, he/she will not have to guess whether the program runs into an infinite loop or the program just takes a long time to complete execution, thus avoiding unnecessary waiting for the program to complete execution or undesirable interrupting of program execution. This is particularly true for production systems whose rule firing patterns depend on initial working memory contents.

Unfortunately, rule-based expert systems are computationally expensive and slow. Moreover, they are considered less predictable and analyzable because of their context-sensitive control flow and possible nondeterminism. To remedy this problem, two solutions are proposed in the literature. The first is to reduce the execution time via parallelism in the matching phase and/or firing phase of the MRA [Brownston et al., 1986] cycle. Several approaches [Cheng, 1993b; Ishida, 1994; Kuo and

Moldovan, 1991; Pasik, 1992; Schmolze, 1991] have been provided to achieve this goal. The other solution is to optimize the expert system by modifying or resynthesizing the rule base if the response time is found to be inadequate [Zupan and Cheng, 1994a; Zupan and Cheng, 1998].

In this chapter, we present more approaches for the response-time analysis of rule-based systems. In particular, we study the timing properties of programs written in the predicate-logic-based OPS5 language [Forgy, 1981] (and other OPS5-style languages), which is not designed for real-time purposes although it has been widely adopted in practice. In chapter 10, we introduced the propositional-logic-based rule-based language EQL (equational rule-based language), for real-time applications. EQL is a simple, rule-based language with well-defined semantics. It has been used to program a number of practical real-time applications.

OPS5 exhibits an incremental increase in expressiveness over MRL [Wang, Mok, and Cheng, 1990; Wang, 1990a] but it is not as complex as more recent object-oriented rule-based languages. OPS5 has been successfully used in a variety of applications [Forgy, 1985]. MRL is designed to be an extension of EQL. It includes set variables (working memories) and logical quantifiers over set variables. However, MRL does not include the timing tags in its working memory, so many conflict resolution strategies, such as LEX and MEA, cannot be applied to MRL programs. It is entirely the programmer's responsibility to guarantee that any firing sequence is a normal execution flow. Under this situation, the programmer usually needs to avoid interference among rules; otherwise, the program may be hard to debug and maintain.

OPS5 has been used to implement several industrial expert systems, including MILEX (The Mitsui Real Time Expert System) and XCON/R1, which is generally considered the first commercially successful expert system [Forgy, 1985].

Our goal is to obtain a tighter bound on the execution time that is close to the real upper bound. We consider the case where an OPS5 expert-system program forms the decision module of a real-time monitoring and controlling system [Payton and Bihari, 1991]. This real-time system takes sensor input readings periodically, and the embedded expert system must produce, based on these input values and state values from previous invocations of the expert system, an output decision that ensures the safety and progress of the real-time system and its environment prior to the taking of the next sensor input values. Thus, the upper bound on the expert system's execution time cannot exceed the length of the period between two consecutive sensor input readings [Cheng et al., 1993; Chen and Cheng, 1995b]. Therefore, our goal is to determine, before run-time, a tight upper bound on the execution time of the expert system in every invocation following each reading of sensor input values.

To analyze the timing behavior of an OPS5 program, we first formalize a graphical representation of rule-based programs. This high-level data-dependency graph captures all possible logical control paths in a program. Based on this graph, we design a termination detection algorithm to determine whether an OPS5 program always terminates in bounded time. If an OPS5 program is not detected to terminate for all initial program states, then the "culprit" conditions that cause nontermination are extracted to assist programmers in correcting the program. They then modify the program to ensure program termination. Note that this modification is performed off-line, prior to the execution of the expert system, and the modified version must still satisfy the logical correctness constraints. On the other hand, if the termination of an OPS5 program is guaranteed, we proceed to determine an upper bound on its execution time. Instead of using static analysis, we build a tool to aid timing analysis of OPS5 expert systems. This tool generates a set of working memory elements (WMEs) which cause the program to consume maximum time. We take this set of WMEs as the initial working memory (WM) and test the program to determine the maximum execution time. In real applications, the initial WM is usually restricted to a certain domain. The OPS5 programs can execute only normally with this restriction. So, we also take this information into consideration. Users can then provide their requirements of the initial WM to our tool, making it possible to reduce the size of the WMEs we generate and thus produce more accurate analysis results.

We briefly introduce the OPS5 language in the next section. Then we describe the Cheng–Tsai analysis methodology, partially based on the graphical representation of the control paths of OPS5 programs. Next we present the Cheng–Chen analysis methodology, based on a different set of quantitative algorithms.

11.1 THE OPS5 LANGUAGE

This section provides an overview of the OPS5 language, with examples, and describes the Rete matching network for determining instantiations of rules.

11.1.1 Overview

An OPS5 rule-based program [Forgy, 1981; Brownston et al., 1986; Cooper and Wogrin, 1988] consists of a finite set of rules, each of which is of the form

```
(p rule-name
   (condition-element-1)
   (condition-element-2)
            :
   (condition-element-m)
 -->
   (action-1)
        :
   (action-n))
```

and a database of assertions, each of which is of the form

```
(class-name      ^attribute-1  value-1
                 ^attribute-2  value-2
                        :
                 ^attribute-p  value-p)
```

The symbol "^" means there is an attribute name following it. The set of rules is called the *production memory* (PM) and the database of assertions is called the *working memory* (WM). Each assertion is called a *working memory element* (WME). A rule has three parts:

- the name of the rule, `rule-name`;
- the left-hand-side (LHS), that is, a conjunction of the condition elements, each of which can be either a positive condition element or negative condition element; and
- the right-hand-side (RHS), that is, the actions, each of which may make, modify, or delete a WME, perform I/O, or halt.

All atoms are literals unless put in variable brackets <>. The scope of variables is a single rule. A WME is an instance of an *element class*. An element class defines a WME structure in the same way a C data type defines the structure of entities in a C program. An element class is the template from which instances are made. It is identified by `class-name` and by a collection of attributes describing characteristics relevant to the entity. The following is an OPS5 rule for processing sensor information from a radar system:

```
(p radar-scan                          ; an OPS5 rule
  (region-scan1 ^sensor object) ; positive condition element
  (region-scan2 ^sensor object) ; positive condition element
  (status-check ^status normal) ; positive condition element
 - (interrupt ^status on)                ; negative condition element
 { <Uninitialized-configuration> ; positive condition element
  (configuration ^object-detected 0) }
  -->
  (modify <Uninitialized-configuration> ^object-detected 1))     ; action
```

If both radars, (`region-scan1`) and (`region-scan2`), detect an object, the status of the radar system is normal, there is no interrupt, and the attribute `object-detected` in the element class `configuration` is 0, then assign 1 to `object-detected`. The notation `<name>` WME is used to name the matching WME for use in this action. Hence, `<Uninitialized-configuration>` refers to the "configuration" WME matched in the LHS. Otherwise, the number of the matching conditions in the LHS may be used in modify and delete commands. Comments are given following the semicolon. When the working memory contains the WMEs

```
(region-scan1 ^sensor object)
(region-scan2 ^sensor object)
(status-check ^status normal)
(configuration ^object-detected 0)
```

but does not contain the WME (`interrupt ^status on`), the above rule is said to have a successful matching. More precisely, a rule is enabled if each of its positive condition elements is matched with a WME in the working memory and each of its negative condition elements is not matched by any WME in the working memory. A rule firing is the execution of the RHS actions in the order they appear in the rule. The above rule fires by modifying the attribute `object-detected` in the element class `configuration` to have the value 1.

A condition element can consist of value tests, other than equality, that a matching WME value must satisfy. These tests may be specified using the following components. Consider the WME

```
(airport ^airport-terminals 3 ^vacancies 3),
```

which is an instance of the element class `airport`.

- Variables: variables are specified in brackets and are used for matching values in the WMEs, or for defining a relationship between two values. Variables are implicitly existentially quantified over the rule LHS and RHS. Note that the following example requires the same value for the attributes `airport-terminals` and `vacancies`.

  ```
  ^airport-terminals <terminals-available> ^vacancies <terminals-available>
  ```

- Predicate operators: for restricting the range of values that can match.

  ```
  ^airport-terminals > 0
  ```

- Disjunctions: for specifying a list of values, one of which must be equal to the value in the WME.

  ```
  ^airport-terminals << 1 2 3 >>
  ```

- Conjunctions: for specifying a group of value tests that must be satisfied by one WME value.

  ```
  ^airport-terminals { > 1 <> nil }
  ```

- Variable semantic restrictions: any variable may be further qualified using these predicates by inclusion in the braces, as in

  ```
  (airport ^airport-terminals { <terminals-available> > 0 }).
  ```

The execution of the OPS5 program is known as the MRA cycle [Brownston et al., 1986] and is executed by the inference engine. The MRA cycle consists of three phases:

- Match: for each rule, determine all sets of WMEs that match the condition elements of the rule. Note that a rule may have more than one matching. The result of a successful match is called an instantiation. The set of all satisfied rule instantiations is called the conflict set.
- Resolve (Select): a single rule instantiation is selected from the conflict set according to some conflict-resolution strategies. Two common strategies are *LEX* (lexicographic ordering) and *MEA* (means-end analysis).
- Act: the selected rule instantiation is executed in the act phase. The actions in the selected rule are executed sequentially in the order they appear in the rule.

The production system repeats the MRA cycle until the conflict set is empty or an explicit halt command is executed.

11.1.2 The Rete Network

Of these three phases, the match phase is by far the most expensive, accounting for more than 90 percent of execution time in some experiments [Forgy, 1982; Gupta, 1987; Ishida, 1994]. Therefore, to maximize the efficiency of an OPS5 program, a fast match algorithm is necessary. The Rete match algorithm was first introduced in [Forgy, 1982] and it has become the standard sequential match algorithm. A new version called Rete II was introduced in [Forgy, 1985].

The Rete algorithm compiles the LHS patterns of the production rules into a discrimination network in the form of an augmented dataflow network [Miranker, 1987]. The state of all matches is stored in the memory nodes of the Rete network. Since a limited number of changes are made to the working memory after the firing of a rule instantiation, only a small part of the state of all matches needs to be changed. Thus,

```
(p p1
   (c1 ^a1 <x> ^a2 10)
   (c2 ^a1 <x>)
-->
   (remove 2))
```

```
(p p2
   (c1 ^a1 <y> ^a2 10)
   (c3 ^a1 2 ^a2 <y>)
  -(c4 ^a1 <y>)
   -->
   (modify 1 ^attri 4))
```

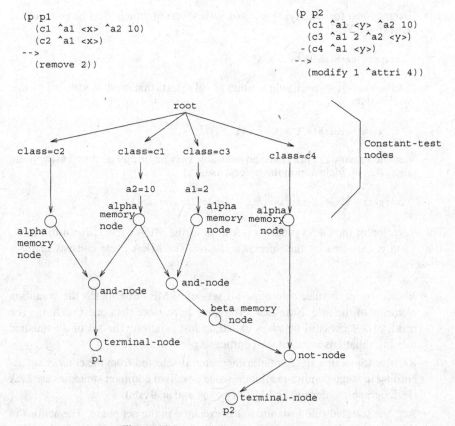

Figure 11.1 An example of a Rete network.

rather than checking every rule to determine which rules are matched by the WM in each recognize–act cycle, Rete maintains a list of matched rules and determines how these matches change due to the modification of the WM by the firing of a rule instantiation. The top portion of the Rete network contains chains of tests that perform the select operations. Tokens passing through these chains partially match a particular condition element and are stored in alpha-memory nodes. The alpha-memory nodes are connected to the two input nodes that find the partial binding between condition elements. Tokens with consistent variable bindings are stored in beta-memory nodes. At the end of the two input nodes are the terminal nodes, which signify that a consistent binding for a particular rule is found. The terminal nodes send the rule bindings to the conflict set. An example of a Rete network is shown in Figure 11.1.

11.2 CHENG–TSAI TIMING ANALYSIS METHODOLOGY

11.2.1 Static Analysis of Control Paths in OPS5

Several graphical representations of procedural programs have been developed for testing and debugging purposes. An intuitive representation is a *physical rule flow graph*. In such a graph, nodes represent rules, and an edge from node a to b implies rule b is executed immediately after rule a is executed. This graph is not appropriate for rule-based programs because the execution order of OPS5 programs cannot be determined statically. On the other hand, the control flow of rule-based programs should be thought of in terms of logical paths. A physical rule flow graph does not present the most appropriate abstraction. Another approach to represent the control paths is a causality graph. Here, too, nodes represent rules, but an edge from node a to node b implies rule a causes rule b to fire. The RHS assertions of rule a match all the LHS condition elements of rule b. This graph is not sufficient to capture all the logical paths since the LHS conditions of a rule are usually generated from the RHS actions of many rules; that is, a combination of several rules may "cause" another single rule to fire. This leads to the definition of a graph called the *enable rule* (ER) graph, which is adapted from [Cheng and Wang, 1990] and [Kiper, 1992]. The control information among rules in an OPS5 program is represented by the ER graph. To define the ER graph, we need to first define the *state-space graph*.

Definition 1. The state-space graph of an OPS5 program is a labeled directed graph $G = (V, E)$. V is a distinct set of nodes, each of which represents a distinct set of WMEs. We say that a rule is enabled at node i if and only if its enabling condition is satisfied by the WMEs at node i. E is a set of edges, each of which denotes the firing of a rule such that an edge (i, j) connects node i to node j if and only if a rule R is enabled at node i, and firing R will modify the WM to become the set of WMEs at node j.

Definition 2. Rule a is said to potentially enable rule b if and only if there exists at least one reachable state in the state-space graph of the program where (1) the

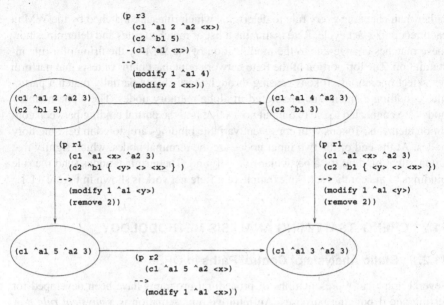

Figure 11.2 State-space graph of an OPS5 program.

enabling condition of rule b is false, (2) the enabling condition of rule a is true, and (3) firing rule a causes the enabling condition of rule b to become true.

Figure 11.2 shows the state-space graph of an OPS5 program. Rule $r1$ potentially enables rule $r2$, and rule $r3$ potentially enables rule $r1$. Suppose we have m different attributes in all classes, each attribute has n data items, and each WME is a unit in the WM, then we have n^m possible WMEs. In the state-space graph, 2^{n^m} states would exist.

Since the state-space graph cannot be derived without running the program for all allowable initial states, we use symbolic pattern matching to determine the potentially enabling relation between rules. Rule a potentially enables rule b if and only if the symbolic form of a WME modified by the actions in rule a matches *one* of the enabling condition elements of rule b. Here the symbolic form represents a set of WMEs and is of the form

```
(classname ^attribute1 v1 ^attribute2 v2 ... ^attributen vn)
```

where v1, v2..., and vn are either variables or constant values and each attribute can be omitted. For example, (class ^a1 3 ^a2 <x>) can be a symbolic form of the following WMEs.

```
(class ^a1 3 ^a2 4)
(class ^a1 3 ^a2 8 ^a3 4)
(class ^a1 3 ^a2 <y> ^a3 <z>)
```

Note that to determine with certainty whether a rule enables rather than potentially enables another rule, and thus determine whether the condition elements of a rule actually have a matching, would require us to know the contents of the working memory at run-time. This a priori knowledge of the WM cannot be obtained statically. Therefore, the above approximation of the potentially enabling relation is used instead. Example 1 illustrates the potentially enabling relation. Rule a potentially enables rule b because the first action of rule a creates a WME (class_c ^c1 off ^c2 <x>), which symbolically matches the enabling condition (class_c ^c1 <y>) of rule b. Notice, incidentally, that the second action of rule a does not match the first enabling condition (class_a ^a1 <x> ^a2 off) of rule b because variable <y> ranges in <<open close>>.

Example 1. An example of a potentially enabling b.

```
(p a
    (class_a ^a1 <x> ^a2 3)
    (class_b ^b1 <x> ^b2 {<y> <<open close>>})
-->
    (make class_c ^c1 off ^c2 <x>)
    (modify 1 ^a2 <y>))
```

```
(p b
    (class_a ^a1 <x> ^a2 off)
    (class_c ^c1 <y>)
-->
    (modify 1 ^a2 open))
```

The symbolic matching method actually detects the enabling relation by checking the attribute ranges. This information can be found by analyzing the semantics of the rules.

Definition 3. The (ER) graph of a set of rules is a labeled directed graph $G = (V, E)$. V is a set of vertices such that there is a vertex for each rule. E is a set of edges such that an edge connects vertex a to vertex b if and only if rule a potentially enables rule b.

Note that an edge from a to b in the ER graph does not mean that rule b will fire immediately after rule a. The fact that rule b is potentially enabled only implies that the instantiation of rule b may be added to the conflict set to be fired.

The previous analysis is useful since it does not require us to know the contents of working memory that cannot be obtained statically.

11.2.2 Termination Analysis

As described in the introduction, the upper bound on a real-time expert system's execution time cannot exceed the length of the period between two consecutive sensor input readings [Cheng et al., 1993; Chen and Cheng, 1995b]. Therefore, our goal is to determine before run-time a tight upper bound on the execution time of the expert system in every invocation following each reading of sensor input values. The first analysis step is to determine whether the expert system terminates. Since a rule-based expert system program is data-driven, it is not designed for all possible data domains. Certain input data are required to direct the control flows in the program. Many control techniques are implemented in this manner, and the absence of certain WMEs or a specific ordering of WMEs is required to generate the initial WM. If these WMEs are not present in the expected data domain, abnormal program behavior will occur, usually leading to a cycle in the program flow.

Ullman [Ullman and Van Gelder, 1988] studied recursive relations and described termination conditions in backward-chaining programs. Here, we consider the termination conditions for forward-chaining rule-based programs. We examine the ER graph of an OPS5 program to detect the termination conditions. If the OPS5 program is found not to terminate for all initial program states, the culprit conditions that cause nontermination are extracted to assist programmers in correcting the program.

Termination Detection   An OPS5 program is *terminating* if the maximal number of its rule firings is finite. Thus the maximal number of times a rule in a terminating program can fire is also finite. A rule is said to be *terminating* if its number of firings is always finite. To detect program termination, we use the ER graph, which provides information about the logical paths of an OPS5 program. In particular, we use this graph to trace the control flows of the program. Because we know the potentially enabling relation between rules, we can detect if the firing of each rule in an OPS5 program can terminate. The following definitions are needed to describe the conditions under which a rule will terminate.

Definition 4. Suppose rule *a* potentially enables rule *b*. Then there is an edge from node *a* to node *b* in the ER graph. A *matched* condition element of rule *b* is one of the enabling condition elements of rule *b*, which may be matched by executing an action of rule *a*. Here, rule *a* is called the enabling rule of the *matched* condition element.

Definition 5. An *unmatched* condition element is one of the enabling condition elements of a rule, which cannot be matched by firing any rule.

Note that an unmatched condition can still be matched by the initial working memory.

Example 2. *Matched* and *unmatched* condition elements

```
(p a
   (c1 ^a1 5)
   (c2 ^a2 <x> ^a3 2)
-->
   (modify 2 ^a2 3))
(p b
   (c2 ^a2 <x>)
   (c3 ^a4 <x> ^a5 <y>)
-->
   (modify 1 ^a2 <y>))
```

In example 2, suppose the firing of any other rule cannot match the second condition element of rule a. In the ER graph, rule b will *potentially enable* rule a. The first condition element (c2 ^a2 <x>) of rule a is a *matched* condition element because it may be matched by firing rule b. The second condition element (c3 ^a4 <x> ^a5 <y>) of rule a is an *unmatched* condition element because it cannot be matched by firing other rules.

An important property of OPS5 rule-based systems is called *refraction*, which ensures that the same instantiation is never executed more than once. Two instantiations are considered the same if they have the same rule name and the same WMEs matching to the same condition elements.

Next, we derive a theorem to detect the termination of a program. One way to predict the termination condition is to make sure that every state in the state-space graph cannot be reached more than once. However, since it is computationally expensive to expand the whole state-space graph, we use the ER graph to detect this property.

Theorem 1. A rule r will terminate (terminate in finite firings) if one of the following conditions holds:

C0. No rule potentially enables rule r.

C1. The actions of rule r modify or remove at least one of the *unmatched* condition elements of rule r.

C2. The actions of rule r modify or remove at least one of the *matched* condition elements of rule r, and all of the enabling rules of the *matched* condition elements can terminate in finite firings.

C3. Every rule that enables rule r can terminate in finite firings.

Note that condition (C1) is not necessary for OPS5 rules because refraction in OPS5 prevents a rule from firing again immediately after firing once. Also, if rule r is self-enabling, condition (C2) is not satisfied.

Proof

C0. If no rule potentially enables rule r, the instantiations of rule r can be formed only from the initial WM. Since the number of WMEs in the initial WM is finite, the number of firings of rule r is also finite.

C1. Since the firing of any rule cannot match the *unmatched* condition elements, the only WMEs that can match the *unmatched* condition elements are the initial WMEs. Moreover, since the actions of rule r change the contents of these WMEs, the WMEs cannot match the *unmatched* condition elements again after rule r is fired. Otherwise, the *unmatched* condition elements will be matched by firing rule r. This contradicts the definition of *unmatched* condition elements. Each initial WME matching the *unmatched* condition element can cause rule r to fire at most once since we have a finite number of initial WMEs. Thus rule r can terminate in finite firings.

C2. Since the enabling rules of the *matched* condition elements can terminate in finite firings, by removing these rules the *matched* condition elements can be treated as *unmatched* condition elements. According to (C1), rule r can terminate in finite firings.

C3. All rules that enable rule r can terminate in finite firings. After these rules terminate, no other rule can trigger rule r to fire. Thus rule r can terminate as well. □

Example 3. A rule can terminate in finite firings.

```
(p a
  (c1 ^a1 1 ^a2 <x>)
  (c2 ^a1 4 ^a2 <x>)
-->
  (modify 2 ^a1 3))
```

In example 3, suppose the second condition element (c2 ^a1 4 ^a2 <x>) cannot be matched by firing any rule, including this rule itself. Then this condition element is an *unmatched* condition element. Suppose three WMEs are in the initial working memory matching this condition element. Then this condition element can be matched by at most three WMEs. The actions of rule a modify these three WMEs when rule a fires. As a result, rule a can fire at most three times.

Example 4. Two rules with a cycle embedded.

```
(p p1
  (class1 ^a11 { <x> <> 1 } )
  (class2 ^a21 <y>)
-->
  (modify 1 ^a11 <y>))
(p p2
  (class1 ^a11 <x>)
  (class2 ^a21 { <x> << 2 3 >> } ^a22 <y>)
-->
  (modify 1 ^a11 <y>))
```

Example 5. Example 4 with modified variables.

```
(p p1
  (class1 ^a11 { <x-1> <> 1 } )
  (class2 ^a21 <y-1>)
-->
  (modify 1 ^a11 <y-1>))
(p p2
  (class1 ^a11 <x-2>)
  (class2 ^a21 { <x-2> << 2 3 >> } ^a22 <y-2>)
-->
  (modify 1 ^a11 <y-2>))
```

Enabling Conditions of a Cycle We use the above termination-detection algorithm to determine whether an OPS5 program always terminates in bounded time by inspecting the ER graph of the program. If no cycle exists in the ER graph or every cycle can be broken, that is, each cycle can be exited as a result of the firing of a rule that disables one or more LHSs of rules in this cycle [Cheng et al., 1993], then the firings of every rule in the OPS5 program are finite, and thus termination is detected. However, if the OPS5 program is not detected to terminate for all initial program states, then the culprit conditions that cause nontermination are extracted to assist programmers in correcting the program. This is done by inspecting the cycles with no exit conditions in the ER graph. Again, note that cycles composed entirely of rules that terminate in finite firings (and hence have exit conditions) do not need to be examined.

We now discuss the conditions under which a cyclic sequence of rule firings occurs. Suppose rules $p_1, p_2 \ldots, p_n$ form a cycle in the ER graph, W is a set of WMEs, and W causes rules $p_1, p_2 \ldots, p_n$ to fire in that order. If firing $p_1, p_2 \ldots, p_n$ in that order will produce W again, then W is called an enabling condition of the cycle. We can use symbolic tracing to find W if the data of each attribute are literal. Example 4 illustrates the idea.

Rules p_1 and p_2 form a cycle in the ER graph. To distinguish different variables in different rules, we assign different names to variables. Thus, the program is rewritten as in example 5. A symbol table is built for each variable, which is bound according to the semantics of the enabling conditions. Here, Table A is the symbol table, where the Binding Space refers to the restrictions imposed by the semantics of the constraints on the variables from the rule conditions.

In order to derive an acceptable enabling condition of the cycle, the algorithm below first postulates it to be the set of all enabling conditions of the rules of the cycle. Then it removes redundant conditions to arrive at a condition suitable for examination by the programmer, to see if the cycle should be broken by introducing further conditions into the LHSs of the rule. Thus W is

```
(class1 ^a11 <x-1>)
(class2 ^a21 <y-1>)
(class1 ^a11 <x-2>)
(class2 ^a21 <x-2> ^a22 <y-2>)
```

Each variable occurs once in the symbol table.

Now we trace the execution by firing p_1 first; p_1 enables p_2 by matching the first condition. Since the first condition of rule p_2 can be generated from rule p_1, it can

TABLE A	
Variable	Binding space
x-1	<>1
y-1	none
x-2	2,3
y-2	none

TABLE B	
Variable	Binding space
x-1	<>1
y-1	2,3
x-2	2,3
y-2	none

TABLE C	
Variable	Binding space
x-1	<>1
y-1	2,3
x-2	2,3
y-2	<>1

be removed from W. Variable x-2 is now replaced by y-1. W is

```
(class1 ^a11 <x-1>)
(class2 ^a21 <y-1>)
(class2 ^a21 <y-1> ^a22 <y-2>)
```

Since x-2 is bound with 2 and 3, y-1 is bound with the same items. The symbol table is modified (Table B). In general, the conjunction of the binding-space restrictions is substituted.

After executing the action of rule p_2, W is now

```
(class1 ^a11 <y-2>)
(class2 ^a21 <y-1>)
(class2 ^a21 <y-1> ^a22 <y-2>)
```

To make this WM trigger p_1 and p_2 in that order again, the WME (class1 ^a11 <y-2>) must match the first condition of p_1. Thus variable y-2 is bound with the binding space of x-1. Table C is the symbol table. W is

```
(class1 ^a11 <y-2>)
(class2 ^a21 <y-1>)
(class2 ^a21 <y-1> ^a22 <y-2>)
     where y-2<>1 and y-1=2,3
```

The detailed algorithm for detecting the enabling conditions of cycles is described next.

Algorithm 1. The detection of enabling conditions of cycles.

Premise: The data domain of each attribute is literal.

Purpose: Rules $p_1, p_2 \ldots, p_n$ form a cycle in the ER graph. Find a set of WMEs, W, that fires $p_1, p_2 \ldots, p_n$ in that order such that these firings cannot terminate in finite firings.

1. Assign different names to the variables in different rules.
2. Initialize W to the set of all enabling conditions of $p_1, p_2 \ldots, p_n$.
3. Build a symbol table for variables. Each variable's binding set is limited to the restriction specified in the rule enabling conditions.
4. Simulate the firing of $p_1, p_2 \ldots, p_n$ in that order.

    Each enabling condition of rule p_i is matched from the initial WM, unless it can be generated from rule p_{i-1}.

    If the enabling condition element w of rule p_i can be generated by firing p_{i-1}, then remove w from W. Substitute p_{i-1}'s variables v_{i-1} for corresponding variables v_i in p_i.

    Modify v_{i-1}'s binding space in the symbol table to the conjunction of the restrictions on v_i and v_{i-1}.

5. If p_1's enabling condition elements can be generated by p_n, substitute p_n's variables v_n for corresponding variables v_1 in p_1. Modify v_n's binding space in the symbol table.

6. In steps 4 and 5, while substituting p_{i-1}'s variables for p_i's variables, check the intersection of the binding spaces of p_i's and p_{i-1}'s variables. If the intersection is empty, then terminate the algorithm: the loops terminates in finite firings.

7. Suppose W_n is the WM after firing $p_1, p_2 \ldots, p_n$. If W_n can match W, then W is an enabling condition of the cycle $p_1, p_2 \ldots, p_n$.

Note that certain conditions are subsets of others, as explained in section 4.4.

Prevention of Cycles   If the OPS5 program is not detected to terminate for all initial program states, then the culprit conditions that cause nontermination are used to assist programmers in correcting the program. After detecting the enabling conditions, W, of a cycle, we add rule r', with W as the enabling conditions of r'. By doing so, once the working memory has the WMEs matching the enabling conditions of a cycle, the control flow can be switched from the cycle to r'. In example 4, r' is

```
(p loop-rule1
  (class1 ^a11 { <y-2> <>1 } )
  (class2 ^a21 { <y-1> << 2 3 >> } )
  (class2 ^a21 <y-1> ^a22 <y-2>)
-->
  action ...
```

If the cycle is not an infinite loop or desirable (e.g., in periodic control and monitoring applications), we may not want to add rule r'. The action of r', determined by the application, depends on how the application needs to react when the program flow is going to enter a cycle. The simplest way to escape from the cycles is to halt.

To ensure the program flow switches out of the cycles, the *extra* rules r' should have higher priorities than the regular ones. To achieve this goal, we use the MEA control strategy and modify the enabling conditions of each regular rule.

At the beginning of the program, two WMEs are added to the WM and the MEA strategy is enforced.

```
(startup
  ......
  (strategy mea)
  (make control ^rule regular)
  (make control ^rule extra))
```

The condition (control ^rule regular) is added to each regular rule as the first enabling condition element. (control ^rule extra) is added to each extra rule as the first enabling condition element too. Since the MEA strategy is enforced, the order of instantiations is based on the recency of the *first* time tag. The recency of the condition (control ^rule regular) is lower than that of the condition (control ^rule extra). Thus, the instantiations of the extra rules are chosen for execution earlier than those of the regular rules. Example 6 is the modified result of example 4.

Example 6. The modified result of example 4.

```
(startup
  (strategy mea)
  (make control ^rule regular)
  (make control ^rule extra))
(p p1
  (control ^rule regular)
  (class1 ^a11 { <x> <> 1 } )
  (class2 ^a21 <y>)
-->
  (modify 2 ^a11 <y>))
(p p2
  (control ^rule regular)
  (class1 ^a11 <x>)
  (class2 ^a21 { <x> << 2 3 >> } ^a22 <y>)
-->
  (modify 2 ^a11 <y>))
(p loop-rule1
  (control ^rule extra)
  (class1 ^a11 { <y-2> <> 1 } )
  (class2 ^a21 { <y-1> << 2 3 >> } )
  (class2 ^a21 <y-1> ^a22 <y-2>)
-->
  (halt))
```

Usually, a cycle is not expected for an application. Thus, once the entrance of a cycle is detected, the program can be abandoned. Hence, after all cycles in the ER graph are found, the program is guaranteed to terminate. In example 6, the action of the extra rule can be

```
(remove 2 3 4)
```

Since the WMEs that match the enabling condition of a cycle are removed, the instantiations in the cycle are also removed. Then, other instantiations in the agenda can be triggered to fire.

Another example of program modification is shown in the analysis of the Space Shuttle Orbital Maneuvering and Reaction Control Systems' Valve and Switch Classification Expert System (OMS) [Barry and Lowe, 1990]. A non-terminating rule is modified in order to break a cycle, thus guaranteeing the termination of this rule and the program.

Program Refinement Due to its complexity, the ER graph usually contains many cycles. Furthermore, even for a single cycle, more than one enabling condition may exist to trigger the cycle. This leads to a large number of extra rules in the modified programs and thus reduces their run-time performance. To tackle this problem, redundant conditions and rules must be removed after the modification.

Redundant Conditions In algorithm 1, after symbolic tracing, some variables will be substituted and the binding spaces may be changed too. This may cause subset relationships among the enabling condition elements of a cycle. In an extra rule, if condition element C_i is a subset of condition element C_j, then C_j can be omitted to simplify the enabling condition. In example 6, the condition (class2 ^a21 <y-1> ^a22 <y-2>) is a subset of (class2 ^a21 <y-1>). Hence, (class2 ^a21 <y-1>) can be omitted.

```
(p loop-rule1
   (control ^rule extra)
   (class1 ^a11 { <y-2> <>1 } )
;    (class2 ^a21 { <y-1> << 2 3 >> } )   ;omitted
   (class2 ^a21  <y-1> << 2 3 >> ^a22 <y-2>)
 -->
   (halt))
```

Redundant Extra Rules In certain situations, we can remove some extra rules if the actions of these extra rules can be ignored. For example, extra rules with action "halt" or "print" can be ignored. Since each cycle is analyzed independently, the extra rules correspond to cycles with different enabling conditions. If the enabling condition of rule r_i is a subset of the enabling condition of rule r_j, then rule r_i can be removed since firing r_i will definitely fire r_j. The cycling information of rule r_j contains that of rule r_i. Thus, it is sufficient to just provide more general information. In many cases, if the set of nodes P_i which forms a cycle C_i is a subset of the set P_j which forms a cycle C_j, then the enabling condition of C_j is a subset of C_i's enabling condition. The situation becomes apparent when the cycle consists of many nodes. Hence, we can expect to remove the extra rules whose enabling conditions are derived from large cycles.

In example 7, the first and third condition elements of rule 1 are identical to the first and fourth condition elements, respectively, of rule 3. WMEs matching the second condition element of rule 3 also match the second condition element of rule 1, but not vice versa. The third condition element of rule 3 is not in rule 1, making the LHS of rule 3 more restrictive than the LHS of rule 1. Thus the enabling condition of rule 3 is a subset of the enabling condition of rule 1. Similarly, the first, second, and fourth condition elements of rule 2 are identical to the first, second, and fifth condition elements, respectively, of rule 4. WMEs matching the third condition element of rule 4 also match the third condition element of rule 2, but not vice versa. The fourth condition element of rule 4 is not in rule 2, making the LHS of rule 4 more restrictive than the LHS of rule 2. Thus the enabling condition of rule 4 is a subset of the enabling condition of rule 2. Therefore, rules 3 and 4 can be removed.

Example 7. Redundant rules.

```
(p 1
   (control ^rule extra)
   (class1 ^a13 { <y-1> <> 1 } )
   (class2 ^a22 <y-1>)
```

```
-->
  action ...
(p 2
  (control ^rule extra)
  (class1 ^a13 { <x-1> <> 1 } )
  (class2 ^a22 <y-1>)
  (class4 ^a41 2 ^a42 <x-3>)
-->
  action ...

(p 3                      ; redundant rule of rule 1
  (control ^rule extra)
  (class1 ^a13 { <y-1> << 2 3 >> } )
  (class4 ^a41 { <y-4> <> 1 } ^a42 <y-1>)
  (class2 ^a22 <y-1>)
-->
  action ...
(p 4                      ; redundant rule of rule 2
  (control ^rule extra)
  (class1 ^a13 { <x-1> <> 1} )
  (class2 ^a22 { <y-1> << 2 3 >> }
  (class4 ^a41 <y-4> ^a42 <y-1>)
  (class4 ^a41 2 ^a42 <x-3>)
-->
  action ...
```

An Example   Now we apply our technique to a complete example.

Example 8.   An OPS5 program with cycles embedded in the ER graph.

```
(p p1
  (class1 ^a13 { <x> <> 1 } )
  (class2 ^a22 <y>)
-->
  (modify 1 ^a13 <y>))
(p p2
  (class3 ^a31 <x> ^a32 <y>)
  (class4 ^a41 <x> ^a42 <y>)
-->
  (modify 1 ^a31 2 ^a32 <x>)
  (make class1 ^a11 1 ^a12 2 ^a13 3))
(p p3
  (class1 ^a11 <x> ^a12 <y>)
  (class4 ^a41 2 ^a42 <x>)
-->
  (modify 1 ^a11 <y>))
(p p4
  (class1 ^a13 { <x> << 2 3 >> } )
  (class4 ^a41 <y> ^a42 <x>)
-->
  (modify 1 ^a13 <y>))
```

```
(p p5
  (class1 ^a11 <x>)
  (class3 ^a31 1 ^a32 <y>)
-->
  (modify 2 ^a31 2 ^a32 <x>)
  (make class2 ^a21 2 ^a22 3))
```

First, we detect if the program can terminate in finite firings. We find rule *p5* can terminate since it contains an *unmatched condition*. Next, the enabling condition of each cycle is found and extra rules are added to the program (Example 9). Here, the actions of all extra rules are `halt`. Hence, we remove the redundant rules without considering the interference among the extra rules. After removing the redundant rules, the number of extra rules is reduced from 16 to 9.

Example 9. Extra rules of example 8 (including redundant rules).

```
(p loop-rule1        ;cycle: 4
 (control ^rule extra)
 (class1 ^a13 {<y-4> << 3 2 >>} )
 (class4 ^a41 <y-4> ^a42 <y-4> )
-->
 ; cycle information
(p loop-rule2        ;cycle: 3
 (control ^rule extra)
 (class1 ^a11 <y-3> ^a12 <y-3> )
 (class4 ^a41 2 ^a42 <y-3> )
-->
 ; cycle information
(p loop-rule3        ;cycle: 2
 (control ^rule extra)
 (class3 ^a31 2 ^a32 2)
 (class4 ^a41 2 ^a42 2)
-->
 ; cycle information
(p loop-rule4        ;cycle: 1
 (control ^rule extra)
 (class1 ^a13 {<y-1> <> 1} )
 (class2 ^a22 <y-1> )
-->
 ; cycle information
(p loop-rule5        ;cycle: 3 4
 (control ^rule extra)
 (class1 ^a11 <x-3> ^a12 <y-3> )
 (class4 ^a41 2 ^a42 <x-3> )
 (class4 ^a41 <y-4> ^a42 {<x-4> << 3 2 >>} )
-->
 ; cycle information
(p loop-rule6        ;cycle: 1 4
 (control ^rule extra)
 (class1 ^a13 {<y-4> <> 1} )
 (class2 ^a22 {<y-1> << 3 2 >>} )
 (class4 ^a41 <y-4> ^a42 <y-1> )
-->
 ; cycle information
(p loop-rule7        ;cycle: 4 3
 (control ^rule extra)
 (class1 ^a13 <x-4> << 3 2 >> )
 (class4 ^a41 <y-4> ^a42 <x-4> )
 (class4 ^a41 2 ^a42 <x-3> )
-->
 ; cycle information
```

```
(p loop-rule8          ;cycle: 1 3
 (control ^rule extra)
 (class1 ^a13 {<x-1> <> 1} )
 (class2 ^a22 <y-1> )
 (class4 ^a41 2 ^a42 <x-3> )
-->
; cycle information
(p loop-rule9          ;cycle: 4 1
 (control ^rule extra)  ;redundant with loop-rule1
 (class1 ^a13 {<y-1> << 3 2>>} )
 (class4 ^a41 {<y-4> <> 1} ^a42 <y-1> )
 (class2 ^a22 <y-1> )
-->
; cycle information
(p loop-rule10         ;cycle: 3 1
 (control ^rule extra)
 (class1 ^a11 <x-3> ^a12 <y-3> )
 (class4 ^a41 2 ^a42 <x-3> )
 (class2 ^a22 <y-1> )
-->
; cycle information
(p loop-rule11         ;cycle: 1 4 3
 (control ^rule extra)  ;redundant with loop-rule8
 (class1 ^a13 {<x-1> <>1} )
 (class2 ^a22 {<y-1> << 3 2 >>} )
 (class4 ^a41 <y-4> ^a42 <y-1> )
 (class4 ^a41 2 ^a42 <x-3> )
-->
; cycle information
(p loop-rule12         ;cycle: 3 4 1
 (control ^rule extra)  ;redundant with loop-rule10
 (class1 ^a11 <x-3> ^a12 <y-3> )
 (class4 ^a41 2 ^a42 <x-3> )
 (class4 ^a41 {<y-4> <> 1} ^a42 {<x-4> << 3 2 >>} )
 (class2 ^a22 <y-1> )
-->
; cycle information
(p loop-rule13         ;cycle: 1 3 4
 (control ^rule extra)  ;redundant with loop-rule8
 (class1 ^a13 {<y-4> <> 1} )
 (class2 ^a22 <y-1> )
 (class4 ^a41 2 ^a42 <x-3> )
 (class4 ^a41 <y-4> ^a42 {<x-4> << 3 2 >>} )
-->
; cycle information
(p loop-rule14         ;cycle: 4 3 1
 (control ^rule extra)  ;redundant with loop-rule7
 (class1 ^a13 {<y-1> << 3 2 >>} )
 (class4 ^a41 <y-4> ^a42 <y-1> )
 (class4 ^a41 2 ^a42 <x-3> )
 (class2 ^a22 <y-1> )
-->
; cycle information
(p loop-rule15         ;cycle: 3 1 4
 (control ^rule extra)  ;redundant with loop-rule5
 (class1 ^a11 <x-3> ^a12 <y-3> )
 (class4 ^a41 2 ^a42 <x-3> )
 (class2 ^a22 {<y-1> << 3 2 >>} )
 (class4 ^a41 <y-4> ^a42 <y-1> )
-->
; cycle information
(p loop-rule16         ;cycle: 4 1 3
 (control ^rule extra)  ;redundant with loop-rule7
 (class1 ^a13 {<x-4> << 3 2 >>} )
 (class4 ^a41 {<y-4> <> 1} ^a42 <x-4> )
 (class2 ^a22 <y-1> )
 (class4 ^a41 2 ^a42 <x-3> )
-->
; cycle information
```

Implementation and Complexity For an OPS5 program with n rules, potentially $O(n!)$ cycles are embedded in the ER graph. However, we found that cycles do not contain a large number of nodes in actual real-time expert systems we examined. If it is detected that no path contains m nodes in the ER graph, there is no need to test cycles with more than m nodes. This reduces both the computational complexity and the memory space.

To further reduce the computation time in identifying cycles, we store information about rules that do not form a path in certain orders. This non-path is called an impossible path. If there is no path consisting of rules $p_1, p_2 \ldots, p_n$ executing in this order, then there is no cycle containing these rules. Thus, we do not need to examine the cycles with an embedded path consisting of the rules in the above order (an impossible path). Since the ER graph actually represents all possible paths between two rules, we can construct a linear list to store all impossible paths with more than two rules. Since storage of these impossible paths requires space, we are in fact trading space with time. In our tool, we store impossible paths with up to nine nodes.

This tool has been implemented on a DEC 5000/240 workstation running RISC/Ultrix. Two real-world expert systems are examined. Ongoing work applies this tool to more actual and synthetic OPS5 expert systems in order to evaluate the run-time performance and scalability of this tool.

Industrial Example: Experiment on the ISA Expert System The purpose of the Integrated Status Assessment (ISA) Expert System [Marsh, 1988] is to determine the faulty components in a network. It contains 15 production rules and some Lisp function definitions. A component can be either an *entity* (node) or a *relationship* (link). A relationship is a directed edge connecting two entities. Components are in one of three states: nominal, suspect, or failed. A failed entity can be replaced by an available backup entity. This expert system makes use of simple strategies to trace failed components in a network.

One rule is found to terminate in a finite number of firings. One hundred twenty five cycles are detected. After removing the redundant rules, four cycles remain.

Industrial Example: Experiment on the OMS Expert System The purpose of the OMS Expert System [Barry and Lowe, 1990] is to classify setting valves and switches. It recognizes special patterns of settings and creates intermediate assertions. With settings and new assertions, it infers more and creates more assertions until no more assertions can be derived. Finally, the settings and assertions are compared with the expected values supplied by the user. All matches or mismatches are reported.

No rule is reported to terminate in finite firings. However, after checking all possible paths, only one cycle is found. The enabling condition of the cycle, shown below, is in rule `loop-rule1`.

```
(control ^rule extra)
(device ^mode {<x-4> <> void } ^domain <y-4>
        ^compnt <v-4> ^desc {<w-4> << closed open >>} )
(valve_groups ^vtype <v-4> ^valve_a <v-4> ^valve_b <v-4> )
```

This cycle contains only the fourth rule. It implies the other rules can terminate in finite firings. The fourth rule is

```
(p check-group
  (device ^mode { <x> <> void } ^domain <y>
          ^compnt <z1> ^desc { <w> << open closed >> })
  (device ^mode <x> ^domain <y> ^compnt  <z2> ^desc <w>)
  (valve_groups ^vtype <v> ^valve_a <z1> ^valve_b <z2>)
-->
  (modify 1 ^compnt <v>)
  (modify 2 ^mode void))
```

We then examine the non-terminating rule with the enabling condition of the cycle. We find that the program flow can enter the cycle when variable <z1> is equal to variable <z2> in the rule check-group. This situation is not expected as a normal execution flow. Hence, we modify the LHS of this rule such that variable <z1> is not equal to variable <z2>.

```
(p check-group
  (device ^mode { <x> <> void } ^domain <y>
          ^compnt <z1> ^desc { <w> << open closed >> })
  (device ^mode <x> ^domain <y> ^compnt  { <z2> <> <z1> } ^desc <w>)
  (valve_groups ^vtype <v> ^valve_a <z1> ^valve_b <z2>)
-->
  (modify 1 ^compnt <v>)
  (modify 2 ^mode void))
```

This modification breaks the cycle, thus guaranteeing the termination of this rule and the program. In the next section, we introduce techniques for determining the execution time of OPS5 programs.

11.2.3 Timing Analysis

Now we introduce techniques for analyzing the timing properties of OPS5 programs and discuss a static-analytic method to predict the timing bound on program execution time. The ER graph is the basic structure of our static analysis. We predict the timing in terms of the number of rule firings. Similar work has been done for MRL in [Wang and Mok, 1993]. We will indicate the problems of static analysis and describe a tool to facilitate the timing analysis and to assist programmers in analyzing run-time performance.

Before we analyze the problem, we need to make the following assumptions:

- The program can terminate.
- The data domains of all attributes are finite.
- No duplicate WMEs are in the WM.

The first assumption is obvious since no timing bound can be found for a program with infinite firings. The second assumption is based on the fact that the analysis problem is in general undecidable for programs with infinite domains. The third assumption is actually an extension of the second assumption. Unlike MRL, OPS5's WMEs are identified not only by their contents but also by their time tags. Thus, the following two WMEs are identified as different items in OPS5; the first WME is generated earlier than the second WME. However, identical WMEs cannot co-exist in the WM in MRL.

```
time tag        WMEs
-----------------------------------
  #3            (class ^a1 3 ^a2 4)
  #6            (class ^a1 3 ^a2 4)
```

An OPS5 system can use a hash table to quickly locate the duplicate WMEs in the WM and prevent redundancy in every cycle. If a set of WMEs satisfies the enabling condition of the first firing rule, we can generate the same WMEs as many times as we want. In other words, we can fire the first-firing rule as many times as we want. This indicates that no upper bound exists for this rule's firings, and thus the program cannot terminate in a finite number of rule firings. Therefore, we need to enforce the third assumption to facilitate our analysis.

11.2.4 Static Analysis

Prediction of the Number of Rule Firings Since the execution of rule-based programs is data-driven, the WM is used to predict the number of rule firings. To predict the number of each rule's firings, we estimate the number of instantiations in the conflict set. The maximum number of instantiations of a rule can be estimated, as in example 10.

Example 10. An example with a maximum number of instantiations.

```
(p a
  (class_a ^a1 <x> ^a2 <y>)
  (class_b ^b1 <x> ^b2 <z>)
  (class_c ^c1 <z>)
-->
  action without changing the instantiations of rule a ...
```

Assume the domains of <x>,<y>, and <z> contain at most x, y, and z instances, respectively. Then, we have at most xyz instantiations of rule a in the conflict set. Suppose the action of rule a does not remove any instantiations of rule a. There are two situations in which rule a can be fired: (1) the initial WM contains rule a's instantiations, or (2) rule a is triggered by other rules.

In the first situation, we have at most xyz instantiations in the initial WM. Thus rule a can fire at most xyz times before rule a is triggered by other rules.

In the second situation, another rule creates or modifies WME w which matches one or more enabling condition elements of rule a. If the WME w matches the first condition element, (class_a ^a1 <x> ^a2 <y>), at most z of rule a instantiations will be added into the conflict set because variables <x> and <y> are bound with the values of w's attributes. Thus rule a can fire at most z times before it is again triggered by other rules. Similarly, if w matches (class_b ^b1 <x> ^b2 <z>) or (class_c ^c1 <z>), rule a can fire at most y or xy times, respectively, before another rule triggers rule a again.

Also, the action part of a rule can affect the rule's instantiations. For example, the rule in example 10 can be

```
(p a
  (class_a ^a1 <x> ^a2 <y>)
  (class_b ^b1 <x> ^b2 <z>)
  (class_c ^c1 <z>)
-->
  (modify 3 ^c1 <y>))
```

Once the value of attribute ^c1 is changed, the instantiations associated with the third condition element, (class_c ^c1 <z>), will be removed. Thus the maximum number of firings is the number of instances of <z>, that is, z. Also, we reduce the maximum number of firings from xyz to z. If rule a is triggered with the match of the third condition element, (class_c ^c1 <z>), rule a can fire at most once before another trigger.

Algorithm 2. Detection of the upper bound on the number of firings of rule r.

Premise: rule r can be detected to terminate in bounded time by using the termination detection algorithm 1.

Suppose we have up to I_r instantiations of rule r in the initial WM. The upper bound on the firings of rule r can be estimated according to the following conditions.

1. Rule r satisfies condition 1 of theorem 1: the upper bound on the firings of rule r is I_r. The maximum number of the initial WMEs is bounded by the domain size of each attribute.

2. Rule r satisfies condition 2 of theorem 1: rules $r_1, r_2, \ldots, r_n$ are enabling rules of the matched condition elements of rule r. These rules can terminate in $f_1, f_2, \ldots, f_n$ firings, respectively. Rule r has at most $I_1, I_2, \ldots, I_n$ instantiations when triggered by $r_1, r_2, \ldots, r_n$. The upper bound on the number of firings of rule r is

$$I_r + \sum_{j=1}^{n}(f_j \times I_j)$$

3. Rule r satisfies condition 3 of theorem 1: rules $r_1, r_2, \ldots, r_m$, which point to rule r in the ER graph can terminate in $f_1, f_2, \ldots, f_m$ firings, respectively. Rule r has at most $I_1, I_2, \ldots, I_m$ instantiations when triggered by

$r_1, r_2, \ldots, r_m$. The upper bound on the number of firings of rule r is

$$I_r + \sum_{j=1}^{m}(f_j \times I_j)$$

Example 3 illustrates condition 1 of this algorithm. Example 11 illustrates condition 2 of this algorithm.

Example 11. A rule satisfying condition 2 of algorithm 2.

```
(p a
  (c1 ^a1 1 ^a2 <y>)
  (c2 ^a1 <x> ^a2 <y>)
-->
  (modify 2 ^a2 <x>))
```

Suppose variables `<x>` and `<y>` have x and y items. The second condition element, `(c2 ^a1 <x> ^a2 <y>)`, is the matched condition element. The enabling rules of this condition element can terminate in $f_1, f_2, \ldots, f_m$ firings, respectively. We have up to I_a instantiations of rule a in the initial WM. Since the action does not affect the WMEs that satisfy the first condition element, `(c1 ^a1 1 ^a2 <y>)`, there would be at most y instantiations when this rule is triggered by one of the enabling rules. The upper bound on the number of firings of rule a is

$$I_a + \sum_{j=1}^{n}(f_j \times y)$$

Problems Algorithm 2 is based on the ER graph. However, in the ER graph, we use the symbolic matching method to detect the enabling relations. Since the contents and interrelationship of WMEs cannot be determined statically, it is likely to cause a pessimistic prediction, as in example 12.

Example 12. A rule with pessimistic estimation.

```
(p a
  (class_a ^a1 7 ^a2 <x>)
  (class_b ^b1 <x> ^b2 6)
-->
  (make class_b ^b1 5 ^b2 4))
(p b
  (class_a ^a1 { <x> <> <y> } ^a2 <y>)
 -(class_a ^a1 <y> ^a2 <x>)
  (class_b ^b1 <x> ^b2 <y>)
  (class_b ^b1 <y> ^b2 <x>)
-->
  (modify 3 ^b2 <x>))
```

First, the enabling conditions of rule *b* are quite restricted. They actually imply tight relationships among the WMEs of class_a and class_b. The probability of firing this rule is relatively low compared to other rules. However, we still need to say that rule *a* potentially enables rule *b* since rule *a* creates a WME (class_b ^b1 5 ^b2 4), which can individually match the third and fourth condition elements of rule *b*.

Second, it is unlikely that the WME modified by rule *a* can match the second condition element of rule *b*, (class_b ^b1 <x> ^b2 6), because of the constant restriction on attribute ^b2. However, since variable <x> in rule *a* is not semantically bounded, the enabling relation still weakly holds.

In addition, algorithm 2 does not take the control strategies (LEX or MEA) into consideration. These control strategies require the time tag of each WME in the WM to determine the priorities of each instantiation in the conflict set. The time tags of WMEs are hard to predict before run-time. Without knowing the time tag of the WMEs, it is difficult to predict the interference among instantiations. Thus we must assume no interference among instantiations to make a conservative estimation. If the domain is too large, our estimation becomes pessimistic. Figure 11.3 illustrates the situation. For example, rule *c* can be triggered by rules *e*, *f*, *g*, and *h*. It is rare or even impossible that instantiations of these four rules triggering rule *c* co-exist in the conflict set because firing one of these rules may prevent other rules from firing. For example, firing instantiations of rule *e* may remove the instantiations of rule *f*. Since we cannot predict the interference relation among rules *e*, *f*, *g*, and *h*, we must assume all instantiations of these four rules can be executed. The same condition applies to rules *a*, *b*, and *d*. As we can see, rule *b* inherits the firing bounds of rules

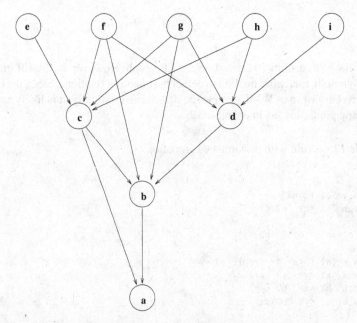

Figure 11.3   Enabling relation with pessimistic estimation.

c and *d*, which are already pessimistic firing estimations. It makes the prediction of rule *b*'s firing bound looser. The estimation of rule *a*'s firings is even worse than that of rule *b*'s. Generally, the greater the number of nodes chained before node *v* in the ER graph, the worse the estimation of node *v*'s firings. Hence, we may not expect a tight estimation from static analysis. We propose another technique in the following section.

11.2.5 WM Generation

Instead of using static analysis, we generate a set of WMEs as the initial WM which maximizes the program execution time. In this manner, we are not only providing the timing bound of the OPS5 programs but also finding the most time-consuming part from the timing report generated in the OPS5 environment. This report can assist programmers in the optimization of programs through the modification of rules that are computationally expensive. Preliminary results in the automated optimization of rule-based systems can be found in [Zupan and Cheng, 1994a; Zupan and Cheng, 1998].

Maximizing Matching Time   The set of WMEs that can maximize matching time is the set of all possible WMEs in the data domain. In the Rete network, the most expensive computation is to compare the WMEs in the left input node of a two-input node to the WMEs in the right input node. This is the so-called *cross-product* effect [Kuo and Moldovan, 1992]. If each one-input node that is at the top level of the Rete network has a maximum number of tuples, we can ensure the beta memories are full. Thus each two-input node will have the highest timing consumption.

Maximizing Rule Firings   To trigger the program to have a maximum number of rule firings, one way is to generate an initial WM that satisfies the LHS condition of each rule as many times as possible. The initial WM can be formed as the union of all positive condition elements of each rule. Consider the following rules:

```
(p p1
  (c1 ^a1 <x> ^a2 <y>)
  (c2 ^a1 3)
 -(c3 ^a1 <y> ^a2 <z>)
-->
  action ...
(p p1a
  (c1 ^a1 <x> ^a2 <y>)
  (c2 ^a1 3)
-->
  action ...
```

The LHS condition of rule p1 is a subset of that of rule p1a. We take rule p1a instead of rule p1 as our test rule. In this way, we are making a conservative estimation since the number of firings of p1a is at least that of p1.

Example 13. An example of the union of positive condition elements.

```
(p p1
  (c1 ^a1 <x> ^a2 { <y> << 1 2 >> } )
  (c2 ^a1 3 ^a2 <x>)
-->
  action ...
(p p2
  (c1 ^a1 3 ^a2 1)
 -(c2 ^a1 <x> ^a2 2)
-->
  action ...
```

In example 13, the union of the positive condition elements of the above two rules is

```
(c1 ^a1 <x> ^a2 { <y> << 1 2 >> } )
(c2 ^a1 3 ^a2 <x>)
```

These are the symbolic forms of the initial WM. The actual WMEs are obtained by expanding the variables according to the attributes' domains. For example, if the domain of attribute ^a1 in class c1 ranges over a, b, and c, and the domain of attribute ^a2 in class c1 ranges over b and c, the WMEs are generated as follows:

```
(c1 ^a1 b ^a2 1)
(c1 ^a1 b ^a2 2)
(c1 ^a1 c ^a2 1)
(c1 ^a1 c ^a2 2)
(c2 ^a1 3 ^a2 b)
(c2 ^a1 3 ^a2 c)
```

Note that attribute ^a1 in class c1 does not generate value a because its variable <x> is bound with the value of attribute ^a2 in class c2, which ranges over b and c.

The WMEs we generate can match all positive condition elements of the program. However, some of the WMEs may not be used during execution since the instantiations they are associated with may be removed by firing other instantiations. Consider the following rule.

```
(p a
  (c1 ^a1 <x> ^a2 1)
  (c2 ^b1 <z> ^b2 <y> ^b3 <x>)
  (c3 ^c1 <y> ^c2 4)
-->
  (remove 2)
  (modify 1 ^a2 <x>))
```

Suppose variables <x>, <y>, and <z> each have 10 items. Potentially, 10, 1000, and 10 WMEs match the first, second, and third condition elements, respectively. Let w be one of the 10 WMEs matching the first condition element, (c1 ^a1 <x> ^a2 1). So, w actually associates with 100 instantiations of this rule. After the first instantiation associated with w executes, the first action removes those WMEs, W_2, which match the second condition element. Thus, at most 10 instantiations of this rule in the initial

WM can be executed. The second action of this rule changes w's content. Variables <y> and <z> actually do not affect the timing properties of this rule. Since we do not have negative condition elements in our test programs, this action to remove W_2 will not cause additional rule firings. Thus, it is unnecessary to generate all WMEs satisfying the second condition element, (c2 ^b1 <z> ^b2 <y> ^b3 <x>). The action of rule a does not modify those WMEs, W_3, which match the third condition element. If W_3 also matches other positive condition elements of rule b, W_3 can be generated in rule b. Otherwise, there is no need to generate all WMEs satisfying (c3 ^c1 <y> ^c2 4).

From the above analysis, we know that we need only to expand <x> to generate the needed WMEs. Variables <y> and <z> can be changed to any constant value in their data domain. The positive condition elements of rule a are rewritten as

```
(c1 ^a1 <x> ^a2 1)
(c2 ^b1 7 ^b2 5 ^b3 <x>)
(c3 ^c1 5 ^c2 4)
```

Variables <y> and <z> are changed to 5 and 7, respectively. There are 10, 10, and 1 WMEs associated with these three condition elements, respectively.

We now describe the algorithm to generate the initial WM. We limit the data type to literal, since most rule-based programs are used in symbolic data applications.

Algorithm 3. Generating WMEs to cause a maximum number of rule firings.

Premise: The data domain of each attribute is "literal."

Purpose: Given an OPS5 program P, find a set of positive condition elements C. Expand the set C to a set of WMEs, W, that causes P to have a maximum number of rule firings.

1. Initialize C to the empty set.
2. For each rule r, do the following:
   For each positive condition element c of rule r, if c is not a subset of any element in C, do the following steps:
   (a) if the action of rule r does not modify the WMEs that satisfy c, then for each variable v associated with attribute a in c, if v does not appear in the action part of rule r, change v to a constant x, where x is in the data domain of attribute a.
   (b) add c to C.
   (c) for every element pc in C, if pc is a subset of c, remove pc from C.
3. Expand the positive condition elements in C to W.

In cases where rules do not generate any instantiations but they have a very high match cost, the match time must be examined with techniques proposed in [Chen and Cheng, 1995a]. Note that the critical point in this algorithm is step (a).

Complexity and Space Reduction   We now analyze the complexity of algorithm 3. In general, $O(n^2)$ is needed to generate the positive condition elements C with n positive condition elements in the program since we check the subset relationship each time we insert a new positive condition element c into C.

The size of the set of WMEs, W, is in general exponential. If W has k variables and each variable has m data items, we will have m^k WMEs as our initial WM. This size can be reduced as described in algorithm 3.

In our analysis, we consider the entire domain of each variable. However, in a real application, it is unlikely that the initial WM ranges over the whole data domain. Since rule-based programs are data-driven, certain input data are required to direct the control flows in the programs. Programmers usually embed control techniques that require the absence of or a specific order of WMEs in the program. Hence, it is more helpful if we can know the timing order of the initial WMEs or which WMEs should not appear in the initial WM.

Our solution to this is ad hoc. We allow the programmer to provide this information in terms of negative condition elements, causing the algorithm to remove the WMEs associated with these condition elements from the initially generated WM, and hence to reduce the size of the initial WM. In addition to providing negative condition elements, programmers can directly (manually) eliminate some of the WMEs we generate before their use in determining the firing sequence.

The Ordering of the Initial WMEs   To find the maximal execution time (in terms of the number of rule firings and match time) of a rule base, we need to determine the firing sequences of the rules, given an initial WM. Since the strategy of selecting an instantiation from the conflict set is based on the recency of WMEs, the order in which the initial WMEs are generated becomes a factor in determining the firing sequence unless the LHS conditions of each rule are independent. Consider the following example:

```
(p p1
  (c1 ^a1 <x> ^a2 <y>)
  (c2 ^a1 3 ^a2 <x>)
-->
  (remove 1))
(p p2
  (c1 ^a1 <x> ^a2 1)
  (c2 ^a1 <x> ^a2 <y>)
-->
  (modify 1 ^a2 <y>))
```

Suppose I_1 and I_2 are two instantiations of rules p1 and p2, respectively. The WME (c1 ^a1 1 ^a2 1) associates with both I_1 and I_2. Firing one of these two instantiations will remove the other from the conflict set. Deciding which rule to fire first depends on the time tag of WMEs satisfying the second condition element of both rules, that is, (c2 ^a1 3 ^a2 <x>) and (c2 ^a1 <x> ^a2 <y>). Hence, different timing analysis results are produced if we generate the WMEs satisfying these two condition elements in different orders.

However, when programmers design their systems, it is unlikely that they take time tags of WMEs into consideration. If programmers do know the property of the time tags, they should know the generating order of WMEs in the initial WM. We can directly arrange them manually. Usually some control techniques are involved to determine which instantiation is chosen to execute. In the above two rules, if programmers cannot predict the properties of time tags of WMEs, they would not know which rule's instantiation should be executed. Without knowing the control flow of the program, this will lead to a debugging and maintenance problem. Several control techniques [Brownston et al., 1986; Cooper and Wogrin, 1988] have been proposed and implemented in many applications. Many of them require additional WMEs which are called *control WMEs*. These WMEs do not belong to the data domain of the application but direct the program flow by their time tags or by their presence or absence. The information of the *control WMEs* should be known a priori and given to the timing analyzer. We can either put the information in the user's negative condition elements as we generate the initial WM, or directly edit the initial WM after we generate it.

11.2.6 Implementation and Experiment

This tool has been implemented on a DEC 5000/240 workstation. The programs are tested under the RISC/Ultrix OPS5 environment.

Implementation   Given an OPS5 program in the file *file.ops*, this tool first asks for the number of possible data of each attribute. If the data items of each attribute are given in the file *file.dom*, the domain of the attributes of the WMEs will be based on it. The description of *file.dom* is

domain ::= entity[+]
entity   ::= classname attribute constant[+] *#*

An example is given as follows.

```
entity name R-A-0 R-A-1 T-A-0 T-A-1 #
entity state nominal failed suspect #
entity mode on off #
entity backup R-A-0 R-A-1 T-A-0 T-A-1 #
relationship from R-A-0 R-A-1 T-A-0 T-A-1 #
relationship to R-A-0 R-A-1 T-A-0 T-A-1 #
relationship state nominal failed suspect #
relationship mode on off #
relationship type direct #
problem entity R-A-0 R-A-1 T-A-0 T-A-1 #
answer name R-A-0 R-A-1 T-A-0 T-A-1 #
answer ans yes no #
step label find_bad_things printed_good #
```

If *file.dom* is not found, the tool automatically searches the possible data items of each attribute from the semantic restrictions of the program. Each constant appearing as the value of attribute *attri* will be assigned as a data item of attribute *attri*. For example, in the following rule

```
(p p1
  (a ^a1 A ^a2 <x>)
  (a ^a1 B ^a2 <x>)
-->
  (make b ^b1 C ^b2 D)
  (modify 1 ^a1 C))
```

A, B, and C are assigned as the data items of attribute a1 because they appear as the values of this attribute. C is also assigned to the data items of attribute b1. D is assigned to attribute b2.

If the number of data items is less than the input number, the tool generates arbitrary constants as the remaining data items. For example, if we input five data items of attribute a1 in class a, then we have three items in a1's domain. The other two items are arbitrarily generated as &a1-1 and &a1-2. These arbitrary constants do not affect the timing properties since they only match LHS variables. All LHS constant data items can be generated from the previous search.

The user's negative condition elements are given in a separate file, *file.usr*. The Backus-Naur Form (BNF) description of the negative condition elements and variable range is given below.

neg-cond-elements ::= -(classname attributes-values*)
attributes-values   ::= ↑attribute op value | ↑attribute value
op   ::= = | ⟨⟩
value   ::= variable | constant

variable-range   ::= variable constant⁺ #

Several terms have been left undefined. *classname* and *attribute* must be defined in the declaration of the original program. *variable*, defined in *variable-range*, must be defined in *value*. *neg-cond-elements* specifies the negative condition elements. *variable-range* specifies the boundary of variables.

Three files are generated by this tool: *file.WM*, *file.All*, and *filetest.ops*. File *file.WM* contains the set of initial WMEs that is the union of all LHS condition elements. File *file.All* contains all possible WMEs in the data domain. Neither file includes the WMEs satisfying the user's negative condition elements. The set of WMEs in *file.All* causes maximum matching time and should also cause maximum rule firings. Users can modify *file.WM* and *file.All* to remove unnecessary WMEs or rearrange the order of these WMEs. File *filetest.ops* is the test program, which eliminates the negative condition elements and modifies corresponding condition numbers on the RHS of rules.

Industrial Example: Experiments on the OMS OPS5 Program   No data are given in *oms.dom*, so the tool searches possible data items from the semantics

RULE NAME	# FIRINGS	LHS TIME	RHS TIME
CHECK-GROUP	333	228	130
CHECK-GROUP-MANIFOLDS	0	5	0
SECURE-ARCS	0	1	0
VALVE-CL	190	17	109
RCS-REGS	7	11	12
VALVE-OP	187	5	80
OMS-REGS	7	1	3
SWITCH-ON	190	12	49
	914	280	383

Figure 11.4   CPU timing report of the OMS expert system.

automatically. *oms.WM* generatres 6192 WMEs. The timing report of rule firings and CPU time is given in Figure 11.4.

The LHS time is determined by measuring the amount of CPU time spent at each two-input node that leads to that rule's instantiation, regardless of how many times the rule has fired. Therefore, a high LHS time may mean that the rule does efficient matching to produce instantiations, or may indicate that a large amount of partial, perhaps unnecessary, matching is taking place [Cooper and Wogrin, 1988].

The RHS time for a rule is the sum of the CPU time spent for all firings of that rule. The time spent on the RHS is measured by the total matching time incurred from the actions on the RHS of the rule. The RHS time divided by the number of times the rule has fired gives the average time for firing this rule [Cooper and Wogrin, 1988].

Five sets of WMEs are randomly generated as test data. Figure 11.5 shows the results of the timing analysis.

11.3   CHENG–CHEN TIMING ANALYSIS METHODOLOGY

Now we describe another approach for determining a priori the maximal response time of predicate-logic rule-based programs. Given a program p, the *response-time analysis problem* is to determine the maximal response time of p. Again, we study

# WMEs	Firings	LHS Time	RHS Time
6192	914	280	383
1150	738	150	226
917	500	108	205
3874	545	109	189
1132	730	254	354
205	50	9	17

Figure 11.5   Test results of the OMS expert system.

this problem in the context of OPS5 production systems. Two aspects of the response time of a program are considered, the maximal number of rule firings and the maximal number of basic comparisons made by the Rete network during the execution of the program.

The response-time analysis problem is in general undecidable. However, a program terminates in a finite time if the rule triggering pattern of this program satisfies certain conditions. Here we present four such termination conditions for OPS5 production systems. An algorithm for computing an upper bound on the number of rule firings is then given. To have a better idea of the time required during execution, we present an algorithm that computes the maximal time required during the match phase in terms of the number of comparisons made by the Rete network. This measurement is sufficient since the match phase consumes about 90% of the execution time.

11.3.1 Introduction

Although the response-time analysis problem is in general undecidable, we observe that, through appropriate classification, several classes of production systems exist for which the property of termination is guaranteed. Each of these classes of production systems is characterized by an execution termination condition. Hence, we tackle the response-time analysis problem by first determining whether the given system is in one of the classes with the property of execution termination and then computing an upper bound on the maximal response time, if possible.

A graph, called the *potential instantiation graph*, showing the potential rule triggering patterns, is defined to be used as the basis to classify OPS5 programs. We show that a program always terminates in a bounded number of recognize–act cycles if its potential instantiation graph is acyclic. An algorithm, Algorithm_A, used to compute an upper bound on the number of recognize–act cycles during program execution is then given. This algorithm also computes the respective maximal numbers of working memory elements that may match the individual condition elements of rules during the execution of a program. These numbers are crucial in determining the time required in the match phase during the execution. We present an algorithm, Algorithm_M, to utilize these numbers to compute the maximal number of comparisons made by the Rete network in the match phase, since it is well known that the match phase consumes about 90% of the execution time [Ishida, 1994]. Furthermore, several classes of programs with cyclic potential instantiation graphs have been found to also have bounded response times. We will show how we can apply these algorithms to programs in one of these acyclic classes.

On the other hand, the response time of programs with cyclic potential rule firing patterns usually depends on the value of run-time data, which cannot be known in advance. It is not realistic to try to develop an algorithm to predict the response time upper bounds of a program with cyclic potential rule firing patterns. Determining whether a given program with cyclic potential rule firing patterns always terminates is the most we can do at this time.

The property of termination of a given program depends on whether all of its potential rule firing cycles terminate. Due to the lack of run-time information that is crucial in determining the satisfiability of condition elements, a conservative approach has to be taken in static analysis to determine whether a condition element can be satisfied by a working memory element whose value/content cannot be known in advance. The potential instantiation graph produced as a result of the static analysis usually contains many edges that are nonexistent. This in turn means that many cycles found in the potential instantiation graph are nonexistent. With the help of the programmer, some of these nonexistent edges/cycles can be detected and removed from the potential instantiation graph. We will discuss later how the programmer can help improve/adjust the potential instantiation graph.

When knowledge-based or production systems are used in time-critical applications, it is essential to predict, prior to their execution, their worst-case response time during actual execution. This static timing analysis problem is extremely difficult even for propositional-logic-based rule-based systems such as EQL [Cheng et al., 1993]. For predicate-logic-based rule-based systems such as those implemented in OPS5 and OPS5-style languages, very few practical static analysis approaches are available. Together with the Cheng–Tsai approach, this approach thus makes a significant contribution to the state-of-the-art for solving this static timing analysis problem by presenting a formal framework and a useful tool set for worst-case response-time prediction of a class of OPS5 and OPS5-style production systems. The proposed analysis techniques are based on (1) the detection of termination conditions, which can be checked by a semantic analysis of the relationships among rules in a rulebase, and (2) the systematic trace of tokens in the match network. These techniques are more efficient than those that rely on longest-path analysis in a state-transition system corresponding to a given rule-based system.

The remainder of this section is organized as follows. We first define the potential instantiation graph and then classify OPS5 programs using this graph. Then we present the response-time analysis of the OPS5 production systems. We first show the property of termination of programs with acyclic potential instantiation graphs. Two algorithms to compute the response time of OPS5 production systems of this class are then introduced. Next, the programs with cyclic potential instantiation graphs are investigated. We show how we can apply the proposed algorithms to one class of programs with cyclic potential instantiation graphs. Then two more cyclic classes of programs with the property of termination will also be introduced. Finally, we describe the experimental results.

11.3.2 Classification of OPS5 Programs

Let r_1 and r_2 denote two OPS5 rules, A denote an action in the RHS of r_1, and e denote a condition element in the LHS of r_2. Action A *matches* the condition element e if the execution of A produces/removes a WME that matches e. Based on the types of A and e, four cases exist in which A matches e.

M1 The execution of *A produces* a WME that matches the *nonnegated* condition element *e*. In this case, r_2 may be instantiated as a result of the firing of r_1.

M2 The execution of *A produces* a WME that matches the *negated* condition element *e*. If this is the case, the system will be in a state where r_2 cannot be instantiated immediately after the firing of r_1.

M3 The execution of *A removes* a WME that matches the *nonnegated* condition element *e*. In this case, r_2 may still be instantiated after the firing of r_1 if there are more than one WME matching *e* before the firing. On the other hand, if r_2 is not instantiated before the firing of r_1, it cannot be instantiated immediately after the firing of r_1.

M4 The execution of *A removes* a WME that matches the *negated* condition element *e*. In this case, r_2 may be instantiated as a result of the firing of r_1.

r_1 is said to *dis-instantiate* r_2 if no instantiation of r_2 exists at each state reached as a result of the firing of r_1. Of the four cases above, only case M2 guarantees that r_2 cannot be instantiated as a result of the firing of r_1. Hence, r_1 dis-instantiates r_2 if and only if the RHS of r_1 contains an action that produces a WME matching a negated condition element in the LHS of r_2. r_1 is said to *potentially instantiate* r_2 if an instantiation of r_2 exists as a result of a firing of r_1. Hence, r_1 potentially instantiates r_2 if case M2 does not occur and either M1 or M4 occurs. That is,

- the RHS of r_1 does not contain an action that produces a WME matching a negated condition element in the LHS of r_2, and
- the RHS of r_1 contains an action that either produces a WME matching a non-negated condition element of r_2 or removes a WME matching a negated condition element in the LHS of r_2.

Definition 6 (Potential Instantiation graph). Let *p* denote a set of production rules. The potential instantiation (PI) graph, $G_p^{PI} = (V, E)$, is a directed graph demonstrating the potential rule-triggering pattern of *p*. *V* is a set of vertices, each of which represents a rule such that *V* contains a vertex labeled *r* if and only if a rule named *r* is in *p*. *E* is a set of directed edges such that *E* contains the edge $\langle r_1, r_2 \rangle$ if and only if the rule r_1 potentially instantiates the rule r_2.

Definition 7 (Cycle classification). Let $\langle r_1, r_2 \rangle$ denote an edge in G_p^{PI}. The edge $\langle r_1, r_2 \rangle$ is classified as a

- *p*(ositive)-type edge if r_1 does not contain an action that removes a WME matching a negated condition element of r_2,
- *n*(egative)-type edge if r_1 does not contain an action that produces a WME matching a nonnegated condition element of r_2, or
- *m*(ixed)-type edge if it is neither a *p*-type edge nor an *n*-type edge.

A *path* is denoted as $\langle r_i, r_{i+1}, \ldots, r_k \rangle$, where $\langle r_j, r_{j+1} \rangle \in G_p^{PI}$ and $j = i \ldots$ $k - 1$. A *cycle* is a path $\langle r_i, r_{i+1}, \ldots, r_k \rangle$ and $r_i = r_k$. A cycle $C \in G_p^{PI}$ is an *n*-type

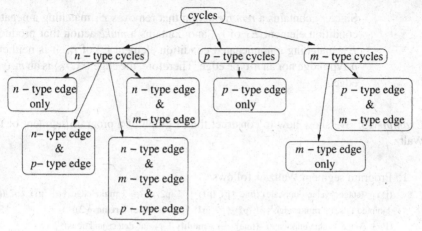

Figure 11.6 PI graph cycle classification.

cycle if it contains an n-type edge, a p-type cycle if it contains only p-type edges or an m-type cycle if it is neither an n-type cycle nor a p-type cycle, as shown in Figure 11.6.

Example 14. Consider the following three cases, each of which represents a different edge type.

Case 1: (P r_1 ($E_1 \cdots$) ($E_2 \cdots$) $\longrightarrow$ (**make** E_3 ↑name ⟨N1⟩ ↑state good) (**remove** 1))
(P r_2 ($E_2 \cdots$) (E_3 ↑state good) $\longrightarrow$ ($\cdots$) ($\cdots$))
r_1 does not contain an action that produces a WME matching a negated condition element of r_2. Furthermore, the firing of r_1 produces a WME of the class E_3 that matches one of the nonnegated condition elements of r_2, and r_1 does not contain an action that removes a WME matching a negated condition element of r_2. Hence, r_1 potentially instantiates r_2. G_p^{PI} contains the p-type edge ⟨r_1, r_2⟩.

Case 2: (P r_3 (E_1 ↑dept Math)($E_2 \cdots$) $\longrightarrow$ (**make** $E_3 \cdots$) (**modify** $E_2 \cdots$) (**remove** 1))
(P r_4 ($E_4 \cdots$) –(E_1 ↑dept Math) $\longrightarrow$ ($\cdots$) ($\cdots$))
The firing of r_3 produces a WME of the class E_3 that does not match the nonnegated condition element E_4 of r_4. Furthermore, r_3 contains a *modify* action that deletes the old WME E_2 and produces the new WME E_2 and does not match a nonnegated condition element E_4 of r_4. So, the edge ⟨r_3, r_4⟩ is an n-type edge.

Case 3: (P r_5 (E_1 ↑dept Math) $\longrightarrow$ (**make** E_3 ↑name N1↑state good) (**remove** 1))
(P r_6 ($E_2 \cdots$) –(E_1 ↑dept Math)(E_3 ↑state good) $\longrightarrow$ ($\cdots$) ($\cdots$))

Since r_5 contains a *remove* action that removes E_1 matching a negated condition element E_1 of r_6, and contains a *make* action that produces E_3, matching a nonnegated condition element E3 of r_6, it is neither a p-type edge nor an n-type edge. Therefore, the edge $\langle r_5, r_6 \rangle$ is an m-type edge.

Example 15. We show how to construct the PI graph of a program segment of the Waltz.

1. Program segment Waltz as follows:

   (P r_1 (stage ↑value duplicate) (line ↑p1 ⟨p1⟩ ↑p2 ⟨p2⟩) ⟶ (**make** edge ↑p1 ⟨p1⟩ ↑p2 ⟨p2⟩ ↑jointed false) (**make** edge ↑p1 ⟨p2⟩ ↑p2 ⟨p1⟩ ↑jointed false) (**remove** 2))

   (P r_2 (stage ↑value duplicate) –(line) ⟶ (**modify** 1 ↑value detect_junctions))

   (P r_3 (stage ↑value detect_junctions) (edge ↑p1 ⟨base_point⟩ ↑p2 ⟨p1⟩ ↑jointed false) (edge ↑p1 ⟨base_point⟩ ↑p2 {⟨p2⟩ ⟨⟩ ⟨p1⟩} ↑jointed false) (edge ↑p1 ⟨base_point⟩ ↑p2 {⟨p3⟩ ⟨⟩ ⟨p1⟩ ⟨⟩ ⟨p2⟩} ↑jointed false) ⟶ (**make** junction ↑type arrow ↑base_point ⟨base_point⟩) (**modify** 2 ↑jointed true) (**modify** 3 ↑jointed true) (**modify** 4 ↑jointed true))

   (P r_4 (stage ↑value detect_junctions) (edge ↑p1 ⟨base_point⟩ ↑p2 ⟨p1⟩ ↑jointed false) (edge ↑p1 ⟨base_point⟩ ↑p2 {⟨p2⟩ ⟨⟩ ⟨p1⟩} ↑jointed false) –(edge ↑p1 ⟨base_point⟩ ↑p2 {⟨⟩ ⟨p1⟩ ⟨⟩ ⟨p2⟩}) ⟶ (**make** junction ↑type L ↑base_point ⟨base_point⟩ ↑p1 ⟨p1⟩ ↑p2 ⟨p2⟩) (**modify** 2 ↑jointed true) (**modify** 3 ↑jointed true))

   (P r_5 (stage ↑value detect_junctions) – (edge ↑jointed false) ⟶ (**modify** 1 ↑value find_initial_boundary))

   (P r_6 (stage ↑value find_initial_boundary) (junction ↑type L ↑base_point ⟨base_point⟩ ↑p1 ⟨p1⟩ ↑p2 ⟨p2⟩) (edge ↑p1 ⟨base_point⟩ ↑p2 ⟨p1⟩ ↑label nil) (edge ↑p1 ⟨base_point⟩ ↑p2 ⟨p2⟩ ↑label nil) –(junction ↑base_point > ⟨base_point⟩) ⟶ (**modify** 3 ↑label B) (**modify** 4 ↑label B) (**modify** 1 ↑value find_second_boundary))

   (P r_7 (stage ↑value find_initial_boundary) (junction ↑type arrow ↑base_point ⟨bp⟩ ↑p1 ⟨p1⟩ ↑p2 ⟨p2⟩ ↑p3 ⟨p3⟩) (edge ↑p1 ⟨bp⟩ ↑p2 ⟨p1⟩ ↑label nil) (edge ↑p1 ⟨bp⟩ ↑p2 ⟨p2⟩ ↑label nil) (edge ↑p1 ⟨bp⟩ ↑p2 ⟨p3⟩ ↑label nil) –(junction ↑base_point > ⟨bp⟩) ⟶ (**modify** 3 ↑label B) (**modify** 4 ↑label plus) (**modify** 5 ↑label B) (**modify** 1 ↑value find_second_boundary))

   (P r_8 (stage ↑value find_second_boundary) (junction ↑type L ↑base_point ⟨base_point⟩ ↑p1 ⟨p1⟩ ↑p2 ⟨p2⟩) (edge ↑p1 ⟨base_point⟩ ↑p2 ⟨p1⟩ ↑label nil) (edge ↑p1 ⟨base_point⟩ ↑p2 ⟨p2⟩ ↑label nil) –(junction ↑base_point < ⟨base_point⟩) ⟶ (**modify** 3 ↑label B) (**modify** 4 ↑label B) (**modify** 1 ↑value labeling))

   (P r_9 (stage ↑value find_second_boundary) (junction ↑type arrow ↑base_point ⟨bp⟨ ↑p1 ⟨p1⟩ ↑p2 ⟨p2⟩ ↑p3 ⟨p3⟩) (edge ↑p1 ⟨bp⟩ ↑p2 ⟨p1⟩ ↑label nil) (edge ↑p1 ⟨bp⟩ ↑p2 ⟨p2⟩ ↑label nil) (edge ↑p1 ⟨b⟩ ↑p2 ⟨p3⟩ ↑label nil) –(junction ↑base_point < ⟨bp⟩) ⟶ (**modify** 3 ↑label B) (**modify** 4 ↑label plus) (**modify** 5 ↑label B) (**modify** 1 ↑value labeling))

   (P r_{10} (stage ↑value labeling) (edge ↑p1 ⟨p1⟩ ↑p2 ⟨p2⟩ ↑label {⟨label⟩ ⟨plus minus B⟩} ↑plotted nil) (edge ↑p1 ⟨p2⟩ ↑p2 ⟨p1⟩ ↑label nil ↑plotted nil) ⟶ (**modify** 2 ↑plotted t) (**modify** 3 ↑label ⟨label⟩ ↑plotted t))

2. We translate these rules into a potential instantiation graph based on definition 6 and definition 7.

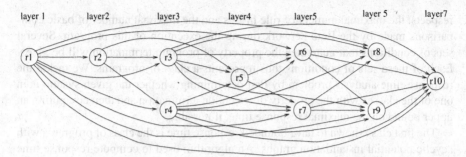

Figure 11.7   PI graph of Waltz program segment.

3. The PI graph of the Waltz program segment is:

	r_1	r_2	r_3	r_4	r_5	r_6	r_7	r_8	r_9	r_{10}
r_1	-	m	p	p	-	p	p	p	p	p
r_2	-	-	p	p	p	-	-	-	-	-
r_3	-	-	-	-	m	p	p	p	p	p
r_4	-	-	-	-	m	p	p	p	p	p
r_5	-	-	-	-	-	p	p	-	-	-
r_6	-	-	-	-	-	-	-	p	p	p
r_7	-	-	-	-	-	-	-	p	p	p
r_8	-	-	-	-	-	-	-	-	-	p
r_9	-	-	-	-	-	-	-	-	-	p
r_{10}	-	-	-	-	-	-	-	-	-	-

"p" stands for the existence of a p-type edge, "m" the existence of an m-type edge, and "-" no edge at all. For example, $\langle r_1, r_2 \rangle$ is an m-type edge and $\langle r_5, r_6 \rangle$ is a p-type edge.

4. We then transform the PI graph into an n-partite PI graph (shown in Figure 11.7).

Our analysis tool constructs the PI graph of the program automatically.

Our framework for static timing analysis of OPS5 programs is as follows. We first extract the semantic relationships among rules in a program by representing it as a potential instantiation graph. Then, based on the type of the constructed PI graph, we determine whether the program satisfies a termination condition. If it does, we proceed to check its worst-case execution time in terms of the number of rule firings and match comparisons. For programs with potential cycles, we show how the programmer can provide assistance in computing a conservative response time upper bound.

11.3.3   Response Time of OPS5 Systems

In this section, we study the response-time analysis problem in the context of OPS5 production systems. The response time of an OPS5 program is investigated in two respects: the maximal number of rule firings and the maximal number of basic comparisons made by the Rete network during the execution of this program. Several sets of conditions that guarantee the property of program termination will be given. Each of these sets of conditions thus represents a class of programs. We tackle the response-time analysis problem by first determining whether the given system is in one of the classes with the property of execution termination and then computing an upper bound on the maximal response time, if possible.

The first class shown to have bounded response time is the class of programs with acyclic potential instantiation graphs. An algorithm used to compute response time upper bounds of programs in this class is introduced.

Theorem 2. Let p denote a set of rules. The execution of p always terminates in a bounded number of recognize–act cycles if the potential instantiation graph G_p^{PI} is acyclic.

Proof. The proof is simliar to the proof of termination in [Aiken, Widom, and Hellerstein, 1992]. Basically, the potential instantiation graph has similar behavior as the triggering graph in [Aiken, Widom, and Hellerstein, 1992]. □

Corollary 1. Let p denote a set of rules. If the execution of p will not terminate in a bounded number of recognize–act cycles, a cycle C exists in the potential instantiation graph G_p^{PI}. Let $C = \langle r_1, \ldots, r_k, r_{k+1} \rangle$ and $r_1 = r_{k+1}$. r_i potentially instantiates r_{i+1}, where $i = 1 \ldots k$, and r_i will fire infinitely often.

We now present a response-time upper bound algorithm that computes the maximal number of instantiations that may exist during the execution and returns this number as the maximal number of rule firings. A direct result of this strategy is that the upper bound obtained is not affected by the resolution strategy used in the select phase of the recognize–act cycle. No matter what resolution strategy is used, no more than the maximal number of instantiations may exist during the execution. Hence, the maximal number of instantiations that may exist is an upper bound on the number of recognize–act cycles during the execution.

Number of Rule Firings   One of the major characteristics of production systems is that the execution time depends on the content of the initial working memory. Not only do the classes (or types) of initial WMEs affect the execution time, but also the number of WMEs of each class plays a role in required execution time. For example, an initial working memory with three WMEs of a certain class and an initial working memory with 30 WMEs of the same class may require different amounts of time for the production system to complete execution. Furthermore, different executions may apply to different sets of initial working memory.

Although the numbers and classes of initial WMEs can only be known at runtime, it is reasonable to assume that the experienced software developer (or user) has an idea of the maximal possible number of initial WMEs of each class in which the application domain may result. In addition, the proposed response-time upper bound algorithm is based on counting the maximal number of instantiations, which is increasing with respect to the number of WMEs of each class. The response time upper bound obtained by applying the proposed algorithm to an initial working memory consisting of the maximal possible number of WMEs of each class is a response time upper bound of the system, since all of the executions cannot have a larger number of WMEs than the (already known) maximal possible number of WMEs. Hence, to obtain a response time upper bound of an OPS5 production system, the developers (or users) need to apply the proposed algorithm to an initial working memory consisting of the maximal possible number of WMEs of each class.

Let r denote a rule of p with acyclic PI graph and c_r^i denote the ith nonnegated condition element in the LHS of r. To simplify the explanations later, a working memory element is classified as an *old* WME if it exists at the invocation; otherwise, it is a *new* WME since it is produced as a result of rule firings. The WMEs matching c_r^i are called *matching WMEs of c_r^i*. A WME is a *matching WME of r* if it is a matching WME of one of the condition elements in the LHS of r.

r can be fired only if it is instantiated, and each instantiation of r can be fired at most once. According to theorem 2, the execution of p always terminates in a bounded number of recognize–act cycles. r can thus be fired at most only a bounded number of times. Hence, only a bounded number of instantiations of r must exist during the execution of p. This means that there are only a bounded number of matching WMEs matching to r during the execution of p. There are only two kinds of matching WMEs of r: *old matching WMEs of r*, which exist at the invocation, and *new matching WMEs of r*, which result from the firings of rules during the execution. The number of matching WMEs of r is equal to the number of old matching WMEs of r plus the number of new matching WMEs of r. Hence, the number of old matching WMEs of r plus an upper bound on the number of new matching WMEs of r is an upper bound on the number of matching WMEs of r.

Since G_p^{PI} is acyclic, new matching WMEs of r result from the firings of its predecessors in G_p^{PI}. To find the number of new matching WMEs, G_p^{PI} is drawn as an *n-partite* graph from left to right. Assume there are n layers in G_p^{PI}. The layers in G_p^{PI} are labeled from left to right as *layer 1, layer 2, ..., layer n*. For each i, $1 \leq i \leq n$, let p_i denote the set of rules in layer i, where n is the number of layers in G_p^{PI} (as shown in Figure 11.7). Suppose r is in layer i. If $i = 1$, no new matching WMEs of r can be produced as a result of rule firings. If $i > 1$, only the firings of those rules in layer 1 through layer $i - 1$ can possibly produce new matching WMEs of r. If the numbers of new WMEs to r, respectively resulting from the firings of rules in layer 1 through layer $i - 1$, have all been calculated, the number of matching WMEs of r can be easily calculated. Once we obtain the number of matching WMEs of r, we can calculate an upper bound on the number of firings by r. Furthermore, if $i < n$, we can compute upper bounds on the numbers of new WMEs, resulting from the firing(s) of r, to rules in layer $i + 1$ through layer n. Hence, the numbers of matching WMEs of individual rules and the upper bounds on the numbers of rule firings are computed in the order corresponding to positions of the rules in G_p^{PI}. From left to right, the numbers of matching WMEs (and the upper bounds on the numbers of firings) to rules in layer 1 are computed first, then to rules in layer 2, and so on.

An Upper Bound on the Number of Firings by *r*   Assume there are k non-negated condition elements (ignore the negated condition elements) in the LHS of r. For each $i, 1 \leq i \leq k$, let N_r^i denote the number of matching WMEs of c_r^i, and d_r^i denote the number of matching WMEs of c_r^i that are removed from the working memory as a result of *one firing* of r. There are at most $N_r^1 * N_r^2 * \cdots * N_r^k$ instantiations of r with respect to this working memory. However, if d_r^i is not equal to 0, there can be at most $\lceil N_r^i / d_r^i \rceil$ firings of r before all of the matching WMEs of c_r^i are deleted as a result of these firings. This means that there can be at most

$$I_r = \min(N_r^1 * N_r^2 * \cdots * N_r^k, \lceil N_r^1/d_r^1 \rceil, \lceil N_r^2/d_r^2 \rceil, \ldots, \lceil N_r^k/d_r^k \rceil) \qquad (11.1)$$

firings of r, unless the firings of rules result in new WMEs that result in new instantiation(s) of r. Note that $\lceil N_r^i/d_r^i \rceil \equiv \infty$ if d_r^i is equal to 0.

Example 16. Assume there are three WMEs of the class E_1, four WMEs of the class E_2, and three WMEs of the class E_3 in the current working memory. Consider the following two rules in the production memory.

$$(\text{P } r_1 \; (E_1 \cdots) \; (E_2 \cdots) \; (E_2 \cdots) \; -(E_3 \cdots) \; \longrightarrow \; (\text{make} \cdots) (\text{make} \cdots) \,)$$

$$(\text{P } r_2 \; (E_1 \cdots) \; (E_2 \cdots) \; (E_3 \cdots) \; \longrightarrow \; (\text{make } E_4 \cdots) (\text{remove } 2) \,)$$

Without knowing the contents of these WMEs, there are at most $N_{r_1}^1 * N_{r_1}^2 * N_{r_1}^3 = 3 * 4 * 4 = 48$ instantiations of r_1 with respect to this working memory. Since each firing of r_1 does not delete any WME, at most 48 firings of r_1 exist. Similarly, at most $N_{r_2}^1 * N_{r_2}^2 * N_{r_2}^3 = 3*4*3 = 36$ instantiations of r_2 exist with respect to this working memory. However, each firing of r_2 removes a WME of the class E_2. Hence, there are at most $\min(36, \lceil 4/1 \rceil) = 4$ firings of r_2 with respect to this working memory.

Maximal Numbers of New Matching WMEs   Assume it has been determined (by the above method) that there are at most I_r possible instantiations/firings of r during the execution of p. An RHS action with the command **make** results in a new WME and increases the number of WMEs of the specified class by one, an RHS action with the command **modify** modifies the content of a WME and does not changes the number of WMEs of the specified class, and an RHS action with the command **remove** removes a WME and decreases the number of WMEs of the specified class by one. Since there are at most I_r possible instantiations of r, r can be fired a total of 0 to I_r times. It is possible that none of the I_r *possible* instantiations exists. If this is the case, r will not be fired. This means that the number of WMEs of each class will not be affected by r in the worst case in terms of the capability of reducing the number of WMEs even though the RHS of r contains an action(s) with the command **remove**. On the other hand, if the RHS of r contains x actions with the command **make** on the class E, then each firing of r results in x new WMEs of the class E. This means that a maximum of $x * I_r$ new WMEs of the class E may be created as a result of the firings of r. Therefore, for the purpose of obtaining the maximal number of WMEs that may affect the instantiatibility of rules, only the actions with the command **make** need to be considered. Let $\overline{N_E^r}$ denote the number of actions, in the RHS of r, with the command **make** that produce WMEs of the class E.

Example 17. Assume there are two WMEs of class E_1, 2 WMEs of class E_2, and one WMEs of class E_3 in the current working memory. Let r_3 below be one of the rules in the production memory.

$$(P\ r_3\ (E_1 \cdots)\ (E_2 \cdots)\ (E_2 \cdots) \longrightarrow (\textbf{modify } 1 \cdots)\ (\textbf{remove } 2)\ (\textbf{make } E_3 \cdots)\ )$$

There are at most $\min(2*2*2, \lceil 2/1 \rceil) = 2$ firings of r_3 with respect to this working memory. Each firing of r_3 produces a new WME of the class E_3. There are at most $m_{r_3}^3 * I_{r_3} = 1 * 2 = 2$ new WMEs of the class E_3 as a result of these firings of r_3. Hence, there are at most two WMEs of class E_1, two WMEs of class E_2, and three WMEs of class E_3 after these firings of r_3.

For each rule r in layer i, we compute the maximal number of new WMEs that result from the firing(s) of r for each working memory element class. For each class E, the sum of those maximal numbers of new WMEs of E, respectively produced by the firings of rules in layer i, is an upper bound on the number of new WMEs of E produced by layer i. Applying the above method, we can find the maximal number of new WMEs of each class produced as a result of the firings of each rule. However, not all of the new WMEs produced as a result of the firings of one rule, say r_1, may be new matching WMEs of all of the other rules. Let r_1 denote a rule whose RHS contains an action that matches one of the nonnegated condition elements in the LHS of r_2. If r_1 is in a layer higher than r_2, those WMEs produced as a result of the firings of r_1 cannot be used to instantiate r_2; otherwise there would be a path from r_1 to r_2 in G_p^{PI}, meaning that r_1 would be in a layer lower than r_2. Hence, the firings of rules can produce new matching WMEs only to rules in higher levels.

Assume r_1 is in a layer lower than r_2. A new matching WME of the nonnegated condition element $c_{r_2}^i$ in the LHS of r_2 may result from an action, say $a_{r_1}^j$, that matches $c_{r_2}^i$, with the command **make** or **modify** in the RHS of r_1. If $a_{r_1}^j$ is a **make** action, the resulting WME is a new matching WME of $c_{r_2}^i$. This means that the number of new matching WMEs of $c_{r_2}^i$ should be increased by one due to $a_{r_1}^j$, as a result of each firing of r_1. If the RHS of r_1 contains x **make** actions that match $c_{r_2}^i$, the number of new matching WMEs of $c_{r_2}^i$ should be increased by $x * I_{r_1}$ as a result of the firings of r_1.

If $a_{r_1}^j$ is a **modify** action on a WME that matches $c_{r_2}^i$, the presence of $a_{r_1}^j$ does not change the number of matching WMEs of $c_{r_2}^i$. If $a_{r_1}^j$ is a **modify** action on a WME that does not match $c_{r_2}^i$, the resulting WME is a new matching WME of $c_{r_2}^i$. This means that the number of new matching WMEs of $c_{r_2}^i$ should also be increased by one due to $a_{r_1}^j$, as a result of each firing of r_1. If the RHS of r_1 contains x **modify** actions that (1) match $c_{r_2}^i$ and (2) modify WMEs that do not match $c_{r_2}^i$, the number

Input An OPS5 program, p.

Output An upper bound, B, on the number of firings by p.

---

1. Set B to 0, and, for each class E_c, let N_{E_c} be the number of old WMEs.
2. For each rule $r \in$ layer 1, initialize N_r^k for each k condition element.
3. Determine all of the $\overline{N_{r_j, r_i}^k}$s and all of the $\overline{N_E^{r_i}}$s.
4. Construct the PI graph G_p^{PI}. Let n be the number of layers in G_p^{PI}.
5. For $l := 1$ to n, Do
   For each rule $r_i \in$ layer l, Do
   (a) $I_{r_i} := \min(N_{r_i}^1 * N_{r_i}^2 * \cdots * N_{r_i}^k, \lceil N_{r_i}^1 / d_{r_i}^1 \rceil, \lceil N_{r_i}^2 / d_{r_i}^2 \rceil, \ldots, \lceil N_{r_i}^k / d_{r_i}^k \rceil)$;
   (b) $B := B + I_{r_i}$;
   (c) For each class E_c, Do $N_{E_c} := N_{E_c} + I_{r_i} * \overline{N_{E_c}^{r_i}}$;
   (d) For each rule $r_j \in$ layer m, $m > l$, Do $N_{r_j}^k := N_{r_j}^k + \overline{N_{r_j, r_i}^k} * I_{r_i}$, for all k.
6. Output(B).

Figure 11.8 Algorithm_A.

---

of new matching WMEs of $c_{r_2}^i$ should be increased by $x * I_{r_1}$ as a result of the firings of r_1.

Algorithm_A Based on the strategy described above, we have developed the following algorithm, Algorithm_A (see Figure 11.8), to compute an upper bound on the number of recognize–act cycles during the execution of OPS5 programs. Note that $N_{i,j}^k$ denotes the number of new matching WMEs of the kth condition element of r_i produced as a result of *one firing* of r_j.

An Example We now show the analysis of a program segment of *Waltz*, an expert system that implements the *Waltz labeling* [Winston, 1977] algorithm. This program analyzes the lines of a two-dimensional drawing, and labels them as if they were edges in a three-dimensional object. The analyzed program segment is a subset of 10 rules of Waltz, which has 33 rules, to demonstrate the proposed algorithm. These rules perform the task of finding the boundaries and junctions of objects. For the sole purpose of demonstrating the proposed analysis algorithm, the understanding of the semantics of the Waltz algorithm (or program) is not necessary.

Assume, at the invocation, the working memory consists of 20 WMEs of the class *line* and the following WME: *(stage duplicate)*. Following Algorithm_A, the potential instantiation graph of this program segment is built and shown in Figure 11.7. Tables 11.1 and 11.2 show some of the characteristics of this program segment. For each condition element $c_{r_i}^j$ of each rule r_i, the number of removed matching WMEs

TABLE 11.1   Program characteristics—1 of Waltz program segment

	Matching WMEs removed					WMEs increment			
	$d_{r_i}^1$	$d_{r_i}^2$	$d_{r_i}^3$	$d_{r_i}^4$	$d_{r_i}^5$	$\overline{N_{E_s}^{r_i}}$	$\overline{N_{E_l}^{r_i}}$	$\overline{N_{E_e}^{r_i}}$	$\overline{N_{E_j}^{r_i}}$
r_1	0	1				0	0	2	0
r_2	1					0	0	0	0
r_3	0	3	3	3		0	0	0	1
r_4	0	2	2			0	0	0	1
r_5	1					0	0	0	0
r_6	1	0	2	2		0	0	0	0
r_7	1	0	3	3	3	0	0	0	0
r_8	1	0	2	2		0	0	0	0
r_9	1	0	3	3	3	0	0	0	0
r_{10}	0	2	2			0	0	0	0

of $c_{r_i}^j$ as a result of one firing of r_i is shown. Also shown are the respective numbers of new WMEs of each class and respective numbers of new matching WMEs of condition elements of rules respectively produced as a result of each firing of individual rules. For example, Table 11.1 indicates that each firing of r_4 removes two matching WMEs from both the second and the third condition elements of r_4. It is also shown that each firing of r_4 may increase the number of WMEs of the class junction by one.

TABLE 11.2   Program characteristics—2 of Waltz program segment

	Number of new matching WMEs produced per rule firing
r_1	$N_{r_3,r_1}^2, N_{r_3,r_1}^3, N_{r_3,r_1}^4, N_{r_4,r_1}^2, N_{r_4,r_1}^3, N_{r_6,r_1}^3, N_{r_6,r_1}^4, N_{r_7,r_1}^3, N_{r_7,r_1}^4,$
	$N_{r_7,r_1}^5, N_{r_8,r_1}^3, N_{r_8,r_1}^4, N_{r_9,r_1}^3, N_{r_9,r_1}^4, N_{r_9,r_1}^5, N_{r_{10},r_1}^2, N_{r_{10},r_1}^3 : 2$
r_2	$N_{r_3,r_2}^1, N_{r_4,r_2}^1, N_{r_5,r_2}^1 : 1$
r_3	$N_{r_7,r_3}^2, N_{r_9,r_3}^2 : 1$
r_4	$N_{r_6,r_4}^2, N_{r_8,r_4}^2 : 1$
r_5	$N_{r_6,r_5}^1, N_{r_7,r_5}^1 : 1$
r_6	$N_{r_8,r_6}^1, N_{r_9,r_6}^1 : 1 \quad N_{r_{10},r_6}^2 : 2$
r_7	$N_{r_8,r_7}^1, N_{r_9,r_7}^1 : 1 \quad N_{r_{10},r_7}^2 : 3$
r_8	$N_{r_{10},r_8}^1 : 1 \quad N_{r_{10},r_8}^2 : 2$
r_9	$N_{r_{10},r_9}^1 : 1 \quad N_{r_{10},r_9}^2 : 3$
r_{10}	

TABLE 11.3   **Analysis results**

		Number of matching WMEs					Number of WMEs after firings				Number of firings	
		$N_{r_i}^1$	$N_{r_i}^2$	$N_{r_i}^3$	$N_{r_i}^4$	$N_{r_i}^5$	N_{E_s}	N_{E_l}	N_{E_e}	N_{E_j}	I_{r_i}	B
Invocation							1	20	0	0		
Layer 1	r_1	1	20				1	20	40	0	20	20
Layer 2	r_2	1					1	20	40	0	1	21
Layer 3	r_3	1	40	40	40		1	20	40	14	14	
	r_4	1	40	40			1	20	40	20	20	
							1	20	40	34	55	
Layer 4	r_5	1					1	20	40	34	1	56
Layer 5	r_6	1	20	40	40		1	20	40	34	1	
	r_7	1	14	40	40	40	1	20	40	34	1	
							1	20	40	34	58	
Layer 6	r_8	2	20	40	40		1	20	40	34	2	
	r_9	2	14	40	40	40	1	20	40	34	2	
							1	20	40	34	62	
Layer 7	r_{10}	4	55	40			1	20	40	34	20	82

Another table showing the initial values of N_r^ks for all rules and k is created. This table will be modified throughout the analysis process. Due to space limitation, it is not shown in this dissertation. Instead, we incorporate the final values of N_r^ks in Table 11.3, which shows the analysis results. From this table, Algorithm_A determines that there are at most 82 rule firings by this program segment during the execution if there are only 1 WME of the class stage and 20 WMEs of the class line at the invocation.

Match Time   In this section, we compute an upper bound on the time required during the match phase in terms of the number of comparisons made by the Rete algorithm [Forgy, 1982]. Each comparison is a basic testing operation, such as testing whether the value of the attribute $\uparrow$age is greater than 20, whether the value of $\uparrow$sex is M, and so on.

The Rete Network   The Rete Match algorithm is an algorithm to compare a set of LHSs to a set of elements to discover all the instantiations. The given OPS5 program is compiled into a Rete network which receives as input the changes to the working memory and produces as output the modifications to the conflict set. The descriptions of the working memory changes are called tokens. A token consists of a tag and a working memory element. The tag of a token is used to indicate the addition or deletion of the working memory element of the token. When an element is modified, two tokens are sent to the network: one token with tag − indicates that the old element has been deleted from working memory and one token with tag + indicates that the new element has been added. The Rete algorithm uses a tree-structured network (refer to Figure 11.9). Each Rete network has a root node and several terminal nodes. The root node distributes to other nodes the tokens that are passed to the net-

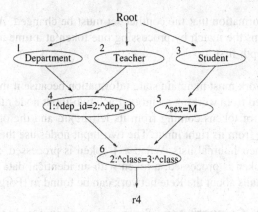

Figure 11.9 The Rete network for r_4.

work. Each of the terminal nodes reports the satisfaction of the LHS of some rule. Other than the root node and terminal nodes, two types of nodes are present in the Rete network: one-input nodes and two-input nodes. Each one-input node tests for the presence of one intra-element feature, while each two-input node tests the inter-element feature(s) applying to the elements it processes. Each of the intra-element features involves only one working memory element. The inter-element features are the conditions involving more than one working memory element.

Example 18. Consider the following rule.

(P r_4
   (Department ↑dep_id⟨D⟩)
   (Teacher ↑dep_id⟨D⟩ ↑class⟨C⟩)
   (Student ↑sex M ↑class⟨C⟩)
  →
  ...)

Rule r_4 is compiled into a Rete network and shown in Figure 11.9. In this figure, the Root node of the network receives the tokens that are sent to this network and passes copies of the tokens to of all its successors. The successors of the Root node are class-checking nodes, which are nodes 1, 2, and 3. Tokens satisfying the class-checking test are passed to the Root node's successors (test that the class of the element is Department, Teacher, or Student). The successors of class-checking nodes are a one-input node (node 5) and a two-input node (node 4). The one-input node tests the intra-element feature (tests the attribute of ↑sex) and sends the tokens to its successors. The two-input node compares tokens from different paths and joins them to create bigger tokens if they satisfy the inter-element constraints of the LHS (test the attribute of ↑dep_id). Node 6 is a two-input node that joins tokens from node 4 and node 5 if they satisfy the inter-element feature (test the attribute of ↑class). The terminal node (node r_4) will receive tokens that instantiate the LHS of r_4. The terminal node sends out the information that the conflict set must be changed. Actually, the Rete algorithm performs the match by processing one token at a time and traversing the entire network depth-first.

The Rete network must maintain state information because it must know what is added to or deleted from working memory. Each two-input node maintains two lists, one called *L-list*, of tokens coming from its left input, and the other called *R-list*, of tokens coming from its right input. The two-input nodes use the tag to determine how to modify their internal lists. When a + token is processed, it is stored in the list. When a − token is processed, a token with an identical data part in the list is deleted. More details about the Rete network can be found in [Forgy, 1982].

The Number of Comparisons Since each one-input node tests for the presence of one intra-element feature, one comparison is conducted whenever a token is passed to a one-input node. On the other hand, a two-input node may conduct many comparisons, since many pairs of tokens may have to be checked whenever a token is passed to this node. Each pair of tokens consists of the incoming token and one of the tokens in the maintained list corresponding to the other input. Hence, for each two-input node, we need to know the maximal number of tokens in each of the two maintained lists.

Assume v is a two-input node that checks the presence of v_x inter-element features, meaning that v conducts v_x comparisons for each pair of tokens. Let L_v and R_v respectively denote the maximal number of tokens in the L-list and R-list maintained by v. Hence, if a token enters the left-input of v, a maximum of R_v pairs of tokens need to be checked. This in turn means that a maximum of $R_v * v_x$ comparisons needs to be conducted whenever a token enters the left-input of v. If a token enters the right-input of v, a maximum of L_v pairs of tokens needs to be checked, meaning that a maximum of $L_v * v_x$ comparisons needs to be conducted. Furthermore, the L-list of each of v's successors has a maximal number of $R_v * L_v$ tokens.

If the tokens entering the right-input of v are of the class E, the value of R_v is equal to the maximal number of WMEs of the class E that may exist during the execution. If the left-input of v receives tokens from a one-input node that checks tokens of some class, say E', the value of L_v is equal to the maximal number of WMEs of class E' that may exist during the execution. If the left-input of v receives tokens from a two-input node, say v', the value of L_v is equal to the value of $R_{v'} * L_{v'}$.

Example 19. Assume there are at most 50 WMEs of the class Student, 20 WMEs of the class Teacher and 5 WMEs of the class Department in the working memory during the execution. Hence, $L_4 = 5$ and $R_4 = 20$, $L_6 = 100$, $R_6 = 50$ (see Figure 11.9). We compute the maximum number of comparisons by a token of class Department passing to the Rete network as follows. For a token of class Department entering the left-input of node 6, a maximum of 50 tokens of class Student need to be checked, and there is one comparison (to check the attribute of ↑class) in node 6, meaning that a maximum of $50 * 1$ comparisons needs to be conducted. The same applies to node 4. Then it is a maximum of $20 * 1$ comparisons (this one comparison check is for the attribute ↑ dep_id) performed, and these 20 tokens then enter the left-input of node 6. So, the maximum number of comparisons for a token of class Department passing from node 4 to node 6 is $20 + 20 * 50 = 1020$. There are three class-checking nodes. A maximum of 1023 comparisons will be conducted by a token of class Department passing to this Rete network. Therefore, a maximum of 258 and 104 comparisons will be conducted by the same network if a token of the class Teacher and class Student is passed to this network. Furthermore, a token of any class other than Student, Teacher, and Department results in only three comparisons by the network since the token will be discarded at the three class-checking nodes.

Based on the discussion above, we compute an upper bound on the number of comparisons made in the match phase as follows. Assume p is an n-rule OPS5 program. For each rule r, let R_r represent the Rete sub-network that corresponds to r. For each class α of tokens, we first compute an upper bound on the number of comparisons made by R_r during the match phase. Let T_r^α denote this upper bound. The sum of T_r^αs, one for each rule $r \in p$, is an upper bound on the number of comparisons made by the Rete network when a token of class α is processed by the network. Let T^α denote this upper bound. That is,

$$T^\alpha = \sum_{r \in p} T_r^\alpha. \tag{11.2}$$

Since there are only a finite number of actions in the RHS of each rule, each firing of a rule produces only a finite number of tokens. Each of these tokens is then passed to and processed by the Rete network. Having obtained all of the T^αs, we can compute, for each rule $r \in p$, an upper bound on the number of comparisons made by the network as a result of the firing of r by summing up $(n_r^\alpha * T^\alpha)$s where, for each α, n_r^α denotes the number of tokens of the class α added or deleted as a result of the firing of r. For example, assume there are three classes of WMEs, E_1, E_2, and E_3.

(P r_1
  (E_1 ↑ value duplicate)
  (E_2 ↑ p1⟨P1⟩ ↑ p2⟨P2⟩)
⟶
  (make E_3 ↑ p1⟨P⟩ ↑ p2⟨P2⟩)
  (make E_3 ↑ p1⟨P2⟩ ↑ p2⟨P1⟩)
  (modify 1 ↑ value detect_junctions)
  (remove 2))

Then $n_{r_1}^{E_1}$ is 2, $n_{r_1}^{E_2}$ is 1, $n_{r_1}^{E_3}$ is 2 as a result of firing r_1. $n_{r_1}^{E_1}$ is 2 because when an element of class E_1 is modified, two tokens are produced, one token indicating that the old form of the element has been deleted from WM, and the other token indicating that the new form of the element has been added to WM. $n_{r_1}^{E_2}$ is 1 since an element of class E_2 is removed from WM, and one token is produced to indicate deletion. $n_{r_1}^{E_3}$ is 2 because two elements have been added to WM, and two tokens are produced to indicate addition. Let T_r denote this upper bound. That is,

$$T_r = \sum_\alpha n_r^\alpha * T^\alpha. \tag{11.3}$$

In this case, we can obtain T_{r_1} from expression (11.3) by computing $T_{r_1} = n_{r_1}^{E_1} * T^{E_1} + n_{r_2}^{E_2} * T^{E_2} + n_{r_3}^{E_3} * T^{E_3}$. Let T_p denote an upper bound on the number of comparisons made by the Rete network during the execution. Since the maximal number of firings by each rule can be obtained by applying Algorithm_A, we can easily compute the value of T_p. That is,

$$T_p = \sum_{r \in p} I_r * T_r. \tag{11.4}$$

Algorithm_M To compute the maximal number of comparisons made by the Rete network R_p in each recognize–act cycle when a token is passed to and processed by R_p, we need to add the numbers of comparisons respectively performed by individual nodes in R_p. Assume a token of class α is passed to R_p. The token passes to the network from top to bottom, but the computing of T_r^α is from bottom to top of the Rete network. The function *comparisons_of_children* adds the largest number of comparisons to T_r^α, when some children nodes have different types of the same attribute for each class. Because of the different types of the same attribute, the condition is exclusive and it exists one at a time, such as ↑ Grade_year. For example, if you are a freshman, then you cannot be a junior or at another level. (Algorithm_M is shown in Figure 11.10.)

Analysis of Waltz We now apply Algorithm_M to the aforementioned Waltz program segment. The corresponding Rete network is shown in Figure 11.11. Note that Table 11.3 shows the respective maximal numbers of matching WMEs of condition elements of individual rules. Each of these numbers corresponds to the maximal number of tokens entering one of the one-input node sequences. Hence, these numbers can be used to determine the respective sizes of L-lists and R-lists in two-input nodes. For negated condition elements, the respective maximal numbers of WMEs of individual classes are used.

Applying these values, step 1 determines the maximal numbers of tokens in the lists maintained by each node, as shown in Table 11.4. For each token class, step 2 computes the maximal number of comparisons performed if a token of this class is passed to the Rete network. We obtain $T^{E_s} = 19{,}757{,}929$, $T^{E_l} = 4$, $T^{E_e} = 1{,}416{,}364$, and $T^{E_j} = 2{,}822{,}566$. Step 3 determines the number of tokens produced as a result of the firing of individual rules. It then computes the maximal number of comparisons made by the Rete network as a result of one firing of individual rules, as shown in Table 11.5. Together with the respective maximal numbers of firings by individual rules during execution, as shown in Table 11.3, step 4 determines that there are at most about 293 million comparisons performed by the Rete network during the execution.

Input The Rete network, R_p, of the OPS5 program p.

Output An upper bound, T_p, on the number of comparisons made by the Rete network.

---

1. Let T_r^α be the maximum number of comparisons of class α performed by rule r.
2. For each token class α passing in R_p,
   - (a) For each rule r,
     - 2.1.1 Set 0 to T_r^α.
     - 2.1.2 Let X_V be the number of comparisons in node V.
     - 2.1.3 For each two-input node V, if α enters V from right-input, NT_V is assigned to the number of tokens that enter V from left-input; otherwise, NT_V is assigned to the number of tokens that enter V from right-input.
     - 2.1.4 Let *comparisons_of_children*(V) be a function that computes the number of comparisons of node V's children, $V_1, \ldots, V_k$. Let C_V be the maximum number of comparisons in V and D_j be the number of comparisons for each distinct checking attribute in $V_1, \ldots, V_k$, where $1 \leq j \leq k$, and $D_j = MAX(C_{V_a}, C_{V_{a+1}}, \ldots, C_{V_{a+\ell}})$, where the attribute checked in node $V_a, \ldots, V_{a+\ell}$ is the same.
       comparisons_of_children$(V) = \sum_j D_j$.
     - 2.1.5 Traverse R_p from bottom to top, for each node V,
       - 2.1.5.1 If V is a two-input node and has no child, compute $C_V = X_V * NT_V$.
       - 2.1.5.2 If V is a two-input node and has children $V_1, \ldots, V_k$, compute $C_V = (X_V + \text{comparisons\_of\_children}(V)) * NT_V$.
       - 2.1.5.3 If V is a one-input node and has children $V_1, \ldots, V_k$, compute $C_V = \text{comparisons\_of\_children}(V) + X_V$.
       - 2.1.5.4 If V is a class-checking node and has children $V_1, \ldots, V_k$, let X be the number of class-checking nodes and compute $T_r^\alpha = T_r^\alpha + \text{comparisons\_of\_children}(V) + X$.
   - 2.2 Compute $T^\alpha = \sum_{r \in P} T_r^\alpha$.
3. For each rule $r \in p$, compute $T_r = \sum_\alpha n_r^\alpha * T^\alpha$.
4. Output$(T_p = \sum_{r \in p} I_r * T_r)$.

Figure 11.10 Algorithm_M.

The Class of Cyclic Programs In this subsection, we investigate the class of programs with cyclic potential instantiation graphs. This class will be further divided into subclasses. We show that three of these subclasses also possess the property of execution termination.

Theorem 3. Let p denote a set of rules. The execution of p always terminates in a bounded number of recognize–act cycles if the potential instantiation graph G_p^{PI} contains only n-type cycles.

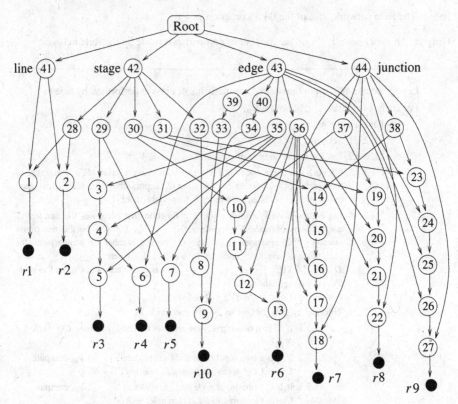

Figure 11.11 The Rete network for the Waltz program segment.

TABLE 11.4 Numbers of tokens maintained by nodes of Waltz program segment

Node #	1	2	3	4	5	6	7	8	9	10	11	12	13	14	15
Comp.	0	0	0	2	3	3	0	0	2	0	2	2	1	0	2
L-list	20	20	1	40	1600	1600	1	1	55	1	20	800	32000	1	14
R-list	1	1	40	40	40	40	40	55	40	20	40	40	20	14	40

Node #	16	17	18	19	20	21	22	23	24	25	26	27
Comp.	2	2	1	0	2	2	1	0	2	2	2	1
L-list	40	40	896000	2	40	40	64000	2	40	40	40	1792000
R-list	560	22400	20	20	40	1600	20	14	28	1120	44800	20

TABLE 11.5   Numbers of comparisons made as a result of rule firings

	Stage(19,757,929)	Line(4)	Edge(1,416,364)	Junction(2,822,566)	Total
$r1$	0	1	2	0	2,832,732
$r2$	2	0	0	0	39,515,858
$r3$	0	0	6	1	11,320,750
$r4$	0	0	4	1	8,488,022
$r5$	2	0	0	0	39,515,858
$r6$	2	0	4	0	45,181,314
$r7$	2	0	6	0	48,014,042
$r8$	2	0	4	0	45,181,314
$r9$	2	0	6	0	48,014,042
$r10$	0	0	4	0	5,665,456

Proof. Assume the potential instantiation graph G_p^{PI} contains only n-type cycles, but the execution of p does not always terminate in a bounded number of cycles. Based on corollary 1, we can find a cycle C in G_p^{PI}. Let $C = \langle r_1, \ldots, r_k, r_{k+1} \rangle$ and $r_1 = r_{k+1}$. r_i potentially instantiates r_{i+1}, where $i = 1 \ldots k$. Since all rules in C will fire infinitely often, r_i will produce new matching WMEs of r_{i+1} which result in new instantiations of r_{i+1}. So every edge in G_p^{PI} is not an n-type edge. Then C is not an n-type cycle, contradicting the assumption that G_p^{PI} contains only n-type cycles.

Therefore, we conclude that if the potential instantiation graph G_p^{PI} contains only n-type cycles, the execution of p always terminates in a bounded number of cycles.

□

Theorem 4. Let p denote a set of rules. The execution of p always terminates in a bounded number of recognize–act cycles if, for each cycle $C \in G_p^{PI}$, (1) C is a p-type cycle and (2) C contains a pair of rules, r_1 and r_2, such that r_1 dis-instantiates r_2.

Proof. Assume G_p^{PI} satisfies conditions (1) and (2) but the execution of p does not always terminate in a bounded number of cycles. Based on corollary 1, we can find a cycle C in G_p^{PI}. Let $C = \langle r_1, \ldots, r_k, r_{k+1} \rangle$ and $r_1 = r_{k+1}$. r_i potentially instantiates r_{i+1}, where $i = 1 \ldots k$. According to condition (1), every edge in G_p^{PI} is a p-type edge.

According to condition (2), C contains a rule, say r_i, that dis-instantiates another rule, say r_j, which is also in C. Hence, every time r_i is fired, it produces a new WME, say **w**, which matches a negated condition element of r_j.

Since C is a p-type cycle according to condition (1), the rule preceding r_j in C does not remove **w**. There must be a rule, g_1, that potentially instantiates r_j and is fired infinitely often such that the firing of g_1 removes those **w**s, as shown in either Figure 11.12(a) or (b). This means that G_p^{PI} contains the edge $\langle g_1, r_j \rangle$ that is not a p-type edge. Furthermore, there must be a path $\langle r_i, \ldots, g_1 \rangle$ in G_p^{PI} with the property that each of the rules potentially instantiates its immediate successor in this path.

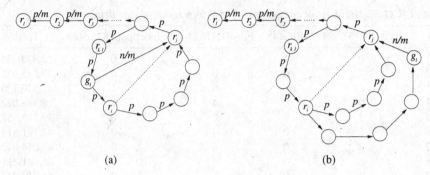

Figure 11.12 r_i dis-instantiates r_j.

A non-p-type cycle in G_p^{PI} shall be found, as shown in Figure 11.12, contradicting condition (1). Therefore, we conclude that the execution of p always terminates in a bounded number of recognize–act cycles if, for each cycle $C \in G_p^{PI}$, C is a p-type cycle and contains a pair of rules, r_1 and r_2, such that r_1 dis-instantiates r_2.   □

Theorem 5. Let p denote a set of rules. The execution of p always terminates in a bounded number of recognize–act cycles if, for each cycle $C \in G_p^{PI}$, C contains a pair of rules, r_i and r_j, such that (1) the firing of r_i removes a WME matching a nonnegated condition element of r_j and (2) no rule in C can produce a new matching WME of r_j.

Proof. Assume each cycle $C \in G_p^{PI}$ contains a pair of rules, r_i and r_j, that satisfy conditions (1) and (2), but the execution of p does not always terminate in a bounded number of cycles. Based on corollary 1, we can find a cycle C in G_p^{PI}. Let $C = \langle r_1, \ldots, r_k, r_{k+1} \rangle$ and $r_1 = r_{k+1}$. r_i potentially instantiates r_{i+1}, where $i = 1 \ldots k$.

C contains a rule, r_i, that removes a WME matching a nonnegated condition element, e_{r_j}, of some rule $r_j \in C$. Furthermore, no rule in C produces a WME matching e_{r_j}. Every time r_i is fired, one of the WMEs matching e_{r_j} is removed. If we consider C alone, eventually there is no WME matching e_{r_j}, and r_j will stop firing.

Since r_i is fired infinitely often, there must be some rule, g_1, whose firings result in new WMEs matching e_{r_j}. Since no rule in C produces a WME matching e_{r_j}, g_1 is not contained in C. We can find that $\langle g_1, r_j \rangle$ is either in another cycle C_1 or a part of path $\langle h_a, h_{a-1}, \ldots, g_1, r_j \rangle$ and $\langle h_a, h_{a-1} \rangle$ is in some cycle C_2 (as shown in Figures 11.13 (a) and (b), respectively). We continue to apply the same argument to rules and cycles found as we did to r_i and g_1. Eventually, since only a finite number of rules exist in p, we will encounter a rule that is in both cases mentioned above and the cycle that produces infinite number of WMEs matching this rule violates the assumption.

Hence, we conclude that the execution of p always terminates in a bounded number of recognize–act cycles if, for each cycle $C \in G_p^{PI}$, C contains a pair of rules, r_i and r_j, such that the firing of r_i removes a WME matching a nonnegated condition element of r_j and no rule in C can produce a new matching WME of r_j.   □

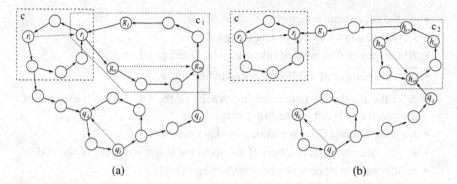

(a)   (b)

Figure 11.13   A cycle violates the assumption if p does not have a bounded response time.

Response Time   In order to use Algorithm_A and Algorithm_M to compute the maximal number of rule firings and comparisons, PI graph G_p^{PI} must be acyclic. We have proved that these three subclasses of cyclic programs possess the property of execution termination in theorems 3, 4, and 5. Suppose that the PI graph G_p^{PI} contains only n-type cycles. Let $\langle r_1, r_2 \rangle \in G_p^{PI}$ denote an n-type edge. According to definition 7, the RHS of r_1 does not contain an action that produces a WME matching a nonnegated condition element of r_2. New WMEs to r_2 cannot result from the firings of r_1. Hence, the edge $\langle r_1, r_2 \rangle$ should be removed from G_p^{PI}. Since each cycle in G_p^{PI} is an n-type cycle, there is at least one n-type edge in each cycle. This in turns means that at least one edge is removed from each cycle in G_p^{PI}. All of the cycles in G_p^{PI} are thus broken and the resulting graph is acyclic. In theorem 4, we conclude that G_p^{PI} contains only p-type cycles, and for each cycle $C \in G_p^{PI}$ and C contains a pair of rules, r_i and r_j, such that r_i dis-instantiates r_j. This means that every time r_i is fired, the firing of r_j produces a WME that matches a negated condition element of r_j. Then one edge can be removed from each cycle and all of the cycles are thus broken. In theorem 5, we conclude that the execution of p always terminates in a bounded number of recognize–act cycles if, for each cycle $C \in G_p^{PI}$, C contains a pair of rules, r_i and r_j, such that the firing of r_i removes a WME matching a nonnegated condition element of r_j, and no rule in C can produce a new matching WME of r_j. So, we can apply Algorithm_A and Algorithm_M to any one of these subclasses of programs.

11.3.4   List of Symbols

We summarize the symbols used below:

- G_p^{PI}: a potential instantiation graph of OPS5 program p.
- N_r^i: the number of matching WMEs of c_r^i.
- d_r^i: the number of matching WMEs of c_r^i that are removed from the working memory as a result of one firing of rule r.

- c_r^i: the ith condition element of rule r.
- I_r: the maximal number of rule firings of r.
- B: the maximal number of rule firings by OPS5 program p.
- $\overline{N_E^{r_i}}$: the number of WMEs produced by the rule r_i.
- $N_{i,j}^k$: the number of new matching WMEs of the kth condition element of r_i produced as a result of one firing of rule r_j.
- N_{E_c}: the number of each working memory element.
- R_v, L_v: the maximal numbers of tokens in the R-list and L-list of the node v.
- v_x: the number of comparisons conducting in node v.
- T_r^α: the maximal number of comparisons of class α conducted by rule r, when a token of the class α is processed by the Rete network.
- T^α: the maximal number of comparisons made in the Rete network and in one recognize–act cycle when a token of the class α is processed by the whole network.
- n_r^α: the number of tokens of the class α added or deleted as a result of the firing of rule r.
- T_r: the maximal number of comparisons made by the Rete network as the result of the firing of rule r.
- T_p: the maximal number of comparisons made by the Rete network during the execution.
- R_p: the Rete network.

11.3.5 Experimental Results

In this section we present the results of experiments on OPS5 programs Callin, Manners, and Waltz in Table 11.6. We run these three OPS5 programs on a DEC 5000/240 workstation that supports DEC OPS5 Version 4.0. We also run our analysis tool using these programs. Callin is to compute $\lfloor \log_2 N \rfloor$. Waltz is a benchmark labeling algorithm and Manners is a benchmark program that assign seats to people around a table. Table 11.6 shows that the actual number of rule firings of Callin using the DEC is greater than that produced by our analysis tool, because there is a rule firing cycle in the Callin program. So, it is not appropriate to use our analysis tool for a cyclic OPS5 program because its result may not be correct. For the Manners program, we

TABLE 11.6 Experimental results using Algorithm_A and Algorithm_M

	DEC		Analysis tool	
	Number of rule firings	Number of comparisons	Number of rule firings	Number of comparisons
Callin	7	44	2	14
Manners	7	315	9	365
Waltz	47	27,3367	82	293 million

invoke three WMEs of the class *Guest*, one WME of the class *Seating*, one WME of the class *Context*, and one WME of the class *Count*. The actual number of rule firings we observed from DEC is seven. Our analysis tool shows the number of rule firings is nine. For program Waltz, each initial WME consists of one WME of the class *Stage* and 20 WMEs of the class *Line*. The actual number of rule firings from these executions is 47, and our tool produces 82. The tightness of the upper bound predicted by algorithm_A is shown in the Manners and Waltz experimental results. DEC does not provide a function to generate the number of comparisons. So, we obtain the number of comparisons by manually simulating how it operates in DEC. In the Manners program, the actual number of comparisons is 315, and our tool shows 365. When we run this program using the actual number of initial WMEs of each class, the results for both cases are very close. In the Waltz program, the number of actual comparisons is 273,367, and our tool shows 293 million. This is because we assume the maximal possible number of initial WMEs of each class. Though the difference between them is quite large, we think it is acceptable as an upper bound on the number of comparisons considering that our tool employs pre-run-time static analysis.

11.3.6   Removing Cycles with the Help of the Programmer

We have implemented an analysis tool to predict the upper bounds on the numbers of rule firings for OPS5 programs with acyclic potential instantiation graphs. However, a real-world OPS5 program usually contains cycles of potential instantiations. Some types of cycles do not change the property of termination, while others do. Our tool can automatically remove only a certain type of cycles at this time.

The response time of programs with cyclic potential rule firing patterns usually depends on the value of run-time data that cannot be known in advance. For example, consider the following rule.

```
(p make_new_data2
   (upperlimit ↑value⟨n⟩)
   (data1 ↑xvalue{⟨x1⟩⟨n⟩})
⟶
   (modify 2 ↑xvalue (compute ⟨x⟩ + 1))
   (make data2 ↑yvalue⟨x1⟩))
```

The value of the attribute ↑value can only be known at run-time. There is no way to know in advance how many times this rule will be fired, although it is clear that this rule will always terminate.

It is not realistic to try to develop an algorithm to predict the response time upper bounds of programs with cyclic potential rule firing patterns. The most we can do at this time is to determine the property of termination for some of the programs with cyclic potential rule firing patterns.

The property of termination of a given program depends on whether all of its potential rule firing cycles terminate. Hence, it is necessary to check each cycle to see if it always terminates. Due to the lack of run-time information, which is very crucial in determining the satisfiability of condition elements, a conservative approach has to be taken in static analysis to determine whether a condition element can be satisfied by a working memory element whose value/content cannot be known in advance. The potential instantiation graph produced as a result of the static analysis usually contains a lot of edges that are nonexistent. This in turn means that a lot of cycles found in the potential instantiation graph are nonexistent. With the help of the programmer, a large number of these nonexistent edges/cycles can be detected and removed from the potential instantiation graph.

It is usually the case that a special purpose working memory element is used to control the progress of program execution. Frequently, an OPS5 production system contains a working memory element of the form

$$(\text{stage } \uparrow\text{value}),$$

where the attribute $\uparrow$value contains the value of "stage1", "stage2," ..., or "stage n." Meanwhile, each of the rules in the program contains a condition element thatz matches this special working memory element. Rules to be fired in different phases request different values of the attribute $\uparrow$value of the above working memory element.

Our tool does not know that the above special working memory element is used to control the flow of the execution and, as a result of this function, eliminate a lot of potential cycles. The analysis tool cannot assume that a certain working memory element and certain condition elements of rules provide special function and should be treated differently. All of the working memory elements and all of the condition elements must be treated equally by the analysis tool. On the other hand, the programmer can easily recognize that this particular working memory element is used to control the progress of execution and determine that the existence of some potential rule firing cycles is actually not possible.

For example, when the entire Waltz program is analyzed by our tool, many potential cycles of rule firings are found to be nonexistent, as follows. This program uses the aforementioned special working memory element to control the flow of program execution. Rules are numbered from 0 to 32. Figure 11.14 shows the matrix representation of the potential instantiation graph, where "p" stands for the existence of a p-type edge, "n" stands for the existence of an n-type edge, and "-" stands for the existence of no edge at all. One p-type cycle that was detected is $\langle r_1, r_6 \rangle$, $\langle r_6, r_3 \rangle$, and $\langle r_3, r_6 \rangle$ (see Figure 11.14). This type of cycle cannot be removed by our analysis tool. A programmer can determine if some of these edges can be removed.

It is clear from this graph that many potential rule firing cycles occur during the execution. Many of these potential cycles can be removed by the programmer. Our tool finds all of these cycles and prompts a message to the programmer for each detected potential cycle. The programmer then checks each potential cycle and determines whether a special purpose working memory element breaks it.

For instance, the graph shows that there is a potential cycle involving only rule 6 and rule 7, which, respectively, are

	r_0	r_1	r_2	r_3	r_4	r_5	r_6	r_7	r_8	r_9	r_{10}	r_{11}	r_{12}	r_{13}	r_{14}	r_{15}	r_{16}	r_{17}	r_{18}	r_{19}	r_{20}	r_{21}	r_{22}	r_{23}	r_{24}	r_{25}	r_{26}	r_{27}	r_{28}	r_{29}	r_{30}	r_{31}	r_{32}
r_0	-	p	p	-	-	-	-	-	-	-	-	-	-	-	-	-	-	-	-	-	-	-	-	-	-	-	-	-	-	-	-	-	-
r_1	-	-	n	p	p	-	p	p	p	p	p	p	p	p	p	p	p	p	p	p	p	p	p	p	p	p	p	-	p	p	p	-	-
r_2	-	-	-	p	p	p	-	-	-	-	-	-	-	-	-	-	-	-	-	-	-	-	-	-	-	-	-	-	-	-	-	-	-
r_3	-	-	-	-	-	n	p	p	p	p	p	p	p	p	p	p	p	p	p	p	p	p	p	p	p	p	p	-	p	p	p	-	-
r_4	-	-	-	-	-	n	p	p	p	p	p	p	p	p	p	p	p	p	p	p	p	p	p	p	p	p	p	-	p	p	p	-	-
r_5	-	-	-	-	-	-	p	p	-	-	-	-	-	-	-	-	-	-	-	-	-	-	-	-	-	-	-	-	-	-	-	-	-
r_6	-	-	-	p	p	-	-	p	p	p	-	p	p	p	p	p	-	p	p	p	p	p	p	p	p	p	p	-	p	-	p	-	-
r_7	-	-	-	p	p	-	p	-	p	p	p	p	p	p	p	p	-	p	p	p	p	p	p	p	p	p	p	-	p	-	p	-	-
r_8	-	-	-	p	p	-	p	p	-	p	p	p	p	p	p	p	p	p	p	p	p	p	p	p	p	p	p	p	p	-	p	-	-
r_9	-	-	-	p	p	-	p	p	p	-	p	p	p	p	p	p	p	p	p	p	p	p	p	p	p	p	p	p	p	-	p	-	-
r_{10}	-	-	-	p	p	-	p	p	p	p	-	p	p	p	p	p	-	p	p	p	p	p	p	p	p	p	p	-	p	-	p	-	-
r_{11}	-	-	-	p	p	-	p	p	p	p	-	-	p	p	p	p	-	p	p	p	p	p	p	p	p	p	p	-	p	-	p	-	-
r_{12}	-	-	-	p	p	-	p	p	p	p	-	p	-	p	p	p	-	p	p	p	p	p	p	p	p	p	p	-	p	-	p	-	-
r_{13}	-	-	-	p	p	-	p	p	p	p	p	p	p	-	-	-	-	p	p	p	p	p	p	p	p	p	p	-	p	-	p	-	-
r_{14}	-	-	-	p	p	-	p	p	p	p	-	p	p	p	-	p	-	p	p	p	p	p	p	p	p	p	p	-	p	-	p	-	-
r_{15}	-	-	-	p	p	-	p	p	p	p	-	p	p	p	p	-	p	p	p	p	p	p	p	p	p	p	p	-	p	-	p	-	-
r_{16}	-	-	-	p	p	-	p	p	p	p	-	p	p	p	p	-	-	p	p	p	p	p	p	p	p	p	p	-	p	-	p	-	-
r_{17}	-	-	-	p	p	-	p	p	p	p	p	p	p	p	p	p	-	-	p	p	p	p	p	p	p	p	p	-	p	-	p	-	-
r_{18}	-	-	-	p	p	-	p	p	p	p	p	p	p	p	p	p	-	p	-	p	p	p	p	p	p	p	p	-	p	-	p	-	-
r_{19}	-	-	-	p	p	-	p	p	p	p	p	p	p	p	-	-	-	p	p	-	p	p	p	p	p	p	p	-	p	-	p	-	-
r_{20}	-	-	-	p	p	-	p	p	p	p	p	p	p	p	-	-	-	p	p	p	-	p	p	p	p	p	p	-	p	-	p	-	-
r_{21}	-	-	-	p	p	-	p	p	p	p	p	p	p	p	p	-	p	p	p	p	p	-	p	p	p	p	p	-	p	-	p	-	-
r_{22}	-	-	-	p	p	-	p	p	p	p	p	p	p	p	p	-	p	p	p	p	p	p	-	p	p	p	p	-	p	-	p	-	-
r_{23}	-	-	-	p	p	-	p	p	p	p	p	p	p	p	p	-	p	p	p	p	p	p	p	-	p	p	p	-	p	-	p	-	-
r_{24}	-	-	-	p	p	-	p	p	p	p	p	p	p	p	p	-	p	p	p	p	p	p	p	p	-	p	p	-	p	-	p	-	-
r_{25}	-	-	-	p	p	-	p	p	p	p	p	p	p	p	-	-	-	p	p	p	p	p	p	p	p	-	p	-	p	-	p	-	-
r_{26}	-	-	-	p	p	-	p	p	p	p	p	p	p	p	-	-	-	p	p	p	p	p	p	p	p	p	-	-	p	-	p	-	-
r_{27}	-	-	-	-	-	-	-	-	-	-	-	-	-	-	-	-	-	-	-	-	-	-	-	-	-	-	-	-	p	p	-	p	-
r_{28}	-	-	-	p	p	-	p	p	p	p	p	p	p	p	p	p	p	p	p	p	p	p	p	p	p	p	p	-	-	-	p	n	-
r_{29}	-	-	-	p	p	-	p	p	p	p	p	p	p	p	p	p	p	p	p	p	p	p	p	p	p	p	p	-	-	-	p	n	-
r_{30}	-	-	-	p	p	-	p	p	p	p	-	p	p	p	-	-	-	p	p	p	p	p	p	p	p	p	p	-	-	-	-	n	-
r_{31}	-	-	-	-	-	-	-	-	-	-	-	-	-	-	-	-	-	-	-	-	-	-	-	-	-	-	-	-	-	-	-	-	p
r_{32}	-	-	-	-	-	-	-	-	-	-	-	-	-	-	-	-	-	-	-	-	-	-	-	-	-	-	-	-	-	-	-	-	-

Figure 11.14 Old PI graph of Waltz.

(p initial_boundary_junction_L ; rule #6
   (stage ↑value find_initial_boundary)
   (junction ↑type L ↑base_point ⟨base_point⟩ ↑p1 ⟨p1⟩ ↑p2 ⟨p2⟩)
   (edge ↑ p1 ⟨base_point⟩ ↑ p2⟨p⟩)
   (edge ↑ p1 ⟨base_point⟩ ↑ p2⟨p2⟩)
   − (junction ↑ base_point > ⟨base_point⟩)
⟶
   (modify 3 ↑label B)
   (modify 4 ↑label B)
   (modify 1 ↑value find_second_boundary))
and
(p initial_boundary_junction_arrow ; rule #7
   (stage ↑value find_initial_boundary)
   (junction ↑type arrow ↑base_point ⟨bp⟩ ↑ p1⟨p1⟩ ↑ p2⟨p2⟩ ↑ p3⟨p3⟩)
   (edge ↑ p1 ⟨bp⟩ ↑ p2⟨p1⟩)
   (edge ↑ p1 ⟨bp⟩ ↑ p2⟨p2⟩)
   (edge ↑ p1 ⟨bp⟩ ↑ p2⟨p3⟩)
   − (junction ↑ base_point > ⟨bp⟩)
⟶
   (modify 3 ↑label B)
   (modify 4 ↑label P)
   (modify 5 ↑label B)
   (modify 1 ↑value find_second_boundary))

Whenever either one of these two rules is fired, the execution enters the next phase since the attribute ↑value of the flow-controlling working memory element is set to the value that initiates the next phase of the execution. Hence, it is not possible for these two rules to be cyclically fired. The dependency analysis performed by our tool cannot detect this fact, since the tool cannot assume the existence of a flow-controlling working memory element.

The programmer can help the analysis tool recognize this fact by rewriting (but not changing the semantic of) these two rules. After a closer look at these two rules, coupled with the understanding of the Waltz algorithm, it is not difficult for the programmer to realize that some condition elements of these rules are reasonably simplified due to the use of the flow-controlling working memory element. For example, the working memory elements matching the third condition element of rule 6 are actually of the form

(edge ↑ p1 ⟨base_point⟩ ↑ p2⟨p1⟩ ↑ label nil ↑ plotted nil).

Because of the use of the flow-controlling working memory element, the condition element considered does not explicitly specify the required values for the last two attributes. Any working memory element of the class edge with the value of ↑label being B or P will not be used to produce an instantiation of rule 6, since the program execution enters the next phase after the attribute ↑label of this working memory element is set to B or P as a result of the firing of either rule 6 or rule 7. So, the rewritten rule 6 and rule 7 are as follows:

(p initial_boundary_junction_L ; rule 6
  (stage ↑value find_initial_boundary)
  (junction ↑type L ↑base_point ⟨base_point⟩ ↑p1⟨p1⟩ ↑p2⟨p2⟩)
  (edge ↑p1⟨base_point⟩ ↑p2⟨p1⟩ ↑label nil ↑ plotted nil)
  (edge ↑p1⟨base_point⟩ ↑p2⟨p2⟩HERE ↑label nil ↑plotted nil)
  – (junction ↑ base_point > ⟨base_point⟩)
⟶
  (modify 3 ↑label B)
  (modify 4 ↑label B)
  (modify 1 ↑value find_second_boundary))
and
(p initial_boundary_junction_arrow ; rule #7
  (stage ↑value find_initial_boundary)
  (junction ↑type arrow ↑base_point ⟨bp⟩ ↑p1 ⟨p1⟩ ↑p2 ⟨p2⟩ ↑p3 ⟨p3⟩)
  (edge ↑p1 ⟨b⟩ ↑p2 ⟨p1⟩ ↑label nil ↑plotted nil)
  (edge ↑p1 ⟨bp⟩ ↑p2 ⟨p2⟩ ↑label nil ↑plotted nil)
  (edge ↑p1 ⟨bp⟩ ↑p2 ⟨p3⟩ ↑label nil ↑plotted nil)
  – (junction ↑ base_point > ⟨bp⟩)
⟶
  (modify 3 ↑label B)
  (modify 4 ↑label P)
  (modify 5 ↑label B)
  (modify 1 ↑value find_second_boundary))

We check each cycle and, if possible, rewrite rules by explicitly specifying the required values of attributes for each condition element. Figure 11.15 shows the new potential instantiation graph obtained when the resulting program is analyzed. There are still many cycles, which need to be analyzed by a more sophisticated method, but the number of cycles has been remarkably reduced in comparison with the number of cycles in the old PI graph in Figure 11.14.

The programmer can further help by exploiting his/her understanding of the semantics of program flow. The programmer can determine that some cycles are terminating. For example, a cycle that consumes a certain class of working memory elements will eventually terminate if only a limited number of working memory elements of that class exist during the execution.

Example 20. The following is the output produced by our analysis tool when analyzing the benchmark program called Manners, which assigns seats to people around a table. Note that some cycles are broken as a result of removing some edges by the programmer with the understanding of the semantics of program flow. The upper bound obtained is very loose because it suffers from the conservative approach taken.

Figure 11.15 New PI graph of Waltz.

```
*************** Analysis results **************

***PI graph

   r0 r1 r2 r3 r4 r5 r6 r7
r0 - p  p  -  p  -  p  -
r1 - p  p  p  p  -  p  -
r2 - -  p  -  -  -  p  -
r3 - p  -  -  p  p  p  -
r4 - -  -  -  -  -  p  p
r5 - p  -  -  -  -  -  -
r6 - n  n  -  -  -  -  -
r7 - -  -  -  -  -  -  -


After removing n-type cycles...

***PI graph

   r0 r1 r2 r3 r4 r5 r6 r7
r0 - p  p  -  p  -  p  -
r1 - p  p  p  p  -  p  -
r2 - -  p  -  -  -  p  -
r3 - p  -  -  p  p  p  -
r4 - -  -  -  -  -  p  p
r5 - p  -  -  -  -  -  -
r6 - -  -  -  -  -  -  -
r7 - -  -  -  -  -  -  -


Do you want to break cycles manually? (y/n) y
1 -- 1
Remove edge <1,1>? y
2 -- 2
Remove edge <2,2>? y
1 -- 3 -- 1
Remove edge <1,3>? n
Remove edge <3,1>? y
1 -- 3 -- 5 -- 1
Remove edge <1,3>? n
Remove edge <3,5>? n
Remove edge <5,1>? y

***PI graph
   r0 r1 r2 r3 r4 r5 r6 r7
r0 - p  p  -  p  -  p  -
r1 - -  p  p  p  -  p  -
r2 - -  -  -  -  -  p  -
r3 - -  -  -  p  p  p  -
r4 - -  -  -  -  -  p  p
r5 - -  -  -  -  -  -  -
```

```
r6 - - - - - - - -
r7 - - - - - - - -

----npartite-------
0
1
2 3
4 5
6 7

after layer #0 (r0 )  B = 1
numbers of classes of WMEs
3 0 2 1 1 0 1

after layer #1 (r1 )  B = 2
numbers of classes of WMEs
3 0 3 1 2 1 1

after layer #2 (r2 r3 )  B = 5
numbers of classes of WMEs
3 0 3 1 4 1 1

after layer #3 (r4 r5 )  B = 7
numbers of classes of WMEs
3 0 3 1 4 1 1

after layer #4 (r6 r7 )  B = 9
numbers of classes of WMEs
3 0 3 1 4 1 1

*** maximal number of rule firings = 9
```

11.4 HISTORICAL PERSPECTIVE AND RELATED WORK

Expert system researchers have studied the issues of meeting real-time constraints in expert systems. [O'Reilly and Cromarty, 1985] were among the first to explain that increasing execution speed does not necessarily guarantee that an expert system can meet real-time performance constraints. [Laffey et al., 1988] provided an overview of real-time expert systems and described techniques for ensuring real-time performance. However, they did not present details of these techniques nor did they evaluate their performance. [Strosnider and Paul, 1994] considered the work of Laffey et al. coincidentally real-time and attempted to provide a more structured way to design smart real-time systems. However, no response-time analysis of rule-based systems was given. [Benda, 1987] and [Koch et al., 1986] described the requirements of real-time knowledge-based systems in the aerospace industry. [Payton and Bihari, 1991] argued that different levels of an intelligent control system must cooperate closely to achieve real-time performance and adaptivity.

[Barachini et al., 1988; Barachini, 1994] presented several run-time prediction methods, as opposed to pre-run-time prediction in our approach, to evaluate the time required for actions in the right-hand sides of rules to be executed. The time required by the Rete network, when a token is passed to it, is estimated. They showed that execution time prediction of embedded expert systems can be performed with finer granularity, such as in the action level. However, in his opinion, the prediction of the execution time of the entire expert system is not achievable in a tractable manner.

However, few attempts have been made to formally address the response-time analysis problem. [Abiteboul and Simon, 1991], among others, have discussed the property of termination in the context of Datalog and its extensions and showed that this property is in general undecidable. Although they have addressed the issue of whether all programs of a given language possesses the property of termination, the issue of determining whether a given program possess the property of termination is not addressed. [Lark et al., 1990] considered the design and implementation issues in the development of Lockheed Pilot's Associate system. They advocateed using experimentation and analysis to guarantee timeliness by requiring the application programmer to set an upper bound on process duration by extensive experimentation but did not show how to verify that the system would satisfy this upper bound. [Aiken, Widom, and Hellerstein, 1992] presented a static analysis method to determine whether arbitrary sets of database production rules satisfied certain properties, including termination. A directed graph demonstrating the triggering relationship among rules is checked to see if the corresponding set of rules is guaranteed to terminate. Some conditions that guaranteed the property of termination were introduced. We derive one property of rule behavior from this idea.

[Wang and Mok, 1995] studied the response time bounded in the context of EQL rule-based systems with a fixed-size working memory. They stated that the use of more general expert systems with dynamically varying working memories for time-critical application was not feasible at this time because of the lack of a tool for analyzing those systems to predict their response time.

In this chapter, we considered a class of expert systems with dynamically varying working memories and proposed pre-run-time static analysis algorithms to predict the response time of these systems. Few attempts have been made to formalize the question of whether a rule-based program has bounded response time. The first formal frameworks were introduced in [Browne, Cheng, and Mok, 1988; Cheng et al., 1993; Cheng and Wang, 1990; Wang, Mok, and Cheng, 1990]. In [Wang and Mok, 1993], a formal analysis was introduced to predict the timing behavior of MRL programs. [Wang, 1989] and [Shaw, 1992] proposed a method to translate OPS5 programs into MRL programs for response-time bound analysis. However, the timing prediction in [Wang, Mok, and Emerson, 1993b] is based on static analysis, whose results are too pessimistic to approximate the actual bound on execution time. Note that worst-case analysis is still essential for an expert system running in a real-time environment [Musliner et al., 1995]. We have developed the two analysis approaches [Tsai and Cheng, 1994; Cheng and Chen, 2000] described in this chapter.

11.5 SUMMARY

The main focus of this chapter is on addressing the timing properties of predicate-logic expert systems. As more knowledge-based systems are used in real-time applications demanding guaranteed response time, it is essential to predict before run-time their worst-case response time during actual execution. As we have seen in chapter 10, this static timing analysis problem is extremely difficult, even for propositional-logic-based rule-based systems, such as EQL. For predicate-logic-based rule-based systems such as those implemented in OPS5 and OPS5-style languages, very few practical static analysis approaches exist.

In our first approach, the Cheng–Tsai timing analysis methodology for OPS5 systems, a data dependency graph (ER graph) is used to facilitate most parts of the analysis. The ER graph captures all of the logical paths of a rule-based program. We use the ER graph to detect if an OPS5 program can terminate in finite execution time. More specifically, our technique detects rules that have a finite number of firings. Once nontermination is detected, we extract every cycle in the ER graph and determine the enabling conditions of the cycles. Providing the programmer with these "culprit" conditions allows extra rules to be added to correct the program.

The programmer has the option of correcting the program to remove the cycles based on these conditions, or the analysis tool can automatically add cycle-breaking rules to the program. If the programmer chooses the latter, then after finding the enabling conditions, W, of a cycle, the tool adds rule r' with W as the enabling condition to the program. By doing so, once the working memory has the WMEs matching the enabling condition of a cycle, the control flow can be switched out of the cycle to r'. However, to ensure that the program flow switches to r', it is modified such that r' has higher priority than the regular rules. The extra rules are further refined to remove redundant conditions and rules. Note that this modification is performed off-line, prior to the execution of the expert system, and the modified version must still satisfy the logical correctness constraints.

The timing analysis problem is in general undecidable and is PSPACE-complete for programs with finite domains, as we showed in chapter 10. A static analysis strategy for tackling the analysis problem is addressed. Similar strategies have been successfully applied to the EQL language [Browne, Cheng, and Mok, 1988; Cheng et al., 1993; Cheng and Wang, 1990]. However, for complex languages such as MRL and OPS5 which have dynamic data domain size, static timing analysis may not be suitable. We developed a tool to aid in the determination of the upper bound on the program execution time. This tool has been implemented to generate a set of WMEs that cause an OPS5 program to have maximum time consumption. A selection strategy is embedded in the tool that avoids generating timing-irrelevant WMEs.

The tool also accepts users' data to ensure that normal program flows are followed. The set of WMEs with the timing reports generated by the OPS5 system can assist the programmer in improving the timing performance. The proposed approach requires substantial programmer assistance in examining the potential cycles. In addition, the modification of the rule base to ensure termination may not be feasible in some cases. However, our approach represents a significant step toward a methodology for the response-time analysis of real-time rule-based systems satisfying the constraints in this chapter. Special forms may be used to characterize the class of OPS5 programs that can be successfully analyzed by the proposed tool. This classification is based on techniques developed for EQL programs [Cheng et al., 1993].

Many approaches have been proposed to improve the performance of production systems. They may be divided into three categories [Kuo and Moldovan, 1992]: (1) speeding up the match phase by faster sequential match algorithms, (2) speeding up the match phase by parallel processing techniques, and (3) making parallel the act phase by firing multiple-rule instantiations in a production cycle. Most of these approaches either change the architecture of the production system or support parallel hardware and software to distribute the rule sets into different processors. The results of these approaches are supposed to yield a significant speedup. This high performance would then allow the production system to meet the stringent response-time requirements although formal verification is lacking. However, parallel production systems are still in an early stage of development. Most of these approaches are evaluated only with simulation results, without actual implementation. The ability of these parallel systems to satisfy timing constraints remains unclear, so more research needs to be done.

Since our timing analysis is based on the semantic structure of the program, our strategies should also apply to these parallel architectures in order to understand their timing behaviors. A formal verification of the timing requirement of the parallel models can be based on our analysis approach. Furthermore, few attempts have been made [Zupan and Cheng, 1994a; Zupan and Cheng, 1998] to formalize the question of whether a rule-based program can be optimized. The optimization of a rule-based program is considered much cheaper than the implementation of parallel models, although we may not expect that it can gain as much speedup as the parallel models can. It also should be an important research issue.

Another issue is to extend the proposed techniques to analyze expert systems implemented in more recent and powerful rule-based languages. These newer languages [Forgy, 1985] incorporate new conflict resolution strategies and procedural/object-oriented styles similar to non-rule-based languages. Our initial assessment is that modification of the proposed techniques is needed to handle different conflict resolution strategies. However, procedural and object-oriented expert systems, by introducing abstraction and by making certain control flows explicit, are easier to analyze [Shaw, 1989] than pure rule-based expert systems.

Our second approach, the Cheng–Chen timing analysis methodology, makes a significant contribution to the state-of-the-art for solving this static timing analysis problem by presenting a formal framework for worst-case response-time prediction of a class of OPS5 and OPS5-style production systems. The proposed analysis techniques are based on (1) the detection of termination conditions, which can be checked by a semantic analysis of the relationships among rules in a rulebase, and (2) the systematic trace of tokens in the match network. These techniques are more efficient than those that rely on longest-path analysis in a state-transition system corresponding to a given rule-based system.

Considering the difficulty of the timing analysis problem, this methodology provides a collection of practical techniques, implemented as a tool set, to determine an upper bound on the execution time of a class of OPS5 and OPS5-style rule-based programs. This upper bound is expressed in terms of the number of total rule firings and in terms of the number of comparisons made during each matching to determine fireable rules. The second metric is particularly important since 90% of the execution time is spent in the match phase. The execution time analysis is performed without actually running the program being analyzed. The predicted execution times and associated results can be used to optimize the program to speed its execution. In general, this analysis problem is undecidable. The fact that we are able to analyze standard benchmark programs indicates the tool set's practicality. As a first significant step to solve the static analysis problem for OPS5 programs, we present four termination conditions for OPS5 programs which are used to determine whether a program terminates in a finite time. These conditions can be checked by a fast semantic analysis rather than a state-space analysis of the programs. Then we analyze the response time only when a program has been found to be acyclic (no loop(s) in the program).

In particular, it is found that if the rule-triggering pattern of an OPS5 program satisfies one of the observed conditions, the execution of this program always terminates in bounded time. An algorithm used to compute upper bounds on the number of recognize–act cycles during the executions of programs with acyclic rule triggering patterns has been developed. We also present an algorithm to compute upper bounds on the numbers of comparisons made by the Rete network during execution. From our experience, the upper bounds obtained by Algorithm_A seem to be fairly good, but the same statement cannot be made of Algorithm_M. A more accurate estimation method of the numbers of tokens maintained in two-input nodes needs to be developed.

We also show how the proposed algorithms can be applied to a class of programs with cyclic rule-triggering patterns. Due to the lack of run-time information, our analysis tool takes a conservative approach in determining the satisfiability of condition elements, and, as a result of this approach, the potential instantiation graph produced by our tool usually contains a large number of nonexistent edges/cycles. Furthermore, for the same reason, it is not realistic to try to develop an algorithm to compute the response time of OPS5 programs with cyclic potential rule firing patterns. Instead, we show how the programmer can help detect nonexistent edges/cycles in the potential instantiation graph. Given that fully automated analysis tools are extremely difficult to develop, our tool set assists the programmer by focusing on rule sets with potentially high run-time costs.

We are currently looking at other characteristics of production systems, such as rule dis-triggering patterns, to see if these characteristics can be exploited to improve the presented algorithms. We plan to expand the applicability of the algorithm to programs with cyclic rule-triggering patterns. The development of new termination conditions is also under way. Furthermore, we also plan to extend Algorithm_M to analyze the execution time of the recently introduced Rete II match algorithm used in OPS/R2 [Forgy, 1985]. We believe that the way in which Algorithm_M painstakingly checks the movement of the tokens in the Rete network can also be applied to Rete II, which more efficiently handles complex LHS conditions and large numbers of WMEs but still retains the basic network structure.

EXERCISES

1. Why is the timing analysis of rule-based systems more difficult than that of sequential programs?

2. How does the use of pattern (structured) variables in predicate-logic rule-based systems make the timing analysis more difficult than in the case of propositional-logic rule-based systems? How does the use of these pattern variables complicate the matching process when compared to the case of simple (non-structured) variables used in propositional-logic rule-based systems?

3. Construct the state-space graphs corresponding to the rule-based programs in the examples.

4. How can a model-checking algorithm, such as the one for the computation tree logic, be used to analyze the response time of rule-based systems with finite-domain variables?

5. Can a program written in a predicate-logic rule-based language such as OPS5 be rewritten as a propositional-logic rule-based program such as EQL? If the answer is yes, can this translation always be performed, or only under certain conditions? Explain.

6. Outline the similarities and the differences between the Cheng–Tsai analysis methodology and the Cheng–Chen analysis methodology.

CHAPTER 12

OPTIMIZATION OF RULE-BASED SYSTEMS

As we have seen in chapters 10 and 11, embedded rule-based expert systems must satisfy stringent timing constraints when applied to real-time environments. We now describe a novel approach to reduce the response time of rule-based expert systems. This optimization is needed when a rule-based system does not meet the specified response-time constraints. Our optimization method is based on a construction of the reduced cycle-free finite-state space-graph. In contrast with traditional state-space graph derivation algorithms, our optimization algorithm starts from the final states (fixed points) and gradually expands the state-space graph until all of the states with a reachable fixed point are found. The new and optimized rule-based system is then synthesized from the constructed state-space graph. We present several algorithms implementing the optimization method. They vary in complexity as well as in the usage of concurrency and state-equivalence, both targeting to minimize the size of the optimized state-space graph.

The optimized rule based systems generally (1) have better response time, that is, require fewer number of rule firings to reach the fixed point, (2) are stable, that is, have no cycles that would result in the instability of execution, and (3) include no redundant rules. The actual results of the optimization depend on the algorithm used. We also address the issue of deterministic execution and propose optimization algorithms that generate the rule bases with a single corresponding fixed point for every initial state.

The synthesis method also determines a tight response-time bound of the new system and can identify unstable states in the original rule base. No information other than the rule-based real-time decision program itself is given to the optimization method. The optimized system is guaranteed to compute correct results independent of the scheduling strategy and execution environment.

12.1 INTRODUCTION

Embedded rule-based systems must also satisfy stringent environmental timing constraints which impose a deadline on the decision/reaction time of the rule base. The result of missing a deadline in these systems may be harmful. The task of verification is to prove that the system can deliver an adequate performance in bounded time [Browne, Cheng, and Mok, 1988]. If this is not the case or if the real-time expert system is too complex to analyze, the system has to be resynthesized.

We present a novel optimization method for rule-based real-time systems. The optimization is based on the derivation of a reduced, optimized, and cycle-free state-space graph for each independent set of rules in the rule-based program. Once the state space graph is derived, no further reduction and/or optimization is required, and it can then be directly used for resynthesis of the new and optimized rule-based program.

The optimization makes use of several approaches and techniques previously used for the analysis and parallel execution of real-time rule-based systems. It also employs several known techniques originated from protocol validation to minimize the number of states in state-space graphs. In particular:

- The complexity of the optimization is reduced by optimizing each independent set of rules separately. This technique originates from [Cheng et al., 1993], where the same approach was used to lower the complexity of analysis of real-time rule-based systems.
- The state-space graph representation of the execution of real-time rule-based system was introduced in [Browne, Cheng, and Mok, 1988]. It was used for the analysis of rule-based systems, but, because of the possible state explosion, the approach may be used solely for systems with few variables. We show how this representation also may be used for larger systems if the reduced state-space graphs are used instead. To reduce the number of states, known methods from protocol analysis (representation of a set of equivalent states with a single vertex of the state-space graph) and from rule-based system analysis (parallel firing of rules within independent rule sets) are employed.

Specific to the optimization method proposed here are reduction and optimization of the state-space graph while it is derived from a set of rules. Also specific are bottom-up derivation and resynthesis of a new and optimized rule-based system. In particular:

- The derivation of the state-space graph starts with the identification of the final states (fixed points) of the system, and gradually expands the state-space graph until all of the states with a reachable fixed point are found. This bottom-up approach combined with a breadth-first search finds only the minimal-length paths to the fixed points.
- Rather than first deriving the state-space graph and then reducing the number of states, the reduced state-space graph is built directly. We identify the techniques that, while building the state space graph, allow us to group the equivalent states

into a single vertex of a graph and exploit the concurrency by labeling a single edge of a graph with a set of rules fired in parallel.

- The derivation of the state-space graph is constrained so that it does not introduce any cycles. The new rule-based system constructed from such a graph is cycle-free (stable).
- The derived state-space graph does not require any further reduction of states and/or optimization, and it can be directly used to resynthesize an optimized real-time rule-based program.

In this chapter, several state space derivation techniques are described, addressing:

- *response-time optimization*: the optimized programs require the same or fewer numbers of rules to fire from some state to reach a final state;
- *response-time estimation*: it is of crucial importance for real-time rule-based systems not only to speed up the execution time but also to at least estimate its upper bounds [Browne, Cheng, and Mok, 1988; Chen and Cheng, 1995b];
- *stability*: all cycles of the original rule-based systems that make the system unstable are removed;
- *determinism and confluence*: if more than one rule is enabled to be fired at a certain stage of the execution, the final state is independent of the execution order.

The algorithms presented here were developed for a two-valued version of the equational rule-based language EQL described in chapter 10. The language was initially developed to study the rule-based systems in a real-time environment. In contrast with popular expert systems languages such as OPS5, where the interpretation of the language is defined by the recognize–act cycle [Forgy, 1981], EQL's interpretation is defined as fixed point convergence. For EQL programs, a number of tools for analysis exist and are described in chapter 10.

12.2   BACKGROUND

Validation and verification is an important phase in the life cycle of every rule-based system [Eliot, 1992]. For real-time rule-based systems, we define the validation and verification as an *analysis problem*, which is to decide if a given rule-based system meets the specified integrity and timing constraints. Here, we focus on the latter.

To determine if a system satisfies the specified timing constraints, one has to have an adequate performance measure and a method to estimate it. We define the *response time* of a rule-based program in terms of the computation paths leading to fixed points. These paths can be obtained from a *state-space representation*, where a vertex uniquely defines a state of the real-time system and a transition identifies a single firing of a rule. An upper bound on the response time is then assessed by the maximum length of a path from an initial (launch) state to a fixed point. We show that even for the rule-based systems that use variables with finite domains, such an approach in the worst case requires exponential computation time as a function of the number of variables in the program [Browne, Cheng, and Mok, 1988].

We have implemented the methods on a class of real-time decision systems where decisions are computed by an *equational rule-based* (EQL) *program.* Corresponding analysis tools were developed to estimate the time responses for programs written in other production languages, for example, MRL [Wang and Mok, 1993] and OPS5 [Chen and Cheng, 1995a].

Within the deductive database research, similar concepts are presented by [Abiteboul and Simon, 1991]. They discuss the *totalness* and *loop-freeness* of a deductive system, which, in the terminology of rule-based systems, describes the stability of the systems in terms of the initial points reaching their fixed points in finite time.

If the analysis finds that the given real-time rule-based program meets the integrity but not the timing constraints, the program has to be optimized. We define this as the *synthesis problem*, which has to determine whether an extension of the original real-time system exists that would meet both timing and integrity constraints. The solution may be achieved by either (1) transforming the given equational rule-based program or (2) optimizing the scheduler to select the rules to fire such that some fixed point is always reached within the response-time constraint. The latter assumes that there is at least one sufficiently short path from a launch state to every one of its end points. In chapter 10, we gave an example for both solutions, but did not propose a corresponding algorithm.

In our definition of the synthesis problem, the original program is supposed to satisfy the integrity constraints. To obtain the optimized program satisfying the same constraints, we require that each launch state of the optimized program has the same set of corresponding fixed points as the original program. We believe that the optimization can benefit highly by easing this constraint, so that for each launch state the optimized program would have only a single corresponding fixed point taken from the set of fixed points of the unoptimized system. Such system has a *deterministic* behavior. [Aiken, Widom, and Hellerstein, 1992] formalize this concept for database production rules and discuss the *observable determinism of a rule set*. The rule set is observably deterministic if the execution order does not make any difference in the order of appearance of the observable actions. Similar concepts can be found in the process-algebraic approach described in chapter 9.

The chapter is organized as follows. We first review the necessary background and discuss in more detail the analysis and synthesis problem of real-time rule-based systems. Next we review the EQL rule-based language, its execution model and its state-space representation. Several optimization algorithms are then presented. We next experimentally evaluate these optimization algorithms. The methods—their limitations and possible extensions—are finally discussed.

12.3 BASIC DEFINITIONS

The real-time programs considered here belong to the class of EQL programs. Here we define the syntax of EQL programs and its execution model, define the measure for the response time of the EQL system, and formally introduce their state-space graphs.

12.3.1 EQL Program

An EQL program is given in the form of n rules $(r_1, \ldots, r_n)$ that operate over the set of m variables $(x_1, \ldots, x_m)$. Each rule has action and condition parts. Formally,

$$F_k(s) \quad \text{IF} \quad EC_k(s)$$

where $k \in \{1, \ldots, n\}$, $EC_k(s)$ is an enabling condition of rule k, and $F_k(s)$ is an action. Both the enabling condition and the action are defined over the state s of a system. Each state s is expressed as a tuple, $s = (x_1, \ldots, x_m)$, where x_i represents a value of ith variable. An action F_k is given as a series of $n_k \geq 1$ subactions separated by "!":

$$F_k \equiv L_{k,1} := R_{k,1}(x_1, \ldots, x_m) ! \ldots !$$

$$L_{k,n_k} := R_{k,n_k}(x_1, \ldots, x_m)$$

The subactions are interpreted from left to right. Each subaction sets the value of variable $L_{k,i} \in \{x_1, \ldots, x_m\}$ to the value returned by the function $R_{k,i}, i \in \{1, \ldots, n_k\}$. The enabling condition $EC_k(s)$ is a two-valued function that evaluates to TRUE for the states where rules can fire.

Throughout the chapter we will use two-valued variables only, that is, $x_i \in \{0, 1\}$. We will identify this subset of EQL by EQL(B). Any EQL program with a predefined set of possible values of the variables can be converted into the EQL(B). Due to the simplicity of such conversion, here we show only an example. Consider the following rules:

```
i := 2 IF j < 2 AND i = 3
[] j := i IF i = 2
```

where i and j are four-valued variables with their values $i, j \in \{0, 1, 2, 3\}$. The corresponding EQL(B) rules using two-valued variables i1, i2, j1, and j2 are:

```
i0 := TRUE ! i1 := FALSE
    IF (NOT j0 AND NOT j1) OR
       (NOT j0 AND j1) AND (i0 AND i1)
[] j0 := i0 ! j1 := i1
    IF (i0 AND NOT i1)
```

Furthermore, we constrain EQL(B) to use only constant assignments in the subactions of rules, that is, $R_{i,j} \in \{0, 1\}$. This can potentially reduce the complexity of optimization algorithms (see Section 12.3.4).

An example of an EQL(B) program is given in Figure 12.1. This program will be used in the following sections to demonstrate the various effects of the optimization. For clarity, the example program is intentionally kept simple. In practice, our method can be used for the systems of much higher complexity, possibly consisting of several hundred rules.

```
PROGRAM an_eql_b_program;
VAR
  a, b, c, d : BOOLEAN;
RULES
(* 1 *)         c:=1 IF a=0 AND b=0 AND d=0
(* 2 *) []      b:=1 IF d=0 AND (a=1 OR c=1)
(* 3 *) []      a:=1 ! c:=1 IF a=0 AND d=0 AND (b=1 OR c=1)
(* 4 *) []      b:=0 ! c:=0 IF d=0 AND b=1 AND
                                  (a=0 AND c=1 OR a=1 AND c=0)
(* 5 *) []      d:=0 ! a:=1 IF a=1 AND c=1 AND d=1
END.
```

Figure 12.1   An example of the EQL(B) rule-based expert system.

12.3.2 Execution Model of a Real-Time Decision System Based on an EQL Program Paradigm

Real-time decision systems based on the EQL program paradigm interact with the environment through sensor readings. Readings are then represented as the values of variables used in the EQL program that implements the decision system. The variables derived directly from sensor readings are called input variables. All other variables are called system variables. After the input variables are set the EQL program is invoked. Repeatedly, among the enabled rules a conflict resolution strategy is used to select a rule to fire. This (possibly) changes the state of the system, and

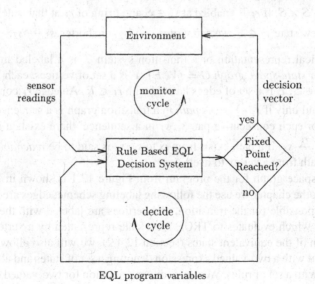

EQL program variables

Figure 12.2   An EQL program-based decision system.

the whole process of firing is repeated until either no more rules are enabled or rule firing does not change the system's state. The resulting state is called a *fixed point*. The values of the variables are then communicated back to the environment.

The process of reading the sensor variables, invoking the EQL program, and communicating back the values of the fixed point is called the *monitor cycle*. A fixed point is determined in a repetitive EQL invocation named the *decide cycle* (Figure 12.2).

As described in chapter 10, EQL's *response time* is the time an EQL system spends to reach a fixed point, or, equivalently, the time spent in the decide cycle. A real-time decision system is said to satisfy the timing constraints if the response time is smaller or equal to the smallest time interval between two sensor readings. A response time can be assessed by a maximum number of rules to be fired to reach a fixed point. The conversion from number of rule firings to response time can be done if one knows the time spent for identification of a rule to fire and the time spent for firing the rule itself. These times depend on the specific architecture of an implementation and will not be discussed here.

12.3.3 State-Space Representation

In order to develop an optimization method, we view an EQL(B) system as a *transition system* T, which is a triple, $(S, R, \rightarrow)$, where

1. S is a finite set of states. Assuming a finite set V of two-valued variables $x_1, x_2, \ldots, x_m$ and an ordering of V, S is the set of all 2^m possible Cartesian products of the values of variables;

2. R is a set of rules $r_1, r_2, \ldots, r_n$ in the system's rule base;

3. $\rightarrow$ is a mapping associated with each $r_k \in R$, that is, a transition relation $\overset{r_k}{\rightarrow} \subseteq S \times S$. If r_k is enabled at $s_1 \in S$ and firing of r_k at that state s_1 results in the new state $s_2 \in S$, we can write $s_1 \overset{r_k}{\rightarrow} s_2$, or shorter, $s_1 \overset{k}{\rightarrow} s_2$.

A graphical representation of a transition system T is a labeled finite directed *transition* or *state-space graph* $G = (V, E)$. V is a set of vertices, each labeled with the states $s \in S$. E is a set of edges labeled with $r_k \in R$. An edge r_k connects vertex s_1 to s_2 if and only if $s_1 \overset{r_k}{\rightarrow} s_2$. A *path* in a transition graph is a sequence of vertices such that for each consecutive pair s_i, s_j in a sequence, there exists a rule $r_k \in R$ such that $s_i \overset{r_k}{\rightarrow} s_j$. If a path exists from s_i to s_j, s_j is said to be *reachable* from s_i. A *cycle* is a path from a vertex to itself.

A state-space graph for the program from Figure 12.1 is shown in Figure 12.3. Throughout the chapter we use the following labeling scheme: edges are labeled with the rule responsible for the transition, and vertices are labeled with the two-valued expression, which evaluates to TRUE for a state represented by a vertex. After the introduction of the equivalent states (section 12.4.2), we will also allow the vertices to be labeled with a two-valued expression denoting a set of states and allow edges to be labeled with a set of rules. We use a compact notation for two-valued expressions. For example, ab represents a conjunction of a and b, a+b denotes a disjunction of a and b, and $\bar{a}$ represents a negation of a.

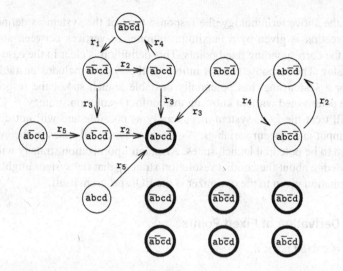

Figure 12.3 State-space graph for the EQL(B) program in Figure 12.1.

Each state may belong to one or more categories of states, which are:

- *fixed point*: A state is said to be a *fixed-point* state if it does not have any out-edges or if all of the out-edges are self-loops. For the state-space graph in Figure 12.3, an example of fixed points are $abc\overline{d}$, $\overline{a}bcd$, and $ab\overline{c}d$.
- *unstable*: A state is unstable if no fixed point is reachable from it. Because such states have to have out-edges (or else it would be a fixed point state), it either has to be involved in a cycle or has to have reachable a state involved in a cycle. States $ab\overline{c}\overline{d}$ and $ab\overline{c}\overline{d}$ from Figure 12.3 are unstable.
- *potentially unstable*: A potentially unstable state is either an unstable state or a state with a reachable fixed point, and either is involved in a cycle or has a path to the state involved in a cycle. States $\overline{a}b\overline{c}\overline{d}$, $\overline{a}b\overline{c}d$, and $\overline{a}bc\overline{d}$ from Figure 12.3 are potentially unstable.
- *stable*: A stable state is either a fixed point or a state from which no unstable or potentially unstable state is reachable. For example, states $\overline{a}bcd$ and $abc\overline{d}$ from Figure 12.3 are stable, while $\overline{a}bc\overline{d}$ is not.
- *potentially stable*: A potentially stable state is one with a reachable fixed point or is a fixed point itself. For example, states $\overline{a}b\overline{c}\overline{d}$ and $\overline{a}bc\overline{d}$ from Figure 12.3 are potentially stable.
- *launch*: The state in which the program is invoked is called the launch state.

Stable states are a subset of potentially stable states. Unstable states are a subset of potentially unstable states. No unstable state is potentially stable. Any valid state is either potentially stable or unstable.

Using the above terminology, the response time of the system as defined in the previous section is given by a maximum number of vertices between any launch state and the corresponding fixed points. This definition is clear in the case of stable launch states. The response time is infinite if the system includes unstable launch states. For a system that has potentially unstable launch states, the response time cannot be determined without knowing the conflict resolution strategy.

We will treat the EQL system as generally as possible and will not distinguish between input and system variables. As a consequence, all states in the system are considered to be potential launch states. Also, our optimization strategy will not use any knowledge about the conflict resolution strategy that the system might use. The sole information given to the optimizer is the EQL program itself.

12.3.4 Derivation of Fixed Points

A state s is a fixed point if:

F1. no rule is enabled at s, or
F2. for all the rules that are enabled at s, firing each of the rules will again result in the same state s.

We can consider the enabling condition to be an assertion over states, deriving TRUE if the rule is enabled or FALSE if it is disabled at a certain state. Our method does not find the fixed points explicitly (this would require an exhaustive search over all 2^m legal states), but rather constructs an assertion that would derive TRUE for fixed points and FALSE for all other states.

The assertion for fixed points for (F1) is defined as

$$FP_1 := \bigwedge_{i=1}^{n} \overline{EC_i}$$

To derive an assertion for (F2) (see Figure 12.4), we have to use an important property of the EQL(B) programs: a rule with constant assignments cannot be consecutively fired more than once so as to derive different states. That is, $a \xrightarrow{r} b \xrightarrow{r} c$ for $a \neq b \neq c$ does not exist. Furthermore, for each rule r_i we define a *destination assertion* D_i. D_i evaluates to TRUE for all states that may result from firing rule r_i and evaluates to FALSE otherwise. In other words, D_i is TRUE for state s if and only if there exists s', so that $s' \xrightarrow{r_i} s$. If such s' exists, s is called a *destination state* of rule r_i.

The assertion FP_2 is initially FALSE, that is, initially the set of states of type (F2) is empty. Then, for every rule r_i, an assertion S is constructed that is TRUE only for the states that both are destination states of that rule and enable the same rule (outmost **For** loop in Figure 12.4). Next, this assertion is checked against all other rules r_j (inmost **For** loop): the algorithm specializes the assertion S to exclude all the states that are not r_j's destination states and that enable r_j. For every rule, the

```
Procedure Derive_FP₂
Begin
    FP₂ := FALSE
    For i := 1 To n Do
        S = Dᵢ ∧ ECᵢ
        If S ≠ FALSE Then
            For j := 1 To n Do
                If i ≠ j and ECⱼ ∧ S Then
                    S := (S ∧ ‾ECⱼ) ∨ (S ∧ ECⱼ ∧ Dⱼ)
                End If
            End For
        End If
        FP₂ := S ∨ FP₂
    End For
End
```

Figure 12.4   Derivation of fixed-point assertion FP_2.

assertion S is disjuncted with current FP_2 to form a new FP_2. In other words, the states of type (F2) found for rule r_i are added to the set of fixed points.

Finally, an assertion for the fixed points is a disjunction, $FP = FP_1 \vee FP_2$. In the following discussions we use this assertion implicitly, meaning that when we assign a vertex to include all the fixed points, the vertex actually stores the assertion rather than the set of states. Due to the substantial number of details involved, here we omit the associated proofs and algorithms, which can be found in [Zupan, 1993].

12.4   OPTIMIZATION ALGORITHM

Our optimization method consists of two main steps: construction of an optimized finite-state-space graph and synthesis of a new EQL rule-based expert system from it. The potential exponential complexity of these two phases [Cheng, 1993b] is reduced by optimizing only one independent rule-set at a time. The optimization schema is depicted in Figure 12.5.

In this section we first present the EQL(B) rule-base decomposition technique. We then propose different optimization methods, all of which have in common the idea of generating the transition system from fixed points up and vary in the complexity of vertices and edges in the generated state-space graphs. Methods that are simpler in the implementation but potentially more complex in the execution are presented first. The section concludes with the algorithm that uses the generated state-space graph to synthesize the optimized EQL(B) program.

12.4.1   Decomposition of an EQL(B) Program

We use a decomposition algorithm for EQL as given in [Cheng, 1993b] and modify it for the EQL(B) case. The algorithm is based on the notion of *rule independence*.

Procedure *Optimize*
Begin
      Read in the original EQL(B) program $\mathcal{P}$
      Construct high level dependency (HLD) graph
      Using HLD graph, identify independent rule-sets in $\mathcal{P}$
      Forall independent rule-sets in $\mathcal{P}$ **Do**
            Construct optimized state-space graph $\mathcal{T}$
            Synthesize optimized EQL(B) program $\mathcal{O}$ from $\mathcal{T}$
            Output $\mathcal{O}$
      End Forall
End

Figure 12.5   General optimization schema.

The decomposition algorithm uses the set L_k of variables appearing in the left-hand side of the multiple assignment statement of rule k (e.g., for the EQL(B) program in Figure 12.1, $L_5 = \{a, d\}$). Rule a is said to be *independent* from rule b if $(\text{D1a} \vee \text{D1b}) \wedge \text{D2}$ holds, where:

D1a. $L_a \cap L_b = \emptyset$,

D1b. $L_a \cap L_b \neq \emptyset$ and for every variable $v \in L_a \cap L_b$, the same expression must be assigned to v in both rules a and b, and

D2. rule a does not potentially enable rule b, that is, a state does not exist where a is enabled and b is disabled, and firing a enables b.

The algorithm first constructs the rule-dependency graph. This consists of vertices (one for every rule) and directed edges. A directed edge connects a vertex a to b if rule a is not independent from rule b. All vertices that belong to the same strongly connected component are then grouped into a single vertex. The derived graph is called a *high-level dependency graph* and each vertex stores the *forward-independent rule-set*. Figure 12.6 shows an example of a HLD graph for the EQL(B) program given in Figure 12.1.

Rules can now be fired by following the topological ordering of the vertices (rule sets). For each vertex the corresponding rules are fired until a fixed point is reached. If the EQL program is guaranteed to reach the fixed point from every launch state, the above rule schedule will guarantee the program will reach a fixed point as well [Cheng, 1993b].

If the optimization technique maintains the assertion about fixed-point reachability for every independent rule-set, each rule-set can be optimized independently. The above decomposition method was evaluated in [Cheng, 1993b] and the results encourage us to use it to substantially reduce the complexity of the optimization process.

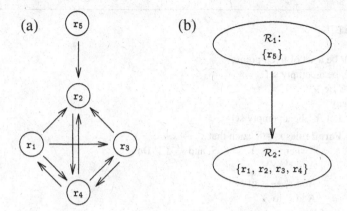

Figure 12.6 Rule-dependency graph (a) and a corresponding high-level dependency graph (b) for the EQL(B) program in Figure 12.1.

12.4.2   Derivation of an Optimized State-Space Graph

The core of EQL(B) optimization is a construction of a corresponding state-space graph. We use a bottom-up approach and start the derivation from the fixed points. We show that the main advantage of this approach is its simplicity to remove the cycles and to identify the paths with the minimal number of rules to fire to reach the fixed points.

Here, no notion of conflict resolution strategy is used. For each stable or potentially unstable state, all corresponding fixed points are treated as equivalent. In other words, the EQL(B) execution is valid if for each launch state the system converges to a fixed point arbitrarily selected from a set of corresponding fixed points.

Bottom-Up Derivation   The optimized transition system is derived directly from the set of EQL(B) rules. The derivation algorithm combines the bottom-up and breadth-first search strategies. It starts at the fixed points and gradually expands each fixed point until all stable and potentially unstable states are found. Note that the stable and potentially unstable states constitute the set of all states that have one or more reachable fixed points.

We will refer to the algorithm step of adding a new vertex s' and a new edge r to a state-space graph as an *expansion*. The state s for which $s' \xrightarrow{r} s$ is referred to as an *expanded state*.

The optimization algorithm BU (Figure 12.7) uses the variables $\mathcal{V}$ and $\mathcal{E}$ to store the vertices and edges of the current state-space graph. The fixed points are determined by using the fixed point assertion (section 12.3.4). Rather than scanning the whole state space (2^m states) to find the fixed points, the algorithm examines the fixed-point assertion and directly determines the corresponding states. For example, rule-set $R_1 = \{r_1, r_2, r_3, r_4\}$ by itself has $FP = $ a AND b AND c OR d. In the first term the variable d is free, so the fixed points are abcd and abcd̄. The fixed points

Procedure BU
Begin
    Let $\mathcal{V}$ be a set of fixed points
    Let $\mathcal{E}$ be an empty set
    Let $\mathcal{X}$ be $\mathcal{V}$
    Repeat
        Let $\mathcal{X}^*$ be an empty set
        Forall rules $r \in \mathcal{R}$ such that $s' \xrightarrow{r} s$,
            where $s \in \mathcal{X}$, $s' \in \mathcal{S}$, and $s' \notin \mathcal{V}$ **Do**
            Add s' to $\mathcal{V}$
            Add $s' \xrightarrow{r} s$ to $\mathcal{E}$
            Add s' to $\mathcal{X}^*$
        End Forall
        Let $\mathcal{X}$ be $\mathcal{X}^*$
    Until $\mathcal{X}$ is an empty set
End

Figure 12.7 Bottom-up generation of an optimized transition system.

derived from the second term are composed of value 1 for d combined with all combinations of values for variables a, b, and c, yielding $2^3 = 8$ different fixed points.

The optimized state-space graphs have no cycles. This is a result of constraining the states in the system to have at most one out-transition; that is, no two rules $r_1, r_2 \in \mathcal{R}$ exist such that $s' \xrightarrow{r_1} s_1$ and $s' \xrightarrow{r_2} s_2$. Consequently, each state in the resulting system will have exactly one reachable fixed point.

The breadth-first search uses two sets, $\mathcal{X}$ and $\mathcal{X}^*$. $\mathcal{X}$ stores the states that are potential candidates for expansion. The states used in the expansion of states in $\mathcal{X}$ are added to $\mathcal{X}^*$. After the states in $\mathcal{X}$ are exhausted, the expansion is continued for the states that have been stored in $\mathcal{X}^*$. Note that at any time instant each set stores the states that are equally distant from the fixed point; that is, a fixed point can be reached by firing the same number of rules.

A breadth-first search guarantees that all the fixed points in the resulting system are reached with a minimal number of rules to be fired. In other words, for each state that is not unstable in the original system, the only reachable fixed point in the new system will be the closest one with respect to the number of rules to fire.

The bottom-up approach discovers only the states that are either stable or potentially unstable. All unstable states, as well as cycles that they are a part of, are removed from the system.

Figure 12.8 shows a possible optimized transition system derived for our EQL(B) example program. Comparison with Figure 12.3 reveals that the optimization eliminates the cycles $\overline{a}\overline{b}c\overline{d} \xrightarrow{2} \overline{a}bc\overline{d} \xrightarrow{4} \overline{a}\overline{b}\overline{c}\overline{d} \xrightarrow{1} \overline{a}\overline{b}c\overline{d}$ and $a\overline{b}\overline{c}\overline{d} \xrightarrow{2} ab\overline{c}\overline{d} \xrightarrow{4} a\overline{b}\overline{c}\overline{d}$ and removes unstable states $\overline{a}b\overline{c}\overline{d}$ and $ab\overline{c}\overline{d}$. The optimization arbitrarily breaks the tie of which rule to use for expansion, and thus an alternative system with equivalent response time could have a transition $\overline{a}\overline{b}c\overline{d} \xrightarrow{3} a\overline{b}c\overline{d}$ instead of $\overline{a}\overline{b}c\overline{d} \xrightarrow{2} \overline{a}bc\overline{d}$.

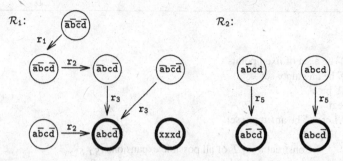

Figure 12.8   State-space graphs for independent rule-sets $\mathcal{R}_1$ and $\mathcal{R}_2$ as generated from the EQL(B) program in Figure 12.1 using the BU algorithm. xxxd denotes all eight states for which the value of variable d is equal to 1.

Equivalence of States   Although the plain bottom-up derivation of the state-space graph approach outlined above reduces the number of examined states by excluding the unstable states, the number of vertices in the state space graph remains potentially high and further reductions are necessary. The idea is to join the equivalent states. The new optimization algorithm derives a state-space graph with vertices representing one or more equivalent states. These vertices are labeled with the expression that identifies the equivalent states of the vertex.

To distinguish the labeling of a vertex with a single state and with the set of states, we will use the symbols s and S, respectively. Thus, for a vertex S, $S = \{s : s \in \mathcal{S}\}$, all s in S are *equivalent*. Also, the transition r from a set S_i to a set S_j would mean that for any state in S_i there is a transition $s_i \xrightarrow{r} s_j$ such that $s_i \in S_i$ and $s_j \in S_j$.

Figure 12.9 shows the recursive algorithm that transforms a state-space graph as derived in section 12.4.2 to a graph with equivalent states. Note that the transforma-

---

Procedure *Join_Equivalent_States(vertex S)*
Begin
    Forall rules $r \in \mathcal{R}$ such that $s \xrightarrow{r} S$ exists **Do**
        Let S^* be a set of all states s, for which $s \xrightarrow{r} S$
        Call *Join_Equivalent_States(S*)*
    End Forall
End

Procedure *Transform_BU*
Begin
    Let S_f be a set of fixed points
    Call *Join_Equivalent_States(S_f)*
End

Figure 12.9   Transformation of the state-space graph generated with the BU algorithm to the graph with grouped equivalent states. Equivalence is based on an equally labeled single-rule transition to a single state. The transformation is initiated with a call to *Transform_BU*.

Procedure ES
Begin
    Let $\mathcal{V}$ be a set of fixed points
    Let $\mathcal{E}$ be an empty set
    Let $\mathcal{X}$ be $\mathcal{V}$
    Repeat
        Let $\mathcal{X}^*$ be an empty set
        Repeat
            Construct a set $\mathcal{T}$ of all possible expansions t_{S,r,S^*},
                such that for every t_{S,r,S^*} and every $s \in S$:
                • $s \notin S'$ if $S' \in \mathcal{V}$ and
                • $s \xrightarrow{r} s^*$, where $s^* \in S^*$ and $S^* \in \mathcal{X}$.
            If set $\mathcal{T}$ is not empty **Then**
                Choose t_{S,r,S^*} from $\mathcal{T}$ such that S includes
                    the biggest number of states
                Add S to $\mathcal{V}$
                Add $S \xrightarrow{r} S^*$ to $\mathcal{E}$
                Add S to $\mathcal{X}^*$
        End If
        Until $\mathcal{T}$ is an empty set
        Let $\mathcal{X}$ be $\mathcal{X}^*$
    Until $\mathcal{X}$ is an empty set
End

Figure 12.10   Bottom-up generation of an optimized transition system with derivation of equivalent states.

---

tion process uses the operator $s' \xrightarrow{r} S$, which means that a transition $s' \xrightarrow{r} s$ exists for $s \in S$.

Rather than transforming the optimized state-space graph, we use the ES algorithm that directly derives the system with equivalent states (Figure 12.10). Again, the algorithm uses the bottom-up approach starting from the fixed-point states and the breadth-first search approach to derive the optimal system with respect to the number of rules to fire. Each time the algorithm expands the system with a new vertex, all possible expansions are considered and the vertex with the biggest number of equivalent states is chosen. This greedy approach may contribute to further minimization of the size of the state-space graph.

For example, suppose there are two states, S_1 and S_2, that are considered for expansion. Let there be two states, s_a and s_b, that are not yet included in the state-space graph such that $s_a \xrightarrow{r} s_1$, $s_b \xrightarrow{r} s_1$, $s_b \xrightarrow{r} s_2$, where $s_1 \in S_1$ and $s_2 \in S_2$. The greedy algorithm will generate a set $S_3 = \{s_a, s_b\}$ and establish a transition $S_3 \xrightarrow{r} S_1$ instead of using the expansion of S_2 with $S_3 = \{s_b\}$.

Figure 12.11 shows a state-space graph with equivalent states constructed using the ES optimization algorithm. Note that instead of the states $\overline{a}bc\overline{d}$ and $\overline{a}b\overline{c}\overline{d}$ there is a new state $\overline{a}b\overline{d}$ (besides joining the fixed points into a single vertex, two equivalent

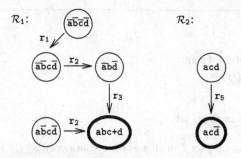

Figure 12.11   State-space graphs for independent rule-sets $\mathcal{R}_1$ and $\mathcal{R}_2$ as generated from the EQL(B) program in Figure 12.1, using the ES algorithm.

states have been found) and that the number of states for R_2 has halved (two pairs of equivalent states have been identified).

Multiple-Rule Transitions   To further reduce the number of vertices in the state-space graphs, we use the technique that originates from the notion of *intra-rule-set parallelism* [Cheng, 1993b] and from the idea of utilizing the concurrency for preventing the state explosion [Godefroid, Holzmann, and Pirottin, 1992]. In contrast with the BU and ES algorithms, here we allow transitions to be labeled with a set of rules, R, rather than with a single rule, r.

For every vertex S in the state-space graph considered for expansion, we find all possible rule-sets so that for a particular set R, each of the rules $r \in R$ can be used to expand S. In other words, for all rules $r \in R$ there should exist S' such that $S' \xrightarrow{r} S$ and none of the states in S' is yet included in the transition system.

Furthermore, for every pair of rules $r_i, r_j \in R, r_i \neq r_j$, the following conditions should hold:

M1. rules r_i and r_j do not potentially disable each other.

M2. $L_{r_i} \cap L_{r_j} = \emptyset$, or $L_{r_i} \cap L_{r_j} \neq \emptyset$ and rule r_i and r_j assign the same values to the variables of the subset $L_{r_i} \cap L_{r_j}$.

(M1) follows the idea of intra-rule-set parallelism [Cheng, 1993b]. Rule r_i potentially disables r_j if a state exists where both rules are enabled and firing r_i results in a state where r_j is disabled. (M2) guarantees the cycle-free firing of rules in R for the states in S', where $S' \xrightarrow{R} S$. (For a detailed proof, see [Zupan, 1993].)

The algorithm (Figure 12.12) exploits both equivalency of states and allows multiple-rule transitions. It uses the bottom-up approach and breadth-first search. The method is greedy and at each step adds the biggest set of equivalent states to the evolving graph.

For our example EQL(B) program, an optimized state-space graph using the ESM algorithm is shown in Figure 12.13. Note that for rule-set R_1 the number of vertices is reduced to three, and the rules r_2 and r_3 can fire in parallel.

Procedure ESM
Begin
  Let $\mathcal{V}$ be a set of fixed points
  Let $\mathcal{E}$ be an empty set
  Let $\mathcal{X}$ be $\mathcal{V}$
  Repeat
    Let $\mathcal{X}^*$ be an empty set
    Repeat
      Construct a set $\mathcal{T}$ of all possible expansions t_{S,R,S^*},
        such that for every t_{S,R,S^*} and every $s \in S$
        • $s \notin S'$ if $S' \in \mathcal{V}$,
        • rules in $\bar{R}$ can fire in parallel, and
        • forall $r \in R$, $s \xrightarrow{r} s^*$, where $s^* \in S^*$
          and $S^* \in \mathcal{X}$.
      If set $\mathcal{T}$ is not empty **Then**
        Choose t_{S,R,S^*} from $\mathcal{T}$ such that S includes
          the biggest number of states
        Add S to $\mathcal{V}$
        Add $S \xrightarrow{R} S^*$ to $\mathcal{E}$
        Add S to $\mathcal{X}^*$
      End If
    Until $\mathcal{T}$ is an empty set
    Let $\mathcal{X}$ be $\mathcal{X}^*$
  Until $\mathcal{X}$ is an empty set
End

Figure 12.12 Bottom-up generation of an optimized transition system with generation of equivalent states and multiple-rule transitions.

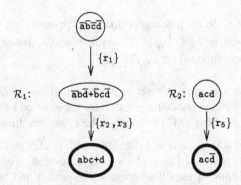

Figure 12.13 State-space graphs for independent rule-sets $\mathcal{R}_1$ and $\mathcal{R}_2$ as generated from the EQL(B) program in Figure 12.1, using the ESM algorithm.

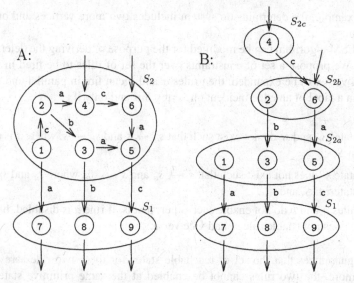

Figure 12.14 An example of a non-deterministic section of a transition system $S_2 \xrightarrow{\{a,b,c\}} S_1$(a) and its corresponding deterministic system $S_{2c} \xrightarrow{\{c\}} S_{2b} \xrightarrow{\{b,a\}} S_{2a} \xrightarrow{\{a,b,c\}} S_1$(b).

While the introduction of multiple-rule transitions minimizes the number of states in the transition system, such a system loses its determinism. A two-vertex section of an imaginary state-space graph shown in Figure 12.14(a) explains the point. Vertex S_2 combines six states, and uses three rules $R = \{a, b, c\}$ that can fire in parallel such that $S' \xrightarrow{R} S$. Both rules a and b are enabled at states 2 and 3 and, for example, from launch state 2, two different states 8 and 9 are reachable and can potentially lead to two different stable states (fixed points).

The ESM algorithm does not guarantee the minimal response time for the state-space graphs it generates. This is because ESM does not optimize the rule firings for the states in the same vertex. This shortcoming can be overcome by additionally optimizing each vertex with the ES method. The optimized graph would then be equivalent to the one using the ES method alone. This shows a potential use of the combination of these two methods, when the approach using the ES method is prohibitively expensive because of the large size of the state-space graph.

Deterministic State Graphs With Multiple-Rule Transitions   To preserve the determinism in the state graphs with multiple rules labeling a single edge, additional constraints have to be imposed. The constraints should enforce the mutual exclusivity of the enabling conditions of the resulting rules; that is, in each state of the optimized transition system no more than one rule can fire. For example, a system from Figure 12.14(a) can have a corresponding deterministic system shown in Figure 12.14(b). The tradeoff is the increased complexity of the state-space graph:

in our example, the deterministic system includes two more vertices and one more transition.

The ESM algorithm can be modified for the purpose of deriving the deterministic system. We propose a set of constraints over the set of rules to be fired in parallel. If S is a vertex to be expanded, then rules a and b can fire in parallel and together appear in a label of an edge incident on vertex S if and only if:

I1. states s_a and s_b do not exist such that $s_a \xrightarrow{a} s$ and $s_b \xrightarrow{b} s$, where s is the state in S,

I2. state s' does not exist such that $s' \xrightarrow{a} s_a$ and $s' \xrightarrow{b} s_b$, where s_a and s_b are the states in S, and

I3. rules a and b do not enable each other; that is, if rule a is disabled, firing rule b does not enable rule a, and vice versa.

(I1) guarantees that the set of reachable states for these two rules are disjoint. Furthermore, the two rules cannot be enabled at the same primitive states of S', $S' \xrightarrow{R} S$ and $a, b \in R$, because of the constraints (I2) and (I3). We will refer to this modified algorithm as ESMD.

We believe that in addition to the set of constraints mentioned above, other similar sets exist that could possibly lead to similar or better results. Future research work dealing with the determinism of the transition system should address this issue.

12.4.3 Synthesis of an Optimized EQL(B) Program

A new EQL(B) program is synthesized from the constructed optimized transition system. For each rule in the independent rule-set, the new enabling condition is determined by scanning through the state space graph so that for rule r_i the new enabling condition is.

$$EC_i^{New} = \left(\bigvee_{S \xrightarrow{R} S', \, r_i \in R} S \right) \wedge EC_i.$$

S and S' are labels of two vertices in the state-space graph that are connected with the edge labeled with r_i or with the set that includes r_i. In the case of the state-space graph having all edges labeled with a single rule, the conjunctive term EC_i can be omitted in the above expression.

The new rules are then formed with the same assignment parts as the original rules and the new enabling conditions. Rules not included in any constructed state-space graph are redundant and are not added to the new rule base.

The optimized EQL(B) program constructed using the optimization algorithm BU or ES is shown in Figure 12.15. Because of the inclusion of state $\overline{a}\overline{b}c\overline{d}$ to the enabling condition of rule r_3, the optimization algorithm ESM derives a slightly different re-

```
PROGRAM an_optimized_eql_b_program_1;
VAR
    a, b, c, d : BOOLEAN;
RULES
(* 1 *)          c:=1 IF a=0 AND b=0 AND c=0 AND d=0
(* 2 *) []       b:=1 IF b=0 AND c=1 AND d=0
(* 3 *) []       a:=1 ! c:=1 IF a=0 AND b=1 AND d=0
(* 5 *) []       d:=0 ! a:=1 IF a=1 AND c=1 AND d=1
END.
```

Figure 12.15   An optimized EQL(B) program derived from the program in Figure 12.1, using either the BU or ES algorithm.

```
PROGRAM an_optimized_eql_b_program_2;
VAR
    a, b, c, d : BOOLEAN;
RULES
(* 1 *)          c:=1 IF a=0 AND b=0 AND c=0 AND d=0
(* 2 *) []       b:=1 IF b=0 AND c=1 AND d=0
(* 3 *) []       a:=1 ! c:=1 IF a=0 AND b=1 AND d=0 OR
                                a=0 AND c=1 AND d=0
(* 5 *) []       d:=0 ! a:=1 IF a=1 AND c=1 AND d=1
END.
```

Figure 12.16   An optimized EQL(B) program derived from the program in Figure 12.1, using the ESM algorithm.

sult (Figure 12.16). Note that rule r_4 was found to be redundant and does not appear in any of the resulting programs.

12.5   EXPERIMENTAL EVALUATION

We have implemented three of the four optimization algorithms presented here, and intentionally bypass the implementation of the BU algorithm due to the possible combinatorial complexity of state-space graph generation. This section attempts to experimentally evaluate the performance of these optimization algorithms on two sets of computer-generated EQL programs and on a commercial rule-based expert system.

Because of the general unavailability of analysis tools for real-time rule-based systems, it is hard to assess the performance of optimization methods proposed here. Such analysis tools should derive the number of rules to be fired to reach a fixed point for both original and optimized rule-based programs and should analyze the stability of the programs. For EQL rule-based programs, the Estella analysis tool (described in chapter 10) has the potential to estimate both. Estella can discover potential cycles, and, when no cycles exist, Estella can estimate an upper bound of the number of rules to fire to reach a fixed point. Unfortunately, Estella imposes several constraints to rules in EQL programs it can analyze, and even if these constraints are met, it might discover a potential cycle even if one does not exist. Estella's assessment of stability is sufficient, but not necessary. That is, if no potential cycles are found, the program is guaranteed to be stable, but the discovery of a potential cycle might not ensure that one really exists.

To clearly state the difference between the original and optimized programs, a precise upper bound of the number of rules to fire to reach a fixed point is required. For this purpose, we have built a system like the one described in [Browne, Cheng, and Mok, 1988] that takes an EQL program, converts it to a C-language routine, and then uses it to build an exact state-space graph. Next, the system performs an exhaustive search to find if the EQL program is stable and to derive a precise upper bound of the number of rules to fire to reach a fixed point. In case of cycles, such a bound is given as a maximum number of rules to fire to reach a fixed point from some state without going into a firing cycle. On one side, such estimation of the bound is pessimistic, because it assumes a rule-firing scheduler to select the rules to fire so that it does not find an optimal and shortest path to a fixed point. On the other side, such estimation may be very optimistic, since it assumes the scheduler would avoid any cycle.

Although the analysis method described above is general and could be used with any EQL(B) program, due to substantial computer resources required and high time complexity, it works only with EQL(B) programs that use only a few variables. For this reason, two sets of relatively simple EQL(B) programs that allow for such analysis but that are still complex enough to show the advantages and disadvantages of the proposed optimization methods were computer-generated.

12.5.1   EQL(B) Programs without Cycles

A set of five cycle-free EQL(B) programs were computer-generated. The generator is given the number of rules and variables in the program, and the desired average complexity of the action and condition parts. The action part complexity is proportional to the number of assignments and the enabling condition complexity is proportional to the number of Boolean operations in the rules' enabling conditions. All test programs were generated to consist of only one independent rule-set. Additional constraints were imposed for the programs to meet one of the special form requirements and therefore to be acceptable for analysis with the Estella tool. Both Estella and the exact state-space graph–based analysis described above were then used to, respectively, estimate and derive the precise upper bound of the number of rules to fire.

Table 12.1 presents the results of the analysis of generated EQL(B) programs and their corresponding optimized versions. Algorithms ES and ESM were used for the optimization. We observed the following:

- Optimization always resulted in a program with the same (P2 and P4) or lower number (P1, P3, and P5) of rule firings to reach a fixed point.

TABLE 12.1   Analysis results for unoptimized (U) programs P1 . . . P5 and their corresponding optimized programs using ES and ESM optimization algorithms

	#R			#V	#rules to fire			#oper/rule			#vars/rule			#vertices	
	U	ES	ESM		U	ES	ESM	U	ES	ESM	U	ES	ESM	ES	ESM
P1	5	4	3	5	3(5)	2(4)	2(5)	1.8	10.0	13.0	1.8	4.7	4.3	6	4
P2	5	5	4	5	3(4)	3(3)	3(4)	7.2	7.8	10.0	3.8	3.8	4.0	12	4
P3	5	5	4	5	4(5)	3(3)	3(4)	1.5	11.8	8.6	1.6	4.7	4.8	9	3
P4	10	9	7	5	4(5)	4(5)	4(5)	2.3	11.7	8.0	2.1	5.0	4.0	18	2
P5	10	9	8	10	6(7)	5(7)	4(7)	7.2	114.4	143.7	4.5	9.6	9.9	37	6

#R = number of rules in a program. #V = number of variables used in a program. #rules to fire = maximum number of rules to fire to reach a fixed point (a precise number of rules to fire is given, a number estimated by Estella is given in parentheses). #oper/rule = average number of logical AND, OR, and NOT operations required to evaluate an enabling condition of a rule. #vars/rule = average number of variables used in enabling condition of a rule. #vertices = number of vertices in the state-space graph derived by optimization algorithm.

- For every example program, the optimization found some rules to be redundant.
- The complexity metrics for enabling conditions of the rules (#oper/rule and #vars/rule) indicate that the optimized programs have more complex enabling conditions. The reason for this is that the optimization is actually a process of removing the unstable states with transitions that lead into cycles. After optimization, the enabling conditions are satisfied for equal or usually fewer states than in the original program. Even though we have applied Boolean minimization to the resulting enabling conditions, the increased specialization usually leads to increased complexity of enabling conditions.
- As expected, compared to algorithm ES, algorithm ESM always found a more compact state-space graph with fewer vertices.
- All optimized programs satisfy Estella constraints and enable Estella to be used for analysis. This is a rather special case, and although cycle-free, the optimized programs do not always satisfy Estella constraints. Furthermore, because of the approximate nature of Estella analysis, this may not be sufficient to judge the optimization of an upper bound of the number of rules to fire to reach a fixed state. For example, based on the sole analysis of Estella, one could conclude that algorithm ES optimized program P2 but did not optimize P5, which is in contradiction with a finding based on derivation of the precise upper bound of the number of rules to fire. In all cases, however, Estella found the optimized programs to be stable—the result expected due to the nature of our optimization method.

12.5.2   EQL(B) Programs with Cycles

Similar to programs from Table 12.1, a set of six unstable EQL(B) programs were generated (Table 12.2). These programs have state-space graphs that include unstable and potentially unstable states. An upper bound of the number of rules to fire to reach

TABLE 12.2 Analysis results for unoptimized (U) programs S1 ... S6 and their corresponding optimized programs using ES and ESM optimization algorithms

	#R			#V	#rules to fire			#oper/rule			#vars/rule			#vertices		
	U	ES	ESM		U	ES	ESM	U	ES	ESM	U	ES	ESM	ES	ESM	%pus
S1	5	3	2	4	2	1(1)	1(1)	6.2	5.7	6.5	2.8	4.0	4.0	3	2	50
S2	9	9	5	5	7	4	3(4)	5.7	5.7	8.2	3.9	3.9	4.2	8	2	87.5
S3	5	5	4	5	5	3	3	1.8	11.2	10.5	1.8	4.6	4.7	7	5	28.1
S4	5	3	3	5	4	2	2	1.8	10.7	10.7	1.8	5.0	5.0	5	4	52.5
S5	10	9	8	10	10	4	4	7.2	97.6	58.7	4.5	9.6	9.6	24	4	69.9
S6	10	6	8	5	8	4	4(5)	2.3	11.0	9.2	2.1	5.0	4.5	15	2	50.0

%pus = number of potentially unstable states as a percent of all states in unoptimized program. For an explanation of other abbreviations used, see Table 12.1.

a fixed point was derived for original and optimized programs as described in the previous section.

From experimental results shown in Table 12.2, similar conclusions to those in the previous section can be drawn. Most important, optimization always reduced the number of rules to fire to reach a fixed point. Again, compared to ES, algorithm ESM derived the state-space graphs with considerably fewer numbers of vertices. Also, due to the specialization of rules, optimized rules have more complex enabling conditions than unoptimized rules.

A number of the optimized programs (S1, S2, and S6) satisfied Estella's constraints and enabled Estella to estimate the upper bound of the number of rules to be fired. The effect of optimization to enable this particular use of the Estella tool is not general, but one might find it useful when it takes place.

The programs in both Tables 12.1 and 12.2 were also optimized using algorithm ESMD. This gave similar results as when algorithm ES was used, resulting in state-space graphs with much higher numbers of vertices than in those generated by algorithm ESM. This is due to the high specificity of constraints that algorithm ESMD imposes over the rules to fire in parallel in order to derive a deterministic state-space graph.

12.5.3 Industrial Example: Optimization of the Integrated Status Assessment Expert System

To demonstrate the applicability of the proposed optimization techniques, we used it to optimize the *Integrated Status Assessment Expert System* (ISA) [Marsh, 1988]. This real-time expert system, originally written by Mitre in OPS5, identifies the faulty components in the planned NASA Space Station. Its EQL equivalent is described in [Cheng et al., 1993], and for the purpose here we have converted it to an EQL(B) program that consists of 35 rules and 46 variables.

In the first optimization step, ISA is decomposed into 17 independent rule-sets. The analysis with the Estella tool shows that for only four rule-sets, either the potential number of firings to reach the fixed point is greater than one, the rule-set has a

TABLE 12.3   Independent rule-sets of ISA with cycle (ISA1), with more than one rule to fire to reach a fixed point (ISA2 and ISA3), or not conforming to constraints to be analyzable by Estella (ISA4)

	IDs of rules in a subset	#vars
ISA1	#3, #6, #18, #34, #35	40
ISA2	#11, #19	9
ISA3	#9, #17	6
ISA4	#8, #16, #32, #33	16

#vars = number of variables used in a rule set.

cycle, or the rules in the set are not analyzable with Estella. Table 12.3 lists the IDs of rules in these sets and gives the number of variables used within each set.

For rule set ISA1, the Estella analysis tool identifies a possible cycle involving rules #34, #10, and #18 (see [Cheng et al., 1993] for the similar analysis that discovered a potential cycle in ISA). For ISA2 and ISA3, Estella estimated the upper bound of rule firings to reach a fixed point to be 2. Rules in ISA4 do not meet Estella's constraints and could not be further analyzed with Estella.

As for EQL(B) computer-generated programs that were presented in this section, the derivation of the precise upper bound of the number of rules to fire to reach a fixed point is needed to clearly evaluate the effects of the optimization. Due to the relatively low number of variables used, the analysis for ISA2, ISA3, and ISA4 that uses the exact derivation of the complete state-space graph as described in the beginning of this section is possible. To make such exact analysis possible for ISA1, we have changed its rules to obtain an equivalent but analyzable system. Namely, we have observed that several variables appear in ISA1 only in the enabling conditions, and we have found that some pairs of such variables could be replaced by a single variable. For example, if the expressions a=TRUE AND b=TRUE and a=FALSE AND b=FALSE are the only ones that involve a and b and are found among rules in a specific subset, a new variable c may be introduced and used instead of a and b, so that c=FALSE indicates that both a and b are FALSE and c=TRUE indicates that both a and b are TRUE. Two expressions involving a and b, respectively, are then changed to c=TRUE and c=FALSE. Such manual alteration of rules reduced the number of variables used in ISA1 to 14.

The optimization algorithms ES and ESM were then used on the four ISA rule-sets mentioned. The exact analysis with the use of the complete state-space graph shows that:

- For ISA1, as Estella analysis suggested, the unoptimized set of rules really is unstable. The longest path from some state to a fixed point that does not involve a cycle requires firing four rules. A corresponding optimized rule set is cycle-free and takes a maximum of three rules to be fired to reach a fixed point. The average number of logical AND, OR, and NOT operations to evaluate an enabling condition of a rule increased from 15.6 to 58.8. Algorithms ES and ESM derived the graph with five vertices.

- For ISA4, the unoptimized rule-set is cycle-free and requires a maximum of five rules to be fired to reach a fixed point. A corresponding optimized set required a maximum of four rules to be fired. The average number of operations to evaluate an enabling condition increased from four to 24. While algorithm ESM derived a state space consisting of nine vertices, the one derived by ES used 14 vertices.

- In the case of ISA2 and ISA3, an optimal rule-set would still need a maximum of two rule firings to reach a fixed state, so no optimization of the original rule-set is required.

12.6   COMMENTS ON OPTIMIZATION METHODS

This section provides a qualitative comparison of the optimization methods, comments on the constraints over EQL language required by optimization algorithms, and considers the optimization of other real-time rule-based systems.

12.6.1   Qualitative Comparison of Optimization Methods

In the previous section we presented several techniques for the optimization of rule-based systems. They were all based on a bottom-up approach for derivation of an optimized state-space graph. All remove the unstable states and generate a state graph with only stable states. Potentially unstable states of the unoptimized program are transformed into stable states in the optimized system by removing the transitions that were responsible for cycles. Optimization alters the enabling condition part of rules, leaving the action part unchanged. Although these methods exhibit many similarities, they vary in complexity (execution time and required memory space) and in the optimization results they achieve.

Table 12.4 qualitatively compares the optimization methods. It shows the trade-off between minimizing the number of rules to fire and minimizing the size of the state-space graphs. While BU and ES can guarantee minimization of rule firings, the number of vertices in the state-space graph generated by ESM is expected to be

TABLE 12.4   Optimization algorithms and their features

Features	Optimization algorithm			
	BU	ES	ESM	ESMD
Exploits equivalence of states	no	yes	yes	yes
Exploits rule-firing concurrency	no	no	yes	yes
Removes cycles and unstable states	yes	yes	yes	yes
Stabilizes potentially unstable states	yes	yes	yes	yes
Minimizes number of rules to fire	yes	yes	no	yes
Generates deterministic transition system	yes	yes	no	yes

lower. ESMD minimizes the number of the rule firings, but as shown in the following discussion, does not perform well with respect to the state-space graph complexity minimization.

12.6.2   On Constraints over EQL Language Required by Optimization Algorithms

To enable the use of the proposed optimization techniques, several constraints were imposed on EQL rule-based programs. First, a two-valued (Boolean) EQL(B) variant of the EQL language is used. In section 12.3.1 we showed that the conversion from multi-valued EQL program to corresponding two-valued EQL(B) is straightforward. EQL(B) rules are further constrained to use only constant assignments in the sub-actions (section 12.3.1). This simplifies the derivation of fixed points and is then implicitly used also in the conditions for rule-based decomposition (D1a), (D1b), and (D2), section 12.4.1) and for parallel rule firing (M1) and (M2), section 12.4.2). To use the proposed optimization technique also for EQL(B) programs with noncon-stant assignments, a possible solution is to convert them to corresponding programs with constant assignments. Such a conversion is straightforward and we illustrate it through an example. Consider the following rule:

```
v1 := Exp1 ! v2 := Exp2 IF EC
```

where Exp1 and Exp2 are nonconstant expressions and EC is the enabling condition. This rule can be converted to its constant-assignment equivalent:

```
   v1 := TRUE  ! v2 := TRUE
          IF  Exp1 AND Exp2 AND EC
[] v1 := TRUE  ! v2 := FALSE
          IF  Exp1 AND (NOT Exp2) AND EC
[] v1 := FALSE ! v2 := TRUE
          IF  (NOT Exp1) AND Exp2 AND EC
[] v1 := FALSE ! v2 := FALSE
          IF  (NOT Exp1) AND (NOT Exp2) AND EC
```

In general, for a rule with k nonconstant assignments, such a conversion would replace this rule with 2^k new rules with constant assignments.

A different approach would be to allow EQL(B) programs to have noncon-stant assignments, but to change the optimization algorithm to handle such cases as well. This would require a more sophisticated fixed point derivation algorithm, $Derive\_FP_2$ (section 12.3.4). New constraints that would handle rules with noncon-stant assignments for decomposition and parallel rule firing could then be adapted from existing ones used for analysis and parallelization of such rule-bases as described in [Cheng et al., 1993] and [Cheng, 1993b].

Several restrictions were imposed that influenced the generation of state-space graphs and defined which state may be merged in a single vertex and thus reduce the number of vertices in state-space graphs. Through experimental evaluation (section 12.5), we have shown that this restriction may still allow the construction of a reduced state-space graph of relatively low complexity.

12.6.3 Optimization of Other Real-Time Rule-Based Systems

The equational rule-based EQL language was initially developed to study the rule-based systems in a real-time environment. EQL's simplicity is due to its use of zero-order logic. To increase the expressive power of such production language, a similar fixed-point interpretable Macro Rule–based language (MRL) that uses first-order logic was derived from EQL [Wang, Mok, and Cheng, 1990]. Consequently, many algorithms for decomposition, response-time analysis, and parallelization of EQL (see [Cheng et al., 1993; Chen and Cheng, 1995b; Cheng, 1993b]) were then reimplemented for MRL [Wang and Mok, 1993]. It was shown that the expressive power of MRL and a popular production language, OPS5, is the same, and to enable the use of response-time analysis tools for OPS5, translation methods from OPS5 to MRL and vice versa were proposed [Wang, 1990c]. Furthermore, the analysis tools that originated from those of EQL and consequently from those of MRL were recently developed for OPS5 as well (see chapter 11).

The importance of the above-mentioned work for the generality of the methods proposed here is that the concepts used for decomposition, response-time analysis, and parallelization of EQL, most of which were adopted and used here, were then defined and used for MRL and OPS5 production systems. For example, the optimization of MRL might as well use state-space graphs that would be derived starting from the fixed points and would gradually be expanded to exclude the cycles. Again, a breadth-first search would optimize the response time of MRL assessed through the number of rules to fire to reach a fixed point. The main difficulty in implementing such optimization is due to different logics used in EQL and MRL: while EQL is zero-order-logic-based, MRL uses first-order logic. In other words, the major task of adapting the optimization methods used for EQL to those for MRL would be the reimplementation of symbolic manipulation routines that handle expressions (logical operators, minimization). This may be a difficult task, but once accomplished it would enable the development of proposed optimization methodology for MRL and for similar first-order-logic-based production languages.

12.7 HISTORICAL PERSPECTIVE AND RELATED WORK

The timing analysis problem is similar to that of *protocol reachability analysis*. Reachability analysis tries to generate and inspect all the states of a system that are reachable from a given set of initial states [Holzmann, 1991]. This *top-down approach* requires that either a set of initial states is given, or, as advocated by [Valmari and Jokela, 1989], the model of the environment is known from which the initial states are derived. Reachability analysis tools use algorithms such as *hashing without collision*, *state-space hashing*, and similar techniques to reduce the number of the states stored in the working memory. These methods are used only for analysis and limit their usability in synthesis and optimization because they generate only a part of the state-space graph. [Bouajjani, Fernandez, and Halbwachs, 1991; Bouajjani et al., 1992] presented a useful method to reduce the complexity of state-space graphs that is based on the identification of equivalent states. [Godefroid, Holzmann, and Pirottin, 1992] showed that most of the state explosion due to the modeling of concurrency can be avoided. They annotated the vertices of a state-space graph with *sleep sets*. If the rule that is enabled in a certain state is also in the sleep set of the same state, its firing would result in a state that was already checked in the earlier stage of the reachability analysis.

To overcome the prohibitive complexity of state-space graphs in the analysis problem, [Cheng et al., 1993] presented the static analysis method which determines if a program has a finite response time. They have identified several special forms of rules: if all rules belong to one of such forms, the program's response time is finite. Recent work of [Chen and Cheng, 1995b] focused on the methods that extend this approach by further estimating the program's response time in terms of the number of rules to fire to reach a fixed point.

[Cheng, 1993b] proposed an approach to decompose the rule-based system into independent rule-sets. This allows for independent analysis of each such rule-set. The overall response time is then derived from the response times of the independent rule-sets. A similar modular approach in the analysis and synthesis of rule-based systems is also advocated in [Browne et al., 1994].

A different approach to response-time optimization is to speed up the rule-based system by a parallel-rule execution. For example, [Kuo and Moldovan, 1991] proposed a parallel OPS5 rule firing model. They used a notion of context, which groups the rules that interfere with each other. Several contexts can be executed in parallel if they are mutually independent. [Cheng, 1993b] proposed a similar rule-firing model for EQL programs and further investigated the possibility of parallel firing of the rules that belong to the same context. In terms of the synthesis problem, a rule-base can be rewritten to increase the parallelism. [Pasik, 1992] introduced the constraint copies of so-called culprit rules, thus balancing the work performed in parallel and reducing the amount of work done sequentially. Culprit rules are rules that require substantially more computation time, which is due to their condition elements that require comparisons to many more working elements than other rules. While the culprit rules have a modified condition part, their action part is the same as that of the rules they are derived from. Another example of speeding up the execution of the production system is Ishida's algorithm [Ishida, 1994], which enumerates possible joint structures for OPS-like systems and selects the best one.

Although Pasik and Ishida both addressed the execution time, their methods do not explicitly addressed problem of fulfillment of the timing constraints and do not estimate the upper bound of execution time. Increased parallelization and execution speedup as proposed above can thus be used to reduce the execution time, but does not give an adequate solution to synthesis and optimization problems for real-time systems as stated in [Browne, Cheng, and Mok, 1988]. [Zupan and Cheng, 1994a; Zupan and Cheng, 1994b] first propose the optimization techniques described here, which are refined and extended in [Zupan and Cheng, 1998].

12.8 SUMMARY

We have presented a novel approach to the optimization of rule-based expert systems. We proposed several methods, all based on a construction of the reduced state-space graph corresponding to the input rule-based system. The optimization methods focus on changing the rules' enabling conditions while leaving their assignment parts unchanged.

The new and optimized rule-based expert systems are synthesized from the derived state graph. The vertices of the state graph are mutually exclusive. This, together with the cycle-free nature of the state graph, contributes to the special properties of the rule-based system constructed from it. In comparison with the original system, the optimized rule-based systems have the same or fewer numbers of rule firings to reach the fixed point. They contain no cycles and are thus inherently stable. Redundant rules present in the original systems are removed. Three of the four optimization methods proposed derive a deterministic system; that is, each launch state in a system will always have a single corresponding fixed point. This is obtained by enforcing only a single rule to be enabled at each state. For the same reason, the use of the conflict resolution for such systems becomes obsolete.

The proposed optimization strategies can also be used for analysis purposes. Namely, they all implicitly reveal the unstable states in the system. All stable and originally potentially unstable states are included in the enabling conditions of optimized rules. Subtracting these from the states included in the enabling conditions of the unoptimized rules identifies the unstable states.

In this chapter, we have constrained the class of EQL programs to have constant assignments only. For unconstrained programs, the same approach can be used. The only major difference is the identification of fixed points. To avoid an exhaustive search of the state space, we show in [Zupan, 1993] that a low-complexity fixed-point derivation algorithm exists if the rule-sets belong to a specific special form. This is a much lesser constraint than in the constant assignments case. Ongoing work is being performed to identify different algorithms to find fixed points for the rules belonging to different special forms.

No information other than the EQL program itself is given to the optimization method. The methods would possibly benefit from environmental and execution constraints, for example, the knowledge about impossible or prohibited states or the knowledge of prohibited sequences of rule firings. Such constraints could be effective in reducing both the execution complexity of optimization and the complexity of the resulting state-space graphs.

The optimization methods were evaluated on several randomly generated rule-based programs and on the real-time rule-based expert system developed by Mitre [Marsh, 1988]. The experiments confirm that optimization techniques proposed may indeed reduce the number of rules needed to fire and stabilize the rule-based system. The experiments also suggest that proposed optimization methods should not be used alone, but rather in combination with the analysis tools. Optimization of rule-based systems should then be an iterative process of discovering which rule-set (or even which set of rules in a rule-set) to optimize, and, depending on the desired properties or the specific bias in the optimization, which optimization method to use.

EXERCISES

1. Describe two approaches for optimizing rule-based systems.
2. How does the high-level dependency (HLD) graph group related rules together into vertices consisting of a set of rules?
3. Transform the following EQL programs into equivalent EQL(B) programs. Let all the variables be four-valued variables with their values $\in \{-1, 0, 1, 2\}$.

```
PROGRAM EQL1
INPUTVAR
       a,b : INTEGER;
VAR
       c : INTEGER;
INIT
       c:=0
RULES
       (*r1*)    c:=1 IF a>0 and b>0
       (*r2*)[] c:=2 IF a>0 and b<=0
END.
```

```
PROGRAM EQL2
INPUTVAR
       a : INTEGER;
VAR
       d,g,h : INTEGER;
INIT
       d:=0,g:=0,h:=0
RULES
       (*r1*)    d:=2 IF a<=0
       (*r2*)[] g:=1!h:=1 IF a>1 and b>1
       (*r3*)[] g:=2!h:=2 IF a<=1
END.
```

4. Construct the state-space graph of the EQL(B) programs obtained in exercise 2.
5. Construct the rule-dependency graph and the HLD graph corresponding to the EQL(B) programs obtained in exercise 2.
6. Describe extensions to the optimization algorithms or propose new algorithms for EQL(B) programs with nonconstant assignments.

BIBLIOGRAPHY

[Abadi and Lamport, 1991] M. Abadi and L. Lamport, "An Old-Fashioned Recipe for Real-Time," pp. 1–27 of *Proc. REX Workshop "Real-Time: Theory in Practice,"* LNCS 600, Mook, The Netherlands, June 1991.

[Abdeddaim and Maler, 2001] Y. Abdeddaim and O. Maler, "Job-Shop Scheduling Using Timed Automata," *13th Conference on Computer Aided Verification*, Paris, France, July 18–23, 2001.

[Abiteboul and Simon, 1991] S. Abiteboul and E. Simon, "Fundamental Properties of Deterministic and Nondeterministic Extensions of Datalog," *Theoretical Computer Science*, vol. 78, pp. 137–158, 1991.

[Aceto and Murphy, 1993] L. Aceto and D. Murphy, "On the Ill-Timed but Well-Caused," *Proc. CONCUR Intl. Conf. on Concurrency Theory*, LNCS 715, August 1993.

[Aceto and Murphy, 1996] L. Aceto and D. Murphy, "Timing and Causality in Process Algebra," *Acta Informatica*, vol. 33, pp. 317–350, June 1996.

[Aho, Hopcroft, and Ullman, 1974] A. V. Aho, J. E. Hopcroft, and J. D. Ullman, "The Design and Analysis of Computer Algorithms," Addison-Wesley, Reading, MA, 1974.

[Aiken, Widom, and Hellerstein, 1992] A. Aiken, J. Widom, and J. M. Hellerstein, "Behavior of Database Production Rules: Termination, Confluence and Observable Determinism," in *Proc. 1992 ACM SIGMOD Int'l Conf. on Management of Data*, San Diego, CA, June 1992, pp. 59–68. Also in IBM Research Report RJ 8562, IBM Almaden Research Center, San Jose, CA, January 1992.

[Akers, 1978] S. Akers, "Binary Decision Diagrams," *IEEE Trans. on Computers*, vol. C-27, pp. 509–516, 1978.

[Allan, Ashby, and Hodge, 1998] D. W. Allan, N. Ashby, and C. Hodge, "Fine-tuning Time in the Space Age," *IEEE Spectrum*, March 1998, pp 42–51.

[Allen, 1993] J. F. Allen, "Maintaining Knowledge about Temporal Intervals," *Communications of the ACM*, vol. 26, no. 11, pp. 832–843, November 1983.

[Alur, 1991] R. Alur, "Techniques for Automatic Verification of Real-Time Systems," Ph.D. thesis, Stanford University, 1991.

[Alur, Courcoubetis, and Dill, 1990] R. Alur, C. Courcoubetis, and D. L. Dill, "Model Checking for Real-Time Systems," *Proc. 5th IEEE Symp. on Logic in Computer Science*, Washington, D.C., pp. 414–425, June 1990.

[Alur, Courcoubetis, and Dill, 1993] R. Alur, C. Courcoubetis, and D. L. Dill, "Model Checking in Dense Real Time," *Information and Computation*, vol. 104, no. 1, pp. 2–34, 1993.

[Alur, Courcoubetis, and Henzinger, 1993] R. Alur, C. Courcoubetis, and T. A. Henzinger, "Computing Accumulated Delays in Real-Time Systems," *Proc. 5th Intl. Conf. on Computer-Aided Verification*, Elounda, Greece, pp. 181–193, June 1993.

[Alur and Dill, 1990] R. Alur and D. L. Dill, "Automata for Modeling Real-Time Systems," *Proc. 17th ICALP*, LNCS 443, Springer-Verlag, 1990.

[Alur and Dill, 1994] R. Alur and D. L. Dill, "A Theory of Timed Automata," *Theoretical Computer Science*, 126(2): pp. 183–235, 1994.

[Alur, Dill, and Wong-Toi, 1992] R. Alur, D. Dill, and H. Wong-Toi, "An Implementation of Three Algorithms for Timing Verification Based on Automata Emptiness," *Proc. 13th Real-Time Systems Symposium*, Phoenix, AZ, pp. 157–166, December 1992.

[Alur, Feder, and Henzinger, 1991] R. Alur, T. Feder, and T. A. Henzinger, "The Benefits of Relaxing Punctuality," *Proc. 10th ACM Symp. on Principles of Distributed Computing*, pp. 139–152, 1991.

[Alur, Fix, and Henzinger, 1994] R. Alur, L. Fix, and T. A. Henzinger, "A Determinizable Class of Timed Automata," *Proc. 6th Intl. Conf. on Computer-Aided Verification*, Stanford, CA, pp. 1–13, June 1994.

[Alur and Henzinger, 1989] R. Alur and T. A. Henzinger, "A Really Temporal Logic," *Proc. 30th Symp. on Foundations of Computer Science*, New York, pp. 164–169, 1989.

[Alur and Henzinger, 1990] R. Alur and T. A. Henzinger, "Real-Time Logics: Complexity and Expressiveness," *Proc. 5th IEEE Symp. on Logic in Computer Science*, Washington, D.C., pp. 390–401, June 1990.

[Alur and Henzinger, 1992] R. Alur and T. A. Henzinger, "Back to the Future: Towards a Theory of Timed Regular Languages," *Proc. 33rd IEEE Symposium on Foundations of Computer Science*, pp. 177–186, 1992.

[Alur and Henzinger, 1994] R. Alur and T. A. Henzinger, "A Really Temporal Logic," *Journal of the ACM*, vol. 41, no. 1, pp. 181–204, 1994.

[Alur and Henzinger, 1995] R. Alur and T. A. Henzinger, "Local Fairness for Compositional Modeling of Fair Reactive Systems," *Proc. 7th Intl. Conf. on Computer-Aided Verification*, Liege, Belgium, pp. 166–179, June 1995.

[Alur, Henzinger, and Ho, 1993] R. Alur, T. A. Henzinger, and P.-H. Ho, "Automatic Symbolic Verification of Embedded Systems," *Proc. 14th Real-Time Systems Symposium*, Raleigh-Durham, NC, pp. 2–11, December 1993.

[Alur, Henzinger, and Ho, 1996] R. Alur, T. A. Henzinger, and P.-H. Ho, "Automatic Symbolic Verification of Embedded Systems," *IEEE Trans. Software Engineering*, vol. 22, no. 3, pp. 181–201, March 1996.

[Alur, Henzinger, and Kupferman, 1997] R. Alur, T.A. Henzinger, and O. Kupferman, "Alternating-Time Temporal Logic," *Proceedings of the 38th IEEE Symposium on Foundations of Computer Science*, 1997.

[Alur, Henzinger, and Vardi, 1993] R. Alur, T.A. Henzinger, and M. Y. Vardi, "Parametric Real-Time Reasoning," *Proc. 25th ACM Symp. Theory of Computing (STOC)*, pp. 592–601, 1993.

[Alur and Kurshan, 1996] R. Alur and R. P. Kurshan, "Timing Analysis in COSPAN," *Hybrid Systems III: Verification and Control*, LNCS 1066, pp. 220–231, 1996.

[Alur, Kurshan and Viswanathan, 1998] R. Alur and R. P. Kurshan and M. Viswanathan, "Membership Questions for Timed and Hybrid Automata," *Proc. 19th IEEE-CS Real-Time Systems Symposium*, Madrid, Spain, December 2–4, 1998.

[Alur et al., 1992a] R. Alur et al., "Minimization of Timed Transition Systems," *Proc. CONCUR*, LNCS 630, 1992.

[Alur et al., 1992b] R. Alur et al., "Timing Verification by Successive Approximation," *Proc. 4th Intl. Conf. on Computer-Aided Verification*, Montreal, Canada, pp. 137–150, June 1992.

[Alur et al., 1995a] R. Alur et al., "The Algorithmic Analysis of Hybrid Systems," *Theoretical Computer Science*, vol. 138, pp. 3–34, 1995.

[Alur et al., 1995b] R. Alur et al., "Timing Verification by Successive Approximation," *Information and Computation*, vol. 118, no. 1, pp. 142–157, 1995.

[Amla and Emerson, 2001] N. Amla, E. A. Emerson, R. P. Kurshan, and K. Namjoshi, "RTDT: A Front-End for Efficient Model Checking of Synchronous Timing Diagrams," *13th Conference on Computer Aided Verification*, Paris, France, July 18–23, 2001.

[Archinoff, 1990] G. Archinoff, "Verification of the Shutdown System Software at the Darlington Nuclear Generating System," *Proc. Intl. Conf. on Control and Instrumentation in Nuclear Installations*, Glasgow, Scotland, May 1990.

[Ardis et al., 1996] M. A. Ardis, J. A. Chaves, L. J. Jagadeesan, P. Mataga, C. Puchol, M. G. Staskauskas, and J. Von Olnhausen, "A Framework for Evaluating Specification Methods for Reactive Systems: Experience Report," *IEEE Transactions on Software Engineering*, vol. 22, no. 6, pp. 378–389, June 1996.

[Attiya and Lynch, 1989] H. Attiya and N. A. Lynch, "Time Bounds for Real-Time Process Control in the Presence of Timing Uncertainty," *Proc. 10th Real-Time Systems Symposium*, Santa Monica, CA, pp. 268–284, December 1989.

[Auernheimer and Kemmerer, 1986] B. Auernheimer and R. A. Kemmerer, "RT-ASLAN: A Specification Language for Real-Time Systems," *IEEE Trans. Software Engineering*, vol. SE-12, no. 9, pp. 879–889, September 1986.

[Avrunin et al., 1994] G. S. Avrunin et al., "Automated Derivation of Time Bounds in Uniprocessor Concurrent Systems," *IEEE Trans. Software Engineering*, vol. SE-20, no. 9, pp. 708–719, September 1994.

[Aziz et al., 1994] A. Aziz, F. Balarin, R. K. Brayton, S.-T. Cheng, R. Hojati, T. Kam, S. C. Krishnan, R. K. Ranjan, A. L. Sangiovanni-Vincentelli, T. R. Shiple, V. Singhal, S. Tasiran, and H.-Y. Wang, "HSIS: A BDD-Based Environment for Formal Verification," *ACM/IEEE Design Automation Conference*, San Diego, CA, June 1994.

[Baeten and Bergstra, 1991] J. C. M. Baeten and J. A. Bergstra, "Real-Time Process Algebra," *Formal Aspects of Computing*, vol. 3, no. 2, pp. 142–188, 1991.

[Baker et al., 1995] N. Baker, W. Harris, J.-M. Le Goff, R. McClatchey, and C. Wallace, "Modelling a Real-Time Control System Based on Distributed Objects," *Proc. 16th Real-Time Systems Symposium*, Pisa, Italy, December 1995.

[Balaji et al., 1992] S, Balaji et al., "S-Nets: A Petri Net Based Model for Performance Evaluation of Real-Time Scheduling Algorithms," *Journal of Parallel and Distributed Computing*, vol. 15, pp. 225–235, 1992.

[Balarin, 1996] F. Balarin, "Approximate Reachability Analysis of Timed Automata," *Proc. 17th Real-Time Systems Symposium*, Washington, D.C., December 1996.

[Balarin and Sangiovanni-Vincentelli, 1993] F. Balarin and A. L. Sangiovanni-Vincentelli, "A Verification Strategy for Timing Constrained Systems," *Proc. 4th Intl. Conf. on Computer-Aided Verification*, Montreal, Canada, pp. 151–163, June 1993.

[Balarin and Sangiovanni-Vincentelli, 1994] F. Balarin and A. L. Sangiovanni-Vincentelli, "Iterative Algorithms for Formal Verification of Embedded Real-Time Systems," *Proc. Intl. Conf. on Computer-Aided Design*, San Jose, CA, 1994.

[Barachini, 1994] F. Barachini, "Frontiers in Run-Time Prediction for the Production System Paradigm," *AI Magazine*, 15(3):47–61, Fall 1994.

[Barachini et al., 1988] F. Barachini et al., "The challenge of Real-Time Process Control for Production Systems," *Proc. AAAI Conference*, pp. 705–712, 1988.

[Barbacci and Wing, 1987] M. R. Barbacci and J. M. Wing, "Specifying Functional and Timing Behavior of Real-Time Systems," *Proc. of Conf. on Parallel Architectures and Languages Europe*, LNCS 259, June 1987.

[Barry and Lowe, 1990] M. R. Barry and C. M. Lowe, "Analyzing Spacecraft Configurations through Specialization and Default Reasoning," *Proc. of the Goddard Conference on Space Applications of Artificial Intelligence*, pp. 165–179, NASA, 1990.

[Baruah, Mok, and Rosier, 1990] S. K. Baruah, A. K. Mok, and L. E. Rosier, "Preemptively Scheduling Hard-Real-Time Sporadic Tasks on One Processor," *Proc. 11th IEEE-CS Real-Time Systems Symposium*, Lake Buena Vista, FL, pp. 182–190, December 1990.

[Beaven et al., 1991] M. Beaven et al., "VERT—Verification of Real-Time Programs," *Proc. 15th Intl. IEEE Computer Software and Applications Conf.*, pp. 618–625, 1991.

[Ben-Abdallah, 1996] H. Ben-Abdallah, "GCSR: A Graphical Language for the Specification, Refinement, and Analysis of Real-Time Systems," Ph.D. dissertation, Department of Computer and Information Science, University of Pennsylvania, August 1996.

[Ben-Abdallah and Lee, 1998] H. Ben-Abdallah and I. Lee, "A Graphical Language for Specifying and Analyzing Real-Time Systems," *Special Issue of Integrated Computer-Aided Engineering on Real-time Engineering Systems*, Vol. 5, No. 4, pp. 279–302, 1998.

[Ben-Abdallah, Lee, and Choi, 1995] H. Ben-Abdallah, I. Lee, and J.-Y. Choi, "A Graphical Language with Formal Semantics for the Specification and Analysis of Real-Time Systems," *Proc. 16th Real-Time Systems Symposium*, Pisa, Italy, pp. 276–286, December 1995.

[Ben-Abdallah et al., 1998] H. Ben-Abdallah, J.-Y. Choi, D. Clarke, Y. Kim, I. Lee, and H.-L. Xie, "A Process Algebraic Approach to the Schedulability Analysis of Real-Time Systems," *J. Real-Time Systems*, vol. 15, no. 3, pp. 189–219, 1998.

[Benda, 1987] M. Benda, "Real-Time Applications of AI in the Aerospace Industry," Presentation at the Fall School on Artificial Intelligence, The Research Institute of Ecole Normal Superieure, France, September 4, 1987.

[Bergstra and Klop, 1985] J. A. Bergstra and J. W. Klop, "Algebra of Communicating Processes with Abstraction," *Journal of Theoretical Computer Science*, vol. 37, pp. 77–121, 1985.

[Bernstein and Harter, 1981] A. Bernstein and P. K. Harter, "Proving Real-Time Properties of Programs with Temporal Logic," *Proc. 8th ACM Symp. on Operating Systems Principles*, pp. 1–11, 1981.

[Berthomieu and Diaz, 1991] B. Berthomieu and M. Diaz, "Modeling and Verification of Time Dependent Systems Using Time Petri Nets," *IEEE Trans. on Software Eng.*, vol. 17, no. 3, pp. 259–273, March 1991.

[Bestavros, 1991] A. Bestavros, "Specification and Verification of Real-Time Embedded Systems Using Time-Constrained Reactive Automata," *Proc. 12th Real-Time Systems Symposium*, San Antonio, TX, pp. 244–253, December 1991.

[Bjorner et al., 1996] N. Bjorner et al., "STeP: Deductiver-Algorithmic Verification of Reactive and Real-Time Systems," *Proc. 8th Intl. Conf. on Computer-Aided Verification*, LNCS 1102, pp. 415–418, July 1996.

[Bolognesi and Brinksma, 1987] T. Bolognesi and E. Brinksma, "Introduction to the ISO Specification Language LOTOS," *Computer Networks and ISDN Systems*, 14(1):25–59, January 1987.

[Bosscher, Polak, and Vaandrager, 1994] D. Bosscher, I. Polak, and F. Vaandrager, "Verification of an Audio Control Protocol," *Proc. Formal Techniques in Real-Time and Fault-Tolerant Systems*, LNCS 863, pp. 170–192, 1994.

[Bouajjani, Echahed, and Sifakis, 1993] A. Bouajjani, R. Echahed, and J. Sifakis, "On Model Checking for Real-Time Properties with Durations," *Proc. 8th IEEE Symp. on Logic in Computer Science*, pp. 147–159, June 1993.

[Bouajjani, Fernandez, and Halbwachs, 1991] A. Bouajjani, J.-C. Fernandez, and N. Halbwachs. "Minimal Model Generation," *Proc. 3rd Intl. Conf. on Computer-Aided Verification*, Aalborg, Denmark, pp. 197–203, July 1991.

[Bouajjani et al., 1992] A. Bouajjani et al., "Minimal State Graph Generation," *Science of Computer Programming*, vol. 18, no. 3, pp. 247–269, June 1992.

[Boussinot and De Simone, 1991] F. Boussinot and R. De Simone, "The Esterel Language," *Proc. IEEE*, vol. 79, no. 9, pp. 1293–1304, September 1991.

[Bowen and Stavridou, 1993] J. Bowen and V. Stavridou, "Safety-Critical Systems, Formal Methods and Standards," *Software Engineering Journal*, vol. 8, no. 4, pp. 189–209, July 1993.

[Boyer, 1971] R. S. Boyer, "Locking: A Restriction of Resolution," Ph.D. thesis, University of Texas at Austin, 1971.

[Braberman and Hung, 1998] V. A. Braberman and D. V. Hung, "On Checking Timed Automata for Linear Duration Invariants," *Proc. 19th IEEE-CS Real-Time Systems Symposium*, Madrid, Spain, December 2–4, 1998.

[Bradfield, 1992] J. C. Bradfield, "A Proof Assistant for Symbolic Model-Checking," *Proc. 4th Intl. Conf. on Computer-Aided Verification*, Montreal, Canada, pp. 316–329, June 1992.

[Brant et al., 1991] D. A. Brant, T. Grose, B. Lofaso, and D. P. Miranker, "Effects of Database Size on Rule System Performance: Five Case Studies," *Proceedings of the 17th International Conference on Very Large Data Bases*, Barcelona, Spain, pp. 287–296, September 1991.

[Brat and Garg, 1998] G. P. Brat and V. K. Garg, "Analyzing Non-Deterministic Real-Time Systems with (MAX,+) Algebra," *Proc. 19th IEEE-CS Real-Time Systems Symposium*, Madrid, Spain, December 2–4, 1998.

[Bremond-Gregoire, 1994] P. Bremond-Gregoire, "A Process Algebra of Communicating Shared Resources with Dense Time and Priorities," Ph.D. thesis, University of Pennsylvania, 1994.

[Bremond-Gregoire, Ben-Abdallah, and Lee, 1996] P. Bremond-Gregoire, H. Ben-Abdallah, and I. Lee, "Ordering Processes in a Real-Time Process Algebra," *Proceedings of AMAST 3rd International Workshop on Real-Time Systems*, Salt Lake City, UT, March 1996.

[Bremond-Gregoire and Lee, 1997] P. Bremond-Gregoire and I. Lee, "A Process Algebra of Communicating Shared Resources with Dense Time and Priorities," *Theoretical Computer Science*, vol. 189, nos. 1–2, pp. 179–219, December 1997.

[Bretz, 2001] E. A. Bretz, "By-Wire Cars: Turn the Corner," *IEEE Spectrum*, vol. 38, no. 4, pp. 68–73, April 2001.

[Bretz, 2002] E. A. Bretz, "Clear Skies Ahead," *IEEE Spectrum*, vol. 39, no. 1, pp. 78-81, January 2002.

[Brockmeyer et al., 1996] M. Brockmeyer, F. Jahanian, C. Heitmeyer, and B. Labaw, "An Approach to Monitoring and Assertion-Checking Distributed Real-Time Systems," *Proc. Workshop on Parallel and Distributed Real-Time Systems*, Honolulu, Hawaii, April 1996.

[Brockmeyer et al., 1997a] M. Brockmeyer, F. Jahanian, C. Heitmeyer and B. Labaw, "A Flexible, Extensible Simulation Environment for Testing Real-Time Specifications," *3rd IEEE Real-Time Technology and Applications Symposium*, Montreal, Canada, June 1997.

[Brockmeyer et al., 1997b] M. Brockmeyer, F. Jahanian, E. Winner, C. Heitmeyer and B. Labaw, "A Software Environment for Custom Simulation and Monitoring of Real-Time Specifications," *Proc. High Assurance Systems Workshop (HASE)*, August 1997.

[Brockmeyer and Wittich, 1998] U. Brockmeyer and G. Wittich, "Real-Time Verification of STATEMATE Designs—Tool-Paper, pp. 537–541 of *Computer Aided Verification*, A. J. Hu and M. Y. Vardi, eds., LNCS 1427, New York, Springer-Verlag, 1998.

[Brockmeyer et al., 2000] M. Brockmeyer, F. Jahanian, C. Heitmeyer, and E. Winner, "A Flexible, Extensible Simulation Environment for Testing Real-Time Specifications," *IEEE Transactions on Computers*, vol. 49, no. 11, pp. 1184–1201, November 2000.

[Browne, Cheng, and Mok, 1988] J. C. Browne, A. M. K. Cheng, and A. K. Mok, "Computer-Aided Design of Real-Time Rule-Based Decision Systems," Technical report, Department of Computer Science, University of Texas at Austin, 1988. Also to appear in *IEEE Trans. on Software Engineering*.

[Browne et al., 1994] J. C. Browne et al., "A New Approach to Modularity in Rule-Based Programming," in *Proc. 6th Int'l Conf. on Tools with Artificial Intelligence, TAI'94*, pp. 18–25, November 1994.

[Brownston et al., 1986] L. Brownston, R. Farrel, E. Kant, and N. Martin, "Programming Expert Systems in OPS5: An Introduction to Rule-based Programming," Addison-Wesley, Reading, MA, 1986.

[Bruno et al., 1993a] G. Bruno et al., "A New Petri Net Based Formalism for Specification, Design and Analysis of Real-Time Systems," *Proc. 14th Real-Time Systems Symposium*, Raleigh-Durham, NC, pp. 294–301, December 1993.

[Bruno et al., 1993b] G. Bruno et al., "Temporal Analysis of Extended Marked Graphs for Real-Time Applications," *Proc. 1st Workshop on Real-Time Applications*, New York, pp. 66–70, May 1993.

[Bryant, 1986] R. E. Bryant, "Graph-Based Algorithms for Boolean Function Manipulation," *IEEE Transactions on Computers*, vol. C-35, no. 8, pp. 677–691, August 1986.

[Bucci and Vicario, 1995] G. Bucci and E. Vicario, "Compositional Validation of Time-Critical Systems Using Communicating Time Petri Nets," *IEEE Trans. Soft. Eng.*, vol. 21, no. 12, pp. 969–992, December 1995.

[Burch, 1989a] J. R. Burch, "Combining CTL, Trace Theory and Timing Models," *Proc. Intl. Workshop on Automatic Verification Methods for Finite State Systems*, LNCS 407, Grenoble, France, pp. 334–348, 1989.

[Burch, 1989b] J. R. Burch, "Modeling Timing Assumptions with Trace Theory," *Proc. IEEE Intl. Conf. on Computer Design*, Silver Spring, MD, pp. 208–211, October 1989.

[Burch, 1992] J. R. Burch, "Trace Algebra for Automatic Verification of Real-Time Concurrent Systems," Ph.D. Thesis, Carnegie-Mellon University, August 1992.

[Burch et al., 1990a] J. R. Burch et al., "Sequential Circuit Verification Using Symbolic Model Checking," *Proc. 27th ACM/IEEE Design Automation Conf.*, Orlando, FL, 1990.

[Burch et al., 1990a] J. R. Burch et al., "Symbolic Model Checking with Partitioned Transition Systems," *Proc. VLSI*, Edinburgh, Scotland, 1990.

[Burch et al., 1990c] J. R. Burch, E. M. Clarke, K. L. McMillan, D. L. Dill, and L. H. Hwang, "Symbolic Model Checking: 10^{20} states and Beyond," *Proc. 5th IEEE Intl. Symp. on Logic in Computer Science*, pp. 428–439,1990.

[Burch et al., 1994] J. R. Burch et al., "Symbolic Model Checking for Sequential Circuit Verification," *IEEE Trans. on Computer-Aided Design of Integrated Circuits and Systems*, vol. 13, no. 4, pp. 401–424, April 1994.

[Burns and Edgar, 2000] A. Burns and S. Edgar, "Predicting Computation Time for Advanced Processor Architectures," *Proceedings of the 12th Euromicro Conference on Real-Time Systems* (EUROMICRO-RTS), 2000.

[Burns and Wellings, 1990] A. Burns and A. J. Wellings, "Real-Time Systems and Their Programming Languages," Addison-Wesley, Wokingham, England, 1990.

[Burns and Wellings, 1994] A. Burns and A. J. Wellings, "HRT-HOOD: A Structured Design Method for Hard Real-Time Systems," *Journal of Real-Time Systems*, vol. 6, no. 1, pp. 73–114, January 1994.

[Burns and Wellings, 1996] A. Burns and A. J. Wellings, "Real-Time Systems and Programming Languages," 2nd Edition, Addison-Wesley, Harlow, England, 1996.

[Butler and Finelli, 1993] R. W. Butler and G. B. Finelli, "The Infeasibility of Quantifying the Reliability of Life-Critical Real-Time Software," *IEEE Trans. on Software Engineering*, vol. 19, no. 1, pp. 3–12, January 1993.

[Cameron and Lin, 1991] E. J. Cameron and Y.-J. Lin, "A Real-Time Transition Model for Analysis of Behavioral Compatibility of Telecommunications Services," *Proc. ACM SIGSOFT Conf. on Software for Critical Systems*, pp. 101–111, 1991.

[Campos and Clarke, 1993] S. V. Campos and E.M. Clarke, "Real-time symbolic model checking for discrete time models," *Proc. 1st AMAST Intl. Workshop on Real-Time Systems*, 1993.

[Campos and Clarke, 1995] S. V. Campos and E. M. Clarke, "Real-Time Symbolic Model Checking for Discrete Time Models," C. Rattray and T. Rus, eds., *AMAST Series in Computing: Theories and Experiences for Real-Time System Development*, 1995.

[Campos and Clarke, 1997] S. Campos and E. Clarke, "The Verus Language: Representing Time Efficiently with BDDs," *Proc. Fourth AMAST Workshop on Real-Time Systems, Concurrent, and Distributed Software*, 1997.

[Campos, Clarke, and Minea, 1997a] S. Campos, E. Clarke and M. Minea, "Symbolic Techniques for Formally Verifying Industrial Systems," *Science of Computer Programming*, special issue on Industrially Relevant Applications of Formal Analysis Techniques, vol. 29, pp. 79–98, Elsevier Science, 1997.

[Campos, Clarke, and Minea, 1997a] S. Campos, E. Clarke and M. Minea, "The Verus tool: a quantitative approach to the formal verification of real-time systems," *Proc. Conference on Computer Aided Verification*, 1997.

[Campos et al., 1994] S. Campos, E. Clarke, W. Marrero, M. Minea and H. Hiraishi, "Computing Quantitative Characteristics of Finite-State Real-Time Systems," *Proc. 15th IEEE Real-Time Systems Symp.*, San Juan, Puerto Rico, pp. 266–270, December 1994.

[Campos et al., 1995a] S. Campos et al., "Timing Analysis of Industrial Real-Time Systems," *Proc. Workshop on Industrial-Strength Formal Specification Techniques*, 1995.

[Campos et al., 1995b] S. V. Campos, E. M. Clarke, W. Marrero and M. Minea, "Verifying the Performance of the PCI Local Bus Using Symbolic Techniques," *Proc. International Conference on Computer Design*, 1995.

[Campos et al., 1995c] S. Campos, E. Clarke, W. Marrero and M. Minea, "Verus: a Tool for Quantitative Analysis of Finite-State Real-Time Systems," *Proc. Workshop on Languages, Compilers and Tools for Real-Time Systems*, 1995.

[Cantone, 1993] G. Cantone, "Temporal Properties of the Timed D-Graphs of Distributed Processes," *Proc. 1st Workshop on Real-Time Applications*, New York, New York, pp. 136–141, May 1993.

[Cass, 2001] S. Cass, "2001: A Mars Odyssey," *IEEE Spectrum*, vol. 38, no. 4, April 2001.

[Cerans, 1992] K. Cerans, "Decidability of Bisimulation Equivalences for Parallel Timer Processes," *Proc. 4th Intl. Conf. on Computer-Aided Verification*, Montreal, Canada, pp. 302–315, June 1992.

[Cerans, Godskesen, and Larsen, 1993] K. Cerans, J. C. Godskesen and K. G. Larsen, "Timed Model Specification—Theory and Tools," *Proc. 5th Intl. Conf. on Computer-Aided Verification*, Elounda, Greece, pp. 253–267, June 1993.

[Ceri and Widom, 1991] S. Ceri and J. Widom, "Deriving Production Rules for Constraint Maintenance," *Proceedings of the 16th VLDB Conference*, Brisbane, Australia, pp. 566–577, 1990.

[Chang, 1970] C.-L. Chang, "The Unit Proof and the Input Proof in Theorem Proving," *Journal of the ACM*, vol. 17 (4), pp. 698–707, October 1970.

[Chang and Lee, 1973] C.-L. Chang and R. Lee, "Symbolic Logic and Mechanical Theorem Proving," Academic Press, 1973.

[Chapman, Burns, and Wellings, 1996] R. Chapman, A. Burns, and A. Wellings, "Combining Static Worst-Case Timing Analysis and Program Proof," *Journal of Real-Time Systems*, 11(2): pp. 145–171, September 1996.

[Chen and Cheng, 1994] J.-R. Chen and A. M. K. Cheng, "Predicting the Response Time of Real-Time Rule-Based Programs with Variable-Expression Assignments," *Proc. 6th IEEE-CS Intl. Conf. on Tools with Artificial Intelligence*, New Orleans, LA, pp. 297–303, November 1994.

[Chen and Cheng, 1995a] J.-R. Chen and A. M. K. Cheng, "Predicting the Response Time of OPS5-style Production Systems," *Proc. IEEE-CS Conf. on Artificial Intelligence for Applications*, Los Angeles, CA, pp. 203–209, February 1995.

[Chen and Cheng, 1995b] J.-R. Chen and A. M. K. Cheng, "Response Time Analysis of EQL Real-Time Rule-Based Systems," *IEEE Trans. on Knowledge and Data Engineering*, vol. 7, no. 1, pp. 26–43, February 1995.

[Cheng, 1992a] A. M. K. Cheng, "Fast Static Timing Analysis of Real-Time Systems," *Proc. 25th Hawaii International Conference on System Sciences (HICSS-25)*, January 1992.

[Cheng, 1992b] A. M. K. Cheng, "Self-Stabilizing Real-Time Rule-Based Systems," *Proc. 11th IEEE-CS Symp. on Reliable Distributed Systems*, Houston, TX, pp. 172–179, October 1992.

[Cheng, 1993a] A. M. K. Cheng, "A New Complexity Metric for OPS5 Rule-Based Systems," *Proc. IEEE-CS Intl. Conf. on Software Engineering and Knowledge Engineering*, San Francisco, CA, June 1993.

[Cheng, 1993b] A. M. K. Cheng, "Parallel Execution of Real-Time Rule-Based Systems," *Proc. IEEE Intl. Parallel Processing Symposium*, Newport Beach, CA, pp. 779–786, April 1993.

[Cheng, 1996] A. M. K. Cheng, "Measuring the Structural Complexity of OPS5 Rule-Based Programs," *Proc. 20th IEEE-CS Computer Software and Applications (COMPSAC) Conf.*, Seoul, Korea, August 1996.

[Cheng and Chen, 1992] A. M. K. Cheng and C.-H. Chen, "Efficient Response Time Bound Analysis of Real-Time Rule-Based Systems," *Proc. 7th IEEE Conf. on Computer Assurance*, U.S. National Institute of Standards and Technology, Gaithersburg, MD, pp. 63–76, June 1992.

[Cheng and Chen, 2000] A. M. K. Cheng and J.-R. Chen, "Response Time Analysis of OPS5 Production Systems," *IEEE Transactions on Knowledge and Data Engineering*, vol. 12, no. 3, pp. 391–409, May/June 2000.

[Cheng and Fujii, 2000] A. M. K. Cheng and S. Fujii, "Bounded-Response-Time Self-Stabilizing Real-Time Rule Systems," *Proc. IEEE-CS Intl. Parallel and Distributed Processing Symp.*, Cancun, Mexico, May 2000.

[Cheng and Rao, 2002] A. M. K. Cheng and S. Rao, "Real-Time Multimedia Traffic Scheduling and Routing in Packet-Switched Networks," to appear in Special Issue on Multimedia Communications, *Journal of VLSI Signal Processing—Systems for Signal, Image and Video Technology*, Kluwer Academic Publishers, vol. 32, no. 3, 2002.

[Cheng and Tsai, 2002] A. M. K. Cheng and H. Tsai, "A Graph-Based Approach for Timing Analysis and Refinement of OPS5 Knowledge-Based Systems," to appear in *IEEE Transactions on Knowledge and Data Engineering*, 2001.

[Cheng and Wang, 1990] A. M. K. Cheng and C.-K. Wang, "Fast Static Analysis of Real-Time Rule-Based Systems to Verify Their Fixed Point Convergence," *Proc. 5th Annual IEEE Conf. on Computer Assurance*, National Institute of Standards and Technology, Gaithersburg, Maryland, pp. 46–56, June 1990.

[Cheng et al., 1991] A. M. K. Cheng, J. C. Browne, A. K. Mok, and R.-H. Wang, "Estella: A Language for Specifying Behavioral Constraint Assertions in Real-Time Rule-Based Systems," *Proc. 6th IEEE Conf. on Computer Assurance*, U.S. National Institute of Standards and Technology, Gaithersburg, MD, pp. 107–123, June 1991.

[Cheng et al., 1993] A. M. K. Cheng, J. C. Browne, A. K. Mok, and R.-H. Wang, "Analysis of Real-Time Rule-Based System with Behavioral Constraint Assertions Specified in Estella," *IEEE Trans. on Software Eng.*, 19(9):863–885, September 1993.

[Chodrow, Jahanian, and Donner, 1991] S. E. Chodrow, F. Jahanian, and M. Donner, "Run-Time Monitoring of Real-Time Systems," *Proc. IEEE-CS Real-Time Systems Symp.*, pp. 74–83, December 1991.

[Choi and Kang, 1994] J.-Y. Choi and I. Kang, "Translation of Modechart Specification to Algebra of Communicating Shared Resources," *Proceedings of the First International Workshop on Real-Time Computing Systems and Applications*, Seoul, Korea, 1994.

[Choi, Lee, and Xie, 1995] J.-Y. Choi, I. Lee, and H.-L. Xie, "The Specification and Schedulability Analysis of Real-Time Systems Using ACSR," *Proc. 16th Real-Time Systems Symposium*, Pisa, Italy, pp. 266–275, December 1995.

[Choudhary, et al., 1995] A. Choudhary, V. Gehlot, B. Narahari, M. Benincasa, and R. Metzger, "A specification language for parallel real-time systems," *Proc. of Third Workshop on Parallel and Distributed Real-time Systems*, pp. 165–173, April 1995.

[Chu, Sit, and Leung, 1991] W. W. Chu, C.-M. Sit, and K. K. Leung, "Task Response Time for Real-Time Distributed Systems with Resource Constraints," *IEEE Trans. on Software Engineering*, vol. 17, no. 10, pp. 1077–1092, October 1991.

[Church, 1936] A. Church, "An Unsolvable Problem of Elementary Number Theory," *American Journal of Mathematics*, vol. 58, pp. 345–363, 1936.

[Cimatti et al., 1999] A. Cimatti, E. Clarke, F. Giunchiglia, and M. Roveri, "NUSMV: A New Symbolic Model Verifier," in N. Halbwachs and D. Peled, eds., *Proc. of the Eleventh Conference on Computer-Aided Verification (CAV'99)*, LNCS 1633, pp. 495–499. Trento, Italy, Springer, 1999.

[Clarke and Emerson, 1981] E. M. Clarke and E. A. Emerson, "Design and Synthesis of Synchronization Skeletons Using Branching-Time Temporal Logic," *Workshop on Logic of Programs*, LNCS 131, 1981.

[Clarke, Emerson, and Sistla, 1983] E. M. Clarke, E. A. Emerson, and A. P. Sistla, "Automatic Verification of Finite-State Concurrent Systems Using Temporal Logic Specifications: A Practical Approach," *Proc. 10th Annual Symp. of Programming Languages*, 1983.

[Clarke, Emerson, and Sistla, 1986] E. M. Clarke, E. A. Emerson, and A. P. Sistla, "Automatic Verification of Finite State Concurrent Programs Using Temporal Logic: A Practical Approach," *ACM Transactions on Programming Languages and Systems*, vol. 8, no. 2, pp. 244–263, April 1986.

[Clarke, Filkorn, and Jha, 1993] E. M. Clarke, M. Filkorn, and T. Jha, "Exploiting Symmetry in Temporal Logic Model Checking," *Proc. 5th Intl. Conf. on Computer-Aided Verification*, Elounda, Greece, June 1993.

[Clarke and Grumberg, 1987] E. M. Clarke and O. Grumberg, "Avoiding the State Explosion Problem in Temporal Logic Model-Checking Algorithms," *Proc. 6th ACM Symp. on Principles of Distributed Computing*, Vancouver, BC, pp. 294–303, August 1997.

[Clarke, Grumberg, and Peled, 1999] E. M. Clarke, O. Grumberg, and D. Peled, *Model Checking*, Cambridge, MA: MIT Press, 314 pp., December 1999.

[Clarke, Lee, and Xie, 1995] D. Clarke, I. Lee, and H.-L. Xie, "VERSA: A Tool for the Specification and Analysis of Resource-Bound Real-Time Systems," *Journal of Computer and Software Engineering*, vol. 3, no. 2, 1995.

[Clarke et al., 1985] E. M. Clarke et al., "Using Temporal Logic for Automatic Verification of Finite State Systems," K. R. Apt, ed., *Logics and Model of Concurrent Systems*, pp. 3–26, Berlin, Springer-Verlag, 1985.

[Clarke et al., 1993] E. M. Clarke, O. Grumberg, H. Hiraishi, S. Jha, D. E. Long, K. L. McMillan, and L. A. Ness, "Verification of the Futurebus+ Cache Coherence Protocol," *Proc. Intl. Symp. Computer Hardware Description Languages and Their Applications*, April 1993.

[Cleaveland, Parrow, and Steffen, 1993] R. Cleaveland, J. Parrow, and B. Steffen, "The Concurrency Workbench: A Semantics-Based Tool for the Verification of Concurrent Systems," *ACM Transactions on Programming Languages and Systems*, vol. 15, pp. 36–72, 1993.

[Cleaveland et al., 1994] R. Cleaveland et al., "The Concurrency Factory—Practical Tools for Specification, Simulation, Verification, and Implementation of Concurrent Systems,"

Proc. DIMACS Workshop on Specification Techniques for Concurrent Systems, Princeton, NJ, 1994.

[Clements, 1993] P. Clements, "Requirements Definition Languages for Real-Time Embedded Systems," Ph.D. thesis, University of Texas at Austin, 1993.

[Clements et al., 1993a] P. Clements et al., "Applying Formal Methods to an Embedded Real-Time Avionics System," *Proc. 1st Workshop on Real-Time Applications*, New York, pp. 46–49, May 1993.

[Clements et al., 1993b] P. Clements et al., "MT: A Toolset for Specifying and Analyzing Real-Time Systems," *Proc. 14th Real-Time Systems Symposium*, Raleigh-Durham, NC, pp. 12–22, December 1993.

[Closse, et al., 2001] E. Closse, M. Poize, and J. Pulou, J. Sifakis, P. Venier, D. Weil, and S. Yovine, "TAXYS: A Tool for the Development and Verification of Real-Time Embedded Systems," *13th Conference on Computer Aided Verification*, Paris, France, July 18–23, 2001.

[Coen-Porisini, Ghezzi, and Kemmerer, 1997] A. Coen-Porisini, C. Ghezzi, and R. A. Kemmerer, "Specification of Realtime Systems Using ASTRAL," *IEEE Trans. Software Engineering*, vol. SE-23, no. 9, pp. 572–598, September 1997.

[Comon and Jurski, 1999] Hubert Comon and Yan Jurski, "Timed Automata and the Theory of Real Numbers," *Proc. 10th Int. Conf. Concurrency Theory (CONCUR'99)*, LNCS 1664, New York, Springer-Verlag, 1999.

[Coolahan and Roussopoulus, 1983] J. Coolahan and N. Roussopoulus, "Timing Requirements for Time-Driven Systems Using Augmented Petri Nets," *Transactions on Software Engineering*, vol. SE-9(5), pp. 603–616, September 1983.

[Cooper and Wogrin, 1988] T. Cooper and N. Wogrin, *Rule-based Programming with OPS5*, Morgan Kaufmann Publishers, Inc., San Mateo, CA, 1988.

[Corbett, 1994] J. C. Corbett, "Modeling and Analysis of Real-Time Ada Tasking Programs," *Proc. 15th IEEE Real-Time Systems Symp.*, San Juan, Puerto Rico, pp. 132–141, December 1994.

[Corbett, 1996] J. C. Corbett, "Timing Analysis of Ada Tasking Programs," *IEEE Trans. on Software Eng.*, vol. 22, no. 7, pp. 461–483, July 1996.

[Coudert, Mader, and Berthet, 1990] O. Coudert, J. C. Mader, and C. Berthet, "Verifying Temporal Properties of Sequential Machines Without Building Their State Diagrams," *Proc. 2nd Intl. Conf. on Computer-Aided Verification*, June 1990.

[Courcoubetis, Damm, and Josko, 1993] C. Courcoubetis, W. Damm and B. Josko, "Verification of Timing Properties of VHDL," *Proc. 5th Intl. Conf. on Computer-Aided Verification*, Elounda, Greece, pp. 225–236, June 1993.

[Courcoubetis and Yannakakis, 1991] C. Courcoubetis and M. Yannakakis, "Minimum and Maximum Delay Problems in Real-Time Systems," *Proc. 3rd Intl. Conf. on Computer-Aided Verification*, Aalborg, Denmark, pp. 399–409, July 1991.

[Courcoubetis and Yannakakis, 1992] C. Courcoubetis and M. Yannakakis, "Minimum and Maximum Delay Problems in Real-Time Systems," *Formal Methods in System Design*, pp. 385–415, 1992.

[Courcoubetis et al., 1992a] C. Courcoubetis, M. Vardi, P. Wolper, and M. Yannakakis, "Memory Efficient Algorithms for the Verification of Temporal Properties," *Formal Methods in System Design*, vol. 275–288, 1992.

[Courcoubetis et al., 1992b]   C. Courcoubetis et al., "Verification with Real-Time COSPAN," *Proc. 4th Intl. Conf. on Computer-Aided Verification*, Montreal, Canada, pp. 274–287, June 1992.

[Craigen, Gerhart, and Ralston, 1994]   D. Craigen, S. Gerhart, and T. Ralston, "Formal Methods in Critical Systems," *IEEE Software*, vol. 11, no. 1, January 1994.

[Dahl, Dijkstra, and Hoare, 1972]   O.-J. Dahl, E. W. Dijkstra, and C. A. R. Hoare, *Structured Programming*, APIC Studies in Data Processing, no. 8, Academic Press, 1972.

[Dang, 2001]   Z. Dang, "Binary Reachability Analysis of Pushdown Timed Automata with Dense Clocks," *13th Conference on Computer Aided Verification*, Paris, France, July 18–23, 2001.

[Dasarathy, 1985]   B. Dasarathy, "Timing Constraints of Real-Time Systems: Constructs for Expressing Them, Methods for Validating Them," *IEEE Trans. on Software Engineering*, vol. SE-11a, no. 1, pp. 80–86, January 1985.

[Davies, 1993]   J. Davies, *Specification and Proof in Real-Time CSP*, Cambridge University Press, 1993.

[Davis, 1983]   M. Davis, "The Prehistory and Early History of Automated Deduction," Automation of Reasoning, Classical Papers on Computational Logic, 1957–1966, Jörg Siekmann and Graham Wrightson (eds), Springer Verlag, 1983.

[Davis and Putnam, 1960]   M. Davis and H. Putnam, "A Computing Procedure for Quantification Theory," *Journal of the ACM*, vol.7, no. 3, pp. 201–215, 1960.

[Daws and Yovine, 1995]   C. Daws and S. Yovine, "Two Examples of Verification of Multirate Time Automata with Kronos," *Proc. 16th Real-Time Systems Symposium*, Pisa, Italy, pp. 66–75, December 1995.

[Daws and Yovine, 1996]   C. Daws and S. Yovine, "Getting Rid of Useless Clocks, Reducing the Number of Clock Variables of Timed Automata," *Proc. 17th Real-Time Systems Symposium*, Washington, D.C., December 1996.

[de Alfaro et al., 1997]   L. de Alfaro, Z. Manna, H. B. Sipma, and T. E. Uribe, "Visual Verification of Reactive Systems," *Proc. of TACAS*, vol. 1217 of LNCS, pp. 334–350, New York, Springer-Verlag, 1997.

[De-Leon and Grumberg, 1992]   H. De-Leon and O. Grumberg, "Modular Abstractions for Verifying Real-Time Distributed Systems," *Proc. 4th Intl. Conf. on Computer-Aided Verification*, Montreal, Canada, pp. 2–15, June 1992.

[De Nicola, Inverardi, and Nesi, 1990]   R. De Nicola, P. Inverardi, and M. Nesi, "Using Axiomatic Presentation of Behavioural Equivalences for Manipulating CCS Specifications," J. Sifakis, ed., *Automatic Verification Methods for Finite State Systems*, LNCS 407, New York, Springer-Verlag, pp. 54–67, 1990.

[Dertouzos and Mok, 1989]   M. L. Dertouzos and A. K. Mok, "Multiprocessor On-line Scheduling of Hard-real-time Tasks," *IEEE Trans. Software Engineering*, vol. 15, pp. 1497–1506, December 1989.

[Dill, 1988]   D. L. Dill, "Trace Theory for Automatic Hierarchical Verification of Speed-Independent Circuits," Ph.D. thesis, Carnegie-Mellon University, February 1988.

[Dill, 1989]   D. L. Dill, "Timing Assumptions and Verification of Finite-State Concurrent Systems," *Proc. 1st Intl. Conf. on Computer-Aided Verification*, July 1989.

[Dill and Wong-Toi, 1995]   D. L. Dill and H. Wong-Toi, "Verification of Real-Time Systems by Successive Over and Under Approximation," *Proc. 7th Intl. Conf. on Computer-Aided Verification*, Liege, Belgium, pp. 409–422, July 1995.

[Dodd and Ravishankar, 1992] P. S. Dodd and C. V. Ravishankar, "Monitoring and Debugging Distributed Real-Time Programs," *Software: Practice and Experience*, vol. 22, no. 10, pp. 863–877, October 1992.

[Dutertre and Stavridou, 1997] B. Dutertre and V. Stavridou, "Formal Requirements Analysis of an Avionics Control Systems," *IEEE Trans. on Software Engineering*, vol. 23, no. 5, pp. 267-278, May 1997.

[Edgar and Burns, 2001] S. Edgar and A. Burns "Statistical Analysis of WCET for Scheduling," *Proc. 22nd Real-Time Systems Symposium*, London, UK, December 2001.

[Eliot, 1992] L. B. Eliot, "If It Works, Is It Good?," *AI Expert*, vol. 7, no. 6, pp. 9–11, June 1992.

[Elseaidy, Cleaveland, and Baugh, 1994] W. M. Elseaidy, R. Cleaveland and J.W. Baugh, Jr., "Verifying an Intelligent Structure Control System: A Case Study," *Proc. 15th IEEE Real-Time Systems Symp.*, San Juan, Puerto Rico, pp. 132–141, December 1994.

[Emerson, 1991] E. A. Emerson, "Real-Time and the Mu-Calculus," *Real-Time: Theory in Practice*, LNCS 600, 1991.

[Emerson and Halpern, 1982] E. A. Emerson and J. Y. Halpern, "Sometimes and Not Never Revisited: On Branching Time versus Linear Time Temporal Logic," *Proc. ACM Symp. on Principles of Programming Languages*, Austin, TX, January 1982.

[Emerson and Sistla, 1993] E. A. Emerson and A. P. Sistla, "Symmetry and Model Checking," *Proc. 5th Intl. Conf. on Computer-Aided Verification*, Elounda, Greece, June 1993.

[Emerson and Sistla, 1995] E. A. Emerson and A. P. Sistla, "Using Symmetry when Model Checking Under Fairness Assumptions: An Automata-Theoretic Approach," *Proc. 7th Intl. Conf. on Computer-Aided Verification*, Liege, Belgium, pp. 309–324, July 1995.

[Emerson et al., 1989] E. A. Emerson et al., "Quantitative Temporal Reasoning," *Proc. Intl. Workshop on Automatic Verification Methods for Finite-State Systems*, Grenoble, France, June 1989.

[Emerson et al., 1990] E. A. Emerson et al., "Quantitative Temporal Reasoning," *Proc. 2nd Intl. Conf. on Computer-Aided Verification*, New Brunswick, NJ, pp. 136–145, June 1990.

[Emerson et al., 1992] E. A. Emerson, A. K. Mok, A. P. Sistla, and J. Srinivasan, "Quantitative Temporal Reasoning," *Journal of Real Time Systems*, vol. 4, pp. 331–352, 1992.

[En-Nouaary et al., 1998] A. En-Nouaary, R. Dssouli, F. Khendek and A. Elqortobi, "Timed Test Cases Generation Based on State Characterisation Technique," *Proc. 19th IEEE-CS Real-Time Systems Symposium*, Madrid, Spain, December 2–4, 1998.

[Faulk, et al., 1992] S. Faulk, J. Brackett, P. Ward, J.Kirby, "The Core Method for Real-Time Requirements," *IEEE Software*, September 1992.

[Felder, Mandrioli, and Morzenti, 1994] M. Felder, D. Mandrioli, and A. Morzenti, "Proving Properties of Real-Time Systems Through Logical Specifications and Petri Net Models," *IEEE Trans. on Software Engineering*, vol. 20, no. 2, pp. 127–141, February 1994.

[Felder and Morzenti, 1994] M. Felder and A. Morzenti, "Validating Real-Time Systems by History Checking TRIO Specifications," *ACM Trans. on Software Engineering and Methodologies*, vol. 3, no. 4, October 1994.

[Ferdinand and Wilhelm, 1999] C. Ferdinand and R. Wilhelm, "Efficient and Precise Cache Behavior Prediction for Real-Time Systems," *Journal of Real-Time Systems*, 17(2/3):131–181, November 1999.

[Fidge, Kearney, and Utting, 1995] C. Fidge, P. Kearney, and M. Utting, "Interactively Verifying a Simple Real-Time Scheduler," *Proc. 7th Intl. Conf. on Computer-Aided Verification*, Liege, Belgium, pp. 394–408, July 1995.

[Forgy, 1981] C. L. Forgy, Ops5 Users Manual, Technical report, Department of Computer Science, Carnegie-Mellon University, 1981.

[Forgy, 1982] C. L. Forgy, "Rete: A Fast Algorithm for Many Pattern/Many Object Pattern Match Problem," *Artif. Intell.*, vol. 19, no. 1, pp. 17–37, 1982.

[Forgy, 1985] C L. Forgy, "The OPS Languages: An Historical Overview," *PC AI*, 9(5):16–21, September 1995.

[Franklin and Gabrielian, 1989] M. K. Franklin and A. Gabrielian, "A Transformational Method for Verifying Safety Properties in Real-Time Systems," *Proc. 10th Real-Time Systems Symposium*, Santa Monica, CA, pp. 112–123, December 1995.

[Fredette, 1993] A. N. Fredette, "A Generalized Approach to the Analysis of Real-Time Computer Systems," Ph.D. thesis, North Carolina State University, March 1993.

[Fredette and Cleaveland, 1993] A. N. Fredette and R. Cleaveland, "RTSL: A Language for Real-Time Schedulability Analysis," *Proc. 14th Real-Time Systems Symposium*, Raleigh-Durham, NC, pp. 274–283, December 1993.

[Frossl, Gerlach, and Kropf, 1996] J. Frossl, J. Gerlach, and T. Kropf, "An Efficient Algorithm for Real-Time Symbolic Model Checking," *Proc. EDTC*, 1996.

[Gabrielian and Franklin, 1991] A. Gabrielian and M. K. Franklin, "Multilevel Specification of Real-Time Systems," *Communications of the ACM*, vol. 34, pp. 51–60, May 1991.

[Gabrielian and Iyer, 1991] A. Gabrielian and R. Iyer, "Verifying Properties of HMS Machine Specifications of Real-Time Systems," *Proc. 3rd Intl. Conf. on Computer-Aided Verification*, Aalborg, Denmark, pp. 421–431, July 1991.

[Gallmeister, 1995] B. Gallmeister, *POSIX.4: Programming for the Real World*, 1st ed., Sebastopol, CA, O'Reilly, 1995.

[Gallmeister and Lanier, 1991] B. O. Gallmeister and C. Lanier, "Early Experience with POSIX 1003.4 and POSIX 1003.4A," *Proc. IEEE Real-Time Systems Symposium*, pp. 190–198, 1991.

[Gangopadhyay and Mitra, 1993] D. Gangopadhyay and S. Mitra, "ObjChart: Tangible Specification of Reactive Object Behavior," pp. 432–457 of *European Conf. on Object-Oriented Prog.* (ECOOP 93) O. M. Nierstrasz, ed., LNCS 707, New York, Springer-Verlag, 1993.

[Garbay et al., 1980] D. Garbay et al., "The Temporal Analysis of Fairness," *Proc. 7th ACM Symp. on Principles of Programming Languages*, Las Vegas, NV, pp. 163–173, January 1980.

[Garey and Johnson, 1979] M. R. Garey and D. S. Johnson, *Computers and Intractability: A Guide to the Theory of NP-Completeness*, New York, Freeman, 1979.

[Garland and Guttag, 1991] S. J. Garland and J. V. Guttag, "A Guide to LP, the Larch Prover," MIT Laboratory for Computer Science, December 1991. Also available as Digital Equipment Corporation Systems Research Center Research Report 82.

[Garvey and Lesser, 1994] A. Garvey and V. Lesser, "A Survey of Research in Deliberative Real-Time Artificial Intelligence," *Journal of Real-Time Systems*, vol. 6, no. 3, May 1994.

[Gavrila et al., 2001] D. M. Gavrila et al., "Real-Time Vision for Intelligent Vehicles," *IEEE Instrumentation*, vol. 4, no. 2, June 2001.

[Genrich, 1987] H. Genrich, "Predicate/Transition Nets," in *Advances in Petri Nets*, W. Reisg and G. Rozemberg, eds., LNCS 254-255, Berlin-New York, Springer-Verlag, 1987.

[Gerber, 1991] R. Gerber, "Communicating Shared Resources: A Model for Distributed Real-Time Systems," Ph.D. thesis, University of Pennsylvania, 1991.

[Gerber and Hong, 1995] R. Gerber and S. Hong, "Compiling Real-Time Programs with Timing Constraint Refinement and Structural Code Motion," *IEEE Transactions on Software Engineering*, vol. 21, no. 5, May 1995.

[Gerber, Hong, and Saksena, 1994] R. Gerber, S. Hong, and M. Saksena, "Guaranteeing End-to-End Timing Constraints by Calibrating Intermediate Processes," *Proc. IEEE-CS Real-Time Systems Symp.*, pp. 192–203, December 1994.

[Gerber and Lee, 1989] R. Gerber and I. Lee, "Communicating Shared Resources: A Model for Distributed Real-Time Systems," *Proc. 10th Real-Time Systems Symposium*, Santa Monica, CA, pp. 68–78, December 1989.

[Gerber and Lee, 1994] R. Gerber and I. Lee, "A Resource-Based Prioritized Bisimulation for Real-Time Systems," *Information and Computation*, vol. 113, no. 1, pp. 102–142, 1994.

[Gerber and Lee, 1990] R. Gerber and I. Lee, "CCSR: A Calculus for Communicating Shared Resources," *Proc. CONCUR Intl. Conf. on Concurrency Theory*, LNCS 458, August 1990.

[Gerber and Lee, 1990a] R. Gerber and I. Lee, "A Proof System for Communicating Shared Resources," *Proc. 11th IEEE Real-Time Systems Symposium*, Orlando, FL, pp. 288–299, December 1990.

[Gerber and Lee, 1992] R. Gerber and I. Lee, "A Layered Approach to Automating the Verification of Real-Time Systems," *IEEE Trans. on Software Engineering*, 18(9):768–784, September 1992.

[Gerth and Boucher, 1987] R. Gerth and A. Boucher, "A Timed Failure Semantics for Extended Communicating Processes," *Proc. ICALP*, LNCS 267, 1987.

[Ghezzi, Mandrioli, and Morzenti, 1990] C. Ghezzi, D. Mandrioli, and A. Morzenti, "TRIO: A Logic Language for Executable Specifications Real-Time Systems," *Journal of Systems Software*, vol. 12, pp. 107–123, 1990.

[Ghezzi, Morasca, and Pezze, 1994] C. Ghezzi, S. Morasca, and M. Pezze, "Timing Analysis of Time Basic Nets," *Journal of Systems and Software*, vol. 27, no. 7, pp. 97–117, November 1994.

[Ghezzi et al., 1991] C. Ghezzi et al., "A Unified High-Level Petri Net Formalism for Time-Critical Systems," *IEEE Trans. on Software Engineering*, vol. 17, no. 2, pp. 160–172, February 1991.

[Gilmore, 1960] P. C. Gilmore, "A Proof Method for Quantification Theory," *IBM J. Res. Develop.* 4, pp. 28–35, 1960.

[Godefroid, Holzmann, and Pirottin, 1992] P. Godefroid, G. J. Holzmann, and D. Pirottin, "State Space Caching Revisited," *Proc. 4th Workshop on Computer Aided Verification*, Montreal, Canada, June 1992, pp. 178–191.

[Gonzalez-Harbour, Klein, and Lehoczky, 1994] M. Gonzalez-Harbour, M. H. Klein, and J. P. Lehoczky, "Timing Analysis for Fixed-Priority Scheduling of Hard Real-Time Systems," *IEEE Trans. on Software Engineering*, vol. 20, no. 1, pp. 13–28, January 1994.

[Gordon and Finkel, 1988] A. J. Gordon and R. A. Finkel, "Handling Timing Errors in Distributed Programs," *IEEE Trans. on Software Engineering*, vol. 14, no. 10, pp. 1525–1535, October 1988.

[Gorlick, 1991] M. M. Gorlick, "The Flight Recorder: An Architectural Aid for System Monitoring," *Proc. ACM-ONR Workshop on Parallel and Distributed Debugging*, pp. 175–183, 1991.

[Gorrieri and Siliprandi, 1994] R. Gorrieri and G. Siliprandi, "Real-Time System Verification Using PT Nets," *Proc. 6th Intl. Conf. on Computer-Aided Verification*, Stanford, CA, pp. 14–26, June 1994.

[Govindaraju and Dill, 1999] S. Govindaraju and D. L. Dill, "Approximate Symbolic Model Checking Using Overlapping Projections," *First International Workshop on Symbolic Model Checking (SMC99) at Federated Logic Conference (FLOC)*, July 1999.

[Green, 1982] T. R. G. Green, "Pictures of Programs and Other Processes, or How to do Things with Lines," *Behavior Inform. Tech.*, vol. 1, pp. 9–32, 1982.

[Grossman et al., 1993] R. L. Grossman et al., eds., *Hybrid Systems*, LNCS 736, 1993.

[Gupta, 1987] A. Gupta, "Parallelism in Production Systems," Ph.D. thesis, Carnegie-Mellon University, 1987.

[Haban and Shin, 1990] D. Haban and K. G. Shin, "Applications of Real-Time Monitoring to Scheduling Tasks with Random Execution Times," *IEEE Trans. on Software Engineering*, vol. 16, no. 12, pp. 1374–1389, December 1990.

[Haddawy, 1986] P. Haddawy, "Implementation of and Experiments with a Variable Precision Logic Inference System," *Proceedings of the AAAI Conference*, pp. 238–242, 1986.

[Haddawy, 1987] P. Haddawy, "A Variable Precision Logic Inference system Employing the Dempster-Shafer Uncertainty Calculus," M.S. thesis, Department of Computer Science, University of Illinois, Urbana, 1987.

[Halbwachs, 1993] N. Halbwachs, "Delay Analysis in Synchronous Programs," *Proc. 5th Intl. Conf. on Computer-Aided Verification*, Elounda, Greece, pp. 333–346, June 1993.

[Halbwachs, Raymond, and Proy, 1994] N. Halbwachs, P. Raymond, and Y.-E. Proy, "Verification of Linear Hybrid Systems by Means of Convex Approximations," *Proc. Static Analysis Symp.*, LNCS 864, pp. 223–237, 1994.

[Halbwachs et al., 1992] N. Halbwachs et al., "Programming and Verifying Real-Time Systems by Means of the Synchronous Data-Flow Language LUSTRE," *IEEE Trans. on Software Engineering*, vol. 18, no. 9, pp. 785–793, September 1992.

[Halpern and Shoham, 1991] J. Y. Halpern and Y. Shoham, "A Propositional Modal Logic of Time Intervals," *Journal of the ACM*, vol. 38, no. 4, pp. 935–962, 1991.

[Hamaguchi et al., 1991] K. Hamaguchi et al., "Verification of Speed-Dependent Asynchronous Circuits Using Symbolic Model Checking of Branching Time Regular Temporal Logic," *Proc. 3rd Intl. Conf. on Computer-Aided Verification*, Aalborg, Denmark, pp. 410–420, July 1991.

[Hamilton et al., 2001] L. Hamilton et al., "Vision Sensors and the Intelligent Vehicle," *Automotive Engineering International*, vol. 109, no. 10, October 2001.

[Hansson and Jonsson, 1989] H. Hansson and B. Jonsson, "A Framework for Reasoning about Time and Reliability," *Proc. 10th Real-Time Systems Symposium*, Santa Monica, CA, pp. 102–111, December 1989.

[Hansson and Jonsson, 1990] H. Hansson and B. Jonsson, "A Calculus for Communicating Systems with Time and Probabilities," *Proc. 11th Real-Time Systems Symposium*, Orlando, FL, pp. 278–287, December 1990.

[Harel, 1980] D. Harel, "On Visual Formalism," *Communications of the ACM*, vol. 31, no. 5, pp. 514–530, 1980.

[Harel, 1987] D. Harel, "Statecharts: A Visual Formalism for Complex Systems," *Science of Computer Programming*, vol. 8, pp. 231–274, 1987.

[Harel and Gery, 1997] D. Harel and E. Gery, "Executable Object Modeling with State-charts," *IEEE Computer*, vol. 30, no. 7, pp. 31–42, July 1997.

[Harel and Naamad, 1996] D. Harel and A. Naamad, "The STATEMATE Semantics of Stat-echarts," *ACM Trans. on Software Eng. and Methodology*, vol. 5, no. 4, pp. 292–333, October 1996.

[Harel and Politi, 1998] D. Harel and M. Politi, *Modeling Reactive Systems with Statecharts: The STATEMATE Approach*, New York, McGraw-Hill, 1998.

[Harel et al., 1987] D. Harel et al., "On the Formal Semantics of Statecharts," *Proc. 2nd IEEE Symp. on Logic in Computer Science*, pp. 54–64, 1987.

[Harel et al., 1990a] D. Harel et al., "Explicit Clock Temporal Logic," *Proc. 5th IEEE Symp. on Logic in Computer Science*, Washington, D.C., pp. 402–413, June 1990.

[Harel et al., 1990b] D. Harel, H. Lachover, A. Naamad, A. Pnueli, M. Politi, R. Sherman, A. Shtull-Trauring, and M. Trakhtenbrot, "STATEMATE: A Working Environment for the Development of Complex Reactive Systems," *IEEE Trans. on Software Eng.*, vol. 16, no. 4, pp. 403–414, April 1990.

[Harmon, Baker, and Whalley, 1994] M. G. Harmon, T. P. Baker, and D. B. Whalley, "A Re-targetable Technique for Predicting Execution Time of Code Segements," *Journal of Real-Time Systems*, vol. 7, no. 2, pp. 159–182, September 1994.

[Harter, 1987] P. K. Harter, Jr., "Response Times in Level-Structured Systems," *ACM Trans. on Computer Systems*, vol. 5, no. 3, pp. 232–248, August 1987.

[Hatley, 1985] D. J. Hatley, "A Structured Analysis Method for Real-Time Systems," *Proc. DECUS Symp.*. December 1985.

[Hatley and Pirbhai, 1987] D. J. Hatley and I. Pirbhai, *Strategies for Real-Time System Spec-ification*, New York, Dorset, 1987.

[Havelund, Lowry, and Penix, 2001] K. Havelund, M. Lowry, and J. Penix, "Formal Analysis of a Space-Craft Controller Using SPIN," *IEEE Transactions on Software Engineering*, vol. 27, no. 8, August 2001.

[Healy and Whalley, 1999a] C. Healy and D. Whalley, "Bounding Pipeline and Instruction Cache Performance," *IEEE Transactions on Computers*, pp. 53–70, January 1999.

[Healy and Whalley, 1999b] C. Healy and D. Whalley, "Tighter Timing Predictions by Auto-matic Detection and Exploitation of Value-Dependent Constraints," *Proceedings of the 5th IEEE Real-Time Technology and Applications Symposium*, Vancouver, BC, Canada, June 1999.

[Healy, Whalley, and Harmon, 1995] C. A. Healy, D. B. Whalley, and M. G. Harmon, "Inte-grating the Timing Analysis of Pipelining and Instruction Caching," *Proc. 16th Real-Time Systems Symposium*, Pisa, Italy, December 1995.

[Healy et al., 1999] C. Healy, M. Sjodin, V. Rustagi, D. Whalley, and R. van Engelen, "Sup-porting Timing Analysis by Automatic Bounding of Loop Iterations," *Journal of Real-Time Systems*, pp. 121–148, May 2000.

[Heimdahl, 1994] M. P. E. Heimdahl, "Static Analysis of State-Based Requirements: Analy-sis for Completeness and Consistency," Ph.D. thesis, University of California, Irvine, 1994.

[Heimdahl and Leveson, 1996] M. P. E. Heimdahl and N. G. Leveson, "Completeness and Consistency in Hierarchical State-Based Requirements," *IEEE Trans. Software Engineer-ing*, vol. SE-22, no. 6, pp. 363–377, June 1986.

[Heitmeyer, Jeffords, and Labaw, 1993] C. Heitmeyer, R. D. Jeffords, and B. Labaw, "A Benchmark for Comparing Different Approaches for Specifying and Verifying Real-Time

Systems," *Proc. 10th IEEE Workshop on Real-Time Operating Systems and Software*, May 1993.

[Heitmeyer and Lynch, 1994] C. Heitmeyer and N. Lynch, "The Generalized Railroad Crossing: A Case Study in Formal Verification of Real-Time Systems," *Proc. 15th IEEE Real-Time Systems Symp.*, San Juan, Puerto Rico, pp. 120–131, December 1994.

[Heitmeyer et al., 1992] C. Heitmeyer et al., "Engineering CASE Tools to Support Formal Methods for Real-Time Software Development," *Proc. 5th Intl. Workshop on Computer-Aided Software Engineering*, July 1992.

[Heitmeyer et al., 1995] C. Heitmeyer, A. Bull, C. Gasarch, and B. Labaw, "SCR*: A Toolset for Specifying and Analyzing Requirements," *Proc. 10 th Annual Conf. on Computer Assurance (COMPASS '95)*, June 1995.

[Helly, 1984] J. J. Helly, "Distributed Expert System for Space Shuttle Flight Control," Ph.D. dissertation, Department of Computer Science, UCLA, 1984.

[Heninger, 1980] K. L. Heninger, "Specifying Software Requirements for Complex Systems: New Techniques and Their Applications," *IEEE Trans. Software Engineering*, vol. SE-6, no. 1, pp. 2–13, January 1980.

[Henzinger, 1991] T. A. Henzinger, "The Temporal Specification and Verification of Real-Time Systems," Ph.D. thesis, Stanford University, August 1991.

[Henzinger, 1995] T. A. Henzinger, "Hybrid Automata with Finite Bisimulations," *Proc. Intl. Conf. on Automata, Languages, and Programming*, LNCS 944, pp. 324–335, 1995.

[Henzinger, 1996] T. A. Henzinger, "The Theory of Hybrid Automata," *Proceedings of the 11th Annual IEEE Symposium on Logic in Computer Science*, pp. 278–292, 1996.

[Henzinger, Henzinger, and Kopke, 1995] M. R. Henzinger, T. A. Henzinger, and P. W. Kopke, "Computing Simulations on Finite and Infinite Graphs," *Proc. 36th Annual Symp. on Foundations of Computer Science*, pp. 453–462, 1995.

[Henzinger and Ho, 1995] T. A. Henzinger and P.-H. Ho, "Algorithmic Analysis of Nonlinear Hybrid Systems," *Proc. 7th Intl. Conf. on Computer-Aided Verification*, Liege, Belgium, pp. 225–238, July 1995.

[Henzinger, Ho, and Wong-Toi, 1995] T. A. Henzinger, P.-H. Ho, and H. Wong-Toi, "HYTECH: The Next Generation," *Proc. 16th Real-Time Systems Symposium*, Pisa, Italy, pp. 56–65, December 1995.

[Henzinger, Ho, and Wong-Toi, 1997] T. A. Henzinger, P.-H. Ho, and H. Wong-Toi, "HyTech: A Model Checker for Hybrid Systems," *Journal of Software Tools for Technology Transfer*, vol. 1, pp. 110–122, 1997.

[Henzinger, Kupferman, and Vardi, 1996] T. A. Henzinger, O. Kupferman, M. Y. Vardi, "A Space-Efficient On-the-fly Algorithm for Real-Time Model Checking," *Proceedings of International Conference on Concurrency Theory (CONCUR'96)*, LNCS 1119, pp. 514–529, 1996.

[Henzinger and Majumdar, 2000] T. A. Henzinger and R. Majumdar, "Symbolic Model Checking for Rectangular Hybrid Systems," pp. 142–156 of *Proceedings of the Sixth International Workshop on Tools and Algorithms for the Construction and Analysis of Systems (TACAS 2000)*, LNCS 1785, New York, Springer-Verlag, 2000.

[Henzinger, Manna, and Pnueli, 1991] T. A. Henzinger, Z. Manna, and A. Pnueli, "Temporal Proof Methodologies for Real-Time Systems," *Proc. 18th ACM Symp. on Principles of Programming Languages*, 1991.

[Henzinger, Manna, and Pnueli, 1992] T. A. Henzinger, Z. Manna, and A. Pnueli, "What Good Are Digital Clocks," *Proc. ICALP*, LNCS 623, 1992.

[Henzinger et al., 1992] T. A. Henzinger, X. Nicollin, J. Sifakis, and S. Yovine, "Symbolic Model Checking for Real-Time Systems," *Proc. 7th IEEE Symp. on Logic in Computer Science*, June 1992.

[Henzinger et al., 1994] T. A. Henzinger, X. Nicollin, J. Sifakis, and S. Yovine, "Symbolic Model Checking for Real-Time Systems," *Information and Computation*, vol. 111, no. 2, 1994.

[Henzinger et al., 1995] T. A. Henzinger et al., "What's Decidable about Hybrid Automata?," *Proc. 27th ACM Annual Symp. on Thoery of Computing*, pp. 373–382, 1995.

[Herbrand, 1930] J. Herbrand, "Recherches sur la Théorie de la Démonstration," *Travaux de la Société des Sciences et des Lettres de Varsovie*, Classe III, 33(128), also Ph.D. thesis, University of Paris, 1930.

[Hilbert, 1927] D. Hilbert, The Foundations of Mathematics (original in German), *From Frege to Godel: A Source Book in Mathematical Logic*, Cambridge, MA, Harvard University Press, pp. 464–479, 1927.

[Ho, 1995] P.-H. Ho, "Automatic Analysis of Hybrid Systems," Ph.D. thesis, Cornell University, 1995.

[Ho and Wong-Toi, 1995] P.-H. Ho and H. Wong-Toi, "Automated Analysis of an Audio Control Protocol," *Proc. 7th Intl. Conf. on Computer-Aided Verification*, Liege, Belgium, pp. 381–394, July 1995.

[Hoare, 1978] C. A. R. Hoare, "Communicating Sequential Processes," *Communications of the ACM*, vol. 21, no. 8, pp. 666–677, August 1978.

[Hoare, 1985] C. A. R. Hoare, *Communicating Sequential Processes*, englewood Cliffs, NJ, Prentice Hall, 1985.

[Holliday and Vernon, 1987] M. A. Holliday and M. K. Vernon, "A Generalized Timed Petri Net Model for Performance Analysis," *IEEE Trans. on Software Engineering*, vol. 13, no. 12, pp. 1297–1310, December 1987.

[Holmer, Larsen, and Yi, 1991] U. Holmer, K. Larsen, and W. Yi, "Deciding Properties of Regular Real Timed Processes," *Proc. 3rd Intl. Conf. on Computer-Aided Verification*, Aalborg, Denmark, pp. 443–453, July 1991.

[Holzmann, 1991] G. J. Holzmann, *Design and Validation of Computer Protocols*, chapter Protocol validation, pp. 217–244, London, Prentice Hall, 1991.

[Hooman, 1991] J. Hooman, "Compositional Verification of Real-Time Systems Using Extended Hoare Triples," *Proc. REX Workshop "Real-Time: Theory in Practice,"* LNCS 600, Mook, The Netherlands, June 1991.

[Hooman, 1993] J. Hooman, "Specification and Verification of a Distributed Real-Time Arbitration Protocol," *Proc. 14th Real-Time Systems Symposium*, Raleigh-Durham, NC, pp. 284–293, December 1993.

[Hopcroft and Ullman, 1979] J. E. Hopcroft and J. D. Ullman, "Introduction to Automata Theory, Languages, and Computation," Addison-Wesley, Reading, MA, 1979.

[Hsieh, 1989] C. S. Hsieh, "Timing Analysis of Cyclic Concurrent Programs," *Proc. IEEE Intl. Conf. on Software Engineering*, pp. 312–318, 1989.

[Huang and Cheng, 1995] X. Huang and A. M. K. Cheng, "Applying Imprecise Algorithms to Real-Time Image and Video Transmission," *Proc. IEEE-CS Real-Time Technology and Applications Symp.*, Chicago, IL, pp. 96–101, May 1995.

[Hulgaard and Burns, 1995] H. Hulgaard and S. M. Burns, "Efficient Timing Analysis of a Class of Petri Nets," *Proc. 7th Intl. Conf. on Computer-Aided Verification*, Liege, Belgium, pp. 423–436, July 1995.

[Hur, et al., 1995] Y. Hur, Y.H. Bae, S.-S. Lim, S.-K. Kim, B.-D. Rhee, S.L. Min, C.Y. Park, M. Lee, H. Shin, and C.S. Kim, "Worst Case Timing Analysis of RISC Processors: R3000/R3010 Case Study," *Proc. 16th Real-Time Systems Symposium*, Pisa, Italy, December 1995.

[Huth and Kwiatkowska, 1997] M. Huth and M. Kwiatkowska, "Quantitative Analysis and Model Checking," *Proc. LICS*, IEEE Computer Society Press, 1997.

[i-Logix, 1993] i-Logix, Inc., *STATEMATE: Analyzer Reference Manual, Version 5.0*, Burlington, MA, June 1993.

[Inal, 1994] R. Inal, "Modular Specification of Real-Time Systems," *Proc. Euromicro Workshop on Real-Time Systems*, 1994.

[Ishida, 1991] T. Ishida, "Parallel Rule Firing in Production Systems," *IEEE Transactions on Knowledge and Data Engineering*, 3(1), March 1991.

[Ishida, 1994] T. Ishida, "An Optimization Algorithm for Production Systems," *IEEE Transactions on Knowledge and Data Engineering*, vol. 6, no. 4, pp. 549–558, August 1994.

[Ishida and S. Stolfo, 1985] T. Ishida and S. Stolfo, "Towards the Parallel Execution of Rules in Production System Programs," *Proc. IEEE Intl. Conf. on Parallel Processing*, 1985.

[Iversen et al., 2000] T. K. Iversen, K. J. Kristoffersen, K. G. Larsen, M. Laursen, R. G. Madsen, S. K. Mortensen, P. Pettersson, and C. B. Thomasen, "Model-Checking Real-Time Control Programs," *Proceedings of the 12th Euromicro Conference on Real-Time Systems (ECRTS'2000)*, Stockholm, Sweden, pp. 147–155, June 19–21, 2000.

[Jaffe et al., 1991] M. S. Jaffe et al., "Software Requirements Analysis for Real-Time Process-Control Systems," *IEEE Trans. Software Engineering*, vol. SE-17, no. 3, pp. 241–258, March 1991.

[Jahanian, 1989] F. Jahanian, "Verifying Properties of Systems with Variable Timing Constraints," *Proc. 10th IEEE Real-Time Systems Symp.*, Santa Monica, CA, pp. 319–328, December 1989.

[Jahanian and Goyal, 1990] F. Jahanian and A. Goyal, "A Formalism for Monitoring Real-Time Constraints at Run-Time," *Proc. IEEE-CS Fault Tolerance Symp.*, pp. 148–155, 1990.

[Jahanian, Lee, and Mok, 1988] F. Jahanian, R. Lee, and A. K. Mok, "Semantics of Modechart in Real Time Logic," *21st Hawaii International Conf. Systems Science*, January 1988.

[Jahanian and Mok, 1986] F. Jahanian and A. K. Mok, "Safety Analysis of Timing Properties in Real-Time Systems," *IEEE Trans. Software Engineering*, vol. SE-12, no. 9, pp. 890–904, September 1986.

[Jahanian and Mok, 1987] F. Jahanian and A. K. Mok, "A Graph-Theoretic Approach for Timing Analysis and Its Implementation," *IEEE Trans. Computers*, vol. C-36, no. 8, pp. 961–975, August 1987.

[Jahanian and Mok, 1994] F. Jahanian and A. K. Mok, "Modechart: A Specification Language for Real-Time Systems," *IEEE Trans. Software Engineering*, vol. SE-20, no. 12, pp. 933–947, December 1994.

[Jahanian and Rajkumar, 1991] F. Jahanian and R. Rajkumar, "An Integrated Approach to Monitoring and Scheduling in Real-Time Systems," *Proc. IEEE Workshop on Real-Time Operating Systems and Software*, 1991.

[Jahanian and Stuart, 1988] F. Jahanian and D. A. Stuart, "A Method for Verifying Properties of Modechart Specification," *Proc. 9th IEEE Real-Time Systems Symp.*, pp. 12–21, December 1988.

[Jeffrey, 1991] A. Jeffrey, "A Linear Time Process Algebra," *Proc. 3rd Intl. Conf. on Computer-Aided Verification*, Aalborg, Denmark, pp. 432–442, July 1991.

[Jensen, 1987] K. Jensen, "Colored Petri Nets," in *Advances in Petri Nets*, W. Reisg and G. Rozemberg, eds., LNCS 254-255, Berlin-New York, Springer-Verlag, 1987.

[Jones, 2002] W. D. Jones, "Building Safer Cars," *IEEE Spectrum*, vol. 39, no. 1, pp. 82–85, January 2002.

[Joseph and Goswami, 1988] M. Joseph and A. Goswami, "What's 'Real' about Real-Time Systems?" *Proc. 9th IEEE Real-Time Systems Symp.*, December 1988.

[Jones, Landweber, and Lien, 1977] N. D. Jones, L. H. Landweber, and Y. E. Lien, "Complexity of Some Problems in Petri Nets" *Theoretical Computer Science*, vol. 4, pp. 277–299, 1977.

[Jourdan, Maraninchi, and Olivero, 1993] M. Jourdan, F. Maraninchi, and A. Olivero, "Verifying Quantitative Properties of Synchronous Programs," *Proc. 5th Intl. Conf. on Computer-Aided Verification*, Elounda, Greece, pp. 346–358, June 1993.

[Kang and Lee, 1994] I. Kang and I. Lee, "State Minimization for Concurrent System Analysis Based on State Space Exploration," *Proceedings of Conference on Computer Assurance*, 1994.

[Kang, Lee, and Kim, 2000] I. Kang, I. Lee, and Y.-S. Kim, "An Efficient State Space Generation for the Analysis of Real-time Systems," *IEEE Transactions of Software Engineering*, vol. 26, no. 5, 2000.

[Katcher, Arakawa, and Strosnider, 1993] D. I. Katcher, H. Arakawa, and J. K. Strosnider, "Engineering and Analysis of Fixed Priority Schedulers" *IEEE Trans. Software Engineering*, vol. SE-19, no. 9, pp. 920–934, September 1993.

[Kemmerer, 1985] R. A. Kemmerer, "Testing Formal Specifications to Detect Design Errors," *IEEE Trans. Software Engineering*, vol. SE-11, no. 1, pp. 32–43, January 1985.

[Kesten, Manna, and Pnueli, 1996] Y. Kesten, Z. Manna, and A. Pnueli, "Verifying Clocked Transition Systems," pp. 13–40 of *Hybrid Systems III*, LNCS 1066, New York, Springer-Verlag, 1996.

[Kiper, 1992] J. D. Kiper, "Structural Testing of Rule-Based Expert Systems," *ACM Transactions on Software Engineering and Methodology*, vol. 1, no. 2, April 1992.

[Kleene, 1956] S. C. Kleene, "Representation of Events by Nerve Nets," Shannon and McCarthy eds., *Automata Studies*, Princeton, NJ, Princeton University Press, pp. 3–42, 1956.

[Klein, Lehoczky, and Rajkumar, 1994] M. Klein, J. Lehoczky, and R. Rajkumar, "Rate-Monotonic Analysis for Real-Time Industrial Computing," *IEEE Computer*, vol. 27, no. 1, pp. 24-33, January 1994.

[Koch et al., 1986] D. Koch, K. Morris, C. Giffin, and T. Reid, "Avionic Sensor-based Safing System Technology," Presentation at the Tri-Service Software System Safety Working Group in association with *IEEE COMPASS Conference*, 1986.

[Kolano, 1999] P. Z. Kolano, "Proof Assistance for Real-Time Systems Using an Interactive Theorem Prover," J.-P. Katoen, ed., *Proceedings of the 5th International AMAST Workshop on Real-Time and Probabilistic Systems (ARTS'99)*, LNCS 1601, pp. 315–333, New York, Springer, 1999.

[Kowalski and Hayes, 1969] R. Kowalski and P. J. Hayes, "Semantic Trees in Automatic Theorem-Proving," Meltzer and Michie, eds., *Machine Intelligence*, Edinburgh University Press, Edinburgh, vol. 4, pp. 87–101, 1969.

[Koymans, 1989] R. Koymans, "Specifying Message-Passing and Time-Critical Systems with Temporal Logic," Ph.D. thesis, Eindhoven University of Technology, 1989.

[Koymans, 1990a] R. Koymans, "Specifying Message-Passing and Time-Critical Systems with Temporal Logic," *Journal of Real-Time Systems*, November 1990.

[Koymans, 1990b] R. Koymans, "Specifying Real-Time Properties with Metric Temporal Logic," *Journal of Real-Time Systems*, pp. 255–299, 1990.

[Krishna and Shin, 1997] C. M. Krishna and K. G. Shin, *Real-Time Systems*, New York, McGraw-Hill, 1997.

[Kuo and Moldovan, 1991] S. Kuo and D. Moldovan, "Implementation of Multiple Rule Firing Production System on Hypercube," *J. Parallel and Distr. Computing*, 13(4):383–394, December 1991.

[Kuo and Moldovan, 1992] S. Kuo and D. Moldovan, "The State of the Art in Parallel Production Systems," *J. Parallel and Distr. Computing*, 15:1–26, 1992.

[Kupferman and Vardi, 2000] O. Kupferman and M. Y. Vardi, "An Automata-theoretic Approach to Modular Model Checking," *ACM Transactions on Programming Languages and Systems*, vol. 22, pp. 87–128, 2000.

[Kupferman, Vardi, and Wolper, 2000] O. Kupferman, M. Y. Vardi, and P. Wolper, "An Automata-Theoretic Approach to Branching-Time Model Checking," *Journal of the ACM*, vol. 47, pp. 312–360, 2000.

[Kwak, Lee, and Sokolsky, 1998] H.-H. Kwak, I. Lee, and O. Sokolsky, "Parametric Approach to the Specification and Analysis of Real-time System Designs Based on ACSR-VP," *Proceedings 1998 ARO/ONR/NSF/DARPA Monterey Workshop on Engineering Automation for Computer Based Systems*, Camel-By-The-Sea, CA, October 27–29, 1998.

[Kwak et al., 1998] H.-H. Kwak, J.-. Choi, I. Lee, A. Philippou, and O. Sokolsky, "Symbolic Schedulability Analysis of Real-Time Systems," *Proc. 19th IEEE-CS Real-Time Systems Symposium*, Madrid, Spain, December 2–4, 1998.

[Laffey et al., 1988] T. J. Laffey, P. A. Cox, J. L. Schmidt, S. M. Kao, and J. Y. Read, "Real-Time Knowledge-Based Systems," *AI Magazine*, vol. 9, no. 1, pp. 27–45, Spring 1988.

[Lagnier, Raymond, and Dubois, 1995] F. Lagnier, P. Raymond, and C. Dubois, "Formal Verification of a Critical System Written in Saga/Lustre," *Proc. Workshop on Formal Methods, Modelling and Simulation for System Engineering*, St. Quentin en Yvelines, France, February 1995.

[Lam and Brayton, 1993] W. K. C. Lam and R. K. Brayton, "Alternating RQ Timed Automata," *Proc. 5th Intl. Conf. on Computer-Aided Verification*, Elounda, Greece, pp. 237–252, June 1993.

[Lam and Brayton, 1994] W. K. C. Lam and R. K. Brayton, "Criteria for the Simple Path Property in Timed Automata," *Proc. 6th Intl. Conf. on Computer-Aided Verification*, Stanford, CA, pp. 27–40, June 1994.

[Lamport, 1978] L. Lamport, "Time, Clocks, and the Ordering of Events in a Distributed System," *CACM*, vol. 21, no. 7, pp. 558–564, July 1978.

[Lamport, Shostak, and Pease, 1982] L. Lamport, R. Shostak, and M. Pease, "The Byzantine Generals Problem," *ACM Transactions on Programming Languages and Systems*, vol.4, no.3, pp. 382–401, July 1982.

[Lark et al., 1990] J. S. Lark, L. D. Erman, S. Forrest, K. P. Gostelow, F. Hayes-Roth, and D. M. Smith, "Concepts, Methods, and Languages for Building Timely Intelligent Systems," *J. Real-Time Systems*, vol. 2, pp. 127–148, May 1990.

[Larsen, Pettersson, and Yi, 1995] K. G. Larsen, P. Pettersson, and W. Yi, "Compositional and Symbolic Model-Checking of Real-Time Systems," *Proc. 16th Real-Time Systems Symposium*, Pisa, Italy, pp. 76–87, December 1995.

[Larsen et al., 1997] K. G. Larsen, F. Larsson, P. Pettersson and W. Yi, "Efficient Verification of Real-Time Systems: Compact Data Structure and State-Space Reduction," *Proceedings of the 18th IEEE Real-Time Systems Symposium*, San Francisco, CA, pp. 14–24, 3–5 December 1997.

[Larsen et al., 2001] K. G. Larsen, G. Behrmann, E. Brinksma, A. Fehnker, T. Hune, P. Pettersson, and J. Romijn, "As Cheap as Possible: Efficient Cost-Optimal Reachability for Priced Timed Automata," *Procceedings of the 13th Conference on Computer Aided Verification (CAV'01)*, Paris, France, July 18, 2001.

[Lavi and Winokur, 1989] J. Z. Lavi and M. Winokur, "ECSAM-A Method for the Analysis of Complex Embedded Systems and Their Software," *Proc. Structured Techniques Association Conf. STA5*, Chicago, IL, pp. 50–63, May 1989.

[Lee, 1959] C. Y. Lee, "Representation of Switching Circuits by Binary Decision Programs," *Bell Systems Technical Journal*, vol. 38, pp. 985–999, 1959.

[Lee, Bremond-Gregoire, and Gerber, 1994] I. Lee, P. Bremond-Gregoire, and R. Gerber, "A Process Algebraic Approach to the Specification and Analysis of Resource-Bound Real-Time Systems," *Proc. IEEE*, pp. 158–171, January 1994.

[Lee and Cheng, 1994] T. Lee and A. M. K. Cheng, "Multiprocessor Scheduling of Hard-Real-Time Periodic Tasks with Task Migration Constraints," *Proc. IEEE-CS Workshop on Real-Time Computing Systems and Applications*, Seoul, Korea, December 1994.

[Lee and Cheng, 2000] Y.-H. Lee and A. M. K. Cheng, "Run-Time Dynamic Optimization of Real-Time Rule-Based Systems," *Proc. IEEE-CS Real-Time Technology and Applications Symposium*, Washington, D.C., May–June 2000.

[Lee and Gehlot, 1985] I. Lee and V. Gehlot, "Language Constructs for Distributed Real-Time Programming," *Proc. 6th IEEE Real-Time Systems Symposium*, December 1985.

[Lee et al., 1996] C. Lee et al., "Analysis of Cache-related Preemption Delay in Fixed-Priority Preemptive Scheduling," *Proc. 17th Real-Time Systems Symposium*, Washington, D.C., December 1996.

[Lehoczky, 1990] J. P. Lehoczky, "Fixed Priority Scheduling of Periodic Task Sets with Arbitrary Deadlines," *Proc. 11th IEEE-CS Real-Time Systems Symposium*, Lake Buena Vista, FL, pp. 201–213, December 1990.

[Lehoczky, Sha, and Ding, 1989] J. P. Lehoczky, L. Sha, and Y. Ding, "The Rate Monotonic Scheduling Algorithm: Exact Characterization and Average Case Behavior," *IEEE Real-Time Systems Symposium*, pp. 166–171, December 1989.

[Lehoczky, Sha, and Strosnider, 1987] J. P. Lehoczky, L. Sha, and J. K. Strosnider, "Enhanced Aperiodic Responsiveness in Hard Real-Time Environments," *Proc. 8th IEEE-CS Real-Time Systems Symposium*, pp. 261–270, 1987.

[Leveson, 1991] N. G. Leveson, "Software Safety in Embedded Computer Systems," *Communications of the ACM*, vol. 34, no. 2, pp. 34–47, February 1991.

[Leveson and Stolzy, 1987] N. G. Leveson and J. Stolzy, "Safety Analysis Using Petri Nets," *IEEE Trans. on Software Engineering*, vol. 13, no. 3, pp. 386–397, March 1987.

[Leveson et al., 1994] N. G. Leveson et al., "Requirements Specification for Process-Control Systems," *IEEE Trans. on Software Engineering*, vol. 20, no. 9, pp. 684–707, September 1994.

[Lewis, 1990] H. Lewis, "A Logic of Concrete Time Intervals," *Proc. 5th IEEE Symp. on Logic in Computer Science*, Washington, D.C., pp. 380–389, June 1990.

[Lewis and Papadimitriou, 1981] H. Lewis and C. Papadimitriou, *Elements of the Theory of Computation*, Englewood Cliffs, NJ, Prentice Hall, 1981.

[Lewis and Papadimitriou, 1998] H. Lewis and C. Papadimitriou, *Elements of the Theory of Computation*, 2nd edition, Upper Saddle River, NJ, Prentice Hall, 1998.

[Li, Malik, and Wolfe, 1995] Y.-T. S. Li, S. Malik, and A. Wolfe, "Efficient Microarchitecture Modeling and Path Analysis for Real-Time Software," *Proc. 16th Real-Time Systems Symposium*, Pisa, Italy, December 1995.

[Lim et al., 1995] S.-S. Lim et al., "An Accurate Worst Case Timing Analysis for RISC Processors," *IEEE Trans. Software Engineering*, vol. SE-21, no. 7, pp. 593–604, July 1995.

[Lin, Liu, and Natarajan, 1987] K. Lin, J. Liu, and S. Natarajan, "Scheduling Real-Time, Periodic Jobs Using Imprecise Results," *Proceedings of the Real-Time Systems Symposium*, San Fransisco, CA, December 1987.

[Liu, 2000] J. W. S. Liu, *Real-Time Systems*, Upper Saddle River, NJ, Prentice Hall, 2000.

[Liu and Ha, 1994] J. W. S. Liu and R. Ha, "Efficient Methods of Validating Timing Constraints," pp. 199–224 of *Advances in Real-Time Systems*, S. H. Son, ed., Prentice Hall, 1994.

[Liu and Layland, 1973] C. L. Liu and J. Layland, "Scheduling Algorithms for Multiprogramming in a Hard-Real-Time Environment," *Journal of the ACM*, vol. 20, no. 1, pp. 46–61, January 1973.

[Liu and Shyamasundar, 1990] L. Y. Liu and R. K. Shyamasundar, "Static Analysis of Temporal Behavior of Programs in CSP-R Real-Time Distributed Language," *IEEE Trans. Software Engineering*, vol. SE-16, no. 4, pp. 373–388, April 1990.

[Loveland, 1970] D. W. Loveland, "A Linear Format for Resolution," pp. 147–162 of *Proc. IRIA Symposium on Automatic Demonstration*, Lecture Notes in Mathematics, Volume 125, New York, Springer-Verlag, 1970.

[Luckham, 1970] D. Luckham, "Refinement Theorem in Resolution Theory," pp. 163–190 of *Proc. IRIA Symposium on Automatic Demonstration*, Lecture Notes in Mathematics, Volume 125, New York, Springer-Verlag, 1970.

[Lundqvist and Stenstrvm, 1999] T. Lundqvist and P. Stenstrvm, "An Integrated Path and Timing Analysis Method based on Cycle-Level Symbolic Execution," *Journal of Real-Time Systems*, 17(2/3): 183–207, November 1999.

[Lynch, 1993] N. A. Lynch, "Simulation Techniques for Proving Properties of Real-Time Systems," *Proc. REX Workshop "Real-Time: Theory in Practice,"* Mook, The Netherlands, June 1993.

[Lynch and Attiya, 1992] N. A. Lynch and H. Attiya, "Using Mappings to Prove Timing Properties," *Distributed Computing*, vol. 6, no. 2, pp. 121–139, 1992.

[Lynch and Vaandrager, 1991] N. A. Lynch and Vaandrager, "Forward and Backward Simulations for Timing-Based Systems," *Proc. REX Workshop "Real-Time: Theory in Practice,"* LNCS 600, Mook, The Netherlands, pp. 397–446, June 1991.

[Lynch and Vaandrager, 1992] N. A. Lynch and F. Vaandrager, "Action Transducers and Timed Automata," *Proc. CONCUR*, LNCS 630, pp. 436–455, 1992.

[Lyttle and Ford, 1990] D. Lyttle and R. Ford, "A symbolic Debugger for Real-Time Embedded Ada Software," *Software: Practice and Experience*, vol. 20, no. 5, pp. 499–514, May 1990.

[MacEwen and Skillicorn, 1988] G. H. MacEwen and D. B. Skillicorn, "Using Higher-Order Logic for Modular Specification of Real-Time Distributed Systems," *Proc. Formal Techniques in Real-Time and Fault-Tolerant Systems*, University of Warwick, UK, pp. 36–66, September 1988.

[Maler, Manna, and Pnueli, 1992] O. Maler, Z. Manna, and A. Pnueli, "From Timed to Hybrid Systems," *Proc. REX Workshop, in "Real-Time: Theory in Practice,"* LNCS 600, Mook, The Netherlands, pp. 447–484, 1992.

[Mandrioli, Morasca, and Morzenti, 1995] D. Mandrioli, S. Morasca, and A. Morzenti, "Generating Test Cases for Real-Time Systems from Logic Specifications," *ACM Trans. on Computer Systems*, Volume 13, no. 4, pp. 365–398, November 1995.

[Manna and Pnueli, 1992] Z. Manna and A. Pnueli, *Temporal Logic of Reactive and Concurrent Systems: Specification*, New York, Springer-Verlag, 1992.

[Manna and Pnueli, 1993] Z. Manna and A. Pnueli, "Verififying Hybrid Systems," pp. 4–35 of *Hybrid Systems*, R. L. Grossman et al., eds., New York, Springer-Verlag, 1993.

[Marlowe, 1994] T. J. Marlowe, "Schedulability-Analyzable Execution Handling for Fault-Tolerant Real-Time Languages," *Journal of Real-Time Systems*, vol. 7, no. 2, pp. 183–212, September 1994.

[Marsh, 1988] C. A. Marsh, "The ISA Expert System: A Prototype System for Failure Diagnosis on the Space Station," MITRE Report, The MITRE Corporation, Houston, TX, 1988.

[Marzullo, 1984] K. Marzullo, "Maintaining the Time in a Distributed System," Ph.D. thesis, Department of Electrical Engineering, Stanford University, June 1984.

[Marzullo and Owicki, 1985] K. Marzullo and S. Owicki, "Maintaining the Time in a Distributed System," *ACM Operating Systems Review*, 19(3):44–54, July 1985.

[Mataga and Zave, 1995] P. Mataga and P. Zave, "Multiparadigm Specification of an AT&T Switching System," in M. G. Hinchey and J. P. Bowen, eds., *Applications of Formal Methods*, Englewoods Cliffs, NJ, Prentice Hall, pp. 375–398, 1995.

[Mattolini and Nesi, 2001] R. Mattolini and P. Nesi, "An Interval Logic for Real-Time System Specification," *IEEE Transactions on Software Engineering*, vol. 27, no. 3, March 2001.

[McMillan, 1992] K. L. McMillan, "Symbolic Model Checking—An Approach for the State Explosion Problem," Ph.D. thesis, Carnegie-Mellon University, 1992.

[Mealy, 1955] G. H. Mealy, "A Method for Synthesizing Sequential Circuits," *Bell System Technical Journal*, vol. 34, no. 5, pp. 1045–1079, 1955.

[Merlin and Farber, 1976] P. M. Merlin and D. J. Farber, "Recoverability of Communication Protocols—Implications of a Theoretical Study," *IEEE Trans. on Communications*, vol. COM-24, no. 9, September 1976.

[Merritt, Modugno, and Tuttle, 1991] M. Merritt, F. Modugno, and M. Tuttle, "Time-Constrained Automata," *Proc. CONCUR Workshop on Theory of Concurrency: Unification and Extension*, Amsterdam, The Netherlands, August 1991.

[Meyer and Wong-Toi, 1991] M. J. Meyer and H. Wong-Toi, "Verification of Scheduling Policies for a Class of Simple CONCURRENT PROCESSES," *Proc. 19th IEEE-CS Real-Time Systems Symposium*, Madrid, Spain, December 2–4, 1998.

[Michalski and Winston, 1986] R. S. Michalski and P. H. Winston, "Variable Precision Logic," *Artificial Intelligence Journal*, vol. 29, no. 2, pp. 121–146, 1986.

[Milner, 1980] R. Milner, *A Calculus of Commuincating Systems*, LNCS 92, New York, Springer-Verlag, 1980.

[Milner, 1983] R. Milner, "Calculi for Synchrony and Asynchrony," *Journal of Theoretical Computer Science*, vol. 25, pp. 267–310, 1983.

[Milner, 1989] R. Milner, *Communication and Concurrency*, Englewood Cliffs, NJ, Prentice Hall, 1989.

[Miranker, 1987] D. P. Miranker, *TREAT: A New and Efficient Algorithm for AI Production Systems*. Ph.D. thesis, Columbia University, 1987.

[Mok, 1984] A. K. Mok, "The Design of Real-Time Programming Systems Based on Process Models," *Proc. IEEE-CS Real-Time Systems Symp.*, 1984.

[Mok and Liu, 1997] A. Mok and G. Liu, "Efficient Run-Time Monitoring of Timing Constraints," *3rd IEEE Real-Time Technology and Applications Symposium*, Montreal, Canada, June 1997.

[Mok and Tsou, 1996] A. K. Mok and D.-C. Tsou, "The MSP.RTL Real-Time Scheduler Synthesis Tool," *Proc. 17th Real-Time Systems Symposium*, Washington, D.C., December 1996.

[Mok et al., 1989] A. K. Mok et al., "Evaluating Tight Execution Time Bounds of Programs by Annotations," *Proc. 6th IEEE Workshop on Real-Time Operating System and Software*, pp. 74–80, May 1989.

[Moller and Tofts, 1990] F. Moller and C. Tofts, "A Temporal Calculus of Communicating Systems," *Proc. CONCUR Intl. Conf. on Concurrency Theory*, LNCS 458, pp. 401–415, August 1990.

[Moore, 1956] E. F. Moore, "Gedanken-Experiments on Sequential Machines," C. E. Shannon and J. McCarthy, eds., in *Automata Studies*, Princeton, NJ, Princeton University Press, pp. 129–153, 1956.

[Moore, 2002] S. K. Moore, "Extending Heathcare's Reach," *IEEE Spectrum*, vol. 39, no. 1, pp. 66–71, January 2002.

[Morzenti and San Pietro, 1994] A. Morzenti and P. San Pietro, "Object-Oriented Logic Specifications of Time-Critical Systems," *ACM Trans. on Software Engineering Methodology*, vol. 3, no. 1, January 1994.

[Moser and Melliar-Smith, 1990] L. E. Moser and P. M. Melliar-Smith, "Formal Verification of Safety-Critical Systems," *Software: Practice and Experience*, vol. 20, no. 8, pp. 799–821, August 1990.

[Muntz and Lichota, 1991] A. H. Muntz and R. W. Lichota, "A Requirements Specifications for Adaptive Real-Time Systems," *Proc. 11th IEEE Real-Time Systems Symp.*, San Antonio, TX, pp. 264–273, December 1991.

[Musliner et al., 1995] D. J. Musliner et al., "The Challenges of Real-Time AI," *IEEE Computer*, 28(1):58–66, January 1995.

[Nadjm-Tehrani and Stromberg, 1995] S. Nadjm-Tehrani and J.-E. Stromberg, "Proving Dynamic Properties in an Aerospace Application," *Proc. 16th Real-Time Systems Symposium*, Pisa, Italy, pp. 2–10, December 1995.

[Naik and Sistla, 1994] V. G. Naik and A. P. Sistla, "Modeling and Verification of a Real Life Protocol Using Symbolic Model Checking," *Proc. 6th Intl. Conf. on Computer-Aided Verification*, Stanford, CA, June 1994.

[Narayana and Aaby, 1988] K. T. Narayana and A. A. Aaby, "Specificaton of Real-Time Systems in Real-Time Temporal Interval Logic," *Proc. 9th Real-Time Systems Symposium*, pp. 86–95, December 1988.

[Natrajan and Cleaveland, 1996] V. Natrajan and R. Cleaveland, "Predictability of Real-Time Systems: A Process-Algebraic Approach," *Proc. 17th Real-Time Systems Symposium*, Washington, D.C., December 1996.

[Nicollin and Sifakis, 1991] X. Nicollin and J. Sifakis, "An Overview and Synthesis on Timed Process Algebra," *Proc. 3rd Intl. Conf. on Computer-Aided Verification*, Aalborg, Denmark, pp. 376–398, July 1991.

[Nicollin and Sifakis, 1994] X. Nicollin and J. Sifakis, "The Algebra of Timed Processes ATP: Theory and Application," *Information and Computation*, vol. 114, no. 1, pp. 131–178, October 1994.

[Nicollin, Sifakis, and Yovine, 1992] X. Nicollin, J. Sifakis, and S. Yovine, "Compiling Real-Time Specifications into Extended Automata," *IEEE Trans. on Software Eng.*, 18(9):794–804, September 1992.

[Nicollin, Sifakis, and Yovine, 1993] X. Nicollin, J. Sifakis, and S. Yovine, "From ATP to Timed Graphs and Hybrid Systems," *Acta Informatica*, vol. 30, pp. 181–202, 1993.

[Nicollin et al., 1990] X. Nicollin et al., "ATP: An Algebra for Timed Processes," *Proc. IFIP TC2 Working Conf. on Programming Concepts and Methods*, Israel, 1990.

[Nielsen, 1987] H. R. Nielsen, "A Hoare-like Proof System for Analyzing the Computation Time of Programs," *Science of Computer Programming*, vol. 9, no. 1, pp. 107–136, August 1987.

[Oettinger, 1961] A. G. Oettinger, "Automatic syntactic analysis and the pushdown store," *Proceedings of the 12th Symposia in Applied Mathematics*, Providence, RI: American Mathematical Society, pp. 104–109, 1961.

[Olivero, Sifakis, and Yovine, 1994] A. Olivero, J. Sifakis, and S. Yovine, "Using Abstractions for the Verification of Linear Hybrid Systems," *Proc. 6th Intl. Conf. on Computer-Aided Verification*, Stanford, CA, pp. 81–94, June 1994.

[O'Reilly and Cromarty, 1985] C. A. O'Reilly and A. S. Cromarty, "'Fast' is not 'Real-time': Designing Effective Real-time AI Systems," *Applications of Artificial Intelligence*, John F. Gilmore, ed., *Proceedings of SPIE*, no. 485.

[Oshisanwo and Dasiewicz, 1987] A. O. Oshisanwo and P. P. Dasiewicz, "A Parallel Model and Architecture for Production Systems," *Proceedings of International Conference on Parallel Processing*, 1987, pp. 147–153.

[Ostroff, 1989] J. S. Ostroff, "Real-Time Temporal Logic Decision Procedures," *Proc. 10th Real-Time Systems Symposium*, Santa Monica, CA, pp. 92–101, December 1989.

[Ostroff, 1990a] J. S. Ostroff, "Deciding Properties of Timed Transition Models," *IEEE Trans. on Parallel and Distributed Systems*, vol. 1, no. 2, pp. 170–183, April 1990.

[Ostroff, 1990b] J. S. Ostroff, *Temporal Logic of Real-Time Systems*, Research Studies Press, 1990.

[Ostroff, 1992a] J. Ostroff, "Formal Methods for the Specification and Design of Real-Time Safety-Critical Systems," *Journal of Systems and Software*, vol. 33, no. 60, pp. 890–904, April 1992.

[Ostroff, 1992b] J. Ostroff, "Verification of Safety Critical Systems Using TTNRTTL," *Proc. REX Workshop* in *"Real-Time: Theory in Practice,"* LNCS 600, 1992.

[Ostroff, 1992c] J. Ostroff, "A Verifier for Real-Time Properties," *Journal of Real-Time Systems*, vol. 4, pp. 5–35, 1992.

[Ostroff, 1994] J. Ostroff, "Visual Tools for Verifying Real-Time Systems," in T. Rus and C. Rattray, eds., *Theories and Exepriences for Real-Time System Development*, AMAST Series in Computing, vol. 2, pp. 83–101, Singapore, World Scientific Publishing Co., 1994.

[Ostroff and Wonham, 1987] J. Ostroff and W. Wonham, "Modeling, Specifying, and Verifying Real-Time Embedded Computing Systems," *Proc. 8th Real-Time Systems Symposium*, pp. 124–132, December 1987.

[Park, 1981] D. Park, "A Timed Failure Semantics for Extended Communicating Processes," *Proc. 5th GI Conf.*, LNCS 104, 1981.

[Park, 1992] C. Park, "Predicting Deterministic Execution Times of Real-Time Programs," Ph.D. thesis, University of Washington, August 1992.

[Park, 1993] C. Park, "Predicting Program Execution Times by Analyzing Static and Dynamic Program Paths," *Journal of Real-Time Systems*, 1993.

[Park and Shaw, 1990] C. Park and A. Shaw, "Experiments with a Program Timing Tool Based on Source-Level Timing Schema," *Proc. 11th IEEE Real-Time Systems Symposium*, pp. 72–81, December 1990.

[Park et al., 1998] D. Y. W. Park, J. U. Skakkebk, M. P. E. Heimdahl, B. J. Czerny, and D. L. Dill, "Checking Properties of Safety Critical Specifications Using Efficient Decision Procedures," *Proc. Second Workshop on Formal Methods in Software Practice (FMSP'98)*, March 1998.

[Parnas, van Schouwen, and Kwan, 1990] D. Parnas, J. van Schouwen, and S. Kwan, "Evaluation of Safety-Critical Software," *Communications of the ACM*, vol. 33, no. 9, pp. 636–648, June 1990.

[Pasik, 1992] A. J. Pasik, "A Source-to-Source Transformation for Increasing Rule-Based System Parallelism," *IEEE Transactions on Knowledge and Data Engineering*, vol. 4, no. 4, pp. 336–343, August 1992.

[Passino, 1995] K. M. Passino, "Intelligent Control for Autonomous Systems," *IEEE Spectrum*, vol. 32, no. 6, pp. 55–63, June 1995.

[Passino, Yurkovich, and Moudgal, 1994] K. M. Passino, S. Yurkovich, and V. G. Moudgal, "Rule-Based Control for a Flexible-Link Robot," *IEEE Transactions on Control Systems Technology*, vol. 2, no. 4, pp. 392–405, December 1994.

[Paul et al., 1991] C. J. Paul et al., "Reducing Problem-Solving Variance to Improve Predictability," *Communications of the ACM*, vol. 34, no. 8, pp. 81–93, August 1991.

[Paulson, 2001] L. D. Paulson, "NASA Satellites will use AI," *IEEE Computer*, vol. 34, no. 8, August 2001.

[Payton and Bihari, 1991] D. W. Payton and T. E. Bihari, "Intelligent real-time control of robotic vehicles," *Communications of the ACM*, vol. 34, no. 8, pp. 48–63, August 1991.

[Peano, 1889] G. Peano, Principles of Arithmetic, Presented by a New Method, 1889. [Transl. in From Frege to Gödel, van Heijenoort, Harvard Univ. Press, 1971.]

[Pease, Shostak, and Lamport, 1980] M. Pease, R. Shostak, and L. Lamport, "Reaching agreement in the presence of faults," *Journal of the ACM*, 27(2):228–234, April 1980.

[Peleg and Dori, 2000] M. Peleg and D. Dori, "The Model Multiplicity Problem: Experimenting with Real-Time Specification Methods," *IEEE Transactions on Software Engineering*, vol. 26, no. 8, pp. 742–759, August 2000.

[Petersohn and Urbina, 1997] C. Petersohn and L. Urbina, "A Timed Semantics for the STATEMATE Implementation of Statecharts," pp. 553–572 of *Industrial Applications and Strengthened Foundations of Formal Methods* (FME 97), J. Fitzgerald, C. B. Jones, and P. Lucas, eds., LNCS 1313, New York, Springer-Verlag, 1997.

[Peterson, 1977] J. L. Peterson, "Petri Nets," *Computing Surveys*, vol. 9, no. 3, pp. 223–248, 1977.

[Peterson, 1981] J. L. Peterson, *Petri Net Theory and the Modeling of Systems*, Englewood Cliffs, NJ, Prentice Hall, 1981.

[Pettersson, 1999] Paul Pettersson, "Modelling and Verification of Real-Time Systems Using Timed Automata: Theory and Practice," Ph.D. thesis, Technical Report DoCS 99/101, Department of Computer Systems, Uppsala University, February 1999.

[Plattner, 1984] B. Plattner, "Real-Time Execution Monitoring," *IEEE Tran. on Software Engineering*, vol. 10, no. 6, pp. 756–764, November 1984.

[Pnueli and Harel, 1988] A. Pnueli and D. Harel, "Applications of Temporal Logic to the Specification of Real Time Systems," *Proc. Formal Techniques in Real-Time and Fault-Tolerant Systems*, University of Warwick, UK, pp. 84–98, September 1988.

[Posix] http://standards.ieee.org/catalog/posix.html.

[Post, 1936] E. L. Post, "Finite Combinatory Processes—Formulation 1," *Journal of Symbolic Logic*, no. 1, pp. 103–105, 1936.

[Probst and Li, 1992] D. K. Probst and H. F. Li, "Verifying Timed Behavior Automata with Nonbinary Delay Constraints," *Proc. 4th Intl. Conf. on Computer-Aided Verification*, Montreal, Canada, pp. 123–136, June 1992.

[Puchol, Mok, and Douglas, 1995] C. Puchol, A. K. Mok, and D. A. Douglas, "Compiling Modechart Specifications," *Proc. 16th Real-Time Systems Symposium*, Pisa, Italy, pp. 256–265, December 1995.

[Puri and Varaiya, 1994] A. Puri and P. Varaiya, "Decidability of Hybrid Systems with Rectangular Differential Inclusions," *Proc. 6th Intl. Conf. on Computer-Aided Verification*, Stanford, CA, pp. 95–104, June 1994.

[Puschner and Koza, 1989] P. Puschner and C. Koza, "Calculating the Maximum Execution Time of Real-Time Programs," *Journal of Real-Time Systems*, vol. 1, no. 2, pp. 159–176, September 1989.

[Quemada and Fernandez, 1987] J. Quemada and A. Fernandez, "Introduction of Quantitative Relative Time into LOTOS," *Proc. IFIP WG6.1 7th Intl. Symp. on Protocol Specification, Testing, and Verification*, pp. 105–121, 1987.

[Quielle and Sifakis, 1981] J. P. Quielle and J. Sifakis, "Specification and Verification of Concurrent Systems in CESAR," *Proc. 5th Intl. Symp. on Programming*, LNCS 137, New York, Springer-Verlag, pp. 337–350, 1981.

[Quielle and Sifakis, 1982] J. P. Quielle and J. Sifakis, "Fairness and Related Properties in Transition Systems," *IMAG 292*, University of Grenoble, March 1982.

[Raju, Rajkumar, and Jahanian, 1992] S. C. V. Raju, R. Rajkumar, and F. Jahanian, "Timing Constraints Monitoring in Distributed Real-Time Systems," *Proc. IEEE-CS Real-Time Systems Symp.*, pp. 57–67, December 1990.

[Raju and Shaw, 1992] S. Raju and A. Shaw, "A Prototyping Environment for Specifying, Executing, and Checking Real-Time State Machines," *Software: Practice and Experience*, 1992.

[Ramakrishna et al., 1993] Y. S. Ramakrishna et al., "Really Visual Temporal Reasoning," *Proc. 14th Real-Time Systems Symposium*, Raleigh-Durham, NC, pp. 262–273, December 1993.

[Ramamoorthy and Ho, 1980] C. V. Ramamoorthy and G. S. Ho, "Performance Evaluation of Asynchronous Concurrent Systems Using Petri Nets," *IEEE Transactions on Software Engineering*, vol. 6, September 1980.

[Ramchandani, 1974] C. Ramchandani, "Analysis of Asynchronous Concurrent Systems by Timed Petri Nets," Ph.D. thesis (Technical Report 120), MIT, Project MAC, February 1974.

[Ratel, Hakbwachs, and Raymond, 1991] C. Ratel, N. Hakbwachs, and P. Raymond, "Programming and Verifying Critical Systems by Means of the Synchronous Data-Flow Programming Language Lustre," *Proc. ACM Sigsoft Conf. on Software for Critical Systems*, December 1991.

[Ravn, Rischel, and Hansen, 1993] A. P. Ravn, H. Rischel, and K. M. Hansen, "Specifying and Verifying Requirements of Real-Time Systems," *IEEE Trans. Software Engineering*, vol. SE-19, no. 1, pp. 41–55, January 1993.

[Raymond et al., 1998] P. Raymond, X. Nicollin, N. Halbwachs, and D. Weber, "Automatic Testing of Reactive Systems," *Proc. 19th IEEE-CS Real-Time Systems Symposium*, Madrid, Spain, December 2–4, 1998.

[Razouk and Gorlick, 1989] R. R. Razouk and M. M. Gorlick, "A Real-Time Interval Logic for Reasoning about Executions of Real-Time Programs," *Proc. 3rd ACM SIGSOFT Symp. on Software Testing, Analysis, and Verification*, pp. 10–19, 1989.

[Reed and Roscoe, 1987] G. M. Reed and A. W. Roscoe, Metric Spaces as Models for Real-Time Concurrency," *Proc. Mathematical Foundations of Computer Science*, LNCS 298, 1987.

[Reed and Roscoe, 1988] G. M. Reed and A. W. Roscoe, "A Timed Model for Communicating Sequential Processes," *Theoretical Computer Science*, vol. 58, pp. 249–261, 1988.

[Rice and Cheng, 1999] L. E. P. Rice and A. M. K. Cheng, "Timing Analysis of the X-38 Space Station Crew Return Vehicle Avionics," *Proc. IEEE-CS Real-Time Technology and Applications Symposium*, Vancouver, Canada, June 2–4, 1999.

[Richter, 1985] G. Richter, "Clocks and Their Use for Time Modeling," *Proc. TFAIS*, IFIP TC 8.1, 1985.

[Rico, Bochmann, and Cherkaoui, 1992] N. Rico, G. V. Bochmann, and O. Cherkaoui, "Model Checking for Real-Time Systems Specified in Lotos," *Proc. 4th Intl. Conf. on Computer-Aided Verification*, Montreal, Canada, pp. 288–301, June 1992.

[Robinson, 1965] J. A. Robinson, "A Machine-Oriented Logic Based on the Resolution Principle," *Journal of the ACM*, Volume 12, issue 1, pp. 23–41, 1965.

[Robinson, 1968] J. A. Robinson, "The Generalized Resolution Principle," *Machine Intelligence* 3, ed. Dale and Michie, Oliver and Boyd, Edinburgh, pp. 77–93, 1968.

[Rose, Perez, and Clements, 1994] A. T. Rose, M. A. Perez, and P.C. Clements, "Modechart Toolset User's Guide," Center for High Assurance Computer Systems, Naval Research Laboratory Memorandum Report NRL/MR/5540-94-7427, February 1994.

[Rushby and von Henke, 1991] J. Rushby and F. von Henke, "Formal Verification of Algorithms for Critical Systems," *Proc. ACM SIGSOFT Conf. on Software for Critical Systems*, pp. 1–15, December 1991.

[Rushby and von Henke, 1993] J. Rushby and F. von Henke, "Formal Verification of Algorithms for Critical Systems," *IEEE Trans. on Software Engineering*, vol. SE-19, no. 1, pp. 13–23, January 1993.

[Schenke, 1994] M. Schenke, "A Timed Specification Language for Concurrent Reactive Systems," *Proc. Workshops in Computing "Semantics of Specification Languages,"* pp. 152–167, 1994.

[Schmolze, 1991] J. G. Schmolze, "Guaranteeing Serializable Results in Synchronous Parallel Production Systems," *J. Parallel and Distr. Computing*, 13(4), December 1991.

[Schneider, 1999] S. Schneider, "Concurrent and Real-time Systems: The CSP Approach," 526 pp., Wiley, New York, NY, November 1999.

[Schneider, Bloom, and Marzullo, 1991] F. Schneider, B. Bloom, and K. Marzullo, "Putting Time into Proof Outlines," *Proc. REX Workshop "Real-Time: Theory in Practice,"* LNCS 600, Mook, The Netherlands, pp. 618–639, June 1991.

[Schruben, 1983] L. Schruben, "Simulation Modeling with Event Graphs," *Communications of the ACM*, vol. 26, no. 11, pp. 957–963, November 1983.

[Schutz, 1990] W. Schutz, "A Test Strategy for the Distributed Real-Time System MARS," *Proc. IEEE CompEuro Conf. on Computer Systemsa and Software Engineering*, Tel Aviv, Israel, pp. 20–27, May 1990.

[Schutz, 1991] W. Schutz, "On the Testability of Distributed Real-Time Systems," *Proc. 10th IEEE Symp. on Relaible Distributed Systems*, Pisa, Italy, pp. 52–61, September 1991.

[Schutz, 1993] W. Schutz, *The Testability of Distributed Real-Time Systems*, Kluwer Academic Publishers, 1993.

[Schutz, 1994] W. Schutz, "Fundamental Issues in Testing Distributed Real-Time Systems," *Journal of Real-Time Systems*, vol. 7, no. 2, pp. 129–158, September 1994.

[Schwartz, Melliar-Smith, and Vogt, 1983] R. L. Schwartz, P. M. Melliar-Smith, and F. H. Vogt, "An Interval Logic for Higher Level Temporal Reasoning," *Proc. 2nd Annual ACM Symp. on Principles of Distributed Computing*, pp. 173–186, 1983.

[Selic, Gullekson, and Ward, 1994] B. Selic, G. Gullekson, and P. Ward, *Real-Time Object Modeling*, New York, Wiley, 1994.

[Sha, Rajkumar, and Lehoczky, 1990] L. Sha, R. Rajkumar, and J. P. Lehoczky, "Priority Inheritance Protocols: An Approach to Real-Time Synchronization," *IEEE Transactions on Computers*, 39(9):1175–1185, 1990.

[Shah, 1992] S. C. Shah, "Automated Conversion of OPS5 Program into MRL Programs for Response Time Bound Analysis," Master's thesis, University of Houston, 1992.

[Shankar, 1992] A. U. Shankar, "A Simple Assertional Proof System for Real-Time Systems," *Proc. 13th Real-Time Systems Symposium*, Phoenix, AZ, pp. 167–176, December 1992.

[Shankar, 1993] N. Shankar, "Verification of Real-Time Systems Using PVS," *Proc. 5th Intl. Conf. on Computer-Aided Verification*, Elounda, Greece, pp. 280–291, June 1993.

[Shaw, 1989] A. C. Shaw, "Reasoning about Time in Higher-Level Language Software," *IEEE Trans. on Software Eng.*, 15(7):875–889, July 1989.

[Shaw, 1991] A. C. Shaw, "Deterministic Timing Schema for Parallel Programs," *Proc. 5th IEEE Intl. Parallel Processing Symposium*, Newport Beach, CA, pp. 56–63, April 1991.

[Shaw, 1992] A. C. Shaw, "Communicating Real-Time State Machines," *IEEE Trans. on Software Eng.*, 18(9):805–816, September 1992.

[Shaw, 2001] A. C. Shaw, *Real-Time Systems and Software*, New York, Wiley, 2001.

[Sjodin and Hansson, 1998] M. Sjodin and H. Hansson, "Improved Response Time Analysis Calculations," *Proc. 19th IEEE-CS Real-Time Systems Symposium*, Madrid, Spain, December 2–4, 1998.

[Skakkebaek et al., 1992] J. U. Skakkebaek et al., "Specification of Embedded, Real-Time Systems," *Proc. IEEE Euromicro Workshop on Real-Time Systems*, 1992.

[Slagle, 1967] J. R. Slagle, "Automatic Theorem Proving with Renamable and Semantic Resolution," *J. the ACM* 14(4):687–697, 1967.

[Smailagic, Siewiorek, and Reilly, 2001] A. Smailagic, D. Siewiorek, and D. Reilly, "CMU Wearable Computers for Real-Time Speech Translation," *IEEE Personal Communications*, vol. 8, no. 2, April 2001.

[Smith and Gerhart, 1988] S. L. Smith and S. L. Gerhart, "STATEMATE and Cruise Control: A Case Study," *Proc. 12th Intl. IEEE Computer Software and Applications Conf.*, pp. 49–56, 1988.

[Sokolsky, Lee, and Ben-Abdallah, 1999] O. Sokolsky, I. Lee, and H. Ben-Abdallah, "Specification and Analysis of Real-Time Systems with PARAGON," *Annals of Software Engineering*, vol. 7, 1999.

[Sokolsky and Smolka, 1994] O. Sokolsky and S. A. Smolka, "Incremental Model Checking in the Modal Mu-Calculus," *Proc. 6th Intl. Conf. on Computer-Aided Verification*, Stanford, CA, pp. 351–363, 1994.

[Sokolsky and Smolka, 1995] O. V. Sokolsky and S. A. Smolka, "Local Model Checking for Real Time Systems," *Proc. 7th Intl. Conf. on Computer-Aided Verification*, Liege, Belgium, pp. 211–224, July 1995.

[Sokolsky et al., 1998] O. Sokolsky, M. Younis, I. Lee, H.-H. Kwak, and J. Zhou, "Verification of the Redundancy Management System for Space Launch Vehicle," *Proc. IEEE-CS Real-Time Technology and Applications Symposium*, June 1998.

[Sowmya and Ramesh, 1998] A. Sowmya and S. Ramesh, "Extending Statecharts with Temporal Logic," *IEEE Trans. on Software Engineering*, vol. 24, no. 3, pp. 216–231, March 1998.

[Stotts and Pratt, 1985] P. D. Stotts, Jr. and T. W. Pratt, "Hierarchical Modeling of Software Systems with Timed Petri Nets," *Proc. 1st Intl. Workshop on Timed Petri Nets*, Torino, Italy, July 1985.

[Stoyenko, 1987] A. D. Stoyenko, "A Real-Time Language with a Schedulability Analyzer," Ph.D. thesis, University of Toronto, December 1987.

[Stoyenko, Hamacher, and Holt, 1991] A. D. Stoyenko, V. C. Hamacher, and R. C. Holt, "Analyzing Hard-Real-Time Programs for Guaranteed Schedulability," *IEEE Trans. on Software Eng.*, vol. 17, no. 8, pp. 737–750, August 1991.

[Strosnider, Lehoczky, and Sha, 1995] J. K. Strosnider, J. P. Lehoczky, and L. Sha, "The Deferrable Server Algorithm for Enhanced Aperiodic Responsiveness in Hard Real-time Environment," *IEEE Transactions on Computers*, vol. 4, pp. 1405–1419, 1995.

[Strosnider and Paul, 1994] J. K. Strosnider and C. J. Paul, "A Structured View of Real-Time Problem Solving," *AI Magazine*, 15(2):45–66, Summer 1994.

[Stuart, 1990] D. A. Stuart, "Implementing a Verifier for Real-Time Systems," *Proc. 11th IEEE Real-Time Systems Symp.*, Orlando, FL, pp. 62–71, December 1990.

[Stuart and Clements, 1991] D. A. Stuart and P. C. Clements, "Clairvoyance, Capricious Timing Constraints, Causality, and Real-Time Specifications," *Proc. 11th IEEE Real-Time Systems Symp.*, San Antonio, TX, pp. 254–263, December 1991.

[Stuart et al., 2001] D.A. Stuart, M. Brockmeyer, A.K. Mok, and F. Jahanian, "Simulation-Verification: Biting at the State Explosion Problem," *IEEE Transactions on Software Engineering*, vol. 27, 2001.

[Suberek, 1980] W. Suberek, "Timed Petri Nets and Performance Evaluation," *Proc. 7th Annual Symp. on Computer Architecture*, May 1980.

[Sun and Liu, 1996] J. Sun and J. Liu, "Bounding Completion Times of Jobs with Arbitrary Release Times and Variable Execution Times," *Proc. Real-Time Systems Symposium*, pp. 2–12, 1996.

[Tarjan, 1972] R. E. Tarjan, "Depth First Search and Linear Graph Algorithms," *SIAM J. Computing*, vol. 1, pp. 146–160, 1972.

[Tindell, Burns, and Wellings, 1994] K. Tindell, A. Burns, and A. Wellings, "An Extendible Approach for Analysing Fixed Priority Hard Real-Time Tasks," *Journal of Real-Time Systems*, vol. 6, no. 2, pp. 133–152, March 1994.

[Tokuda and Kotera, 1988] H. Tokuda and M. Kotera, "Scheduler 1-2-3: An Interactive Schedulability Analyzer for Guaranteed Schedulability," *Proc. 12th IEEE Intl. Computer Software and Applications Conf.*, pp. 211–219, 1988.

[Tokuda, Kotera, and Mercer, 1988] H. Tokuda, M. Kotera, and C. W. Mercer, "A Real-Time Monitor for a Distributed Real-Time Operating Systems," *Proc. ACM Workshop on Parallel and Distributed Debugging*, pp. 68–77, 1988.

[Tripakis, 1999] S. Tripakis, "Verifying Progress in Timed Systems," pp. 299–314 of *Proceedings of the 5th International AMAST Workshop on Real-Time and Probabilistic Systems (ARTS'99)*, J.-P. Katoen, ed., LNCS 1601, Springer-Verlag, 1999.

[Tsai and Cheng, 1994] H.-Y. Tsai and A. M. K. Cheng, "Termination Analysis of OPS5 Expert Systems," *Proc. 12th National Conf. on Artificial Intelligence (AAAI)*, Seattle, WA, pp. 193–198, August 1994.

[Tsai, Fang, and Chen, 1990] J. J. P. Tsai, K.-Y. Fang, and H.-Y. Chen, "A Noninvasive Architecture to Monitor Real-Time Distributed Systems," *IEEE Computer*, vol. 23, no. 3, pp. 11–23, March 1990.

[Tsai and Yang, 1995] J. J. P. Tsai and S. J. H. Yang, eds., *Monitoring and Debugging of Distributed Real-Time Systems*, Los Alamitos, CA, IEEE Press, 1995.

[Tsai, Yang, and Chang, 1995] J. J. P. Tsai, S. J. H. Yang, and Y. H. Chang, "Timing Constraint Petri Nets and Their Applications to Schedulability Analysis of Real-Time Systems Specifications," *IEEE Trans. on Software Engineering*, vol. 21, no. 2, pp. 449–459, February 1995.

[Tsai et al., 1996] J. J. P. Tsai, Y. Bi, S. J. H. Yang, and R. A. W. Smith, "Distributed Real-Time Systems: Monitoring, Visualization, Debugging, and Analysis," 336 pp., Wiley, New York, NY, July 1996.

[Turing, 1936] A. M. Turing, "On Computable Numbers, with an Application to the Entscheidungsproblem," *Proceedings of the London Mathematical Society*, Series 2, no. 42 (1936–37), pp. 230–265, 1936.

[Ullman and Van Gelder, 1988] J. D. Ullman and A. Van Gelder, "Efficient Tests for Top-Down Termination of Logical Rules," *Journal of the ACM*, 35(2), April 1988.

[Valmari, 1990] A. Valmari, "A Stubborn Attack on the State Explosion Problem," *Proc. 2nd Intl. Conf. on Computer-Aided Verification*, June 1990.

[Valmari and Jokela, 1989] A. A. Valmari and T. M. Jokela, "Embedded Software Validation through State Space Generation," in *Proc. 2nd Int'l Conf. on Software Engineering for Real-Time Systems*, Cirencester, England, pp. 278–282, 1989.

[van der Aalst, 1993] W. M. P. van der Aalst, "Interval Timed Coloured Petri Nets and Their Analysis," pp. 453–472 of *Application and Theory of Petri Nets*, M. Ajmone Marsan, ed., LNCS 691, Springer-Verlag, Berlin, 1993.

[Vardanega, 1996] T. Vardanega, "Tool Support for the Construction of Statically Analyzable Hard Real-Time Ada Systems," *Proc. 17th Real-Time Systems Symposium*, Washington, D.C., December 1996.

[Vestal, 2000] S. Vestal, "Formal Verification of the MetaH Executive Using Linear Hybrid Automata," *6th IEEE Real-Time Technology and Applications Symposium*, Washington, D.C., May–June 2000.

[Vicario, 2001] E. Vicario, "Static Analysis and Dynamic Steering of Time-Dependent Systems," *IEEE Transactions on Software Engineering*, vol. 27, no. 8, August 2001.

[Vilain, 1982] M. Vilain, "A System for Reasoning about Time," *Proc. American Association for Artificial Intelligence Conf.*, Pittsburgh, PA, August 1982.

[VIS, 1996] The VIS Group, "VIS: A System for Verification and Synthesis," pp. 428–432 of *Proceedings of the 8th International Conference on Computer Aided Verification*, R. Alur and T. Henzinger, eds., LNCS 1102, New York, Springer-Verlag, 1996.

[Volz and Mudge, 1987] R. A. Volz and T. N. Mudge, "Timing Issues in the Distributed Execution of Ada Programs," *IEEE Trans. on Computers*, vol. C-361, no. 4, pp. 449–459, April 1987.

[von der Beek, 1994] M. von der Beek, "A Comparison of Statechart Variants," pp. 128–148 of *Formal Techniques in Real-Time and Fault-Tolerant Systems*, L. De Roever and J. Vytopil, eds., LNCS 863, New York, Springer-Verlag, 1994.

[Wang et al., 1991] R.-H. Wang et al., "Automated Analysis of Bounded Response Time for Two NASA Expert Systems," *Proc. ACM SIGSOFT Conf. on Software for Critical Systems*, pp. 147–161, 1991.

[Wang, 1989] C.-K. Wang, "Translation between OPS5 and MRL Rule-Based Programs," Technical report, Department of Computer Science, University of Texas at Austin, August 1989.

[Wang, 1990a] C.-K. Wang, "MRL: The Language," Technical Report, Department of Computer Science, University of Texas at Austin, August 1990.

[Wang, 1990b] Y. Wang, "Real Time Behavior of Asynchronous Agents," *Proc. CONCUR*, LNCS 458, 1990.

[Wang, 1990c] C.-K. Wang, "Translation between OPS5 and MRL Rule-Based Programs," Technical Representative, Department of Computer Science, University of Texas at Austin, August 1990.

[Wang, 1991a] Y. Wang, "A Calculus of Real Time Systems," Ph.D. thesis, Chalmers University of Technology, 1991.

[Wang, 1991b] Y. Wang, "CCS + Time = An Interleaving Model for Real Time Systems," *Proc. Intl. Conf. on Automata, Languages and Programming*, July 1991.

[Wang and Cheng, 1999] J.-C. Wang and A. M. K. Cheng, "A State-Space-Based Approach for Optimizing MRL Rule-Based Programs," *Proc. Intl. Conf. on Parallel and Distributed Computer Systems*, MIT: Cambridge, MA, November 1999

[Wang and Cheng, 2002] R. Wang and A. M. K. Cheng, "A New Schedulability Test and Compensation Strategy for Imprecise Computation," Technical Report, Department of Computer Science, University of Houston, submitted to *IEEE-CS Real-Time Technology and Applications Symposium*, September 2002.

[Wang and Mok, 1993] C.-K. Wang and A. K. Mok, "Timing Analysis of MRL: A Real-Time Rule-Based SAystem," *Journal of Real-Time Systems*, vol. 5, no. 1, pp. 89–128, March 1993.

[Wang and Mok, 1995] R.-H. Wang and A.K. Mok, "Response-Time Bounds of EQL Rule-Based Programs Under Rule Priority Structure," *IEEE Trans. Software Engineering*, vol. 21, no. 7, pp. 605–614, July 1995.

[Wang, Mok, and Cheng, 1990] C.-K. Wang, A. K. Mok, and A. M. K. Cheng, "MRL—A Real-Time Rule-Based Production System," *Proc. IEEE Real-Time Systems Symposium*, Lake Buena Vista, FlL, pp. 267–276, December 1990.

[Wang, Mok, and Emerson, 1992] F. Wang, A. K. Mok, and E. A. Emerson, "Formal Specification of Asynchronous Distributed Real-Time Systems by APTL," *Proc. 14th ACM Intl. Conf. on Software Engineering*, pp. 188–198, 1992.

[Wang, Mok, and Emerson, 1993a] F. Wang, A. K. Mok, and E. A. Emerson, "Distributed Real-Time System Specification and Verification in APTL," *ACM Transactions on Software Engineering and Methodology*, vol. 2, no. 4, pp. 346–378, 1993.

[Wang, Mok, and Emerson, 1993b] F. Wang, A. K. Mok, and E. A. Emerson, "Symbolic Model Checking for Distributed Real-Time Systems," *FME*, pp. 632–651, 1993.

[Want and Schilit, 2001] R. Want and B. Schilit, "Expanding the Horizons of Location-Aware Computing," *IEEE Computer*, vol. 34, no. 8, August 2001.

[Ward, 1986] P. Ward, "The Transformation Schema: An Extension of the Data Flow Diagram to Represent Control and Timing," *IEEE Trans. Software Engineering*, vol. SE-12, pp. 198–210, 1986.

[Ward and Mellor, 1985] P. Ward and S. Mellor, *Structure Development for Real-Time Systems*, New York, Yourdon, 1985.

[Weinberg and Lynch, 1996] H. B. Weinberg and N. Lynch, "Correctness of Vehicle Control Systems," *Proc. 17th Real-Time Systems Symposium*, Washington, D.C., December 1996.

[Weinberg and Zuck, 1992] H. B. Weinberg and L. D. Zuck, "Timed Ethernet: Real-Time Formal Specification of Ethernet," *Proc. 3rd CONCUR*, LNCS 630, 1992.

[Welch et al., 1992] L. R. Welch, B. Ravindran, B. A. Shirazi, and C. Bruggeman, "Specification and Modeling of Dynamic, Distributed Real-Time Systems," *Proc. 19th IEEE-CS Real-Time Systems Symposium*, Madrid, Spain, December 2–4, 1998.

[White et al., 1999] R. T. White, F. Mueller, C. Healy, D. Whalley, and M. Harmon, "Timing Analysis for Data and Wrap-Around Fill Caches," *Journal of Real-Time Systems*, 17(2/3):209–233, November 1999.

[Williams et al., 2000] P. F. Williams, A. Biere, E. M. Clarke, and A. Gupta, "Combining Decision Diagrams and SAT Procedures for Efficient Symbolic Model Checking," *Proc. 12 th Int. Conf. on Computer Aided Verification*, 2000.

[Winston, 1977] P. H. Winston, *Artificial Intelligence*, Reading, MA, Addison-Wesley, 1977.

[Wong and Cheng, 1997] C. Wong and A. M. K. Cheng, "An Approach for Imprecise Transmission of TIFF Image Files Through Congested Real-Time ATM Networks," *Proc. 22nd Intl. Conf. on Local Computer Networks*, Minneapolis, MN, November 1997.

[Wong-Toi, 1994] H. Wong-Toi, "Symbolic Approximations for Verifying Real-Time Systems," Ph.D. Thesis, Stanford University, December 1994.

[Wood and Wood, 1989] D. P. Wood and W. G. Wood, "Comparative Evaluations of Four Specification Methods for Real-Time Systems," Software Engineering Institute, Carnegie-Mellon University, CMU-SEI-89-TR-36, December 1989.

[Xu and Parnas, 1990] J. Xu and D. L. Parnas, "Scheduling Processes with Release Times, Deadlines, Precedence, and Exclusion Relations," *IEEE Trans. on Software Engineering*, vol. 16, no. 3, pp. 360–369, March 1990.

[Xu and Parnas, 1993] J. Xu and D. L. Parnas, "On Satisfying Timing Constraints in Hard-Real-Time Systems," *IEEE Trans. on Software Engineering*, vol. 19, no. 1, pp. 70–84, January 1993.

[Yang, Mok, and Wang, 1993] J. Yang, A. K. Mok, and F. Wang, "Symbolic Model Checking for Event-Driven Real-Time Systems," *Proc. 14th Real-Time Systems Symposium*, Raleigh-Durham, NC, pp. 23–33, December 1993.

[Yannakakis and Lee, 1993] M. Yannakakis and D. Lee, "An Efficient Algorithm for Minimizing Real-Time Transition Systems," *Proc. 5th Intl. Conf. on Computer-Aided Verification*, Elounda, Greece, pp. 210–224, June 1993.

[Yeh, 1998] Y. C. B. Yeh, "Design Considerations in Boeing 777 Fly-By-Wire Computers," *Proceedings of the 3rd IEEE International High-Assurance Systems Engineering Symposium*, 1998.

[Yi, 1991] W. Yi, "A Calculus of Real Time Systems," Ph.D. thesis, Chalmers University of Technology, S-412 96 Goteborg, Sweden, 1991.

[Yodaiken and Ramamritham, 1990] V. Yodaiken and K. Ramamritham, "Specifying and Verifying a Real-Time Priority Queue with Modal Algebra," *Proc. 11th IEEE Real-Time Systems Symposium*, Orlando, FL, pp. 300–310, December 1990.

[Yoneda et al., 1991] T. Yoneda et al., "Acceleration of Timing Verification Method Based on Time Petri Nets," *Systems and Computers in Japan*, vol. 22, no. 12, pp. 37–52, 1991.

[Yoneda et al., 1993b] T. Yoneda et al., "Efficient Verification of Parallel Real-Time Systems," *Proc. 5th Intl. Conf. on Computer-Aided Verification*, Elounda, Greece, pp. 321–332, June 1993.

[Yovine, 1997] S. Yovine, "Kronos: A Verification Tool for Real-Time Systems," *Journal of Software Tools for Technology Transfer*, vol. 1, no. 1–2, October 1997.

[Zhao, Ramamritham, and Stankovic, 1987] W. Zhao, K. Ramamritham, and J. Stankovic, "Scheduling Tasks with Resource Requirements in Hard Real-Time Systems," *IEEE Trans. Software Engineering*, vol. SE-13, no. 5, pp. 564–577, May 1987.

[Zhou, Hoare, and Hansen, 1993] C. Zhou, C. A. R. Hoare, and M. R. Hansen, "An Extended Duration Calculus for Hybrid Real-Time Systems," R. L. Grossman et al., eds., *Hybrid Systems*, New York, Springer-Verlag, pp. 36–59, 1993.

[Zhou, Hoare, and Ravn, 1991] C. Zhou, C. A. R. Hoare, and A. P. Ravn, "A Calculus of Durations," *Information Processing Letters*, vol. 40, pp. 269–276, 1991.

[Zhou and Hooman, 1992] P. Zhou and J. Hooman, "A Proof Theory for Asynchronous Communicating Real-Time Systems," *Proc. 13th Real-Time Systems Symposium*, Phoenix, AZ, pp. 177–186, December 1992.

[Zupan, 1993] B. Zupan, "Optimization of Real-Time Rule-Based Systems Using State-Space Diagrams," Master's thesis, University of Houston, Department of Computer Science, 1993.

[Zupan and Cheng, 1994a] B. Zupan and A. M. K. Cheng, "Optimization of Rule-Based Expert Systems Via State Transition System Construction," *Proc. IEEE Conference on Artificial Intelligence for Application*, pp. 320–326, 1994.

[Zupan and Cheng, 1994b] B. Zupan and A. M. K. Cheng, "Response Time Optimization of Rule-Based Expert Systems," *Proc. SPIE OEAerospace Sensing Conference on Knowledge-Based Artificial Intelligence Systems in Aerospace and Industry*, Orlando, FL, pp. 240–248, April 1994.

[Zupan and Cheng, 1998] B. Zupan and A. M. K. Cheng, "Optimization of Rule-Based Systems Using State Space Graphs," *IEEE Trans. on Knowledge and Data Eng.*, vol. 10, no. 2, pp. 238–254, March/April 1998.

[Zupan, Cheng, and Bohanec, 1995a] B. Zupan, A. M. K. Cheng, and M. Bohanec, "Stability Analysis of Real-Time Systems: Porting Crisp Methods to Fuzzy," *Electrotechnical Review: Journal for Electrical Engineering and Computer Science*, vol. 62, no. 3–4, pp. 163–170, 1995.

[Zupan, Cheng, and Bohanec, 1995b] B. Zupan, A. M. K. Cheng, and M. Bohanec, "Static Stability Analysis Method for Fuzzy Rule-Chaining Real-Time Systems," *Proc. IFAC Conf. on Artificial Intelligence in Real-Time Control*, Slovenia, November 1995.

[Zwarico, 1988] A. Zwarico, "Timed Acceptance: An Algebra of Time Dependent Computing," Ph.D. thesis, University of Pennsylvania, 1988.

[Zwarico and Lee, 1985] A. Zwarico and I. Lee, "Proving a Network of Real-Time Processes Correct," *Proc. 6th Real-Time Systems Symposium*, pp. 169–177, December 1985.

INDEX